# EQUATIONS, MODELS, AND PROGRAMS

## A Mathematical Introduction

## to

## Computer Science

*THOMAS J. MYERS*

*Colgate University*

PRENTICE-HALL SOFTWARE SERIES
Brian W. Kernighan, Series Advisor

PRENTICE HALL, Englewood Cliffs, New Jersey 07630

*Library of Congress Cataloging-in-Publication Data*
Myers, Thomas J.,
   Equations, models, and programs.

   Bibliography: p.
   Includes index.
   1. Electronic data processing—Mathematics.
I. Title.
QA76.9.M35M94      1988      004'.01'51       87-36114
005.74—dc19
ISBN 0-13-283474-X

Editorial / production supervision and
   interior design: *Gertrude Szyferblatt*
Cover design: *Lundgren Graphics, Ltd.*
Manufacturing buyer: *Ed O'Dougherty*

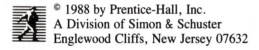 © 1988 by Prentice-Hall, Inc.
A Division of Simon & Schuster
Englewood Cliffs, New Jersey 07632

Printed in the United States of America

10 9 8 7 6 5 4 3 2 1

ISBN 0-13-283474-X

Prentice-Hall International (UK) Limited, *London*
Prentice-Hall of Australia Pty. Limited, *Sydney*
Prentice-Hall Canada Inc., *Toronto*
Prentice-Hall Hispanoamericana, S.A., *Mexico*
Prentice-Hall of India Private Limited, *New Delhi*
Prentice-Hall of Japan, Inc., *Tokyo*
Simon and Schuster Asia Pte. Ltd., *Singapore*
Editora Prentice-Hall do Brasil, Ltda., *Rio de Janeiro*

This book is dedicated to GALILEO GALILEI, who showed what a mathematical world-view could add to the effectiveness of experiment—and to the fun of experimentation.

Philosophy is written in this grand book—I mean the universe—which stands continually open to our gaze, but it cannot be understood unless one first learns to comprehend the language and interpret the characters in which it is written. It is written in the language of mathematics, and the characters are triangles, circles, and other geometrical figures, without which it is humanly impossible to understand a single word of it; without these, one is wandering about in a dark labyrinth.

*Il Saggiatore* (*The Assayer*) [1623]

# Contents

## 7  PROOFS: REASONING CAREFULLY THROUGH PROGRAM DESIGN                              297

# Preface

Computer science creates new worlds for us each year: environments for work and play, for study and experimentation, for science and art and philosophy, as well as the often-forgotten background to our lives in which we have increasingly "intelligent" cars and watches and toaster-ovens. That does not automatically mean that you need computer literacy, any more than you need automotive literacy or photocopier literacy in order to drive a car or copy a document. It does, however, suggest that unless you're short on curiosity about the world around you—and your own place in it—you'll have some motivation for learning about the worlds within computer science itself. Computers are machines whose behavior is quite different from the behavior of any machines previously known to man. What are the basic concepts? (This book will tell you.) How can they do what they do? (This book will tell you.) Is there anything they can't do? (See the end of Chapter 1.) What will they do next? (This book won't tell you that, but you'll understand the basis for possibilities.) Computers sometimes appear to "know" and even to "understand," even—or especially—abstract mathematical concepts. How can that be? (You'll learn the computer's view in Chapter 1, and you'll see the implementation from electric wires to algebra problems in Chapter 10.) What—if anything—does it suggest about the basis for our own knowledge and understanding? (That you'll have to answer for yourself, but at least you'll understand one possible partial answer well.) Can a machine think? (Look at the last few exercises in the book.)

Besides sheer curiosity, there are other motives for studying computer science. Computer programming is a useful skill, even if you're not going to be a professional programmer. Of course, you can learn to write programs as a hobbyist without learning much (if anything) about computer science. You need a computer, a programming language implementation, a manual, and some programming examples which you can run and alter and rerun and alter and rerun and alter...; that's a lot of fun, but it's not what this book is about. In fact, if you have gone through that kind of learning process, you probably have a lot to unlearn: the habits you've picked up are likely to be good for small problems, but bad for large problems (or for writing programs which other people will use). If you're going to take programming seriously, then you need to understand the objects of computer science and the operations which work on them, and then you need to understand the way we build large objects and operations out of smaller ones. If your programs are to work with someone else's programs, you both need to agree on a precise description of what those programs do and how much space and time they'll need to do it; you need a common vocabulary for those descriptions, and a "pretty good" description just isn't good enough. Let's put it another way. If you want to make a table for yourself, you can get by with a carpenter's rule and scribbled measurements. If you want to build a house or start manufacturing thousands of tables, you'd better be able to work with a plan, and you'd better understand the concepts underlying the world of that plan—even if sheer curiosity isn't a good enough motive.

The worlds of computer science are mathematical worlds, with differences. First, they're usually much more concrete than most of the worlds which mathematicians create for us. They have to be: these are worlds of "programs" which take "input" and compute for a while before producing "output"; if we can't write the input or the output or even the program as a sequence of letters, digits, or other symbols, then we start to lose interest. (Even if the output controls a robot's motion, the signals must be sequences of symbols.) Second, the worlds of computer science are more dynamic—more interactive—than most mathematical worlds: once you get that program written, it goes by itself and you get to play with it.

Unfortunately, these two remarks could just as well have been put quite differently. First, the worlds of computer science are usually much more rigid than most of the worlds of mathematics: everything must be just so, and not otherwise. If you make a little mistake, you're probably in big trouble, because your program is being interpreted by a dumb machine rather than by a human who'll say "Oh, she meant to say..." Second, the worlds of computer science are less manageable than most mathematical worlds: once you get that program written, it goes by itself and you've lost control.

Both of these points of view are true. One objective of the book is to make program design (and debugging and revision) an easier, more natural, and more intelligible process by helping you to bring a mathematical point of view to concrete problems and the programs which solve them. Mathematics guides the experiments; the experiments provide the structure for the mathematics. Beyond that, the experiments provide the basis for learning the mathematics, because you're learning about computation rather than proof.

First, you need some general ideas about computer science. These are best expressed as pictures, and you'll find them in the Introduction. Then you need a language for precise descriptions of objects and computations—an equational language, extending ordinary algebra in a straightforward way, supplemented with words and pictures. As you learn the language, you learn to compute—with a pencil and paper, no electronic gadgets required. (You can use a "real" programming language at the same time, but you'll have major problems unless you stick to the parts of it which correspond closely to equations; that generally means that you can't write very efficient programs yet.) That's Part 1, on *Equations*. After that, you can look at several kinds of precise descriptions involving different mathematical concepts in Part 2, on *Models*. Part 2 closes with a chapter on proof; if you're ready for it, read it, but it is not required for the later chapters. Finally, Part 3, on *Programs*, shows you how to turn your equations into programs and then use your notions of models to build representations in the programming languages. The examples given are in *Modula-2*; the language structure makes it possible for me to provide "modules" with the book which you can use (without understanding them) at the beginning of Part 3 or even earlier. You can analyze or replace them later on. We'll move steadily down from simple and elegant outlines to the low-level concepts of the machine. At the end, we can go over the concepts and many details of the implementation of a *Modula-2* system... and of a higher level system which "understands" the equations we started with. We end where we began, but—for an ever-increasing range of purposes—we're no longer alone.

*Tom Myers*

# Acknowledgments

I would like to thank the people who helped develop this material from an idea into lecture notes and then into book form. Most of the computer science faculty at the University of Delaware argued about the ideas at their inception; Toni Cohen was probably the most vociferous, at least after Ralph Weischedel went to BBN. Bob Caviness (as chairman) provided a great deal of support for the direction of the course, pushed for summer funding for the initial lecture notes and course-related software, and pushed for an eventual book formulation from the beginning. Dave Saunders and Franz Winkler criticized the early lecture notes; Franz then used (and continued to criticize) them. After major revisions, they were used again—and Sandee Carberry provided more criticism. Graduate students were kept very busy helping to debug the course: Art Smith set up the initial programming environment for the programming parts of it, and Madhu Murthy (and other teaching assistants) did a great deal to make that environment grow. Many of the students worked at checking over the lecture notes as well as providing more immediate feedback: Bill Doerner, Rob Elkins, Doug Latimer, and Jim Morgan were very helpful. (They and many others collected the plastic "Creepy Creature Awards" for mistakes found in the lecture notes.) Finally, I must acknowledge the support—and further criticism—of my new colleagues at Colgate University. Allen Tucker and Tom Brackett in particular have changed my approaches to several issues in the text.

# Introduction

## I.1 GOALS

This introduction is intended to help a potential reader (or instructor) decide what she might be getting into by starting this book, and whether or not that's a good idea. There are three sections (not counting this one):

- *About Computer Science*: what sort of subject you're starting.

- *About Life*: how computer science relates to other things.

- *Notes for the Instructor*: how the subject is to be presented. This part is really an instructor's preface, but even if you're not an instructor—for yourself or anyone else—you may still like to scan it and see what you can get out of it. Among other things, this is the section which examines the contrast between this book and more conventional introductory courses in computer science.

At the end of the introduction (if you're still with me) you'll have mental pictures for the book itself, for the computer, for the program design process, and for the range of topics in computer science. You'll also have a general feeling for what I meant by the title and subtitle of this book.

Even without reading the whole introduction, you can define the goals of the book pretty well. Let's talk about you—specifically, let's go over the *precondition* and *postcondition* for the course. The *precondition* is the situation at the start: your expected background. The *postcondition* is the situation at the end: the intended goal.

### I.1.1  Expected Background

The course is subtitled *A Mathematical Introduction to Computer Science*. As you might expect, the prerequisites are in computing and in mathematics—a little bit of computing and quite a bit of mathematics.

Ideally, you should already have had some elementary programming experience: most likely *BASIC* in high school, but preferably *LOGO* or even *Pascal.* You shouldn't need to be told what a terminal is or how to use one. More important, you should have some feeling for the fact that bugs are hard to find and fix. If you've never seen how picky a computer can be, you may not understand why we work so hard at planning to avoid all mistakes and simultaneously at planning to find all the mistakes that we'll make anyway. Still, if your computing experience is limited to the use of a word processor, you need not despair: you are starting with a handicap but not necessarily a major one. Of course, if you're in a class where everyone else has a lot of experience, you may find yourself falling behind because the discussion relies on examples and vocabulary you're not used to.

The mathematical background I'm expecting is also common in high school. You should already have done a fair amount of careful paper-and-pencil symbolic manipulation: at least algebra and geometry, and preferably trigonometry and analytic geometry. If you have never studied algebra, you will not be able to succeed in this course, because it begins by developing a model of simple programs which is based on your prior understanding of algebra. We are going to plan and describe programs precisely before we implement them; in particular, we will go back over the procedures of elementary-school arithmetic and express them as collections of algebraic rules. What I mean by that is that the first-grader's observation that "to add 7 and 5, I just start at 7 and count up 5 times" can be reexpressed as

$$7 + 5 = 8 + 4 = 9 + 3 = 10 + 2 = 11 + 1 = 12 + 0 = 12$$

which is justified by two algebraic identities: $x + (y+1) = (x+1) + y$ for the first five steps, and $x + 0 = x$ for the last. We'll go over this very slowly and carefully, but if this is the first time you've ever seen such formulas, then you should start with another book before this one. This sort of handicap is not just major: it's almost inevitably fatal.

It is *not* required that you feel happy with mathematics as you've learned it, or that you think that it's fun. Most of the mathematics learned by most of the prospective readers of this book has been a combination of memorization and proof, but neither of these is of great importance in what you'll be seeing here. The approach taken to mathematics in this book is experimental: you'll be learning about the properties of mathematical objects (equations, for the most part) by computing with them to see what happens, and by trying to find analogies between different kinds of objects in order to use one as a representation of another. (For more detailed discussion, look at the *Notes for the Instructor* which end this introduction.) If you happen to remember how to derive

$$x = \frac{-b \pm \sqrt{b^2 - 4ac}}{2a} \quad \text{from} \quad ax^2 + bx + c = 0$$

then I'm proud of you, but you have no need for that knowledge in this course. You will need the beginnings of an understanding of mathematical expressions, which can only partly be supplied within any one book. If you don't have such an understanding, it's worth a lot of effort for you to achieve it; don't give up easily.

Of course, it's possible that you feel quite willing but unable to deal with mathematics; you may have been taught badly, or you may simply need more help than you've been given. Don't give up, and don't think you need to take mathematics courses: there are many books on "math for those who think they hate it," and some of them are very well-written. They go as far as you need to begin this book, and you'll find a selection in any well-stocked library.

## I.1.2  Intended Results

Suppose you finish this book. What will you gain, and what options will open? Some of the intended results will not make sense to you until after you finish. Still, I can describe two kinds of results: you'll learn skills relevant to large-scale programming and project design, and on the other hand you'll learn ways of thinking which have led many people into new ideas about what it means to think, to know, or even to learn.

**Large-scale Programming**    Professional programmers work on programs which are large, which last for a long time, which have to be understood by several (or perhaps by many) people, which have to be used by people who don't understand them, and which go through many versions. Professionals also work on programs which are small but very confusing. Planning and understanding these two kinds of programs is not the same as planning and understanding small, simple programs. Training which is appropriate for either purpose is not necessarily appropriate for the other. Most introductory courses (at the time of this writing) are oriented towards teaching students to write small-scale programs fairly quickly, with little if any time for planning before the programs are to be written; they would have you do more programming than we can do here, but less planning. (For a more careful comparison, see the *Notes for the Instructor* at the end of this introduction; you may not understand everything, but much of the section should make sense.)

You will learn to design and analyze (and revise) programs rather than just write them, and you will learn some of the mathematical material which is basic to specification and analysis. Some of this is only of use to the professional programmer; other parts are relevant to anyone who tries to work with large-scale programming projects in any capacity, and still others are relevant to anyone who thinks about complex projects or structures of any sort.

> Reading maketh a full man, writing an exact man, and conference a ready man.
>
> Francis Bacon, *Of Studies*

Writing programs maketh a much more exact man (or woman) than writing English prose, but writing specifications can carry the idea even further because you can use the ideas you learn in areas far from programming.

If this is where your interest lies, there are many books which might be helpful even at this early stage of development. Some will deserve rereading later, perhaps more than once. Brooks's *Mythical Man-Month*[2] will give you an idea of the joys and dangers of large-project development, and the justification for Brooks's Law: *Adding programmers to a late project makes it later.* Weinberg's *Introduction to General Systems Thinking* [15] is not limited to computer science. If you want to think carefully about the behavior of systems of computer programs, cars, ants, birds, or people, you should have some of the ideas of "general systems theory," and this is a very good starting place. The same author has applied the same kind of thinking—and very readable writing—to the people that you're thinking of joining, in *Psychology of Computer Programming* [16]. There are parts of that which you probably can't make much of yet, but if you skip back and forth between anecdotes and analysis, you should find the experience worthwhile.

**Thinking about Thinking**    Of course, you may not want to be a professional programmer or technical designer of any kind; you may be more interested in philosophy or psychology or religion. If so, you may want to classify computers along with the invention of the printing press, the steam engine, television, the Arabic numbering system, or other technical achievements that changed the fabric of the human world, turning the unimaginable into the routine. Indeed, you might want to learn some of the fundamental concepts of computer science just to keep track of the world around you. I'm not talking about learning specific applications of computers (such as spreadsheets, database programs, the word-processing system with which I'm writing this book, or a hundred other applications that no one's thought of yet). I'm not talking about learning the rudiments of a programming language, either. The world has changed in that large parts of it are becoming more mechanical, and you should have some feeling for what that means.

However, there's a reason that goes beyond that, that applies to none of the historical examples I just gave you but does apply to computer science along with Darwin's theory of evolution, Copernicus's theory that the earth revolves around the sun, and a very small number of other ideas in human history. These are ideas that changed our ideas of ourselves— of our inner nature or of our place in the Universe—in a fundamental way. Computers are different from steam engines or televisions or other traditional "machines": they appear to think, to know, to search for answers, to understand, and even to learn.

Do they, or can they, really think? This book is not going to answer that question, but we will spend a lot of time working mechanically—computationally— with symbolic expressions. You will begin to see how some kinds of "thought" are in effect mechanical. After that, you may want to join those who study how far the mechanization of thought can go. Cognitive science  mixes computer science, psychology, philosophy, logic, and linguistics, and there are many related books which you can read with little or no prior experience of computer science. Pamela McCorduck's *Machines Who Think* [12] gives the viewpoint of a nontechnical person who became deeply involved in these ideas, and several quite readable books have been written by professionals. Douglas Hofstadter's *Gödel, Escher, Bach: An Eternal Golden Braid* [10] won a Pulitzer award for its literary quality—but it's not easy reading. John Haugeland's *Artificial Intelligence: The Very Idea* [9] is easier to get through (but then, it has more limited objectives). Other titles can be found at many bookstores and libraries; go look for them.

**Summary**    The following description of intended results doesn't give you a very concrete list of goals; however, I'll provide one of those too. I suggest that you reread the list of goals occasionally: it will slowly come to make sense.

- To develop your understanding of high school algebra, to the point where you can compute with expressions describing the basic data objects and structures of computer science, not just with numbers. Beyond this, you should be able to experiment with a definition and analyze what its behavior will be.

- To build up your understanding of the idea of a model, to the point where you find it natural to answer a question by translating it into some simpler context, answering the translation, and then retranslating the answer.

- To develop your understanding of a state-space of possible situations, with associated operations, as a natural model of a great variety of problems, and of a state-space search as a natural model of a variety of solutions.

- To give you a feeling for the kinds of mathematics used in developing computational models: the laws of small, large, and medium numbers.

- To extend your ability to work with descriptions into the beginning of an understanding of mathematical proof.

- To use a specification as a guide in program development and debugging, even to the extent of developing many programs as models of the symbolic computation learned in the first part of the book.

## I.2 ABOUT COMPUTER SCIENCE

Before studying computer science, we'd better develop some idea of what it is we'll be studying. There's no one right answer, but there's a great deal to think about, and there are a number of ways to approach the problem.

### I.2.1 Look It Up in the Dictionary

Some people will tell you that a "computer" is an electronic device. They may even quote a dictionary such as the *American Heritage Dictionary of the English Language* [3] and say that a computer is

> A device that computes; especially, an electronic machine that performs high-speed mathematical or logical calculations or that assembles, stores, correlates, or otherwise processes and prints information derived from coded data in accordance with a predetermined program [see].

That's an important definition, and those are certainly important devices, but actually I'm cheating. That was definition (2), coming after definition (1) had explained that a computer is

> A person who computes.

The *Oxford English Dictionary* [4] (1933, compact edition copyright 1971) antedates electronics, and describes a computer as

> One who computes: a calculator, reckoner; spec. a person employed to make calculations in an observatory, in surveying, etc.

It mentions that Browne wrote of *"the Calendars of these computers"* in 1646. The process of computing can be performed by machines (electronic, electromechanical, simply mechanical, hydraulic, optical...) or by people. There were computers before there were electronic devices, there were computers before there was an English language, and there may even have been computers before there were calendars. What, then, does it mean to compute? Quite simply,

> To determine by mathematics, especially by numerical methods.

(That's from *American Heritage* again.) There were no computers before there were mathematical systems in which computational methods could be described.

**Computation Is a Mathematical Concept**   Computer science, for the purposes of this book, has to do with the precise description of abstract objects and of processes which manipulate abstract objects. The physical nature of the machine which carries out these processes is (almost) of no interest whatsoever; what counts is that we develop an image of the computer which we can work with and plan with, and then that the machine behaves in such a way that this image doesn't cause us to make mistakes. To serve that purpose, the image should be a mathematical one.

That doesn't mean that you shouldn't open the box. Opening the box is fine, fun, and highly educational; all computer science students should do it on many occasions, but what you find inside is not "the computer" any more than what you find inside a person's skin is the person. "The computer" would still be the same computer if we replaced all the circuits by some new technology, as long as it behaved in the same way. What's more, if you're going to be a good programmer, your programs had better run well after that new technology comes in; that is, they should be "machine independent." For this to happen, you should have some way of understanding what a program does, independently of how the machine does it. The first part of this book should get you started in that direction.

**Mathematics Is Abstract**    So what does it mean to "determine by mathematics"? What is mathematics? Back to the dictionary: it seems to be

> The study of number, form, arrangement, and associated relationships, using rigorously defined literal, numerical, and operational symbols.

A different slant on the same definition comes from the mathematician and philosopher Bertrand Russell:

> Mathematics may be defined as the subject in which we never know what we are talking about, nor whether what we are saying is true.

To be able to see that $5 + 3 = 3 + 5$, you have to stop asking whether we're counting five ripe apples or five grimy fingers. $5+3 = 3+5$ is an abstract statement, and it holds good no matter what we're talking about. We don't need to know what particular things are involved, or even whether any particular things are involved. "Fiveness" is a property shared by all collections of five things; specifically... well, specifically it's the property that causes you to get to "5" when you count them.

Such abstractions dominate this book, and they are not always easy to learn. "Abstract" does mean "considered apart from concrete existence," but it also means "not easily understood; abstruse." You do have the assurance that you've managed to learn abstractions before, and not only or even primarily the numbers:

> To the child the letter A would seem terribly abstract, so we give him familiar conceptions along with it: "A was an Archer who shot at a frog." This tides over his immediate difficulty; but he cannot make serious progress with word-building so long as Archers, Butchers, Captains, dance round the letters. The letters are abstract, and sooner or later he has to realize it.
>
> Arthur Eddington. *The Nature of The Physical World*, xvi [5]

The child learns A, B, C and 1, 2, 3 by such simple examples of their use; eventually that child learns to deal with $5 + 3$, beginning with examples like five apples plus three apples but later learning to deal with abstract written numbers using rigid rules. That same child later learns to deal with $x + y$, beginning with examples like $5 + 3$ but later learning to deal with abstract written formulas using rigid rules. An important component in dealing with the abstractions is to start from an example; another important component is to keep everything explicitly written. A third important component, conflicting with the second, is to avoid writing details that would just confuse us.

So, what is a computer? How should we imagine its workings so that we don't make (too many) mistakes? For the purpose of this course, we'll use the idea of a (mechanical) moron as indistinguishable from a human, limited in very peculiar ways.

- He sits at a desk in a locked room.

- He gets messages and sends messages through holes in the wall, sometimes called "ports."

  - Some holes communicate with the outside world.
  - Some holes communicate with a file clerk who has a lot of cabinets with plenty of space for folders.

- The desk is for graph paper— one gigantic piece of graph paper. There is a place for every square, and each square is in its place.

- Everything he knows is on that paper: one letter, digit, or other symbol for each square. There are no pictures except for what can be represented by letters and digits, there is no music except for what can be represented by letters and digits, and there are no intuitions or emotions except for what can be represented by letters and digits.

- Even to deal with numbers, he has to be careful: to write 9999999999 takes 10 spaces of graph paper, and if that's all the space he left himself to write down a number in, then 9999999999+1 won't fit, because there's no room for it. That's an "integer overflow" error.

**Abstraction Requires Examples**   We don't want to deal with all the details at once, so we won't yet imagine our hypothetical moron to be as stupid as an electronic device really is. Instead, we'll suppose that he can deal with high-school algebra, to some extent. If you give him the explicit rules that $0 + 1 = 1, 1 + 1 = 2, 1 + 3 = 4$, and so on up to $9 + 1 = 0$ with a carry into the next column to the left, and if you then give him explicit rules for doing the same thing over again, he can count. We can imagine his doing it by actually taking a sheet of scratch paper (one of his pieces of graph paper that isn't being used for anything else at the moment) and writing

$$
\begin{aligned}
[3, 4, 9, 2, 9, 9 + 1] &= [3, 4, 9, 2, 9 + 1, 0] \\
&= [3, 4, 9, 2 + 1, 0, 0] \\
&= [3, 4, 9, 3, 0, 0]
\end{aligned}
$$

Then he would copy 349300 to wherever he was supposed to write 349299+1. (Notice that the rules are not stated on this page; we don't even have a notation in which they could be stated, except to someone who already understood what was going on. One of our tasks is to develop such notations.) If you give him another set of rules, including $9 - 1 = 8, 8 - 1 = 7$, etc., he can probably count down. If you then give him explicit rules such as $(x + 1) + y = x + (y + 1)$, he can now discover that $3 + 3 = 2 + 4 = 1 + 5 = 0 + 6$, and if you remember to give him a rule saying $0 + x = x$ he can finish the sequence, discovering that $3 + 3 = 6$.

If you give him rules that are sufficiently precise, then he will apply them as given to any problem description you give him. The problem doesn't have to be one of arithmetic: once we learn how to make precise descriptions of problems in archaeology and art, botany and beekeeping, $\ldots$, zoology and zymurgy, we can get him to solve those. The only restriction is that the descriptions must be symbolic: he only works on letters and digits. Problems of positions, angles, motions, and emotions can only be given to him to the extent that they can be put into symbolic form. Perhaps there are some problems which cannot ever be expressed in symbols, or perhaps not. For now, one of our major goals is to learn to express rules so precisely that even a mechanical moron can perform some tasks we learned as children (and some tasks that we didn't).

The moron doesn't have to understand the rules, but we do. Of course, there are different levels of understanding. If we are going to describe the multiplication $22 * 19$, we can fill out a table like this one:

| A | 22 | 11 | 5 | 2 | 1 |
|---|----|----|----|----|----|
| B | 19 | 38 | 76 | 152 | 304 |
| C | 0 | 38 | 76 | 0 | 304 |
| D | 0 | 38 | 114 | 114 | 418 |

As you can see, the rows labelled $A$ and $B$ begin with 22 and 19 respectively, and the row labelled $D$ ends with 418, which just happens to be $22 * 19$. It is possible for us to give rules for the process represented by this table:

1. The first item in row $A$ is 22. Each later item is half the one before it (ignoring remainders). Stop when you reach 1.

2. The first item in row $B$ is 19. Each later item is double the one before it. Stop under the 1 in row $A$.

3. Each item in row $C$ is 0 if it's under an even number in $A$. If not, it's a copy of the entry in row $B$ above it.

4. The first item in row $D$ is a copy of the first in row $C$. Each later item comes from adding the previous item in $D$ to the next in $C$. (So $114 = 38 + 76$.)

5. The last item in $D$ is the answer.

This works, and the process works for any positive whole numbers, but even if it didn't a computer would be happy to go through the steps. If you carry out rules like this precisely, without deviation or understanding, then *you* are becoming a computer. We'll spend some time practicing that (with much more precisely stated rules), but our long-range objective is for you to understand the rules and the computer, not to follow the rules or be the computer.

### I.2.2 Nobody Has a Good Definition for "Computer Science"

Or perhaps somebody out there does, but if so, they haven't gotten much agreement from computer scientists. Maybe that's because the subject hasn't existed for long, or maybe there really is no such science. You might think that "computer science" is just the use of computers for solving particular problems, so that there is no single area to be called computer science. If so, perhaps we should teach computer applications in biology, physics, medicine, and so on, each in complete isolation from the rest.

I don't think that's true, mainly because the skills required for developing computer applications in biology and physics often have more in common with each other than they do with the skills required for dealing with other aspects of biology. I do not mean the use of particular programming languages: once you have learned to plan your programs, you can put them into almost any language you want. I'm talking about the process of design.

I'll try to give you some feeling for what computer science is about, using a collection of diagrams.

**The Software Life Cycle**  The figure on the following page illustrates a (slightly simplified) picture of what goes on in constructing a programming project.

In the diagram, program design begins with a description of the problem and of its context: requirements analysis. Here we might say "we want a chess-playing program for an Apple IIe; it can't use more memory than the usual 128K ($128 \times 1024 = 131072$ graph-paper squares, each with one letter or digit); it has to have levels for beginners and experts, with maybe a few in between; it must be profitable selling for less than \$200...". Requirements analysis does mean somewhat different things to different people, but you should have some idea of the flavor of the problems being addressed: we're trying to figure out what sort of program might possibly be worth designing, writing, and selling.

After we agree on what we're talking about, we can work out a specification. This is a blueprint, a very precise description of *what* the program does which never mentions *how* it does it (nor even what programming language is to be used). With requirements in hand, we choose the kinds of objects we'll have in our specification: board positions, pieces, saved games, and precalculated openings as well as disk drives, printers, and pictures. We also have to choose the operations to be provided:

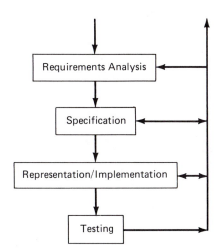

display a piece in a given position, move a piece in accordance with the rules, change the level of play. These operations have to be tied to specific commands, and the exact results must be stated. The specification could be used as a manual, except that it may be too detailed and hard to read for the average user.

With a good specification, we can predict the program's behavior perfectly (except where the specification carefully says "if you try to save a game with no disk in the drive, results are unpredictable.") If two readers of the specification disagree about what the program should do in some situation, then the specification is bad. Try again. Sometimes in writing the specification you can already see that there's something wrong with the requirements analysis; then you take a step backwards and try again.

The program can now be written. "Data structures" are laid out on the moron's graph paper to *represent* the specified objects. "Algorithms"—lists of rules—are described to *implement* the specified operations. If the programmers aren't sure what the moron should do, then the specification was bad: take a step backwards and try again.

From the specification, we write tests for the program to see if it works. Of course, it won't: take a step backwards and try again.

If (by some miracle) everything ends up working correctly, it looks as if we might escape the diagram by the arrow on the upper right. Before we do that, someone will discover a need for a new version of the program. Take several step backwards and several deep breaths, and try again.

Of course, this diagram is too simple to be true to life; the separation of development into stages for requirements, specifications, etc., is an idealization which will be seen differently in different organizations and at different scales of complexity. Nonetheless, something resembling these stages will be needed for all but the smallest projects, and they are worth describing in more detail.

**Process Charts and Data Streams**   I can't give you a helpful diagram of the requirements analysis process, as I've described it. (Well, a sketch of a happy customer handing over money might help.) On the other hand, specifications are often strongly pictorial. Let's look at the "objects" involved in describing a chess-playing program:

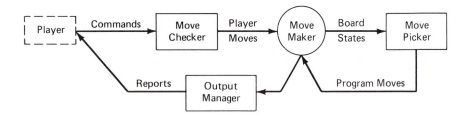

The player is in a dashed-line box: she won't be part of the program, but she provides commands and receives reports. A *MoveChecker* subprogram takes the commands and makes sure that they are acceptable moves in the game, a *MovePicker* subprogram looks over a state of the board and chooses the program's moves, and a *MoveMaker* subprogram actually keeps track of the board. (It's circled because it needs to remember what it did from one move to the next.) The picture doesn't say whether the reports will be in words, symbols, or pictures, nor does it say whether commands will come from a keyboard or a mouse. It just tells us what things are called and how they are connected, just as the following description does:

$$
\begin{aligned}
PlayerMoves &= MoveChecker(Commands); \\
Reports &= OutputManager(BoardStates); \\
BoardStates &= MoveMaker(ProgramMoves, PlayerMoves); \\
ProgramMoves &= MovePicker(BoardStates);
\end{aligned}
$$

That first line says that there are objects (streams of data) called *PlayerMoves* and *Commands*, and that the function of *MoveChecker* is to generate the moves from the commands; it's equivalent to the line in the picture. The picture is certainly easier to read, but it's actually incomplete: did you notice that there's no label on the data stream from *MoveMaker* to *OutputManager*? That kind of mistake is somewhat harder to make when writing equations, while other mistakes are harder with pictures or even words. Pictures, words, and equations are all important; each serves to clarify the others in some respects.

**Abstraction and Representation**    Suppose that we have the specification all worked out, with all the objects and operations defined. How do we get to a program? There is a conventional picture of the programmer's movement from an abstract description to a representation and implementation; it looks like this:

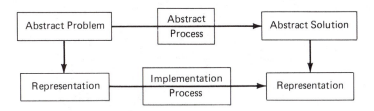

The idea is simple, basic, and extremely important. You're finding a correspondence between two things, so that one can represent another as a map might represent a country or as a verbal description might represent a map. Then when you have a problem of finding your way in the country, you can translate it into a problem of working with the map, or translate that into one of studying the verbal description. A lot of this book's material will fit into that structure, because a lot of what you'll be learning is to develop representations.

Usually, it's just too difficult to represent what you want directly in terms of what you have: you couldn't possibly keep track of chess pieces by direct use of the moron's squares of graph paper. However, you can build up layers of abstraction: you can say how you want to use squares of graph paper to represent numbers, and then you can say how you want to use groups of numbers to represent chess pieces and positions, and how you want to use groups of chess pieces and positions to represent situations in a game, and how you want to use groups of situations and responses to them to represent strategies, and so on. Every computer system is designed as a hierarchy of layers as indicated in the diagram at the top of the following page.

The overall goal may be to have a system of glass, plastic, and metal play chess, but we don't want to think that way any more than we think of teaching tissue and bones to write programs, or of driving a (larger) system of glass, plastic, and metal to work in the morning. Such hierarchies exist in all of nature: a tree is made up of structures like branches and roots, which are made up of layers with fancy Latin names, which are made up of cells, which are made up of molecules. . . . The point should be a familiar one, but computer programmers tend to deal with more layers simultaneously than most people, and the definitions of the layers have to be very precise.

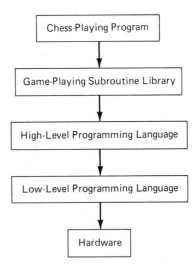

Looking closely, we see that one item in a layer is made up of several items at the next layer down: your body is made of many systems (circulatory, respiratory, etc.), each of which contains many components, each of which contains many cells, each of which contains many parts each containing many molecules and so on. The same idea applies to the structure of a book, a city, a car, or a computer. Even "structures" such as the possible outcomes of a design process or of a chess game are similar: for each choice there are several choices to follow, each of which has several possibilities to follow it, and so on until we reach success or failure. This is represented by a special kind of hierarchy called a *tree*. Ever since Aristotle, a large part of the information available to humanity has been organized this way:

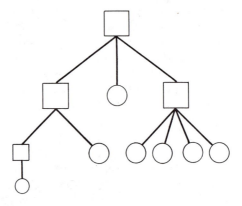

This tree is left empty (with no words in it) for a very good reason: in computer science we use trees to work with so many different kinds of information that we often worry about the trees themselves more than about the information they carry. Other disciplines can have the information; we keep track of the **structure** of the information, keep it organized, and find for them the answers implicit in their input. It is not up to us to check that their ideas make sense.

## I.3  LIFE, THE UNIVERSE, AND EVERYTHING

Of course, the view with which the last section closed is somewhat exaggerated, and I'd better say something here about professional ethics. I'm talking now to my (numerically) primary audience: college students thinking about "majoring" in computer science. This is a very nontechnical subsection, and it won't hurt my feelings if you skip it, but in some ways it may be the most important in the book.

If you become a professional, you'll almost certainly join a society of professionals (such as the Association for Computing Machinery or the Institute for Electrical and Electronic Engineering). Professional societies (like all societies) tend to have codes of conduct for their members, but that's not what I mean. No human society can exist without codes of conduct, but prior to that comes a sense of responsibility for the foreseeable consequences of your own choices. Notice that I didn't say "all consequences of your own actions": you're not responsible for what you can't help or couldn't rationally foresee as a (probable or at least possible) consequence of your decisions. So what choices are we talking about?

### I.3.1  Take a Look Around You

Technical problem solving is important. Your friends in political science are going to be very busy studying the "art of the possible" and your other friends in philosophy will be even busier studying the impossible, but you're thinking of becoming a technical person: one of those who shift things from impossible to possible, as technical people have done ever since one of them figured out how to keep fire going and use it. When you think about fire as the paradigmatic technical advance (hey, where's the dictionary? What's "paradigmatic"?), you may conclude that technical advance is progress and progress is obviously good. That's a very risky assumption. Many people are inclined to think of the nuclear bomb as the paradigmatic technical advance and to conclude that technology is bad. That's a risky assumption, too. Many others will argue that bombs, guns, fire, penicillin, computers, and safety pins are "morally neutral," neither good nor bad. That may well be the riskiest assumption of all: it is likely to lead computer science students, among others, into a "good Nazi" syndrome, a feeling that they are tools rather than people, ready to build anything for anyone who wants to hire them.

### I.3.2  You Will Hurt People

Inevitably, some of your technical decisions will hurt people, in at least two fundamentally different ways.

You might make a thoughtful, careful, conscientious decision based on all the knowledge you could reasonably bring to bear on the problem, and have it go horribly wrong. If you want to go build missile guidance systems for third-world countries because you think that nuclear proliferation is the world's best hope for peace, then I disagree and I'd like to talk to you about it while I teach you about real-time programming. You might bring disaster on us all, but on the other hand you might be right and I certainly don't have any good alternatives in hand. Good luck! Unfortunately, there's another possibility, which is far more likely to bring disaster on any level: you might make a decision based on nothing at all but the convenience of the moment. If you want to go work for whoever pays you best, if you want to solve reasonably interesting technical problems, if you want to live in an area with nice restaurants and with resorts not too far off, and if you just couldn't care less about what you leave behind you, then you're a dangerous lunatic and I really don't want you as a student.

No, I'm not urging you to become a super-liberal or ultra-conservative, I'm not asking you to write to computer scientists (in the Soviet Union or elsewhere) who are victims of human rights violations, and I'm not asking for contributions to the American Civil Liberties Union, Oxfam-America, Amnesty International or even the Association for Computing Machinery. I am asking you to spend some time *now* and more time later thinking about the people whose lives you'll change. I'd like you to read books like Weinberg's *Rethinking Systems Analysis and Design* [17], Florman's *Blaming Technology* [7], and Weizenbaum's *Computer Power and Human Reason* [18]. None of these are beyond you now, and most of them are fun to read. Even more, you might want to read Pirsig's novel, *Zen and the Art of Motorcycle Maintenance* [14]: even if you disagree with the protagonist (after all, he's crazy), you might learn something.

> The Buddha, the Godhead, resides quite as comfortably in the circuits of a digital computer or in the gears of a cycle transmission as he does at the top of a mountain or in the petals of a flower. To think otherwise is to demean the Buddha—which is to demean oneself.
>
> R. Pirsig, *Zen and the Art of Motorcycle Maintenance*

Eventually, you will probably realize the importance of the context in which you work: reading the U.S. Constitution is not a bad idea, and time spent with Locke and Hume and the Federalist Papers is not wasted time. Adam Smith is relevant, and so is Karl Marx.

## Exercises

**I.3-1** Who wrote the books *Worldly Philosophers, Two Cheers for Capitalism*, and *Freedom to Choose*?

**I.3-2** What do they have in common?

### I.3.3  To Think About Ethics, Study Cases

Ethical problems will pop up at various times in your life; one good way to be ready for them is to think about examples that might be somewhat similar. It may worry you that there are no agreed-upon right answers and no algorithms for solving these problems. If that stimulates you to spend some time studying philosophy, theology, or literature, so much the better. Here's an example to start out with.

**The Case:**  Once upon a time, there was a computer club (the FangsALot Club) full of bright, hardworking, deserving young people who wanted to do lots of things with computers. They didn't have much money, and they thought computer software prices were outrageous, so they rarely paid for what they used; it was more fun to copy it, anyway. They didn't think of this as theft: obviously the software companies weren't hurt by someone making a copy, so why worry?

**The Principle:**  the author of a book clearly isn't hurt by your making a copy of it, right? An actor isn't hurt by your watching him without paying for the privilege, right? Baseball players get ridiculous salaries, and it's much more fun to slip into the stadium without paying. The owner of a lawn isn't hurt by your picnicking on it without permission, right? The owner of a car isn't hurt by your borrowing it for a little while, right? It doesn't hurt you if I read your mail, does it? What harm does it do you if I eavesdrop on your conversations? (Hey, speak up, I can hardly hear what you're telling her.)

Obviously, many people sincerely disagree about whether copying software without paying for it is a crime. Perhaps equally obviously, your author doesn't think much of the principle usually given as a justification.

### Exercises

**I.3-3**  Can you think of another justification for copying software without the author's permission? If so, try to apply it to other situations; just how much does it seem to justify?

**I.3-4**  Would art, science, and engineering do better or worse in a society without copyright and patent protection? Justify your answer. (I. e., in either case you must consider what freedom you are granting to whom; what sacrifices you are expecting from whom.)

**I.3-5**  Suppose that a software company sells a program at a particular price and then raises the price because so many copies are pirated that the company is unable to meet its payroll costs. Demand then drops due to the overpricing, and the company goes bankrupt. Are the copiers stealing from the company's investors, from the employees, from the customers who paid for their copies, from the customers who would have paid for copies if the company had survived, or from some combination of these?

**I.3-6**   Suppose that the company does not go bankrupt, but is forced to drop some projects for development of new software. Who has been robbed, and of what?

## I.3.4 Planning Ahead

Some students make very bad choices, right at the beginning, without ever realizing that they were making choices at all. You can't act responsibly without a reasonable effort to foresee consequences, and that means a plan. Here are some suggestions; they're not compulsory, but some students find them helpful.

**Study College Survival Skills (Study Studying)**   You don't have to plan your approach to all your courses, just the ones you want to pass. Remember that all of your classmates were probably among the better students in high school: the competition is stiffer than it was.

1. Make a schedule for your work, play, eating, and even sleeping. Include about three hours of study time for each hour of lecture, or more when in difficulty.

2. Look over the text at the beginning of the course: it probably talks about related books. You should study the table of contents and index. (Won't you feel silly when you find that the assignment you couldn't do was just like an example you didn't read?)

3. Look over (and mark up) the text before, during, and after each class. Draw diagrams of the ideas.

4. Take notes in class, and ask questions; don't assume that everybody else knows what's going on. If it makes you feel better, you can make deals with each other to alternate asking "dumb" questions.

5. Rewrite your notes after each class; organize them so that you'll be able to study from the notes later, and use them to add to a list of probable exam questions, a list of words or phrases to look up in the text or elsewhere, and even a list of books to read.

6. Begin each assignment on the day it is assigned, without waiting for a better explanation. If you don't understand the assignment at all, make a list of questions to ask about it and **ask them**.

7. Use all available consulting hours, with people on the computing center staff, your instructor, your teaching assistant, and the guy down the hall in your dorm who took this course last year.

8. Visit the library frequently to find books which explain things better than this one does.

9. Read a college survival manual.

10. Add to this list.

**Think About the Skills You'll Need**    Programming is not the only skill you need to be a programmer, even if that's all you'll ever be. To work with the machines you'll need math, to deal with people you'll need some communications skills, to deal with the world in general you'll need to learn something about it, and to deal with yourself you'll need to grow a little. (You don't need to grow? You're as grown up as you'll ever be? Then you're already dead, so please stop reading this.)

**You Need to Learn Some Mathematics**    The math you'll need tends to come in three major flavors. If we're going to hang a picture or send up a rocket, we try to describe all we need to know with just a few numbers such as distances, weights, and times. The mathematics of small-number systems, of "organized simplicity," is calculus. A lot of physics is based on it, and you'll need some. If you're going to study whole populations of people or insects or atoms, there are many, many, many numbers in the problem, but you don't really want to know about them individually: no single item makes much of a difference. The mathematics of large-number systems, of "disorganized complexity," is statistics. You'll need some. Finally, if you have a computer or a computer program or a business or a human mind or an ant's thorax or a large molecule to analyze, there may well be many measurements needed to describe what's going on in a system, and each of them individually makes a difference. If the number is really large, you're stuck: it can't be done. If you can reduce it somehow by considering the problem's structure, then you are working in the mathematics of medium-number systems, of "organized complexity," which is discrete mathematics. You need some.

**You Need to Be Able to Write**    Unfortunately, you will soon see many badly written manuals even if you never saw one before. Errors in spelling and grammar are usually just irritating: you can figure out what was intended, although more slowly than otherwise. However, there is almost sure to be some such error which actually conceals an answer you need. Clear writing adds value to your programs: a few toll-free calls for clarification from each user of a program can turn a profit into a loss. Practice writing at whatever level you can manage, in English courses naturally, but also in history and philosophy and wherever else you can find someone to criticize your prose.

**You Need to Know Something about the World**    Computing exists within a world and changes it; parts of that world change computing right back. If you know nothing of history and philosophy and politics, if you know nothing of economics and poetry and sociology, then you won't know why you're doing whatever you do. If you don't want to know why, you're either more or less than human, and I think I know which is more common.

**You Need to Know Something about Yourself**    There are things you will learn only by fencing or running or playing chess or joining a drama group or joining a glee club or painting pictures. Don't leave them out of your plan for your education. Don't leave them out of your life. As the Red Queen instructed Alice: "Speak in French when you can't think of the English for a thing—turn out your toes when you walk—and *remember who you are!*" If you can.

## I.4 NOTES FOR THE INSTRUCTOR

As the title implies, this section is mainly directed at the instructor, but some readers may be their own instructors. I will make as much as possible as widely accessible as I can.

### I.4.1 This Is Not a Conventional Introduction

The technical objective for this book is to prepare students for a program development process in which

1. Programs are designed as sets of modules, each with a visible specification and an invisible implementation.

2. Program specification is both precise and abstract, using formulas and diagrams as well as words.

3. Algorithms and data structures are designed from the specification.

4. Test cases are selected to reflect properties of the specification.

5. Debugging is based on assertions found in the specification.

6. Specifications and their implementations go through versions, with implementations altered frequently and independently, but specifications altered only with great caution after considering other modules which may be affected.

The basis for development is the specification, which may be very close to the first (prototype) version of the program but is not required to be executable. A typical introductory course sequence doesn't lead students toward that kind of thought. In contrast, it teaches by example that

1. A program is a single block in a block-structured procedural language.

2. The only unambiguous description of the program's behavior is the program itself.

3. The control and data structures of the given language are the starting points for "top-down" design.

4. Test cases are selected arbitrarily at the last minute.

5. Debugging is a black art.

6. The program will be thrown away after completion.

Of course, some will object to this description, with phrases like "We teach language-independent problem solving." This normally means that programs are first outlined in a pseudo-code which strongly resembles *Pascal, Algol, Ada, PL/I,* or *Modula-2* but not *Lisp, APL, Prolog,* or *ML.* Pidgin Pascal is no more language independent than Pidgin APL would be; it may well be more useful, but neither is a specification language. The crucial omission in the typical course is specification: there is none, nor do the students learn any language in which specifications could be written.

In Part I of this book, high-school algebra is extended to describe operations on all the elementary data structures of computer science. Proof is not important here; the algebra is used experimentally to guide computations and describe results. In Part II, modeling and problem solving are studied, still without commitment to any particular kind of programming language. Finally, in Part III we develop implementations and representations as directly as possible from the specifications.

The danger of such an approach is that it could easily become too abstract. Students might learn mathematics interspersed with some computer jargon, rather than a mathematical introduction to computer science. I can't deny that risk: if this approach or one like it ever becomes the conventional introduction to computer science, I expect that some schools will in fact go in that direction, which I see as wrong (for computer science departments). However, I see it as a reasonably small risk, one which can be minimized and one which can be justified. In the remainder of this section, I want to talk about minimizing the risk and about justifying it, and then I want to sketch possible courses to be based on this book.

### I.4.2 Mathematics and Experiment

To avoid excessive abstraction in a mathematical introduction, we don't remove the mathematics; instead, we make it concrete. I'll illustrate with a short parable.

Once there were three teachers whose students needed to use and understand the Pythagorean theorem: given any right triangle with sides $a$, $b$, and $c$, the last being the side opposite the right angle, $a^2 + b^2 = c^2$. All of them drew this picture:

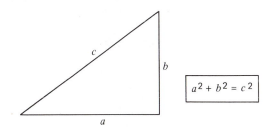

One of the three began by reciting the appropriate geometric axioms, wrote the steps of a proof on the blackboard, stopped for questions at the end of the proof, and then went on to the next subject. The second teacher began by drawing several pictures and then made a clever diagram of triangles and rectangles which could be rearranged to fill up (exactly) either a square of side-length $c$ or the other two squares together; he argued briefly that things filled by the same things were equal to each other and went on to the next subject. The third teacher had her students measure many triangles. She had the class suggest different groupings for them (acute, obtuse, right angled, equilateral, triangles whose height and base are equal, and so on). She asked them to find relationships between the lengths of the sides, the areas of the triangles, and the areas of other figures. After a while, she told them to draw some right triangles and make a table somewhat like this:

| $a$ | $b$ | $c$ | $a+b$ | $a+c$ | $b+c$ | $a/c$ | $b/c$ | $a^2$ | $b^2$ | $c^2$ |
|-----|-----|-----|-------|-------|-------|-------|-------|-------|-------|-------|
| 1 | 1 | 1.4 | 2 | 2.4 | 2.4 | .7 | .7 | 1 | 1 | 1.96 |
| 1 | 2 | 2.3 | 3 | 3.3 | 4.3 | .4 | .9 | 1 | 4 | 5.23 |

After the table had a fairly large number of entries and they had drawn graphs of the results, they found the Pythagorean theorem as one of the consequences. She wanted to present a proof as well, but there wasn't time so she left it for a later course.

The first teacher's students learned the rule, and something about formal proof. They believed that what they had learned was good for them, but they were upset on rereading their notes and finding that the teacher had copied a previous theorem incorrectly; perhaps the Pythagorean rule was wrong, too. The second teacher's students learned the rule, and something about informal proof, but they were equally upset when a particularly obnoxious classmate started showing similar "proofs" from a puzzle book, proving obviously false statements. The third teacher's students learned the rule, and a lot about selecting examples for study and asking reasonable questions about them. It was unfortunate that they didn't learn much about proof, but they did learn how to work with, classify, and think about abstract geometric objects. They used a lot of paper, many thought it was fun, and they were ready to study proof later.[1]

Similarly, if you want to teach students that

$$\sum_{i=1}^{n} = 1 + 2 + \ldots + (n-2) + (n-1) + n = \frac{n(n+1)}{2}$$

[1] At this point I should acknowledge the help of my son Toby, who at age 9 came up with the Pythagorean theorem from guidance like that of the third teacher in my parable. (I knew he would need it for some programs he wanted to write, so I tried to put him in a situation where he couldn't help but discover it.)

then you can certainly use this as an introductory example of an inductive argument, but it's also possible to make another table:

| $n$ | $A = \sum_{i=1}^{n}$ | $A/n$ | $A - n$ | $n^2$ | $n^2 - A$ |
|---|---|---|---|---|---|
| 0 | 0 | – – | 0 | 0 | 0 |
| 1 | 1 | 1 | 0 | 1 | 0 |
| 2 | 3 | 1.5 | 1 | 4 | 1 |
| 3 | 6 | 2 | 3 | 9 | 3 |
| 4 | 10 | 2.5 | 6 | 16 | 6 |
| 5 | 15 | 3 | 10 | 25 | 10 |

One of many observations you can make from this is that $A - n$ is the same as $n^2 - A$, so $A$ is halfway between $n$ and $n^2$, i.e. the formula works. For this example, the pictorial approach is still better: the area of the boxes in

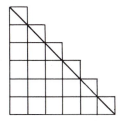

is obviously that of the triangle plus half the area of the diagonal elements, which again confirms the formula. I am not pretending that such experiments and discoveries will take the place of inductive proof; there is a chapter on proof in this book. However, I do believe that they can be used to make mathematics concrete and computational, and that this is one right way (not *the* one right way, but one right way) to approach mathematics in computer science.

### I.4.3  A Tale of Two Schools

Granted that the risk can be brought downwards, and students made less allergic to mathematics; the risk is still not zero. Is it worthwhile? I'll try to answer with another parable. This one is longer.

Once upon a time, there were two academies of bridge-building. The Hard-Knock School of Practical Construction believed that a student should begin by building a bridge, should continue by building bridges, should finish by building bridges, and then would be well prepared for a career spent as a member of bridge-building teams. Members of the LookBeforeYouLeapFromThe Ivory Tower School believed that a student should begin by describing bridges, should continue by working on parts of bridge plans and parts of bridge construction, should finish by developing (but perhaps not constructing) a full bridge plan, and then would be well-prepared for a career spent as a member of bridge-building teams. Representatives of each school could offer good arguments for their philosophies.

The HardKnock School of Practical Construction put entering students into classes where they listened to lectures, then into laboratories where they were issued shovels, hammers, nails, and wooden planks. Each student constructed a small wooden bridge over a ditch. Naturally, the bridges were mostly badly done, but it didn't matter since they were to be thrown away at the end of the semester. The project gave students a strong sense of achievement, of skills acquired and immediately used in a highly visible way. The students were told to plan ahead and were warned that the habit of planning ahead was of enormous importance; they were even required to submit plans for their bridges. Actually, however, with bridges this size, it was easiest to knock together a bridge, tear it apart and put it together again until it seemed all right, and finally write a "plan" for the finished product. In later classes, HardKnock students would construct larger bridges, bridges of different materials, and bridges over different obstacles. As the students reached greater levels of maturity, they were also given lectures on structural analysis, materials analysis, and so on: they were told that professionally built bridges had to be planned very carefully for a long time before construction. Some students who had done well up to here turned out to lack the aptitudes for abstract thinking, and dropped out; others did well. In the end, all the surviving students had a fairly full exposure to the techniques of large-scale bridge-building.

In the Ivory Tower, new students were required to walk around on small and medium-sized bridges, and were taught to describe them and to work with plans for them. Instead of having a completely individual project, each student would join a small group, and the group would be given the task of finishing a small bridge (including a plan) from which some essential parts had been removed by the professor. Some students who would have built wooden bridges very well dropped out immediately. In later classes, students would tackle progressively larger components of progressively larger and more complex bridges (of many kinds); sometimes they would assume the existence of complete plans and would be working only with construction techniques, other times they would assume the existence of a construction team and would work only on the mathematical techniques required for the plans. In the end, all the surviving students had a fairly full exposure to the techniques of large-scale bridge-building.

**HardKnock:** There are many students who cannot cope with much abstraction as freshmen, but whose problem is maturity rather than aptitude. We can keep these students, but they could not have survived the Ivory Tower.

**Ivory Tower:** That's true as far as it goes, *if* they always start as freshmen. On the other hand, a student who has aptitudes (whether for abstract mathematics, art, or zoology) but lacks the maturity to match them, is a student who shouldn't specialize yet. It seems to me you're saying that a freshman who enjoys knocking together a wooden bridge across a ditch should be encouraged to choose a career in which he will never use the same skills or problem-solving approaches, just because he might grow up a little and be able to help build big bridges. I don't like the reasoning.

**HK:** So? I can pack more into a four-year curriculum than you can into a curriculum that can be started by a sophomore. Besides, if you think about students who have only done part of our program and compare them with those who have only done part of yours, I think you'll find that our dropouts are more employable than yours at the end of the sophomore year. They may not be much use in a large-scale or medium-scale project, but they have learned to hack together small bridges that don't require much planning.

**IT:** That's true: a "minor in bridge-building" for your students may be a direct route to a job, all by itself. I think a city planner or an executive in a civil engineering firm would be better served by our first few semesters if she could handle the mathematics, but she wouldn't be able to help much in building actual bridges. The main weakness of your position here is that the kind of thinking your students are required to do is going to change in midstream, and that means that some of your best students of early classes may do quite badly later. We should have more students who drop out early, but fewer who invest years and large chunks of family (or scholarship) money and then drop out in the middle; let's compare statistics some time.

**HK:** Actually, I don't think we do have that many midstream dropouts, because plenty of students who really can't handle the math do go all the way through our program and get good jobs. You're exaggerating the importance of planning in industry. Standards aren't always what they might be, and a lot of bridges will be poorly planned or will have good plans which are poorly used. We tell students how important planning is, maybe we even exaggerate a little, but we don't teach courses in such a way that some students will be forced to drop out when we could teach the same course so that they'll go on to successful careers.

**IT:** Excuse me if I'm being rude, but it sounds as if you're bragging that you get good jobs for students who will build bad bridges.

**HK:** You have to be realistic about these things; we're in the business of training students to be able to get good jobs, and what we produce is what industry wants. As long as our students have plenty of offers, I'm not worried.

**IT:** I am; you're perpetuating a bad situation. First, you're letting some students through who would never make it through our school because they don't have the aptitude for analysis and design. Second, you teach students to see small-project ways of approaching problems as natural, and then you don't really require that they change. That means that some students who would have learned to be good planners in the Ivory Tower will learn to be bad planners at HardKnock.

**HK:** Good planners, bad planners ... look, there's no universal agreement on what constitutes good planning anyway. There are so many different opinions about the right way to set up a job, that if you teach them all, you're really teaching nothing but confusion. What makes you so sure that your methods of planning are the right ones?

**IT:** I'm not sure that our design methods are best; it's perfectly possible that someone, somewhere, is teaching a better design method. I'm sure that our methods are better than no methods at all, and I'm pretty sure that any worthwhile method will be based on the preparation of a collection of documents (blueprints with all their symbols, materials descriptions, parts lists, and so on) which exactly describes what's going on.

**Author's Bias**   It should be obvious by now that this book is being perpetrated by an adherent of the LookBeforeYouLeapFromThe Ivory Tower, and that what has been said about bridge-building is intended to apply just as well to program design and analysis. There are a few differences: our bridges will sometimes change size and shape many times each second in response to changes in traffic loading, water level, wind velocity and so on; our bridges will be moved from river to canyon to underwater locations, and will be expected to keep on working; our bridges will be expected to test themselves for possible collapse, since most of their workings will be invisible. None of these differences, however, seem to make careful planning and description less relevant.

This book is not intended to teach students to be "as good as" the professional programmers of the day. Instead, it is intended to provide basic tools by which they teach themselves to be better.

### The State of the Art of Programming
**Q:** What's wrong with conventional teaching?

**A:** The conventional method of teaching programming, as expressed in most introductory programming textbooks and courses, is that of teaching the student to "think like a computer": to write down what the computer should do first, then to write down what it should do next, and so on. The only really precise description of *what* the program does is the program itself. The basic failure of this method is that although it works well with small problems, it works very badly with large problems. A careful preliminary description of a wooden footbridge is probably a waste of time; it will be easier to use the bridge as its own description and change it as required. A careful description of a single span of a large bridge is essential; if it weighs too much or too little, if it is too flexible or too rigid, if it is smaller or larger than is expected by the team working on the next span over, then the bridge may be dangerously unstable.

**Q:** I suppose I can see that the HardKnock people really ought to require good plans from their advanced students, but what's wrong with having introductory students work without plans?

**A:** There are two problems, both partly expressed in the dialogue above. First, you're giving your introductory students a false impression of what their job should be, and even what aptitudes are needed. They make career decisions based on those false impressions. Later on, they're told that they must develop completely different skills, and some won't be able to do it. That's unfair. Second, we learn from observations by students of human nature from Ovid (a Roman poet who commented that "Nothing is stronger than habit") to B. F. Skinner (principal spokesman for the theory of behaviorism) that it is much easier to teach a bad method than to dislodge it later on. In programming, "We think that [the conventional method of program development] works because it worked for the first program that we wrote. . . . In recent years many programmers have tried to improve their working methods using a variety of software design approaches. However, when they get down to writing executable programs, they revert to the conventional way of thinking." [13]

**Q:** It still seems pretty radical to demand that students be taught how to describe programs before they ever write any. Do you believe it's practical?

**A:** No; six-year-old children are being taught to write simple programs, and I see no point in writing a book to teach them how to describe such programs precisely. Nor is there much point in writing a book at the usual high-school level, although it could be done; most of those students are building footbridges, just for fun, and will never build anything larger. The typical "introductory" student in computer science has already written several programs in an unsystematic way; this has advantages and disadvantages, but in any case it is the situation to which this book is adapted.

### I.4.4 Possible Outlines

The book is divided into three parts. The first three chapters work with a language for explicit program description. The next four cover examples of modeling and problem solving (with the notions of a state-space and of state-space search as central theme). The last three chapters work out techniques for developing programs from specifications.

There are two basic plans for using the full book as primary text for a one-year course. First, it is possible to teach the chapters in order, in which case little conventional programming can be done in the first semester. Some programming in a language which strongly supports recursive equations can be done at any time: the students are learning to work with specifications, and can learn easily that some specifications are executable programs. The crucial point here is that the students are *not* learning programming apart from specification: if it is already necessary to introduce imperative constructs of the language then the wrong language (or the wrong example) is being used. *Scheme* is perhaps the best choice for this kind of programming, since it is suitable for a wide range of later work, but relatively little-known languages such as *ML* and *Hope* or *KRC* are closer to the specification language given, and *Logo* could (somewhat awkwardly) be used. If one of these is used in the first semester, the second semester can introduce a conventional programming language for the last three chapters. In this plan, it would be reasonable to have a first-semester project involving specification (e.g, of a text editor) with a prototype implementation, and a second-semester project implementing the same project.

An alternative plan is to avoid programming altogether until the students have finished the first three chapters, and then skip almost directly to Chapter 8. At this point, the students are ready to implement functions they have specified in Chapter 3, within specified (and almost-completed) modules of a text editor project. In the second semester, these students study the modeling concepts of Chapters 4–7, and then deal with alternative representations in Chapters 9 and 10. Both of these plans (with variations) have been used at the University of Delaware.

A compromise plan is also possible: with *Modula-2*, it is quite possible to use library modules supporting abstract types like SequenceOfInteger and SequenceOf-String with operations just like those used in the specification notation, and have students write programs which at first are just transcriptions of specifications into *Modula* syntax. The first few sections of Chapter 8 can be used to support this. One crucial *caveat*: if you start using assignment statements, iterative constructs, or indeed anything procedural beyond input/output, then your students will not be able to make the connections between the specifications and the programs which they're working with; they don't yet have the tools. As long as their programs correspond directly to equations, they have a simple computation model of the moron with his graph paper using algebraic substitutions. If you add nonequational material prematurely, you'll lose coherence.

# PART I
# EQUATIONS

# 1

# An Algebraic View
# of Computation

## 1.1 EXAMPLES AND MOTIVATION

In the three chapters of Part I, you will be learning to work with precise descriptions of computations and the objects they work on. In Chapter 1, the focus will be on the computational process and the equations which are used for it. You'll learn to analyze expressions, to manipulate them, to use them as programs, and to analyze the behavior—and ultimate limits—of such programs. In Chapter 2, the emphasis will be on testable properties of programs which work on the simple objects of computer science: the cardinal numbers 0, 1, 2, ...; the integers, rationals, and real numbers; the logical values *True* and *False*; characters in an alphabet and "enumerations" such as the days of the week or denominations of coin. All of these form similar patterns which you can use in designing and debugging programs, and the patterns carry over into Chapter 3, where they can be used on sequences of characters, sequences of numbers, sequences of sequences, and other structures such as "bags" and "sets." At the same time, you'll see how each new kind of object can be represented by the old—and vice-versa. At the end, you'll be ready to develop a specification of a word-processing system, a game-playing program, or any program whose underlying concepts you already understand, and you'll also be able to describe the tests which each component must pass. You won't be ready to write the programs, unless you have a programming system which allows an equational style of program development.

Let's expand on that for this chapter. We will be developing an understanding of computation as an activity to be carried out with paper and pencil, or on a blackboard; we will be computing by hand rather than with machines. After studying the chapter, you will be able

1. To analyze mathematical expressions into their parts,

2. To use groups of equations as algorithms,

3. To describe a computation in terms of *invariant assertions*, which are true at every step, and

4. To analyze the space and time requirements of some of these algorithms.

You'll also see one of the fundamental limitations of our programming abilities: a simple-to-describe and highly desirable program which will never be written.

## 1.1.1 A Simple Sample Computation

To begin with, we will think about multiplication. If we know how to count down and how to add a pair of numbers, we can multiply:

| | | | | | | |
|---|---|---|---|---|---|---|
| 1. | $5 * 3$ | $=$ | $5 * 3 + 0$ | $4 * 4$ | $=$ | $4 * 4 + 0$ |
| 2. | | $=$ | $4 * 3 + 3$ | | $=$ | $3 * 4 + 4$ |
| 3. | | $=$ | $3 * 3 + 6$ | | $=$ | $2 * 4 + 8$ |
| 4. | | $=$ | $2 * 3 + 9$ | | $=$ | $1 * 4 + 12$ |
| 5. | | $=$ | $1 * 3 + 12$ | | $=$ | $0 * 4 + 16$ |
| 6. | | $=$ | $0 * 3 + 15$ | | $=$ | $16$ |
| 7. | | $=$ | $15$ | | | |

Can you see what happened? Look at the left-hand problem, in which we find $5 * 3$. The leftmost number (the multiplier) began as 5 but shrank by 1 at each step, the middle number (the multiplicand) was always 3, and the rightmost number (partial result) began at 0 but grew by 3 at each step. There was a beginning step to have a partial result of 0, a final step to state the overall result of 15, and five intermediate steps to bring the 5 down to 0.

Now look at the right-hand problem, $4 * 4$. The multiplier now begins at 4 but shrinks by 1 each time, the multiplicand is fixed, and the partial result again begins at 0 but now grows by 4 each time. How many steps are there? Again we have a beginning step to have a partial result of 0, a final step to state the overall result of 16, and four intermediate steps.

Think what will happen if we use this method on $5000 * 6$: the multiplier will begin at 5000 but then shrink by 1 with each step, the multiplicand will always be 6, and the partial result will begin at 0 but grow by 6 each time. There will be a total of 5002 steps: an initial step, a final step, and 5000 intermediate steps to bring the 5000 down to 0.

## Exercises

**1.1-1**   Apply the method to $3 * 3$; to $5 * 1$; to $1 * 5$.

**1.1-2**   How many steps will be needed for $1000000 * 1$? For $1 * 1000000$? For $1000000 * 1000000$?

### 1.1.2 An Informal Algorithm

There are several ways of formalizing this intuitive process. One is to write out an "algorithm," a step-by-step procedure for applying the method.

1. Let the Addend be 0
2. ——The desired result is Multiplier $*$ Multiplicand$+$Addend
    2.1 If Multiplier is 0, then produce Addend as answer; stop.
    2.2 Add the Multiplicand to the Addend.
    2.3 reduce the Multiplier by 1.
    2.4 repeat from the beginning of step 2.

Make sure that you understand the algorithm description: think about what it tells you to do in order to find $5 * 0$, $0 * 5$, and $4 * 6$.

Notice that the beginning of step 2 is an assertion, not an action. The assertion is true as we begin with Multiplier $= 5$, Multiplicand $= 3$, Addend $= 0$. It continues to be true as we go on with Multiplier $= 4$, Multiplicand $= 3$, Addend $= 3$. It is still true with Multiplier $= 3$, Multiplicand $= 3$, Addend $= 6$; it continues to be unchangingly, *invariantly* true throughout the computation, and will still be true when we have Multiplier $= 0$, Multiplicand $= 3$, Addend $= 15$. There is a sense in which this *invariant assertion* expresses what the procedure is all about, and another sense in which the idea of an invariant expression is what this course is all about.

An equivalent way to describe the same solution is to describe Multiplier, Multiplicand and Addend as sequences of values.

In order to find Multiplier $*$ Multiplicand, we describe the sequences

1.  $a =$ Multiplier, Multiplier $-1$, Multiplier $-2, \ldots 3, 2, 1, 0$. (The sequence has Multiplier $+1$ items, the last being 0).

2.  $b =$ Multiplicand, Multiplicand, $\ldots$ Multiplicand (which is just as long as the first sequence, but all the items in it are the same).

3.  $c = 0$, Multiplicand, Multiplicand $+$ Multiplicand, $\ldots$ which is the same as the sequence $0*$ Multiplicand, $1*$ Multiplicand, $2*$ Multiplicand, $\ldots$ and which is also just as long as the first sequence. The tenth item in it is $9*$ Multiplicand, and the last item in it is Multiplier $*$ Multiplicand which is the answer.

To describe the invariant, it will help to give names to the items in the sequence. The Multiplier sequence is $a = a_1, a_2 \ldots$ so that $a_3$ is the value of the Multiplier after the third step. Similarly, the Multiplicand sequence is $b = b_1, b_2, \ldots$ so that $b_3$ is the value of the Multiplicand after the third step. Finally, the Addend sequence is $c = c_1, c_2, \ldots$ in the same way. If we find the first step $s$ where $a_s = 0$, that's the end of the problem, and $c_s$ is the answer. Meanwhile, the invariant is simply that no matter what $i$ may happen to be, $a_i * b_i + c_i = \text{Multiplier} * \text{Multiplicand}$.

### 1.1.3 An Improved Method for the Same Problem

Of course, it does seem somewhat silly to need so many steps for such simple examples. Perhaps we should say that if we are multiplying $5000 * 6$, we should begin by switching the two numbers; then we have only eight steps needed.

That would work, but what about $5000 * 5000$? Why should that require 5002 steps? We really need a different method. Try this one:

| | | | | | | |
|---|---|---|---|---|---|---|
| 1. | $4 * 4$ | $=$ | $4 * 4 + 0$ | $5 * 3$ | $=$ | $5 * 3 + 0$ |
| 2. | | $=$ | $2 * 8 + 0$ | | $=$ | $2 * 6 + 3$ |
| 3. | | $=$ | $1 * 16 + 0$ | | $=$ | $1 * 12 + 3$ |
| 4. | | $=$ | $0 * 32 + 16$ | | $=$ | $0 * 24 + 15$ |
| 5. | | $=$ | $16$ | | $=$ | $15$ |

What's going on? Look at the left-hand problem: it's really saying that you can solve $4 * 4$ if you can solve $2 * 8$; that you can solve $2 * 8$ if you can solve $1 * 16$, and that you can solve $1 * 16$ if you can solve $0 * 32$. The multiplier is cut in half with each step, the multiplicand is doubled, and the partial result doesn't always change. Similarly, in $5 * 3$ we find that the multiplier is cut in half each time, the multiplicand is doubled, and the partial result doesn't always change. If we wrote this method as an algorithm description, we could have the same invariant assertion as with the other method: at each intermediate stage (or state), we find that $\text{Multiplier} * \text{Multiplicand} + \text{Addend}$ is the desired result. The big difference between the methods is the fact that the Multiplier is shrinking much faster. If we use this method on $5000 * 5000$, the series of multipliers will be 5000, 2500, 1250, 625, 312, 156, 78, 39, 19, 9, 4, 2, 1, 0. That is certainly awkward, but 16 steps is enormously better than 5002 steps, even if each of the 16 steps is harder than any of the 5002 steps.

### Exercises

**1.1-3** Apply the same method to $8 * 9$, $6 * 7$, and $7 * 8$.

**1.1-4** How many steps will be required for $1000000 * 1$? For $1 * 1000000$? For $1000000 * 1000000$?

In fact, this method is quite appropriate for electronic computers. They find it easy to multiply and divide by 2, just as we find it easy to multiply and divide by 10, because they (almost invariably) use base-2 arithmetic just as we use base-10 arithmetic. For a human computer, it is easier to say

| | | | | | | |
|---|---|---|---|---|---|---|
| 1. | $5000 * 5000$ | $=$ | $5000 * 5000 + 0$ | $367 * 249$ | $=$ | $367 * 249 + 0$ |
| 2. | | $=$ | $500 * 50000 + 0$ | | $=$ | $36 * 2490 + 7 * 249$ |
| 3. | | $=$ | $50 * 500000 + 0$ | | $=$ | $3*24900+6*2490$ |
| | | | | | | $+7*249$ |
| 4. | | $=$ | $5 * 5000000 + 0$ | | | |

To find the answer to either of these problems, we must know how to multiply a multidigit number by a single-digit number. For an electronic computer, that does not require much special knowledge because the only single-digit numbers in base-2 arithmetic are 0 and 1. In base 10 it requires steps such as

| | | | |
|---|---|---|---|
| 1. | $7 * 249$ | $=$ | $(7 * 249) * 1 + 0$ |
| 2. | | $=$ | $(7 * 24) * 10 + 7 * 9$ |
| 3. | | $=$ | $(7 * 2) * 100 + 7 * 4 * 10 + 7 * 9$ |

To find the value of this last line, we must know how to (a) multiply a pair of digits, as in $7 * 2$ and $7 * 4$, (b) multiply a number by a power of 10, and (c) add. In elementary school, first you learn (c), then (a), then (b); then you can multiply a long number by a digit, and finally you learn "long multiplication." The details are different because humans use position to indicate the multiplication and division by 10, we memorize the products of any two digits, and we do the addition step by step, carrying along a partial result from each column to the next. Basically, however, the binary and decimal methods are the same.

The first multiplication algorithm was based on the relationship between $n*m$ and $(n + 1) * m$; it led to a very simple approach which was very slow. The second algorithm was based on the relationship between $n * m$ and $(2 * n) * m$; this is more complicated, but leads to a much faster algorithm. There is a principle here which can be applied in many areas: *Try to cut the problem in half with each step.* If we are telling the moron how to look up "Smith, John" in a telephone book of 1000000 entries, we can have him look at the first name (which leaves 999999 to go), then the second (which leaves 999998), and so on; at the tenth step he will have 999990 names left to go. Think of this as a sequence of telephone books, each of which is smaller than the one before by one name. As an improved algorithm, we can point out that the telephone book is in alphabetical order. Thus, if the *middle* entry (not the first) is "Smith, John" then stop; otherwise cut the problem in half. If the middle entry comes before him, then throw away everything before it. If the middle entry comes after him, then throw away everything after it. In either case, the next telephone book in the series is half the size of the current one. Repeat this cutting in half until you find "Smith, John" or the whole book is on the floor.

Again, we see the series 1000000, 500000, 250000, 125000, ... which comes down to 0 quite quickly.

### 1.1.4 Algorithms and Algebra

How can we justify such methods? How can we discover new methods? How can we know that two methods will produce the same result? How can we estimate how long a given method will take and how much space (scratch paper) it will require? Each of those questions can be answered in many ways, but the answer of this chapter is "through algebraic manipulation." We will begin with the algebra of numbers merely because it's familiar; then we will work on the algebra of truth and falsity (Boolean algebra), and then on the algebras of sequences, sets, relations, and even expressions. In each case, we will be working on ways to write explicit expressions which can (we hope) be used to justify our programming techniques.

For example, let us justify each step of the simple multiplication $5 * 3$, by writing an appropriate general rule to the right of the step.

| | | | | | | |
|---|---|---|---|---|---|---|
| 1. | $5 * 3$ | $=$ | $5 * 3 + 0$ | $n * m$ | $=$ | $n * m + 0$ |
| 2. | | $=$ | $4 * 3 + 3$ | $(n + 1) * m + a$ | $=$ | $n * m + (m + a)$ |
| 3. | | $=$ | $3 * 3 + 6$ | $(n + 1) * m + a$ | $=$ | $n * m + (m + a)$ |
| 4. | | $=$ | $2 * 3 + 9$ | $(n + 1) * m + a$ | $=$ | $n * m + (m + a)$ |
| 5. | | $=$ | $1 * 3 + 12$ | $(n + 1) * m + a$ | $=$ | $n * m + (m + a)$ |
| 6. | | $=$ | $0 * 3 + 15$ | $(n + 1) * m + a$ | $=$ | $n * m + (m + a)$ |
| 7. | | $=$ | $15$ | $0 * m + a$ | $=$ | $a$ |

IF you find the rules obvious,
  THEN much of this chapter will be review for you
  AND much of the rest will be pretty easy; congratulations.

IF you don't really see that they have anything to do with the problem,
  THEN you may have serious difficulty with this book;
  AND perhaps you should work on a review of elementary algebra first.

IF you see the resemblance between left and right (you realize that
  $2 * 3 + 9 = 1 * 3 + 12$ does "match" $(n + 1) * m + a = n * m + (m + a)$,
  but it wouldn't match $0 * m + a = a$ at all),
AND you don't really think you could have come up with the rules or
  used them comfortably yourself,
THEN you're ready for this chapter, and you need it.

**Exercises**   Match the rules with the steps.(I.e., fill in the appropriate letter in each blank space.)

$$
\begin{aligned}
(a) && n * m &= n * m + 0 \\
(b) && (2n) * m + a &= n * (2m) + a \\
(c) && (2n + 1) * m + a &= n * (2m) + (m + a) \\
(d) && 0 * m + a &= a
\end{aligned}
$$

**1.1-5**

$$
\begin{aligned}
1. \quad 4 * 1 &= 4 * 1 + 0 \quad && 1.\underline{\qquad} \\
2. \quad &= 2 * 2 + 0 \quad && 2.\underline{\qquad} \\
3. \quad &= 1 * 4 + 0 \quad && 3.\underline{\qquad} \\
4. \quad &= 0 * 8 + 4 \quad && 4.\underline{\qquad} \\
5. \quad &= 4 \quad && 5.\underline{\qquad}
\end{aligned}
$$

**1.1-6**

$$
\begin{aligned}
1. \quad 18 * 7 &= 18 * 7 + 0 \quad && 1.\underline{\qquad} \\
2. \quad &= 9 * 14 + 0 \quad && 2.\underline{\qquad} \\
3. \quad &= 4 * 28 + 14 \quad && 3.\underline{\qquad} \\
4. \quad &= 2 * 56 + 14 \quad && 4.\underline{\qquad} \\
5. \quad &= 1 * 112 + 14 \quad && 5.\underline{\qquad} \\
6. \quad &= 0 * 112 + 126 \quad && 6.\underline{\qquad}
\end{aligned}
$$

## 1.2 EXPRESSIONS AND RULES HAVE STRUCTURE

Throughout this course, we will be dealing with expressions, with the rules which work on them, and with the expressions that make up those rules. In order to make this work, we will have to study the components of rules and expressions and learn how those components fit together.

### 1.2.1 Expressions Can Be Simple
###       or Composite

Before we can talk intelligently about $x * y = x * y + 0$, we must first be able to deal with its parts: the expressions $x * y$ and $x * y + 0$. Here, as in most of computer science, we deal with the problem by distinguishing simple cases from composite ones. 573 is a simple expression, as is $x$, as is 3.14159; $x * y$ is a composite expression, a product built from the simple expressions $x$ and $y$; $n + 1$ is a composite expression, a sum built from the simple expressions $n$ and 1; and $x * y + x * z$ is a composite expression, a sum built from the composite expressions $x * y$ and $x * z$.

Thus far, a simple expression is either a name or a number, and a composite expression is either a sum or a product of two expressions. We are not yet going to define "name" or "number," except to say that "name" is a name, and "number" is a name, and 537 is a number, as is 3.14159. Sometimes in this course we will use names which themselves seem to be structures.

For example, if we want to describe a point $p$ as a position $(x, y)$ on a grid, we may simply treat $p_x$ and $p_y$ as distinct names for the horizontal and vertical distances; in programming languages such composite names are usually written $p.x$

and $p.y$, so we don't have to worry about printing (or typing) small letters below the line. Similarly, if we want to describe a sequence $S$ of 8 numbers, we may talk about the eight distinct names $S_1, S_2, \ldots S_8$ (or $S[1], S[2], \ldots S[8]$), each of which is a name for a number. For now, however, we will just deal with simple names as simple expressions which may form parts of other expressions.

**Exercises** For each simple expression, say which kind of simple expression it is; for each composite expression, say which kind of expression it is and what expressions (simple or composite) it is made from:

**1.2-1** 700092

**1.2-2** $z * 3$

**1.2-3** $95 + 44$

**1.2-4** $73 * x + y * 5$

We can extend our list of expressions by including quotients and differences as well. Thus, $3 - x$ and $99/6 + 17 * y$ are expressions. Including these operations makes little difference; if we call $*, +, -$, and $/$ "infix operators" we can just say that "a composite expression is a pair of expressions with an infix operator written in between." A more important extension comes when we notice that we can't tell which are the components of $1 + 2 + 3 + 4$; is it made from 1 and $2 + 3 + 4$, or from $1 + 2$ and $3 + 4$, or from $1 + 2 + 3$ and 4? For addition, of course, it doesn't make much difference, but it makes a lot of difference when we have to say what $12/3 * 2$ is supposed to mean: is it the quotient of 12 and $3 * 2$, or the product of $12/3$ and 2? It is always safer to put in parentheses: we really want $(12/3) * 2$ or $12/(3 * 2)$. If the parentheses are omitted, it's usual to "associate to the left," which means that we read $12/3 * 2$ as if it were $(12/3) * 2$ and we read $5 * 3 * 7 * 6$ as if it were $((5 * 3) * 7) * 6$. Now let's look at the definition again:

> **A composite expression is either a pair of expressions with an infix operator between them, or it is an expression with parentheses around it.**

## 1.2.2 Diagrams Help Keep Track of Composite Expressions

Now we can say that $12/(3 * 2)$ is a composite expression, a quotient whose components are the simple expression (number) 12 and the composite expression $(3 * 2)$. $(3 * 2)$ is a parenthesized expression whose sole component is the composite expression $3 * 2$. $3 * 2$ is a composite expression, a product whose components are the simple expressions 3 and 2. Got it? This is a complete breakdown of the original expression $12/(3 * 2)$. It may help to draw a simplified picture of the structure; try to see which of the diagrams in Figure 1.1 is correct before going on.

These pictures are called "abstract syntax trees." The logical structure that was implicit in $12/(3 * 2)$ because we knew the grammar is explicitly shown in the

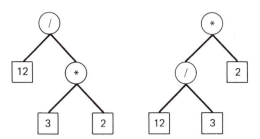

**Figure 1.1** Abstract Syntax Trees for Simple Arithmetic Expressions

picture on the left. The parentheses are no longer needed, because the structure of $(12/3) * 2$ is that of the picture on the right.

**Q:** If that's an abstract syntax tree, what's a concrete syntax tree?
**A:** That would be a "full parse tree", one which identifies all the concepts employed in analyzing the expression. The full parse tree of the same expression is in Figure 1.2.

You can read this tree as a collection of assertions, from bottom to top. 12 is a number, so it is a simple expression, so it is an expression; the same applies to 3 and to 2, while / and * are infix operators. $3 * 2$ is therefore an expression followed by an infix operator followed by an expression, so it is a composite expression, so it is an expression. $(3 * 2)$ is therefore an expression between parentheses, so it is a composite expression, so it is an expression; $12/(3 * 2)$ is therefore a pair of expressions separated by an infix operator, so it is a composite expression, so it is an expression. (Whew!!)

**Exercises**

**1.2-5**    Give abstract syntax trees for
    **(a)**   $12 * (3 + 4)$      **(b)**   $(5 - x) * (y + 3)$      **(c)**   $1 + 2 + 3 + 4 + 5$
    Remember to associate to the left.
**1.2-6**    For the expression $x + 1$, give
    **(a)**    an abstract syntax tree   **(b)**    a full parse tree.

**Q:** What about an expression like $x + 2 * y$? Are we really supposed to read that as $(x+2)*y$? I thought that we were supposed to do multiplication and division before addition or subtraction.
    **A:** Yes; $1 * 2 * 3 + 4 - 5 + 6 * 7/8/9 + 10 + 11 * 12$ is grouped as $(1 * 2 * 3) + 4 - 5 + (6 * 7/8/9) + 10 + (11 * 12)$. Within groups, it is associated to the left to get

$$(((((((1 * 2) * 3) + 4) - 5) + (((6 * 7)/8)/9)) + 10) + (11 * 12).$$

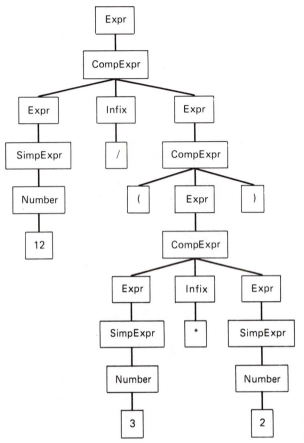

**Figure 1.2**  Full Parse Tree for a Simple Arithmetic Expression

That's called *precedence*: multiplication and division have higher precedence than addition and subtraction.

**Exercise**

**1.2-7**  Write an abstract syntax tree for $1 * 2 * 3 + 4 - 5 + 6 * 7/8/9 + 10 + 11 * 12$.

### 1.2.3 Named Functions Can Also Build Expressions

It seems that we have now re-created the familiar language of algebra. Is it complete yet? Not quite; the familiar collection of infix operators is not enough. For suppose we are writing a program which finds the area of a triangle, half the product of the base and height. Then we would need to give the operation a name and a rule, something like

$$TriangleArea(base, height) = (base * height)/2$$

Suppose again we are writing a program which finds one of the roots of a quadratic equation $Ax**2 + Bx + C = 0$. Then we would need to give the operation a name and a rule, something like

$$QuadRoot(A, B, C) = ((0 - B) + SqrRt(B * B - 4 * A * C))/2 * A$$

To be able to talk about $SqrRt(n)$, $TriangleArea(x, y)$, or $QuadRoot(x, y, z)$, we have to accept them as expressions too; $SqrRt$, $TriangleArea$, and $QuadRoot$ are just names, but the full expressions here also include a list of "arguments," which are expressions. These functions are called *prefix* functions because they are fixed in front of their arguments just as the infix operators are fixed in between their arguments. For prefix functions, the arguments are separated by commas and the list is surrounded by parentheses.

**Q:** How would you draw trees for those?
**A:** For an abstract syntax tree (which is all we generally want), it's really pretty much like the trees for expressions with infix operators, as you see in Figure 1.3.

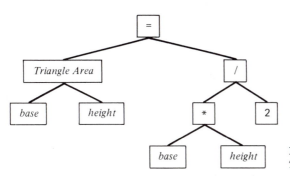

**Figure 1.3** Abstract Syntax Tree for *TriangleArea* definition

I've used rectangular boxes for all the positions, or *nodes*, in the tree just to blur the distinctions between names, numbers, and the infix operator symbols. In fact, looking at the abstract syntax tree won't tell you whether $*$ is an infix function, or just a function of two arguments used in the form $*(base, height)$. Every abstract syntax tree corresponds directly to a prefix expression. Thus the abstract syntax tree for $(base * height)/2$ can be written in prefix form as $Quotient(Product(base, height), 2)$, or even as $/(*(base, height), 2)$. The *TriangleArea* definition above could have been written as

$$= (TriangleArea(base, height), /(*(base, height), 2))$$

although we would usually leave the "=" as infix and write

$$TriangleArea(base, height) = /(*(base, height), 2))$$

Since any tree can be written as a prefix formula, we can even do it with a full parse tree. Let me abbreviate *Expr, CompExpr, SimpExpr, Infix* and *Number* as *E, C, S, I* and *N* respectively. Thus, we can now abbreviate the full parse tree for $3 * 2$ as $E(C(E(S(N(3))), I(*), E(S(N(2))))))$. This is even worse than the tree itself, but studying it may give you a feeling for formulas as relating to trees.

**Exercises**

**1.2-8**    Write an abstract syntax tree for $x + h(x, y, z * w + 3) = 17$ as a picture.

**1.2-9**    Rewrite your solution as a prefix formula.

Let's summarize:

An expression is
     a simple expression, or
     a composite expression.

A simple expression is
     a name, or
     a number.

A composite expression is
     a pair of expressions separated by an infix operator, or
     an expression surrounded by parentheses, or
     a function name followed by an argument list.

An argument list is
     a left parenthesis, and
     a series of expressions separated by commas, and
     a right parenthesis.

Now we can definitely say that "this is an expression" is a lie, at least in our current context: we have no rule allowing such a construction, and no way to build a parse tree. On the other hand, $IsAnExpr(this)$ actually *is* an expression, even though we have no rule to say what it means: "this" is a name, which is a simple expression, which is an expression; therefore, "(this)" is an argument list. And "IsAnExpr" is a name, so we know that the whole thing is a composite expression made from the simple expression "this".

**Exercises**    Give full parse trees for

**1.2-10** $SqrRt(x * x)$

**1.2-11** $TriangleArea(54, zip - zap)$

There is a useful mathematical shorthand for these descriptions of expressions. Look at the rules which follow, and try to make sense of them before going on.

$$
\begin{array}{rcl}
Exp & ::= & CompExp \mid SimpExp \ ; \\
CompExp & ::= & Exp\ InfixOp\ Exp \mid \text{``(''}\ Exp\ \text{``)''}\ ; \\
SimpExp & ::= & Name \mid Number \ ; \\
InfixOp & ::= & \text{``*''} \mid \text{``+''} \mid \text{``-''} \mid \text{``/''} \mid \ldots \ ; \\
Name & ::= & \textbf{``John''} \mid \textbf{``f''} \mid \textbf{``x''} \mid \textbf{``phooey''} \mid \ldots \ ; \\
Number & ::= & 3.5 \mid 99997 \mid -523.973 \mid 0 \mid \ldots \ ;
\end{array}
$$

The first three rules are fully formal; the last three are lists of examples. In either case, you read the vertical bar as "or" because it separates alternatives. You can read the first rule as "An *Exp* is either a *CompExp* or a *SimpExp*" and the second as "A *CompExp* is either an *Exp* followed by an *InfixOp* followed by an *Exp*, or ...." Sound familiar? We will not make heavy use of this notation for some time, but it is the standard notation for describing programming languages—the BNF (for *Backus-Naur Form*) grammatical notation.

**Q:** But you didn't add any rules for prefix formulas. Can you do that?

**A:** Yes; it's just necessary to extend the rule for *CompExp* with one more alternative, and then to add rules to define the alternative:

$$
\begin{array}{rcl}
CompExp & ::= & Exp\ InfixOp\ Exp \mid \text{``(''}\ Exp\ \text{``)''} \mid Name\ ArgList\ ; \\
ArgList & ::= & \text{``()''} \mid \text{``(''}\ ExpSeq\ \text{``)''}\ ; \\
ExpSeq & ::= & Exp \mid Exp\ \text{``,''}\ ExpSeq\ ;
\end{array}
$$

**Exercises**

**1.2-12** Find out about John Backus and Peter Naur. How does an idea like BNF come into existence?

**1.2-13** Write a full parse tree for $f(x, g(a, b, x))$.

The same idea can be used for (partial) descriptions of English:

| | | |
|---|---|---|
| *Sentence* | ::= | *NP Verb NP* \| *NP Verb*; |
| *NP* | ::= | *Article AdjP* \| *AdjP*; |
| *AdjP* | ::= | *Adjective AdjP* \| *Noun* ; |
| *Article* | ::= | **"THE"** \| **"A"** \| **"AN"** ; |
| *Adjective* | ::= | **"BIG"** \| **"LITTLE"** \| **"COWARDLY"** ; |
| *Noun* | ::= | **"LION"** \| **"TOE"** \| **"TOTO"** ; |
| *Verb* | ::= | **"JUMPED"** \| **"HIT"** \| **"BIT"** ; |

According to this grammar, **TOTO** is a *Noun*, so it must also be an *AdjP*, and since **LITTLE** is an *Adjective* we see that **LITTLE TOTO** is also an *AdjP* and therefore is an *NP*. Similarly, **THE BIG COWARDLY LION** is an *NP*, so **LITTLE TOTO BIT THE BIG COWARDLY LION** is a *Sentence* and so is **THE BIG COWARDLY LITTLE TOE JUMPED** (There is nothing in the grammar to require that sentences be sensible.)

**Exercises**    Which of the four sentences which follow are *Sentences*? Justify your claims.

**1.2-14 THE LION HIT**

**1.2-15 AN BIG BIG BIG BIG BIG TOE BIT**

**1.2-16 THE LION JUMPS**

**1.2-17 A COWARDLY LITTLE LION HIT A LITTLE BIG TOE**

**1.2-18** Draw a full parse tree of **THE COWARDLY TOE JUMPED**.

Now that we have a more or less adequate notion of how to break an expression into pieces, the next problem is to think about the meaning of an expression, as found through rules.

### 1.2.4 Rules Are Made From Expressions

A rule is a pair of expressions connected with an "=" sign; it is a *valid* rule if the two expressions are always equal, and an *invalid* rule otherwise. For example, $3 + 4 = 7$ is always *True*, so the rule is valid; so is $9 + 8 = SqrRt(289)$. On the other hand, $0 = 1$ is always *False*; we don't want it around. Rules with variables could be always *True*, like $x = x$; that's a valid rule. They could be always *False*, like $x = x + 1$, which is invalid. Finally, they could be sometimes *True* and sometimes *False*, like $x = y$; that is an invalid rule also.

**Exercises**    State which rules are valid and which are invalid; explain briefly.

**1.2-19** $SqrRt(5 * 5) = 5$

**1.2-20**  $3 + 4 = 2 * 3$

**1.2-21**  $7 + 9 = 4 * 4$

**1.2-22**  $(x + 9)/4 = x/4 + 2$

**1.2-23**  $((2 * n + 3) * (2 + 3) + 9)/2 = 5 * n + 12$

Of course, a rule can be valid and still be quite useless; it is hard to imagine wanting to use $9 + 8 = SqrRt(289)$ as a rule, and even $SqrRt(289) = 17$ is not something that you want to know every day of your life. A useful rule should be applicable to many cases, like the rule of commutativity $x + y = y + x$ which tells us that $3 + 4 = 4 + 3$, but also tells us that $SqrRt(289) + x = x + SqrRt(289)$ and even that $SqrRt((x + 1) * (1 + x)) = SqrRt((x + 1) * (x + 1))$. (Of course, then we need another rule to tell us that $SqrRt((x + 1) * (x + 1)) = (x + 1)$.) Our next problem is to learn just how to tell when a rule is applicable and how to interpret its result.

## 1.3  RULES WORK THROUGH SUBSTITUTION

How do we deduce that $3 + 4 = 4 + 3$ follows from the general rule $x + y = y + x$? We *substitute* values (numbers) for the variables (names) in the general rule: 3 for x and 4 for y. What we are saying is simply that if $x + y = y + x$ is *always* true, it must be true even when $x = 3$ and $y = 4$. The expression $3 + 4 = 4 + 3$ is called an *instance*, or more specifically a *substitution instance*, of the law. In this section, we will be working on finding instances of laws or recognizing them when they are given.

### Exercises

**1.3-1**    Substitute 9 for $x$, 7 for $y$, and 3 for $z$ in
  (a)  $x + y = y + x$          (b)  $x + 0 = x$          (c)  $x + (y + z) = (x + y) + z$

**1.3-2**    What must you substitute for $x$ and $y$ to verify that
  (a)  $3 + 5 = 5 + 3$          (b)  $9 + 0 = 0 + 9$
  are instances of the commutative law?

A substitution pattern like $\{x = 3, y = 4\}$ defines the values of variables; it is called a *state* or an *environment*, and it is one of the fundamental concepts of computer science.

### 1.3.1  We Can Substitute Expressions
for Variables

In these examples, we've been substituting numbers for the variables. That's usually the way it works: if we had a rule that said $x + 0 = x$, we certainly would **not** want to argue that $3 + 5 = 3$ by substituting 3 for $x$ and 5 for 0; we're not allowed to substitute for numbers at all. Of course, we're not limited to substituting numbers.

What if $x = (a + b), y = b, z = SqrRt(a)$? In that case, the commutative law tells us that $(a + b) + b = b + (a + b)$, and the associative law tells us that $(a + b) + (b + SqrRt(a)) = ((a + b) + b) + SqrRt(a)$.

## Exercises

**1.3-3**   Substitute $(3 * a)$ for $x$, $(a * 3)$ for $y$, and $(a * a)$ for $z$ in
    **(a)**   the associative law   **(b)**   the commutative law

**1.3-4**   What must you substitute for x, y, and z to verify that
$$(a * b) + (SqrRt(a) + (c * c)) = ((a * b) + SqrRt(a)) + (c * c)$$
is an instance of the associative law?

## 1.3.2 We Can Substitute Expressions
##       for Expressions

We have been substituting expressions for variables in a rule, and that's always safe: the whole idea of having a rule like $x + 0 = x$ is that it works no matter what you substitute for $x$, so of course $5 + 0 = 5$. Another way of looking at it is that the rule tells us that we can substitute $x$ for any instance of $x + 0$ that we happen to see. This way of looking at it lets us see that $5 * (x + 0) = 5 * x$. Similarly, the commutative law tells us that $a + (b + c) = a + (c + b)$ by substitution of $b$ for $x$ and $c$ for $y$, just as it tells us that $a + (b + c) = (b + c) + a$ by substitution of $a$ for $x$ and $(b + c)$ for $y$.

As a matter of terminology, we will say that IF we notice that part of an expression is an instance of the left-hand side of a rule, AND we then choose to replace that part with the corresponding instance of the right-hand side, THEN this is one **direct use** of that rule on the expression. We can use the rule $x + 0 = x$ in two ways on $(5 + 0) * 3 + 0$: we could use it on the inner addition to get $5 * 3 + 0$, or on the outer addition to get $(5 + 0) * 3$. These are two different direct uses, with different instantiations of the left-hand side of the rule.

Again, given the expression $3 + SqrRt(a + 7)$, the commutative law has two direct uses: it can generate $3 + SqrRt(7 + a)$, or it can generate $SqrRt(a + 7) + 3$. From either of those direct uses, we can get back where we started or go on—as an **indirect use** of commutativity—to $SqrRt(7 + a) + 3$. That makes four possibilities, as you see in Figure 1.4.

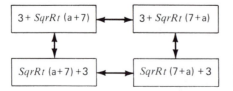

Figure 1.4   Substitution with Commutativity

There is a seemingly trivial but actually quite fundamental point to see in this diagram: the commutative law will take us along any side of this rectangle, but it will *not* take us directly along a diagonal. There are only two direct uses of the law on the original expression.

## Exercises

**1.3-5**   List all the direct uses of the commutative law on
   **(a)**   $3 + (7 + 5)$      **(b)**   $(a + b) + (b + c)$      **(c)**   $SqrRt(5 + 8)$
**1.3-6**   List one direct use of the commutative law for each of the results from the previous problem, on
   **(a)**   Part a      **(b)**   Part b      **(c)**   Part c

What does it mean, then, to use a law $A = B$ on an expression $C$? For example, what does it mean to use $x * 1 = x$ on $((5 * 1) + 1) * 1$, to simplify it into $(5 + 1) * 1$ or into $(5 * 1) + 1$? In this case, $A = x * 1$, $B = x$, and $C = ((5 * 1) + 1) * 1$.

1. We start by finding an instance of $A$ within $C$; call it $D$. In this case, we are looking for an instance of $x * 1$, and we find one: $5 * 1$ comes from $x * 1$ by $\{x = 5\}$, so $D = 5 * 1$ is all right.

2. Next, we apply the same substitution $\{x = 5\}$ to $B$, creating a new expression; call it $E$. In this case, substituting 5 for $x$ in the expression $x$ just produces 5. Since the same substitution was applied, we know that $D = E$ is an instance of the valid rule $A = B$, so $D = E$ (which is $5 * 1 = 5$) must be true.

3. Go back to the original expression $C$ which contained $D$. Since $D = E$, we can replace $D$ with $E$, constructing a simplified version of $C$ which we can call $F$: the final result, $(5 + 1) * 1$.

## Exercise

**1.3-7**   Draw abstract syntax trees for $A, B, C, D, E$, and $F$.

The abstract syntax trees should help you see what's going on. Draw them on separate transparent sheets of plastic (or pretend that you've done so). Slide the sheet with $A$ around on the sheet with $C$. If you've drawn your trees to the same scale, you should find that $A$ fits neatly on top of $D$. In fact, they are the same except that where $A$ has $x$, $D$ has 5. Now slide $B$ over on top of $E$. They are the same, except that $E$ has 5 where $B$ has $x$. Finally, put $C$ on top of $F$. Again they are the same, except that $C$ has $D$ where $F$ has $E$. You will find that these relationships are always true.

As another example, we'll apply the associative law $(x + y) * z = (x * z + y * z)$ to the expression $(2 * n + 1) * m + a$. Here, $A = (x + y) * z$, $B = (x * z + y * z)$, and $C$ is the expression.

1. We start by finding an instance of $A$ within $C$; call it $D$. In this case, we are looking for an instance of $(x + y) * z$, and we find one: $(2 * n + 1) * m$ comes from it by the substitution $\{x = 2 * n, y = 1, z = m\}$.

2. Next, we apply the same substitution to $B$, creating $E$. In this case, the result is $(2 * n) * m + 1 * m$. Again, $D = E$ is an instance of the valid rule $A = B$, so $D = E$ must be true.

3. Go back to the original expression $C$ which contained $D$. Since $D = E$, we can replace $D$ with $E$, constructing a simplified version of $C$ which we can call $F$: the final result of this application, in this case $((2 * n) * m + 1 * m) + a$.

### Exercise

**1.3-8**   Draw abstract syntax trees for $A, B, C, D, E$, and $F$.

Let's try another example: we'll apply the commutative law $x + y = y + x$ to the associative law, phrased as $(u + (v + w)) = ((u + v) + w)$. Here, $A = x + y$, $B = y + x$, and $C = (u + (v + w)) = ((u + v) + w)$.

1. We start by finding an instance of $A$ within $C$; call it $D$. We find that $u+(v+w)$ comes from $x + y$ by the substitution $\{x = u, y = (v + w)\}$.

2. Next, we apply the same substitution to $B$, creating $E$, which in this case is $(v + w) + u$. As always, $D = E$ is a substitution instance of $A = B$.

3. Finally, we go back to the original expression $C$ and replace $D$ with $E$, to yield $F$; the final result, which is $((v + w) + u) = ((u + v) + w)$.

### Exercises

**1.3-9**   Draw abstract syntax trees for $A, B, C, D, E$, and $F$ in the last example.

**1.3-10**  In the first example, with $C = ((5 * 1) + 1) * 1$, we could also have chosen $D$ to be the whole expression $C$, with $\{x = (5 * 1) + 1\}$. Write out $A, B, E$, and $F$, and draw their abstract syntax trees.

**1.3-11**  Show the three steps involved in using the law $(2 * n) * m = n * (2 * m)$ in all possible ways (direct uses only) on the expressions
    **(a)**   $(a * b) * c + (2 * a) * c$          **(b)**   $(2 * ((2 * a) * b)) * c$

### 1.3.3  We Can Substitute for Expressions with Overlapping Variables

Another serious problem arises with substitution. So far we have had substitutions that can be thought of simply as equations: to justify $a + b = b + a$, we just use the rule $x + y = y + x$ while thinking that $x = a$ and $y = b$. That seems simple.

Suppose now we want to say $2 + x = x + 2$, no matter what $x$ may be. That is an obvious application of the rule, isn't it? How do we apply the rule here? Should we assume that $x = 2$ and $y = x$? If so, we could end up replacing $2 + x$ with $2 + 2$, which is not what we wanted at all; we were trying to talk about any value of $x$, and ended up restricting ourselves to 2.

**Q:** Huh? I thought I was following, but you just blew me away altogether. What's going on?

**A:** Is it true that $x + (y + z) = x + (z + y)$, no matter what $x$, $y$, and $z$ may be?

**Q:** Yes, of course; that's just an application of commutativity to the $y + z$ expression. So what?

**A:** Good; now what did you substitute into the commutative law $x + y = y + x$ to get $y + z = z + y$?

**Q:** Well, I substituted $y$ for $x$, and $z$ for $y$. Hey, that's not right... or is it?

**A:** If you took the commutative law and substituted $y$ for $x$, you would get $y + y = y + y$; now substitute $z$ for $y$ and you get $z + z = z + z$. Is that what you meant?

**Q:** No, I guess not; I'm not sure any more. Can't we start writing programs? I'm much better at that, and I don't see that this has anything to do with programming.

**A:** What we're getting into is the concept of the "scope" of a name, which you really must understand in order to write substantial programs in a high-level programming language. (That's slightly exaggerated; older versions of *BASIC* and *COBOL* have very limited control of scope, which is one reason that they make it relatively difficult to build large programs from small programs.) When I write the rule $x + y = y + x$, I'm really talking about *any* possible $x$ and *any* possible $y$. $x$ and $y$ are *local variables* which do not refer to anything outside of that one short rule. If, somewhere else, I write the expression $x + (y + z)$, there is absolutely no connection between the two uses of $x$ or the two uses of $y$ except that they have the same name; it is like having two different people named Joe. On the other hand, if I write a *single* rule like $x + x = 2 * x$, all three occurrences of $x$ must refer to the same object, because they're all occurring in the same local context (the same rule).

**Q:** But how is that supposed to help? If I write down $x + x$ somewhere, how can I possibly keep track of the fact that the first $x$ comes from one context and the second $x$ comes from another?

**A:** Just as you keep track of two guys named Joe in a class: you can keep track of them either by adding something to the name, e.g. by calling the one from the Jones family "Joe J." and the one from the Smith family "Joe S.," or you can just rename them: call the weight-lifter "Tiny" and the one from Brooklyn "Tex." For instance, if I think of the $x$ within the commutativity rule as being one of a family, I might call it $x_C$, and the $y$ would become $y_C$. Then when I started working on $x + (y + z)$, I would say $x_C = y, y_C = z$ and then I'd find that $y + z = z + y$ makes perfect sense.

**Q:** All right, that is sort of like using a full name, but it's pretty inconvenient. How would you do it by giving them nicknames?

**A:** I would say that the $x$ and $y$ in the rule $x + y = y + x$ should be nicknamed $u$ and $v$, so that the rule is written as $u + v = v + u$. That's the same rule, because all I've done is switch to names that aren't used elsewhere and won't get me confused. Similarly, $u + (v + w) = (u + v) + w$ is the same associative law as the one which talked about $x, y,$ and $z$, and so is

$$zippo + (hippo + blippo) = (zippo + hippo) + blippo.$$

**Q:** In algebra we usually used $u, v, w, x, y,$ and $z$ as variable names. Do you mean you can use anything at all? Can I say $Joe + Fred = Fred + Joe$? Can I say

$$John \; Jones \; the \; third \; + \; King \; Philip = King \; Philip + John \; Jones \; the \; third?$$

**A:** It would get rather hard to read if you did that; it's better to use "names" which do not include blank spaces, so that you can be sure where they begin and end. (The programming languages $BASIC$ and $FORTRAN$ normally do allow–and ignore–blank spaces inside names; programs which take advantage of this feature can be frighteningly unreadable.) Mathematicians often use variables with only one letter, so that "$xyz$" means "$x * y * z$" rather than being a three-letter variable name. They start out with a convention that has the letters you mentioned being used for arbitrary variables, the letters $i, j, k, l, m,$ and $n$ being used for whole-number variables, the letters $f, g,$ and $h$ being used for functions, and so on. We will use that convention some of the time, but we will not be completely rigid about it. In English, a capitalized name like $Joe, John,$ or $Mary$ normally refers to a specific person, where a word like "person" is like a variable in that it can refer to any one of a large collection of people. We will sometimes make use of that convention, too. For now, you are better off using the familiar one-letter symbols of traditional mathematics.

## Exercises

**1.3-12** Find all the uses of commutativity on
    **(a)** $x + (y + x)$      **(b)** $(u + x) + (x + u)$      **(c)** $(j + x) + u$

**1.3-13** Find all the uses of $x + 0 = x$ on
    **(a)** $5 + 0$      **(b)** $(5 + 0) + 0$      **(c)** $((x + 0) + (y + 0)) + x$

Actually, it is safe to get $x + (y + z) = (x + y) + z$ by substituting $y$ for $x$ and $z$ for $y$ in $x + y = y + x$, provided you do the substitutions all at once. We will worry about "simultaneous substitution" later on; for now, depend on inventing unique "nicknames" for the variables whenever you start to get confused.

### 1.3.4 We Can Sometimes Recognize Numbers as Patterns

There is still one problem with recognizing instances of laws. If you go back to the previous section, you will see that we said (in effect) that $5*3 = 5*3+0$ is justified by $n*m = n*m + 0$, i.e., that $5*3$ is an instance of $n*m$. That's quite true: we just have to substitute 5 for $n$ and 3 for $m$. The closing rule was just as easy: we said that $0*3 + 15 = 15$ was justified by $0*n + m = m$, and you should certainly be able to see what substitution is required to find $0*3 + 15$ as an instance of $0*n + m$. However, the steps in between required that we say, for example, that $5*3+0 = 4*3 + 3$ is justified by $(x+1)*y + z = x*y + (y+z)$, so that $5*3+0$ must be an instance of $(x+1)*y + z$.

We are substituting 5 for $x+1$, 3 for $y$, and 0 for $z$. How can we substitute 5 for $x+1$? The answer is clearly to make $x = 4$, but is this a substitution? Worse yet, the improved multiplication rules say that $5*3+0$ is an instance of $(2x+1)*y + z$. Here the answer is to make $x = 2$, but how can this be substitution at all?

We are not about to give a full answer to this here; we are just going to stretch the idea of substitution a little, while being careful not to stretch it too far. We'll assume that if you're looking for an instance of "$x+1$," you can recognize that 5 is all right provided that $x = 4$, or that 1 is all right provided that $x = 0$, but that (until we deal with negative numbers) 0 is just plain wrong; it is not an instance of $x + 1$. That means that we're classifying the nonnegative whole numbers: 0 sits all by itself, and everything else is said to be an instance of $n+1$ for some $n$. Similarly, we could introduce a classification of the nonnegative whole numbers into 0 (again sitting all by itself), the odd numbers $1, 3, 5, 7, \ldots$ and the nonzero even numbers $2, 4, 6, 8, \ldots$; that classification would let us say that any number was either 0, an instance of $2*n + 1$, or an instance of $2*n$.

**Q:** But suppose that I'm looking for an instance of "$n*n$"; is it all right to use 9, provided that $n = 3$?

**A:** Certainly, provided that you have introduced a classification that fits; we might say that 0 sits as usual by itself, that we have the exact nonzero squares $1, 4, 9, 16, 25, \ldots$ as one class matching $n*n$, that we then have the numbers $2, 5, 10, 17, 26 \ldots$ as a class matching $n*n + 1$, that the numbers $3, 6, 11, 18, 27, \ldots$ match $n*n + 2$, that $7, 12, 19, 28, \ldots$ match $n*n + 3$, and so on. In this case, 190 is an instance of $13*13 + 21$, while 21 is an instance of $4*4 + 5$, 13 is an instance of $3*3 + 4$, and so on.

It is important to avoid having more than one classification idea at a time; we will usually stick with 0 vs. $n+1$ or else with 0 vs. $2*n$ vs. $2*n + 1$.

It may help to think of the expression "3" as an abbreviation. In many contexts it will be an abbreviation for "$2 + 1$", where "2" is an abbreviation for "$1 + 1$", and an isolated "1" is an abbreviation for "$0 + 1$". In other contexts 3 will be an abbreviation for "$2*1+1$", where an isolated "1" is an abbreviation for "$2*0+1$".

**Exercises**

**1.3-14** I want to classify numbers as $0$, $2*n$, or $2*n+1$. Classify the numbers $5, 4, 3, 2, 1, 0$, giving the value for $n$ in each case.

**1.3-15** Given the same classification as in the previous problem, I could add an even number to an odd number with the rule $(2 * n) + (2 * m + 1) = 2 * (n + m) + 1$, which tells me that $4 + 5 = 2 * (2 + 2) + 1$. Make up a rule for adding two even numbers, and give an example.

## 1.4 SIMPLIFICATION

Given that you can manipulate expressions and match rules to them, you're reaching the point where you can carry out one step of an algorithm. We're now going to work on the process of using a collection of rules to reach a goal.

### 1.4.1 You Need to Learn to Simplify Expressions by Using Rules

In our first multiplication problem, we used three rules to simplify the expression $5 * 3$ into the equivalent expression $15$. The rules were

$$
\begin{aligned}
x * y &= x * y + 0 \\
(x + 1) * y + z &= x * y + (y + z) \\
0 * y + z &= z
\end{aligned}
$$

In this section, you will be learning to use explicit lists of rules to solve simple problems involving operations like multiplication. Just as important, you will learn about separating implicit knowledge from explicit knowledge. As an inexperienced programmer, you may often find it difficult to tell exactly how much "knowledge" you have put into a program. Sometimes your programs will generate surprising results, because you forget that the program doesn't know that addition is commutative unless you tell it so by giving it a rule of the right form.

You must bring yourself to the point where you can take a collection of rules and apply them mechanically to a problem without worrying about what they mean, just as in elementary school you had to multiply numbers without thinking of what the stages meant. Learning this will help you in two ways. First, it will greatly increase your general ability to handle formulas, so that you will be able to recognize significant patterns in mathematical notation (and in the related parts of programming languages), just as study of the grammar of a foreign language gradually enables you to read a book in that language without ever thinking about the grammar itself. Second, it will give you a midway point between program specification (the careful description of what a program is supposed to do) and algorithm design (the careful description of how it is to be done.)

## 1.4.2 An Expression Is Simplified By Using Rules and Skills

Given a particular set of rules, we can describe a *fully simplified* expression as one which cannot be simplified any further because none of these rules matches it. With our three rules above for multiplication, 5 is fully simplified but $5 * 3$ is not because the rule $n * m = n * m + 0$ can be applied to it to get a new expression. If we had no rules which would work on it at all, then we would have to call it "simplified" even though it is a composite expression. The game we are playing forbids us to use our actual understanding of multiplication; we can only use the rules. For example, $(x + y) * 5$ is fully simplified, because we cannot tell whether to classify $x + y$ as 0 or as $n + 1$ for some value of $n$, so there is no rule to be applied.

**Q:** Why can't I simplify it to $x * 5 + y * 5$?

**A:** Because we don't yet have any explicit rule to justify that step. At any given moment, you have some explicit rules, and that's what you should use to work on the given problem. When you think of another rule that should be used instead, first add it to your "program," which is your list of explicit rules.

**Exercises**    Given the multiplication rules, which of the following are fully simplified? (For each one which is not fully simplified, state which rule could be used.)

**1.4-1**    $3 * 7$

**1.4-2**    $15/5$

**1.4-3**    $3 * (9/3)$

Thus, $12 - 8$ seems to be a fully simplified expression and so does $12 + 8$, because none of our explicit rules match either of these expressions. In practice, some rules are always implicit. We would be perfectly willing to say that $(9 - 2) * (2 + 9) = 7 * 11 + 0$ is a use of rule 1. In order to recognize that $9 - 2 = 7$ and $2 + 9 = 11$, we have to use our skills of addition and subtraction. In other words, the rules and procedures for these operations are so familiar (we hope) that everyone knows them, and it isn't necessary to write lists of rules for them.

**Q:** But how do you know which rules you're supposed to list?

**A:** In an ideal world, all the rules would always be explicitly listed. In practice, we usually have some things that we take for granted because it's much easier to use them than to describe them and we think (often wrongly) that this will not confuse anyone. These will be described as "skills" rather than as rules. A "skill" is a collection of rules inside a black box, like a calculator. As we go through examples, we will often refer to skills by name, but sometimes they will be taken for granted. That always creates a risk of misunderstanding; the benefit is an improved chance of actually reaching the end of the example without either falling asleep or losing track of all the details.

### 1.4.3 Using Simple Rules

A simple rule is a rule which can be "matched" just using substitutions for variables, without thinking much about anything. For example,

$$Incr(n) = n + 1 \qquad Decr(n) = n - 1$$
$$Half(n) = n/2 \qquad Sqr(m) = m * m$$
$$Double(n) = n + n \qquad Cube(n) = n * Sqr(n)$$
$$Distance(x1, y1, x2, y2) = SqrRt(Sqr(x2 - x1) + Sqr(y2 - y1))$$
$$TriangleArea(base, height) = (base * height)/2$$
$$RectangleArea(base, height) = base * height$$
$$RectanglePerimeter(base, height) = Double(base + height)$$

All of these are "simple" rules not because they are familiar from ordinary arithmetic and geometry, but because of the form of their left-hand sides. A simple rule in this sense is one whose left-hand side is a prefix expression whose argument list contains only names, like $f(x, y, z)$ or $TriangleArea(base, height)$. A rule whose left-hand side is $Decr(Incr(x))$ is not a simple rule, because the argument list contains $Incr(x)$, which is not a name. All of the names must be distinct, so $RectangleArea(x, x) = Sqr(x)$ is not a simple rule. Most programming languages require that procedures be defined in a form that resembles this. Any instance of the left-hand side is supposed to be replaced by the corresponding instance of the right-hand side. We should easily find $Distance(0, 0, 3, 4)$, just by listing a series of steps with justifications for each step:

$$
\begin{aligned}
Distance(0, 0, 3, 4) \quad &= \quad SqrRt(Sqr(3 - 0) + Sqr(4 - 0)) \quad &\textit{Distance} \text{ Rule} \\
&= \quad SqrRt(Sqr(3) + Sqr(4)) \quad &\text{Subtraction} \\
&= \quad SqrRt(3 * 3 + 4 * 4) \quad &\textit{Sqr} \text{ Rule} \\
&= \quad SqrRt(9 + 16) \quad &\text{Multiplication} \\
&= \quad SqrRt(25) \quad &\text{Addition} \\
&= \quad 5 \quad &\textit{SqrRt} \text{ Rule}
\end{aligned}
$$

The *Distance* rule and the *Sqr* rule for the first and third steps are explicit, but none of the others are justified in the current collection of rules. Subtraction, Multiplication, Addition, and finding a *SqrRt* are all assumed as skills; if you don't have them, you can't finish this computation. In fact, addition is often assumed as a skill prior to subtraction as well as prior to multiplication, and multiplication and division are usually used as skills in defining *SqrRt*.

## Exercises

**1.4-4**   List the steps and justifications for *Distance*(2,3,14,16).

**1.4-5**   List the steps and justifications for *TriangleArea*(5,*Cube*(*Decr*(3))).

### 1.4.4  Using Classification Rules

You've seen one way to calculate the square of a number: just use the rule $Sqr(n) = n * n$, and assume that multiplication is known as a skill. But suppose that it isn't. Suppose that our computer (human or mechanical) doesn't know how to multiply. Even if the computer can multiply, there might be a better way to solve the problem; for example, it might be possible to find the square of a number with fewer steps than the general-purpose multiplication rules would use. What choices do we have?

A different way to calculate is to classify the numbers and work out the value of $Sqr(n)$ for each possible value of $n$. For example, if we classify numbers into 0 and $m + 1$, then we might find that

$$
\begin{aligned}
Sqr(0) \quad &= \quad 0 \quad &(1)\\
Sqr(m + 1) \quad & \quad [= (m + 1) * (m + 1)\\
& \quad = m * m + 2 * m + 1]\\
&= \quad Sqr(m) + (m + m + 1) \quad &(2)
\end{aligned}
$$

To *understand* the second rule here, you must understand the distributive law of multiplication over addition, you must understand the associative and commutative laws of addition, and so on. To *apply* it, you just need to classify numbers correctly so that you'll know when to use which rule. Thus,

$$
\begin{aligned}
Sqr(5) \quad &= \quad Sqr(4) + (4 + 4 + 1) & \text{Rule 2 for } Sqr\\
&= \quad (Sqr(3) + (3 + 3 + 1)) + 9 & \text{Rule 2, 2 additions}\\
&= \quad ((Sqr(2) + (2 + 2 + 1)) + 7) + 9 & \text{Rule 2, 2 additions}\\
&= \quad (((Sqr(1) + (1 + 1 + 1)) + 5) + 7) + 9 & \text{Rule 2, 2 additions}\\
&= \quad ((((Sqr(0) + (0 + 0 + 1)) + 3) + 5) + 7) + 9 & \text{Rule 2, 2 additions}\\
&= \quad ((((0 + 1) + 3) + 5) + 7) + 9 & \text{Rule 1, 2 additions}\\
&= \quad 25 & \text{5 additions}
\end{aligned}
$$

**Q:** These rules are generating more and more terms, even though you do some additions along the way. Why can't we add those terms together as we go along? Then we would only write

$$
\begin{aligned}
Sqr(5) \quad &= \quad Sqr(4) + 4 + 4 + 1\\
&= \quad (Sqr(3) + 3 + 3 + 1) + 9\\
&= \quad (Sqr(2) + 2 + 2 + 1) + 16\\
&= \quad (Sqr(1) + 1 + 1 + 1) + 21\\
&= \quad (Sqr(0) + 0 + 0 + 1) + 24 = 25
\end{aligned}
$$

Here the first step uses rule 2, the next uses rule 2 and two additions, the next three use rule 2 and three additions each, and the last uses rule 1 and four additions. What's wrong with that?

**A:** Only that your steps are not instances of the given rules. It's all right to assume that the moron has the *skill* to do addition, but that's not the same as the *knowledge* that addition is associative. When you write programs for a human computer, you can generally assume that he or she has that knowledge, but a mechanical computer generally won't. (There are exceptions in both cases.) If you want to take your algebraic knowledge and put it into a form that's usable as an algorithm, you'll need to make that knowledge explicit by embedding it in a rule, as was done for multiplication previously. You'll have to stop talking about what $Sqr(n)$ equals when it is all alone, and start worrying about what $Sqr(n) + m$ is equal to:

$$
\begin{array}{llcl}
1. & Sqr(n) & = & Sqr(n) + 0 \\
2. & Sqr(0) + m & = & m \\
3. & Sqr(n + 1) + m & = & Sqr(n) + (n + n + 1 + m)
\end{array}
$$

### Exercises

**1.4-6**   Write the steps and justifications for $Sqr(4)$ using these rules.

**1.4-7**   Write steps and justifications for $Sqr(4)$ using the previous rules.

**1.4-8**   Write the abstract syntax trees for each step of the last problem.

As usual, the use of abstract syntax trees should give you a better feeling for the structure of the process you're carrying out. Only a piece of the abstract syntax tree changes with each step.

Rules using classifications sometimes make it easy to clarify what we're thinking about, even when the classification style doesn't seem necessary. If we are only working with nonnegative whole numbers, then the rule $Decr(n) = n - 1$ is misleading; it makes it seem that $Decr(0)$ is meaningful. The problem is more obvious when we express this as $Decr(n + 1) = n$, and simply note that there is no rule to use on the expression $Decr(0)$.

Two even more familiar examples should help with that idea and with classification rules in general: addition and subtraction.

$$
\begin{array}{llcl}
1. & Add(0, n) & = & n \\
2. & Add(m + 1, n) & = & Add(m, n + 1)
\end{array}
$$

Here it seems clear that given any two nonnegative numbers, the first of the pair will be either zero or positive, so one rule or the other will be usable.

$$
\begin{array}{llcl}
1. & Sub(n, 0) & = & n \\
2. & Sub(n + 1, m + 1) & = & Sub(n, m)
\end{array}
$$

Here we have no such assurance. Given a pair of nonnegative numbers, if the second is zero or if neither is zero we have a rule, but if we are given the problem $Sub(3, 9)$, we will eventually simplify it down to $Sub(0, 6)$, which cannot be simplified any further with these rules.

**Exercises**   Show steps and justifications for

**1.4-9**   $Add(5, 5)$
**1.4-10**  $Sub(3, 9)$
**1.4-11**  $Sub(9, 3)$
**1.4-12**  $Decr(Sub(Add(4, 2), 2))$

You should now be getting comfortable with the uses of rules, separate from their meaning. Let's try this out on some silly rules. Suppose that we're given the rules $Foop(0) = 3$ and $Foop(n + 1) = 2 + Foop(n)$. Now we can find

$$
\begin{aligned}
Foop(4) \quad &= \quad 2 + Foop(3) & \text{Foop rule 2} \\
&= \quad 2 + (2 + Foop(2)) & " \\
&= \quad 2 + (2 + (2 + Foop(1))) & " \\
&= \quad 2 + (2 + (2 + (2 + Foop(0)))) & " \\
&= \quad 2 + (2 + (2 + (2 + 3))) & \text{Foop rule 1} \\
&= \quad 11 & \text{Four additions}
\end{aligned}
$$

Of course, you may see immediately that $Foop(n) = 2 * n + 3$, but all that you have to be able to see now is that

(a) The definition given enables you to find $Foop(4)$ with the steps and justifications given;

(b) It enables you to find $Foop(399)$ using rule 2 399 times, using rule 1 once, and then doing 399 additions; and

(c) Within those 399 steps, the first step contains a single "2" written out, the second step has two of them, and so on; the longest line will be the 399th, which will be $2 + (2 + (2 + (2 + (2 + \ldots + Foop(0) \ldots))))$ and will have 399 "2"s.

**Exercises**   For each of the following rule sets, you are given two problems. Write out

**1.4-13**  The steps and justifications for solving the first problem,
**1.4-14**  The number of each kind of step required to solve the second problem, and

**1.4-15** The description of the longest line in the sequence of steps.

| Rules | Problems |
|---|---|
| a. $F1(0) = 0,$     $F1(n+1) = n - F1(n);$ | $F1(5),$    $F1(500).$ |
| b.   $F2(0) = 1,$     $F2(n+1) = (n+1)*F2(n);$ | $F2(4),$    $F2(3000).$ |
| c. $F3(0,n) = n,$ $F3(m+1,n) = F3(m, n+m);$ | $F3(4,9),$ $F3(30,200).$ |
| d. $F4(n,0) = n,$ $F4(n, m+1) = F4(n*(m+1), m);$ | $F4(1,4),$ $F4(1,3000).$ |

We will often use classification rules in specification, but they are not as common as simple rules for programming. There are some programming languages with constructs like classification rules, but you are not very likely to have heard of them; *PROLOG, Hope, ML, SNOBOL, SASL,* and *KRC* are at least fairly well known. Most of the languages you will see, however, require procedure definitions in the simple-rule form which we have already dealt with. They achieve (and surpass) the effect of classification by allowing you to give two or more alternative rules and some way of deciding which rule is correct for a given case. In specifications, we will use a simple "conditional rule" construction.

### 1.4.5  Using Conditional Rules
###         For Classification

A *conditional rule* is one which applies only if certain conditions are satisfied. For example, we can say in English that "IF John is Joe's father, THEN Joe is John's son," or "IF you get through this section, THEN you will have learned something about conditional rules." All of the rules based on classification can be expressed through conditions:

$$
\begin{aligned}
Foop(n) \quad &= \quad 3, &&\text{if } n = 0 \\
&= \quad 2 + Foop(n-1) &&\text{otherwise}
\end{aligned}
$$

$$
\begin{aligned}
F2(n) \quad &= \quad 1, &&\text{if } n = 0 \\
&= \quad n * F2(n-1), &&\text{otherwise}
\end{aligned}
$$

$$
\begin{aligned}
F4(n,m) \quad &= \quad n &&\text{if } m = 0 \\
&= \quad F4(n*m, m-1) &&\text{otherwise}
\end{aligned}
$$

We have six rules here, but each rule has an associated condition. Thus, $Foop(n) = 3$ is to be applied whenever $n = 0$, and $Foop(n) = 2 + Foop(n-1)$ is only to be applied when $n = 0$ is false, i.e., when $n \neq 0$. Thus, for example, we find steps and *conditional* reasons for Foop(3):

| | | | |
|---|---|---|---|
| 1. | $Foop(3)$ | $= \quad 2 + Foop(2)$ | Foop rule 2, $3 \neq 0$ |
| 2. | | $= \quad 2 + (2 + Foop(1))$ | "     , $2 \neq 0$ |
| 3. | | $= \quad 2 + (2 + (2 + Foop(0)))$ | "     , $1 \neq 0$ |
| 4. | | $= \quad 2 + (2 + (2 + 3))$ | Foop rule 1, $0 = 0$ |
| 5. | | $= \quad 9$ | three additions |

## Exercises

**1.4-16**  Write conditional rules for the prefix functions F1 and F3.

**1.4-17**  Write steps and conditional justifications for F2(3) and F4(1,3).

### 1.4.6  Using Conditional Rules in General

In dealing with a function for which you have a sequence of conditional rules, you should simply try them one after another. If the first condition is true, use the first rule. If not, and if the second is true, use the second rule. To use a famous example which will appear again later,

$$
\begin{array}{llll}
1. & gcd(x,y) & = & y & \text{if } x = 0 \\
2. & & = & x & \text{if } y = 0 \\
3. & & = & gcd(x - y, y) & \text{if } x > y \\
4. & & = & gcd(x, y - x) & \text{otherwise}
\end{array}
$$

Suppose we want to simplify $gcd(24, 15)$. First we try rule 1, but $24 \neq 0$. Next we try rule 2, but $15 \neq 0$. Then we check rule 3, and find that $24 > 15$ so we can use this rule; we don't need to look at the last. We thus get

$$
\begin{array}{lllll}
1. & gcd(24,15) & = & gcd(9,15) & \text{gcd rule 3} \\
2. & & = & gcd(9,6) & \text{gcd rule 4} \\
3. & & = & gcd(3,6) & \text{gcd rule 3} \\
4. & & = & gcd(3,3) & \text{gcd rule 4} \\
5. & & = & gcd(3,0) & \text{gcd rule 4} \\
6. & & = & 3 & \text{gcd rule 1}
\end{array}
$$

The $gcd$ function as defined here produces the "greatest common divisor" of its arguments, i.e., the largest number which divides both of them evenly. For example, $gcd(24, 18) = 6$, $gcd(1000, 375) = 125$, and $gcd(12, 25) = 1$.

## Exercise

**1.4-18**  Find the steps and justifications for $gcd(28, 77)$.

Similarly, we can write conditional rules for a variety of simple functions:

$$
\begin{array}{llll}
mod(n,m) & = & n, & \text{if } n < m \\
 & = & mod(n-m,m) & \text{otherwise} \\
\\
div(n,m) & = & DivAcc(n,m,0) & \\
DivAcc(n,m,a) & = & a, & \text{if } n < m \\
 & = & DivAcc(n-m,m,a+1) & \text{otherwise} \\
\\
mul(n,m) & = & MulAcc(n,m,0) & \\
MulAcc(n,m,a) & = & a, & \text{if } n \neq 0 \\
 & = & MulAcc(n-1,m,m+a) & \text{otherwise} \\
\\
SqrRt(n) & = & SqrRtApprox(1,1,n) & \\
SqrRtApprox(i,s,n) & = & i-1, & \text{if } s > n \\
 & = & SqrRtApprox(i+1,s+i+i+1,n) & \text{otherwise}
\end{array}
$$

**Exercises**    Show all steps and justifications for

**1.4-19**   $3 * div(19,3) + mod(19,3)$

**1.4-20**   $SqrRt(9) + Sqr(SqrRt(8))$

### 1.4.7 What Are Conditions?

We started working on expressions and rules by defining carefully what they are. We're now using conditions attached to rules, but we haven't given any definition of them. What's a condition? So far, conditions have been written as pairs of expressions with rather special infix operators connecting them: $x = 0$, $n > m$, $x \neq 0$. The usual operators are $=, \neq, <, \leq, >$, and $\geq$; these are called respectively "Equal," "NotEqual," "LessThan," "LessOrEqual," "GreaterThan," and "GreaterOrEqual." Collectively, we can refer to them as *conditional infix operators*. Basically, a condition is just like an expression except that its value is *True* or *False* instead of being a number. Thus $5 > 3$ is *True*, $5 < 3$ is *False*, $5 = 5$ is *True* and $5 = 4 + 2$ is *False*. However, *True* + *False* is simply meaningless: "+" works on numbers, and *True* and *False* are not numbers. In English we can often use one kind of word where another would be expected, as when you say "Please hammer the mail" or "Please mail the hammer"; this usually creates some confusion, but in context can make sense. In formally defined languages, the same principle can be applied. *True* = *True* is *True* and *True* = *False* is *False*, so we can also say that

$$( \mathit{True} = \mathit{False} ) = \mathit{False}$$

is *True*. By convention, we can also say that *False* < *True*. If it's true, it must be *True*, so (*False* < *True*) = *True*. That looks like a rule, and it's certainly valid;

if we apply it to the "*True*" within (*True* > *False*), then we can observe that ((*False* < *True*) > *False*) is *True*.

**Exercises**  For each valid expression or conditional expression, write a value; for each invalid expression or conditional expression, show what's wrong:

**1.4-21**  $(4 + 5) < 9$

**1.4-22**  $(3 < 5) < 6$

**1.4-23**  $(3 < 5) < False$

**1.4-24**  *False* + 9

**1.4-25**  *True* > (3 > *False*)

We can summarize what we have so far by saying that a conditional expression either is *True*, or is *False*, or is a pair of expressions joined by a conditional infix operator, or is a pair of conditional expressions joined by a conditional infix operator. Thus, 0 > *False* is not a conditional expression because it doesn't match any of these alternatives: 0 is an expression, and *False* is a conditional expression, and they are not comparable. On the other hand, (5 > 3) > *False*) is a conditional expression with value *True*, while *True* > (*True* > *True*) is a conditional expression with value *True*, and (*True* > *True*) > *True* is a conditional expression with value *False*.

### 1.4.8  What if Conditions Have Unknown Variables?

Conditions as used in conditional rules should be somewhat restricted. Consider the use of "if $n = 2 * k$" within the following:

$$
\begin{array}{lll}
mul(n, m) & = & MulAcc2(n, m, 0) \\
MulAcc2(n, m, a) & = & a, & \text{if } n = 0 \\
& = & MulAcc2(k, m + m, a), & \text{if } n = 2 * k \\
& = & MulAcc2(k, m + m, a + m), & \text{if } n = 2 * k + 1
\end{array}
$$

For example,

$$
\begin{array}{lll}
mul(6, 2) & = & MulAcc2(6, 2, 0) \\
& = & MulAcc2(3, 4, 0) \\
& = & MulAcc2(1, 8, 4) \\
& = & MulAcc2(0, 16, 12) \\
& = & 12
\end{array}
$$

We are supposed to apply the first rule if its condition is true; fine, we look to see if $n = 0$. If not, we look to see if the second rule's condition is true. Is $n = 2 * k$? Evidently, that depends on $k$. The intent should be clear: we want to say that for every value of $k$ for which $n = 2 * k$, it is true that $MulAcc2(n, m, a) = MulAcc2(k, m + m, a)$. Try to find a value for $k$; if you fail, go on to the next rule, but if you find it, then substitute that value into $MulAcc2(k, m + m, a)$. The problem with this as a recipe for computation is that it requires that we start from $n$ and find the $k$ satisfying $n = 2 * k$. But we have not yet described any mechanical way to solve problems like that. Instead, we should write something like

$$
\begin{aligned}
MulAcc2(n, m, a) \quad &= \quad a, & \text{if } n = 0 \\
&= \quad MulAcc2(Half(n), m + m, a), & \text{if } n \text{ is even} \\
&= \quad MulAcc2(Half(n), m + m, m + a) & \text{otherwise}
\end{aligned}
$$

Now we need a formal expression which is *True* if $n$ is even and *False* otherwise; "$mod(n, 2) = 0$" will do fine.

**Q:** Can't we ever have new variables inside a condition?

**A:** Not in most programming languages. Still, there is one usage which is quite easy to handle as describing a computation. Suppose that the second line said

$$
= \quad MulAcc2(k, m + m, a), \quad \text{if } mod(n, 2) = 0 \text{ and } k = Half(n)
$$

Here the *logical* meaning is unchanged, but the *computational* meaning is now simple: if you find that $mod(n, 2) = 0$, and if you find the value of $Half(n)$ and call that value $k$, then you can substitute that value into $MulAcc2(k, m + m, a)$ to get what you need.

## 1.5 RULE USAGE: TOP DOWN AND BOTTOM UP

You can now use rules on an expression to simplify it, but there are some fine points to be considered. Suppose that you have an expression like $(1 * 2) * (3 * 4)$. There are three multiplications here; which one should be done first? Look at the abstract syntax tree in Figure 1.5.

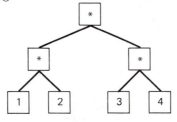

**Figure 1.5** Tree for Bottom=Up Evaluation

**Q:** Isn't it obvious? You can do either $1 * 2$ or $3 * 4$ first, but you have to do both of them before you can start on $2 * 12$.

**A:** That is in fact the usual approach, and it's called **bottom-up** evaluation; to be more precise, we usually do **bottom-up, left-to-right** evaluation, which does first $1 * 2$, then $3 * 4$, and finally $2 * 12$. Most programming languages are implemented so that they always work this way. Now look at another example: $0 * (SqrRt((4793 + 95) * 613))$, in Figure 1.6.

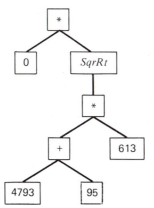

**Figure 1.6**    Tree for Top-Down Evaluation

Quick, what's the answer?

**Q:** 0, of course.

**A:** Now, did you find $SqrRt((4793 + 95) * 613)$ in order to come out with that?

**Q:** No, I didn't need to. Just looking at the top of the abstract syntax tree is enough to make it clear that I don't need to know anything about the lower parts.

**A:** You were using a **top-down** evaluation strategy. Some programming languages are implemented to work that way.

**Q:** I thought **top-down** and **bottom-up** were ways of designing programs.

**A:** They are; in fact, they are ways of solving problems. Every problem (unless it's completely trivial) is made out of subproblems. To work bottom-up means to solve all the subproblems before you start thinking about the "big picture" at all. To work top-down means to think about the overall context first, before you solve the subproblems. In practice, top-down solutions usually include some bottom-up work because you usually have to put the subproblems' solutions together after you find them. In any case, top-down means to work from top to bottom of an abstract syntax tree, and bottom-up means—

**Q:** To work from bottom to top, right?

**A:** Right. Later we will go over other uses of this distinction, but for now it should be pretty clear what is meant.

**Q:** Does it make a lot of difference?

**A:** Not usually. For most problem descriptions, both of them work, and the bottom-up strategy works somewhat faster. That's because looking at the top usually just tells you that you need to solve all subproblems, so you've lost a little time for no gain. For some kinds of problem descriptions, they both work, but the top-down works a lot faster just because looking at the top tells you that you don't need to solve a subproblem. For a few kinds of problem descriptions, the top-down strategy works and the bottom-up strategy doesn't work at all, because the subproblem that you don't need to solve is a subproblem that you can't solve.

**Q:** You mean that you have to use different programming languages to solve different problems?

**A:** Not really, although it's often a good idea (for several reasons). You may find that you can write rules which enable you to solve a problem, but which don't seem to work bottom-up. Don't despair: there is always a way to change your problem description so that your solution will still work. It may not be easy to find, but it exists.

**Q:** I think I see what you're talking about, but how much of this do I really have to understand now?

**A:** Given a particular composite expression, and a particular list of rules, you should be able to try applying the rules to the expression either in strictly bottom-up order or top-down (which usually requires some bottom-up work).

**Q:** Why is that important? Isn't it just built into the programming language anyway? Why should I be able to apply it?

**A:** For two reasons. First, so that you can see what's going wrong when something does go wrong. That's "when," not "if"; things will go wrong, and you'll need to understand the process which got the computer into a mess. Secondly, understanding the top-down and bottom-up use of rules on dependency trees will help you rephrase your rules so that the computer will work efficiently towards a solution.

**Q:** What are dependency trees?

**A:** A dependency tree is a collection of expressions, some of which depend on others. For example, if I describe multiplication as

$$\begin{aligned} Mul(0, y) &= 0 \\ Mul(x+1, y) &= y + Mul(x, y) \end{aligned}$$

then $Mul(3,5)$ turns into a dependency tree: $Mul(3,5)$ depends upon 5, and upon $Mul(2,5)$ which depends upon 5, and upon $Mul(1,5)$ which depends upon 5, and upon $Mul(0,5)$. We can write that as a single large expression:

$$\text{``Mul(3,5)"}\,(5, \text{``Mul(2,5)"}\,(5, \text{``Mul(1,5)"}\,(5, \text{``Mul(0,5)"}\,())))$$

**Exercises**

**1.5-1**   Draw an abstract syntax tree for the preceding "dependency expression." This is the "dependency tree" in this case. Explain why larger problems are at the top and smaller ones down below.

**1.5-2**   Draw a dependency tree for $mod(8, 3)$.

### 1.5.1 Rules, Strategies, and Sequences

To examine the differences between top-down and bottom-up strategies more carefully, we'll need a more complex example. The one we'll be using is called Pascal's Triangle, and it has many applications, but we're only interested in it as an example of a kind of equation which has many possible rule-use choices.

$$
\begin{aligned}
P(i,j) \quad &= \quad 1, & \text{if } i = 0 \\
&= \quad 1, & \text{if } j = 0 \\
&= \quad P(i-1,j) + P(i,j-1) & \text{otherwise}
\end{aligned}
$$

This gives us a dependency tree in which $P(i+1, j+1)$ depends on $P(i, j+1)$ and simultaneously on $P(i+1, j)$.

### Exercises

**1.5-3**  Draw the dependency tree for $P(5,1)$.

**1.5-4**  Draw the dependency tree for $P(3,3)$.

There's an important observation you can make about the dependency tree for $P(3,3)$: it contains two copies of the dependency tree for $P(2,2)$. (If it doesn't, go back and try again.) If you weren't pretending to be a moron, you would only figure out the value of $P(2,2)$ once and then remember it until the next time. Actually, we don't want a dependency tree here: we want a dependency *graph*, in which several different items up high could depend on items down low. To make a computer deal with this, we would need to describe more complicated rules (for saving values). That can be done, but we won't worry about it for a while: right now our job is just to apply rules systematically until we get an answer. We can evaluate $P(3,3)$ in many different orders; here's one:

$$
\begin{aligned}
P(3,3) \quad &= \quad P(2,3) + P(3,2) \\
&= \quad (P(1,3) + P(2,2)) + P(3,2) \\
&= \quad ((P(0,3) + P(1,2)) + P(2,2)) + P(3,2) \\
&= \quad ((1 + P(1,2)) + P(2,2)) + P(3,2) \\
&= \quad ((1 + (P(0,2) + P(1,1))) + P(2,2)) + P(3,2) \\
&= \quad ((1 + (1 + P(1,1))) + P(2,2)) + P(3,2) \\
&= \quad ((1 + (1 + (P(0,1) + P(1,0)))) + P(2,2)) + P(3,2) \\
&= \quad ((1 + (1 + (1 + P(1,0)))) + P(2,2)) + P(3,2) \\
&= \quad (4 + P(2,2)) + P(3,2) \\
&= \quad \vdots
\end{aligned}
$$

Clearly, we are just doing the leftmost "reduction" with each step, and following immediately with any possible simplifications. Top-down and bottom-up don't appear to matter in this case, because there is never any job inside of another.

**Exercises**

**1.5-5**  Finish the calculation of $P(3,3)$, continuing to do the leftmost reduction with each step.

**1.5-6**  Repeat the exercise, picking the rightmost reduction each time. Does it make any difference? What difference can picking the rightmost rather than leftmost reduction ever make? Justify your answer.

**1.5-7**  Draw the abstract syntax trees for the first four steps of the calculation of $P(3,3)$.

In other cases, top-down and bottom-up matter a great deal. Suppose we have defined the three silly functions which follow:

$$
\begin{aligned}
f(x) &= g(x, x^{**}x)) \\
g(x,y) &= x \\
h(x) &= g(f(x), f(x+x))
\end{aligned}
$$

Now, if we want to evaluate $h(3)$, we can go through a top-down sequence in which we always replace the leftmost function:

$$
\begin{aligned}
h(3) &= g(f(3), f(6)) \\
&= f(3) \\
&= g(3, 3^{**}3) \\
&= 3
\end{aligned}
$$

Notice that we never tried to figure out what the righthand arguments to $g$ came out to be. The expression $g(f(3), f(6))$ has a "$g$" on the left, so we use the rule for "$g$". A bottom-up rule would require that we find out what $f(3)$ and $f(6)$ are *before* using the rule for "$g$". In this case, that would mean that we proceed as follows:

$$
\begin{aligned}
h(3) &= g(f(3), f(6)) \\
&= g(g(3, 3^{**}3), f(6)) \\
&= g(g(3, 27), f(6)) \\
&= g(3, f(6)) \\
&= g(3, g(6, 6^{**}6)) \\
&= g(3, g(6, 46656)) \\
&= g(3, 6) \\
&= 3
\end{aligned}
$$

The top-down strategy simply takes the leftmost of all the operations and applies its rule to the arguments of that operation, as expressions. This is sometimes called *call-by-name*. The bottom-up strategy takes the leftmost of those operations whose arguments are all values, ignoring those which may have arguments that are expressions; it applies its rule to the arguments as values. This is often called *call-by-value*, and it is the usual rule for programming languages.

## Exercises

**1.5-8**   Given the same function definitions as before, apply top-down and bottom-up evaluation to the expression $g(h(1), f(3))$.

**1.5-9**   Take the function definitions above, and change the definition of $f(x)$ to $g(x, h(x))$. Now try the top-down and bottom-up strategies on $f(2)$. What happens?

**1.5-10**  In these examples, top-down looked good and bottom-up looked bad. It is also possible for bottom-up to look good: use both strategies to evaluate $f(f(2))$ with the definitions

$$
\begin{aligned}
f(x)    &=& g(x, x+1) \\
g(x, y) &=& (x + x) * (y + y)
\end{aligned}
$$

Why does top-down look so bad here?

Understanding the way that rules work often helps us redesign rules to work better. The simplest rules for the computer to handle are those which tell it exactly what to do: those which define a simple computation sequence in which the line doesn't lengthen, i.e., a fixed number of spaces are used.

### 1.5.2  Rephrasing Rules as Simple Recurrences

We have been using some rules which change the length of a line, and others which don't. For example, $Mul(x+1, y) = y + Mul(x, y)$ says in effect that the problem $5 * 4$ can be replaced by the problem $4 * 4$ if we remember that we must add 4 to the result; $MulAcc(x+1, y, a) = MulAcc(x, y, y+a)$ says in effect that the problem $5 * 4 + 20$ can be replaced by the problem $4 * 4 + 24$, with no further work to be done. Thus, using the first definition causes us to go through a computation sequence of longer and longer lines, while the second lets us use a sequence of lines, each of which says "$MulAcc(x, y, a)$" for some values of $x$, $y$, and $a$. Rules like the rule for $MulAcc$ which look like $f(x, y, z) = f(x', y', z')$, so that a problem is replaced by another of exactly the same form, are called *simple recurrences*.

## Exercises

**1.5-11**  Find three functions in the last few sections which are simple recurrences like our rule for $MulAcc$; i.e., the line doesn't grow.

**1.5-12**  Find three which are not simple recurrences; i.e., the line grows.

Simple recurrences are very important in computer science. In fact, a few special kinds of simple recurrence are included as constructs in most programming languages. Look at the following rules, for example:

$$
\begin{aligned}
While(prob) &=& While(Simpler(prob)), & \text{if } Complex(prob) \\
            &=& prob, & \text{otherwise}
\end{aligned}
$$

This rule takes us through the sequence $prob_1, prob_2, \ldots prob_N$, where each *problem* is somewhat simpler than the last, but only the final one is indivisible. This form is called *"while"*, and is usually associated with some syntax such as

$$WHILE\ Complex(prob)\ DO\ prob := Simpler(prob)\ END;$$

If you think of the *problem* to be solved as having three components, *prob.n, prob.m,* and *prob.a,* then *MulAcc* fits into this form quite nicely. *Complex(prob)* is a test for *prob.n*> 0, and *Simpler(prob)* is another problem with components $n' = n - 1$, $m' = m$, and $a' = a + m$. Surprisingly, any program which can be written at all can be written with *while* as the sole source of repetition.

Still, there are other simple recurrences which are often provided. One of the most specialized, but still very useful, is

$$
\begin{aligned}
For(prob, l, h) &= For(Next(prob, l), a + 1, h), &&\text{if } l \le h \\
&= prob, &&\text{otherwise}
\end{aligned}
$$

**Exercise**

**1.5-13** Describe the sequence of *problem* values (and any other sequences) involved in the preceding recurrence.

The syntax associated with this is something like

$$FOR\ i := l\ TO\ h\ DO\ prob := Next(prob, i)\ END$$

*MulAcc* still fits into this form: all we have to do is let *Next(a,i)* be $m + a$ and we find that *Mul(n, m)* performed by *For(0, 1, n)*. Simple recurrences are computationally simpler to handle than rules like $Mul(n, m) = m + Mul(n - 1, m)$, but the more complex rule is easier to relate to the fundamental properties of arithmetic. We would like to have some way of getting from the more obviously correct forms to the more computationally tractable forms.

Basically, we find simple recurrences by drawing pictures and thinking about them; in this case the pictures will be dependency trees. We start at the top, with $Mul(x, y)$; then we have to have $y$ and $Mul(x - 1, y)$; then we have to have $y$ and $y$ and $Mul(x - 2, y)$.... At the bottom we find $Mul(0, y)$, so we produce 0 and start recombining copies of $y$ to produce

$$y + (y + \ldots + (y + y) \ldots))$$

The problem is that we were saving lots of copies of $y$, to add them up backwards. What we need to do is *reassociate* the additions so that we keep a running total instead of adding them up at the end; this produces the *MulAcc* accumulator solution, which is a top-down approach to the dependency tree of our original rules.

**Q:** What do you mean, it's top-down? What does top-down mean now?

**A:** It just means that as we compute with *MulAcc* we are following the dependency tree top-down, using the same values for $x$ and $y$; the only change is that we're explicitly keeping a total in an accumulator rather than implicitly saving it for later use.

**Q:** Well, what about bottom-up then?

**A:** Suppose we just go up from the bottom of the dependency tree to the top; i.e., we find the answers to $Mul(0, y)$, $Mul(1, y)$, and so on in that order. Here's a bottom-up multiplication:

$$
\begin{aligned}
Mul(x, y) &= MulAns(x, y, 0, 0) \\
MulAns(x, y, i, i * y) &= x * y \\
MulAns(x, y, i, ans) &= x * y, &\text{if } i \leq x \text{ and } i * y = ans \\
&= ans, &\text{if } i = x \\
&= MulAns(x, y, i + 1, y + ans) &\text{otherwise}
\end{aligned}
$$

This will carry us through a computation sequence in which $i$ and $y$ continue to increase *while $i \neq x$*.

$$
\begin{aligned}
Mul(5, 5) &= MulAns(5, 5, 0, 0) \\
&= MulAns(5, 5, 1, 5) \\
&= MulAns(5, 5, 2, 10) \\
&= MulAns(5, 5, 3, 15) \\
&= MulAns(5, 5, 4, 20) \\
&= MulAns(5, 5, 5, 25) \\
&= 25
\end{aligned}
$$

**Exercise**

**1.5-14** Describe the sequences of values for $x$, $y$, $i$, and *ans* involved in the preceding recurrence.

This, too, is a simple recurrence; it just defines the values we find as we go up the dependency tree rather than down it, so it's a bottom-up schedule.

**Exercises**

**1.5-15** Find a bottom-up schedule for exponentiation.

**1.5-16** Find top-down and bottom-up schedules for the factorial function, defined as

$$
\begin{aligned}
F(n) &= 1, &&\text{if } n = 0 \\
&= n * F(n-1), &&\text{otherwise}
\end{aligned}
$$

Simple recurrences are very close to iterative programs in conventional programming languages, as you will see in later parts of this course. There are even languages in which simple recurrences are always used instead of iteration. Your ability to find a top-down simple recurrence for a given dependency tree rests on your understanding of properties like associativity; for example, that's what keeping a running total requires. Similarly, your ability to find a bottom-up simple recurrence depends in many cases on your understanding of invertibility: the dependency tree goes from $n$ to $n-1$, so the bottom-up schedule goes from $n-1$ to $n$.

Remember, "simple recurrence" does *not* mean "efficient program"; it just means less bookkeeping than other forms. The rules for $MulAns$ which you just saw are enormously slower than rules such as

$$
\begin{aligned}
Mul(2*n+1, m) &= m + Mul(n, 2*m) \\
Mul(2*n, m) &= Mul(n, 2*m) \\
Mul(0, m) &= 0
\end{aligned}
$$

even though those are not simple recurrences.

**Q:** Is multiplication the only function we're going to study?

**A:** No, it's probably about time to give you a more precise version of the "telephone book" problem, presented earlier in the chapter. Since we're still only working with cardinal numbers, we'll rephrase it. Instead of a structure like

[John Jones:123-4567, Mary Smith:145-0020, Jim Wilson:123-1313]

with a million names (in alphabetical order), we'll just have

[456:1234567, 589:1450020, 632:1231313]

with a million numbers in numerical order. More precisely, we'll pretend that the telephone book is actually two functions: $Nam(i)$ which yields the $i$th "name" in the telephone book; and $Num(i)$, which yields the $i$th telephone number. In the three-name "book" above, we can define $Nam$ and $Num$ with the rules

$$
\begin{array}{llll}
Nam(1) &= 456 & Num(1) &= 1234567 \\
Nam(2) &= 589 & Num(2) &= 1450020 \\
Nam(3) &= 632 & Num(3) &= 1231313
\end{array}
$$

Now we want the $LookUp$ function defined in such a way that $LookUp(456) = 1234567$, $LookUp(589) = 1450020$, and so on; $LookUp(n)$ should produce 0 if $n$ is not in the $Nam$-list at all. We look at two functions: $SS$ for sequential search, and $BS$ for binary search. With a one-million entry telephone book,

$$
\begin{array}{lll}
LookUp(a) & = & SS(a, 1, 1000000) \\
SS(a, lo, hi) & = & 0, & \text{if } lo > hi \\
& = & Num(lo), & \text{if } Nam(lo) = a \\
& = & SS(a, lo + 1, hi), & \text{otherwise}
\end{array}
$$

Alternatively,

$$
\begin{array}{lll}
LookUp(a) & = & BS(a, 1, 500000, 1000000) \\
BS(a, lo, md, hi) & = & 0, & \text{if } lo > hi \\
& = & Num(md), & \text{if } Nam(md) = a \\
& = & BS(a, lo, Half(lo + md), md - 1), & \text{if } (Nam(md) > a \\
& = & BS(a, md + 1, Half(md + hi), hi), & \text{otherwise}
\end{array}
$$

At this point you should be able to see that we're dealing with the same principle that we used in multiplication, but you should also be able to see why we did multiplication first: this is harder. Still, we have defined $LookUp$ through simple recurrences, and you can easily get the feel of the mechanics of a telephone-book program by tracing through a few examples.

**Exercises**    Given the three-entry telephone book on the previous page, show the steps for the four problems following:

**1.5-17** $SS(632, 1, 3)$

**1.5-18** $BS(632, 1, 2, 3)$

**1.5-19** $SS(100, 1, 3)$

**1.5-20** $BS(100, 1, 2, 3)$

**1.5-21** We have talked about a dramatic contrast between the sequential and binary approaches to searching. Do you see it with the previous problems? Discuss briefly.

### 1.5.3 Invariants of a Computation

When we rephrase rules so that they naturally describe a computation sequence, they often are not as easy to understand as the original specification. However, there are several ways of examining the rules and making sense of them. In this subsection, we'll look at different ways of describing a computation sequence, using familiar examples. These descriptions (program *invariants*) turn out to be very helpful in program design, debugging, and maintenance. At the end of the examples, you should be able to write or use invariants of several kinds for many computations.

Let's go back to multiplication: we are trying to define a $Mul$ function so that $Mul(x, y) = x * y$, and in order to achieve that we define a $MulAcc$ function so that $MulAcc(x, y, z) = x * y + z$.

$$
\begin{aligned}
Mul(x, y) &= MulAcc(x, y, 0) & \\
MulAcc(x, y, a) &= a, & \text{if } x = 0 \\
&= MulAcc(Half(x), Double(y), a + y) & \text{if } odd(x) \\
&= MulAcc(Half(x), Double(y), a) & \text{otherwise}
\end{aligned}
$$

This leads us to examples like

$$
\begin{aligned}
Mul(10, 10) &= MulAcc(10, 10, 0) & (S_1) \\
&= MulAcc(5, 20, 0) & (S_2) \\
&= MulAcc(2, 40, 20) & (S_3) \\
&= MulAcc(1, 80, 20) & (S_4) \\
&= MulAcc(0, 160, 100) & (S_5) \\
&= 100
\end{aligned}
$$

Apart from the beginning and end, this computation sequence is just a sequence of situations or *states* in which we are trying to find $MulAcc(x, y, a)$ for particular values of $x$, $y$, and $a$. In state $S_3$, for example, we want $MulAcc(x, y, a)$ for $x = 2$, $y = 40$, and $a = 20$. In state $S_4$ we want to solve the same problem for $x = 1$, $y = 80$, and $a = 20$. Another way of saying this is that $x_1 = 10$, $x_2 = 5$, $y_1 = 10$, $y_2 = 20$, $a_1 = 0$, $a_5 = 100$, and so on.

### Exercises

**1.5-22** Describe $S_2$. What problem are we solving here?

**1.5-23** Find $x_3$, $y_5$, and $a_3$.

An invariant is something that doesn't change; an invariant assertion is one which continues to be true throughout the computation. Certainly, $x = 2$ is not true throughout the computation; in fact, it's only true in state $S_3$. However, $x \leq 10$ is true throughout; it is an invariant assertion, which helps express the fact that $x$ can only decrease from its initial value. Similarly, we can notice that $y \geq 10$, since $y$ can only increase. We could note that $y$ and $a$ are always even, or that $x * y \leq 100$.

### Exercises
For each of the following, tell whether it is always true and state in English what its truth or falsity expresses.

**1.5-24** $mod(y, 10) = 0$.

**1.5-25** $mod(a, 10) = 0$.

**1.5-26** $mod(x, 10) = 0$.

**1.5-27** $x * a \leq 100$.

**1.5-28** $y + a \leq 100$.

A great many such assertions will be invariant for the particular computation we're working on; some help us understand the problem being solved, while others don't. One of the most important is also one of the most obvious:

$$MulAcc(x, y, a) = Mul(x_1, y_1)$$

In this case, that's an abbreviation for five statements:

$$
\begin{aligned}
Mul(x_1, y_1) &= MulAcc(x_1, y_1, a_1) \\
Mul(x_1, y_1) &= MulAcc(x_2, y_2, a_2) \\
Mul(x_1, y_1) &= MulAcc(x_3, y_3, a_3) \\
Mul(x_1, y_1) &= MulAcc(x_4, y_4, a_4) \\
Mul(x_1, y_1) &= MulAcc(x_5, y_5, a_5)
\end{aligned}
$$

This particular invariant is an *adequate invariant*: if it is indeed true for all the states, then the whole computation works correctly because $Mul(x_1, y_1)$ is what we're after. It isn't the most readable of adequate invariants, however: it might be better to say

$$x_1 * y_1 = x * y + a$$

without mentioning named functions at all. Whether we worry about such clarification or not, we are dealing with a *goal-directed invariant*, one which says where we're going from here. In this case and many others, the goal-directed invariant is an equation $G = E$ where $G$ is the original goal (in this case, $x_1 * y_1$) and $E$ is an expression using values from the current state (in this case, $x * y + a$).

Suppose that we chose another example:

$$
\begin{aligned}
H(x) &= f(x, x) \\
f(x, y) &= y - x, &&\text{if } x < 2 \\
&= f(x - 2, y - 1) &&\text{otherwise}
\end{aligned}
$$

We can still write the goal-directed invariant that $H(x_1) = f(x, y)$, even though it won't tell us very much until we try an example like

$$H(9) = f(9, 9) = f(7, 8) = f(5, 7) = f(3, 6) = f(1, 5) = 4$$

After that, we can make observations like

$$
\begin{aligned}
H(x) &= Half(x) \\
f(x, y) &= (y - k) - a, &&\text{if } x = 2 * k + a, a < 2 \\
&= (y - Half(x)) - mod(x, 2) &&\text{so that} \\
f(x, x) &= (x - Half(x)) - mod(x, 2) \\
&= x - (x - Half(x)) \\
&= Half(x)
\end{aligned}
$$

Now we can note that every state satisfies the assertion

$$H(x_1) = Half(x_1) = (y - Half(x)) - mod(x, 2)$$

## Exercises

**1.5-29** Write a computation sequence for $H(93)$, and check the given assertion for each line.

**1.5-30** Write a computation sequence for $Exp(7, 9)$, and formulate a goal-directed invariant for it.

**1.5-31** Repeat the previous exercise for $mod(70, 3)$.


**Q:** You keep saying "goal-directed invariant." What kind of an invariant isn't goal directed? What kind of a sap am I for asking leading questions like this?

**A:** I think I'll ignore the second question. A "goal-directed invariant" is one which says where we're going from here; we could have a "data-directed" or "process-directed" invariant instead, i.e., one which just helps keep track of things as we go along, relating the current state to the original state rather than to the final goal. Actually, invariants like $x \leq x_1$ are "data-directed": if you know that you begin with $x_1$ and go down from there, then this invariant must hold; it doesn't tell you anything about what problem is being solved. Another data-directed invariant would be that $y_i = y_1 * (2**(i - 1))$; we will not use this kind of invariant very much. Another would be $x_1/x \geq y/y_1$.

Sometimes a data-directed invariant is helpful in thinking of a goal-directed invariant. For example, in the function $H(x)$ above, I knew that $H(x)$ was supposed to come out to be $Half(x)$ but I did not see in advance what $f(x, y)$ would do in general; I only knew that $f(x, x)$ should find $Half(x)$ by generating the series

$$[x, x], [x - 2, x - 1], [x - 4, x - 2] \ldots [x - 2 * i, x - i] \ldots$$

I was working out the data-directed invariant $x_i = x_1 - 2 * i, y_i = y_1 - i$, which is equivalent to $y_1 - y = (x_1 - x)/2$, in the belief that this would get me to $[0, Half(x_1)]$.

**Q:** What do you mean? It only does that if $x$ is even. If $x$ is odd it ends up with $[1, Half(x) + 1]$; that's why you have $y - x$ as the result.

**A:** True, but I didn't think of that at first, so my first version of $f$ was wrong for odd values of $x$. I realized that my data-directed invariant was true but not adequate, so I changed the definition.

**Q:** I thought the whole point of this course was that we'd be planning things in advance so you wouldn't have to make mistakes and fix them.

**A:** To err is human, to forgive divine... to debug is technical. Specifications aren't always going to be correct; the advantage of using them is that we can find mistakes like that one more easily than we could with programs. Invariants help you see *what*'s going on without simultaneously remembering *how* it happens; that helps you find mistakes. Anyway, once I found that invariant, I could say that $y = y_1 - (x_1 - x)/2$, so that if I knew that $x_1 = y_1$, I could be sure that $y = (2*x_1 - (x_1 - x))/2 = (x_1 + x)/2$; these are all invariants for the calculation of $H$ by this collection of rules. If $x = 0$, then this invariant means that $y - x = x_1/2$. If $x = 1$, and $x_1$ is odd, then the same invariant means that $y - x = x_1/2$.

**Exercises**    Find and justify invariants for the following:

**1.5-32**  $G(x) = h(x, x)$, $h(x, y) = y - x$ if $x < 3$, $h(x, y) = h(x - 3, y - 1)$ otherwise .

**1.5-33**  $L(n) = f(n, 1)$ where $f(n, a) = a$ if $n < 10$, $f(n, a) = f(n/10, a + 1)$ otherwise.

The invariants that we've talked about all have to do with rules which are not "nested"; it isn't as easy to deal with

$$fib(n) = fib(n - 1) + fib(n - 2), \text{ if } n > 1$$

because the states in the computation sequence are not so simple. Consider, for example,

$$
\begin{aligned}
fib(5) &= fib(4) + fib(3) \\
&= fib(3) + fib(2) + fib(3) \\
&= fib(2) + fib(1) + fib(2) + fib(3) \\
&= \qquad \vdots
\end{aligned}
$$

Here the number of variables changes from line to line. We cannot describe this very usefully yet, but at least for many rules we can now come up with good descriptions of the computations they ought to generate. When you write programs from specifications, you will learn to include these invariants as comments in the code. A variety of mistakes in coding can then be caught by checking to see whether the invariant is true, and then by looking for a reason if it isn't.

**Q:** But how do I check to see if the invariant is true?

**A:** Simple: you'll edit the program to print out the invariant itself and  the values of the variables on which it depends; for example, you'd edit the program which computes $H$ so that if you called $H(9)$ it might print out a series of lines saying

$$
\begin{aligned}
x = 9; \quad & y = 9; \quad & y_1 - y &= (x_1 - x)/2 \\
x = 7; \quad & y = 8; \quad & y_1 - y &= (x_1 - x)/2 \\
x = 5; \quad & y = 7; \quad & y_1 - y &= (x_1 - x)/2 \\
x = 3; \quad & y = 6; \quad & y_1 - y &= (x_1 - x)/2 \\
x = 1; \quad & y = 5; \quad & y_1 - y &= (x_1 - x)/2
\end{aligned}
$$

In each case, the assertion is true, so all is well so far. If there's a problem in the program, it must be in some other part... perhaps you didn't really want $H(9)$ at all, or perhaps the program which gets $H(9)$ does the wrong thing with it.

### 1.5.4 Time and Space

At this point, we have achieved most of the goals of the chapter: you can break down expressions into their parts (and even diagram them), you can use groups of equations as algorithms, and you can describe the properties of those algorithms with invariant assertions. You can use words, formulas, and pictures for all of those. We have also made some progress on understanding time requirements (number of steps) and space requirements (length of longest line), but we went no further than words and numerical examples. That's not enough: we need some way to give an exact description of the time and space requirements for carrying out a given set of rules. We need to compare algorithms with one another, and to tell roughly what kind of performance to expect *before* we have spent large sums on developing a piece of software, just as a bridge-builder has to be able to estimate the strength of a bridge before it's built. Testing is necessary, and we have the advantage that we can (and must) test our product past the failure point and still sell it, but we cannot depend on testing alone.

**Q:** Won't the exact time and space depend on the input? Surely you can't tell just by studying the rules themselves how long they will take in every case, because different rules have different costs and you can't tell in advance which ones will be applied.

**A:** Yes, and we don't try. Normally we don't even try to worry about typical input, or "average-case behavior"; we start with Murphy's Law. If you assume that everything that can go wrong will go wrong, and that the time that the program takes is as long as the program could possibly take, then you're probably still being optimistic (because something will go wrong that you didn't even think of), but you're likely to come pretty close to realism. Time and space analysis of algorithms usually starts with the assumption of "worst-case behavior."

For example, think of the telephone-book algorithms we mentioned in the first section of this chapter, or the *LookUp* rule sets in the previous section. A computer looking up a name by reading names one at a time from front to back might happen to come across it as the first name, after one step. We assume the worst: Murphy will step in and make sure that the name is close to the end, after roughly 1,000,000 other names. If we worried about averages, we might guess that it will really be roughly 500,000, but it is simpler and safer to assume the worst. Suppose that the computer checks names at a rate of 1000 per second; then worst-case analysis suggests about half an hour, best-case analysis suggests 0.001 second, and average-case analysis suggests about 15 minutes.

**Exercises**   Write approximate worst-case, best-case, and average-case times with computer speeds and telephone book sizes as follows:

**1.5-34**  500,000 names processed at 1000 per second

**1.5-35**  500,000 names processed at 10 per second

**1.5-36**  50 names processed at 1000 per second

**1.5-37**  50 names processed at 10 per second

**1.5-38**  5 names processed at 1000 per second

**1.5-39**  5 names processed at 10 per second

If you think about it, you should see that worst-case and average-case analyses are giving you the same warnings about the impracticality of this method for large telephone books. Now let's look at the other method, in which the computer tears (the remainder of the) telephone book in half with each step, always looking in the middle of the book for the name. The sequence of remaining lengths is 1,000,000 followed by 500,000 followed by 125,000 followed by 62,500 ... which comes to an end after 20 steps, but of course the steps are harder, perhaps even 10 times as hard. If the computer can only manage 100 steps per second, then the best-case analysis (which this time means that the name was right in the middle of the book, found on the first step) suggests 0.01 second: twice as long as before. Worst-case analysis, however, suggests limits on Murphy's power: even the 20 steps required on consistent failure will take only 0.2 second to go through a million-name telephone directory. Average-case analysis for this problem is difficult; after you study some probability you can come back and take an algorithms course and find out, but clearly you can see that the worst-case analyses of these two programs gave you a lot of useful information while the best-case analyses were almost worthless. That's usually the way it works out.

**Exercises**  Write approximate worst-case, best-case, and average-case times with computer speeds and telephone book sizes as follows:

**1.5-40**  500,000 names processed at 100 per second

**1.5-41**  500,000 names processed at 1 per second

**1.5-42**  50 names processed at 100 per second

**1.5-43**  50 names processed at 1 per second

**1.5-44**  5 names processed at 100 per second

**1.5-45**  5 names processed at 1 per second

As you can see from the exercises, the "cutting-in-half" or *binary* search is enormously faster for large telephone books, but can actually be slower for small ones. That's a common problem when we try to compare algorithms. It's one of the factors that makes testing dangerous: we usually test a program with problems which are smaller than the problems it will be used on in practice. Again we assume that Murphy is nearby: he will make sure that the problems we get are *very* large, and so analysis emphasizes what happens as problem size gets larger and larger and Larger without any predefined limit at all. This is called asymptotic analysis, and if you go to the dictionary to look up "asymptote," I hope that you'll use a binary search for the word. Compare it with the way you usually look up words in a dictionary. Think about whether the method you usually use when you're starting out (large problem) is the same as the method you use when you're within a few pages (small problem). Become algorithm-conscious!

So how do we describe an algorithm's space and time requirements in terms of problem size? Mostly we use a few simple categories, being very careful to be consistent in our measure of problem size. If we're multiplying two numbers $x * y$ we could say that $x$ will be the size, or that whichever is the larger—or smaller—of $x$ and $y$ is the size, or that the number of digits in the larger—or smaller—of $x$ and $y$ is the size. All of those are fine (at least, some of the time), but when you compare two algorithms for the same kind of problem you'd better use the same measure of problem size.

- There are *constant-time* algorithms, which—despite all Murphy can do—will use a fixed number of steps no matter what the size of the input. Finding the first name of the telephone book is like that. We'll call these $\mathcal{O}(1)$ algorithms; that's pronounced "big-Oh-of-1," or "on the order of 1."

- There are *linear* algorithms, which in the worst case use a number of steps proportional to the size of the input. Finding a particular name in the telephone book by going sequentially through the whole book is like that. We'll call these $\mathcal{O}(n)$ algorithms (where $n$ is the size of the input), and pronounce the name "big-Oh-of-$n$."

- There are *logarithmic* algorithms, which can use a number of steps proportional to the logarithm (base 2) of the size of the input, because they cut the problem in half with each step and the base-2 logarithm of a number is roughly the number of times it can be cut in half before reaching zero. (The logarithm of a number is also proportional to its length: an $n$-digit decimal number can be cut in half about $3n$ times before reaching 0.) We'll call these $\mathcal{O}(\log n)$ algorithms.

- There are *quadratic* algorithms, which can use a number of steps proportional to the square of the size of the input. We'll call these $\mathcal{O}(n^2)$ algorithms.

- Finally, there are *exponential* algorithms, which can use a number of steps proportional to $2 * 2 * 2 \ldots * 2$, with $n$ 2's in the product. These are $\mathcal{O}(2^n)$ algorithms. For example, if I asked you to check all possible sequences of $n$ letters, to find the percentage which would make reasonably pronounceable English words, you would have (roughly) an exponential number of steps to go through.

Of course, there are combinations of these which get more and more complex as your problems get harder and your analysis gets more careful. It turns out that the multiplication process we've been talking about is worthy of very careful analysis indeed, and it's quite complicated when you try to do it as carefully as possible. For most purposes, we will think of multiplication as if it were a constant-time algorithm, but we started with a multiplication algorithm for $n * m$ which is $\mathcal{O}(n)$, unless you want to think of it as a multiplication algorithm for $n$-digit numbers which is $\mathcal{O}(2^n)$. Remember to take care in measuring the problem size! We followed with a multiplication algorithm for $n * m$ which is $\mathcal{O}(\log n)$, unless you want to think of it as a multiplication algorithm for $n$-digit numbers which is $\mathcal{O}(n)$. Of course, that's assuming that addition is a single step. The multiplication of a pair of $n$-digit numbers is actually described as an $\mathcal{O}(n * \log n * \log(\log n))$ algorithm in Theorem 7.8 of Aho, Hopcroft, and Ullman's *Design and Analysis of Computer Algorithms* [1].

For most purposes, we think of having the computer check a single item on his graph paper as $\mathcal{O}(1)$, but if he has a total of $n$ squares of graph paper then an electronic circuit will actually need $\mathcal{O}(\log n)$ steps because of "fanout," which you'll learn about in computer architecture courses, and—even worse, in practical terms— it really needs $\mathcal{O}(\sqrt[3]{n})$ steps because that's how long it takes electrical impulses to travel at the speed of light.

**Q:** You're kidding, aren't you?

**A:** No. An electronic switch can flip in one-billionth of a second (one nanosecond), in which time light travels about one foot. How many cells can you pack in a cubic foot? The number is large, but it's certainly not unlimited... and if you didn't go look up "asymptote" or "asymptotic" before, I suggest you do it now.

**Exercises**    Classify the following as roughly $\mathcal{O}(1)$, $\mathcal{O}(n)$, $\mathcal{O}(\log n)$, $\mathcal{O}(n^2)$, or $\mathcal{O}(2^n)$. Justify your classifications briefly.

**1.5-46**    Adding two numbers, of which the smaller is $n$, by the rules $0 + y = y$, $(x+1) + y = x + (y+1)$.

**1.5-47**    Adding two $n$-digit numbers by the same rules.

**1.5-48**    Finding $P(n, n)$ where $P$ is the Pascal's triangle definition mentioned earlier in the chapter.

**1.5-49**    Finding $TriangleArea(n, m)$ (also mentioned earlier in the chapter) on the assumption that multiplication and division are single steps.

### 1.5.5  The Limits of Analysis

In some cases, the worst case you can find is that the program doesn't halt. Think about this example:

$$
\begin{aligned}
SR(n, m) &= n, & \text{if } n = m \\
&= n + SR(n+1, m), & \text{otherwise}
\end{aligned}
$$

In this case, $SR(1, 100)$ is the sum of the range $1 \ldots 100$, that is, $1 + 2 + 3 + \ldots + 99 + 100 = 5050$, but $f(100, 1)$ would never stop. The function depends on the precondition that $n \leq m$. Given that precondition, the time and space worst-case behavior is $\mathcal{O}(m - n)$, but without it you could only say that it's $\mathcal{O}(\infty)$. Of course, that's better than the program defined by the one rule $f(n) = f(n+1)$, which never halts under any circumstances.

You can't always tell just by studying the rules whether or not they will always halt. I'll give you an example: suppose that I have the function

$$
\begin{aligned}
UD(n) &= 1, & \text{if } n = 1 \\
&= UD(\mathit{Half}(n)) & \text{if } mod(n, 2) = 0 \\
&= UD(\mathit{Half}(3 * n + 1)), & \text{otherwise}
\end{aligned}
$$

This is a simple recurrence, and the length of the longest line is therefore quite short: lines don't build up, unless we worry about the actual length of a number. Goal-directed invariants are also simple. Moreover, we know that *if* the computation of $UD(n)$ ever comes to an end, the value it produces is 1. However, *nobody knows* whether or not there is a number $n$ such that $UD(n)$ never finishes. Watch the sequence.

$$
\begin{aligned}
UD(7) &= UD(11) & \text{by the third rule} \\
&= UD(17) & \text{by the third again} \\
&= UD(26) & \text{by the third} \\
&= UD(13) & \text{by the second} \\
&= UD(20) & \text{by the third} \\
&= UD(10) & \text{by the second} \\
&= UD(5) & \text{by the second} \\
&= UD(8) & \text{by the third} \\
&= UD(4) & \text{by the second} \\
&= UD(2) & \text{by the second} \\
&= UD(1) & \text{by the second} \\
&= 1 & \text{by the first}
\end{aligned}
$$

I've called it the $UD$ function because of the way its computation sequence goes $U$p and $D$own.

**Exercises**   Show the sequence of steps for

**1.5-50**  $UD(15)$

**1.5-51**  $UD(16)$

**1.5-52**  $UD(17)$

Are you confident that the computation sequence for $UD(12345678)$ would ever stop? (I am fairly confident, because I've been told that $UD(n)$ has been found for all values of $n$ up to 100,000,000, but I haven't done it myself.)

**Q:** Well, if you can't predict performance for rules as simple as those, what point is there in worrying about it?

**A:** The performance of a practical program is pretty predictable. Actually, that's a tautology: if the worst-case performance of a program isn't predictable, it's not likely to be very practical. However, there are many cases (like this one) where we don't know whether the program always halts or not, and we do know that in principle the "halting problem"—the problem of predicting whether or not a given program will always halt—can never be solved. More precisely, we know that it's not possible for any program to solve it, and we have no reason to believe that we can do any better ourselves. It's even worse than that: we can't reliably solve the problem of predicting whether or not a program will halt for a particular input. In other words, it's possible to have a rule-set defining $f$ and a particular argument $x$ and be completely unable to tell whether or not $f(x)$ will ever halt. (Of course, you could simply try it, but if the answer is "no," you'll never find out.)

**Q:** That sounds ridiculous. I can understand that there are programs whose performance nobody can predict yet, but how can you say that the problem can never be solved at all?

**A:** It turns out that to solve the problem would generate a logical contradiction. Think for a moment what a solution would be: it would have to be a program *Halts* which takes an expression "**f(x)**" as an argument and says (among other things, perhaps) either "Yes, the evaluation of "**f(x)**" will eventually halt" or "No, the rules defining $f$ will go on forever if started on $x$." Of course, you don't really have a solution unless *Halts* itself is reliable: it has to always halt, so *Halts*("**Halts(e)**") has to say "Yes, this will eventually halt" no matter what $e$ may be. All right so far?

**Q:** Sort of, but I'm not comfortable with the idea of a program which takes an expression as an argument. So far we've only had programs which work on numbers and produce numbers.

**A:** That's a problem, but it can be solved—in fact, you know it has been solved, since the programs which you write are processed by other programs called interpreters or compilers in order to get them to run. Moreover, most of this chapter has been devoted to getting you to work mechanically with expressions. Let's suppose that the argument of *Halts* is actually a number identifying the graph paper square where the expression begins, and *Halts(e)* produces a 1 if $e$ does always halt or a 0 if it doesn't always halt. Now it should be clear that *Halts*("**SR(2,5)**") = 1, while *Halts*("**SR(5,2)**") = 0. Similarly, *Halts*("**UD(123456789012345)**") is either 0 or 1, but we don't know which.

**Q:** All right, where's the paradox?

**A:** Look at the rules which follow:

$$
\begin{array}{lll}
Paradox & = & Loopy(\text{``}\textbf{Loopy}\text{''}), \\
Loopy(e) & = & 1, & \text{if } Halts(\text{``}\textbf{Loopy}(e)\text{''}) = 0 \\
& = & Loopy(e), & \text{otherwise}
\end{array}
$$

Let's see if we can figure out what the *Paradox* here is. The rule to be applied in finding *Loopy*("**Loopy**") depends on the value of *Halts*("**Loopy**("**Loopy**")"), so we think about whether the evaluation of "**Loopy**("**Loopy**")" ever comes to an end.

- Suppose that *Halt* produces a 0, i.e., the evaluation of "**Loopy**("**Loopy**")" never halts. In this case the first rule applies, and *Loopy*("**Loopy**") = 1. Clearly, *Halt* was wrong: the evaluation did halt.

- Suppose that *Halt* produces a 1, i.e., the evaluation of "**Loopy**("**Loopy**")" does halt. In this case the second rule applies, and we go through the sequence

$$
\begin{aligned}
Loopy(\text{``\textbf{Loopy}''}) \quad &= \quad Loopy(\text{``\textbf{Loopy}''}) \quad \text{by the second rule} \\
&= \quad Loopy(\text{``\textbf{Loopy}''}) \\
&= \quad Loopy(\text{``\textbf{Loopy}''}) \\
&= \quad \dots
\end{aligned}
$$

The evaluation doesn't halt: again the *Halt* function was wrong. No matter what it says, *Halt* is giving the wrong answer.

**Exercise**

**1.5-53**  Who was Alan Turing, and why is his name associated with the unsolvability of the "halting problem"?

As it happens, it's perfectly possible to write a limited version of the *Halt* function to check for some of the situations that lead to unbounded evaluation, or to warn you against suspicious circumstances. However, any solution to the *Halt*ing problem in general would be self-contradictory, as you've just seen. No one has written that program; no one ever will. Never. Never. Never. (Sigh...)

# 2

# Working with Formal Descriptions

At this point in your reading, you should be able to work with expressions and rules, acting as a computer. That skill will serve you well in understanding programming languages, because the substitutions and simplifications you can now perform are very much like those which are actually performed by the "abstract machines" which programming language implementations are designed to be. For now, however, we want to expand in a different direction: you will use yourself as an experimental tool to explore the properties of systems of rules, systems which define the various kinds of objects used in computer science. You will not be learning to do mathematical proofs, but you will be using computations.

At the end of the chapter, you should be able to understand and use the fundamental "simple data types" of computer science: numbers of several distinct kinds, the logical values *True* and *False*, symbols in an alphabet, and arbitrary enumerations like (`Monday, Tuesday, ...`). This understanding and use will focus on the properties of operations associated with the data types.

1. You will be familiar with the standard properties (associativity, commutativity, identity elements, and so on) of standard operations on each type, and you'll be ready to use them as guides in programming.

2. You will be able to test such properties for operations defined with rules, and you'll be ready to use them both for debugging and for program modification.

**3.** You will be able to formulate and test nonstandard properties (such as "$f(x, y)$ has to be between $x$ and $y$").

**4.** You will be able to represent simple objects with other simple objects: logical values or real numbers or enumerations with cardinals, cardinals with logical values.

**5.** Within these representations, you will be able to translate operations on objects into operations on their representations.

The presentation is designed to give you a strong sense of *déjà vu* with each new type: each of them has a *system* of operations, these systems are all very similar in many ways, and these similarities are extremely useful in describing and debugging programs as well as in rewriting them for improved performance.

## 2.1 CARDINAL NUMBERS

In the last chapter we used your existing intuitive understanding of the *cardinal* or *natural* numbers, the nonnegative integers $[0, 1, 2, \ldots]$, to give examples of what rules could do. In this section we are turning that around: we will use rules to build a sense of the system formed by the cardinal numbers themselves, and—much more important—a sense of how we can go about describing such systems. We have to learn to describe data of a given form through the operations associated with that form. We have to learn to use heuristics (where's the dictionary?) to guide the process of developing a system of operations. We have to recognize that operations will form certain patterns; patterns which will be found in rules which work on numbers, employees, messages within an electronic mail system, or targets being tracked by radar. Of course, to do these things we'll have to use some ideas which we haven't yet fully developed, and in any case we're working on an essentially creative process which may be learnable but is not really teachable, but that's a common situation: we can still explore.

### 2.1.1  How Can We Describe Data?

When we're computing with rules, the important thing is to have rules for each operation: addition, subtraction, multiplication, and so on. When we're trying to understand the data, the important thing is to have rules which interconnect the operations: how does addition relate to subtraction? We're really trying to use our description of the numbers as a model for describing data in general. Afterwards, we'll use more rules to build a similar understanding of other kinds of data.

**Q:** But it seems that you're saying that in order to talk about algorithms you give rules about operations, and in order to talk about data you give rules about operations. What's the difference?

**A:** Only the emphasis of the rules. In describing algorithms, the most important kind of rule is one like $(x + 1) * y = x * y + y$, which can be applied over and over again, in a simple fixed sequence, to solve a problem. (In the end, the most important kinds are simple rules, which can be directly related to programs in conventional programming languages.) In describing data, the most important kind of rule is one like $x + y = y + x$ or $x * (y + z) = x * y + x * z$, which lets us see the structure of the problem and therefore helps us find analogies between similar problems. Commutative and distributive laws crop up not only in arithmetic and logic, but also in data base manipulations, programming language implementations, graphics, and other seemingly unrelated areas of computer science.

**Q:** I'll have to think about that for a while. My first reaction is that if you've got all kinds of useful examples of what you're teaching, why are you starting out with the counting numbers $0, 1, 2, 3, \ldots$? Why don't you include negatives, fractions, and decimals, as well?

**A:** There are three reasons for starting with the cardinals:

1. The cardinal numbers are very important in computer science applications: you will write many programs in which you have variables which are cardinal numbers and are not allowed to be anything else, usually because the variable actually represents a number of discrete objects.

2. The cardinal numbers are fundamental in computer systems (beneath the hierarchical level of those applications). The moron with his graph paper actually associates a cardinal number as an address with each square, and (as I hinted in the description of the halting problem) he actually uses such addresses to keep track of large objects.

3. The rules for cardinal numbers are somewhat simpler than most, and it's easier to start with something simple.

The description of data (numbers, in this case) is based on the description of possible operations on data and possible conditions. We have to be able to see what operations create the objects we're interested in, what operations use them, what conditions are possible for objects created by those operations, and what rules interconnect them all. Even for a world as simple as that of the cardinal numbers, this involves a description that is just as complicated as we will let it become. That means that we have to figure out what is to be emphasized. Often, this means we stress some small collection of "primitive" operations which are powerful enough so that we can define everything else in terms of them; this helps provide coherence. At other times we stress those operations which are very easy to work with because they strongly resemble something we already know, or because they have properties which we can describe easily. At still other times, we stress those operations which are easy to implement efficiently.

### 2.1.2 Informal Rules for Finding Formal Rules

In looking for the rules which will characterize a kind of object, we need some kind of *heuristics*: rules of thumb, guides for guesswork. Rather than write a list of heuristics, we'll go over the child's discovery of arithmetic and state (in italics) a general rule for each new kind of fact discovered. These general rules will mostly carry over to other kinds of objects.

A preschooler first comes to understand numbers with the operation of counting up from 1, or sometimes from 0: 0 is a closed fist, 1 is one finger raised and the rest down, and so on until we run out of fingers. Alternatively, 0 is an empty space on the floor, we get 1 from 0 by adding a block, we get 2 from 1 by adding a block, and so on until we run out of blocks. More generally, when we go up from 0 we get 1, up from 1 gets us to 2, up from 2 is 3, or in the notation we're using now:

$$
\begin{aligned}
Up(0) &= 1 & Up(4) &= 5 \\
Up(1) &= 2 & Up(5) &= 6 \\
Up(2) &= 3 & Up(6) &= 7 \\
Up(3) &= 4 & Up(7) &= 8
\end{aligned}
$$

and so on.

That answers a very basic question: what is a number? In this case, a number is either 0 or it's $Up(n)$ where $n$ is already a number. That gives us the $[0, 1, 2, 3, 4, 5, 6, 7, \ldots]$ series.

Somewhat later (but still prior to kindergarten) the child learns that the *inverse* of counting up by adding a block is counting down by removing a block: $Down(4) = 3$, $Down(3) = 2$, $Down(2) = 1$, $Down(1) = 0$, but $Down(0)$ is meaningless because you can't go down from 0. At this level, there is a very simple relationship between the two operations: if you add a block and then take a block away, you've got just as many blocks as you started with. If you try to take a block away and then add one, then again you have just as many as before (unless it didn't work because you started with none). Thus, we have

$$
Down(n) \quad = \quad m, \quad \text{if } n = Up(m)
$$

or equivalently

$$
\begin{aligned}
Down(Up(m)) &= m, \\
Up(Down(n)) &= n, \quad \text{if } n \neq 0
\end{aligned}
$$

This is part of a general process that we will be applying to all kinds of objects: *If you have one operation that yields m from n, look for another operation that yields n from m; this is the inverse.*

Naturally, *Up* and *Down* are the same operations we called *Incr* and *Decr* (increment and decrement) previously. Later, the child learns to add two piles of blocks by taking one block at a time from the left-hand pile to the right-hand pile:

$$n + m = Down(n) + Up(m), \quad \text{if } n \neq 0$$
$$0 + m = m$$

or alternatively,

$$n + m = Up(Up(\ldots Up(m)\ldots)), \quad \text{repeated } n \text{ times.}$$

This, too, is a special case of a very general rule for data describers: *If you've found an interesting operation, try describing what happens when you do it over and over again.* In this case, we are thinking of $n+$ as being the operation $Up$ repeated $n$ times, or as being the Shift-Over operation repeated until the left-hand pile is empty.

Later still, the child learns some experimental laws, the Laws of Block Conservation: if you switch the piles and then add them you get the same answer, and if you add three piles you can work from either end.

$$x + y = y + x$$
$$x + (y + z) = (x + y) + z$$

These are the familiar commutative and associative laws for addition: an operation on two objects is *commutative* if the objects may be exchanged without changing the result, and it is *associative* if, when it is to be used to combine a whole sequence of objects, the process can begin at any point in the sequence.

Commutativity and associativity by themselves are quite important in computer science, because there are a lot of operations which are commutative or associative or both. They are of practical value because after you've implemented one of these operations, you can build test functions like these: $NC(n, m)$ (NonCommutative) tests a pair of numbers to see if your your function $f$ is commutative on that test case, $NCR(n, m)$ (NonCommutative Range) tests the left argument $n$ with the range $0 \ldots m$, and $NCC(n, m)$ (NonCommutative Count) tests all possible pairs from the ranges $0 \ldots n$ and $0 \ldots m$.

$$NC(n, m) = 0, \quad \text{if } f(n, m) \neq f(m, n)$$
$$= 1, \quad \text{otherwise}$$

Thus, if $f$ happens to be subtraction, then $NC(2, 2) = 0$ but $NC(2, 1) = 1$.

$$NCR(n, m) = NC(n, m) \qquad \qquad \text{if } m = 0$$
$$= NC(n, m) + NCR(n, m - 1) \quad \text{otherwise}$$

Again, if $f$ is subtraction, then $NCR(2, 2) = NC(2, 2) + NC(2, 1) + NC(2, 0) = 2$.

$$NCC(n, m) = NCR(n, m) \qquad \qquad \text{if } n = 0$$
$$= NCR(n, m) + NCC(n - 1, m) \quad \text{otherwise}$$

Finally, if $f$ is subtraction, $NCC(2,2) = NCR(2,2) + NCR(2,1) + NCR(2,0) = 6$. By using programs like this, you can test your own work to see if it has the properties it's supposed to... without reading very much output.

**Exercises**    Find $NCC$ for the given examples:

**2.1-1**    $f = \text{``+''}, n = 5, m = 5$
**2.1-2**    $f = \text{``--''}, n = 5, m = 5$
**2.1-3**    $f = \text{``--''}, n = 5, m = 0$
**2.1-4**    $f = \text{``--''}, n = 0, m = 5$
**2.1-5**    Given $f$, is $NCC$ (ever or always) a commutative function? Under what circumstances could you use it to test itself?

However, we don't want to focus too much on specific, traditional rules like those for commutativity and associativity. As usual, the rule for the experimentalist is more general: *Shuffle things around and look for rules to describe what doesn't change.* The commutative law tells us that if we can look at $n + m$ as involving an $n+$ operation which repeats the *Up* operation $n$ times, then we can also look at it as involving a $+m$ operation which repeats *Up* $m$ times. Another useful rule is to *look for operations which don't change anything.* We know already that $0 + x = x$, and naturally $x + 0 = x$ also: 0 is an *identity element* for addition because adding 0 to a cardinal number leaves it unchanged.

Our last rule (for now) is to *look for special cases.* Given a formula like $x + y$, that means to think about special values for $x$ and $y$. What if either (or both) should happen to be 0 or 1? What if they just happen to be the same? Here this means trying out possibilities like $1 + 1 = 2$ and $x + x = 2 * x$; the former looks pretty useless, the latter is worth remembering for later. It also means coming up with $x + 1 = Up(x)$.

Now that we know how to add by repeated *Ups*, we look for the result of repeated *Downs*. In $x + y$ and $x - y$, we see the operations $+y$ and $-y$ carried out on $x$, where $+y$ is *Up* carried out $y$ times and $-y$ is *Down* carried out $y$ times. Then we find that

$$
\begin{aligned}
n - m &= Down(Down(\ldots Down(n)\ldots)); \quad \text{repeated m times, so that} \\
(x + y) - y &= x \\
(x - y) + y &= x, \qquad\qquad\qquad\qquad\qquad \text{if } x \geq y
\end{aligned}
$$

We could just as well say that $x - y = z$ if $y + z = x$; subtraction is the inverse of addition.

**Q:** That doesn't make sense. An inverse to producing $z$ from $x$ and $y$ ought to produce $x$ and $y$ from $z$.

**A:** True; it would be more precise to say that the $-x$ operation is the inverse of the $+x$ operation for any number $x$. For now, however, the important point is that when we used the *look for an inverse* rule on addition and the *look at repetitions* rule on *Down*, we got to the same operation (subtraction). The inverse of repeated *Up* is the repetition of inverted *Up*.

**Q:** I don't quite get that last remark; what's it for?

**A:** I'm just summarizing the two ways of getting to subtraction: you can either start with counting *Up*, try repetition to get addition and then try inversion to get subtraction; or else you can start with *Up*, try inversion to get *Down* and then repetition to get subtraction. The reason I phrase it this way is that you will see statements of that general form again: "The inverse of repeated $F$ is the repetition of inverted $F$." Remember it.

$$
\begin{aligned}
n - m &= Down(Down(\ldots Down(n)\ldots)) \quad \text{repeated } m \text{ times, so that} \\
Up(n) - Up(m) &= Down(Down(\ldots Down(Up(n)\ldots)) \quad \text{repeated } Up(m) \text{ times} \\
&= n - m \\
n - 0 &= n
\end{aligned}
$$

Now let's try the rule about shuffling again: what if we try $(x+y)-x$? We don't really see anything new: this has to be $(y + x) - x$ since addition can be shuffled, and we know that that is $y$. $x - (x + y)$ is just not going to work unless $y = 0$, in which case it's not very interesting. Still we can find that $x - (x - y) = y$, if $x \geq y$, and $(x - y) - z = x - (y + z)$.

Looking for operations which change nothing, we find that $x - 0 = x$ is always true, but 0 is not a full identity element for subtraction as it was for addition because $0 - x = x$ is not true unless $0 = x$. One way of saying this is that 0 is a *right identity* for subtraction, and is a *left and right identity* for addition. Turning to special cases, we can find that $x - x = 0$.

### 2.1.3   Old Patterns for New Operations

**Q:** I guess I see the pattern. Next you're going to say that the rule for looking at repetitions will tell you to look at repeating the $+x$ operation for some $x$, and if you do it $y$ times starting with 0, that will be $x * y$; and the inverse of that will be division. Right?

**A:** Exactly, and repeated multiplication gives us exponentiation, with the inverse being logarithms. We can write the rules to make the most of the similarity:

$$
\begin{aligned}
x + 0 &= x \\
x * 0 &= 0 \\
x + (y + 1) &= (x + y) + 1 \\
x * (y + 1) &= (x * y) + x \\
x**0 &= 1 \\
x**(y + 1) &= (x**y) * x \\
x - y &= z, & \text{if } y + z = x \\
x/y &= z, & \text{if } y * z = x \\
\log(x, y) &= z, & \text{if } y**z = x
\end{aligned}
$$

The last line should be read as "The logarithm of $x$ in the base $y$ is $z$, if $y$ raised to the power $z$ is $x$." (We are not dealing with remainders just yet.)

**Exercises**    Evaluate the following:

**2.1-6**    $9 - 3$

**2.1-7**    $20/4$

**2.1-8**    $\log(27, 3)$

We can look for commutativity and associativity as before and find that multiplication has both properties but exponentiation has neither; we can look for identity elements and find that 1 is a left and right identity for multiplication because $x * 1 = 1 * x = x$, and it is a right identity for division and for exponentiation. Shuffling around, we can also find that some of the rules relating addition to subtraction hold just as well for multiplication and division, or even exponentiation and logarithms.

**Exercises**    Evaluate a few examples for each of the following; experiment a little. Based on your experiments, state simplification rules if possible (conditional rules, if necessary). Justify your answers briefly. Don't worry about using the rules as direct justification; you're supposed to be experimental here. (Remember that we are using only cardinal numbers; don't start using decimals.)

**2.1-9**    **(a)** $(x * y)/y$;    **(b)** $x/(x/y)$;    **(c)** $x/x$;    **(d)** $(x/y)/z$

**2.1-10**    **(a)** $log(x**y, x)$;    **(b)** $log(x, log(x, y))$;    **(c)** $log(x, x)$;    **(d)** $log(log(x, y), z)$

In future courses you will learn about repeated exponentiation; it's not very useful here, but has some use in describing algorithms for very difficult problems. It often happens that an extremely difficult problem can be solved only by a program which takes an enormous amount of time and scratch-pad space; analysis of these programs (and problems) can require an understanding of repeated exponentials.

### 2.1.4 Approximate Inverses and Breaking Down Numbers

**Q:** What about remainders? You defined inverses for various things, but there isn't any exact answer to 9/4 within the whole numbers. The same is true for your other functions.

**A:** The complete rule for cardinal-number division and logarithms will be

$$
\begin{aligned}
x/y &= z, & \text{if } y*z \le x \text{ and } y*(z+1) > x \\
log(x,y) &= z, & \text{if } y^{**}z \le x \text{ and } y^{**}(z+1) > x
\end{aligned}
$$

In other words, the quotient and logarithm are the largest numbers which aren't too large to be the inverses; they are pretty good approximations. The same idea applies to the *SqrRt* function defined by

$$
SqrRt(y) = x, \text{ if } Sqr(x) \le y \text{ and } Sqr(x+1) > y
$$

To find such approximations, we could use the strategy suggested already by *SqrRtApprox*, which goes upward through the cardinals until it finds something to match. However, this is usually a very slow strategy. It's often better to adopt some variant of the binary strategy for telephone books, which jumps around but tries to close in on the answer by chopping out pieces as we go. For example, if we're trying to find *SqrRt*(30), we know that the answer has to be in the range $0\ldots30$. We try 15, then 7, then 3, then 5, and we're done.

**Exercises**    Write binary-search rules, and analyze their complexity, for

**2.1-11**  *SqrRt*
**2.1-12**  *div*
**2.1-13**  *log*

To check these approximations, we can also look for the remainders:

$$
\begin{aligned}
mod(x,y) &= x - y*(x/y) \\
LogRem(x,y) &= x - y^{**}log(x,y) \\
SqrRtRem(x) &= x - Sqr(SqrRt(x))
\end{aligned}
$$

*mod*—which we've already seen in Chapter 1—is a very important function, available in most programming languages; it's simply the ordinary remainder, left over after division. The others are used as examples here, but we'll be forgetting them afterwards. In each case, we're defining the "leftover" part of the number: $mod(x, y)$ will be 0 when $x$ is divisible by $y$, $LogRem(x, y)$ will be 0 when $x$ is an exact power of $y$, and $SqrRtRem(x)$ will be 0 when $x$ is a perfect square. Of these, only $mod$ is commonly considered to be important; it is a primitive (sometimes under a different name) in most programming languages. In effect, $mod(x, y)$ is the rightmost digit of the number $x$ when written out in base $y$, and $x/y$ is the rest of the number: $mod(394, 10) = 4$, and $394/10 = 39$.

**Q:** Couldn't I take the leftmost digit instead? Wouldn't that be just as important?

**A:** It could be, but if you think about the methods for arithmetic that you learned as a child, you'll realize that they depend on having the digits placed in fixed columns. That means you can always find the rightmost digit easily, just by looking in the "ones-place" column, but finding the leftmost digit requires figuring out how large it is.

**Q:** You mean counting how many digits there are?

**A:** Right; that is just what the "log" function does. In fact we could say that the leftmost digit of a number $n$ written in base $b$ is

$$LeftMostDigit(n, b) = n/(b** \log(n, b))$$

Thus, the leftmost digit of 560321 in base 10 would have to be 5 and the leftmost digit of the same number in base 100 would have to be 56.

**Q:** But 56 is not a digit. What's going on?

**A:** In base 10, 560321 is a six-place number, having a 1 in the ones column, a 2 in the tens column, a 3 in the hundreds column, and so on; it is $(1 * 10**0) + (2 * 10**1) + (3 * 10**2) + (0 * 10**3) + (6 * 10**4) + (5 * 10**5)$. In base 100, we have a ones place, a hundreds place, and a ten-thousands place: the number is $(21 * 100**0) + (3 * 100**1) + (56**100**2)$. In base 100, there have to be 100 different digits, just as there have to be 10 digits (0,1,2,3,4,5,6,7,8, and 9) in base 10. If you want to invent symbols for them so that the 57th digit will need only a single written space, go ahead. If you use the familiar first 10 digits, then the 26 letters of the alphabet in upper case (so that "A" stands for 10, "Z" for 35, then the lower-case letters (so that "a" stands for 36, "z" for 61) and then go on with other symbols, you'll find that 560321 in base 100 will be written "u3L." Having the $mod$ primitive in programming languages will give you the ability to always check the ones place, no matter what number base you find it convenient to work in; 10 and 2 are the most common, but 16, 8, and 256 are by no means unusual, and other bases are useful in particular problems.

Given a number $n$ and a number base $b$, we can easily imagine writing $n$ out in base $b$ as a series of digits. It is convenient to call the rightmost digit (ones place) "digit 0," the next (tens place) "digit 1," and so on. We can generalize on the *LeftMostDigit* function above to write a function to extract an arbitrary digit from an arbitrary position:

$$Digit(n, b, i) \quad = \quad mod(n, b), \qquad\qquad \text{if } i = 0;$$
$$= \quad Digit(div(n, b), b, i - 1) \quad \text{otherwise}$$

**Exercises**   Show steps and justifications, assuming *mod* and *div* as skills.

**2.1-14**  209 broken down in base 10:

    **(a)**  $Digit(209,10,0)$      **(b)**  $Digit(209,10,1)$
    **(c)**  $Digit(209,10,2)$      **(d)**  $Digit(209,10,3)$

**2.1-15**  209 broken down in base 2:

    **(a)**  $Digit(209,2,0)$      **(b)**  $Digit(209,2,1)$
    **(c)**  $Digit(209,2,2)$      **(d)**  $Digit(209,2,3)$
    **(e)**  $Digit(209,2,4)$      **(f)**  $Digit(209,2,5)$
    **(g)**  $Digit(209,2,6)$      **(h)**  $Digit(209,2,7)$
    **(i)**  $Digit(209,2,8)$

It is important to realize that handling really large numbers requires extra rules and skills: if you want to find 37**453, you need a great deal of patience, a great deal of paper, and some way to deal with numbers that take more than a page to write down. In most cases, we write numbers within columns that are big enough for reasonably big numbers, perhaps 10 digits long. When a number doesn't fit in the columns, we tend to get irritated. Electronic computers have similar problems: any number requiring more than a fixed number of binary digits (usually 8, 16, or 32) needs special treatment. Let's get back to algebra.

### 2.1.5  New Patterns for New Operations

**Q:** So far, you've been using the same ideas for multiplication and exponentiation that you used for addition. Don't they introduce anything fundamentally new? I mean, like new algebraic properties?

    **A:** Well, the idea that division and logarithms are only approximate inverses is new in a way, but there are two kinds of algebraic properties that don't show up at all in addition and subtraction alone.

    First, these operations have "zero" elements as well as "identity" elements. An identity element was one which can be combined with any $x$ to yield $x$ unchanged, as in $1 * x = x * 1 = x**1 = x/1 = x$. Similarly, a zero element is one which can be combined with any $x$ to yield the zero element back again: it is an object for which every *other* object is an identity. Look at these laws:

$$\left. \begin{array}{rcl} x*0 & = & 0 \\ 0*x & = & 0 \\ 0/x & = & 0 \\ 0**x & = & 0 \end{array} \right\} \text{ if } x \neq 0$$

In every case, we are combining an object with 0, but instead of getting the object back we get the 0 back. Notice that 0 should be called a "left and right zero" for multiplication, but it's only a left zero for division and for exponentiation. With other operations, other items will act as 0 does here, and they will be called zeros for those operations, but there is no object which is unchanged by addition or subtraction.

**Q:** Well, if I add anything to infinity or take anything away, I still have infinity, right?

**A:** Yes, and when you put infinity into computations I'll have to worry about that. It is a good question, and it's related to the fact that some programming languages do have zero elements for addition and subtraction, but that's not something we can go into now.

The second new kind of pattern that we get by considering new functions is simply that which comes from combining them with one another.

$$\begin{array}{rcl} x*(y+z) & = & x*y + x*z \\ (x+y)*z & = & x*z + y*z \\ x**(y*z) & = & (x**y)**z \\ (x*y)**z & = & (x**z)*(y**z) \\ x**(y+z) & = & x**y * x**z \end{array}$$

These are *distributive* laws. We distribute left-multiplication or right-multiplication over addition. That is, an addition followed by multiplication is the same as a pair of multiplications followed by an addition. Similarly, we distribute left-exponentiation over multiplication, but we cannot distribute right-exponentiation over multiplication. Thus, a multiplication followed (on the right) by an exponentiation is the same as a pair of exponentiations followed by a multiplication. Finally, we have a kind of distributive law which says that an addition followed (on the left) by exponentiation is the same as two exponentiations followed by a multiplication. Most of the idea is captured by the general distributive law

$$f(g(a,b)) = g(f(a), f(b))$$

For example, in $x*(y+z) = (x*y) + (x*z)$, the function $g$ is addition and the function $f$ is "$x*$", i.e., it is a function which multiplies its argument by $x$.

**Exercises**    Draw abstract syntax trees for

**2.1-16**  The general distributive law.

**2.1-17**  Each of the distributive laws given above.

**2.1-18**  Which of the particular laws doesn't quite fit the general pattern?

**Q:** I see that you're making lots of patterns, but I don't see what use they could possibly be.

**A:** This is not the place to develop the subject in depth, but these rules, and similar rules for other kinds of objects, are of considerable use in algorithm design, and we've been using them all along. Think about the first rule. If we classify numbers as 0 vs. $n + 1$, then we have an obvious match $y = n, z = 1$ and $x * (y + 1) = x * y + x$; this gives us back the algorithm we started with. If instead we classify numbers as $0$, $2 * n$ or $2 * n + 1$, then we should look at the special cases $z = y$ and $z = y + 1$ to find $x * (2 * y) = 2 * (x * y)$ and $x * (2 * y + 1) = 2 * (x * y) + x$. This is already an enormous improvement: if it takes one step to double or halve a number, then it now takes a few dozen steps to find $1,000,000 * 1,000,001$, where previously it took millions of steps. Our first "improved algorithm" was actually a simple application of the distributive law.

**Q:** The equations you just gave aren't quite the same as the ones from the first chapter. In fact, when I try them on a small example, they're pretty messy. First I break down the problem, then I double and add and double and add and double and double and double and add... It's a bore.

**A:** That's true. We can improve it, again by thinking about algebra. Just a little more thought tells us that $x * (2 * y) = (2 * x) * y$ and that $x * (2 * y + 1) = (2 * x) * y + x$; that lets us do the doubling at the same time that we do the halving, instead of letting it wait until the end, and it simply depends on the commutativity of multiplication. A little work beyond that, just using the associativity of addition, brings you back to the rules we used at the end of the first chapter.

**Q:** I suppose so, but don't you think I could have muddled through to a reasonable algorithm for multiplication without learning all this stuff about equations?

**A:** Quite possibly, mostly because other people (centuries ago) did slowly work out algorithms for multiplication, and you learned them. The real payoff comes when you try to solve a similar problem, like exponentiation. The solution is basically just the same, but instead of *Double* you use *Sqr*. Later you'll solve an apparently quite different problem, like sorting a sequence (shuffling it so that the elements appear in order). The same kind of algebraic rule appears, leading you to a fundamentally similar algorithm. Of course, you can't use this kind of thinking if you can't find the rules. That means that you have to be able to take an operation and start thinking about whether or not it is commutative or associative, whether or not it has an identity element, and whether or not it will distribute over some other operation as multiplication distributes over addition (or subtraction) and exponentiation distributes over multiplication (and division). In fact, problem-solving itself often works by distribution: in order to solve a problem put together from components, you solve the components and put the answers together.

There is another use of rules, beyond algorithm design. After you've written your program (efficiently or not), you have to test it. Suppose that you've written a program to perform multiplication. How do you make certain it works? One good method is to list special-case numbers like 0 and 1 and typical numbers like 5 and 37921. You may want to include 9999999999999999 as a special-case number as well, just because it's huge. Now try all possible combinations $x * y$ where $x$ and $y$ are both selected from your list; there are 25 combinations here. Use your program to print out the operations and their results. Then, if you see that $5 * 37921$ gives a different answer than $37921 * 5$, this signals not only a problem, but a different problem than would be suggested by seeing that they gave the same wrong answer. Similarly, you could try structuring your test cases to look for associativity, or for distributivity over addition. At three o'clock in the morning, almost any output looks fine; having an awareness of algebraic patterns and special cases will make bugs easier to find systematically. Later in this chapter, we will go over methods for having a program do this checking for you.

A third use of algebraic rules like these is that they enable you to see your program as a collection of familiar patterns rather than as a structure you've never seen before and will never see again. Often you will find yourself needing to rewrite a confusing collection of expressions in some simpler way; rules like distributivity make it possible to do this systematically.

Now, let's get back to the elementary school student's discovery of the cardinals.

### 2.1.6  Distribution and Simplification

One interesting facet of distribution is that we can change the structure of expressions quite systematically. Any combination of addition and multiplication, for example, can be turned into a simple sum of products like the following

$$
\begin{aligned}
(a + c) * (d * (e + f)) &= a * d * (e + f) + c * d * (e + f) \\
&= a * d * e + a * d * f + c * d * e + c * d * f
\end{aligned}
$$

There are two situations in which this sort of conversion into a "standard form" or "normal form" is extremely useful. First, we may want to look for other simplifications. In a problem with subtraction, for example, we could find that

$$
\begin{aligned}
(a - c) * (d * (c + a)) &= a * d * (c + a) - c * d * (c + a) \\
&= a * d * c + a * d * a - c * d * c - c * d * a \\
&= a * d * a - c * d * c \\
&= d * (a * a - c * c)
\end{aligned}
$$

Remember that we are only using the cardinal numbers, so you must be careful not to subtract any number from a smaller number. This sort of manipulation is more useful when negative numbers, fractions, and decimals are allowed; it is most useful of all when we're working on assertions, as we'll see in the section on Boolean algebra.

Another situation which makes these conversions useful arises when we write very complicated program fragments: it is easy to lose track of what a complex expression or command means, and breaking it down into an appropriate normal form makes analysis easier.

**Exercises**    Convert the following to simple sums of products. Show your steps.

**2.1-19**  $(a + b) * (c + d)$

**2.1-20**  $(a * b) * (c + d + e)$

**2.1-21**  $(a + b) * (c * (d + a) + e)$

### 2.1.7  Problems with Conditional Rules

**Q:** There's one problem with your rules: you've used $\geq$, but there aren't any rules for it yet. Is the poor kid just supposed to tell which is bigger by eye?

**A:** No, I'm just minimizing what I say about conditions until we get to the section on Boolean algebra, where I can talk systematically about orderings like $>$, $<$, $\geq$, and so on without wasting time on each one separately. For now, it's better to see that each one can be dealt with, without worrying about how they fit together. With a little bit of help, you should be able to think of rules for "GreaterThanOrEqualTo" now; for consider the cases

$$
\begin{aligned}
(0 \geq 0) &= \underline{\qquad} \\
(0 \geq (n + 1)) &= \underline{\qquad} \\
((n + 1) \geq 0) &= \underline{\qquad} \\
((n + 1) \geq (m + 1)) &= \underline{\qquad\qquad}
\end{aligned}
$$

For the first three, you can fill in *True* or *False*, just by thinking about one or two examples; $0 \geq (n + 1)$ will be used on $0 \geq 5$ and on $0 \geq 317$, but never on $0 \geq 0$. The last one is harder. Suppose you knew that $n \geq m$ was *True* (or *False*), what would you know about $(n + 1) \geq (m + 1)$? Use your rules to find $5 \geq 4, 2 \geq 2$, and $1 \geq 3$.

**Q:** I can see the first three easily: they're just *True*, *False*, and *True* in that order. Is the last one supposed to be "*True*, if $(n \geq m) = True$"? Don't I need to fill in a line with "*False*, otherwise"?

**A:** That's correct, but not as elegant as it might be: just fill in the blank with "$(n \geq m)$", and you're done.

Are there algebraic rules to be discovered here? Remember that we're working on the cardinal numbers. Obviously, $x \geq y$ is not the same as $y \geq x$, and $x \geq (y \geq z)$ will not even be a condition unless $x$ is a condition rather than an expression. The ideas we've been using don't work very well here, but don't be discouraged; as soon as we've worked a little with the algebra of conditions, we'll be able to find a lot of structure in orderings.

Using conditions is fundamental to another pair of preschool operations on block piles, plates of cookies, and so on. The *min*imum and *max*imum functions just pick the smaller or larger of a pair:

$$
\begin{aligned}
min(x,y) &= x, & \text{if } x \leq y \\
&= y, & \text{otherwise} \\
max(x,y) &= y, & \text{if } x \leq y \\
&= x, & \text{otherwise}
\end{aligned}
$$

## Exercises

**2.1-22** Are max and min commutative? Associative?

**2.1-23** Is $x + max(y,z) = max(x+y, x+z)$? Why or why not?

**2.1-24** What is the identity element for *max*? Is there one for *min*?

**2.1-25** Look back at the *gcd* function described in Chapter 1, and describe its algebraic properties as well as you can. Is it associative or commutative? Does it have an identity element? Does it satisfy any distributive laws with $+, -, *,$ or $/$? Justify your answer.

**2.1-26** Now consider the definition

$$lcm(x,y) = (x * y)/gcd(x,y)$$

Find $lcm(5,9), lcm(8,24)$, and $lcm(12,18)$; now describe the algebraic properties of *lcm* as you did for *gcd* in the previous exercise. [Hint: "*lcm*" stands for "least common multiple".]

**2.1-27** Describe the algebraic properties of exponentiation in the same way.

### 2.1.8 Exploration vs. Accumulation

It is tempting to close off the section on cardinal numbers with a neat list of all the necessary facts about cardinal numbers. The only trouble is that there's no reason to believe that a complete list is possible. In a later chapter, you will see a standard form for writing data descriptions and a sample description of the cardinal numbers, but it will only be a beginning. For now, the most important thing is to get you started thinking algebraically. If given a simple program to write, such as "find the average of two cardinal numbers," you should immediately realize that the operation $ave(x,y) = Half(x + y)$ will be commutative. You should quickly (after a few trials) see that it is not associative, since $ave(0, ave(1,2)) = 0$ but

$ave(ave(0,1),2) = 1$. (Actually, $ave(x, ave(y,z)) \leq ave(ave(x,y),z)$ if $x \leq z$, and the difference between the collective averages is proportional to the difference $z - x$; try a few examples to see why.) It has no identity element, but it does have the useful special cases $ave(x,x) = x$ and $ave(x,0) = Half(x)$. It satisfies the distributive law $x + ave(y,z) = ave(x + y, x + z)$. There is no reason for you to try to memorize these rules: right now, you are trying to learn to invent or check them.

**Q:** I guess I can see myself running down a checklist of questions about associativity, commutativity, identity elements, and distributivity; is that all you mean?

**A:** That's a very large part of it. Still, there is always a possibility that the standard questions don't reveal the most important properties. For example, if I wrote a program that told you that the average of 495969 and 837363 was 7, and that the average of 837363 and 495969 was also 7, it would satisfy the commutative property, but it's obviously wrong. Why is it wrong? (If you find that the only way you can answer me is to work out that the real average is 666666, which is different from 7, then you're too successful as a computer: stop computing and *think*!

**Q:** Well, the average of two numbers has to be between them. Is that something you can say algebraically?

**A:** Certainly: try $ave(x,y) \leq max(x,y)$ and $ave(x,y) \geq min(x,y)$. Another reasonable answer would be that if two numbers end with the digits 9 and 3 respectively, then their sum must end with the digit 2 and half of that must end with the digits 6 or 1; 7 is not a possible last digit for numbers . . . 9 and . . . 3.

**Exercises**    Describe the algebraic properties of each of the following:

**2.1-28**  The *diff*erence function defined by

$$
\begin{aligned}
diff(x,y) &= x - y, \quad \text{if } x \geq y \\
&= y - x, \quad \text{otherwise}
\end{aligned}
$$

**2.1-29**  $mean(x,y) = SqrRt(x * y)$

**2.1-30**  $mod(x,y) = x - (x/y) * y$

**2.1-31**  The *mask* function, defined by the rules

$$
\begin{aligned}
mask(0,x) &= mask(x,0) &&= 0 \\
mask(2*x,y) &= mask(y, 2*x) &&= 2 * mask(x, Half(y)) \\
mask(2*x+1, 2*y+1) &= 2 * mask(x,y) + 1
\end{aligned}
$$

[Note: This is a very important function, present as a built-in instruction on most computers (even those which do not have a built-in multiplication operation). If you can express a few examples as binary numbers, such as turning $mask(12,5) = 4$ into $mask(1100, 101) = 100$ and $mask(18,13) = 0$ into $mask(10010, 1101) = 0$, you may begin to see what the important questions are, but even without that you should be able to find the fundamental algebraic properties.]

## 2.2  ASSERTIONS AND BOOLEAN ALGEBRA

In working with rules and with programs, we must constantly deal with conditional expressions, or assertions, whose values are *True* or *False*. Much of what you will see here was formulated by an English logician named George Boole [1815–1864], and is now called Boolean algebra. We are working with mathematical logic, but the logician's point of view is not the same as the programmer's. For the logician, logic is important simply because it is beautiful. For the programmer, logic is important because it serves as the fundamental guide to calculation. That means that some of the logical constructs used in this book will not be the same as those that would be used in a logic text for logicians; we will sacrifice some symmetries for the sake of computational convenience.

Mainly, I want to get you working with logical expressions, to learn to rephrase a "simple" expression to make it cheaper to evaluate (or vice versa), to use the algebraic properties of logical operators; to translate English problems into logical expressions; to represent logical expressions with expressions about cardinal numbers (and vice versa), and to begin thinking about the properties of relations like "=" and "≤" which produce logical values.

### 2.2.1  Assertions in Computer Science

Here are some assertions, fairly typical of those you will deal with in this course and later ones:

*Multiplier* ∗ *Multiplicand* + *Addend* is the desired result.
The employee file is ordered from lowest to highest salary.
The value of $x$ is always greater than $y$, less than $z$.
If a line begins with "@", then it contains a command;
    otherwise it contains input data.
If a married employee's salary is less than \$20,000,
    then his or her social security number is in the X file;
    otherwise it is only in the master file.
$X \leq A$; and if $X$ is even, then $X \ast B + Z = A \ast B$.
$X$ is even and $Y$ is odd, or $X$ is odd and $Y$ is even, or $X + Y$ is even.
If $X$ is small or $X$ is not an elephant,
    then $X$ is not in the large elephants list.

The key concept here is that of an *assertion, proposition* or *condition*; all of these terms refer to statements which are true or false. "Hit John" is not an assertion, because it is neither true nor false; it is a command, closely related to the assertion "You should hit John." Similarly, "Which way is up?" is not an assertion, again because it is neither true nor false: it is a question, closely related to the assertion "I would like to know which way is up." To test whether or not a sentence is an assertion, just try to imagine it being false.

**Exercises**    Identify the following as assertions or nonassertions:

**2.2-1**    Mary would like to knock John's block off.

**2.2-2**    Why does she want to do that?

**2.2-3**    John said Jim was even dumber than Harold.

**2.2-4**    Go to it, Mary!

To work carefully with assertions, we have to translate each English assertion $S$ into a formula $F$. $F$ represents $S$ correctly if $F = True$ whenever $S$ is true and $F = False$ otherwise. We have to study conditions as we studied numbers, learning when things are $True$ or $False$.

**Q:** I've been checking through this stuff in a discrete mathematics book, and it doesn't use = for $True$ or $False$; it uses $\Longleftrightarrow$, and says that $p \Longleftrightarrow q$ is $True$ if $p$ and $q$ are both $True$ or both $False$. What goes on?

**A:** That's somewhat like using different symbols for "+" when you add real numbers than when you add cardinals. These are different but closely related operations; I'm using the same symbol for both because I want to emphasize the similarity.

The operations = and $\leq$ can be used for comparing numbers or elephants or the Boolean values $True$ and $False$, but of course it requires different rules to deal with different kinds of objects, just as + will require new rules when you .want to add fractions. A new set of rules means that you're carrying out a new operation, so it's perfectly reasonable to call it by a different name. We will stick to calling it = (most programming languages do), but there will be a few places below where it's convenient to remember that $\Longleftrightarrow$ is a Boolean operation, which doesn't know about numbers. When we are thinking about the value of a translation being $True$ or $False$, it doesn't make much difference: all we're concerned with is whether the translation is right or wrong.

There are often many correct translations, just as a given English statement has many translations into French. In translating the statement "The value of x is always greater than y, less than z," we can choose between the expressions "$y < x$" and "$x > y$" for the first condition; in dealing with the cardinal numbers, we could even write "$y \leq x - 1$". Sometimes there is no translation, just as there is probably no word in ancient Greek for "hot dog"; the concept doesn't exist. In that case, it can be the translator's job to invent a word and see that it is defined and used appropriately. For example, in finding the truth or falsity of "The employee file is ordered from highest to lowest salary," we first have to realize that we're evidently talking about a sequence (i.e., a sequential file). Then there are two jobs to be done: finding (the sequence of employees in) the employee file, and testing a given sequence to see if it is ordered (up or down) in a particular way. This could lead to the translation "Ordered(EmployeeFile, Down, Salary)". Now we would need rules defining "Ordered" as a test on sequences. We would try to make those rules sufficiently general so that a translation of the assertion "The telephone book is ordered alphabetically by surname" would end up using the same rules.

## 2.2.2 "If..."

> "If a horse or an ass crosses the threshold of the house
>   [then] the owner of the house will die."
>
>     Assyrian tablets, ca. 1000 BC

We want to work out the meanings of logical operations by thinking about examples and analogies. The basic exploratory method will be the same as it was for numbers, except that not all of our rules for finding rules will apply. In particular, we won't have much use for repeated operations because there are only two Boolean values and a repeated operation could only go back and forth between them. We'll begin by defining some simple operations on numbers; they will be called Boolean operations or *predicates* because their values are always one of the Boolean values *True* and *False*. (They are also called *relations*, because they express the relationships between their arguments.)

$$\begin{aligned}
Divisible(n, m) &= (mod(n, m) = 0) \\
even(n) &= Divisible(n, 2) \\
odd(n) &= (mod(n, 2) = 1) \\
IsSquare(n) &= (n = Sqr(SqrRt(n)))
\end{aligned}$$

Given these rules, you can find that $Divisible(81, 3) = True$ while $Divisible(19, 2) = False$. Similarly, $even(3) = False$ but $even(8) = True$ and $odd(7) = True$, while $IsSquare(9) = True$ and $IsSquare(12) = False$.

The "even" and "odd" functions are often present in programming languages because they make it easy to write conditional rules from the classifications $0, 2 * n, 2 * n + 1$. You have already seen the conversion of the incremental rules

$$\begin{aligned}
n * 0 + a &= a \\
n * (m + 1) + a &= n * m + (n + a)
\end{aligned}$$

into

$$\begin{aligned}
n * m + a &= a, & \text{if } m = 0 \\
&= n * (m - 1) + (n + a), & \text{otherwise}
\end{aligned}$$

Similarly,

$$n * 0 + a \quad = \quad a$$
$$n * (2 * m) + a \quad = \quad (2 * n) * m + a$$
$$n * (2 * m + 1) + a \quad = \quad (2 * n) * m + (n + a)$$

becomes

$$
\begin{aligned}
n * m + a \quad &= \quad a, & &\text{if } m = 0 \\
&= \quad (2 * n) * (m/2) + a, & &\text{if } even(m) \\
&= \quad (2 * n) * (m/2) + (n + a), & &\text{otherwise}
\end{aligned}
$$

The basic logical construction we as programmers are concerned with is "if," borrowed fairly closely from English or as used in our conditional equations. In English it is usually found in assertions of the form "if __ then __ else __," where all three blanks are to be filled in with assertions. For example, "if (the moon is made of green cheese) then (we can eat some) else (we'll have to fall back on the canned supplies)." Often (in English, in logic, and in programs) the "else condition" is left out, but we can deal with that as a special case later. An enormous part of the work of programming comes down to analyzing cases this way and dealing with them one by one. It will help if we have "**if**" defined as an operation:

$$
\begin{aligned}
\mathbf{if}(x, y, z) \quad &= \quad y, \text{ if } x = True \\
&= \quad z, \text{ otherwise}
\end{aligned}
$$

It's more common to write this particular operation out as an English-like construction:

$$
\begin{aligned}
(\ \mathbf{if}\ True\ \mathbf{then}\ y\ \mathbf{else}\ z) \quad &= \quad y \\
(\ \mathbf{if}\ False\ \mathbf{then}\ y\ \mathbf{else}\ z) \quad &= \quad z
\end{aligned}
$$

Let's look at some examples:

**if** $(x > 0)$ **then** $(x - 1 \geq 0)$ **else** $(x = 0)$
**if** $odd(x)$ **then** $x = 2 * (x/2) + 1$ **else** $x = 2 * (x/2)$
**if** $x = 0$ **then** $x * y = 0$ **else** $x * y = (x - 1) * y + y$
**if** $n = 0$ **then** $n * m + a = a$
        **else** ( **if** $even(n)$ **then** $n * m + a = (n/2) * (2 * m) + a$
                **else** $n * m + a = (n/2) * (2 * m) + (m + a))$

Read these examples carefully; each one expresses some information you have already seen in the preceding sections.

**Exercises**   Evaluate the following as *True* or *False*:

**2.2-5**   **if** $(3 > 5)$ **then** $9 = 7$ **else** $19 = 94$

**2.2-6**   if $5 = 15/5$ then $18/3 = 4$ else $3 = mod(10, 7)$
**2.2-7**   if $6 = 9$ then $x > 5$ else *True*
**2.2-8**   if $mod(4, 2) = 0$ then $5 = 18$ else *True*
**2.2-9**   if $x < x + 1$ then $mod(15, 5) = 0$ else *False*

The locution "**if**" has no identity or zero element, it is not commutative or associative, it has no inverse and it doesn't fit the pattern for a simple distribution. Still, it does have some useful properties:

( **if** $p = $ *False* **then** $q$ **else** $r$ ) = ( **if** $p$ **then** $r$ **else** $q$)
( **if** $p$ **then** $q$ **else** $q$ ) = $q$
( **if** $p$ **then** ( **if** $p$ **then** $q$ **else** $r$) **else** $s$ ) = ( **if** $p$ **then** $q$ **else** $s$)

These and other properties like them turn out to be very important in computer science, mainly because they work even when the second and third arguments to **if** are not assertions. "If you are too hot then go jump in the lake else stop talking about the weather" has an assertion ("you are too hot") and two commands ("go jump in the lake" and "stop talking about the weather"). It combines them to form a single conditional command. Most programming languages allow this usage of "**if**". Others allow "**if**" to be used to form expressions—not only assertions, but even numeric expressions: $min(x, y) = $ **if** $x \leq y$ **then** $x$ **else** $y$ and $diff(x, y) = $ **if** $x > y$ **then** $x - y$ **else** $y - x$ are then legitimate definitions, and $5 + ($ **if** *True* **then** $3$ **else** $4) = 8$ is *True*. The primary property to remember for **if** is that everything distributes over the arms of a conditional. Given any operation $Op$, we find that

$$Op( \text{ \textbf{if} } p \text{ \textbf{then} } q \text{ \textbf{else} } r) = \text{ \textbf{if} } p \text{ \textbf{then} } Op(q) \text{ \textbf{else} } Op(r)$$

This still holds true when we use "**if**" with non-Boolean values and with commands, as in most programming languages. Even comparison distributes over conditionals: we could express

**if** $n = 0$   **then** $n * m + a = a$
         **else** ( **if** $even(n)$ **then** $n * m + a = (n/2) * (2 * m) + a$
                 **else** $n * m + a = (n/2) * (2 * m) + (m + a))$

by saying that

$n * m + a = ($ **if** $n = 0$ **then** $a$
                 **else** ( **if** $even(n)$ **then** $(n/2) * (2 * m) + a$
                         **else** $(n/2) * (2 * m) + (m + a)))$

Similarly, any assertion of the form "$x = y$, if $p$; $x = z$, otherwise" can be written either as " **if** $p$ **then** $x = y$ **else** $x = z$" or as "$x =$ **if** $p$ **then** $y$ **else** $z$".

Programmers constantly rearrange Boolean expressions in order to make fewer tests, or to clarify the tests they are making, or to make cheaper tests (and even to avoid making impossible tests). For the present, however, we are just using "**if**" to combine Boolean values and to illustrate the relationships between other Boolean operations such as "and," "or," and "not." The **if** construction itself was not used by Boole; he emphasized functions which were algebraically nicer (but less general) than it, with most or all of the properties (commutativity, associativity, distributivity) used in previous sections.

### 2.2.3  Conventional Boolean Operations

We would like to be able to express the fact that with any number, either it is even or it is odd. Equivalently, we'd like to say that either a number is even or it isn't even. We want to say that the square of an even number is even, and that if a number is a square, and that number is even, then its square root must also be even. We want to say that if $x$ is divisible by $y$ and $y$ is divisible by $z$, then $x$ is divisible by $z$. We even want to be able to say that the sum of two odd numbers is even. Finally, we want to say that $gcd(x, y)$ is the greatest common divisor of $x$ and $y$—a number which divides both of them and is larger than any other number which divides both of them. How can we say these? Like this:

$even(n) \lor odd(n)$

$even(x) \lor \neg even(x)$

$even(n) \Rightarrow even(Sqr(n))$

$(even(n) \land IsSquare(n)) \Rightarrow even(SqrRt(n))$

$(Divisible(x, y) \land Divisible(y, z)) \Rightarrow Divisible(x, z)$

$(odd(n) \land odd(m)) \Rightarrow even(n + m)$

$z = gcd(x, y) \Rightarrow (Divisible(x, z) \land Divisible(y, z) \land$

$(Divisible(x, w) \land Divisible(y, w) \Rightarrow z \geq w))$

The "$\lor$" symbol is called "or," the "$\neg$" symbol is called "not," the "$\land$" symbol is called "and," and the "$\Rightarrow$" symbol is called "if-then." Using them, it is usual to read the statements just given as "Either even of n or odd of n is true"; "If even of n, then even of Square of n"; "If even of n and IsSquare of n are both true, then even of SquareRoot of n is also true"; and so on. Notice that "$p \Rightarrow q$" is used to express " **if** $p$ **then** $q$" with no " **else** ___"; we will sometimes write it that way. The rules defining these symbols—these Boolean operations—are simple (but still quite likely to be confusing at first sight).

$$
\begin{aligned}
\neg p &= \textbf{if}(p,\, False,\, True) \\
p \wedge q &= \textbf{if}(p,\, q,\, False) \\
p \vee q &= \textbf{if}(p,\, True,\, q) \\
p \Rightarrow q &= \textbf{if}(p,\, q,\, True)
\end{aligned}
$$

"$\neg p$" is *True* whenever $p$ is *False*, and is its own inverse:

$$
\begin{aligned}
\neg p &= (p = False) \\
\neg\neg p &= p
\end{aligned}
$$

For example,

$$
\neg\neg True = \neg False = True.
$$

Moreover,

$$
\neg(\ \textbf{if } p \textbf{ then } q \textbf{ else } r) = (\ \textbf{if } p \textbf{ then } \neg q \textbf{ else } \neg r)
$$

The distribution of negation over "**if**" is a special case of the general rule that everything can be distributed over "**if**". "$p \wedge q$" is *True* whenever both $p$ and $q$ are *True*, and *False* if either is *False*. That means that $even(3) \wedge odd(3)$ is *False*, but $even(4) \wedge odd(3)$ is *True*. Since there are only a few possibilities, we can write them all:

$$
\begin{aligned}
True \wedge True &= True \\
True \wedge False &= False \\
False \wedge True &= False \\
False \wedge False &= False
\end{aligned}
$$

The "$\wedge$" operation is commutative and associative, with identity element *True* and zero element *False*. Thinking about repetition and inversion gets us nowhere, but the special case $p \wedge p = p$ is certainly worth remembering. It also relates to "$\neg$" and to our general " **if** " construct:

$p \wedge \neg p = False$
$(\ \textbf{if } p \wedge q \textbf{ then } r \textbf{ else } s) = (\ \textbf{if } p \textbf{ then } (\ \textbf{if } q \textbf{ then } r \textbf{ else } s)$
$\phantom{(\ \textbf{if } p \wedge q \textbf{ then } r \textbf{ else } s) = (\ \textbf{if } p \textbf{ then }} \textbf{else } s)$
$p \wedge (\ \textbf{if } q \textbf{ then } r \textbf{ else } s) = (\ \textbf{if } q \textbf{ then } p \wedge r \textbf{ else } p \wedge s)$

This last rule is another special case of the general rule that everything distributes over " **if** ".

Another way of characterizing "$\wedge$" is to remember our conventional assumption that *False* < *True*. Given that, we can almost immediately see that

$$
p \wedge q = min(p, q).
$$

**Exercises**   Find equivalent (simpler) expressions for

**2.2-10**   if $\neg p$ then $q$ else $r$
**2.2-11**   if $p$ then $q$ else $p$
**2.2-12**   if $p$ then $p$ else $q$
**2.2-13**   if $\neg(p \wedge q)$ then $r$ else $s$
**2.2-14**   if $p \wedge q$ then $p$ else $q$
**2.2-15**   if $p$ then $\neg p$ else $p$

"$p \vee q$" is *True* whenever either $p$ or $q$ (or even both) are *True*, but *False* if both are *False*. That means that $even(3) \vee odd(3)$ is *True*, but $even(3) \vee odd(4)$ is *False*. It also means that $(x \leq y) \vee (y \leq x)$ is *True*, even if $x = y$. Here's another way to say the same thing:

$$p \vee q = max(p, q)$$

**Q:** But if I say "A number is either even or odd," I really mean one or the other, not both. Shouldn't it be *False* if both are *True*?

**A:** In English we go both ways. When the detective observes that "The murder weapon was a heavy blunt instrument, very clumsily swung: it could have been the chair or the printer stand" she doesn't mean that it could have been both. On the other hand, when you say "You'll get an A if you're brilliant or if you work really hard," it's reasonable to assume that brilliant hardworking students are going to get A's. The interpretation depends on context. Most programming languages have "and" and "or" instructions; their interpretation has to be rigid. In practice, the formal meaning of "$\vee$" in mathematical logic and computer science is what I've described.

**Q:** But then what do we say if we mean "one or the other but not both"?

**A:** For a different formal meaning, you need a different formal symbol; the "exclusive-or" or "xor" operation is also important (we'll talk about it more later), but not quite as important to us as "$\vee$" is. The "xor" operation is achieved by a symbol we already have: $p \neq q$, which on Boolean values is true provided that either $p$ is true and $q$ is false, or vice-versa. I'll describe "$\vee$", and then you'll describe "$\neq$".

Disjunction is commutative and associative, with zero element *True* and identity element *False*. It has the special case $p \vee p = p$, inherited from the properties of $max$.

**Exercises**

**2.2-16**   Describe the algebraic properties and special cases of "$\neq$", without considering possible distributivity.
**2.2-17**   Does "$\wedge$" distribute over "$\neq$"? Justify.

**2.2-18** There is an inverse to "$\neq$", i.e., a function $f$ such that $f(x \neq y, y) = x$. What is it?

**2.2-19** Does "$\neq$" distribute over "**if**"? Justify.

Also inherited from $max$ and $min$ are the characteristics of mutual distributivity: conjunction and disjunction distribute over each other, so that

$$p \vee (q \wedge r) \;=\; (p \vee q) \wedge (p \vee r),$$

while

$$p \wedge (q \vee r) \;=\; (p \wedge q) \vee (p \wedge r).$$

(Try to say those aloud: "Either $p$ or both $q$ and $r$" is the same as "Either $p$ or $q$, and also either $p$ or $r$". You can justify that by thinking about the possible cases: if $p = False$, then both statements come down to "$q \wedge r = q \wedge r$"; and if $p = True$, then they are both $True$. Similar reasoning establishes the distribution of "$\wedge$" over "$\vee$".)

These distributions are quite useful, as we will see shortly. Even more useful are the connections between negation, conjunction, and disjunction. Consider: when you deny that "John is tall and Bill is short," you are saying that one of the two must be false, i.e., either John is short or Bill is tall. In algebraic form, this becomes the distributive law

$$\neg(p \wedge q) = (\neg p \vee \neg q)$$

Similarly, if it is not true that "John is tall or Bill is short," then we know that John is short and Bill is tall. Algebraically we write

$$\neg(p \vee q) = (\neg p \wedge \neg q)$$

"$p \Rightarrow q$" is $True$, roughly speaking, if $p = True$ requires that $q = True$; it is therefore $False$ when $p = True$ and $q = False$. For example, $(x = 3) \Rightarrow odd(x)$ should certainly be true no matter what $x$ may be. To achieve that, we need to say at least that

$$((3 = 3) \Rightarrow odd(3)) \;=\; True,$$

i.e.

$$(True \Rightarrow True) \;=\; True$$

we also need

$$((1 = 3) \Rightarrow odd(1)) \;=\; True,$$

i.e.

$$(False \Rightarrow True) \;=\; True$$

which more or less says that "if 1 were 3, 1 would still be odd"; and we still need

$$((0 = 3) \Rightarrow odd(0)) \quad = \quad True,$$

i.e.

$$(False \Rightarrow False \quad = \quad True)$$

which seems to say that "if 0 were 3, 0 would be odd." Finally, as above,

$$(True \Rightarrow False) \quad = \quad False$$

It may be easier to think about "$\Rightarrow$" with "$\land, \lor, \neg$":

$$(p \Rightarrow q) \quad = \quad \neg p \lor q,$$

and

$$\neg(p \Rightarrow q) \quad = \quad p \land \neg q$$

Simplest of all, we can notice that

$$p \Rightarrow q = (p \leq q)$$

"$\leq$" is provided in most programming languages, usually as the two-character symbol "$<=$", so there is no need to include "$\Rightarrow$" as an extra symbol.

**Q:** But isn't it confusing to have the arrow go backwards?

**A:** Yes, it can be, but we're dealing with a basic duality: a stronger (greater) constraint is one which is satisfied by fewer (lesser) objects. Speaking very loosely, when we write $p \leq q$, we mean that $p$ is less true (less often true) than $q$, so it is a stronger constraint than $q$, so when $p$ is true we should find $q$ true also: $p \Rightarrow q$. Be careful, and remember that most programmers prefer to stick with conjunction, disjunction, and negation, with occasional uses of "$=$" and "$\neq$".

Algebraically, we can find that *True* is a left identity and a right zero for "$\Rightarrow$".

### Exercises

**2.2-20** Summarize the other algebraic properties of "$\Rightarrow$". Is it commutative? Associative? Does it distribute over "$\land$" or "$\lor$", or do they distribute over it? (Remember to consider left and right distribution separately if necessary.) Give the examples (if any) which you used to justify your conclusions.

**2.2-21** Transform the following into equivalent expressions which use only "$\vee$", "$\wedge$", and "$\neg$" instead of "$\Rightarrow$":

(a) $(p \Rightarrow q)$     (b) $(p \Rightarrow (q \Rightarrow p))$     (c) $\neg(p \Rightarrow p)$

### 2.2.4 From English to Formalism

Let's consider a few examples of formalizing English statements. The problem is usually that in order to understand them, humans depend heavily on an implicitly shared context and on their ability to bounce from one misunderstanding to another with little lost effort. We'll begin with examples whose translations don't introduce any new terms.

**Simple Numerical Examples**     Suppose we are trying to make a rule to generalize on our observation that $30 * 5 > 30$, $900 * 2 > 900$, $70 * 15 > 70$, and so on. We could try "The product of two numbers is always greater than the first." This is a false assertion, but that won't keep us from translating it. We observe that two objects are mentioned, but neither is specified, so we need variable names for them. We'll call them $x$ and $y$, with $x$ being the first. Their product is formed: that's $x * y$. That product is said to be greater than the first: "$x * y > x$". Remember that when we write this as a rule, we assume that *any* substitutions for $x$ and $y$ will work.

**Exercises**     Translate:

**2.2-22** The sum of two numbers is less than the second.

**2.2-23** The sum of two numbers is at least as big as their difference.

Once we have the statement formalized, we usually have a better chance of criticizing it: the statement "$x * y > x$" is wrong if $y$ is 0 or 1; it's also wrong if $x$ is 0. (It could also be wrong if we included negative numbers or fractions, but those are not included in our formal notion of "number" yet.) One improvement would be "The product of a positive number by a number greater than 1 is greater than the first", which could become "$(x > 0 \wedge y > 1) \Rightarrow (x * y > x)$".

**Exercises**     Translate:

**2.2-24** The sum of two positive numbers is greater than the first.

**2.2-25** The product of any positive number and zero is less than that number.

When we have different cases represented in an English assertion, we simply combine them as disjunctions or conjunctions in the formalization. Thus,

"If either of two numbers is 0, their product is too"
becomes

$(x = 0 \lor y = 0) \Rightarrow x * y = 0.$

"if either of two numbers is 0, then their sum is the other one"

is

$(x = 0 \Rightarrow x + y = y) \land (y = 0 \Rightarrow x + y = y).$

And similarly,

"Things equal to the same thing are equal to each other"

becomes

$(x = z \land y = z) \Rightarrow x = y$

Actually, the phrase "equal to each other" should be translated as "$x = y \land y = x$", just as "John and Mary hate each other" involves both "John hates Mary" and "Mary hates John." Similarly,

"Things greater than the same thing are greater than each other"

becomes

$(x > z \land y > z) \Rightarrow (x > y \land y > x).$

**Exercises**    Translate:

**2.2-26**  If either of two numbers is 1, their product is the other.

**2.2-27**  Things divisible by the same thing are divisible by each other.

When you get confused, it will often help to go back to considering cases individually: "If a number is 0, then multiplying it by anything will produce 0. Otherwise, if we multiply it by something larger than 1, we'll get a larger number. Otherwise, we won't." This can be translated into

**if** $n = 0$ **then** $n * m = 0$
        **else** ( **if** $m > 1$ **then** $n * m > n$
                  **else** $\neg(n * m > n))$

**Exercises**    Translate:

**2.2-28**  The sum of two positive numbers is greater than either.

**2.2-29**  If, considering five numbers, we find that each is divisible by the next, then the first is divisible by the last.

Overall, you should by now be able to deal with a simple English assertion which talks only about operations you already know. Make up names (if necessary) for the objects it needs to be given, use the formal names of the operations, and split up the statement into cases if it uses confusing constructions like "each other" or "either" or sometimes even "both".

**Defining New Operations**    There are two reasons for defining new operations in formalizing a description. First, there may be an actual operation, test, or relationship present in the description which you don't have a formal word for. If you are trying to assert that "John likes Mary" or that "Mary is angry at John", you can assume that "John" and "Mary" are objects like 57 or *True*, but "likes" and "is angry at" don't seem to be objects: they are conditions like ">" and "=". To bring them into the formal world, we could just choose function names, such as

$$Likes(John, Mary);$$
$$IsAngryAt(Mary, John);$$

These new operations, "*Likes*" and "*IsAngryAt*", are still **predicates** like the familiar ones on numbers. They should be easy enough to understand, and even to use within assertions. If I wanted to say that Joe likes everyone who likes him, and that Mary is angry at anyone who Joe likes, and that Jim likes everybody, I could say

$$Likes(x, Joe) \quad \Rightarrow \quad Likes(Joe, x)$$
$$Likes(Joe, x) \quad \Rightarrow \quad IsAngryAt(Mary, x)$$
$$Likes(Jim, x)$$

Think about those assertions. It should be clear that Jim likes Joe, because by substituting "*Joe*" for the variable "*x*" in the third rule you get "*Likes(Jim, Joe)*". Therefore, Joe likes Jim, and therefore Mary is angry at Jim. In fact, Mary is angry at anyone who likes Joe, because Joe likes all such people.

**Q:** I suppose I can see that, but I'm not sure I could come up with new predicates to translate an English sentence that way. How do you do that?

**A:** It is somewhat arbitrary. You think of a name which you think will suggest the condition or operation you're talking about, and then you describe it as a function with one argument for each thing that it depends upon. If we are trying to say "Mary sells seashells," we might write

$$Sells(Mary, SeaShells)$$

In this case, we are committing ourselves to the use of "*Sells*" as a prefix function to be used in the form "*Sells(x, y)*" where "*x*" is a person and "*y*" is a kind of saleable object, like "*HatPins*" or "*Typewriters*". If we really want to say "Mary sells seashells by the seashore to tourists for 59 cents each," it might be preferable to translate it as

$$Sells(Mary, SeaShells, SeaShore, Tourists, 59)$$

Now we want "*Sells*" to be a different prefix function which depends on several things. When you translate, you make the decisions and you live with the consequences. The *IsAngryAt* and *Likes* examples seem pretty simple, but even they could have been translated in a very different way: if we wanted to emphasize that liking and anger were alternative feelings, we could say that *"Liking"* and *"Anger"* are different objects (values), and that

$$Feeling(Mary, John) \quad = \quad Anger;$$
$$Feeling(John, Mary) \quad = \quad Liking;$$

We could even define

$$Likes(x, y) \quad = \quad (Feeling(x, y) = Liking);$$
$$IsAngryAt(x, y) \quad = \quad (Feeling(x, y) = Anger);$$

These are different but closely related translations of the statements we wanted. For some purposes they would be better, because they makes the structure of the emotions more explicit. For other purposes they would be much worse, because it rules out possibilities we might want to deal with. Given this translation, we could immediately conclude that Mary doesn't like John, since her feeling for him is *Anger*, which is a different value than *Liking*. That conclusion might very easily be wrong, since in the real world we can be angry at people we like.

**Exercises**   Find translations for the following. Do not try to figure out whether Mary hates herself.

**2.2-30**  Mary hates John.
**2.2-31**  Mary hates John, and either John likes Joe or Joe isn't angry at Mary.
**2.2-32**  Mary hates everyone who likes her, and likes everyone who hates her.

When we formalize assertions, there is one more reason for inventing a function name. Here is a very simple assertion: "For every number, there is some larger number." Think for a moment of how you could translate it.

**Q:** There are two objects mentioned, call them "$x$" and "$y$"; the operation is just comparison, so the assertion is "$y > x$". There's something wrong with that. Doesn't the formal version imply "$3 > 5$"?

**A:** It does indeed. You're given a number and you call it $x$, but do you really want it to be true for *any* choice of $y$ as larger number?

**Q:** No, I want to pick $y$—the larger number—depending on $x$. How do I do it?

**A:** You must give a name to the operation which is going to produce $y$, and it has to have $x$ as an argument. In effect, you're saying "For every number $x$, there is some larger number $BiggerNumber(x)$"; this becomes

$$BiggerNumber(x) > x$$

**Q:** But the original sentence said absolutely nothing about any "BiggerNumber" operation. Why should I assume that there's anything like that going on?

**A:** Because you see its result, namely the larger number.

**Q:** But what function is "BiggerNumber" anyway?

**A:** It's one of the many functions whose output is larger than its input, but you have no way of knowing which. The original English assertion requires that something like that be used, but doesn't do any more. These rather nebulous functions are called **Skolem** functions, named after the logician who invented them.

Skolem functions are often needed when you see negations. To say that a rule is false is to claim the existence of a counterexample, and therefore of a Skolem function to generate it. The way the negation is done is important here. Suppose you deny that $(x/y) * y = x$; that might mean any of

$$
\begin{aligned}
(x/y) * y &\neq x, &&\text{if } y = NonDivisorOf(x), \\
(x/y) * y &\neq x, &&\text{if } x = NonMultipleOf(y), \\
(x/y) * y &\neq x, &&\text{if } y = NonDiv() \wedge x = NonMult()
\end{aligned}
$$

In the first version, you are saying that for any $x$, there is something which doesn't divide it evenly. In the second, you are saying that for any $y$, there is something which isn't a multiple of it. (Both of these are false; think about 0 and 1.) In the third version, you are only saying that there are some numbers whose division yields a remainder. You're letting these numbers be generated by operations *NonDiv*() and *NonMult*(), which have no arguments at all because they don't have to depend on anything; they can just produce their values independently. The third version is the correct translation.

**Q:** But what if they both produce 5, or something like that which isn't a counterexample?

**A:** Then you chose the wrong functions. As long as you don't say anything about them except that they are operations called on to create the values needed here, you can't really go wrong. Assuming that the functions *NonDiv* and *NonMult* are not mentioned anywhere else, the third rule is logically equivalent to negation of the rule "$(x/y) * y = x$" which we started out with.

**Q:** You mean that it's equivalent to "$\neg((x/y) * y = x)$"?

**A:** No, *No*, **NO!** If you say that "$\neg((x/y) * y = x)$" is a valid rule, you're claiming that all substitution instances of it are true, including "$\neg((4/2) * 2 = 4)$". That's wrong. Neither "$\neg((x/y) * y = x)$" nor the original $(x/y) * y = x$ is a valid rule.

**Q:** But I thought that any statement or its negation has to be true.

**A:** That's right; any substitution instance of

$$((x/y) * y = x) \vee \neg((x/y) * y = x)$$

is *True*. The problem is that a rule is not just an assertion: it's an enormous collection of assertions, namely all of the specific substitution instances of the rule. The rule itself is not really true or false: we describe it as "valid," "good," or "sound" if all of its specific substitution instances are true, and "invalid," "unsound," or "yucchy" if there are any counterexamples. It's perfectly possible to have a rule like $x = y$ which is sometimes right and sometimes wrong, so that neither the rule nor its negation will be valid.

**Q:** But what if I want to assert that the rule $x = y$ is not valid?

**A:** You're claiming the existence of a counterexample. To do that in the notation we have, either provide a particular counterexample, namely $0 \neq 1$, or invent a pair of function names and write (for example) $FigNewton() \neq PruneLeibniz()$.

**Q:** But don't I have to define them?

**A:** No, to define them means that you're actually picking the counterexamples, and you might not be ready to do that. There is an implied promise that you or somebody could someday fill in their definitions, but in logic as in programming we often give names to things we can't yet construct.

Actually, we've already seen an example of this kind of confusion:

$$
\begin{aligned}
MulAcc2(n, m, a) &= a, & \text{if } n = 0 \\
&= MulAcc2(k, m + m, a), & \text{if } n = 2 * k \\
&= MulAcc2(k, m + m, a + m) & \text{if } n = 2 * k + 1
\end{aligned}
$$

In these rules, the expression "$n = 2 * k$" obviously isn't supposed to be true for *all* values of $k$; we wanted it to be true if there were any $k$ for which $n = 2 * k$ holds. In this case we don't need to invent a new name for the function, provided that we realize that an appropriate function already exists; namely, *Half*.

$$
\begin{aligned}
MulAcc2(n, m, a) &= a, & \text{if } n = 0 \\
&= MulAcc2(k, m + m, a), & \text{if } even(n) \wedge k = Half(n) \\
&= MulAcc2(k, m + m, a + m) & \text{if } odd(n) \wedge k = Half(n)
\end{aligned}
$$

It is common to simplify further by writing

$$
MulAcc2(n, m, a) = a, \quad \text{if } n = 0
$$

otherwise let $k = Half(n)$ in

$$
\begin{aligned}
MulAcc2(n, m, a) &= MulAcc2(k, m + m, a), & \text{if } even(n) \\
&= MulAcc2(k, m + m, a + m) & \text{if } odd(n)
\end{aligned}
$$

The difference is simple: in the first description we are talking about solving the equation $n = 2 * k$ for $k$, whereas in the second we are talking about using existing rules to find $Half(n)$ and calling the result $k$. Solving equations requires considerable sophistication; using existing rules requires substitution and simplification.

Rewriting a rule list this way is called Skolemization, even though we are picking an existing function rather than inventing a name for a new one. For computational purposes, Skolemization is not complete until we have a definition for the function which generates $k$.

## Exercises

**2.2-33** The English proverb "All that glitters is not gold" is sometimes taken to mean "Nothing that glitters is gold" and sometimes to mean "There is something which glitters which is not gold." (The latter is the historically correct interpretation of the proverb, but perhaps the former *ought* to be the interpretation. Write translations for both interpretations, assuming that $Gold(x)$ is *True* if $x$ is made of gold. (You must invent one more function.)

**2.2-34** Skolemize the following rule list:

$$
\begin{array}{lll}
exp(n, m) & = & n, & \text{if } m = 0 \\
 & = & Sqr(exp(n, k)) & \text{if } m = k + k \\
 & = & n * Sqr(exp(n, k)) & \text{if } m = 1 + k + k
\end{array}
$$

**2.2-35** Skolemize the following rule list:

$$
\begin{array}{lll}
gcd(n, m) & = & m, & \text{if } n = 0 \\
 & = & gcd(k, m) & \text{if } m + k = n \\
 & = & gcd(m, n) & \text{otherwise}
\end{array}
$$

[Hint: Remember that you're dealing with cardinal numbers; when is there a $k$ such that $m + k = n$, and what is it?]

### 2.2.5 Distribution and Simplification

In dealing with cardinal numbers, we found it possible to turn any combination of addition and multiplication into a sum of products. The same idea applies here: we can turn any combination of disjunctions and conjunctions into a disjunction of conjunctions. Consider the rules which you justified in a previous exercise:

$$
\begin{array}{lll}
(p \vee q) \wedge r & = & (p \wedge r) \vee (q \wedge r) \\
p \wedge (q \vee r) & = & (p \wedge q) \vee (p \wedge r)
\end{array}
$$

We can use these rules to find that

$$
\begin{array}{lll}
p \wedge (q \wedge (\neg p \vee \neg q)) & = & p \wedge ((q \wedge \neg p) \vee (q \wedge \neg q)) \\
 & = & (p \wedge q \wedge \neg p) \vee (p \wedge q \wedge \neg q)
\end{array}
$$

This can easily be simplified further to the constant *False*.

**Exercises**    Simplify the following expressions

**2.2-36**  $(x = y) \wedge (even(x) \vee \neg(x = y))$
**2.2-37**  $\neg((p \vee q) \wedge (\neg p \vee \neg q))$
**2.2-38**  $(p_1 \vee q_1) \wedge (p_2 \vee q_2)$
**2.2-39**  $(p_1 \vee q_1) \wedge (p_2 \vee q_2) \wedge (p_3 \vee q_3)$
**2.2-40**  $(p_1 \vee q_1) \wedge (p_2 \vee q_2) \wedge (p_3 \vee q_3) \wedge (p_4 \vee q_4)$

Used systematically, these rules form an algorithm for "normalizing" Boolean expression. This is often worthwhile because of the simplifications it makes possible. Normalizations of one sort or another are used throughout the hierarchy of computer science, from hardware design (where we have to formulate and simplify logical expressions to describe the functions of circuitry) through complex conventional software (where "decision tables" of normalized expressions are often helpful in keeping track of combinations of circumstances) to artificial intelligence applications (where some methods for mechanical deduction cannot handle expressions unless they have been normalized).

Nonetheless, you should be careful with normalization, and sometimes it's just not practical: the expression you get at the end may be enormously larger than the expression you started with. Imagine the last exercise carried out through $(p_{100} \vee q_{100})$; you begin with a conjunction of 100 disjunctions of two terms each, but you would end up with a disjunction of 2**100 ≈ 10**30 conjunctions of 100 terms each. Supposing that each term required four spaces on the paper, and that each written line has eighty spaces, we would need $(4 * 2 * 100)/80 = 10$ lines to write the input. Supposing that a large page has 100 lines and a fairly thick volume has 500 pages or $5 * 10^{**}4$ lines, the "simplified" version would require about $(4 * 100 * 10^{**}30)/80 = 5 * 10^{**}30$ lines, or $10^{**}26$ fairly thick volumes.

**Q:** Why are you doing all this arithmetic?

**A:** To get you used to the idea of estimating the sizes of things. Once you learn to estimate the number of leaves on a tree, the number of bricks in a house, the number of spaces in a book, the number of volumes in a library and so on, you will be much nearer to readiness for estimating the cost of running a program. Also, I want you to realize that some apparently reasonable problem statements (like "simplify a Boolean expression") are totally impractical for some cases. This kind of impossibility is not really similar to the impossibility of solving halting problem, because in this case the programming is straightforward, and the program will—in principle—handle all inputs. In practice, the program must fail sometimes simply because the job is too big for any possible computer system.

**Exercise**

**2.2-41** Assume that each book weighs one kilogram (1 kg = 2.2 lb); that one cubic meter of water weights $10**3$ kg; that rock is 5 times heavier than water; that the radius of the earth is about $6 * 10**6$ meters; and that the volume of a sphere of radius $r$ meters is about $4 * r**3$ cubic meters. Find the ratio $M_b/M_e$, where $M_b$ is the mass of $10**26$ books and $M_e$ is the mass of the earth.

Of course, this "normalization" algorithm only works on expressions made up of conjunctions and disjunctions to begin with. If we have an expression using implications and negations as well, we can work one simplification after another. For example, let's try to simplify $\neg((p \Rightarrow q) \Rightarrow (\neg q \Rightarrow \neg p))$. First, use the rule $(p \Rightarrow q) = (\neg p \vee q)$ wherever possible:

$$
\begin{aligned}
\neg((p \Rightarrow q) \Rightarrow (\neg q \Rightarrow \neg p)) &= \neg(\neg(p \Rightarrow q) \vee (\neg q \Rightarrow \neg p)) \\
&= \neg(\neg(\neg p \vee q) \vee (\neg q \Rightarrow \neg p)) \\
&= \neg(\neg(\neg p \vee q) \vee (\neg\neg q \vee \neg p))
\end{aligned}
$$

Now we have only negation and disjunction, but there are negations outside of some of the disjunctions as well as outside negations. To simplify negations outside of negations, disjunctions, or conjunctions, we can use the rules $\neg\neg p = p$, $\neg(p \vee q) = (\neg p \wedge \neg q)$, and $\neg(p \wedge q) = (\neg p \vee \neg q)$. In this case, we can use these rules top down to get:

$$
\begin{aligned}
\neg(\neg(\neg p \vee q) \vee (\neg\neg q \vee \neg p)) &= \neg\neg(\neg p \vee q) \wedge \neg(\neg\neg q \vee \neg p) \\
&= (\neg p \vee q) \wedge \neg(\neg\neg q \vee \neg p) \\
&= (\neg p \vee q) \wedge (\neg\neg\neg q \wedge \neg\neg p) \\
&= (\neg p \vee q) \wedge (\neg q \wedge \neg\neg p) \\
&= (\neg p \vee q) \wedge (\neg q \wedge p)
\end{aligned}
$$

Now we can simplify this according to the rules for distributing "$\wedge$" over "$\vee$," and get

$$
\begin{aligned}
(\neg p \vee q) \wedge (\neg q \wedge p) &= (\neg p \wedge \neg q \wedge p) \vee (q \wedge \neg q \wedge p) \\
&= (\neg p \wedge p \wedge \neg q) \vee (q \wedge \neg q \wedge p) \\
&= (False \wedge \neg q) \vee (False \wedge p) \\
&= False \vee False \\
&= False
\end{aligned}
$$

**Exercises**    Use the same methods to simplify these as far as you can:

**2.2-42** $\neg(p \Rightarrow p)$

**2.2-43** $(p \Rightarrow (q \Rightarrow r)) \Rightarrow ((p \Rightarrow q) \Rightarrow (p \Rightarrow r))$

**2.2-44** $\neg((p \Rightarrow (\neg q \vee r)) \Rightarrow ((p \vee q) \wedge (p \vee \neg r)))$

**Q:** Can you do that the same way for $=$ and $\neq$ and so on?

**A:** Yes, as long as I know that I'm talking about operations on Boolean values; we don't want to convert $x = 5$ into $(x \wedge 5 \vee \neg x \wedge \neg 5)$. This is one of the places where it would have been convenient to use $\Longleftrightarrow$ rather than $=$. The expression $x = y$ may be an equation on numbers, in which case it is already simplified. Alternatively, it may be equivalent to $(x \Rightarrow y) \wedge (y \Rightarrow x)$. In order to know which it is, we must know what kinds of things $x$ and $y$ are allowed to be. In most programming languages, we are required to state this explicitly.

### 2.2.6  Difficult Translations

English assertions are often very difficult to formalize. Most of the translations to be considered in elementary computer science applications are reasonably straightforward, but you should realize how easily English can be used to create situations that are all but impossible to handle with confidence. We will close with two well-known examples of hard-to-formalize assertions:

Time flies like an arrow.

Every man seeks a frog.

These are metaphorical, which makes it easier to create difficult situations, but is not a requirement for that.

"Time flies like an arrow" could occur in a context such as "His plans shifted incessantly; one year he studied business, the next he intended to become a great painter, but time flies like an arrow towards the ends of our lives, and none of his plans came to be." This might convey the feeling that events in our lives form a progression which somehow resembles that of an arrow (direct, undeviating, and much too fast). To test it, we need to be able to interpret a word as indicating a sort of progression, and then we need to be able to look at two progressions (or descriptions of progressions) and see whether or not they are similar:

$$Resembles(progression(time), \; progression(arrow))$$

On the other hand, we might be talking about a mythical sort of fly: "Beelzebub, the Lord of the Flies, needed messengers from Below to be like the angels from Above. He created the race of Time flies, to accelerate the progress of entropy among men; they feed upon weapons as other flies on rotten fruit. So we find that infant Time flies like an arrow or spear, and the adults gorge on ICBMs." Here we seem to be saying that if something is a Time fly then it enjoys arrows, and to work with that we need to be able to test whether things are Time flies and whether they like arrows:

$$TimeFly(x) \; \Rightarrow \; Enjoys(x, \; arrow)$$

Finally, we might be running a somewhat improbable race-course, with daily instructions for the timekeepers: "Today we have flyraces and dograces. You will find instructions in the Operations Manual for timing arrows and horses. Time flies like an arrow, and dogs like a horse." In this case, the fragment we are translating is not really an assertion; it's a command. Implicitly, it involves the assertions that there are such things as procedures for timing races, and that

$$TimingProcedure(flies) = TimingProcedure(arrows)$$

**Exercise**

**2.2-45**  Write at least two interpretations for "Flying fields go high."

Our last example of English ambiguity is the assertion that "Every man seeks a frog." Suppose that you were trying to test this. Clearly it is talking about all men, and not about a particular man (or about horses): it must be true of any $x$ which is human. The formal assertion will have to be of the form " **if** $Human(x)$ **then** ...". However, it is not clear whether we are talking about one particular frog, or not. The assertion might mean that there is some one particular frog, $SuperFrog()$, which is sought by all men:

$$Human(x) \Rightarrow Seeks(x, SuperFrog()).$$

Note that this translation removes an ambiguity. It assumes that "all men" includes "all women". Feminists (and others who assume that women have better sense than to seek frogs) may wish to translate differently. It might mean that each man wants his own frog, the one particular frog which he was foreordained to find:

$$Human(x) \Rightarrow Seeks(x, HisFrog(x))$$

In both cases, the $Seeks$ predicate is defined by some test such that $Seeks(m, f)$ is $True$ if the particular man $m$ is looking for the particular frog $f$. Finally, the original statement might mean that each man wants to have some frog, but that he (or she) doesn't care which frog it might be. Now the assertion is that if $m$ is a man and and $f$ is a frog then $m$ $Seeks$ $f$:

$$Human(x) \land Frog(y) \Rightarrow Seeks(x, y)$$

In our notation, these are quite different statements. Nonetheless, it is possible to describe them in terms which make their fundamental similarity clear:

1. There is some $f$ which is a frog, such that
         for every $m$ which is a man,

$m$ seeks $f$.

2. For every $m$ which is a man,
   there is some $f$ which is a frog, such that
   $m$ seeks $f$.
3. For every $m$ which is a man, and
   for every $f$ which is a frog,
   $m$ seeks $f$.

Later in your computer science work, you will need to learn to work with "universal quantification" in statements of the form "For every $x$ which is a $T$, $P(x) = True$". These are usually abbreviated $\forall(x : T)P(x)$. Similarly, "existential quantification" is explicit in statements of the form "There is some $x$ which is a $T$ such that $P(x) = True$," and these are usually abbreviated $\exists(x : T)P(x)$. Each of these latter statements is asserting that something exists: we have been dealing with the Skolem functions which (are promises to) generate that something. Eventually, you may learn to write with explicit quantification and then translate the result mechanically into the kind of statements we have been working with. For the present, it will be easier to stick with what we have: rules which are valid provided that all their substitution instances are true, and explicit names for any implicit functions.

### 2.2.7 Arithmetic and Logic: Representation

In trying to understand and implement objects and their corresponding operations, we always try to see how they could be represented in terms of the objects and operations we already have. In trying to understand and give rules for Boolean values, it is reasonable to see how they could be imitated by computations on the cardinal numbers.

We have treated predicates as functions which always produce *True* or *False* as values. That means that conditional expressions are no different from arithmetic expressions except for the kinds of values they produce. Thus, if we write the number 0 whenever we mean *False*, and 1 whenever we mean *True*, then we can consistently represent logic with numbers. If we think of this representation as being produced by an operation *Rep*, we can see it must satisfy rules like

$$Rep(True) = 1$$
$$Rep(False) = 0$$

Naturally, when we've found our cardinal number which represents the abstract *True* or *False*, we have to translate it back.

$$Ab(n) = False, \quad \text{if } n = 0$$
$$= True, \quad \text{otherwise}$$

Notice that 5 is assumed to represent *True* even though the representation function *Rep* will never generate it. All that we require of *Ab* and *Rep* is that for any abstract

Boolean value $b$,

$$Ab(Rep(b)) \;\; = \;\; b$$

In other words, the Boolean value has to be recoverable from its representation. We **don't** insist that $Rep(Ab(n)) = n$, and in fact that won't usually be the case: $Rep(Ab(5)) = 1$.

Now we can find the implementations of all operations: $\vee$ and $\wedge$ will be represented as $max$ and $min$, $\Rightarrow$ is $\leq$, and $\neg p = 1 - p$ or $\neg p = (p = 0)$.

Of course, the operations "=" and "$\leq$" must now be defined as producing 1 and 0 wherever they would have produced $True$ or $False$ respectively. Thus, the statement $(p \wedge False) \Rightarrow p$ can be represented by $min(p, 0) \leq p$, and

$$
\begin{aligned}
Rep(p \wedge q) &= min(Rep(p), Rep(q)) \\
Rep(p \vee q) &= max(Rep(p), Rep(q)) \\
Rep(\neg p) &= (1 - Rep(p))
\end{aligned}
$$

If we assume that any variable name is translated into itself, we get

$$
\begin{aligned}
Rep(True \wedge (q \vee \neg p)) &= min(Rep(True), Rep(q \vee \neg p)) \\
&= min(1, Rep(q \vee \neg p)) \\
&= min(1, max(Rep(q), Rep(\neg p))) \\
&= min(1, max(q, Rep(\neg p))) \\
&= min(1, max(q, 1 - Rep(p))) \\
&= min(1, max(q, 1 - p))
\end{aligned}
$$

After you think for a while about specific examples, you may want to think about the generalization: for each Boolean operation $Op_B(b_1 \ldots b_k)$, we're trying to find a numeric operation $Op_N(n_1 \ldots k)$ which distributes nicely:

$$Ab(Op_N(n_1, \ldots, n_k)) = Op_B(Ab(n_1), \ldots, Ab(n_k))$$

When that generalization is satisfied (as it is for $Op_B(x, y) = x \wedge y$, for $Op_N(X, Y) = min(X, Y)$, and for the others listed above) then we can say that $Op_B$ is correctly implemented by $Op_N$.

**Exercises**    Translate the following to arithmetic formulae:

**2.2-46**   $p \wedge q = \neg(\neg p \vee \neg q)$
**2.2-47**   $(p \Rightarrow (p \Rightarrow False)) \vee p$

Some programming languages expect you to keep track of $Ab$ and $Rep$ in your head: they represent $True$ and $False$ as 1 and 0, allowing Boolean or arithmetic operations on them. This has the result that programmers using these languages can sometimes write significantly shorter programs to do certain kinds of tasks.

Unfortunately, these programs are often harder to understand and fix than the longer programs of other languages. *C* and *APL* are notable in both respects.

It is also worthwhile to consider representing cardinal numbers with Boolean values; with an electronic computer, that is what happens. Remember (from the discussion of the *Digit* function) that cardinal numbers used internally by electronic computers are restricted to a fixed number of digits; remember also that a binary dig*it*, or *bit*, can only be 0 or 1. If we associate *True* with 1 and *False* with 0, we can represent the number $5 = 2{**}2 + 2{**}0$ by saying that $bit_0(5) = True$ and $bit_2(5) = True$ and all the other bits are *False*. Suppose that we want to represent cardinal numbers from 0 up to $2{**}32 - 1$; we will have $bit_0$, $bit_1$, ..., $bit_3$ as 32 functions to be defined for each operation, and then we can say that $n = bit_0 * 2{**}0 + bit_1 * 2{**}1 + bit_2 * 2{**}2 + \ldots + bit_{31} * 2{**}32$. For example,

$$
\begin{aligned}
bit_i(Up(n)) &= bit_i(n) \neq carry_i(n) \\
carry_0(n) &= True \\
carry_{i+1}(n) &= bit_i(n) \wedge carry_i(n)
\end{aligned}
$$

You can fill that in for each of the 32 values of $i$ and 31 values of $i + 1$, and you will find that $bit_i(Up(5)) = bit_i(6)$ for every possible choice of $i$.

Similarly,

$$
\begin{aligned}
bit_0(Half(n)) &= bit_1(n) \\
bit_1(Half(n)) &= bit_2(n) \\
bit_2(Half(n)) &= bit_3(n) \\
bit_3(Half(n)) &= bit_4(n)
\end{aligned}
$$

The same idea can be extended to deal with addition on cardinal numbers. Here we have two input numbers $a$ and $b$, represented by the bits $a_i$ and $b_i$. We want the sum $s$ of these two, which will be represented by the corresponding bits $s_i$. In between, we have to keep track of the carry bits $c_i$ just as we did in the $Up$ problem: each digit $s_i$ can be thought of as coming from the addition $a_i + b_i + c_i$, and we get a carry if this sum is at least 2, and a resultant bit which is *True* if the sum is 1 or 3.

$$
\begin{aligned}
c_0 &= False \\
c_{i+1} &= (bit_i(a) \wedge bit_i(b)) \vee (bit_i(a) \wedge c_i) \vee (bit_i(b) \wedge c_i)
\end{aligned}
$$

This just means that we carry onwards from any bits with at least two input *Trues*. The resulting function looks a lot stranger:

$$
s_i = (bit_i(a) \neq bit_i(b)) \neq c_i
$$

Check it out in an example... or several.

**Exercises**   Suppose that we are only dealing with four bits, i.e., $bit_0 \ldots bit_3$ of a number. We can abbreviate $b_0 = 1$, $b_1 = 0$, $b_2 = 1$, $b_3 = 0$ as "1010"; this is the ordinary binary representation of the decimal number "5".

**2.2-48**   Use the rules given to find $Up(5)$. (You are simulating a "counter" circuit.)

**2.2-49**   Use the rules given to find $Half(6)$. (You are simulating a "right shift" circuit.)

**2.2-50**   Write rules for $bit_0 \ldots bit_4$ of $Double(n)$ and use them to find $Double(6)$. (You are simulating a "left shift.")

### 2.2.8  Comparison Predicates

We have described parts of the algebraic structure of logic, largely by analogy with the algebraic structure of the cardinal numbers. In doing so, we left a gap between them: we came from cardinals to Boolean values by the comparison operators $=$, $\neq$, $\leq$, $>$, $<$, and $\geq$, but we did not describe these comparison operations as being associative, commutative, etc. except when they were used on Boolean values. In fact, we said that the rule $((x = y) = z) = (x = (y = z))$ was meaningless for cardinal numbers, since $(x = y) = z$ compares a number with *True* or *False*. However, comparisons do have a very orderly algebraic structure. Some of their properties should be familiar:

$$
\begin{aligned}
(x \neq y) &= \neg(x = y) \\
(x \leq y) &= (x < y) \vee (x = y) \\
(x \geq y) &= (x > y) \vee (x = y) \\
(x > y) &= (y < x)
\end{aligned}
$$

We are thus left talking about $=$ and $<$; the others can be considered as abbreviations. What are the basic rules for understanding these? We can work from examples or from intuitions for each.

Intuitively, we expect $x = y$ to mean that $x$ and $y$ are essentially the same: either can be used wherever the other could be. By that reasoning, $x = x$ is obvious; anything can be used wherever it can be used. Moreover, if $x = y$ then we do have a use of each: we could use each where the other is, and immediately find that $y = x$. Finally, if $x = y$ and $y = z$, then we could use $x$ instead of $y$ in the second equation and discover that $x = z$. These three properties are called the properties of *reflexivity*, *symmetry* and *transitivity*.

$$
\begin{aligned}
x &= x \\
(x = y) &\Rightarrow (y = x) \\
(x = y) \wedge (y = z) &\Rightarrow (x = z)
\end{aligned}
$$

Any two-argument predicate with those properties is called an *equivalence relation*. No matter what kind of data we're talking about, there will be equivalence relations worth discussing, and the most important equivalence relation is equality itself, as we've seen it used for the cardinal numbers and for Boolean values. In computer science, however, we often use one construction to represent another, as when we had 1 and 0 to represent *True* and *False*. That was an oversimplification: we could just as well have 0 representing *False* and say that *any other number* will serve to represent *True*. In that case, all the nonzero numbers would be equivalent in that they would represent the same idea, and any one could be substituted for any other. This kind of equivalence will be very important throughout your programming work.

The < comparison is an *ordering* relation: $x < y$ says that $x$ comes before $y$ in some ordering. Intuitively, that means that $x$ cannot be the same as $y$; it also means that if $x$ comes before $y$ and $y$ comes before $z$ then $x$ must come before $z$. We also know that $x$ cannot come before itself. These properties are called *transitivity* and *antisymmetry*:

$$(x > y) \wedge (y > z) \quad \Rightarrow \quad (x > z)$$
$$(x > y) \quad \Rightarrow \quad \neg(y > x)$$

A comparison which has at least these properties will be called a *partial order*.[1] The importance of orderings like this is that they define sequences: $x_1 > x_2 > x_3 > \ldots > x_n$, such as $98 > 17 > 9 > 8 > 7 > 2 > 0$; antisymmetry and transitivity together guarantee that these sequences follow nice patterns and never repeat. Some orderings, like > on the cardinal or Boolean values, also have the *finite termination* property, which says that any such sequence must come to an end; we'll call them *finite orderings*. They're enormously important in computing: when you write a program, you normally want to be pretty sure that its labors will come to an end. With the first rule collection in this chapter, we saw that the multiplication of $n * m$ had to come to an end because the series $n, n-1, \ldots, 0$ must come to an end. With the second, our series was $n, n/2, (n/2)/2, \ldots, 0$. If you find such a series for every program you write, you will avoid many of the problems that bedevil most programmers. Obviously, > on the cardinals provides the right sort of ordering, but so do other predicates.

**Q:** I see why you call it a finite order, but why is it a *partial* order? What's incomplete about it?

**A:** > on the cardinals is actually a *total* (also called *linear*) order, because it has the additional property that you probably learned to call the "trichotomy" property:

$$(x = y) \vee (x > y) \vee (y > x)$$

That tells us that for any $x$ and $y$, either $x = y$ or $x > y$ or $y > x$, and we already know that that no two of these assertions can be true at once. With other orderings,

---

[1]Some books will use the *partial order* term for the complementary relationship "$\leq$", which is transitive and reflexive. They usually call the antisymmetric "$>$" form a *strict* partial order. We are emphasizing the antisymmetric form because it helps in thinking about sequence termination.

it's perfectly possible that none of them will be true: $x$ and $y$ will not be the same, but neither will be greater or less than the other.

**Q:** Huh?

**A:** Think about divisibility. That was the predicate with which we started the discussion of Boolean operations). We have already found that divisibility is transitive; if you know that $Divisible(243, 27)$ and also that $Divisible(27, 9)$, you can be sure that $Divisible(243, 9)$ is true without trying to divide. What about antisymmetry? This property says, for example, that since $Divisible(14, 2)$ is true, we can be sure that $Divisible(2, 14)$ is false. Surely, then, we can say

$$Divisible(x, y) \Rightarrow \neg Divisible(y, x).$$

Right?

**Q:** I don't believe it. What do I do with $Divisible(x, x)$? Isn't that a counterexample?

**A:** You're right: divisibility is not an ordering of the sort I want. Do I give up? No; if I gave up easily, I would be setting a bad example for computer science students. I want to find an ordering which will be based on the definition of divisibility, so I'll just define a $Divides$ predicate which is the same as $Divisible$ except that $Divides(x, y)$ is $False$ when $x = y$. Try to state that formally.

**Q:** Thinking about the cases, I suppose I should say that

$$\begin{aligned} Divides(x, y) \quad &= \quad \textbf{if } (x = y) \textbf{ then } \textit{False} \textbf{ else } \textit{Divisible}(x, y), \text{ or} \\ &= \quad (x \neq y) \wedge Divisible(x, y) \end{aligned}$$

**A:** Exactly. Now we can form sequences like $1728, 864, 432, 48, 8, 2, 1$, each of which is divisible by the next; the $Divides$ predicate is a partial order which guarantees finite termination, because we have to stop at 1 (or at 0, if we started at 0). If you were to write a program which forms such a series and doesn't go beyond the end of that series, then you can be sure it will stop. Nonetheless, it's perfectly possible to have two numbers (like 93 and 74), neither of which divides the other, so the trichotomy property does not hold. It's a very nice property, of course; it means that all possible data objects could be put in a line. Still, we don't need trichotomy to see that a program will terminate, and termination is so important that you should be able to see (and say) exactly what you have to be sure of before you're sure your program isn't going to run forever.

**Exercises**    Justify each answer you give.

**2.2-51** Is $\leq$ a partial ordering by our definition?

**2.2-52** Is $<$ a partial ordering?

**2.2-53** Is $<$ a finite ordering?

**2.2-54** Define $IsSq(x, y) = (x = y * y)$; is $IsSq$ a partial ordering?

**2.2-55** Define $P(x, y) = (x = y^{**}log(x, y))$; is $P$ a partial ordering?

**Q:** I see what you're saying, but again I don't see what good it does. You've made *Divides* into a partial order, but you could just as well have used $>$ since $Divides(x, y) \Rightarrow (x > y)$. What have you gained?

**A:** Simplicity. Actually, any ordering can be translated into the usual $>$ ordering somehow, but often you lose information by making the translation, and it's sometimes confusing. You saw one example in the first chapter: given the expression $(a + b) + (c + d)$, you have an abstract syntax tree of seven boxes. There are three "$+$"-operations and four numbers. Let's think about the dependency relation on boxes: $Dep(x, y)$ is to be *True* if $x$ depends upon $y$ so that $y$ must be evaluated first, but *False* otherwise. If we are trying to design a language implementation which will evaluate these expressions properly, then we need to respect the *Dep* ordering, but we do not have to decide whether $a + b$ will have to be evaluated before $c + d$ or vice versa. In real language implementations, the strict left-to-right ordering I suggested before may sometimes be violated because it may be cheaper to evaluate $c + d$ first.

As another example, think about family trees. Suppose we are trying to write rules for figuring out genealogical information. For each person, we have listed their parents, so we have the primitive functions *Father* and *Mother* such that $Father(x)$ is $x$'s father and $Mother(x)$ is $x$'s mother. We can define the predicate $ParentOf(x, y) = (x = Father(y) \lor x = Mother(y))$, which is rather like an ordering but isn't numeric at all. It is not quite an ordering. Where does it fail, and how could you fix it?

**Q:** It is antisymmetric, but it's not transitive because your parent's parents are not your parents, they're your grandparents. I guess they're all your ancestors, and their ancestors are yours too. Could you make an *Ancestor* predicate that would be an ordering?

**A:** Yes. Try

$$Ancestor(x, y) = ParentOf(x, y)$$
$$\lor Ancestor(x, Father(y)) \lor Ancestor(x, Mother(y))$$

Now let's think of a nonnumeric equivalence relation on the family tree. How about the *Sibling* relation between brothers and sisters. Check it for reflexivity, transitivity, and symmetry.

**Q:** You're not your own brother or sister, so it's not reflexive; your brother's brother is your brother, so it is transitive; you are your own brother's or sister's brother or sister, so it's symmetric. Right?

**A:** No. You're falling into a very common error: as long as you have any siblings, and they have you as a sibling, then transitivity requires that you be your own sibling. Let's avoid the problem by letting you be your own sibling, and just say

$$Sibling(x, y) = (Father(x) = Father(y) \lor Mother(x) = Mother(y))$$

I'm making it disjunctive to throw in half-brothers and half-sisters; it's all in the family anyhow. Is that an equivalence relation? Think of a few examples.

**Q:** No. If my parents had divorced, and then each had remarried and had more children, then you're saying that the both sets of children are my siblings, but that they are not siblings of one another. How do you fix that?

**A:** By throwing out the half-siblings again. Try

$$Sibling(x, y) = (Father(x) = Father(y) \land Mother(x) = Mother(y))$$

Now any sibling has exactly the same parents, and you have the same parents as yourself or as any of your siblings, so this is an equivalence relation.

**Exercises**  Suppose we are organizing a business in which every employee $E$ has a manager $Manager(E)$ (except for the company president; don't worry about her).

**2.2-56**  Define a partial ordering predicate on employees, like Ancestor.

**2.2-57**  Define an equivalence relation on employees, like Sibling.

Partial orders are found all over the place; if you're a member of a team developing a program, you are likely to find that your work can only be finished after that of $X$, which can only be finished after that of $Y$,... and if this isn't a partial order you're in trouble. There are several important partial orders between courses in a computer science (or any other) curriculum, between pieces of a program, between terms in a *BNF* grammar for a programming language (or for a mathematical notation, or for a fragment of English), and between components of an automobile or of a hurricane. Try to be "partial-order-conscious" for the next few days; describe some partial orderings on your favorite cartoon characters or musical themes. Amuse some of your friends—and aggravate others.

## 2.3  MORE KINDS OF NUMBERS

The cardinal numbers provide the foundation for much of computing, but they are not adequate for all purposes. Soon after you learned these "counting" numbers, you learned about negative numbers, about fractions, about decimal numbers on the "real number line," and quite possibly about the complex plane. We will not be dealing with complex numbers here, but we will have something to say about each of the other kinds.

## 2.3.1  Integers

The integers are the whole numbers, written either as $\ldots, -2, -1, 0, 1, 2, \ldots$ or as $0, 1, -1, 2, -2, 3, -3, \ldots$. They include the cardinal numbers and the negative numbers as well. The cardinal numbers were all reached by *Up* from 0; the integers are reached by *Up* or *Down*. Equivalently, we could say that the integers are what we get when we take

$$(x - y) + y = x, \text{ if } x > y$$

and remove the "if $x > 0$" condition. The integers are "closed under subtraction," which means that for any integers $x$ and $y$ we are sure that $x - y$ is an integer, even though it was easy to pick cardinals $x$ and $y$ so that $x - y$ was not a cardinal. For convenience, we define the *negation* of x, written $-x$, to be the same as $0 - x$. We therefore know that

$$0 = (0 - x) + x = -x + x = x + -x = x - x.$$

Negation is totally meaningless for cardinal numbers, but it's not completely unfamiliar. It looks a lot like negation for Boolean values. It is its own inverse, and it distributes over *max* and *min* in exactly the same way Boolean negation distributed over disjunction and conjunction:

$$\begin{aligned} --x &= x \\ -min(x, y) &= max(-x, -y) \\ -max(x, y) &= min(-x, -y) \end{aligned}$$

**Old Functions on New Values**    Negation is the only new idea here, but it has many effects on the old operations. Each needs to be redefined in a consistent way so that it will work on negative values. It turns out that negation distributes over addition, subtraction, multiplication, and division in various ways:

$$\begin{aligned} -(x + y) &= -x + -y & &= -x - y \\ -(x - y) &= -x - -y & &= -x + y = y - x \\ -(x * y) &= (-x) * y & &= x * (-y) \\ -(x/y) &= (-x)/y & &= x/(-y) \end{aligned}$$

**Q:** I know all those, but they're completely arbitrary. Why should they be like that?

**A:** Because no other choice would be consistent with the rules we already have. For example, you know that $x + -x = 0$ from the definition. One instance of that is $-x + --x = 0$. From that it follows that $x = --x$. The other rules can be justified in similar ways. The extension from cardinal numbers into the integers is thus made as consistent as possible, so that almost everything that was true before is still true... but not quite everything.

**Q:** Why? After all, any cardinal number is already an integer, so why should you lose anything at all? Obviously you gain a lot of objects, and you gain some confidence that what you write will mean something, but why should you lose?

**A:** When you permit new situations, you can be fairly sure that some of them will be unpleasant surprises. You don't lose objects here, but you do lose rules and the habits based on those rules. Remember that we had most functions defined by cases such as $0$ vs. $n + 1$. That worked because on the cardinal numbers we know that $x \neq 0 \Rightarrow x \geq 1$. This is not true when negative numbers are included; you must now go back and redefine each of those functions to include a case $-n$ to cover the negation of a positive number: $-n + m = -(n - m)$, $-n - m = -(n + m)$, $-n * m = n * -m$, $-n/m = n/-m$, and so on. Division now appears to be defined by

$$
\begin{aligned}
div(n, m) &= divAcc(n, m, 0), & \text{if } n \geq 0 \\
&= divAcc(-n, -m, 0) & \text{otherwise} \\
divAcc(n, m, a) &= a, & \text{if } n > m \\
&= divAcc(n - m, m, a + 1), & \text{otherwise}
\end{aligned}
$$

Every other function will have a similar statement of what to do when it sees a negative.

**Exercises**   Show steps and justifications for the following (while doing each one, assume that all the others are known as skills):

**2.3-1**   $-2 * 3$

**2.3-2**   $-2 + 3$

**2.3-3**   $-2 - 3$

**2.3-4**   $-5/ - 2$

It is perfectly common to write rules (or subroutines) in this way: first you work on the cardinals, then you extend with some rule to deal with negatives, then you check with an example, then you submit the solution to your instructor or your boss. It is unfortunately very difficult to think of the right examples. In this case, the boss might well say that the division program just given was obviously working, since it had been tested with positive and negative input. Your 319th customer, however, is bound to divide $-5$ by 2. The rule just used would produce

$$
\begin{aligned}
div(-5, 2) &= divAcc(5, -2, 0) \\
&= divAcc(7, -2, 1) \\
&= divAcc(9, -2, 2) \\
&= divAcc(11, -2, 3) \\
&= \ldots
\end{aligned}
$$

The process would never stop, because we have lost two crucial properties that were guaranteed in the cardinals: (1) The particular rule $x > y \Rightarrow x > (x - y)$ is no longer true, and we were implicitly depending on that to let us finish the computation. (2) Worse yet, even if it were true, we have to remember that the $>$ relation is not a finite ordering on the integers, because we can have an infinite series $0 > -1 > -2 > -3 \ldots$ in which every item is greater than the next.

**Q:** But is there any more to it than just finding 5/2 and then negating the answer?

**A:** Not in this case: the problem is to write rules to cover all the cases and then to be sure that you've done so.

**Q:** Well, instead of just classifying the first number, how about classifying both of them?

$$
\begin{aligned}
div(-n, -m) &= divAcc(n, m, 0) \\
div(-n, m) &= -divAcc(n, m, 0) \\
div(n, -m) &= -divAcc(n, m, 0) \\
div(n, m) &= divAcc(n, m, 0)
\end{aligned}
$$

That way, $divAcc$ is always called on cardinal numbers.

**A:** Excellent. Of course, it would be perfectly all right to phrase these as conditional rules:

$$
\begin{aligned}
div(n, m) &= divAcc(-n, -m, 0), &&\text{if } n < 0 \wedge m < 0 \\
&= -divAcc(-n, m, 0), &&\text{if } n < 0 \\
&= -divAcc(n, -m, 0), &&\text{if } m < 0 \\
&= divAcc(n, m, 0), &&\text{otherwise}
\end{aligned}
$$

**Exercises**   Now go and do likewise for these other functions:

**2.3-5**   Multiplication,

**2.3-6**   Subtraction,

**2.3-7**   Addition,

**2.3-8**   Gcd (the result should always be a cardinal number),

**2.3-9**   Mod.

The fact that $-n$ is a reliable additive inverse of $n$ is certainly helpful. In effect, we are throwing away subtraction as a separate operation, so all the nice reshuffling properties of addition become available just from the fact that $x - y = x + -y$. Subtraction itself is not associative, but we do find that $(x + -y) + -z = x + (-y + -z)$, and these correspond to $(x - y) - z$ and $x - (y + z)$ respectively. The old properties of associativity, commutativity, identity, and zeroes are all preserved.

**Q:** Well, of course they are; how could they not be?

**A:** If I had included *max* and *min* in the list, they wouldn't have been. On the cardinal numbers, 0 is an identity for *max* and a zero for *min*, but this doesn't work for the integers.

### 2.3.2  Integer Representation

If we wanted to represent cardinal numbers using integers, that would be easy: just don't use the negatives. If we wanted to represent Boolean values with integers, that would be easy too: just use 0 and 1, and copy the representation ideas from the previous section. If, however, we want to represent integers using cardinals, we have a little bit of thinking to do. Look how an integer is written: 243, 719, $-9$, 0, $-52$, 76. In each case we have a cardinal number, and there may or may not be a "$-$" sign. We can represent an integer by a cardinal number and a predicate to tell whether or not there is a "$-$" sign; we can call these the *abs*olute value function and the *Neg*ation predicate, satisfying

$$
\begin{aligned}
Neg(n) &= n < 0 \\
abs(n) &= -n, && \text{if } Neg(n) \\
&= n, && \text{otherwise}
\end{aligned}
$$

or of course

$$abs(n) = \textbf{if } Neg(n) \quad \textbf{then } -n \textbf{ else } n$$

In mathematics and in programming languages the *Neg* predicate is usually not stated, since it is just as easy to write $n < 0$ as $Neg(n)$. Nonetheless, it is right there on the paper when you write a "$-$", and it is also stored (normally as the leftmost binary digit) on electronic computers. Using these functions, we can give a conditional–equation version of the *div*ision definition above:

$$
\begin{aligned}
div(n, m) &= divAcc(abs(n), abs(m), 0) && \text{if } Neg(n) = Neg(m) \\
&= -divAcc(abs(n), abs(m), 0) && \text{otherwise}
\end{aligned}
$$

**Q:** When you make it that short, the repetition of the *divAcc* expression gets rather irritating. Isn't there a better way to say this?

**A:** There is a shorter way:

$$div(n, m) = \textbf{if } Neg(n) = Neg(m) \textbf{ then } k \textbf{ else } -k$$

where

$$k = divAcc(abs(n), abs(m), 0)$$

**Q:** It's still pretty ugly, as rules go.

**A:** You're right, and it's a good point to make. Often you will find yourself writing a rule or a program which looks ugly; when that happens, try to think of some different way of phrasing the problem. Ugliness usually indicates incoherence, which leads to bugs. The problem here is that we want to attach the signs of $n$ and $m$ to $k$, which makes no difference if both are negative or if both are positive. The *sign* function can do that directly if we define $sign(n) = n/abs(n)$, i.e., $sign(n) = 1$ if $n \geq 0$ and $sign(n) = -1$ otherwise. That definition leads to a clearer version of *div*ision:

$$div(n, m) = sign(n) * sign(m) * divAcc(abs(n), abs(m), 0).$$

Of course, if you don't consider it clearer, then you can go back to the previous version or make up your own. In that case, however, you should spend some time thinking about why the author thinks that this last version is the clearest so far. Clarity is in the eye of the beholder, but a great deal of the point of programming methodology is to create code and documentation in such a way that it will be clear to most of those who have to work on it.

### 2.3.3  Rational Numbers

The rational numbers are the fractions, or ratios between integers; they come from our wish that multiplication had an inverse as addition does. Actually, there cannot be any complete inverse for a function with a zero element, but we can come close by allowing division by anything but 0 and requiring that $n * (m/n) = m * (n/n) = m$, as long as $n \neq 0$.

Fractions are usually represented as pairs of integers like $5/3$, $9/18$, $-4/12$, or even $48/-12$. Of course, it's preferable to keep these ratios as simple as we can, so those four ratios would normally be simplified to $5/3$, $1/2$, $-1/3$, and either $-4/1$ or simply $-4$. The numerator (top) and denominator (bottom) should not have any divisors in common, and the denominator should always be positive.

To have rational numbers within a program, we need some kind of a naming convention for variables which may be rationals and which are therefore "really" represented by two variables each: one for the numerator and one for the denominator. To talk about a rational number $r$, we'll actually use $r.n$ or $r_n$ for the numerator and $r.d$ or $r_d$ for the denominator; whenever we define a rational number, we need to describe both parts. To find the rational number $r$ corresponding to the integer ratio $n/m$, we write

$$Rat(n, m) \quad = \quad r$$

where

$$
\begin{aligned}
r_n &= sign(n) * sign(m) * Red(n) \\
r_d &= Red(m) \\
Red(a) &= abs(a)/gcd(abs(n), abs(m))
\end{aligned}
$$

The product of the signs is positive if and only if the two integers have the same sign; the *Red* function reduces each term by dividing out the greatest common divisor of the two. You should know the normal rules for combining fractions:

$$a/b + c/d \quad = \quad (a*d)/(b*d) + (c*b)/(d*b) = (a*d+c*b)/(d*b)$$
$$(a/b)*(c/d) \quad = \quad (a*c)/(b*d)$$

The first can be rewritten as

$$x + y \quad = \quad r$$

where

$$
\begin{aligned}
r_d &= bot/d \\
r_n &= top/d \\
bot &= x_d * y_d \\
top &= x_d * y_n + y_d * x_n \\
d &= gcd(abs(top), bot)
\end{aligned}
$$

That's a good deal harder to read, but it's much closer to being a program; both of those observations follow from the fact that all the simplification is explicit. (The rewrite also implicitly depends on the fact that $bot$ and $d$ are already positive, so that $r_d$ will certainly be positive.)

We can look for special cases, as always:

$$a/b + c/b \quad = \quad (a+c)/b$$
$$(a/b)*(b/d) \quad = \quad a/d$$

### Exercises

**2.3-10**  Rewrite the rule for multiplication of fractions as a collection of rules defining $r_d$ and $r_n$, where $x*y = r$.

**2.3-11**  Criticize the rule $max(a/b, c/d) = max(a*d, b*c)/b*d$; fix it.

**2.3-12**  State rules for $x - y$ and $x/y$, where $x$ and $y$ are fractions.

Rational numbers are rarely available as primitive constructs in a programming language, except in a very restricted way: a decimal number like 3.14159 is 314159/100000, while 2.718 is 2718/1000. The principle is the same when we use binary digits or any other number base: the binary number 1.0101 is the binary ratio 10101/10000, which in decimal numbers would be written 21/16. Accordingly, we will now talk about real numbers, written as decimal or binary sequences.

### 2.3.4  Real Numbers

The mathematical idea of a real number assumes that you can go on writing digits forever: a real number is the pot of gold at the end of an infinitely long rainbow, where each step along the way has a better approximation.

$$.3, .33, .333, .3333, .33333, .333333, \ldots \quad \rightarrow \quad 1/3$$
$$1., 1.4, 1.41, 1.414, 1.4142, \ldots \quad \rightarrow \quad \sqrt{2}$$

The real numbers, thought of this way, are a very nice extension of the rationals: arithmetic has all (or almost all) of the expected properties, and you can deal with the continuous quantities of the physical world. Every rational number is a real number, but there are more real numbers than rationals. However, the presentation of an infinite series is more ambitious than most programming languages wish to provide. It is not impossible: you can represent an infinite series of digits $.d_1, d_2, \ldots d_i, \ldots$ with a function $D$ defined so that $D(i)$ generates the digit $d_i$. However, that is very difficult, very expensive, and quite unnecessary. The engineer's notion is expressed in *scientific notation*: we usually don't know more than the first few digits, so write those down and provide an exponent. Thus $5.37 * 10^{**}6$ is approximately $5,370,000$; $-99.99938 * 10^{**} - 9$ is approximately $-.00000009999938$. With this restriction, every real number represented is actually rational. When we also restrict the number of digits allowed, we end up with a finite number of quantities which the computer (man or machine) is able to write.

With this restricted notion of a real number, representation is not a major problem: a pair of integers is needed, one to serve as *exponent* and the other as *mantissa*. Thus, to represent the real number $r = 5.37 * 10^{**}17$ we can create $r_m = 537$ and $r_e = 15$, or equivalently $r_m = 5370$ and $r_e = 14$, or $r_m = 537000$ and $r_e = 12$. We'd like to have a normal-form representation just as with the rationals, so that (for example) we could say that two real numbers are equal exactly when their exponents are equal and their mantissas are equal; we'd also like to be able to say that if one number has a smaller exponent than another, then its absolute value must be smaller. Real machines (or programming languages' virtual machines) achieve that by always choosing $r_m$ to be the largest cardinal which wouldn't actually be illegal, and then letting $r_e$ be the corresponding exponent. Addition, subtraction, and so on then work out in much the same way that they did with the rationals, since all of these numbers are rationals. For example, in order to add two reals, we first adjust the exponents (roughly speaking, the denominators) to be equal, then add the resultant mantissas, and then renormalize.

**Exercises**    Write rules for the following real-number operations:

**2.3-13** Addition

**2.3-14** Subtraction

**2.3-15** Multiplication

**2.3-16** *Mini*mum and *Maxi*mum

Unfortunately, the restriction to a finite number of digits turns out to be of much greater practical consequence for ordinary programming with the reals than it was for ordinary programming with the rationals. Many properties which hold on the mathematical real numbers do not reliably hold for the computer representations of them. We will briefly mention some of the problems.

1. Multiplication is only an approximate inverse for division, since we will often find that $3/(1/3) = .9999999999$ or something close to it, just as it is for paper-and-pencil arithmetic on decimal numbers.

2. These small errors can be greatly magnified, because the addition of one approximate number to another approximate number yields an approximation of the sum which can be farther off than either of the arguments. Thus, if we find $c = a + b$, but in fact $a$ was wrong by a quantity $x$ and $b$ was wrong by a quantity $y$, the result may be wrong by as much as $x + y$. Murphy's law guarantees that this maximal error will be often seen.

3. Even a single step can be very wrong: for example, an intuitive or formal understanding of the numbers requires that $(a + b) - a = b$, no matter what $a$ and $b$ may happen to be. In scientific notation, however, we find that

$$
\begin{aligned}
5.3 * 10^{**}50 + 1.7 * 10^{**} - 20 &= 5.30000000000\ldots00000001.7 * 10^{**}50 \\
&= 5.3 * 10^{**}50
\end{aligned}
$$

because the probable error in the first quantity is enormously greater than the whole magnitude of the second. In such cases, we can easily find that $(a + b) - a = 0$ even though $b \neq 0$, at which point we have a computer program with a very hard-to-find error. The problem is that significant digits can become apparently insignificant, and once lost they are gone forever.

4. Equality cannot be correctly implemented. The usual approach is to implement the equality test on approximate numbers as an approximate equality test, e.g., $1.0000000000 = 0.9999999999$ and $0.9999999999 = 0.9999999998$. Those seem reasonable, and they make it possible for $(1/3)*3=1$, but then we find that $1.0000000000 \neq 0.9999999998$, so equality is not transitive. The idea of an implementation of equality in which it is not even an equivalence relation seems strange; this, too, causes many hard-to-find errors in programs.

**Q:** But what am I supposed to do?
**A:** Be careful. Always develop your solutions as far as you can in the paper-and-pencil world where $3 * (1/3) = 1$, where the associative and distribute laws hold, and where equality means what it ought to. When you get to the stage of computing, think about loss of precision; you can often rearrange your formulas to reduce the problem. Usually it's better to avoid testing equality on real numbers; instead, make an explicit decision as to how close you need your approximations to

be. If you want $x = y$ to be considered *True* when their difference is less than $d$, then replace $x = y$ with $abs(x - y) < d$.

**Q:** What will that do?

**A:** Let's look at a pair of examples—a simple one for *SqrRt*, and then some essential routines for a graphics system. Suppose we're applying a binary search to find the square root of a real number: we want the square root of 5.0, which (since $5.0 \geq 1$) lies in the range $1 \ldots 5.0$. We begin with $(1+5)/2=3$, whose square is 9; too large, so we're in the range $1 \ldots 3$. We try $(1+3)/2=2$, whose square is 4; too small, so we're in the range $2 \ldots 3$. We try the $(2+3)/2=2.5$, whose square is 6.25; too large, so we're in the range $2 \ldots 2.5$. We try $(2+2.5)/2=2.25$, whose square is 5.0625: too large, so we're in the range $2 \ldots 2.25$. Next comes 2.125, whose square is 4.5156, then comes .... We will get closer and closer, but the process will *never* stop if we insist on exact equality. If you want $n$ decimal digits of precision, you will need about $3n$ steps; perfect precision requires an infinite number of steps. There are better algorithms than this for finding square roots, but none of them will provide actual equality.

Now let's suppose that we're working on the specification of a graphics system, i.e., a program which will let the customer use a joystick or mouse as a "brush" or "pencil" or "spraygun" or "eraser." Before we get to the level of specifying those, we'd better have a good grip on the specifications of "point," "line," "circle," and so forth.

Our pictures are going to be laid out on a grid, just like the moron's graph paper. (At this point, perhaps you should get a sheet to follow along with sketches.) To specify a point $p$, we'll just take the horizontal and vertical—$x$ and $y$—coordinates and call them $p.x$ and $p.y$, or $p_x$ and $p_y$. (In a mathematics course, we would probably say $x_p$ and $y_p$, but here we're thinking of the coordinates as *components* of an object $p$ which is a "point[2].") In the real world, we'd like these coordinates to be real numbers, but on the grid they'll be cardinals; sorry about that, but that's all we've got. Suppose that we have points $a$ and $b$ with $a_x = b_x = 5$, $a_y = 1$, $b_y = 0$; there are no points in between $a$ and $b$. Euclid wouldn't have liked that, and we aren't going to like some of the consequences, but we're stuck with it. We can now define the operation (on pictures) of "plotting a point $p$": namely, we fill in the square at $(p_x, p_y)$.

So how do we represent a line? (Mathematicians may want to point out that we are really talking about "line segments"; certainly we can't deal with more than a finite part of a line.) Beginning and end points will do it nicely: $l_b$ and $l_e$, each with a pair of coordinates. Thus, a line goes from $(l_{b_x}, l_{b_y})$ to $(l_{e_x}, l_{e_y})$ or—perhaps more readably—from $(l.b.x, l.b.y)$ to $(l.e.x, l.e.y)$. In the outside world, we just put dots on those two points, lay down a ruler, and draw from one to the other. To make a program do that, we go back to equations like $y = mx + b$ or (equivalently)

---

[2]Of course, in a graphics system we might also have components $p.c$ and $p.b$ for color and brightness, but we have enough problems right now.

$\frac{x-x_0}{y-y_0} = \frac{x_1-x_0}{y_1-y_0}$. We can turn those quotients into products by cross-multiplication; that lets us stay in the world of the cardinals. What we want is to plot points at all the points $p$ for which

- $p.x$ is in between $l.b.x$ and $l.e.x$,

- $p.y$ is in between $l.b.y$ and $l.e.y$, and

- $(p.x - l.b.x) * (l.e.y - l.b.y) = (p.y - l.b.y) * (l.e.x - l.b.x)$

(Don't feel worried if you don't remember these formulas, or if you never saw them in this form; do feel worried if you can't see that they're true from the picture in Figure 2.1.)

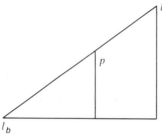

**Figure 2.1** Line Segment Ranges and Ratios

Now suppose that we're actually going to plot each of the points in between $l.b$ and $l.e$. The nasty fact arises that we can have quite a long line, such as the line from (1,1) to (2,100), in which the equality between fractions is *never* exactly true... except at the end points, because the only gridpoints which fall exactly on the line are the end points. Computer graphics is obviously a failure: we cannot even draw straight lines between points.

Of course, we can; one very simple approach (not used in any real graphics systems for straight-line drawing) is to look at every point on the grid and plot every gridpoint which comes close enough to the line. For example, if we draw the line from (1,1) to (2,100) by plotting each point $p$ for which

$$abs((p.x - l.b.x) * (l.e.y - l.b.y) - (p.y - l.b.y) * (l.e.x - l.b.x)) \le d$$

and then play with alternative values for the cardinal number $d$, we'll find that we're plotting all the points "close enough" to the straight line. The same idea will work with circles, ellipses, parabolas, or any other figure defined by an equation on the real numbers.

**Q:** All right, so why isn't it used in real systems?

**A:** There are two very good reasons, which you can find out quickly by trying to do this by hand on a few examples. First, we're talking about a quadratic algorithm: in order to draw a straight line across a $320 \times 200$ medium-resolution grid, you have to test 64,000 points when you only want to draw about 300! That's bad, and of course if you double the resolution then it's four times as bad. Second, the results are rather unattractive: the line you draw will vary in thickness because sometimes there will only be one gridpoint close enough, and at other times there will be more. Curves drawn this way look especially ugly, and nobody wants to buy a graphics system which makes ugly pictures. Still, this might be a very good first draft: you can get it finished in an hour for several sorts of curves and give it to your teammates who are working on the other parts of the system. It will be much easier for them to debug their routines if they can call on (slowly, clumsily, but correctly) working versions of yours than if they have to work around your bugs or work without your code altogether.

As the next version of a line-drawing program, you might start with the assumption that you're drawing a line which slopes upward, so $l.e.x \geq l.b.x$ and $l.e.y \geq l.b.y$. You could also assume that that it slopes upward with an angle no greater than 45°: the horizontal distance $h = l.e.x - l.b.x$ is at least as great as the vertical distance $v = l.e.y - l.b.y$. Those assumptions let you guarantee an even thickness of line, just by plotting one point for each $x$-position between $l.b.x$ and $l.e.x$. You can now write a function $P(i)$ which defines the point to be plotted: $P(0) = l.b$, and $P(h) = l.e$, and in between we have

$$
\begin{aligned}
P(i)_x &= i + l.b.x \\
P(i)_y &= l.b.y + div(v, h) * i
\end{aligned}
$$

This is an enormously faster algorithm, and it also draws nicer lines. You can then generalize it to deal with lines which slope downwards (remember to take care of the case $h = 0$, where $div$ would be undefined), and also to the case where $h < v$ where $P(i)_y = i + l.b.y$. Then you can apply the same idea to curves. First restrict the problem, say to one-eighth of a circle of radius $r$ and center $(0,0)$. We're going from the top center point $(0, r)$ halfway to center right $(r/\sqrt{2}, r/\sqrt{2})$, where the horizontal change is faster than the vertical. Again, we just define the approximate $y$-value to go with each $x$-point, via $P(i)_y = SqrRt(Sqr(r) - Sqr(i))$. And again, the picture is a little better than it was in the first draft, and it goes immensely faster.

## Exercises

**2.3-17** Define a set of rules for an arbitrary line, covering all cases. (Remember to keep looking for simplifications you can apply.)

**2.3-18** Define a set of rules for a full circle around $(0,0)$.

**2.3-19** Define a set of rules for a full circle around $(h, k)$.

**2.3-20** Define a set of rules for an ellipse around $(0,0)$.

**Q:** All right, is that the end? How can you tell?

**A:** You can tell right away that you're getting close to the end: we have what amounts to a constant-time algorithm for finding the coordinates of each point, or a linear algorithm for finding all the coordinates you need. You couldn't possibly have a logarithmic or constant-time algorithm for drawing a whole line by plotting points, because each point-plot action requires at least one step even apart from coordinate calculation. That means that asymptotically, you're doing as well as you can. However, it's still possible to do significantly better than what we've just gone through, and your teammates would have to wait for their third version while you went to a library and studied graphics algorithms. The subject depends heavily on your understanding of the "real" curves through geometry and calculus; it depends just as heavily on your ability to approximate those curves by dealing with cardinals.

Remember that the computer's real numbers are basically unreliable. If your output looks wrong, it may be that your idea is wrong, but it may also be that you have neglected some aspect of the imperfection of our representations. Perhaps by using properties like associativity you can rearrange your abstract specification into something that ought to be equivalent and actually works much better. Before you advertise your program to instructors or employers, test it on reasonable and on completely unreasonable examples, to see if you can make it do something obviously wrong. If you can, try to figure out why. Finally, study numerical analysis at some point in your career; there are many books on the subject, but this isn't one of them.

## 2.4 ENUMERATED OBJECTS

Simple objects in the world of computer science are not restricted to numbers and Boolean values. Before you can write instructions for dealing with any objects, you must have an alphabet to write in, and the alphabet must contain symbols like "carriage return" and "line feed" as well as punctuation marks, letters, and digits. The ideas used for handling alphabets can be used for many analogous constructions: if you know how to deal with ['A', 'B', 'C', ..., 'Z'], you should have a pretty good idea of how to handle [*Sunday, Monday, Tuesday, ..., Saturday*] or [*January, ..., December*] or [*Red, Orange,..., Indigo, Violet*], or even [*Delete, Insert, Substitute, Append, Print, Read, ...*].

### 2.4.1 Character Sets: Letters, Digits, Symbols, and Controls

Here we are trying to represent keystrokes: 'A', 'B', 'C', but also '.', '5', and even ','. For the moment, these are just labels on a keyboard, and we have to keep from getting mixed up between the number "5" (which is the same as "7-2") and the keystroke '5' (which is very different from the sequence of keystrokes '7', '-', and '2'.)

"A" might be the name of a variable or constant or function, but '**A**' is just a letter. For each keystroke, we put its label between single-quotes to indicate that we're talking about one character. For the moment, we'll just talk about ordinary letters of the alphabet. Of course, these can be represented by numbers. My daughter came home from kindergarten recently with a "Break The Code!" assignment: a picture of a snowman, the code shown in Figure 2.2, and the message

20,8,5,__,19,21,14,__9,19,__,13,5,12,20,9,14,7,__,13,5!

| A 1 | B 2 | C 3 | D 4 | E 5 |
|------|------|------|------|------|
| F 6 | G 7 | H 8 | I 9 | J 10 |
| K 11 | L 12 | M 13 | N 14 | O 15 |
| P 16 | Q 17 | R 18 | S 19 | T 20 |
| U 21 | V 22 | W 23 | X 24 | Y 25 |
| Z 26 | | | | |

**Figure 2.2**    The Snowman's Code

## Exercises

**2.4-1**    What is the snowman saying?

**2.4-2**    What would you have to do to let the snowman provide his own spaces and punctuation marks?

We really do need symbols for all of the keys: "Carriage Return" is an English phrase describing a key, but '<Carriage Return>' or '<CR>' is a single symbol for that key.

The standard codes used by computers are the *ASCII* and *EBCDIC* codes. *ASCII* stands for "American Standard Code for Information Interchange."

## Exercises

**2.4-3**    Find out what *EBCDIC* stands for.

**2.4-4**    Find out who was primarily responsible for creating each code.

Other codes have been used, and at times it can make sense to make up your own; no code is perfect for all purposes. For the moment, we will pretend that *ASCII* is the one right answer: it happens to be used by virtually all microcomputers and by virtually all non-IBM mainframes. In *ASCII*, any typewriter key is represented by a number between 0 and 127.

**Q:** What's so special about the range 0...127?

**A:** That's the range of binary numbers 0000000...1111111, which electronic computers handle quite nicely. It doesn't have room for all the characters you could possibly want: it doesn't include any symbols for "$\Rightarrow$" or "$\Longleftrightarrow$" or "$\wedge$," or even "$\neq$", but it includes enough for ordinary typing. (Actually, to make the "$\Longleftrightarrow$" symbol appear here, I have to type ``$\Longleftrightarrow$'' because the program which generates mathematical codes (and other things) as output will only accept *ASCII* symbols as input.

**Q:** All right, what do I have to learn about it?

**A:** You do not need to memorize it, but you should learn enough of the pattern so that you can easily pick up more. There are lowercase letters $a \ldots z$ and uppercase letters $A \ldots Z$; there are punctuation marks like the exclamation point, period, and comma; there are digits $0 \ldots 9$, and finally there are control codes like blank space, tab, carriage return and line-feed, as well as other codes needed for controlling terminals such as an "end of transmission" symbol and an "acknowledge transmission." There is even a "null" symbol, appropriately numbered 0 and found (like vacuums) in empty spaces.

**Q:** But isn't that the same as a blank?

**A:** No, you're confusing the vacuum in someone's head with the volume of air that comes out of his mouth. You can have a blank in between words, but it does not normally make sense to say that there is a null symbol between words. Null is used by programs which count on its not being used for ordinary text, so there isn't any typewriter key for it.

Here's an outline of the *ASCII* code:

$$
\begin{array}{rcl}
0 & = & \text{null} \\
1 \ldots 31 & = & \text{control codes} \\
32 \ldots 47 & = & \text{blank, punctuation marks and symbols} \\
48 \ldots 57 & = & \text{the digits } 0 \ldots 9 \\
58 \ldots 64 & = & \text{more symbols} \\
65 \ldots 90 & = & \text{uppercase letters } A \ldots Z \\
91 \ldots 96 & = & \text{more symbols} \\
97 \ldots 122 & = & \text{lowercase letters } a \ldots z \\
123 \ldots 127 & = & \text{more funny symbols}
\end{array}
$$

**Q:** Isn't that a little bit ridiculous? Why should symbols be scattered all over? Shouldn't you put digits and lowercase letters and uppercase letters next to each other?

**A:** Not necessarily. There is actually a pattern, but it's a binary-number pattern rather than a decimal-number pattern. The 17th uppercase letter (character $96 + 17$) is just the same as the 17th lowercase letter (character $64 + 17$), except that $bit_5$ is 0 rather than 1; the 17th control code (character 17) is the same again, except that $bit_6$ is also 0 where for either letter (or any other letter) it is 1. We are not going to go over all of this carefully, but we will describe the strangest collection of characters, which are the control codes; after that we will worry about functions and predicates on characters.

After null come the control codes, numbered $1 \ldots 31$. Many of these have special keys, but they can also be generated by holding the "control" key down while typing another key. **Control-A** or **CTL-A** or **^A** are all ways of describing *ASCII* character 1, found by holding the control key down while typing the first letter of the alphabet. **^Z** is similarly found as character 26. If your carriage return key (sometimes called *Enter*) is stuck, you can type **^M** instead; this is character 13.

## Exercises

**2.4-5**   Find the numbers for the following keys:
     **(a)**   **^H** (backspace)     **(b)**   **^L** (form feed)
**2.4-6**   Find the keys for the following numbers:
     **(a)**   10 (line feed)     **(b)**   4 (end of transmission)

**Q:** All right, and what about character 27? Is that a control key?

**A:** That's the **^[** key, also called **esc**ape. There are a few more control symbols after that, until we finally get to the blank, which is character 32.

### 2.4.2  Operations on Characters

At this point, we need formal names for functions and predicates. The basic functions are those which convert from a number to its character or from a character to the number which represents it: these are the usual functions $Ab$ and $Rep$. In this case, $Ab$ and $Rep$ are conventionally called $chr$ and $ord$, respectively.

$$chr(65) = \text{`}\mathbf{A}\text{'} \qquad \text{and} \qquad ord(\text{`}\mathbf{A}\text{'}) = 65,$$

More generally, we find that

$$
\begin{aligned}
chr(ord(c)) &= c, \text{ if c is an } ASCII \text{ character} \\
ord(chr(n)) &= n, \text{ if } n \geq 0 \wedge n \leq 127
\end{aligned}
$$

There's not much to say about those two except that they are mutual inverses, as $Ab$ and $Rep$ have to be. There's not much sense in looking for commutativity, associativity, and so forth when talking about functions with only one argument each. Still, once we have them, we can deal with characters by using what we already know about numbers. We can express the basic patterns we've seen by predicates

$$
\begin{aligned}
IsLC(l) &= (ord(l) \geq 97) \wedge (ord(l) \leq 122) \\
IsUC(l) &= (ord(l) \geq 65) \wedge (ord(l) \leq 90) \\
IsLetter(L) &= IsLC(L) \vee IsUC(L) \\
IsDigit(c) &= (ord(c) \geq 48) \wedge (ord(c) \leq 57)
\end{aligned}
$$

We can convert to uppercase letters from lowercase, without changing anything else, or find the numeric value corresponding to a given digit:

$$UC(l) \quad = \quad \textbf{if } IsLC(l) \textbf{ then } chr(ord(l) - 32) \textbf{ else } l$$
$$DigVal(d) \quad = \quad (ord(d) - 48)$$

### Exercises

**2.4-7**   Define a function $LC(L)$ which converts from uppercase to lowercase.

**2.4-8**   Write a function $DigChar$ which finds the character for a cardinal number $n \leq 9$.

We would like to compare letters alphabetically, so that '**A**' < '**C**', '**x**' ≥ '**c**' and so on. That is simple enough; if we compare them by comparing their numeric representations, we'll get the right answers. In effect, we define "<" on characters by the distribution rule

$$a < b = (ord(a) < ord(b))$$

**Q:** But my dictionary has '**A**', then '**a**', then '**B**', then '**b**', and so on. It's not the same at all; your definition of $x > y$ will be wrong whenever $x$ is an uppercase letter which actually comes later in the alphabet than $y$, but before $y$ in the *ASCII* codes because $y$ is lowercase.

**A:** If you want to use that ordering, you'll need to use a different code or else define a function for it, such as

$$LexGreater(\text{a,b}) = \quad \textbf{if } \ IsUC(a) \wedge IsLC(b)$$
$$\textbf{then } \ ord(a) > ord(UC(b)))$$
$$\textbf{else } \ ord(a) > ord(b)$$

Finally, we would like to be able to find the next letter after (or before) a given letter. Here, we can have distribution rules of another kind:

$$ord(Succ(c)) \quad = \quad Up(ord(c)),$$
$$ord(Pred(c)) \quad = \quad Down(ord(c))$$

Here we have the same problem as with ordering: $Succ(c) = chr(ord(c) + 1)$ is correct on the *ASCII* code as a whole, but it works strangely on letters—$Succ('\textbf{A}') = '\textbf{B}'$, but $Succ('\textbf{Z}') = '['$. One alternative is to use

$$NextLetter(\text{L}) = \quad \textbf{if } \ (ord(L) = ord('\textbf{Z}')) \textbf{ then } 'a'$$
$$\textbf{else } ( \ \textbf{if } L = 'z') \textbf{ then } '\textbf{A}'$$
$$\textbf{else } chr(1 + ord(L))$$

## Exercises

**2.4-9**  Write $NextLex$ so that $NextLex(\text{`}\mathbf{A}\text{'}) = \text{`}\mathbf{a}\text{'}$, $NextLex(\text{`}\mathbf{a}\text{'}) = \text{`}\mathbf{B}\text{'}$, and so on, respecting dictionary order. $NextLex(\text{`}\mathbf{z}\text{'})$ need not be defined.

**2.4-10**  Write $PrevLex$ by analogy with $NextLex$ from the previous exercise.

### 2.4.3  Other Enumerations

Given the days of the week or the months of the year or the phases of the moon, we can write them in a list. Given any $n$ items which we can write in a list, we can associate those items with the numbers $0 \ldots n - 1$. That automatically gives us the *ord* function and its inverse, as well as the successor function *succ* and its inverse *pred*; it even gives us $=$, $\leq$, $\geq$, and so on.

Let's try a really different problem, one which doesn't appear to be a cardinal-number problem at all. Imagine a family tree containing five people: [Joe, Mary, Bill, Harry, Richard]. Bill is Joe's first child from his first marriage; Joe later married Mary. Their first child was Harry, and they had no children after. Harry's first child was Richard, who (like Bill) has no children yet.

### Exercise

**2.4-11**  Draw Richard's family tree.

This looks about as far from our arithmetic examples as it could be, but actually we have all the ideas we need to deal with it. The enumeration tells us that $ord(Joe) = 1$, $ord(Mary) = 2$, $\ldots ord(Richard) = 5$. Now I'm going to have a function to express the family tree, called *Child*; *Child* takes a person $p$ (e.g., Joe) and a number $n$ (e.g., 2) and produces the $n$th child of $p$ (e.g., Harry).

$$
\begin{array}{rcll}
Child(Joe, n) & = & Bill, & \text{if } n = 1 \\
& = & Harry, & \text{if } n = 2 \\
& = & Nobody, & \text{otherwise}
\end{array}
$$

$$
\begin{array}{rcll}
Child(Mary, n) & = & Harry, & \text{if } n = 1 \\
& = & Nobody, & \text{otherwise} \\
Child(Bill, n) & = & Nobody &
\end{array}
$$

$$
\begin{array}{rcll}
Child(Harry, n) & = & Richard, & \text{if } n = 1 \\
& = & Nobody, & \text{otherwise} \\
Child(Richard, n) & = & Nobody & \\
Child(Nobody, n) & = & Nobody &
\end{array}
$$

We're creating a quasi-person called *Nobody* as a dummy standing for "Nobody's supposed to be here, so here I am." We'll let his *ord*-value be 0—just for memorability. After all, he is a left zero for the *Child* function.

That's all there is to this particular family data base. You can trace through it, if you like, from Joe to Harry to Richard: all the relationships are present. What can we compute from this particular kind of data base? Well, we might want to check the total number of descendants of any given person in the data base, or we might want to go backwards in the data base to ask for the father or mother of a given person.

Before trying a hard problem, do an easy one: let's first find the total number of children of a given person. One way to do this is with the same idea as we used in *SqrRtApprox* a few sections back: we'll try out the numbers 0,1,2,..., and when we get to a number which is too large we just produce one less:

$$NC(p) \quad = \quad NCA(p, 1),$$

where $NCA(p, i)$ requires that $p$ has at least $i - 1$ children

$$
\begin{aligned}
NCA(p, i) \quad &= \quad i - 1, && \text{if } Child(p, i) = Nobody \\
&= \quad NCA(p, i + 1) && \text{otherwise}
\end{aligned}
$$

**Exercises**   Write the steps and justifications for

**2.4-12**  $NC(Bill)$

**2.4-13**  $NC(Mary)$

**2.4-14**  $NC(Joe)$

Now that you've done a little computation on direct descendants, we'll try all descendants. Still, we'd better look at simple cases first.

- To find the number of descendants of Richard, we note that $Child(Richard, 1) = Nobody$: the answer is 0. The same goes for Bill.

- To find the number of descendants of Harry, we note that $Child(Harry, 1)$ is *Richard* with 0 descendants, and that $Child(Harry, 2)$ is *Nobody*. The answer is 1.

- To find the number of descendants of Mary, we note that her first child is *Harry* with 1 descendant, and that her second child is *Nobody*. The answer is 2.

- To find the number for Joe, we note that his first child is *Bill* with 0 descendants, that his second is *Harry* with 1 descendant, and that his third is *Nobody*. The answer is 3.

Check over that reasoning, comparing it with the steps required for

$$Desc(Nobody) \quad = \quad 0$$
$$Desc(x) \quad = \quad DC(x, 1)$$

where $DC(x, i)$ is the number of descendants of $x$ beginning with the $i$th child.

$$DC(x, i) \quad = \quad 0 \qquad\qquad\qquad\qquad\qquad \text{if } k = Nobody.$$
$$= \quad 1 + Desc(k) + DC(x, i + 1) \quad \text{otherwise}$$

where $k = Child(x, i)$

**Exercises**   Write steps and justifications for

**2.4-15** $Desc(Richard)$.
**2.4-16** $Desc(Joe)$.

Of course, $Desc$ still produces a number as result. However, we can just as well have functions which produce Boolean values, like the function $IsChild(p, c)$, which asks "Is $c$ a child of $p$?":

$$IsChild(p, c) \quad = \quad IC(p, c, 1)$$

where $IC(p, c, i) = $ "Is $c$ an $i$th or later child of $p$?"

$$IC(p, c, i) \quad = \quad False, \qquad \text{if } Child(p, i) = Nobody$$
$$= \quad True, \qquad \text{if } Child(p, i) = c$$
$$= \quad IC(p, c, i + 1) \quad \text{otherwise}$$

**Exercises**   Write steps and justifications for:

**2.4-17** $IsChild(Richard, Harry)$.
**2.4-18** $IsChild(Joe, Harry)$.

As our final example, we'll look at an inverse of the *Child* function:

$$Parent(c) = p \quad \text{if} \quad IsChild(p, c)$$

**Q:** Isn't that impossible? There are two parents for Harry, and you can't produce both.

**A:** True, and so we have to modify the specification: we'll produce whichever one has a higher *ord*-value. (Later, we'll have a formal notation for that.)

$$Parent(c) \quad = \quad PA(Richard, c)$$

where $PA(p, c)$ assumes that $c$ has no parent of higher *ord* than $p$

$$
\begin{aligned}
PA(p, c) \quad &= \quad p, & &\text{if } p = Nobody \lor IsChild(p, c) \\
&= \quad PA(pred(p), c) & &\text{otherwise}
\end{aligned}
$$

**Exercises**    Write steps and justifications for:

**2.4-19**  *Parent(Richard)*

**2.4-20**  *Parent(Harry)*

**2.4-21**  *Parent(Joe)*

Actually, this family "tree" is not really a tree, just because there can be more than one parent for a node. In computer science, we try to deal with structures which are slightly simpler, but sometimes we can't. Still, the problem does have some reasonably nice structure.

**Exercises**

**2.4-22**  Define a partial order which is meaningful on the people in this data base.

**2.4-23**  Define an equivalence relation which is meaningful on the people in this data base.

**2.4-24**  Define a function $Parent(c, i)$ which produces the $i$th parent of child $c$: the first will be highest-*ord* $p$ such that $IsChild(p, c)$, the second will be the next highest, and so on. (Of course, we can hope that there will normally be at most two parents on record, but some families are pretty strange.)

**2.4-25**  Whether or not you wrote the function in the last problem, write some algebraic rules which relate it to *Child*, to *IsChild*, and to the other functions we've looked at.

Of course, all of this is based on the idea that people were encoded as cardinal numbers $p_1 = Joe, \ldots$; that gave us some data to work on. We worked on it with the *Child* function, which simply encoded a sequence of children $c_1, c_2, \ldots$ for each person. When data and operations alike are just encoded sequences, it is past time to study sequences.

# 3

# Structures

You can now work with descriptions of the "scalar" objects of computer science: numbers, truth-values, characters, and simple enumerations. It is time to deal with structures: collections of scalars and collections of structures. Of course, you've already had experience with the idea of groups of variables indicated by special names, as when we represented a point $p$ by its coordinates $p.x$ and $p.y$; when a programming language includes such a convention, we call the "structure" $p$ a *record*. It's nice to be able to say "$p$ is a point" as shorthand for "$p.x$ and $p.y$ are numbers used to represent the $x$ and $y$ coordinates of a point," even if that's all you mean by saying it. Programs organized that way are usually much easier to modify than programs that aren't.

You've also had experience dealing with environments; an environment itself is just a collection of names which you keep together, so it's a sort of record too. If you have two rule-sets $A$ and $B$, each of which contains rules for the function $f$, then we can refer to $A.f$ and $B.f$ to keep them straight whenever confusion might arise; that's a convenience, too. However, we don't need to worry very much about the algebraic properties of records; we could study them algebraically for years, but it's much easier to think of them as a kind of shorthand. Instead, we'll begin with the other kind of structure which we've already promised you: if we want a sequence $S$ of eight items, we can work with the eight names $S_1, S_2, \ldots S_8$ which (to stick with the restrictions of *ASCII* code) we will often call $S[1], S[2], \ldots S[8]$. Sequences can be long, but they are normally quite simple: start at the beginning, do one thing after another until you get to the end, and then stop. (If a sequence *never* stops, then there are some operations which you can't perform on it, like finding the last item. Such sequences are quite useful at times, but we'll start with something easier.)

## 3.1   SEQUENCES OF CHARACTERS: STRINGS

Most of computer science deals with sequences of one kind or another. You will therefore learn to use a variety of notations to describe sequences of different kinds; eventually you'll be ready to talk about the sequence of employee records scattered over different sectors of a disk, or the sequence of databases created (in time) by a sequence of database update commands. We'll begin more prosaically, with a special notation for a special kind of sequence that you're familiar with already.

### 3.1.1   Fundamental String Operations

A document like the one you're reading is a sequence of characters; in computerese, this is called a *string*. It is like a physical piece of twine, with zero or more letter blocks attached to it: "" is a piece of twine with nothing attached to it, "**A**" is a piece holding a letter block '$A$',

$$Alphabet = \text{``}\mathbf{ABCDEFGHIJKLMNOPQRSTUVWXYZ}\text{''}$$

and so on. That means that the letter block '$A$' is a very different object from "**A**": "**A**" contains '$A$', but not vice versa. More precisely, "$\mathbf{A}$"$_1$ = '$\mathbf{A}$'. Let's think of more examples:

$X = \text{``}\mathbf{ThisIsAStringStartingWithT}\text{''}$
$Y = \text{``}\mathbf{This\ is\ a\ string\ of\ 34\ characters.}\text{''}$

($Y$ includes six blanks and the period, but **not** the quotation marks themselves.) There are two obvious things to do with a string: you can count the characters in it, and you can find the character at a given position. Counting characters, we find that $X$ has 26 characters, just like *Alphabet*; $Y$ has 34.

Formally, we need a name for the operation of counting the characters. We call it *Length*: $Length(X) = 26$, and $Length(Y) = 34$. Let's find characters at given positions: the character at the first position of $X$ is '$T$', the character at the seventh position of $Y$ is '$s$'. Formally, we need a name for this operation too. We call it indexing, and we have the two notations for it which we have introduced before: $Y_7 = Y[7] = $ '$s$'. Neither of these is a conventional prefix operation, so we will have a third notation for occasional use: $Get(Y, 7) = Y_7$. In a way, these two operations are all you need to know about any string. Two strings are equal if they have the same length and if each corresponding position is filled by the same character; thus, to say that the two strings $A$ and $B$ are equal is to assert that

$$(Length(A) = Length(B)) \wedge (1 \le i \le Length(A) \Rightarrow (A[i] = B[i])).$$

[Note that the variables in this rule are uppercase letters: we will often use uppercase for names of sequences and other structures, so that when you see a rule involving an expression $F(x, i, S)$ your first guess should be that $x$ is a character or other item, $i$ is an index, and $S$ is the sequence.]

Length and indexing are quite basic: if we can create a string of any given length and put any given character at any given position, then that's all we need to know in order to work with strings.

**Exercises**    Find the values (if any) of the five expressions following:

**3.1-1**    $Length($"abcde"$)$
**3.1-2**    $Length($""$)$
**3.1-3**    $Length($"**This is not a string of Length 8**"$)$
**3.1-4**    "**5**"$[1]$
**3.1-5**    "**Happiness**"$[6]$
**3.1-6**    Explain why $Length('$**A**$')$ and '**A**'$[1]$ and "**A**"$[2]$ are all meaningless.

As a convenient notation, we can refer to a string $S_1, \ldots, S_n$ as $S_{1\ldots N}$. Then, to assert that strings $A_{1\ldots N}$ and $B_{1\ldots M}$ are equal, we can write the rule

$$((N = M) \wedge ((1 \leq i \leq N) \Rightarrow (A_i = B_i)))$$

This test for equality is not a constant-time algorithm unless $N \neq M$: in the worst case we may have to compare every character, and equality testing is $\mathcal{O}(N)$. We can assume the existence of rules like

$$
\begin{aligned}
Eq(A, B) \quad &= \quad False, & &\text{if } Length(A) \neq Length(B) \\
&= \quad Eqq(Length(A)), & &\text{otherwise}
\end{aligned}
$$

where

$$
\begin{aligned}
Eqq(n) \quad &= \quad True, & &\text{if } n = 0 \\
&= \quad False, & &\text{if } A[n] \neq B[n] \\
&= \quad Eqq(n - 1), & &\text{otherwise}
\end{aligned}
$$

The notation $S_{1\ldots n}$ for a string $S$ of length $n$ also suggests a notation for a segment of a string: if $X =$ "**Happiness**", presumably $X_{4\ldots 8} =$ "**pines**"; happiness pines away from four to eight. Again, a restriction to *ASCII* is simple: we can write $X[4 \ldots 8]$ equivalently.

Notice that this is **not** the same as indexing: indexing produces a character, while this segment notation produces a string. For example, "**a**"$_1 = $ '**a**' while "**a**"$_{1\ldots 1} = $ "**a**"; computers get very confused if you mix these up. We may clarify the difference by looking at prefix forms: the segment formation in $S_{a\ldots b}$ is a function of three arguments, and we can write it $Mid(S, a, b)$. Note that

$Length(Mid(S, a, b)) = b + 1 - a$ as long as $Length(S) \geq b$, but $Length(Get(S, a))$ is meaningless since $Get(S, a)$ is not a string.

## Exercises

**3.1-7**  Draw abstract syntax trees for $X[i \ldots j]$ and $X[i]$.

**3.1-8**  Write steps and justifications for $Eq(\textbf{``blow''}, \textbf{``slow''})$.

**3.1-9**  Evaluate $\textbf{``Groucho''}_{3\ldots6}$.

**3.1-10**  Evaluate $Get(\textbf{``character''}_{5\ldots7}, 2) = \text{`a'}$.

   *Length* has no inverse: if we have $n$ and know that $Length(X) = n$, we may be able to construct a string of length $n$ but we'll have no way to be sure that it is really the same as $X$ because it may have different values for indexing. For example, if you know that I have a string $S$ such that $Length(S) = 5$, that doesn't help much in reconstructing $S$.

   Indexing has an almost-inverse: if we know that $X[i] = a$, then given $X$ and $a$ we can try to find $i$. For example, if you know that $\textbf{``abracadabra''}[i] = \text{`c'}$ then you can be sure that $i = 5$, but if you know that $\textbf{``abracadabra''}[j] = \text{`a'}$ then you can't be sure of whether $i$ is 1, 4, 6, 8, or 11. The other almost-inverse doesn't seem to work at all: if you know $a$ and $i$, you can't even begin to guess at $X$. Nonetheless, this almost-inverse is the basis for one of the most fundamental operations of computer programming: the assignment statement. Given a sequence $Y$, a location $i$ in it and a value $v$, the operation *Put* creates a sequence which is just the same as $Y$ except that position $i$ has a copy of value $v$:

$$Put(Y, i, v)[j] = \textbf{ if } i = j \textbf{ then } v \textbf{ else } Y[j]$$

As you can see from trying out an example or two, *Put* takes $i$ and $v$ and creates a sequence whose $i$th item is $v$, but it is only a partial inverse to *Get* because it needs help in deciding what the other items are to be. We won't use *Put* much for a while, because it is rarely the simplest way to describe sequences, but it is crucial in implementation. *Get* and *Put* are basically all that the moron knows how to do: get a scalar item from a numbered square of graph paper, or put a scalar item in a numbered square of graph paper. Like *Get*, *Put* has a "bracketed" notation: we can write $Put(Y, i, v)$ as $Y[i := v]$ or as $Y_{i \leftarrow v}$.

   Enough of notation; we need to learn about strings as we learned about numbers, conditions, and characters. Think about how they can be constructed, combined, and used informally; try to express those combinations and uses with formal operations; and explore the algebraic structure of those operations, looking for inverses, commutativity, associativity, distributivity, special case rules, and repetitions.

### 3.1.2  Building Strings

We'd like to have quite a few operations on strings: we'd like to say that we can combine "**light**" and "**house**" to make "**lighthouse**", we'd like to take the first four letters of "**combine**" to produce "**comb**", and we'd even like to reverse "**Madam, I'm Adam**" and get "**madA m'I ,madaM**". Then we'd like to be able to delete blanks and punctuation marks, convert all letters to uppercase and compare the two strings so that we could then say that "Madam, I'm Adam" is a *palindrome* just like "A man, a plan, a canal—Panama!". The palindrome example is simple enough to serve as an introduction to the basic ideas, complex enough to be interesting. We will build up towards it.

The closest analogue of numeric addition on strings is **concatenation**, often written with a "+" as in "**light**" + "**house**" = "**lighthouse**". For strings $X$ and $Y$, the string $X + Y$ is found as the sequence

$$X_{1...n} + Y_{1...m} \quad = \quad X_1, X_2 \ldots X_n, Y_1, Y_2, \ldots Y_m$$

or equivalently

$$X + Y \quad = \quad X[1], X[2], \ldots, X[Length(X)], Y[1], Y[2], \ldots, Y[Length(Y)]$$

This is associative, has the identity element "", and satisfies the distributive law $Length(A + B) = Length(A) + Length(B)$; it does look very much like addition. However, it is not commutative.

### Exercises

**3.1-11** Give several examples to suggest that $A + (B + C) = (A + B) + C$ for strings $A$, $B$, and $C$.

**3.1-12** Give an example to show that concatenation is not commutative.

**Q:** But now we know that $a + b = b + a$ if $a$ and $b$ are numbers, but not if they're strings. How are we supposed to make use of rules like that?

**A:** That's not really a new idea: $(a - b) + b = a$ was reliable for integers but not for cardinals, and $(a/b) * b = a$ was reliable for rationals but not for integers. When you use a rule, you have to make sure of the kinds of objects it's supposed to be talking about.

In dealing with numbers, the most important special case of addition was $Up$, or addition by 1. With numbers, this was the operation of adding a block to a pile; it gave us a way of classifying numbers so that we could describe simple rules for many operations. A cardinal is either 0, or it is $Up(n)$ for some other cardinal $n$.

Similarly, the most important special case of concatenation is the concatenation of a single item. With twine, this amounts to tying a new letter block to the front of a given string. As with *Up*, this gives us a unique way of classifying strings: a string is either "", or it is $c@s$ for some character $c$ and some string $s$.

$$
\begin{aligned}
\text{"example"} &= \text{'e'@"xample"} \\
\text{"xample"} &= \text{'x'@"ample"} \\
\text{"ample"} &= \text{'a'@"mple"} \\
\text{"mple"} &= \text{'m'@"ple"} \\
\text{"ple"} &= \text{'p'@"le"} \\
\text{"le"} &= \text{'l'@"e"} \\
\text{"e"} &= \text{'e'@""}
\end{aligned}
$$

We'd also like to have some description of what "@" itself does as an operation; here's one way of looking at it:

$$
\begin{aligned}
c@S_1 &= c \\
(c@S_{1\ldots n})_{2\ldots(n+1)} &= S
\end{aligned}
$$

Alternatively, we can describe the operation of tying a string to a single block as that of forming the unit string $Str1(c)$ which contains only that block:

$$
\begin{aligned}
Length(Str1(c)) &= 1 \\
Str1(c)_1 &= c \\
c@S &= Str1(c) + S
\end{aligned}
$$

It can be more convenient to write $Str1(c) + S$ rather than $c@S$. The two are equivalent. However, it is meaningless to talk about the string "**strin**"@'g' or "i"@"t" or 'o'@'k'. In each case, a mechanical moron taught the "@" operation of tying a new letter block at the front of a piece of string would only respond "That's not a letter block" or "That's not a string." **WARNING WARNING WARNING!!!**: this confusion is very common for students, and causes programs to break down catastrophically—or worse, to compute the wrong answer without making any fuss. If it's not clear to you, go get some alphabet blocks, some glue, and some string. Work on it a while.

**Q:** What's so special about adding to the front of the string anyway? Why can't you add to the back?

**A:** You can add to the back if you want to; for example, you can define

$$
\begin{aligned}
AddToBack(S_{1\ldots n}, c)_{n+1} &= c \\
AddToBack(S_{1\ldots n}, c)_{1\ldots n} &= S \\
AddToBack(S, c) &= S + Str1(c)
\end{aligned}
$$

so that

$$
AddToBack(\text{""}, c) = c@\text{""} = Str1(c)
$$

My point is only that "+", "@" and "*AddToBack*" are three different operations: the first connects a pair of sequences, the second puts an item in front of a sequence, the third puts an item at the end of a sequence. Life is somewhat simpler if we take either "@" ∩r "*AddToBack*" as basic; we're taking "@" as the basic one, but for some purposes *AddToBack* is more convenient. Both will be very important in later computer science work. A sequence which is only constructed and classified with "@" (i.e., you *Put* and *Get* items only at the front) is called a *stack*. A sequence which is constructed with "*AddToBack*" but classified with "@" (i.e., you *Put* items onto the back but *Get* them from the front) is called a *queue*. They are often represented in different ways, and algorithms on them have different costs. For now, however, we just want to be able to describe strings.

Having introduced "@", we could describe "+" as the repetition of "@", just as arithmetic addition was the repetition of *Up*. *Length* correspondingly really is the repetition of *Up*:

$$
\begin{aligned}
\text{""} + s &= s \\
(a@X) + Y &= a@(X + Y) \\
Length(\text{""}) &= 0 \\
Length(a@X) &= Up(Length(X)) \\
(a@X)[1] &= a \\
(a@X)[n] &= \textbf{if } n = 1 \textbf{ then } a \textbf{ else } X[n-1]
\end{aligned}
$$

Now our classification of sequences into "" and $a@X$ is usable on *Length* and indexing, so we can compute these incrementally on given strings:

$$
\begin{aligned}
Length(\text{"\textbf{abc}"}) &= Up(Length(\text{"\textbf{bc}"})) \\
&= Up(Up(Length(\text{"\textbf{c}"}))) \\
&= Up(Up(Up(Length(\text{""})))) \\
&= Up(Up(Up(0))) \\
&= 3
\end{aligned}
$$

These classification rules are equivalent to conditional rules, just as they are with the cardinal numbers:

$$
\begin{aligned}
Length(S) &= 0, & \text{if } S = \text{""} \\
&= Up(Length(X)), & \text{if } S = a@X
\end{aligned}
$$

Or of course (Skolemizing) we can find

$$
\begin{aligned}
Length(S) &= 0, & \text{if } S = \text{""} \\
&= Up(Length(Tl(X))), & \text{otherwise}
\end{aligned}
$$

Here, the *Tl* operation is somehow defined to select all of a string except for its first character, by the rule $Tl(a@X) = X$ or $Tl(S_{1...n}) = S_{2...n}$.

We can define other operations incrementally as well. Given a string $S$ of letters, we would like $Capitalize(S)$ to be the corresponding string of all capital letters, formed by applying the $UC$ function to each character in the string. Suppose that we have a string $S$ which has some letters and some nonletters. We would like $Letters(S)$ to be a string of all the letters in $S$, ignoring the nonletters.

$$Letters(\text{``\textbf{Donald E. Knuth}''}) \quad = \quad \text{``\textbf{DonaldEKnuth}''}$$
$$Capitalize(\text{``\textbf{DonaldEKnuth}''}) \quad = \quad \text{``\textbf{DONALDEKNUTH}''}$$

$Capitalize$ has some simple laws, useful for looking for test cases:

$$
\begin{aligned}
Length(Capitalize(X)) &= Length(X) \\
Capitalize(X)[i] &= UC(X[i]) \\
Capitalize(X+Y) &= Capitalize(X) + Capitalize(Y) \\
Capitalize(Capitalize(X)) &= Capitalize(X)
\end{aligned}
$$

The rules for $Letters$ are almost as simple, and some of them are the same:

$$
\begin{aligned}
Letters(X+Y) &= Letters(X) + Letters(Y) \\
Letters(Letters(X)) &= Letters(X) \\
Length(Letters(X)) &\leq Length(X)
\end{aligned}
$$

## Exercises

**3.1-13**  Give one example for each of the preceding rules.

**3.1-14**  Explain why neither $Letters$ nor $Capitalize$ is invertible.

**3.1-15**  List three major contributions to computer science made by Donald E. Knuth.

The most important rules for calculation are the distribution rules, just as they are in arithmetic. With rules like these, it is easy to think of the incremental cases:

$$
\begin{aligned}
Capitalize(\text{``''}) &= \text{``''} \\
Capitalize(c@s) &= UC(c)@Capitalize(s) \\
Letters(\text{``''}) &= \text{``''} \\
Letters(c@s) &= c@Letters(s), &&\text{if } IsLetter(c) \\
&= Letters(s), &&\text{otherwise}
\end{aligned}
$$

$Capitalize$ is defined with two rules: for an empty string and for one with at least one item. Similarly, $Letters$ is defined with three rules: for an empty string, for a string whose first item is a letter, and for a string whose first item is not a letter.

Given those definitions, we can find

$$
\begin{aligned}
Letters(\text{``\textbf{I'm Adam}''}) & = & \text{`I'}@Letters(\text{``'\textbf{m Adam}''}) \\
& = & \text{`I'}@(Letters(\text{``\textbf{m Adam}''})) \\
& = & \text{`I'}@(\text{`m'}@(Letters(\text{`` \textbf{Adam}''}))) \\
& = & \ldots \text{`I'}@(\text{`m'}@(\text{`A'}@(\text{`d'}@(\text{`a'}@(\text{`m'}@\text{``''})))))
\end{aligned}
$$

which in each case is justified by one of the three rules for *Letters*.

## Exercises

**3.1-16**  Find *Letters*(**"23-skiDOO!"**). Show each step.

**3.1-17**  Find *Capitalize*(**"MadamImAdam"**). Show each step.

Finally, we will define *Reverse*. Given $X = $ **"abc"**, we would like to reverse the letters, producing $Reverse(X) = $ **"cba"**. Given $S = $ **"MadamImAdam"**, we would like to find that $Reverse(S) = $ **"madAmImadaM"**. Again, we have simple laws and special cases:

$$
\begin{aligned}
Length(Reverse(X)) & = & Length(X) \\
Reverse(S)[i] & = & S[Length(S) + 1 - i] \\
Reverse(\text{``''}) & = & \text{``''}
\end{aligned}
$$

$$
\begin{aligned}
Reverse(Reverse(X)) & = & X \\
Reverse(X + Y) & = & Reverse(Y) + Reverse(X) \\
Reverse(Str1(a) + X + Str1(b)) & = & Str1(b) + Reverse(X) + Str1(a)
\end{aligned}
$$

Again, the distribution rule is the important one for calculation; we can write

$$
\begin{aligned}
Reverse(\text{``''}) & = & \text{``''} \\
Reverse(c@s) & = & Reverse(s) + Str1(c)
\end{aligned}
$$

The second rule is a special case of the distribution of reversal over concatenation.

**Q:** Don't you mean "$Reverse(c@s) = Reverse(s) + c$"?

**A:** No; remember that the variable "$c$" is a single character, and you can't concatenate to it. Once you understand *Reverse*, you should be able to see that

$$
IsPalindrome(X) \quad = \quad (Y = Reverse(Y))
$$

where

$$
Y \quad = \quad Capitalize(Letters(X))
$$

## Exercises

**3.1-18**  Show all steps for *IsPalindrome*("**1R,d r**").

**3.1-19**  Define (and give algebraic rules for) a function *Digits* which selects the digits of a string as *Letters* selects the letters: *Digits*("**Nov. 23, 1749**") = "**231749**".

**3.1-20**  Define (and give algebraic rules for) a function *Control* which maps a string of letters into a string of control characters: *Control*("**MIIJH**") is a string of one carriage return, two tabs, a linefeed, and a backspace.

**3.1-21**  Define (and give algebraic rules for) a function *SpaceCap* which copies a string of characters but puts a space in front of every capital letter: *SpaceCap*("**GotIt!**") = " **Got It!**"

**3.1-22**  Give an algebraic rule which says that if you concatenate a sequence with its own reversal, you get a palindrome. Is it true?

**3.1-23**  Give an algebraic rule which says that if you add any letter to the front and back of a palindrome, you get a palindrome.

### 3.1.3 Taking Strings Apart

Checking to see whether a given string is or is not a palindrome can be fun, but very few people make their livings that way. We are now ready to build up towards somewhat more practical examples: the descriptions of the operations which find or replace a given string within a larger string. As I write this, I frequently call on programs which perform both of these operations in order to find and fix "**mixspelinks**" and other problems in what I've already written. Nor does the process stop there: what you see as the boldface and quoted "**mixspelinks**" is actually produced by a program which knows how to find the string "\\**Str**" and then replace the sequence "\\**Str**{**mixspelinks**}" with symbols which will cause a printer to generate the right output. To achieve effects like this, we need to take strings apart and put the pieces together again, with other strings inserted.

To take strings apart, we look for functions which invert the effects of "@" and "+". We can easily define two functions to invert "@" on nonempty strings; if we call the first character the *head* and the rest of the string the *tail*, we can define

$$
\begin{aligned}
Hd(a@s) &= a \\
Tl(a@s) &= s
\end{aligned}
$$

Those can be useful, but with strings we'd like something a little more general. These operations take one item or drop off one item; we'd like to be able to take or drop off any number of items.

$$
\begin{aligned}
Take(i, X_{1...i...n}) &= X_{1...i} \\
Drop(i, X_{1...i...n}) &= X_{i+1...n} \\
Take(i, S) &= X, \text{ if } S = X + Y \wedge Length(X) = i \\
Drop(i, S) &= Y, \text{ if } S = X + Y \wedge Length(X) = i
\end{aligned}
$$

If you take the first five characters from a ten-character string, that's what you get. If you drop them, you have all the rest.

**Q:** But what if you take or drop the first ten characters from a five-character string?

**A:** Then you have taken all five or dropped all five, but you can't take more than there are. Even including cases like that, you'll find that

$$
\begin{aligned}
Take(i, s) + Drop(i, s) &= s \\
Length(Take(i, s)) &= min(i, Length(s)) \\
Length(Drop(i, s)) &= max(0, Length(s) - i) \\
Drop(i, Drop(j, s)) &= Drop(i + j, s) \\
Take(i, Take(j, s)) &= Take(min(i, j), s) \\
Drop(i, Take(j, S)) &= Take(j - i, Drop(i, S)) \text{ if } j \geq i
\end{aligned}
$$

Combining these rules makes it possible to see simplifications such as

$$
\begin{aligned}
Drop(i, Take(j, Drop(k, S))) &= Take(j - i, Drop(i, Drop(k, S))) &&\text{if } j \geq i \\
&= Take(j - i, Drop(i + k, S)) &&\text{if } j \geq i
\end{aligned}
$$

Reasoning like this is implicit in the design of many programs, but if you can't state the rules explicitly, you have to keep guessing. Whenever I insert or delete part of a document, I am using *Take* and *Drop*. Suppose that I am editting a document $D$ at position $i$ and want to insert the string $S$ or delete the next $n$ characters. The program I call on will use some version of *Insert* or *Delete*, satisfying the rules

$$
\begin{aligned}
Insert(S, i, D) &= Take(i - 1, D) + S + Drop(i - 1, D) \\
Delete(n, i, D) &= Take(i - 1, D) + Drop(i + n - 1, D) \\
Delete(Length(S), i, Insert(S, i, D)) &= D
\end{aligned}
$$

Some of these expressions are easier to follow when written with dots; thus,

$$
Insert(S, i, D) = D[1 \ldots i - 1] + S + D[i \ldots Length(D)]
$$

is a formula with a picture inside it.

## Exercises

**3.1-24** Finish the incremental rules:
   $Take(0, s) = \underline{\phantom{xx}};$   $Take(i + 1, \text{""}) = \underline{\phantom{xx}};$   $Take(i + 1, c@s) = \underline{\phantom{xx}};$

**3.1-25** Finish the incremental rules:
   $Drop(0, s) = \underline{\phantom{xx}};$   $Drop(i + 1, \text{""}) = \underline{\phantom{xx}};$   $Drop(i + 1, c@s) = \underline{\phantom{xx}};$

**3.1-26** Show all steps for
   $Drop(3, \textbf{"zippety"});$   $Take(15, \textbf{"doo"});$   $Drop(0, \textbf{"dah"});$

**3.1-27** When is $Insert(S, i, Delete(Length(S), i, D)) = D$?

$Insert$ is actually a kind of inverse for $Mid$, which extracts a substring from the middle of a longer string just as $Insert$ inserted it.

$$
\begin{aligned}
Mid(Insert(S, i, D), i, i + Length(S)) &= S \\
Mid(S, i, j) &= Drop(i - 1, Take(j, S)) \\
Mid(\textbf{"zippety"}, 3, 5) &= Drop(2, Take(5, \textbf{"zippety"})) \\
&= Drop(2, \textbf{"zippe"}) \\
&= \textbf{"ppe"} \\
Mid(S, i, j) &= Take(j + 1 - i, Drop(i - 1, S));
\end{aligned}
$$

**Exercises**    Use the rules for $Take$, $Drop$, and $Mid$ to find simplifications for:

**3.1-28** $Mid(Take(i, S), j, k)$

**3.1-29** $Mid(Drop(i, S), j, k)$

**3.1-30** $Take(i, Mid(S, j, k))$

**3.1-31** $Drop(i, Mid(S, j, k))$

The compound $Mid$ operation is the one most directly related to the design and description of computer programs in general, because it enables you to express ideas like "The information on Jones is on lines 3–7 of page 46." To tell a computer where to find something, you must usually identify some region, and then a starting and ending point in that region. Whenever possible, however, we like to use the restricted forms $Take$ and $Drop$ because they give us fewer things to keep track of.

You can now read and use descriptions of operations on strings. Here's a simple Boolean function which checks whether a given string contains a given character:

$$
\begin{aligned}
IsIn(c, S_{1\ldots n}) &= (S_1 = c) \vee \ldots \vee (S_n = c) \\
IsIn(c, S) &= False && \text{if } S = \text{""} \\
&= True && \text{if } Hd(S) = c \\
&= IsIn(c, Tl(S)) && \text{otherwise}
\end{aligned}
$$

**Exercises**    Using the last three rules, show steps and justifications for

**3.1-32** $IsIn(\text{'c'}, \textbf{"cat"})$

**3.1-33** $IsIn(\text{'t'}, \textbf{"cat"})$

**3.1-34** $IsIn(\text{'d'}, \textbf{"cat"})$

As a more sophisticated (and realistic) sample function, let's look for the first occurrence of a given character after a given starting position in a string:

$$Find(c, S, i) \quad = \quad j, \quad \text{if } (S_j = c) \wedge \neg(IsIn(c, S_{i \ldots j-1}))$$

For example,

$$\begin{aligned} Find(\text{`a'}, \text{``cat''}, 1) &= 2 \\ Find(\text{`a'}, \text{``radar''}, 3) &= 4 \\ Find(\text{`a'}, \text{``NoLowA''}, 1) &= 0 \end{aligned}$$

And more generally,

$$\begin{aligned} Find(c, S, i) &= 0, && \text{if } i > Length(S) \\ &= i, && \text{if } S[i] = c \\ &= Find(c, S, i+1) && \text{otherwise} \end{aligned}$$

Thus,

$$\begin{aligned} Find(\text{`a'}, \text{``cat''}, 1) &= Find(\text{`a'}, \text{``cat''}, 2) \\ &= 2 \end{aligned}$$

### Exercises

**3.1-35** Show all steps for $Find(\text{`b'}, \text{``car''}, 1)$.

**3.1-36** *Find* does not distribute neatly. Complete the assertions:

(a) **if** $Find(a, X, 1) = 0$ **then** $Find(a, X + Y, 1) = $ _____.
(b) **if** $Find(a, X, i) > 0$ **then** $Find(a, X + Y, i) = $ _____.

**3.1-37** Define the function $FindPat(P, S, i)$ which looks for the first occurrence of a given string after a given starting position in a string: $FindPat(\text{``cad''}, \text{``abracadabra''}, 1) = 5$ because **cad** does occur beginning at position 5 in **abracadabra**. [Hint: it can be just like *Find* except for the second condition.]

*FindPat* in the last exercise is the function which searches for an occurrence of a given string. Whenever you write a report or a program, the "editor" program which you use makes use of some version of this function to help you move from where you are working to where you want to be. Sometimes that's all you want; a moment ago I scanned backwards to the **"mixspelinks"** string to reread what I had written then. Frequently we want to substitute some new string for the one we've found, as when we instantiate a rule by substituting a string for a variable name. Let's suppose we are at position $i$ in a document $D$; we want to substitute a new string $S$ for an old one $O$ at the very next place it occurs.

$$\begin{aligned} SubstNxt(S, O, D, i) \quad = \quad &\textbf{if } k = 0 \textbf{ then } D \\ &\textbf{else } Insert(S, k, Delete(Length(O), k, D)) \end{aligned}$$

where

$$k \quad = \quad FindPat(O, D, i)$$

Repeated use of this can substitute the new string $S$ for every instance of $O$ after position $i$ in $D$, if needed:

$$SubstAll(S, O, D, i) \quad = \quad \begin{array}{l} \textbf{if } D = D' \textbf{ then } D \\ \textbf{else } SubstAll(S, O, D', i) \end{array}$$

where

$$D' \quad = \quad SubstNxt(S, O, D, i)$$

*SubstAll* is almost a *closure* operation; such operations keep doing something over and over until progress closes off, i.e., until it doesn't seem to make any difference. If we started over again at the beginning each time, we would really have a closure:

$$SubstClo(S, O, D) \quad = \quad \begin{array}{l} \textbf{if } D = D' \textbf{ then } D \\ \textbf{else } SubstCLo(S, O, D') \end{array}$$

where

$$D' \quad = \quad SubstNxt(S, O, D, 1)$$

### Exercises

**3.1-38** Assume *SubstNxt* as a single-step skill; show the steps of
$SubstAll($ "**15**", "**x**", "**x+y=y+x**", 1$)$.

**3.1-39** Explain briefly why it is not possible to calculate any value for
$SubstClo($ "**bigger**", "**big**", "**Zbigniew**", 1$)$. Explain why the same problem arises with *SubstAll*.

**3.1-40** Define the function *SubstEach* so that
$SubstEach($ "**ab**", "**b**", "**bbxbb**", 3$) =$ "**bbxabab**".

**3.1-41** Find the value of $SubstAll($ "**122**", "**11**", "**1111**", 1$)$.

You're getting close to the point where you could define the operations which you learned to carry out at the beginning of the first chapter: given a set of rules written down as a string, and an expression also written as a string, you are almost ready to define an operation which looks for a rule applicable to the expression and either applies it and starts over, or gives up. For simple cases, *SubstAll* already achieves that. There are two obstacles in your way: first, you don't have any way to simplify expressions like "538+93" because you don't have any connection between strings and the things they represent; and second, you don't have a good way to view strings as trees. We can deal with representation now, but we'll have to leave trees for a little later.

### 3.1.4 String Representations

Think of the computer memory as being a huge collection of rules, each defining the contents of one square of graph paper:

$$
\begin{aligned}
Mem(0) &= 12 \\
Mem(1) &= 143 \\
Mem(2) &= 18 \\
Mem(3) &= 99 \\
Mem(4) &= 1 \\
Mem(5) &= 112 \\
&\vdots \\
Mem(999999) &= 46
\end{aligned}
$$

We can put the string $S =$ "**Thinker Toys**" in locations $Mem(130 \ldots 141)$ by making sure that $Mem(130)$ is the *ASCII* code for '**T**', and so on, and then keeping track of two variables: $S.loc = 130$ and $S.len = 12$. That gives us $Length(S) = S.len$ and $Get(S, i) = Mem(S.loc - 1 + i)$, so we would then be able to work with $S$ as a value. Alternatively, we could use many other ways of generating the index and length functions; this will be an important subject for later chapters. At the moment, it is more desirable for us to think of strings as representing scalar values than to try to go in the opposite direction. When we write programs which deal with numbers, they normally have to read (input) numbers and write (output) other numbers (and perhaps some nonnumeric data as well); the same will go for any other kind of information. To read a number is to find the number (if any) corresponding to a given string; to write a number is to invert that function.

To represent a cardinal number by a string, just write it down; to interpret a string as a cardinal number, just read it. Thus, the number 5491 becomes the string "**5491**" of length 4, and the string "**0057**" becomes the number 57. How do we deal with this? As usual, start with the trivial cases (the one-digit numbers), and then work with harder examples and generalize them into rules. For the one-digit numbers, we just use the mutual inverses

$$
\begin{aligned}
DigChr(n) &= Chr(n + Ord(\text{'}\mathbf{0}\text{'})) \\
DigVal(d) &= Ord(n) - Ord(\text{'}\mathbf{0}\text{'})
\end{aligned}
$$

This makes it easy to turn the numbers $0 \ldots 9$ into strings and back. Then we can go on to multidigit numbers.

$$
\begin{aligned}
Rep(5) &= \quad \text{"}\mathbf{5}\text{"} \\
Rep(0) &= \quad \text{"}\mathbf{0}\text{"} \\
Rep(51) &= \quad \text{"}\mathbf{51}\text{"} = Rep(5) + Rep(1) \\
Rep(5791) &= \quad \text{"}\mathbf{5791}\text{"} = Rep(579) + Rep(1)
\end{aligned}
$$

**Q:** Why do you pick $Rep(579)+Rep(1)$ instead of $Rep(5)+Rep(791)$?

**A:** For two reasons. First, because the last digit is the accessible one, just by using $mod$. We can easily write rules now, of the form

$$
\begin{aligned}
Rep(n) \quad &= \quad Str1(DigChr(n)), & \text{if } n < 10 \\
&= \quad Rep(div(n,10)) + Rep(mod(n,10)) & \text{otherwise}
\end{aligned}
$$

This makes some sense, and can easily be checked out by examples:

$$
\begin{aligned}
Rep(50037) \quad &= \quad Rep(5003) + \text{``\textbf{7}''} \text{ (this is actually two steps )} \\
&= \quad Rep(500) + \text{``\textbf{37}''} \text{ (abbreviating again)} \\
&= \quad Rep(50) + \text{``\textbf{037}''} \\
&= \quad Rep(5) + \text{``\textbf{0037}''} \\
&= \quad Rep(0) + \text{``\textbf{50037}''} \\
&= \quad \text{``\textbf{50037}''}
\end{aligned}
$$

## Exercises

**3.1-42** Calculate $Rep(60606)$ using these rules.

**3.1-43** Write rules for $CardStr$ so that $CardStr(n, S) = Rep(n) + S$ just as $MulAcc(n, m, a) = n * m + a$

**Q:** All right, what was the second reason for not picking the leftmost digit?

**A:** Just that it wouldn't work very well: $Rep(500) \neq Rep(5)+Rep(00)$, because $Rep(00) = \text{``0''}$.

Now we can represent numbers with strings; what about inverting the process to form numbers from strings? Think about $Ab(Rep(n)) = n$:

$$
\begin{aligned}
Ab(Str1(DigChr(n))) \quad &= \quad n, & \text{if } n < 10 \\
Ab(Rep(div(n,10)) + Str1(DigChr(mod(n,10)))) \quad &= \quad n, & \text{otherwise}
\end{aligned}
$$

Thus, $Ab(Str1(c)) = DigVal(c)$, and $Ab(S + Str1(c)) = 10 * Ab(n) + DigVal(c)$. If you think about that, it's a scanner like $MinLoc$: it goes from left to right through a sequence.

$$
Ab(S) \quad = \quad f(S, 0, 1)
$$

where

$$
\begin{aligned}
f(S, n, i) \quad &= \quad n, & \text{if } i > Length(S) \\
&= \quad f(S, n * 10 + DigVal(S[i]), i + 1) & \text{otherwise}
\end{aligned}
$$

Alternatively,

$$
Ab(S) \quad = \quad f(S, 0)
$$

where

$$f(S, n) \quad = \quad n, \qquad\qquad\qquad\qquad\qquad\qquad\qquad\qquad \text{if } S = [\,]$$
$$\phantom{f(S, n)} \quad = \quad f(Tail(S), n * 10 + DigVal(Head(S))) \quad \text{otherwise}$$

## Exercises

**3.1-44** What is $Ab(\text{``''})$ with these rules? Does it make sense?

**3.1-45** What is $Ab(\text{``}\mathbf{00009997}\text{''})$?

**3.1-46** In general, when will $Rep(Ab(x)) \neq x$, where $x$ is a string? [Hint: What if $x = Rep(n)$? What if there is no $n$ for which this is true?]

This particular $Rep\text{---}Ab$ pair is important enough to be used in many places; we will call the functions $CardToStr$ and $StrToCard$. They are the basic operations for output and input respectively. We can build other numeric input-output functions on them: if we assume that an integer is always written in the form $\pm C$ where $C$ is the string corresponding to a cardinal, we can write that

$$StrToInt(S) = \text{ if } (Hd(S) = \text{`--'}) \text{ then } 0\text{-}StrToCard(Tl(S))$$
$$\qquad\qquad \text{else if } (Hd(S) = \text{`+'}) \text{ then } StrToCard(Tl(S))$$
$$\qquad\qquad \text{else } StrToCard(S)$$

**Exercises**    Apply the same ideas to write:

**3.1-47** $BoolToStr$ and $StrToBool$ which convert back and forth between *True* and "**TRUE**", and between *False* and "**FALSE**".

**3.1-48** $RealToStr$ and $StrToReal$ which convert back and forth between real numbers and their written forms. You may assume for simplicity that a real number (e.g., "$\mathbf{-5.7896E+12}$" $\rightarrow -5.7896*10**12$)) is always written in the form $\pm d.C_1 \mathbf{E} \pm C_2$, where the decimal point and "**E**" are actual characters, $d$ is a digit, and both $C_1$ and $C_2$ are cardinal numbers.

## 3.2 GENERAL SEQUENCE CONSTRUCTIONS

We have built up a knowledge of strings as sequences of characters, but almost all of it applies to sequences of numbers, sequences of employee records, sequences of Boolean values. More surprisingly, it also applies to sequences of strings, sequences of sequences of numbers, sequences of sequences of sequences of numbers, and so on. What we lack at the moment is a notation for writing such sequences. There are many such notations, but we will use explicit bracketed lists. The list of days of the week can be written

$$Days \quad = \quad [Sun, Mon, Tues, Wed, Thurs, Fri, Sat]$$

The third day is $Days[3] = Tues$. Any sequence can be written this way, even a string: for example,

$$['a', ' ', 's', 't', 'r', 'i', 'n', 'g'] = \text{"a string"}.$$

Indexing, $Hd$, $Tl$, $Mid$, $Take$, and $Drop$ can be used just as well on a sequence of weekdays or a sequence $[2, 3, 5, 7, \ldots]$ of numbers; of course we find that $Capitalize$ and $Letters$ don't mean much, but other functions of similar forms will be important.

### 3.2.1 Familiar House Shapes with New Bricks

Following the pattern of $Letters$, we can write $UpFive$ which filters the numbers $m \geq 5$ from a sequence of cardinal numbers: $UpFive([1, 5, 9, 4, 6, 9]) = [5, 9, 6, 9]$. Looking back at the definition of $Letters$, you can see that

$$
\begin{aligned}
UpFive([]) &= [] \\
UpFive(m@S) &= \textbf{if } m \geq 5 \textbf{ then } m@UpFive(S) \textbf{ else } UpFive(S)
\end{aligned}
$$

$UpFive$ distributes over concatenation and has some other nice properties, but is not very general. It would be better to define it as a special case of a function which works with other numbers as well as 5: $NoLess(n, S)$ should select the numbers $m \geq n$ from the given sequence, just by writing

$$
\begin{aligned}
NoLess(n, []) &= [] \\
NoLess(n, m@S) &= \textbf{if } m \geq n \textbf{ then } m@NoLess(n, S) \textbf{ else } NoLess(n, S)
\end{aligned}
$$

This has other nice properties, such as

$$NoLess(n, (NoLess(m, S))) = NoLess(\min(n, m), S)$$

In exactly the same spirit, we could write $NoMore$ so that $NoMore(n, S)$ would pick the numbers $m \leq n$ from S. Again, we could write $More$ so that $More(n, S)$ would pick the numbers $m > n$ from S. It should be clear that $NoMore(n, NoLess(n, S))$ will be a sequence of copies of $n$ whose length is the number of occurrences of $n$ in $S$, and $More(n, NoMore(n, S)) = []$. Similarly, you should be able to see that $More(n, S)$ contains those items in $S$ that are excluded from $NoMore(n, S)$.

These functions are so trivially simple that you may think them trivially unimportant; that's a confusion that programmers have to keep clear of. One of the most common sources of overdue projects (in and out of school) is overconfidence: we are much too prone to expect things to go right. The more really trivial pieces you can break off of a project, so that they really will go right, the better off you are.

Suppose we needed to write a function $SquareOdds$ which squares the odd numbers in a sequence, but leaves out the evens:

$$SquareOdds([1, 2, 3, 4]) = [1, 9]$$

We could do it in either of two ways. A common method, especially among inexperienced programmers, is to write a few more examples and then start writing a single set of rules to do the whole thing:

$$
\begin{aligned}
SquareOdds([\,]) \quad &= \quad [\,] \\
SquareOdds(n@S) \quad &= \quad (n * n)@SquareOdds(S), \quad \text{if } odd(n) \\
&= \quad SquareOdds(S), \quad\quad\quad\;\; \text{otherwise}
\end{aligned}
$$

Here is a more tedious approach:

$$
\begin{aligned}
Squares([\,]) \quad &= \quad [\,] \\
Squares(n@S) \quad &= \quad (n * n)@Squares(S) \\
Odds([\,]) \quad &= \quad [\,] \\
Odds(n@S) \quad &= \quad n@Odds(S), \quad\quad\;\; \text{if } odd(n) \\
&= \quad Odds(S), \quad\quad\quad\;\;\; \text{otherwise} \\
SquareOdds(S) \quad &= \quad Squares(Odds(S))
\end{aligned}
$$

This second way is more tedious not only for the person writing the rules, but also for the person or machine who has to use them. Both methods are linear-time algorithms, but it takes more steps to find $SquareOdds([3, 1, 4, 1, 5, 9])$ using the second method. Nonetheless, the second method is better when working on a specification—or in the first few versions of an implementation. Think about it:

- Since the pieces of the second method are more trivial, they are more likely to be right on the first try.

- Since are simple, with nice algebraic properties, you can test them more easily—separately.

- Since you know they are more likely to be right, and since you can test them more easily, your attention shifts more quickly to the difficult parts of the program.

- Since they have simple, standard forms, it's quite likely that you have written other programs almost exactly like them; if you'd already written *Letters* and *Capitalize*, then "writing" *Odds* and *Squares* will take at most a few minutes with a text editor. It may not even require that: you may have versions of those programs which treat functions themselves as variables, and then you find that *Letters* and *Odds* are the same program with a different predicate as parameter, while *Capitalize* and *Squares* are the same program with a different function as parameter. The smaller the pieces, the more likely they are to fit exactly into standard forms which you already know how to generate.

## Exercises

**3.2-1**   Define a function *DblAll* which looks just like *Capitalize*, but doubles every number in a sequence: $DblAll([1, 2, 3]) = [2, 4, 6]$.

**3.2-2**   Define a function *Evens* which selects even numbers from a sequence of numbers:
$Evens([1, 2, 3, 4, 4, 12, 5, 6, 7, 8, 9]) = [2, 4, 4, 12, 6, 8]$.
It should look just like *Letters*.

**3.2-3**   Define the functions *More* and *NoMore*.

**3.2-4**   What is $More(n, NoLess(n, S))$?

### 3.2.2  Generation and Accumulation

Many routine programs have the form of *Find*, of *Capitalize*, of *Letters* or of some combination of these.  Programs like *Find* and *FindPat* are *search* programs, which scan through a sequence to find some kind of a value. Programs like *Capitalize* and *DblAll* are *mappings*, which transform each thing in a sequence. Programs like *Letters* and *Evens* are *filters*, which let good things through and stop the bad ones. There are a few other common forms which are worth remembering. One is the *generator*, which repeatedly adds items to a starting value. For example, we might want to make the sequence $[1 \ldots 100]$ or $[128 \ldots 255]$.

$$Range(i, j) \quad = \quad [i \ldots j],$$

as in

$$Range(3, 9) \quad = \quad [3, 4, 5, 6, 7, 8, 9]$$

i.e.

$$Range(i, j) \quad = \quad \textbf{if } i > j \textbf{ then } [] \textbf{ else } i @ Range(i + 1, j).$$

A generator has a stopping condition (in this case $i > j$). It also has something to produce (in this case $i$). Finally, it has something to try next (in this case $i + 1$). *Range* is a very useful generator with simple properties:

$$
\begin{aligned}
Length(Range(i, j)) &= j + 1 - i \\
Range(i, j)[k] &= i + k - 1 \\
Range(i, j) + Range(j + 1, k) &= Range(i, k) \\
Drop(i, Range(j, k)) &= Range(i + j, k) \\
Take(i, Range(j, k)) &= Range(j, \min(i + j - 1, k))
\end{aligned}
$$

Writing $Range(i, j)$ as $[i \ldots j]$ and $Take(i, S)$ as $S[1 \ldots i]$, that last rule becomes

$$[j \ldots k][1 \ldots i] = [j \ldots \min(i + j - 1, k)].$$

This degree of compaction can be confusing, but sometimes it is helpful. In this case it would probably be better to to use either "*Range*" or "*Take*" in prefix form, but not both. (Try them and see.)

Another simple generator is *Repeat*, which produces a sequence of identical elements: $Repeat(\text{'a'}, 5) = $ "**aaaaa**" and $Repeat(3, 2) = [3, 3]$. The definition of *Repeat* is

$$Repeat(x, n) \quad = \quad \textbf{if } n = 0 \textbf{ then } [\,] \textbf{ else } x@Repeat(x, n - 1)$$

so that

$$
\begin{array}{rcll}
Repeat(x, n + m) & = & Repeat(x, n) + Repeat(x, m) & \text{if } x, y \geq 0 \\
Reverse(Repeat(x, n)) & = & Repeat(x, n) & \\
Length(Repeat(a, n)) & = & n & \\
Repeat(a, n)[i] & = & a, & \text{if } 1 \leq i \leq n
\end{array}
$$

Here the stopping condition is different and the continuation is different, but we still have a generator.

### Exercises

**3.2-5**  What *Range* is $Mid(i, j, Range(m, n))$?

**3.2-6**  Simplify $Repeat(x, i) + Repeat(x, j)$.

**3.2-7**  Simplify $Take(i, Repeat(x, i))$.

**3.2-8**  Write a generator $G$ which counts down to 0:
$G(2) = 2@G(1) = 2@(1@(G(0))) = 2@(1@([\,])) = [2, 1]$

(If you have gotten this far, you probably need a rest.)

Another kind of sequence function we often deal with is called an *accumulator*. Here are two examples: *Sum*, which adds up the numbers in a sequence of numbers, and *Count*, which counts the occurrences of a given item in a sequence. Thus, $Sum([4, 5, 6]) = 15$, and $Count(\text{'a'}, \text{"gaga"}) = 2$. Accumulations are often distributive:

$$
\begin{array}{rcl}
Sum(S_1 + S_2) & = & Sum(S_1) + Sum(S_2) \\
Count(c, S_1 + S_2) & = & Count(c, S_1) + Count(c, S_2) \\
Sum([\,]) & = & 0 \\
Sum(n@S) & = & n + Sum(S)
\end{array}
$$

We could define *Count* for computational purposes by means of the rules

$$
\begin{array}{rcll}
Count(x, [\,]) & = & 0 & \\
Count(x, y@S) & = & 1 + Count(x, S) & \text{if } x = y \\
& = & Count(x, S) & \text{otherwise}
\end{array}
$$

On the other hand, we could just go on thinking up interesting facts about *Count* as a function:

$$Count(x, Repeat(y, n)) = \textbf{if } x = y \textbf{ then } n \textbf{ else } 0$$
$$Count(x, S) = Length(NoMore(x, NoLess(x, S)))$$

## Exercises

**3.2-9** Find *Count*('a', "**abracadabra**"). Show your steps.

**3.2-10** Find *Sum*(*Range*(3, 6)). Show your steps.

**3.2-11** Give an algebraic rule saying that the sum of a sequence is not changed by reversing it.

**3.2-12** Give an algebraic rule saying that to double each item in a sequence and then to find the sum is the same as doubling the sum of the sequence. (You must use *DblAll*).

**3.2-13** Define an accumulator which finds the product of a sequence of numbers. [Hint: It should produce 1 for an empty sequence.]

Accumulators can also be used to find the maximal or minimal item of non-empty sequences. The *Min* function is suggested by the rules $Min(S) \le S[i]$ and **if** $S \ne []$ **then** $0 \ne Find(Min(S), S, 1)$, generalizing on the idea that $Min([a, b]) = min(a, b)$. These rules are not particularly adapted for computation. To compute, it helps to realize that *Min* distributes over concatenation and that $Min([n]) = n$. (Notice that $Min([])$ is meaningless, although we could arbitrarily define it as $+\infty$. Similarly, a function to find the maximal element of a sequence cannot work on an empty sequence, but could be arbitrarily defined to produce $-\infty$.)

$$
\begin{aligned}
NoLess(Min(S), S) &= S, & &\text{if } S \ne [] \\
NoMore(Min(S), S)[i] &= Min(S), & &\text{if } i \le Count(Min(S), S) \\
Min(S) &= S[1], & &\text{if } Tl(S) = [] \\
&= min(S[1], Min(Tl(S))), & &\text{otherwise} \\
Min([3, 4, 2]) &= min(3, min(4, 2)) \\
&= 2
\end{aligned}
$$

With *Sum* and *Count* and many other accumulators, it is possible to find the final answer by keeping track of a current sum or current count; similarly, one can find the minimum by keeping track of the smallest so far:

$$Min(S) = MinAcc(Hd(S), Tl(S))$$

where

$$
\begin{aligned}
MinAcc(a, S) &= a, & \text{if } S = [\,] \\
&= MinAcc(\min(a, S[1]), Tl(S)), & \text{otherwise} \\
Min([3, 4, 2]) &= MinAcc(3, [4, 2]) \\
&= MinAcc(3, [2]) \\
&= MinAcc(2, [\,]) \\
&= 2
\end{aligned}
$$

Yet another equivalent definition is worth mentioning; a version of $Min$ which finds the position of the minimal element, starting from position 1, rather than that element itself:

$$
\begin{aligned}
MinLoc(i, S) &= Find(Min(S[i \ldots]), S, i) \\
Min(S) &= S[MinLoc(1, S[2 \ldots])]
\end{aligned}
$$

Suppose that we had the location of the minimal element in $S[2 \ldots]$; it's the 14th item in that sequence, so it's the 15th item in $S$. If it is smaller than $S[1]$, then the answer is 15; otherwise the answer is 1.

That reasoning gives us the following equations:

$$
\begin{aligned}
MinLoc(1, S[2 \ldots]) &= 1, & \text{if } 2 > Length(S) \\
&= 1, & \text{if } S[1] \leq S[n] \\
&= n + 1, & \text{otherwise},
\end{aligned}
$$

where

$$
n = MinLoc(1, Tail(S)[2 \ldots])
$$

The dependency structure for $MinLoc(1, [3, 9, 5])$ thus looks like this:

$$
\text{``}MinLoc\mathbf{(1,[3,9,5])}\text{''}(3, \text{``}MinLoc\mathbf{(1,[9,5])}\text{''}(9, \text{``}MinLoc\mathbf{(1,[5])}\text{''}(\,)))
$$

Using the rules straightforwardly will give a strictly bottom-up calculation. A better way of getting the answer comes from the ideas of $Find$: begin at the first position and consider how to go on from there, but always look for something smaller than the smallest so far.

In other words, $MinLoc(i, S[j \ldots k])$ assumes that $S[i] = Min(1, S[1 \ldots j-1])$ and proceeds from there:

$$
\begin{aligned}
MinLoc(i, S[j \ldots k]) &= i, & \text{if } j > k \\
&= MinLoc(i, S[j + 1 \ldots k]) & \text{if } S[i] \leq S[j] \\
&= MinLoc(j, S[j + 1 \ldots k]) & \text{otherwise}
\end{aligned}
$$

$MinLoc$ is important because it finds the position of the least item as well as its value, so that we could delete it if we wanted to. That lets us talk about the sequence of all *but* the least element, or the sequence formed by putting the minimum element in front:

$$MinFirst(S) \quad = \quad S[k]@Delete(k, 1, S)$$

where

$$k \quad = \quad MinLoc(1, S[2\ldots])$$

Accumulators can also be predicates. To test whether all numbers in a sequence are odd, we could write *AllOdd* as a function satisfying

$$
\begin{aligned}
AllOdd([\,]) &= \quad True \\
AllOdd([n]) &= \quad odd(n) \\
AllOdd(X + Y) &= \quad AllOdd(X) \wedge AllOdd(Y)
\end{aligned}
$$

To test whether a digit occurs anywhere in a string, we could write *HasDigit* as a function satisfying $HasDigit([\,]) = False$, $HasDigit([c]) = IsDigit(c)$ and $HasDigit(X +Y) = HasDigit(X) \vee HasDigit(Y)$. To test whether a sequence has a number bigger than some given $n$, we could write *HasBigger* so that $HasBigger(n, X + Y) = HasBigger(n, X) \vee HasBigger(n, Y)$. To test whether an item occurs anywhere in a sequence, we could write *IsIn* so that $IsIn(x, S) = True$ whenever $Find(x, S, 1) \neq 0$, i.e., if $x$ occurs in $S$. All of these are accumulators.

### Exercises

**3.2-14** Give a rule for $AllOdd(x@S)$ like that defining *Sum*.

**3.2-15** Give a rule for $HasDigit(x@S)$.

**3.2-16** Summarize the algebraic properties of *IsIn*.

**3.2-17** $Find(a, S, 1)$ produces $i \neq 0$ precisely when $S[i] = a$ and no earlier item in $S$ is the same as $a$. Similarly, $FindBigger(a, S, 1)$ should produce $i \neq 0$ precisely when $S[i] > a$ and no earlier item is larger than $a$. Define *FindBigger* by copying the definition of *Find* and changing it a little bit.

### 3.2.3 Invariants with Sequence Calculations

One of the nice things about invariants is that they don't change: the same problems and solutions occur as did with the invariants for simple recurrences on the cardinals.

Suppose we have the familiar equations defining sequence reversal:

$$
\begin{aligned}
Rev(S) &= \quad R(S, [\,]), \\
R(A, B) &= \quad B, & \text{if } A = [\,] \\
&= \quad R(Tail(A), Head(A)@B) & \text{otherwise}
\end{aligned}
$$

Then we can end up with a computation sequence looking like this:

$$
\begin{array}{rcll}
Rev([a,b,c]) & = & R([a,b,c],[\,]) & (S_1) \\
& = & R([b,c],[a]) & (S_2) \\
& = & R([c],[b,a]) & (S_3) \\
& = & R([\,],[c,b,a]) & (S_4) \\
& = & [c,b,a]
\end{array}
$$

There are four states involving the $R$ function, and all of them certainly satisfy the invariant $R(A,B) = Rev(A_1) = Rev(S)$. We can do better than that; even if we don't know the origin of the $R$ function, we can try running it on a silly input like $R([a,b,c],[x,y])$. After five steps we'll come up with $[c,b,a,x,y]$, which is likely to suggest to us that

$$
R(A,B) = Rev(A) + B
$$

This is in fact the case, as you can see from trying more examples and thinking carefully about both rules defining $R$. Once we know that, we can write the invariant as $Rev(A) + B = Rev(A_1)$, which is much more likely to make sense if we see a program printing output like

$$
\begin{array}{ll}
A = [a,b,c]; B = [\,]; & \qquad Rev(A) + B = Rev(A_1) \\
A = [b,c]; B = [a]; & \qquad Rev(A) + B = Rev(A_1) \\
A = [c]; B = [b,a]; & \qquad Rev(A) + B = Rev(A_1) \\
A = [\,]; B = [c,b,a]; & \qquad Rev(A) + B = Rev(A_1)
\end{array}
$$

On each line, the statement made is true. It's working!

As with the examples on cardinal numbers, this was a goal-directed invariant: it states the original goal in terms of the current values. It is also possible to find data-directed invariants such as $Length(A) \leq Length(A_1)$; or $Length(B) \geq Length(B_1)$. We can describe the variables themselves in this particular computation as $A_i = A_1[i\ldots]$ and $B_i = Rev(A_1[1\ldots i-1])$. These depend on the hypothetical variable $i$, but they can be rephrased to avoid that: $B = Rev(A_1[1\ldots Length(B)])$ and $A = A_1[Length(B)+1\ldots]$ are safer formulations. We can twist around the invariant: $A_1 = Rev(B)+A$, which is also data-directed because it relates the current variables to the original state rather than to a goal.

**Exercises**    Provide and discuss goal-directed and data-directed invariants for

**3.2-18**

$$
\begin{array}{rcll}
Min(S) & = & S[MinLoc(1, S[2\ldots Length(S)])] & \\
MinLoc(k, S[i\ldots j]) & = & k, & \text{if } i > j; \\
& = & MinLoc(k, S[i+1\ldots j]) & \text{if } S[k] \leq S[i] \\
& = & MinLoc(i, S[i+1\ldots j]) & \text{if } S[k] \leq S[i]
\end{array}
$$

**3.2-19**

$$Get(S, i) \quad = \quad Head(S), \qquad\qquad \text{if } i = 1$$
$$\qquad\quad = \quad Get(Tail(S), i - 1), \quad \text{otherwise}$$

### 3.2.4 Simple Recurrences Once More

The top-down and bottom-up construction of recurrences is also little changed by changing from scalars to sequences. Suppose we're given a rule like

$$Rev(S[i \ldots j]) = Rev(S[i + 1 \ldots j]) + [S[i]]$$

This can be used to see that $Rev([a, b, c])$ depends upon $[a]$ and upon $Rev([b, c])$, which depends upon $[b]$ and upon $Rev([c])$, which depends upon $[c]$ and upon $Rev([])$. A top-down solution will save $a$, $b$, and $c$ into some sort of accumulator which will hold the answer when we get to the bottom; a bottom-up solution will build $Rev([])$ as $[]$, then add $S[3]$ to it, then add $S[2]$ to the result, then add $S[1]$ and achieve the final goal. We have

$$Rev(S) \quad = \quad RTop(S, [])$$
$$RTop(S, A) \quad = \quad Rev(S) + A,$$

so

$$RTop([], A) \quad = \quad A,$$
$$RTop(x@S, A) \quad = \quad RTop(S, x@A)$$

and

$$Rev(S) \quad = \quad RBot(S, Length(S), [])$$
$$RBot(S, i, A) \quad = \quad A + Rev(S[1 \ldots i]),$$

so

$$RBot(S, 0, A) \quad = \quad A$$
$$RBot(S, i + 1, A) \quad = \quad RBot(S, i, A + [S[i + 1]])$$

Notice that $RTop$ is exactly the simple recurrence we gave before; the only new factor is that now we are thinking about the process of reasoning by which you can come up with a solution like that.

### Exercises

**3.2-20** Write top-down and bottom-up solutions for *Sum* and *Min*. (There are simple recurrences for each of them already; you must identify them as top-down or bottom-up, and design the other solution for each.)

**3.2-21** Write top-down and bottom-up solutions for *Letters* and *Capitalize*.

### 3.2.5 Nested Sequences Form the Branches of Trees

At this point in our notation, there's nothing to stop us from writing

$$[[[[2, `\mathbf{B}'], ``\vee"], ``\neg"], [2], `\mathbf{b}']$$

This is a sequence of three items,

- The first being $[[[2, `\mathbf{B}'], ``\vee"], ``\neg"]$, which is a sequence of two items,
  - The first being $[[2, `\mathbf{B}'], ``\vee"]$, which is a sequence of two items
    * The first being $[2, `\mathbf{B}']$, and
    * The second being $``\vee"$
  - And the second being $``\neg"$,
- The second being $[2]$, and
- The third being $`\mathbf{b}'$.

In fact, we can combine arbitrary things in arbitrarily nested sequences. In much of computer science, we don't do that: we say in advance what kind of nesting will occur, and if we have decided to deal with sequences of sequences of sequences of strings, we don't suddenly insert numbers into them. However, there are many applications where we really want to deal with arbitrary nesting, and you've already seen some of them. It's extremely difficult to deal with expressions without nested sequences, but with them a lot of tasks become easy.

Suppose that you have an expression which you want to describe as a computational structure. First, write it in prefix form: you should remember how to do that. (And you should remember that *any* tree can be written unambiguously as a prefix-form expression.) For example, we rewrite

$$(x + (y * z) * 3 + y)$$

as

$$+(+(x, *(*(y, z), 3)), y)$$

(Draw the abstract syntax tree for this if you're in difficulty.) All the parentheses are now being used to enclose argument lists; none are helping with any kind of precedence control. Let's put the argument lists in square brackets, each preceded by the operation symbol:

$$+[+[x, *[*[y, z], 3]], y]$$

That's not a significant change, and it's certainly reversible. We now have "funny-expressions" which are either simple expressions (names or numbers) or structures of the form $Op[e_1, \ldots e_n]$, with each $e_i$ being a funny-expression. Fine: take each funny-expression and rewrite it with the operation symbol inside the brackets, as $[\text{"\textbf{Op}"}, e_1, \ldots e_n]$. In our specific example, we get

$$S = [\text{"\textbf{+}"}, [\text{"\textbf{+}"}, \text{"\textbf{x}"}, [\text{"\textbf{*}"}, [\text{"\textbf{*}"}, \text{"\textbf{y}"}, \text{"\textbf{z}"}], 3]], \text{"\textbf{y}"}]$$

This is still a tree, but it's also a sequence containing structures which we now know how to handle. For any sequence $S$ formed in this way, $Hd(S)$ is a string indicating an operation and $Tl(S)$ is the sequence of arguments.

**Exercises**   Find the nested sequences to represent

**3.2-22**  $x + 3$

**3.2-23**  $x + 3 * y$

**3.2-24**  $Sqr(Distance(a, b, a + b, 2 * d))$

Suppose that you have an expression and a collection of rules which might be used to simplify it: the expression would become a nested sequence, each rule would become a pair (i.e., a sequence of length two) of nested sequences, and the collection of rules would also be a sequence. We won't go over a full set of rules which could be used to teach the computer-moron how to follow rules,[1] but we'll give an example: to substitute a value for a single variable in a structure, we could write

$$
\begin{aligned}
Subst(val, var, S) \quad &= \quad val, & \text{if } S = var \\
&= \quad S, & \text{if } S = [\,] \vee S \text{ is not a sequence} \\
&= \quad Subst(val, var, S_1) & \text{otherwise} \\
& \quad\; @Subst(val, var, Tl(S))
\end{aligned}
$$

For example, we could find

$$
\begin{aligned}
Subst(5, \text{"\textbf{x}"}, [\text{"\textbf{+}"}, \text{"\textbf{x}"}, 3]) \quad &= \quad Subst(5, \text{"\textbf{x}"}, \text{"\textbf{+}"})@Subst(5, \text{"\textbf{x}"}, [\text{"\textbf{x}"}, 3]) \\
&= \quad \text{"\textbf{+}"}@Subst(5, \text{"\textbf{x}"}, [\text{"\textbf{x}"}, 3]) \\
&= \quad \text{"\textbf{+}"}@(Subst(5, \text{"\textbf{x}"}, \text{"\textbf{x}"})@Subst(5, \text{"\textbf{x}"}, [3]) \\
&= \quad \text{"\textbf{+}"}@(5@Subst(5, \text{"\textbf{x}"}, [3])) \\
&= \quad \text{"\textbf{+}"}@(5@(Subst(5, \text{"\textbf{x}"}, 3)@Subst(5, \text{"\textbf{x}"}, [\,]))) \\
&= \quad \ldots [\text{"\textbf{+}"}, 5, 3]
\end{aligned}
$$

**Exercises**

**3.2-25**  Find steps and justifications for $Subst(7, \text{"\textbf{y}"}, [\text{"\textbf{Half}"}, \text{"\textbf{y}"}])$

---

[1] Does that sound circular? It is, somewhat, but the circle can be broken once you understand it well enough to go around and around and around without getting too dizzy.

**3.2-26** Find steps and justifications for $Subst(7, \text{"}\mathbf{x}\text{"}, Subst(3, \text{"}\mathbf{y}\text{"}, [\text{"}\mathbf{*}\text{"}, \text{"}\mathbf{y}\text{"}, \text{"}\mathbf{x}\text{"}]))$

We will not yet worry about the "parsing" process by which a programming language implementation transforms "$\mathbf{x+3*y}$" into a nested-sequence construction or prints it out again as "$\mathbf{x+3*y}$", but we will try to deal with the simpler problem of specification for the reading and writing operations on nested sequences themselves. We will lead into that by reading and writing sequences which are not nested.

### 3.2.6  Reading and Writing Sequences

The next step up from writing and reading numbers is writing and reading sequences of numbers. We want to convert back and forth between the sequence [5,922,717] of three numbers and the sequence "$\mathbf{[5,922,717]}$" of eleven characters. Again, it is easier to define $Rep$, which takes us from sequences to strings, and then to define $Ab$ which takes us back again: if we write $A = CardToStr(a), B = CardToStr(b),\ldots,$ then

$$
\begin{aligned}
Rep([]) &= \text{"[]"} \\
Rep([a]) &= \text{"["} + A + \text{"]"} \\
Rep([a,b]) &= \text{"["} + A + \text{","} + B + \text{"]"} \\
Rep([a,b,c]) &= \text{"["} + A + \text{","} + B + \text{","} + C + \text{"]"}
\end{aligned}
$$

We look for a pattern in this; the empty sequence seems like a very special case, but after a while we just keep on looking for the end, and either finding it (and writing the closing bracket) or failing to find it (and writing the next comma, followed by a number).

$$
\begin{aligned}
Rep([]) &= \text{"[]"} \\
Rep(a@X) &= \text{"["} + A + f(X)
\end{aligned}
$$

where

$$
\begin{aligned}
f([]) &= \text{"]"} \\
f(a@X) &= \text{","} + A + f(X)
\end{aligned}
$$

Algebraically, these are not very nice functions. You can almost say that

$$Rep(X + Y) = Rep(X) + Rep(Y), \text{ if } X \neq [] \neq Y$$

but it doesn't quite work; you are left with a "][" in the middle instead of a ",". Still, not too much will be required of the representation, because it is just used for storage. All we want is that when we read a sequence which we have printed, we should get the same thing back again: $Ab(Rep(S)) = S$. For that, we need to define $Ab$:

$$
\begin{aligned}
Ab(\text{"[]"}) &= [] \\
Ab(\text{"["} + A + S) &= a@g(S)
\end{aligned}
$$

where

$$g(``]") \quad = \quad []$$
$$g(``," + A + S) \quad = \quad a@g(S)$$

**Q:** Where did $g$ come from?

**A:** $g$ is the inverse of $f$; the definition comes from switching the left-hand and right-hand sides of $f$, so that $g(f(S)) = S$ just as $Ab(Rep(S)) = S$.

**Exercises**    Given the $Ab$ and $Rep$ discussions above, and ignoring blanks altogether, define

**3.2-27** *SeqToStr* as a conditional recurrence, calling on *CardToStr* when necessary.

**3.2-28** *ReadSeq* as a simple conditional recurrence, calling on *StrToCard*. For this one, you will have to *Take* and *Drop* a sequence of digits from the front of a string. Define a function *LastDigit(S)* so that

$$LastDigit(\text{``}\mathbf{9999{,}88888}]\text{''}) \quad = \quad 4,$$

so that

$$Take(4, \text{``}\mathbf{9999{,}88888}]\text{''}) \quad = \quad \text{``}\mathbf{9999}\text{''}$$

These last exercises also prepare you for the input and output of nested sequences. If you want to modify *SeqToStr* so that it will find the string representation of nested sequences, all you have to do is look at the point where it calls *CardToStr* to print out an item. That item might now be a cardinal, a string... or a sequence. Let's ignore strings for the moment; all you need to do to them is put quotation marks around them anyway. To deal with both cardinals and sequences, you must replace *CardToStr(a)* with

**if** *IsSequence(a)* **then** *SeqToStr(a)* **else** *CardToStr(a)*

For *StrToSeq*, you have a similar difficulty, worsened by the fact that if you are reading a sequence from the front of a string, as in "$\mathbf{[2,[3,1]],[4],5}$", you need to find the end of the sequence "$\mathbf{[2,[3,1]]}$" before you can apply *Take* and *StrToSeq*.

**Q:** You mean you have to read it before you can read it?

**A:** No, you just need to find out where the matching bracket is, and you can do that by counting:

```
[ 2 , [ 3 , 1 ] ] , [ 4 ] , 5 ]
1 1 1 2 2 2 2 1 0 0 1 ...
1 2 3 4 5 6 7 8 9 ...
```

The answer we want is 9, which is $Find(0, C, 1)$, where $C$ is given by

$$
\begin{aligned}
C[1] &= 1 \\
C[i+1] &= C[i] + 1, \quad \text{if S[i]='['} \\
&= C[i] - 1, \quad \text{if S[i]=']'} \\
&= C[i] \qquad\quad \text{otherwise}
\end{aligned}
$$

**Exercises**    Using the preceding definitions,

**3.2-29** Define a function which actually finds the matching bracket (notice that I've cheated by defining the sequence $C$ with rules for a function; you should redefine it using a generator.)

**3.2-30** Explain why the resulting *StrToSeq* function will have to be quadratic in the length of the input string. [Hint: Think about very, *very* deeply nested sequences.]

Actually, nested-sequence (or expression) input is normally handled with linear-complexity functions called *parsers*. Such programs produce composite results: not just a tree, but also the residual (unread) input. Thus, if we know we have a string $S$ which begins with a sequence, we might define

$$
ParseSeq(S) \quad = \quad C
$$

where

$$
\begin{aligned}
C.t &= StrToSeq(Take(n, S)) \\
C.r &= Drop(n, S) \\
n &= \text{the position of the ']' matching } S\text{'s opening '['}
\end{aligned}
$$

The reason that *ParseSeq* is a good thing to specify is that it can be computed through rules which compute $C.t$ and $C.r$ together, scanning through the input string once: it is not necessary to count brackets over and over again.

We won't present the rules; they are much easier if written directly from the *BNF* grammar being used, and you're not quite ready for these yet. The analysis required is based on notions of set theory, which we'll get to soon (although we certainly won't cover the techniques of automatic parser generation; this is a foundations course, not a one-book summary of all computer science.) For now, it is time to go on with the basic properties of sequences and the fundamental operations which work on them.

## 3.3 STRUCTURES OF SEQUENCES

In order to deal properly with sequences, you must be able to build them into structures and relate them to other types: you must be able to deal with sequences of sequences, you must be able to find orderings within sequences and between sequences, and you must be able to think of sequences as representations of functions or as being represented by functions. Each of these ideas turns out to lead to important topics within computer science.

### 3.3.1 Sequences of Sequences

Most of the time when we deal with sequences of sequences, they are not trees, and they don't look like expressions. Instead, they are closely analogous to the flat sequences we formed from numbers or characters. We will just give a few examples of them so you can begin to see the idea. The word "**abracadabra**" is said to have come from a medieval cantrip: if you have a cold, you should write "**abracadabra**" above your bed, then the next day write "**bracadabra**", on the third day write "**racadabra**", and so on; your cold will disappear by the time the word does. (It almost always works, too: try it the next time you have a cold.) This is a sequence of strings. To generate it, we can define the *Tails* function so that

$$
\begin{aligned}
Tails(\text{``abcd''}) &= [\text{``abcd''}, \text{``bcd''}, \text{``cd''}, \text{``d''}] \\
Tails([1,2,3]) &= [[1,2,3],[2,3],[3]]
\end{aligned}
$$

*Tails* has simple algebraic properties, such as

$$
\begin{aligned}
Length(Tails(S)) &= Length(S) \\
Tails(S)[i][j] &= S[i+j-1] \\
Hd(Tails(S)) &= S, \text{ if } S \neq []
\end{aligned}
$$

Some of its properties are good (classification) rules for computation:

$$
\begin{aligned}
Tails([]) &= [] \\
Tails(x@S) &= (x@S)@Tails(S)
\end{aligned}
$$

Having created a sequence of sequences, you can manipulate it in various ways. *Tails* has no nice distributive properties, but it does have an inverse: if we describe a function $Heads(S)[i] = S[i][1]$, then $Heads(Tails(S)) = S$.

One kind of sequence of sequences has special importance in computer science: a *looooonnnnngg* sequence of short sequences, where each short sequence describes a step in a computation. For example, we began Chapter 1 with the sequence

$$[[5,3,0],[4,3,3],[3,3,6],\ldots,[0,3,15]]$$

A particularly important group of sequences of this kind are called *Cartesian products*. The Cartesian product operation is rather like multiplication for sequences:

$$
\begin{aligned}
\text{``abc''} * \text{``xy''} &= [\text{``ax''}, \text{``ay''}, \text{``bx''}, \text{``by''}, \text{``cx''}, \text{``cy''}] \\
[1,2] * [9,6] &= [[1,9],[1,6],[2,9],[2,6]] \\
Length(X * Y) &= Length(X) * Length(Y)
\end{aligned}
$$

It has a zero element and reasonable distribution properties:

$$
\begin{aligned}
[\,] * X &= X * [\,] = [\,] \\
X * (Y + Z) &= (X * Y) + (X * Z) \\
(X + Y) * Z &= (X * Z) + (Y * Z) \\
IsIn([a, b], X * Y) &= IsIn(a, X) \wedge IsIn(b, Y) \\
(X * Y)[j + Length(Y) * (i - 1)] &= [X[i], Y[j]]
\end{aligned}
$$

Of course, it is not exactly like multiplication, just as concatenation is not exactly like addition: "$*$" on sequences is neither commutative nor associative, and it has no identity element. It does satisfy other laws which have nothing to do with numbers; e.g., $Reverse(X * Y) = Reverse(X) * Reverse(Y)$.

**Q:** When would you really want to use all possible combinations of anything?
**A:** One good example would be in testing a program; provide a few possible input values and use the Cartesian product to make sure that all the combinations are tested. In order to define Cartesian products, let's first define the specific Cartesian product of the ranges $1 \ldots n$ and $1 \ldots m$: this runs from $[1, 1]$ to $[1, m]$, then from $[2, 1]$ to $[2, m]$, and so on until it finally goes from $[n, 1]$ to $[n, m]$ and stops.

$$Ranges(n, m) \quad = \quad Range(1, n) * Range(1, m)$$

so that

$$Ranges(n, m) \quad = \quad RangeFrom(1, 1)$$

where

$$
\begin{aligned}
RangeFrom(i, j) \quad &= \quad [\,], \text{ if } i > n \\
&= \quad RangeFrom(i + 1, 1), \qquad \text{if } j > m \\
&= \quad [i, j] @ RangeFrom(i, j + 1) \quad \text{otherwise}
\end{aligned}
$$

Notice that $RangeFrom$ is not a function which can be used all by itself; it exists as part of the definition of $Ranges$, and makes use of the values of $n$ and $m$ without changing them. That gives one way to define the Cartesian product:

**if** $Ranges(Length(X), Length(Y))[i] = [j, k]$
   **then** $(X * Y)[i] = [X[j], Y[k]]$

Here is another:

$$X * Y \quad = \quad UpFrom(X, Y)$$

where

$$UpFrom(A, B) \quad = \quad [], \qquad \text{if } A = []$$
$$= \quad UpFrom(Tl(A), Y), \qquad\qquad\qquad \text{if } B = []$$
$$= \quad [Hd(A), Hd(B)] @ UpFrom(A, Tl(B)) \quad \text{otherwise}$$

## Exercises

**3.3-1**  Show all steps in finding "**abc**" ∗ "**xy**".

**3.3-2**  Write a function *Triples* which is just like ∗ except that it makes all possible triples out of three sequences: *Triples*(["**br**", "**ai**", "**ng**"]) will be a sequence of eight three-letter sequences, beginning with "**ban**" and ending with "**rig**".

**3.3-3**  Write a function *IsAssoc*(S) which assumes the existence of a function $f$ and returns *True* if $f$ is associative on all possible combinations of items from $S$: thus if $f(x, y) = x - y$ and $S = [0, 1, 2, 9]$ then *IsAssoc* will form 64 triples, call on $f$ 256 times, and eventually produce *False*. [Hint: Don't write it from scratch; think about filters.]

### 3.3.2 Orderings and Permutations

When we look at sequences and try to apply the notion of ordering, there are two fundamental possibilities: we can try to think about comparison between sequences, or we can try to think about ordering within a sequence.

The usual ordering between sequences is called *lexicographic* ordering because it's the ordering used in dictionaries, encyclopedias, telephone books, and almost everywhere else you see text being used. "**art**" comes before "**car**" because 'a' comes before 'c'; "**ark**" comes before "**artist**" because the first two letters are the same, and 'k' comes before 't'; "**artist**" comes before "**artistic**" because we put shorter sequences first (in effect, putting blanks before letters). The idea of lexicographic ordering, then, is that within sequences you compare the first item, then the second, and so on until you find two corresponding elements that are different or else come to the end of one sequence. Shorter sequences come first, so the empty sequence comes first of all: for any pair $X, Y$ of sequences,

$$X < Y = \text{ if } X = [] \text{ then } (Y \neq [])$$
$$\text{else } (Hd(X) < Hd(Y)) \lor (Tl(X) < Tl(Y))$$

We will have a great deal to do with lexicographic orderings later, but for now if you understand the idea and can use the rule, that's sufficient.

Our second kind of sequential ordering is the ordering within a sequence. This, too, is fairly simple to describe: "**art**" is ordered, "**rat**" is not; $[1, 9, 12]$ is ordered, $[9, 1]$ is not; $[]$ is as ordered as it can be, and so is $[93]$.

One of the principal uses of computers (human and mechanical) has always been to put items into order—to *sort* them. The items could be dictionary entries, library catalogue cards, telephone numbers, or tax returns. For example,

$$Sort([\text{``cat''}, \text{``cart''}, \text{``car''}]) = [\text{``car''}, \text{``cart''}, \text{``cat''}]$$

Similarly, $Sort(\text{``catalepsy''}) = \text{``aacelpsty''}$, and $Sort([3,1,2]) = [1,2,3]$. Often a program will begin by sorting the items it is to work on, so that it can find needed information faster. Obviously, we can say that $Ordered(Sort(S))$ is always *True*, but that doesn't fully describe *Sort*: it doesn't say that the output has anything to do with the input. We know that the output is somehow very similar to the input; it is of the same length, so we can say that $Length(Sort(S)) = Length(S)$. The similarity goes further. Any item which occurs five times in a sequence will still occur five times in the sorted sequence. This is because the sorted sequence is simply a rearrangement or *permutation* of the original: $Count(a, X) = Count(a, Sort(S))$. These two ideas, of ordering and of permutation, are all that you need to understand sorting. To sort a sequence is just to find an ordered permutation of it, i.e., an ordered sequence which contains exactly the same items (and the same number of repetitions of each item). There are two principal kinds of sorting algorithms: those which preserve the items of the original sequence while coming closer and closer to order, and those which construct ordered sequences which come closer and closer to containing all the items of the original sequence. Each different way of analyzing ordering or permutation tends to lead to a different way of sorting.

**Q:** I learned "bubble sort" in high school; why isn't that good enough?
**A:** Because on large data bases it can take literally millions of times longer than other available methods. "Bubble sort" is perpetuated by introductory programming classes; it is never the best method, and is usually one of the worst. However, it is very easy to describe and remember.

**Q:** So why don't you just teach us the best one? Why do we have to learn a lot of analysis?
**A:** There is no one best method; different approaches fit different circumstances. You really need to be able to work with different ways of describing permutations and orderings. How can you tell when one sequence is a permutation of another? How can you tell when a sequence is ordered? What happens to these properties when we combine sequences?

For the moment, we will just give a brief summary of the properties of permutations, in terms of a predicate *Perm* which is so defined that $Perm(A, B)$ is *True* exactly when the rule $Count(a, A) = Count(a, B)$ holds for all values of $a$. There are just two things that you need to know, to start with. First, swapping any two items will produce a permutation:

$$Perm(X + [a] + Y + [b] + Z, X + [b] + Y + [a] + Z)$$

Another way to describe this would use indices and a named function which actually exchanges elements: $Swap(\text{"}\mathbf{tar}\text{"}, 1, 3) = \text{"}\mathbf{rat}\text{"}$. $Swap(S, i, j)$ is meaningless unless $i$ and $j$ are between 1 and $Length(S)$, in which case

$$
\begin{aligned}
Swap(S, i, j)[k] \quad &= \quad S[j], \quad \text{if } k = i \\
&= \quad S[i], \quad \text{if } k = j \\
&= \quad S[k], \quad \text{otherwise}
\end{aligned}
$$

This gives us a number of relationships to count on:

$$
\begin{aligned}
Swap(S, i, j) \quad &= \quad Put(Put(S, i, S[j]), j, S[i]) \\
Length(Swap(S, i, j)) \quad &= \quad Length(S) \\
Swap(S, i, j) \quad &= \quad Swap(S, j, i) \\
Swap(Swap(S, i, j), i, j) \quad &= \quad S
\end{aligned}
$$

Using these, we can restate the permutation rule as $Perm(S, Swap(S, i, j))$. That's not only more concise, but we now have the function $Swap$ with many useful applications. Of course, not all permutations are the result of a single exchange of elements, but it turns out that every permutation can be found by repeated exchanges. "Being a permutation" is an equivalence relation between sequences: $Perm(S_1, S_1)$ holds for all $S_1$, and $Perm(X, Y) \Rightarrow Perm(Y, X)$, and finally $Perm(X, Y) \wedge Perm(Y, Z) \Rightarrow Perm(X, Z)$. Other properties can be derived from those: $Perm(x @ S, Insert(x, i, S))$ may or may not be obvious, but as long as $i$ is a reasonable index in $S$ this is true. We can distribute permutation across concatenation: if $Perm(X, X')$ and $Perm(Y, Y')$ are both true, then so is $Perm(X + Y, X' + Y')$. Of course, concatenation is not the only way to break down a sequence: if you have a filter which takes some of the items, you can also consider taking all of the rest:

$$
Perm(X, NoMore(n, X) + More(n, X))
$$

**Q:** That's not a series of swaps; you're making two separate sequences and then concatenating them.

**A:** I didn't say that every permutation *is* found by repeated exchanges, but only that it *can be*. The items in the concatenation are the same as the items in $X$, just shuffled around.

Separately from learning how $Perm$ works, you can learn to work with ordered sequences: the question of whether or not a sequence is ordered soon leads to techniques for generating ordered sequences.

A sequence is ordered if it has no adjacent items out of order; the assertion $Ordered(S)$ is true if the assertion

$$
(1 \le i \wedge i \le j \wedge j \le Length(S) \Rightarrow S[i] \le S[j])
$$

holds for all values of $i$ and $j$, and false if it doesn't. Since '$\leq$' is a transitive and reflexive relation, we can just as well say

$$0 < i \wedge i < Length(S) \Rightarrow S[i] \leq S[i+1]$$

which comes to the same thing.

**Q:** You mean $Ordered(S) = (0 < i \wedge i < Length(S) \Rightarrow S[i] \leq S[i+1])$?

**A:** No. Such an equation should apply to all values of $S$ and $i$, and it doesn't: try $S = [3, 1, 2]$, $i = 2$. What I'm saying is that when you pick a sequence $S$ and say "$Ordered(S)$", you're making one assertion with one Boolean value (*True* or *False*). When you write the implication involving $i$, you're giving a pattern for a great many such assertions, some of which might be *True* and others *False*. A rule is not simply an expression, as we've said before. If you want to transform a rule into an expression, you can do it by forming the *conjunction* of all of the rule's instances: $(S[1] \leq S[2]) \wedge \ldots \wedge (S[n-1] \leq S[n])$. If there are only a finite number of instances, you can just list them. If not, you need some abbreviation for them all, using something like the "for every" construction which we discussed in the previous chapter's work on Boolean algebra: "For every $M$ which is a man, *Seeks*($M$, *SuperFrog*)" is an expression (in English) which effectively includes a rule. Later in this chapter we'll have an alternative notation which covers the same need. For now, it's important to realize exactly what you lack.

**Q:** But then how do I write rules for *Ordered*?

**A:** We've described many rules as talking about the $Hd$ and $Tl$ of a sequence. In this case, we want to make sure that the $Hd$ is not larger than the second item, and that the $Tl$ is ordered. So

$$Ordered(S) = (Length(S) < 2) \vee ((S[1] \leq S[2]) \wedge Ordered(Tl(S)))$$

If $Ordered(Tl(S))$ is the conjunction of all the instances $S[2] \leq S[3] \wedge \ldots \wedge S[n-1] \leq S[n]$, then you can see that $Ordered(S)$ is really the conjunction we want.

This observation is crucial to the understanding of exchange-sorting algorithms such as the "bubble sort." If we use it as a guide in creating a procedure for "bubble sorting," it will check the first two elements, and if they are out of order it will *Swap* them. Then it will check the second two, possibly exchanging them (so that the first pair may now be out of order). Then the third pair will be put in order and so on until it reaches the end. If the process is repeated until no exchanges are required, the result will be ordered.

$$
\begin{aligned}
Bubble(S) \quad &= \quad S, && \text{if } Length(S) < 2 \\
&= \quad S[1]@Bubble(Tl(S)), && \text{if } S[1] \leq S[2] \\
&= \quad S[2]@Bubble(S[1]@Tl(Tl(S))), && \text{otherwise}
\end{aligned}
$$

We see that after *Bubble* has checked all the places it can:

$$Sort(S) \quad = \quad D, \qquad \text{if } D = S$$
$$= \quad Sort(D), \quad \text{otherwise}$$

Since the *Bubble* routine is evidently linear, *Sort* when defined this way is quadratic.

Another way to describe an ordered sequence is by observing that the *Hd* of the sequence is the smallest item in the sequence, and that the *Tl* is ordered:

$$Ordered(S) = (S = [\,]) \vee (MinLoc(S) = 1 \wedge Ordered(Tl(S)))$$

This is the insight behind selection sorting algorithms. If we *Find* the *Min*imal item in a sequence and put it in front (with *Swap*), we can then sort the remainder:

$$Sort(S) \quad = \quad S[k]@Sort(Delete(1, k, S))$$

where

$$k \quad = \quad MinLoc(S)$$

### Exercise

**3.3-4**   Describe the asymptotic performance of *Sort* when defined this way; compare it with the definition using *Bubble*.

Another *sort* method comes from thinking about when $Insert(x, i, S)$ might be ordered: it is almost true that

$$Ordered(Insert(x, i, S)) = Ordered(S) \wedge (i = FindBigger(x, S, 1))$$

where $FindBigger(x, S, i)$ (as described in an earlier exercise) produces the first location past $i$ in $S$ of an item greater than $x$. This is the basic idea behind insertion sorting: if you insert items into place in an already ordered sequence, you get a slightly larger ordered sequence. If you make space for an empty pile and then insert all the items from your sequence into it according to a rule like the one just stated, then the result will be ordered.

$$Sort(a@X) \quad = \quad Insert(a, i, Y)$$

where

$$Y \quad = \quad Sort(X), \text{and}$$
$$i \quad = \quad FindBigger(a, Y, 1)$$

**Exercises**    The assertions relating *Insert* to *FindBigger* depend upon the precondition *HasBigger*$(x, S)$.

**3.3-5**    How could *FindBigger* be changed to make the assertions always true, without changing *Insert*? [What should it produce instead of 0?]

**3.3-6**    How could *Insert* be changed to make it always true, without changing *FindBigger*? [What should be the value of *Insert*$(x, 0, S)$?]

The heuristic of repetitions tells us to generalize on finding a single minimal element and also on finding a place for a single insertion. Each of our approaches has worked on combining a single element with a sequence; we want to consider operations which involve pairs of sequences, like concatenation. Perhaps we can find many near-minimal elements at once, or perform multiple insertions all together.

*Ordered* does look rather like an accumulation, except that it looks at every item (except the first) twice. If you remember that, you can make sense of a distribution law for *Ordered*:

$$Ordered(X + Y)\ =\ \begin{array}{l} Ordered(X) \wedge Ordered(Y) \\ \wedge(X = [\,] \vee Y = [\,] \vee Max(X) \leq Min(Y)) \end{array}$$

This is a generalization of the very first description, and it leads to an algorithm so much better for large sequences that it is called QuickSort. As with the rules for bubbling, selection and insertion, that distribution law of the test for ordering becomes a distribution law for the creation of ordered permutations. For any $x$, we find that

$$Sort(S)\ =\ Sort(NoMore(x, S)) + Sort(More(x, S))$$

In particular,

$$Sort(S)\ =\ Sort(NoMore(S_1, S_{2...N})) + [S_1] + Sort(More(S_1, S_{2...N}))$$

**Q:** Aren't you equating an assertion with a rule now?

**A:** No, I'm just saying that the above equation is true for any values of $x$ and $S$. Different versions of QuickSort come from picking different values of $x$, usually the first element of $S$ or a random element or even a value which is not in $S$ at all: it doesn't change the truth of the equation, although it will change the performance of QuickSort. If you can always choose an item that will split the sequence in half, then it takes $\mathcal{O}(\log(N))$ sweeps through an input of length $N$ to split it into tiny fragments, as you see in sorting [4,3,7,6,5,2,8,1]:

| | |
|---|---|
| $[4, 3, 7, 6, 5, 2, 8, 1]$ | *We will split it with 4, getting* |
| $[4, 3, 2, 1], [7, 6, 5, 8]$ | *We will split these with 2 and 5* |
| $[2, 1], [4, 3], [6, 5], [7, 8]$ | *We will split these with 1, 3, 5, and 7* |
| $[1], [2], [3], [4], [5], [6], [7], [8]$ | *And now we're done* |

With each sweep we need $\mathcal{O}(N)$ steps for *NoMore* and *More* so overall we need $\mathcal{O}(N * \log(N))$ steps. However, if we choose badly, we may split off only one item with each $\mathcal{O}(N)$ sweep, so that QuickSort can be quadratic; in practice, a few precautions keep this from being a concern.

Each of these methods has basically tried to find pairs which were out of order and swap them. BubbleSort and InsertionSort are slow because they waste a lot of effort swapping pairs which are nearby, so that the items moved don't go anywhere near their final position. QuickSort is fast because each time you move anything, it moves at least half of the distance towards where it's actually going to be when you stop sorting. A sorting method that always goes halfway will have to be $\mathcal{O}(N * \log(N))$.

**Q:** Is it possible to go faster than that?

**A:** Yes, in special cases. Suppose that I'm sorting a pile of papers into A's, B's, C's, D's, F's, and "Please see me". I can just scan through that big pile and create six little ones in $\mathcal{O}(N)$ steps. However, I can't do better than $\mathcal{O}(N * \log(N))$ for the general case of sorting a sequence of $N$ arbitrary integers; at least not with methods which are restricted to "<" and "≤" tests—or any Boolean-valued function—used to control swaps. That's another fundamental limitation on our ability to compute, and the reason for it is actually pretty simple.

First, imagine that the sequence you're sorting is written in a giant telephone book, along with the answer—and all the other permutations. The job of sorting is really just to find the particular permutation which is ordered. Every time you perform a comparison and either swap or don't, you're splitting the book into those permutations you still may have to worry about and those that you don't. That's the most you can do with a yes-or-no test like "≤". The best you can possibly do is to eliminate half of them at each step—to cut the telephone book in half.

**Q:** Why couldn't I eliminate more than half?

**A:** Suppose that you ask a yes-or-no question that splits the book into pieces, one of which is smaller than the other. In the worst case the input was set up by somebody who knew what your questions would be: the demonic Murphy, who carefully chose a sequence whose answer would be in the larger piece. That means that the best strategy you can possibly devise will still require $\mathcal{O}(\log(T))$ steps, where $T$ is the size of the telephone book—the number of permutations of your $N$-element sequence. It just happens that a mathematician named Stirling figured out that this number is approximately $2^{N*\log(N)}$, and since $\log(2^x) = x$, we're stuck with QuickSort as (one of the) best possible comparison-sorting methods.

**Q:** After going over that a few times, I finally realized that you never said that sorting a sequence of arbitrary numbers has to be based on comparison. Does it?

**A:** No, but I don't know for certain that you can do any better with any other method. Think for a moment about looking things up in a telephone book; do you really follow a binary search? I certainly don't; I guess where the name I want should be, and open there. If it starts with '**T**' which is about 4/5 of the way through the alphabet, then I open it somewhere around 4/5 of the way through. This idea doesn't change the form of the binary search, it just means that instead of $(lo + hi)/2$ for a middle element, you calculate a more complicated fraction; and it can lead to a $\mathcal{O}(\log(\log(N))$ algorithm.

**Q:** Could you explain $\mathcal{O}(\log(\log(N)))$, please?

**A:** Sure. If $N$ is a billion, then $\log(N)$ is about 32, and $\log(\log(N))$ is about 5; this is a function which grows so slowly that it's almost a constant.

**Exercises**    Suppose you had a billion names in a phone book and you could check any one of them in 0.001 second.

**3.3-7**   How long for a linear search?

**3.3-8**   How long for a binary search?

**3.3-9**   How long for this "interpolation" search?

Unfortunately, interpolation is worthwhile only for really large sequences, because you have to go to the trouble of making the guess—and guard against the possibility that your guess might be totally wrong. Still, it's a lovely idea and well worth puzzling over.

**Q:** So you mean that you could use interpolation to sort in $\mathcal{O}(N*\log(\log(N)))$, or something like that?

**A:** Personally I doubt it, but I don't know[2]. It seems probable that you could go more than half-way toward the right position, but reaching the right position in $\mathcal{O}(\log(\log(N)))$ steps seems unlikely.

Other approaches to comparison sorting (not so obviously based on swapping) are common; we'll go over a few, briefly. MergeSort merely requires the existence

---

[2]If some reader does, please tell me.

of a *Merge* operation which shuffles ordered sequences together somewhat as you might shuffle cards, so that the resulting sequence is ordered:

$$Merge([1, 2, 7], [2, 3, 9]) = [1, 2, 2, 3, 7, 9]$$

*Merge* is a repeated *Insert* which assumes that the both of its arguments are ordered. *Merge* is commutative and associative, with identity element [ ]; its other important properties include

$$Perm(X + Y, Merge(X, Y))$$
$$Ordered(X) \wedge Ordered(Y) \Rightarrow Ordered(Merge(X, Y))$$
$$Sort(X + Y) = Merge(Sort(X), Sort(Y))$$

If I'm going to sort a large pile of student papers by names or by grades, MergeSort is what I generally use: split the pile into two equal subpiles, sort each subpile, and then *Merge* the pair of ordered sequences by picking off whichever *Hd* I want first until I've got them all. With MergeSort there is no difficulty in making sure that $X$ and $Y$ are each roughly half of the input sequence, and since *Merge* is linear it turns out that MergeSort is always $\mathcal{O}(N * \log(N))$. MergeSort turns out to be a very good method for dealing with sequences when *Hd* and *Tl* (which look only at the front of the sequence) are cheap, but *Get* and *Put* (which may look anywhere) are expensive. This applies to most really enormous sequences, as well as to some of moderate size. QuickSort, however, is generally somewhat better if *Get* and *Put* are cheap.

### Exercises

**3.3-10**  Suppose you know that $Merge(X, b@Y) = Z$. What can you say about $Merge(a@X, b@Y)$ if $a \leq b$? If $a > b$?

**3.3-11**  When is $Merge(X, Y) = X + Y$? When is it $Y + X$?

If we go beyond simple sequence ideas, we can use trees as an aid to sorting. Each tree is either [ ], or it is written in the form $[L, n, R]$, where $n$ is a number, $L$ is a tree containing numbers less than $n$, and $R$ is a tree containing numbers greater than (or equal to) $n$. Here is a sequence of ordered trees, formed by starting with [ ] and successively inserting 5, then 2, then 9, and finally 3:

$$[\,]$$
$$[[\,], \quad 5, \quad [\,]]$$
$$[[[\,], 2, [\,]], \quad 5, \quad [\,]]$$
$$[[[\,], 2, [\,]], \quad 5, \quad [[\,], 9, [\,]]]$$
$$[[[\,], 2, [[\,], 3, [\,]]], \quad 5, \quad [[\,], 9, [\,]]]$$

If you want to make a diagram of this kind of tree, do it with the middle number on top and ignore the "[]" marks, as in Figure 3.1.   Given a tree which has these

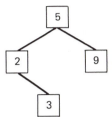

**Figure 3.1**   Ordered Trees of Numbers

properties, we can extract the numbers into an ordered sequence quite easily:

$$
\begin{aligned}
FlatTree([\,]) &= [\,] \\
FlatTree([L, n, R]) &= FlatTree(L) + [n] + FlatTree(R)
\end{aligned}
$$

and that certainly takes only a linear number of operations to get the required sequence.

To sort a sequence $S_{1...n}$, however, we will first need to form the ordered tree containing the items $S_1 \ldots S_n$. We do so by insertion:

$$
\begin{aligned}
InsTree(n, [\,]) &= [[\,], n, [\,]] \\
InsTree(n, [L, m, R]) &= [InsTree(n, L), m, R], \quad \text{if } n < m \\
&= [L, m, InsTree(n, R)], \quad \text{otherwise}
\end{aligned}
$$

This insertion takes a number of steps proportional to the depth of the tree rather than to the number of items in it; that is usually logarithmic, although (as with QuickSort) things can get very bad for some input. If each of $N$ insertions takes about $\mathcal{O}(\log(N))$ steps, then we have $\mathcal{O}(N * \log(N))$ as the overall number of steps for sorting.

**Q:** Why is the depth of the tree logarithmic?

**A:** Another way to say the same thing is that one of these trees, if it has grown to depth $d$, will usually have about $2^{**}d$ numbers in it. That's because the tree $[L, n, R]$ is just one level deeper than $L$ or $R$, but it's as big as both of them put together: if they are about the same size, then you've doubled the size while increasing the depth by 1.

## Exercises

**3.3-12** Define *InsTree* and *FlatTree* without classification rules (conditionals only).

**3.3-13** *InsTree* inserts only one item; define an accumulator function *InsAll(S, T)* which inserts all the numbers in the (unordered) sequence $S$ into the (ordered) tree $T$ so that $Sort(S) = FlatTree(InsAll(S, [\,]))$.

**3.3-14** Explain why this "TreeSort" algorithm is sometimes very bad; describe a "worst-case" input sequence of 1000 items and explain how many steps would be required.

TreeSort is not often used as a "batch" sorting method when all we want to do is take an input sequence, sort it in one big batch, and have the answer. However, such ordered trees are very nice when we want to have a dictionary (environment) which grows, but is always orderly. Suppose that we keep adding definitions, in a series like "$x = 14, y = x + 3, i = 2, n = x/2, \ldots$"; this gives us a series of environments $\{\}, \{x = 14\}, \{x = 14, y = 17\}, \{x = 14, y = 17, i = 2\}$, and so on. In such cases, *InsTree* can be modified slightly so that we have trees which either are $[\,]$ or are $[L, [var, val], R]$, where all the variables in $L$ alphabetically precede $var$, and all those in $R$ alphabetically follow it. Then we write

$$
\begin{aligned}
LookUp(var, [\,]) &= \text{``***ERROR***''} & \\
LookUp(var, [L, [x, v], R]) &= v, & \text{if } var = x \\
&= LookUp(var, L) & \text{if } var < x \\
&= LookUp(var, R) & \text{otherwise}
\end{aligned}
$$

This is logarithmic in insertion *and* access, which is better than we can easily achieve on a straight sequence.

### 3.3.3 Representing Sequences by Functions, and Vice Versa

We can represent a short sequence of digits or Boolean values or even characters by the use of cardinal numbers decomposed with *mod* and *div*, and this is common-place in programming. If we allowed ourselves the use of arbitrarily large cardinal numbers, we could break them down in base 128 to represent arbitrary strings. (This whole book would therefore be represented by a single *very* large number.) However, in most programming situations we think of numbers, Booleans, and characters as being "scalar" or "atomic" items which occupy a single storage space, while sequences can grow arbitrarily large. The only way we can represent sequences in terms of what we have before is to use a function to simulate indexing. To represent $[S_1 \ldots S_n]$, we can write a function

$$
\begin{aligned}
f_S(i) = \ &\textbf{if } i = 1 \ \textbf{then } \ S_1 \\
&\textbf{else } \ \textbf{if } i = 2 \ \textbf{then } \ S_1 \\
&\textbf{else } \ \textbf{if } \ldots \\
&\textbf{else } \ \textbf{if } i = n \ \textbf{then } \ S_n \\
&\textbf{else } \ Illegal\_Index\_Value
\end{aligned}
$$

By the definition we can see that $S[i] = f_S(i)$, and any question about the values of $S$ can be answered by looking at $f$. In programming there is a cost/benefit tradeoff to be studied for almost every sequence and whether to save space by representing the sequence with a function which will calculate the values as required so that they need not be stored all the time. With simple sequences generated by *Range* or *Repeat*, it usually makes sense to do this. With very complicated sequences, it may be a bad idea. Often you deal with sequences which are very orderly in some ways, but disorderly in others: you could save half the space of storing a palindromic sequence just by replacing it with a function which "remembers" only the first half and whether the sequence was odd or even in length. Programs often have to deal with mathematical matrices (sequences of sequences of numbers) which are 0 in all but a few places; some algorithms would be completely impractical if all of those zeros were actually to be written out.

On the other hand, it is not uncommon to represent a function by a sequence of stored values, like a multiplication table or a table of arctangents. In the section on characters and other enumerations we had separate functions to check whether a given character was a digit, a lowercase letter, an uppercase letter, etc. The functions we tried used *ord* and arithmetic comparison. However, it is also common to preserve a sequence *CharClass* of length 128 containing classifications from an enumeration like

[*Ctl, Digit, LBracket, RBracket, LCLetter, UCLetter, ...*]

A classification for $chr(0)$ will be recorded in $CharClass(1)$, and so on through all 128 positions; the classification for $chr(i)$ is found in $CharClass(i+1)$. Positions $[1...32]$ correspond to the *ASCII* characters $chr(0)...chr(31)$, which will be classed as *Ctl* characters. $49...58$ will be classed as *Digits*, and so on. The result of an arithmetic comparison is thus *tabulated* in a sequence. The costs and benefits of this are precisely the converse of what they were for going in the other direction: we may save time, but we lose space. The decision is one of economics, based on the performance and reliability of the computers. When most computers were human, it was cheaper to use tabulated arctangents; since most electronic computers are able to calculate such things quite quickly, the storage space may be better left unused. (Or it may not be: some supercomputers use tabulation to speed up operations as fundamental as division.) The point is that there are no fundamental differences between values that have been stored and values that have been computed by rules; the two ideas are interchangeable.

**Q:** But sequences are limited: you can have operations like addition or multiplication or exponentiation that work on all pairs of cardinals, but you can't store all of those in a sequence. Besides, you can't store the value of the *Sum* operation on sequences at all; this only works for functions on cardinals or enumerations which can be translated into cardinals with *ord*.

**A:** That's true, but there are ways to get at least partly around both of those problems. We may not be able to store the whole range of values of exponentiation, but it can still help to *describe* it as a sequence of sequences satisfying $Exp[i][j] = i**j$. When it comes time to program, it may or may not be desirable to store some values as a help in calculating others.

With the second problem, what we need is a way of storing a dictionary; *InsTree* and *LookUp* of the last section provide that very nicely. They aren't the only method; insertion into a linear list, followed by lookup as described in the first chapter, will also work. Here's one approach.

What we're looking for is a version of *ord* that works on all kinds of objects— even sequences. This is something you've already seen: it's called *Find*. If you want to tabulate the *Length* of strings, you just put the strings into a sequence $S$ of strings and the *Length*s into a corresponding sequence $V$ of cardinals; then you'll find that $Length(x) = V[Find(x, S, 1)]$. This is the basis for many "symbol table" implementations used in all kinds of programming; if you wish to associate symbols with attributes of any kind, you put those symbols into a sequence *Names* in which you can *Find* them again, and then you put the information you want into another sequence *Val* of the same length, so that $Val[Find(x, Names, 1)]$ has the information about the symbol $x$.

## 3.4 BAGS AND SETS: WHEN NOT TO BE SPECIFIC

One problem in dealing with sequences is that they are frequently too specific. It is important to have a description of what you require a program to produce; it is sometimes just as important to make it clear what options are available to the programmer (or even to the computer). If many options are available, and you specify one just for the sake of being specific, you may find (or, worse yet, never learn) that you have ruled out the best solutions. In this section, we'll deal with some ideas for avoiding overspecification of sequences.

### 3.4.1 Bags: Forgetting Order

In many circumstances we would like to say that a program is supposed to produce certain items, but the order doesn't matter. The sequence $[Joe, Joe, Harry]$ is really just the same as $[Joe, Harry, Joe]$, or any other permutation; we would like the program to produce whichever version can be produced most easily. A description of the program which requires that they come out in alphabetical order may make the program easier to test, but it also may make it harder to write and more expensive to run. Computer programmers sometimes find it convenient to imagine that they are putting the items into a shopping bag rather than into a sequence: items may be in some order inside, but you are not allowed to ask about that order. To avoid confusion, we use a notation for mathematical **bags** which is like that for sequences, but implies that they're a little more thoroughly hidden in their containers:

$$\begin{aligned} [\![2,3,5,2]\!] &= [\![2,2,3,5]\!] \\ &\neq [\![2,3,5]\!] \end{aligned}$$

The number of occurrences of 2 is important; their order is not. Watch the notation carefully:

$$[\![1,2,3]\!] \quad \neq \quad [1,2,3] \text{ (it is not a sequence of numbers)}$$
$$\neq \quad [[1,2,3]] \text{ (nor a sequence of sequences)}$$

Suppose that $B = [\![1,2,4,2,9,2]\!]$ is a bag. You cannot really ask for $B[2]$, because $B$ isn't a sequence. You can ask for the minimal item of $B$, which is 1. You can ask for the bag containing all the items greater than 2, which is $[\![4,9]\!]$. You can ask for the sum of the items in $B$, which is 20. You can ask for a *Count* of the 2's in $B$, which is 3.

Two bags $B_1$ and $B_2$ are equal if $Count(x, B_1) = Count(x, B_2)$ for any choice of x—in effect, when a sequence of all items in $B_1$ is a permutation of a sequence of all items in $B_2$. Remember that *Perm* is an equivalence relation: it has all the nice properties of equality, but it says "yes" a little more often than a check on sequences would do. The bag $B$ itself can be thought of as an abstraction representing a class of sequences, the *equivalence class* which contains all permutations of the items in $B$.

In effect, it is reasonable to apply a function to a bag if that function would give the same answer for any permutation of the sequence of items which you see when you write the bag down on a page. A function which might give different answers for different permutations shouldn't be applied to bags, because there's no way of knowing what the answer ought to be. For example, $B[2]$ could produce any item of the bag, and you could even find that $B[2] \neq B[2]$ because if you look at the second position, it changes before you can look at it again. (No, that is not just a silly idea brought in to confuse you: there are common algorithms based on the notion that whenever you look at a particular item in a sequence, you should automatically move it somewhere else.)

**Q:** What about functions that form bags? Can you concatenate them?

**A:** Certainly. All we need to do is reinterpret the operations which create sequences; "@" is the most basic, and we need only say that

$$Count(x, y @ B) \quad = \quad 1 + Count(x, B) \quad \text{if } x = y$$
$$= \quad Count(x, B) \quad\quad \text{otherwise}$$

Thinking about that, you should be able to see that for any bags $A, B$,

$$Count(x, A + B) = Count(x, A) + Count(x, B)$$

just as it did with sequences; you should be able to see that there is no longer any distinction between "@" and *Insert*, or between "+" and *Merge*, or between *Hd* and *Min*. Notice that even though we have lost many properties, we have also gained a few: "+" on bags is a commutative operation.

**Q:** Is it all right to *Reverse* a bag, then?

**A:** Certainly, but $Reverse(B) = B$ for any bag $B$.

### Exercises

**3.4-1**   Is it reasonable to ask about the *Length* of a bag?

**3.4-2**   Is it reasonable to define $f(\llbracket x, y \rrbracket) = x - y$?

### 3.4.2  Representing Bags by Sequences or Functions

If we represent a bag of strings by a function, that function will work on strings and produce cardinal numbers. However, we can't find the *Min*imum item in the bag with just that function, so we need to write other functions to represent operations like that. It is more common to represent bags by sequences; after all, "$\llbracket 1, 2, 4, 1, 4 \rrbracket$" is a sequence of characters, and it looks almost exactly like the sequence $[1, 2, 4, 1, 4]$. Suppose we try to make this well-understood sequence into a bag by some function $Ab$. We know that

$$Ab(X) = Ab(Y) \quad \text{if and only if} \quad Perm(X, Y)$$

We do have a function which works like that: it's called *Sort*. In order to convert a sequence into a bag, we sort it.

**Q:** But I thought the whole point of a bag was that it didn't matter what order things were in.

**A:** That's right, it doesn't, but if we want to be able to test equality of bags then we need some way to deal with $\llbracket 1, 2 \rrbracket = \llbracket 2, 1 \rrbracket$. Actually, we would not usually expect to deal with bags themselves, but with their representations. Rather than converting sequences into bags, we want to convert questions about bags into questions about sequences. In this case, the question about the equivalence of two bags can be translated into a question about the equivalence of two sorted sequences; that may or may not be the best translation.

We can imagine the function $Ab$ as taking a sequence of items and dumping them into a bag; the inverse, which is the representation function $Rep$, should take a bag of items and put them into a sequence. This does have the property that if we take a bag, copy its items into a sequence, and put them into a bag, the resulting bag will be equal to the original: $Ab(Rep(B)) = B$ for any bag $B$. However, if you take a sequence and put its items into a bag, the original ordering is lost and you can never be sure of getting the same sequence back again: $Rep(Ab(S)) = Sort(S)$.

The property we need in *Rep* is that

$$
\begin{aligned}
Rep(\llbracket\,\rrbracket) &= [\,] \\
Rep(\llbracket x \rrbracket) &= [x] \\
Rep(B_1 + B_2) &= Merge(Rep(B_1), Rep(B_2))
\end{aligned}
$$

The "+" operation now joins two bags into a larger one; their representations as ordered sequences are *Merged* into an ordered sequence.

The almost-inverse to *Rep* is

$$
\begin{aligned}
Ab([\,]) &= \llbracket\,\rrbracket \\
Ab([x]) &= \llbracket x \rrbracket \\
Ab(X + Y) &= Ab(X) + Ab(Y)
\end{aligned}
$$

Remember that "+" means different things on left and right of that last equation: "+" on sequences is concatenation, which is associative but not commutative and puts every item in a particular place. "+" on bags is commutative as well as associative, and mainly achieves

$$
\begin{aligned}
Count(x, Ab(S)) &= Count(x, S) \\
Count(x, \llbracket\,\rrbracket) &= 0 \\
Count(x, \llbracket y \rrbracket) &= \textbf{if } x = y \textbf{ then } 1 \textbf{ else } 0 \\
Count(x, B_1 + B_2) &= Count(x, B_1) + Count(x, B_2)
\end{aligned}
$$

In effect, *Count* distributes over *Ab*. So do the one-argument operations *Length*, *Sum*, *Min*, and all the other operations that don't depend on ordering. That's how representation works: $f(Ab(S)) = f'(S)$, where $f'$ is the corresponding operation on the representation type... in these cases, $f'$ and $f$ are the same.

We will not do very much with bags in this course; they are mentioned as a topic which will be important much later, and as a transition between sequences and sets. Rather than saying that a program should produce a bag, we will try to say that it should produce a sequence, but we will also try to avoid saying exactly what that sequence should be.

For example, in the discussion of sorting we described *QuickSort* as dependent on forming

$$
NoMore(x, S) + More(x, S)
$$

or even

$$
NoMore(S_1, S_{2..N}) + [S_1] + More(S_1, S_{2..N})
$$

Actually it's rather awkward to form this sequence as a series of exchanges. If you try to do it on paper or on a tabletop, you'll find yourself scanning through $S$, putting each item in the *NoMore* bag or in the *More* bag, and then putting the bags together. If you force yourself to use only exchanges, you'll have to scan through looking for items near the beginning which are more than $n$, and swapping them with items near the end which are no more than $n$. If you do that systematically, you can easily form a sequence $S_{low} + S_{high}$ in which $S_{low}$ is a permutation of $NoMore(S_1, S)$ and $S_{high}$ is a permutation of $More(S_1, S)$, while $S_1$ has not moved. You just have to start at the beginning *and* at the end simultaneously, and work inwards comparing items with your "partition element" and looking for chances to swap, until you have finally "partitioned" the sequence (split it into subsequences) which have the right items somewhere in the right subsequences. Then at the end, you *Swap* the last item in your $NoMore(S_1, S)$ with $S_1$. Here's an example:

$Partition([5, 2, 9, 4, 2, 5, 1, 3, 6, 1, 8]) =$

| | | |
|---|---|---|
| $=$ | $Split([5, \boxed{2}, 9, 4, 2, 5, 1, 3, 6, 1, \boxed{8}], 2, 11)$ | $S_2 = 2, S_{11} = 8$ |
| $=$ | $Split([5, 2, \boxed{9}, 4, 2, 5, 1, 3, 6, 1, \boxed{8}], 3, 11)$ | $S_3 = 9, S_{11} = 8$ |
| $=$ | $Split([5, 2, \boxed{9}, 4, 2, 5, 1, 3, 6, \boxed{1}, 8], 3, 10)$ | $S_3 = 9, S_{10} = 1$ |
| $=$ | $Split([5, 2, 1, \boxed{4}, 2, 5, 1, 3, \boxed{6}, 9, 8], 4, 9)$ | $S_4 = 4, S_9 = 6$ |
| $=$ | $Split([5, 2, 1, 4, \boxed{2}, 5, 1, 3, \boxed{6}, 9, 8], 5, 9)$ | $S_5 = 2, S_9 = 6$ |
| $=$ | $Split([5, 2, 1, 4, 2, \boxed{5}, 1, 3, \boxed{6}, 9, 8], 6, 9)$ | $S_6 = 5, S_9 = 6$ |
| $=$ | $Split([5, 2, 1, 4, 2, 5, \boxed{1}, 3, \boxed{6}, 9, 8], 7, 9)$ | $S_7 = 1, S_9 = 6$ |
| $=$ | $Split([5, 2, 1, 4, 2, 5, 1, \boxed{3}, \boxed{6}, 9, 8], 8, 9)$ | $S_8 = 3, S_9 = 6$ |
| $=$ | $Split([5, 2, 1, 4, 2, 5, 1, 3, \boxed{6}, 9, 8], 9, 9)$ | $S_9 = 6, S_9 = 6$ |
| $=$ | $r$ | |

where

$$r.pos \;=\; 8$$
$$r.seq \;=\; \boxed{\boxed{3,2,1,4,2,5,1}, \boxed{5}, \boxed{6,9,8}}$$

*Partition* produces a compound result (or two results, if you prefer to think of it that way) because to use the fact that the sequence has been split appropriately, we need to know where the dividing line is. Another way to think of *Partition*'s effect is that it is producing an environment $\{pos = 8, seq = [3, 2, 1, 4, 2, 5, 1, 5, 6, 9, 8]\}$ as its result. At the end, the sequence has the properties required. $Take(r.pos - 1, r.seq)$ is a permutation of $NoMore(S_1, S_{2...N})$, while $r.seq[r.pos]$ is the original $S_1$ and the *More* result is found in $Drop(r.pos, r.seq)$. However, it is certainly not the only sequence with those properties; in fact, any reshuffling of the items up to (but not including) $r.pos$ on the one hand, or of the items after it on the other hand, would be allowable.

To define *Partition* as used above, we need only say

$$Partition(S) = Split(S, 2, Length(S))$$

Of course, the operation $Split(i, j)$ is fairly complex, but if we take it case by case it's not too hard. We know it has to produce a position and a sequence; we know what they are if the subsequence from $i$ to $j$ is empty or contains only one item;

and then we have to start worrying about whether any objects in the subsequence need to be reshuffled.

$$
\begin{aligned}
Split(S, i, j) \;&=\; \ldots \text{``}\{pos, seq\}\text{''} \\
&=\; \{pos = i - 1, seq = Swap(S, 1, i - 1)\} \quad &\text{if } i \geq j \\
&=\; Split(S, i + 1, j) &\text{if } S[i] \leq n \\
&=\; Split(S, i, j - 1) &\text{if } S[j] > n \\
&=\; Split(Swap(S, i, j), i + 1, j - 1) &\text{otherwise}
\end{aligned}
$$

**Q:** Am I really supposed to be able to write things like that?

**A:** Not yet. The point of giving it to you as an example is that you *are* supposed to be able to *use* things like that, and you should be able to follow it through with the given example to get the answer. You're not skipping the examples, are you? You are, I presume, going over each formula either alone or with a friend, thinking up examples of your own?

**Q:** Well, sometimes.

**A:** It's probably all right. You don't have to do that in every technical course, just the ones you want to pass.

In order to think of a function like *Partition*, it can help to understand bags, but in order to describe it without being too specific, we can just use a definition which leaves some options open:

$$
Partition(n, S) \;=\; Lo + Hi
$$

where

$$
Perm(Lo, NoMore(n, S)) \quad \wedge \quad Perm(Hi, More(n, S))
$$

Notice that this is not specific about the output of *Partition*: it says that *Partition* is supposed to have certain properties, and leaves the rest to the imagination. *Partition* is thus a constrained Skolem function. The version of *Partition* given is certainly a solution, but so is

$$
Partition(n, S) = NoMore(n, S) + More(n, S)
$$

as long as we adjust it to keep track of the *pos* component.

The use of partially described functions is more general than that of bags, but it can lead to some confusion. With bags, it is obvious what is being left open, but with partially described functions it is necessary to be very careful that any incompleteness is intentional.

**Q:** When you described *QuickSort* before, you said it might choose any item for partitioning; now you've made it work only on the first. Is that an unintentional incompleteness?

**A:** No, it's an intentional one: I'm trying to give you a feeling for *QuickSort* and for design methods which can lead to comparable solutions to other problems, but I'm not trying to give you the whole story. If it matters, you can choose any item as partition element and still use the *Partition* which I just outlined: choose your item, then *Swap* it with $S_1$, then call on *Partition*.

### 3.4.3 Sets: Forgetting Repetition

With sequences, we could ask which item was at a given position; the indexing function characterized the structure. With bags, that information was lost, but at least we could ask how many repetitions of a given item was to be found in the bag. The *Count* function or *Perm* equivalence relation characterized the structure. Sometimes we are not even interested in *Count*s, except to make sure that they are not zero: you want to know that $IsIn(x, S)$, but as far as you're concerned any two sequences are equivalent if the same items always occurs in them. This, too, is an equivalence relation: the assertion $SameSet(X, Y)$ should be *True* if $IsIn(a, X) = IsIn(a, Y)$ for all possible items $a$, because in that case $X$ and $Y$ both contain the same *set* of items. Sets are used so much that the *IsIn* predicate deserves a special infix operator symbol: $IsIn(a, X)$ is written $a \in X$.

Sets are written with curly braces, so that $\{1, 2, 3\}$ is a set containing 1, 2, and 3; $\{\}$ is the *empty set*, which contains nothing at all; $\{Alaska, Arkansas, ..., Wyoming\}$ is a set of state names; and the environments which we've been using all along are sets of equations.

$\{1, 2, 3\}$ is the same set as $\{3, 2, 1\}$ or $\{1, 2, 3, 2, 1\}$. Clearly, $2 \in \{1, 2, 3, 2, 1\}$.

**WARNING, WARNING, WARNING!!**: Some books will say that since a set has no repetitions, $\{1, 2, 3, 2, 1\}$ is not a set at all, but a bag (sometimes called a *multiset*). That's quite understandable, and it saves on typography because we don't need to worry about funny symbols like '$[\![$'. However, it makes life very difficult if we want to say that the expression $\{a, b\}$ can only be said to be a set *after* we make sure that $a \neq b$. That would rule out some very important manipulations. In what you are about to read, repetitions within the expression describing a set are not illegal, but they're ignored, and when we finally get down to comparing values we must remove the repetitions.

An operation on a set makes sense only when neither reordering nor removal of duplicates will make any difference, as when we note that $a \in [b, c, b] = a \in [b, c]$. *Min* and *Max* have the same flavor: $Min([a, a]) = Min([a])$. If you see an operation like *Sum* applied to a set, you should assume that it is applied *once* to each element (or *member*) of the set: $Sum(\{1, 2, 3, 2, 1\}) = 6$, even though $Sum([\![1, 2, 3, 2, 1]\!])$ and $Sum([1, 2, 3, 2, 1])$ are both 9. Such usages are common but can be confusing, because $Sum([a, a])$ is usually not the same as $Sum([a])$. Similarly, *Length* applied to a set should count each separate item only once: the *Length* of two sets joined together may be less than the sum of their *Length*s.

### 3.4.4 From Sets to Sequences and Back

To be specific about representation, let's suppose that $Ab$ now finds the set represented by a given sequence, so that $Ab(X) = Ab(Y)$ if and only if $X$ and $Y$ are sequences with exactly the same items. Consider the empty structure first:

$$
\begin{aligned}
a \in Ab([\,]) &= IsIn(a, [\,]) = False \\
Ab([\,]) &= \{\}
\end{aligned}
$$

There's nothing surprising about that. Now we can go on to consider the sequence (or set) which contains a single item:

$$
\begin{aligned}
a \in Ab([b]) &= IsIn(a, [b]) = (b = a) \\
Ab([b]) &= \{b\}
\end{aligned}
$$

Finally, we can talk about structures built up from smaller structures:

$$
\begin{aligned}
a \in Ab(X + Y) &= IsIn(a, X + Y) = IsIn(a, X) \vee IsIn(a, Y) \\
Ab(X + Y) &= Ab(X) + Ab(Y)
\end{aligned}
$$

The "+" operation on the left joins sequences; the "+" operation on the right joins sets, in no particular order and with no respect for duplication. With bags, we found that "+" was commutative; with sets it is not only commutative but *idempotent*, in that for any set $S$ we find $S + S = S$. Every set has become an identity for itself under "+", just as it was for max, for min, for $\wedge$, and for $\vee$. It should not be surprising to find that $\{\}$ is a left and right identity for "+".

The converse of abstraction is again representation: *Rep* now converts sets to the sequences which represent them, making sure that each item in the set appears exactly once in the sequence so we can be confident that equivalent sets are turned into equivalent sequences. If we couldn't be sure that $X = Y \Rightarrow Rep(X) = Rep(Y)$, there wouldn't be much we could be sure of.

$$
\begin{aligned}
Rep(\{\}) &= [\,] \\
Rep(\{x\}) &= [x] \\
Rep(X + Y) &= RemDups(Merge(Rep(X), Rep(Y)))
\end{aligned}
$$

Thus you can represent the set of items in a sequence by using that sequence itself, but if you are going to compare sets with one another, it will help to write them in order with no duplications. To achieve this, you can *Sort* them and remove duplicates. To remove duplicates, you pick out an item and remove copies of it; this is a filtering operation.

$$
\begin{aligned}
RemDups([1, 4, 3, 1, 4, 2, 1]) &= [1, 4, 3, 2] \\
Ab(RemDups(S)) &= Ab(S) \\
Rem(1, [4, 3, 1, 4, 2, 1]) &= [4, 3, 4, 2] \\
Ab(a@Rem(a, S)) &= Ab(a@S) \\
RemDups([\,]) &= [\,] \\
RemDups(a@S) &= a@Rem(a, RemDups(S))
\end{aligned}
$$

This gives us properties such as $RemDups(RemDups(X)) = RemDups(X)$, and $RemDups(X + Y) = RemDups(RemDups(X) + RemDups(Y))$.

There are distribution laws, but they always seem to leave something behind. $Rem$ is more fun:

$$
\begin{aligned}
Rem(a, [\,]) &= [\,] \\
Rem(a, [b]) &= \textbf{if } a = b \textbf{ then } [\,] \textbf{ else } [b] \\
Rem(a, X + Y) &= Rem(a, X) + Rem(a, Y) \\
Rem(a, b@S) &= Rem(a, S) && \text{if } a = b \\
&= b@Rem(a, S) && \text{otherwise}
\end{aligned}
$$

$Rem$ is a moderately interesting operation; heuristics from long ago tell us to look for special cases, such as

$Rem(a, Copy(n, b)) = $ **if** $a = b$ **then** $[\,]$ **else** $Copy(n, b)$

We should also look for an inverse (there is none) and for simplifications:

$Rem(a, Rem(b, S)) = Rem(b, Rem(a, S))$
$Rem(a, Rem(a, S)) = Rem(a, S)$

We should also look for generalizations, as by repeated use: $RemAll(X, Y)$ is the sequence formed from $X$ by removing every item in $Y$, and it looks a lot like subtraction.

$RemAll([1, 4, 3], [2, 4, 1]) = Rem(2, Rem(4, Rem(1, [1, 4, 3]))) = [3]$

Let's write $RemAll(A, B)$ as $A - B$ and look for similarities:

$$
\begin{aligned}
[\,] - S &= [\,] \\
S - [\,] &= S \\
X - X &= [\,] \\
S - (X + Y) &= (S - X) - Y \\
(X + Y) - Z &= (X - Z) + (Y - Z)
\end{aligned}
$$

That last one doesn't look very much like subtraction, does it? Nonetheless, $RemAll$ is an algebraically quite well-behaved function, important in dealing with sets and important in describing programs: a simple spelling checker which produces the sequence of misspelled words in a document $D$ is simply $D - Dictionary$. $RemAll$ can be used on a pair of sets to produce a set because

$$a \in (X - Y) = (a \in X \land \neg(a \in Y))$$

and neither permutations nor repetitions change those results:

$$
\begin{aligned}
Sort(X) - Sort(Y) &= Sort(X - Y) \\
RemDups(X) - RemDups(Y) &= RemDups(X - Y) \\
X - Y &= X - RemDups(Y) \\
RemDups(X + Y) &= Z + (Z - Y)
\end{aligned}
$$

where

$$Z = RemDups(X)$$

You also find

$$RemDups(Merge(X, Y)) = RemDups(Merge(X, Y - X))$$

As with sorting, your understanding of rules like these now will help you to develop better programs later; these rules justify removing some duplicates as you merge, so that there's less to do later on.

At this point, you can represent sets with sequences. It turns out that it's just as useful (sometimes) to think of sequences as being represented by sets. We'll do that after we've introduced some notation.

### 3.4.5 Sets and Predicates

The importance of sets is that they correspond exactly to predicates, and the basic operations on sets correspond exactly to the operations of Boolean algebra. Given an arbitrary set $S$, we can represent it as the predicate $P_S(x) = (x \in S)$. Given an arbitrary predicate $Q$, we can encode it in the set $S_Q$ which contains every item $x$ for which $Q(x)$ is true, and no others. For example, if $S = \{1, 3, 2\}$, we can define $P_S(x) = (x = 1 \lor x = 3 \lor x = 2)$. If $Q(x) = IsDigit(x)$, we can define $S_Q(x) = \{`0`, `1`, \ldots `9`\}$. If $P(x) = False$, then $S_P = \{\}$.

**Q:** What about a predicate like *odd*? That has an infinite number of items; do you mean it corresponds to an infinite set?

**A:** Exactly: it corresponds to the set $\{1, 3, 5, \ldots, 2i + 1, \ldots\}$. Much worse is the simple predicate $P(x) = True$: it contains everything in the universe—horses and quasars mixed in with great works of literature. We'll have to have a name for that set: we'll just call it *Universe*. We already noticed that $X + \{\} = X$ for all sets $X$; we should also note that $X + Universe = Universe$, so that this rather large beastie is a zero element. We can also see that $X - Universe = \{\}$.

**Q:** But does it really mean anything to talk about *Universe* as a collection? How can you compute with it?

**A:** You can't really compute with it any more than you can compute with $\infty$ as a cardinal; it's what you get when you go to the limit and keep right on going past it. Really large sets can't be represented as sequences: an infinitely long sequence is still not long enough to hold the *Universe*; it's not even long enough to hold the set of all predicates on the cardinals, but it is long enough to hold the set of all written rules, or programs.

**Q:** But I thought predicates were to be defined by rules.

**A:** All the predicates that we work with are defined by rules. That just means that we work with an infinitesimally small fraction of the possible predicates. Don't worry about it; there's still a lot to do, and right now we have to finish giving rules relating predicates with their sets.

Now suppose that we have a pair of predicates $P$, $Q$ and their corresponding sets $Ab(P)$, $Ab(Q)$. We can put the predicates together with $\wedge, \vee, \neg, \Rightarrow$, and so on. How does this relate to the sets? We know that $P(x) \vee Q(x)$ is true exactly when $x \in Ab(P) + Ab(Q)$; it would be nice to express this as a distribution law, such as

$$Ab(P \vee Q) = Ab(P) + Ab(Q)$$

**Q:** That looks like it ought to be obvious. Certainly it's true that $x \in (A+B) = x \in A \vee x \in B$, but I still don't follow. "$\vee$" connects Boolean values; how can it connect predicates?

**A:** Well, according to all the definitions so far it is absolutely meaningless, and if you use "$\vee$" to connect predicates in a program you will find that it doesn't work at all. However, we can always give it a meaning by writing a definition, and in this case it works out quite nicely if we say that Boolean operations applied to predicates should simply generate predicates according to the rules

$$
\begin{array}{rcl}
(P \vee Q)(x) & = & P(x) \vee Q(x) \\
(P \wedge Q)(x) & = & P(x) \wedge Q(x) \\
(P \Rightarrow Q)(x) & = & P(x) \Rightarrow Q(x) \\
\neg(P)(x) & = & \neg P(x)
\end{array}
$$

That way we find that $(odd \wedge IsSquare)(9)$ is *True* because both of the operations produce *True*. We can use the same idea on predicates with more than one argument:

$$(P \vee Q)(a, b, c) = (P(a, b, c) \vee Q(a, b, c))$$

**Q:** What if $P$ takes one argument and $Q$ takes four?

**A:** Then this idea doesn't work. (Actually it can be made to work fairly well in some programming languages like *FP*, but we won't try; we have a more general solution which will be coming up in the next subsection.)

At any rate, we have a reasonable rule for disjunction and a reasonable interpretation for it. Try negation: $Ab(\neg P)$ should be a set which contains everything which is not in $Ab(P)$—absolutely everything, from anywhere in the universe (horses and quasars included). That should remind you of something:

$$Ab(\neg P) = Universe - Ab(P)$$

Notice that $Universe - (Universe - S) = S$, just as it ought to.

Now try conjunction: $Ab(P \wedge Q)$ should be a set which contains everything which occurs in $Ab(P)$ and in $Ab(Q)$. We don't have such a function, but we can invent one to work on sequences:

$$[1, 3, 5, 7] \& [2, 5, 3, 6] = [3, 5]$$

so that we are filtering the first sequence, selecting those elements which also occur in the second. Hmmmm... That's very much like *RemAll*, but backwards. Look at the example a moment more:

$$[1, 3, 5, 7] - [2, 5, 3, 6] \quad = \quad [1, 7]$$
$$[2, 5, 3, 6] - [1, 3, 5, 7] \quad = \quad [2, 6]$$

Are those any help? [1,7] and [2,6] are exactly the items we *don't* want, within the sets we had. In fact, if we take them away from those sets, we get

$$[1, 3, 5, 7] - [1, 7] \quad = \quad [3, 5]$$
$$[2, 5, 3, 6] - [2, 6] \quad = \quad [5, 3]$$

One way to define & as a sequence operation, then, is

$$X \& Y = (X - (X - Y))$$

On sequences, this is not a commutative operation, but on sets it is, and in fact

$$Ab(P \wedge Q) = Ab(P) \& Ab(Q)$$

which is a rule in the form we wanted. We could also have reached this point by remembering that

$$(P \wedge Q) \quad = \quad \neg(\neg P \vee \neg Q).$$

Often, however, it's easier to work from an example, as we did. In either case we can soon realize that the relationship between + and & is very much like the relationship between max and min, as you might expect of structures which correspond to $\vee$ and $\wedge$, respectively. In fact, if you think about + and & on sets with the elements {} and *Universe*, you can see that they look just like max and min on cardinals with the elements 0 and $\infty$, or like $\vee$ and $\wedge$ on Booleans with the elements *False* and *True*.

The observation that we have a version of max and min in the context of sets leads us to look for an analogue to ordering. Remember that

$$\max(n, m) \quad = \quad \textbf{if } n \leq m \textbf{ then } n \textbf{ else } m$$

was our starting point for max, with a similar equation for min. When will it be true that $X + Y = Y$ or $X\&Y = Y$? By the analogy, we ought to find that $X + Y = Y$ if $X \leq Y$ since $+$ now has the role of max, while $X\&Y = Y$ should be true if $Y \leq X$. Both of these are correct if we interpret $X \leq Y$ to mean that every item in $X$ is also found in $Y$, i.e., if

$$X \leq Y = (X - Y = \{\})$$

If $X \leq Y$ is *True*, then we call $X$ a *subset* of $Y$, and $Y$ is a *superset* of $X$. Given that interpretation, we will also find that we have other properties reminiscent of max and min on the cardinals:

$$
\begin{array}{rcl}
X & \leq & (X + Y) \\
(X\&Y) & \leq & X \\
\{\} & \leq & X \\
X & \leq & \textit{Universe}
\end{array}
$$

However, sets are not cardinal numbers: $\leq$ on sets is a partial ordering but not a total ordering, because it is easy to find a pair of sets (such as $\{1\}$ and $\{2\}$), neither of which is a subset of the other.

### 3.4.6 Notation for Set Operations

The analogies between structures are often important, but it is still confusing to have too many different meanings for "+". We are reaching the point where this practice, commonly called "overloading" in programming languages, is liable to overload the reader. The simplest way to avoid this is to use different symbols. We replace "+" with "$\cup$", called *union* because it brings together all elements from its arguments. (The cup-like shape of the symbol suggests the "$\vee$" which it closely resembles, and also reminds you that if you pour things into the cup, they tend to stay put). Similarly, we replace "$\leq$" with "$\subseteq$" and "$>$" with "$\supset$". The common symbol for "&" is "$\cap$", which strongly suggests the "$\wedge$" operator to which it corresponds. Finally, instead of talking about the *Length* of a set $S$, it is common to refer to the *cardinality* of $S$, specifically defined as the number of distinct elements in it. This is written $|S|$ and can generally be found by rules such as

$$
\begin{array}{rcl}
|\{\}| & = & 0 \\
|\{a\}| & = & 1 \\
|X \cup Y| & = & |X| + |Y| - |X \cap Y|
\end{array}
$$

The biggest notational extension used in set theory, however, is the use of rules within set descriptions. We have deferred these because they distract somewhat from the straightforward algebraic analogies between operations, but they often make it easy to describe operations which are very awkward to deal with without them.

Here are some set descriptions using rules, and expressions using them:

$$
\begin{aligned}
Ab(P) &= \{x : P(x)\} \\
X \cup Y &= \{a : a \in X \lor a \in Y\} \\
Perm(X, Y) &= (\{\} = \{a : Count(a, X) \neq Count(a, Y)\}) \\
Find(a, S) &= Min(\{i : S[i] = a\}) \\
Divisors(x) &= \{y : mod(x, y) = 0\} \\
gcd(x, y) &= Max(Divisors(x) \cap Divisors(y)) \\
Prime(x) &= |Divisors(x)| = 2 \\
SqrRt(n) &= Max(\{i : i * i \leq n\})
\end{aligned}
$$

A set description using a rule has the form $\{E : P\}$; the set described is actually the set of all possible values of $E$ for which the condition $P$ is satisfied. In the first example, you see that the set corresponding to a given predicate is exactly the set containing all variables for which that predicate is true. In the second, you see that "the union of $X$ and $Y$ is the set of all values of $a$ for which $a$ is found in $X$ or in $Y$." That is simple enough, but it solves a problem for which we had to invent a notion of "$\lor$" working on predicates to produce predicates. The third rule says that $X$ is a permutation of $Y$ if the set of all values of $a$ for which $a$ occurs a different number of times in $X$ than in $Y$ is empty. This, too, is simple, but it expresses the idea that the assertion $Perm(X, Y)$ is true if the rule $Count(a, X) = Count(a, Y)$ is valid for all possible $a$; we had to work around that idea.

Then you learn that the location of an item $a$ in a sequence $S$ is the smallest (first) $i$ for which $S[i] = a$. This is a helpful addition to the description given previously, but of course it's not quite true: it doesn't work when the set given is empty.

Then you learn that the set of divisors of a number $x$ contains exactly those values of $y$ for which $mod(x, y) = 0$; and to this is added that the greatest common divisor of two numbers is exactly the greatest member of the intersection of their sets of divisors. This is a much more helpful description of $gcd$ than the ones given previously. (It's reliable, too.)

Set-forming expressions with embedded rules can be used to express many of the notions we've worked with on sequences. Filters, mappings, and generators are quite simple.

Remember the filter *Letters*? It helped us get towards palindromes by taking only the letters from a given input. If we want to select the letters from a set, we need only write

$$Letters(X) = \{c : c \in X \land IsLetter(c)\}$$

Or if we want to capitalize the result, we can write

$$Capitalize(X) = \{UC(c) : c \in X\}$$

These expressions allow us to avoid explicit repetition for mappings or filters, and sometimes for generators:

$$Range(i, j) = \{k : i \leq k \wedge k \leq j\}$$

On rare occasions, you may need to describe a generator through explicit repetition; your ancestors include your parents, and the parents of any ancestors:

$$Ancestors(x) = Parents(x) \cup \{z \in Parents(y) : y \in Ancestors(x)\}$$

### Exercises

**3.4-3**  Rewrite a mapping from the sequence section as a set expression.

**3.4-4**  Rewrite a filter from the sequence section as a set expression.

**3.4-5**  Rewrite a generator from the sequence section as a set expression.

Many of the most important uses of these kinds of expressions produce sets of sequences. For example, in order to describe a predicate with more than one argument, like $x < y$, we would write the set of all pairs for which the predicate holds true:

$$Ab(``<") = \{[x, y] : x < y\}$$

If we had to describe a predicate like *IsSumOf* defined by

$$IsSumOf(x, y, z) = (z = (x + y))$$

we could note that

$$Ab(IsSumOf) = \{[x, y, z] : x + y = z\}$$

This way of looking at things makes it easy for you to *tabulate* predicates as collections of assertions. A collection of tabulated assertions is a data base.

### Exercises

**3.4-6**  Write $Ab(``>")$

**3.4-7**  Write $Ab(``=")$

**3.4-8**  Write a simple equation describing the relationship between the sets $Ab(``>")$, $Ab(``<")$, and $Ab(``=")$.

**3.4-9**   Define $SumSet(a, b) = \{c : [a, b, c] \in Ab(IsSumOf)\}$. What is $SumSet(3, 5)$?

**Q:** Why does this idea of embedding rules in expressions only work on sets? Why can't it be used to describe bags and sequences as well?

**A:** Most books do not use it that way, but it can. If we write $[i : odd(i) \wedge i \leq 10]$, it is reasonable to interpret this as the sequence $[1, 3, 5, 7, 9]$, and we shall so interpret it. Similarly, we could write $Letters(X) = [c : c \in X \wedge IsLetter(c)]$ and insist that the items involved should come out in the result in the same order that they had in $X$. This is a matter of convention; we could insist that the items should come out in the opposite order, but we must be definite. Look at an example:

$$Sort(S) = [a : a \in [\![b : b \in S]\!]]$$

That's a rather nice way to say that if you dump the items from a sequence (in order of appearance) into a bag, and then pull them (in order, as we've discussed) into a sequence, you will get an ordered permutation of the original sequence. Similarly,

$$Merge(Sort(X), Sort(Y)) = [a : a \in ([\![b : b \in X]\!] + [\![b : b \in Y]\!])]$$

Notice that the two embedded rules each used a variable called $b$; these two variables are entirely independent, and you can rename either without affecting the other.

A very important use of expressions like these is to express Cartesian products and operations involving them. The Cartesian product sequence of $S_1$ and $S_2$ is given by

$$[[x, y] : x \in S_1, y \in S_2].$$

For example,

$$[[i, j] : i \in [1, 2, 3] \wedge j \in [5, 6]] = [[1, 5], [1, 6], [2, 5], [2, 6], [3, 5], [3, 6]]$$

Since this is a sequence, ordering is important: "$\wedge$" used as a guide for finding values to try is not commutative. If we switch the order of extraction for the variables, we get

$$[[i, j] : j \in [5, 6] \wedge i \in [1, 2, 3]] = [[1, 5], [2, 5], [3, 5], [1, 6], [2, 6], [3, 6]]$$

In the first equation, you have to imagine yourself taking a value for $i$ out of $[1,2,3]$, then trying all possible values for $j$, then switching to the next value of $i$, and so on. In the second you take a value for $j$ out of $[5, 6]$, then try all possible values for $i$, then switch to the next value for $j$, and so on.

Mappings and filters are easily described with these rules; accumulators and generators are harder, but we'll deal with them soon.

## Exercises

**3.4-10** Pick a sequence mapping from the preceding section and describe it with an embedded rule.

**3.4-11** Pick a sequence filter from the preceding section and describe it with an embedded rule.

Of course, if we find Cartesian product sets by the same kind of construction, the use of $\wedge$ will be commutative:

$$\{[a,b] : a \in S_1 \wedge b \in S_2\} = \{[a,b] : b \in S_2 \wedge a \in S_1\}$$

You will spend a great deal of time thinking about Cartesian products, both as sets and as sequences. A Cartesian product is just a shorthand for thinking about everything that can possibly happen, and Murphy's law guarantees that if you don't think about them all, the ones you forgot will wreck your work.

Suppose we want to use rules to specify a value which is the only one satisfying a certain condition; for example, we may want to use rules to specify the *Max* function itself as producing the one and only value which is as large as any value in a given set or sequence. A clumsy way to say this is

$$\{Max(S)\} = \{i : i \in S, \{\} = \{j \in S : j > i\}\}$$

It certainly works, but the proliferation of set brackets is confusing. We'll use a conventional abbreviation and a useful function:

$$Max(S) \quad = \quad i : i \in S, null(\{j \in S : j > i\})$$

where

$$null(S) \quad = \quad (S = \{\})$$

## Exercise

**3.4-12** Use the same idea to describe the *Min* function.

Similarly, we can assert that 3 is the only (cardinal) number between 2 and 4 by writing

$$3 = i : 2 < i < 4$$

It's common to use this abbreviation in a few other ways as well; especially to pick minimal (first) or maximal (last) values of an expression. To say

$$
\begin{aligned}
SqrRt(n) &= Max(i) : Sqr(i) \leq n \\
&= Min(i-1) : Sqr(i) > n \\
&= i : Sqr(i) \leq n < Sqr(i+1)
\end{aligned}
$$

is useful and reasonably self-explanatory; if you get confused by such a notation, you should be able to translate it back into the rule-based definition for sets or sequences from which it came. We can write very compact descriptions this way, such as

$$
\begin{aligned}
Sum(S) &= f(Length(S)) : f(0) = 0, f(i+1) = f(i) + S[i+1] \\
Min(S) &= f(Length(S)) : f(0) = \infty, f(i+1) = \min(f(i), S[i+1]) \\
gcd(n,m) &= q_{Min(i:r_i=0)} : q_0 = \max(n,m), r_0 = \min(n,m), q_{i+1} = r_i, \\
&\qquad r_{i+1} = mod(q_i, r_i)
\end{aligned}
$$

but we will rarely do so: too much abbreviation is as dangerous as too little.

### 3.4.7 Notations for Generators and Accumulators

The rule notation gives us a very convenient way to write mappings and filters, but it's not so great for generators and accumulators. Generators are not too hard, provided that you're willing to think of repeated function application $f(f(f(...f(x)...)))$ as a form of exponential construction; $f^n(x)$ or $(f^{**}n)(x)$ representing the $n$-times-repeated application of $f$ to $x$. Ancestors are found by repeated application of the *Parents* function; to get the grandparents of $x$, perhaps we could try $(Parents^{**}2)(x)$. Would it work? Think about it before going on.

It's actually almost right, but $Parents(Parents(x))$ is not quite what we want: *Parents* generates a set from a single individual, and we can't apply it to a set. However, we can use rules to construct an *AllP* function which will work:

$$
AllP(S) = \{p \in Parents(x) : x \in S\}
$$

Now we can generate all ancestors of $x$ with

$$
Ancestors(x) = \{p \in (AllP^{**}n)(\{x\}) : n \in 1\ldots\infty\}
$$

This isn't just a notational trick: when you break down a relationship this way, you come closer to seeing what will be involved in generating it with a simple recurrence...or a program, for that matter.

**Exercises**    Write generators for

**3.4-13** The descendants of $x$, assuming that $Children(x)$ is the set of all of $x$'s children.

**3.4-14** $Tails(S)$ as defined earlier in this chapter.

Accumulators offer a similar difficulty, one which mathematicians have re-solved in a rather strange way. Given a set or sequence $S$, we rather often want to accumulate an arithmetic result like $S_1 + S_2 + S_3 + \ldots$ or $S_1 * S + 2 * \ldots$, a Boolean result like $S_1 \vee S_2 \ldots$ or $S_1 \wedge S_2 \ldots$, or a set-construction like $S_1 \cup S_2 \ldots$ or $S_1 \cap S_2 \ldots$. In mathematics, these are indicated by special symbols: $\sum, \prod, \vee, \wedge, \cup,$ and $\cap$, respectively: each symbol is somehow an "enlarged" version of the symbol for the simple binary operation which it accumulates.

We don't really have the option of doing this, because we can't invent a new en-larged symbol for each accumulation: almost every program will accumulate values, often using functions defined only in that particular program. We will sometimes use uppercase for accumulators, as in *Min* being the accumulation corresponding to the binary operation min, but we can't always do that either because we write so many functions with long names that capitalization really shouldn't have such a restricted meaning. There are a few programming languages which actually have a standardized way of forming accumulators. In *APL*, the sum of a sequence is found by the accumulator $/+$ and its cumulative product by $/\times$; if it happens to be a Boolean sequence, we can accumulate $\wedge$ with $/\wedge$. As you can see, *APL* doesn't stick to the *ASCII* character set. Lacking a good solution, we will often take the coward's way out and fake it: if we have to form the cumulative concatenation of all the sequences in a sequence, we'll usually use the expression $S_1 + S_2 \ldots + S_n$, or possibly

$$f(S_1, f(S_2, f(S_3, \ldots f(S_{n-1}, S_n) \ldots$$

Neither is really satisfactory. There is one alternative: we can say that **if** we have rules for a binary function $f(x, y)$, **then** whenever we say $f([a, b, c, d]$ what we really mean is the accumulation of $f$ over the sequence $[a, b, c]$. That's certainly simple, and hardly ever confusing. Even when we write "$+([1, 4, 5, 6])$" it's pretty obvious that there's nothing much we could mean except "16".

One particular use of these notions and notations is to invert the representa-tion process we described before. Previously, we said that sets were represented by sequences (by forgetting some information). Now we'll go the other way.

### 3.4.8 Sequences Can Be Described by Tables.

This doesn't seem possible, at first: sets have less information than sequences. Nonetheless, the idea works. We can represent the sequence $X = [here, there, yonder]$ with a set of assertions: $\{X_1 = here, X_2 = Sumer, X_3 = Babylon\}$. Now we write this as a table:

$$\{[1, here], [2, Sumer], [3, Babylon]\}$$

**Exercise**

**3.4-15** Write such a table for $[this, is, a, sample, sequence]$.

**Q:** Isn't this a little bit ridiculous? Here we had a simple little sequence, something that obviously ought to be written out with one thing after the other until you get to the end, and you're representing it by a set of sequences. How can that possibly help?

**A:** It's complicated, but it's not ridiculous. This way, we get rather nice definitions of the primary functions, which are compact and a little hard to read, but very easy to think about after we get used to them. First we define *Rep* formally:

$$
\begin{aligned}
Rep([]) &= \{\} \\
Rep(S_{1...N}) &= \{[i, S_i] : i \in 1 \ldots N\}
\end{aligned}
$$

The primary functions are now quite neat:

$$
\begin{aligned}
Length(A) &= |Rep(A)| \\
&= Max(0@\{i : [i, x] \in Rep(A)\} \\
Rep(A + B) &= Rep(A) \cup \{[i + Length(A), b] : [i, b] \in Rep(B)\} \\
Find(x, S) &= Min(0@\{j : [j, x] \in Rep(S)\}) \\
S[i] &= x : [i, x] \in Rep(S)
\end{aligned}
$$

**Exercises**    Use these ideas to implement the sequence operations

**3.4-16** "@"

**3.4-17** "Put"

Doing it this way, we find out more about sets even as we set out to find more about sequences.

We could go further, and represent each sequence with a three-place table and a starting point. For example, we could write

$$
\begin{aligned}
&[s3, \quad a, \quad\quad\quad s4] \\
&[s2, \quad is, \quad\quad\quad s3] \\
&[s5, \quad sequence, \quad END] \\
&[s4, \quad sample, \quad\quad s5] \\
&[s1, \quad this, \quad\quad\quad s2]
\end{aligned}
$$

and from the starting point $s1$ we read off $[this, is, a, sample, sequence]$. Now we've found how to represent sequences of arbitrary length in terms of sets of short sequences (or even sets of records—it is easy enough to describe each line as a variable $s$ composed of the two variables $s.Hd$, and $s.Tl$: we thus have a set of 5 variables and the constant *END*).

The advantage to this sort of table is that if we want to insert an item in the middle of the sequence, between *"a"* and *"sample"*, we need only change [$s3, a, s4$] to [$s3, a, s6$] and then create a new entry wherever we have room: [$s6, silly, s4$]. (In terms of records, we are inventing a new variable $s6 = \{Hd = silly, Tl = s4\}$ and changing $s3$ so that $s3. Tl = s6$. Nothing has been copied or moved, but the sequence can now be read off as *[this, is, a, silly, sample, sequence]*.)

When working with a very long sequence, you don't want to move everything when it becomes necessary to insert something in the middle. This choice of representation makes it possible to do insertion in constant time, so that insertion into enormous sequences becomes practical.

**Exercise**

**3.4-18** What change and what additions would now turn S into
[$this, is, a, long, and, silly, sample, sequence$]?

We are far from being finished with the idea of using one format to represent another, but at this point you should feel that you are beginning to be comfortable with some of the interrelationships between sets and sequences as rather abstract entities.

At this point, you have the tools required for the description of almost any conceivable program behavior, provided that you understand the problem it's solving. For example, you could specify the behavior of a chess-playing program, with functions and relations on boards and pieces and moves and colors and players, but only if you know the rules of chess. You don't yet know how to design programs to search for good moves, but that is a later stage of design in any case.

Your algebraic work will not be complete until you stop studying computer science, but you have enough to go on with, and it's time to be going. You could go on directly to Part III, and work on writing programs from specifications. However, it might be more sensible to start working on written models of parts of the world, so that you have some notions of how to think about problems and search for answers. That's Part II.

# 4

# Models, Maps, and Types

In Part I, you learned the essence of "representation": the invertible *Ab* and *Rep* mappings which carry us from one type to another. You also learned to think of a state, or environment, as a collection of values for variables. In the next four chapters, we'll carry these ideas further, toward representations of fragments of the real world...or at least fragments of worlds somewhat like it. In Chapter 4, you work specifically with physical maps; we are dealing with a space containing places described by coordinates and connected by paths. In Chapter 5, the same terminology and extensions of the same techniques are used on problems in which the coordinates are not simply spatial, but may involve anything you can measure. This takes us into three fundamentally different kinds of models, but in each case there is a "state-space" to be explored by the computer—mechanical or human. Chapter 6 develops some of the techniques of systematic state-space search: if you don't know what to do next, try everything (but in some orderly way). Finally, Chapter 7 tries to pull all this together in an introduction to formal reasoning about models and the computations we carry out within them.

Now, let's expand on the ideas to be covered in the chapter.

A model—a map, a globe, a blueprint, a pilot plant, a toy truck, a formula, a prototype—is a scaled-down representation of some part or aspect of the world. You're going to spend a lot of time thinking about models: it will include all the time you spend thinking about programs (because that's what programs are), and it will also include all the time you think about science, mathematics, art, history, and a few other things.

This chapter develops some of the ideas you need to know in order to study models. It's fairly hard work, so we don't begin on models in general. Instead, we think about a particular kind of model: a map.

Throughout the chapter, we will introduce simple ideas about maps by using them. How are they used to answer questions? How they are designed to make such use reasonably easy? How can we describe maps? First we will be thinking about ordinary maps, as drawn on paper; then we'll think about symbolic maps, which could be used by people and which are much easier for computers to work with. We'll also relate these to the mathematical underpinnings of Part I. We'll try to develop the fundamental concepts of models as they are used in science (and in business). We won't actually build anything very complex, but it wouldn't hurt to keep a complex model in mind: a mechanical or chemical system for science, or a desktop with nearby file drawers and wastebasket for business.

## 4.1  READING PICTORIAL GEOMETRIC MAPS

Simple geometric maps are the kind of maps that you've been using all your life. You're not likely to learn anything new about using them from reading this chapter, but you'll think carefully about just how you use them, and about why they work.

### 4.1.1  Modeling Is Translation: There and Back Again

> How many miles to Babylon?
> Three-score miles and ten.
> Can I get there by candle-light?
> Yes, and back again.
>
>   Mother Goose

How do you answer questions like that? Most of us, most of the time, expect that we won't have memorized the answer in advance; we have to look on a map. To find the distance from "here" to Babylon in miles, we go through a sequence of steps, one after another:

1. Find the points on the map which correspond to "here" and to "Babylon" in our world; then

2. Find the distance in inches between those map points; then

3. Find the number of world-miles which correspond to that number of map-inches.

Answering questions with models often has that structure: we translate a question about the world into a question about the model, then we answer the question about the model, and finally we translate back.   The map is a "good" map if it

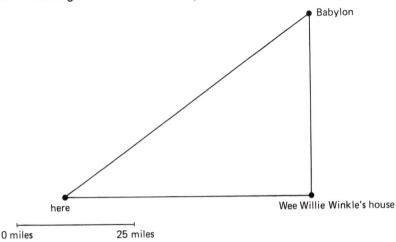

Figure 4.1 "How Many Miles To Babylon?"

is easier to go through those three stages than to answer the original question by measuring the distance to Babylon.

### 4.1.2 Maps and Places

Consider the map structure and our use of it in more detail. A map is generally a map of a region, a set of places—in Figure 4.1 that set is {here, Babylon, Wee Willie Winkie's house}. A subset of the places (a smaller region) has Mother Goose labels: {Babylon, Wee Willie Winkie's house}. An overlapping subset is relevant to this problem: {here, Babylon}. The union of the two subsets is the whole set, and the intersection is the unit set which contains only our destination: {Babylon}.

Notice that these really are sets, not sequences. To check that, look for two properties: a set is an *unordered* collection *without repetitions*. Here, the order we write them in doesn't matter, because a region with labels {Babylon, here, Wee Willie's house} would be just the same. Again, if we combine the two regions {Mother Goose places, relevant places} we don't get two different Babylons in the result; we just get the whole region back again.

The labels make it fairly easy to find the points on the map corresponding to points on the world. The measurement of distance in inches is simple enough with a ruler. For translating back, we have a scale factor in with the key, usually given as a line whose real lengths are in inches but which is marked with lengths in miles. It is a very concise way of expressing the relation between map-inches and world-miles. To use it, we find map-labels ("here", and "Babylon") which match our names for the world-places; then we measure map-inches (2.8 inches) between the map-labels; and finally we multiply by 25 world-miles (per map-inch) to get 70 world-miles.

$$RealDistance(x, y) = Scale * MapDistance(MapPlace(x), MapPlace(y))$$

This formula can be read aloud as "To find the real distance from a real place called $x$ to a real place called $y$, you must first find the map-places for $x$ and $y$, then find the map-distance between the map-places, and then multiply by a scale factor. The product is your answer."

### 4.1.3 Formalization Is Abbreviation

After you've read a lot of such formulas aloud or to yourself, you'll get tired of wordiness, and you'll start saying things like "the RealDistance of x and y is Scale times the MapDistance of the MapPlace of x and the MapPlace of y." You still have to remember that "MapPlace" is a name for a function, a way of finding a location on a map when given a name, that "MapDistance" is another function, a way of finding a distance in inches when given two map-places, and that the Scale for a given map tells how many world-miles are packed into each map-inch. You still have to remember that, but you don't have to remind yourself of it each time you speak the formula.

### 4.1.4 Formalization Is Format

An important issue in keeping track of a model, whether it is a simple one like this or a complex one like those we will see later, is to have a standardized way of checking out answers to questions like

- **TYPES**: What kinds of objects are involved? These could be place names, colors, integers, or employees; in any case, it's important to make the possibilities clear.

- **CONSTANTS**: What special values are important? Perhaps all roads lead to Rome among place names, perhaps black and white are to colors as 0 and 1 are to integers, perhaps we have to remember *SuperFrog*.

- **FUNCTIONS**: How are objects of each kind created and used? Place names are not (in our present problem) created, but they are used; colors may be created by mixing primary colors, integers are generated by + and −, etc. For each operation, what are the types of its arguments and what is the type of its result? Thus, $Up(n : Cardinal) : Cardinal$ is a simple expression indicating that the function $Up$, given a cardinal number, produces a cardinal number.

- **ASSERTIONS**: What facts can I really count on? Examples make useful rules, but they cannot stand alone: general rules are needed. This is the hardest part, and that's one major reason why Part I was all about assertions.

A good way to look at this is that we're filling in a questionnaire—not an essay in which you can really express your feelings, but just a simply formatted set of answers to a restricted list of questions. To make sense of this, you may want to go back to the introduction's discussion of specification. If you're going to write a chess program, you need objects which are chess pieces and boards and players and board-displays and scores and timers and commands and printers and disk files and so on. If you're going to write a program for children to make and print drawings with, you need objects which are pens and erasers and paintbrushes and menus and sprayguns and paint mixes and lines and points and circles and colors and commands and printers and disk files and so on. If you're going to write a telecommunications program, you need objects which are modems and hosts and protocols and packets and messages and telephone numbers and commands and printers and disk files and so on. In each case, you need to describe these types of objects, any particularly important objects of the types, and all the available operations on these types, and you need to do it by making assertions that are unambiguous—and as easy to read as possible. For now, we have a very simple objective (finding the real distance), a simple rule for achieving that, and very few new kinds of objects to think about. Look again at the rule:

$$RealDistance(x, y) = Scale * MapDistance(MapPlace(x), MapPlace(y))$$

What are these things? Let's look at Figure 4.2.

**TYPES**  $PlaceName = \{here, Babylon, WeeWilliesHouse\};$
$MapPosition = ?;$
  —We don't know or care what it really is;
  —maybe rectangular or polar coordinates.
$Distance = Real;$
  —a number like 0.0, .345, −96.72, etc.

**CONSTANTS**  $Scale = 25.0 : Real;$

**FUNCTIONS**  $MapPlace(x : PlaceName) : MapPosition;$
$MapDistance(x : MapPosition, y : MapPosition) : Distance;$

**ASSERTIONS**  **if** $MapPlace(x) = MapPlace(y)$ **then** $x = y;$

  —No two names on our map
    —have the same place.

$MapDistance(x, y) \geq 0.0$

  —There are no negative distances.

$MapDistance(x, x) = 0.0;$

  —The distance from here to here is 0.0.

$MapDistance(x, y) = MapDistance(y, x);$
$MapDistance(x, y) + MapDistance(y, z) \geq MapDistance(x, z);$

**Figure 4.2** Objects and Types in a Map

To understand this, keep looking back at the model and the formula. The function MapPlace takes a place name and produces a map position; the function MapDistance takes a pair of positions and produces a length, and so on. Functions like XCoord are not part of the problem; they're really things we use to help create the solution, so we keep them separate.

If it doesn't really make sense, try looking at a similar layout for something you do understand. Let's put the real numbers in the same layout, as in Figure 4.3.

**TYPES**             $Real = ?;$
**CONSTANTS** :       $1, 0 : Real;$

**FUNCTIONS** :       $"+"(x : Real, y : Real) : Real;$

                      $"*"(x : Real, y : Real) : Real;$
**ASSERTIONS** :      $x + 0 = x$

                      $x + y = y + x$
                      **if** $x > y$ **then** $x + z > y + z$
                      $x * (y + z) = x * y + x * z$
                      $x * 0 = 0$

**Figure 4.3** Objects and Operations for Real Numbers

These functions and assertions for the reals are a very, very brief indication of the kind of thing a programmer needs to know in order to write programs using the reals; the functions and assertions for map places are a little closer to being complete because we haven't yet developed much of a concept of a map, but they're still certainly not all there.

Of course, the final answer we wanted was whether or not you could get there by candlelight: is the time remaining before dark less than the time required to reach Babylon? To find this out, you need to know not only distance but speed, and not only the current time but the time of sunset. We need functions like these:

$$
\begin{array}{rcl}
CanGet(x, y, t) & = & AvailableTime(t) > NeededTime(x, y) \\
AvailableTime(t) & = & SunsetHour - t \\
NeededTime(x, y) & = & RealDistance(x, y)/HighestSpeed
\end{array}
$$

Of course, your interpretation may differ slightly from mine. (I think of the expression "$CanGet(a, b, c)$" as the true-or-false assertion "I can get from $a$ to $b$ starting at time $c$," and of "$AvailableTime(t)$" as being the amount of time in seconds between the time "$t$" and sunset.) Sometimes such differences cause no trouble at all; at other times, they cause programming teams working on different parts of one project to spend months developing programs which fail disastrously when put together. The only way for us to be sure that our interpretations are compatible is for me to explicitly write the assumptions I make about $CanGet$, $AvailableTime$, $NeededTime$, and so on, and for you to do the same; then we trade assumptions and read carefully. As a sample, I might point out my belief that

$$
CanGet(x, y, t) \wedge RealDistance(x, y) > RealDistance(u, v) \rightarrow CanGet(u, v, t)
$$

or that $HighestSpeed > 0$ and $(16.0 \leq SunsetHour \leq 18.0)$. (At this point, you probably realize that I never stated anything about the *units* in which these were to be measured; the assertion given would make sense if times were taken as real numbers between 0.0 (midnight) and 24.0 (the following midnight), but not otherwise. A specification must make such points clear, at whatever cost in boring focus on detail.

## Exercises

**4.1-1**   Expand the formal layout description with **TYPES** *Time* and *Velocity*, and then add the **FUNCTIONS** *CanGet*, *AvailableTime*, and *NeededTime* with appropriate **ASSERTIONS**.

**4.1-2**   "Get there by candlelight" is actually ambiguous: it could mean "get there before dark," as we assumed, or it could mean "get there by the light of one candle," in which case the length and the burning speed of a candle are needed. How much of the formulation just given would be changed? What would it be changed to?

**4.1-3**   For the **TYPE** *Region*, we have the obvious constant {} and the **FUNCTIONS** *Union* and *Intersection*. What are some reasonable **ASSERTIONS**?

### 4.1.5   Computation Is Substitution

In this case, if we were writing (almost) everything down, we could say something like

$$
\begin{aligned}
goal \quad &= \quad RealDistance(here, Babylon) \\
&= \quad Scale * MapDistance(MapPlace(here), \qquad \text{definition} \\
&\qquad\qquad\qquad\qquad\qquad MapPlace(Babylon)) \\
&= \quad Scale * 2.8 \qquad\qquad\qquad\qquad\quad \text{measurement} \\
&= \quad 25 * 2.8 \qquad\qquad\qquad\qquad\qquad \text{map's construction} \\
&= \quad 70 \qquad\qquad\qquad\qquad\qquad\qquad\quad \text{multiplication}
\end{aligned}
$$

The computer can handle the first few lines with no trouble; we've seen that in the previous chapters. However, the "measurement" step looks awkward: how can we tell him what a ruler is? Still, if we get through that somehow, he can look up what the scale is and fill in the fourth line, and he can be taught to multiply, so he can fill in the fifth.

At each point, an expression is replaced with something equivalent, and we go from an initial setup through a sequence of rephrasings and so at the end to a simple number, which is the goal.

**Q:** Why does it work? Why should it say anything about real distances? No matter how many questionnaires we fill out with formal statements, we're still using a piece of paper with pictures and numbers on it to answer questions about the real world, like "Can we get there by candle-light?"

**A:** Well, as I've been saying, the paper with pictures and numbers is a model of some aspect of the real world.

**Q:** Why? What makes it a model? This is a chapter on models, and I still don't know what a model really is.

**A:** Actually, anything can be a model of anything else; it's just that some models are better than others.

**Q:** You're evading my question: why does the map help me solve problems?

### 4.1.6 Translation Depends on Similarity of Structure

**A:** The basic reason is that the map has the same form as the land it represents: it is a same-form image, and it turns out that distance is strictly proportional between structures of the same form. As your high school geometry course probably put it, corresponding sides of similar triangles are proportional.

**Q:** What do similar triangles have to do with it? There's a triangle here, but what's it supposed to be similar to?

**A:** It's similar to the triangle which you could draw on the ground. What's more, it has the same proportion to the scale line that the real triangle would have to a 25-mile "scale line" actually stretched out on the ground.

If you remember enough high-school geometry, you can actually prove that the ratio of the scale line on the map (1 inch) to the scale line in the real world (25 miles) is the same as the ratio of the here–Babylon line on the map (2.8 inches) to the here–Babylon line in the real world (which now has to be 70 miles, or three-score miles and ten). To make it a high-school geometry proof, you would fill in lines from the ends of the scale to "here" and "Babylon," just to make sure that they were all on triangles, but the idea only depends on the assumption that shapes in the real world are actually similar to shapes on the map. All that you need to know is that the map is a "same-form" image. Being in college, we then figure out that Greek for "same" (or just "like") is "homo" and Greek for "form" is "morphos," so we call the map a "homomorphic image" of the land.

MODELS ARE HOMOMORPHIC IMAGES. THEY HAVE TO BE.

**Q:** Whaddaya mean, models have to have the same form as the originals? You know perfectly well that the Earth isn't flat, but I can still have a flat map of it: not perfect, but pretty good.

**A:** Yes, but a form on the curved Earth is still somehow "similar" to a corresponding form on the map. Similar triangles in simple geometry were defined as those which could be matched up against one another by sliding, turning, and shrinking or expanding them. Similarity in a more general context will be defined as matching by more complicated translations. If you have a rule for the translation of the problem (and an inverse rule for retranslation of the answer), and the process gets (close to) the right answers, then the logical structure is similar. If you can't translate, then you are not going to be able to use your model to answer questions.

For example, we can translate English statements about physical laws involving time into Spanish pretty well, because (despite some very real differences) the English "time" corresponds pretty well to Spanish "tiempo." Even ideas like "killing time" can be translated directly.[1] The linguist Benjamin Lee Whorf reported that translation into Hopi doesn't work so well, because there is no closely analogous structure; for one thing, the Hopi concept of time is based not on measurement, but rather on a feeling of intensity.

A homomorphic image is just something into which we can translate.

**Q:** Isn't that a pretty vague definition of "homomorphic image"?

**A:** Yes, but it's true. For our purposes, a homomorphism is a special kind of distribution law: one which has the form

$$f(g(x_1, x_2, \ldots x_n)) = g'(f(x_1), f(x_2), \ldots, f(x_n))$$

In that rule, $f$ is the function which carries us to a representation, $g$ is the abstract function, and $g'$ is the implementation of that abstract function. The basic idea of a homomorphism in mathematics is that it embodies this translation idea: the translation (to the map) of the answer is the answer (in the map) to a translated question. Look at Figure 4.4; the idea is that you can go either way and get the same answer. (If the structure doesn't look familiar, go back to the introduction for a few minutes and look for one like it.)

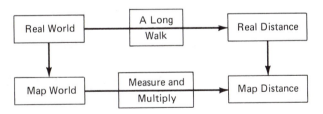

**Figure 4.4** Representing Babylon

If I want to move along the top, finding the distance from here to Babylon in the world, I can instead translate the problem into a map problem, find that distance, and then find the world-distance which would translate into that map-distance.

----

[1]Your author once saw a garage in Mexico with a sign warning that *"No se puede matar al tiempo sin dañar al eternidad"*: you cannot kill time without injuring eternity.

**Q:** What's abstract about a long walk?

**A:** Sorry...the use of the word "abstract" is sometimes a little confusing. Actually, what we're representing is not Babylon, but our idea (some aspect) of Babylon; the abstract process to be represented is not the actual long walk with sweat, stumbles, and the possibility of hitchhiking, but our idea of the long walk. Those are abstractions, and our map is intended to represent them. In ordinary speech we usually get away without that kind of distinction, and we pretend that the map represents Babylon itself.

**Q:** Hey, don't you want to reverse that last arrow? Shouldn't it be translating the map-distance to the world-distance?

**A:** Good point, but I'd rather say that both vertical arrows go downward (they represent translating the world into the map), and I just sometimes have to go backward along an arrow. That way I can think of the picture itself as a map of "places," and say that all these words about translation and retranslation are implicit in the observation that there are two (equivalent) paths from the upper left to the lower right.

Whenever we solve problems, whenever we do mathematical proofs, and most especially whenever we write computer programs, we have this kind of reasoning process to go through: translate, operate, and translate back. We will spend a lot of time trying to make this idea precise. That means that we have to develop a mathematical notion of a translation—of a homomorphism. Other jawbreakers will also keep pushing themselves into the discussion and there there isn't much we can do about it except try to introduce them informally before you have to study them carefully.

## Exercises

**4.1-4**  Going back to high school geometry, use the Euclidean theorems about corresponding triangles to prove that the ratio of distances on the map is equal to the ratio of corresponding distances in the world.

**4.1-5**  Given a perfect 1/100th scale model of a trailer truck, will the angle of the diagonal from the left front wheel to the right rear wheel be the same on the model as on the truck? Why or why not? Will the model (assuming that it's made of the same materials) be able to carry 1/100th as much as the real truck? Why or why not?

**Q:** Okay, I guess I see that you can talk about maps as using translation and back-translation; I can follow it so far. What I don't get is why you're doing it at all. How would you feed this kind of a map into a computer at all?

**A:** Actually, I would prefer not to. (It certainly can be done, but then we are talking about fairly sophisticated programs doing fairly complicated things.)

A better approach would be to find a model which has the same form symbolically instead of geometrically; a "good" model for a computer is made of out of words and numbers.

## 4.2  A MAP CAN BE A TABLE

It's easy for a computer to deal with a table of words and numbers. Instead of storing a picture which you can measure, we just store a list of measurements. If you go back to the image of a mechanical moron working everything out on graph paper, following instructions very explicitly, he can simply write a letter or a digit in each space, and it is pretty easy for him to look up what's in square 53/819, or in the five squares immediately following it to the right. He can even look at the left-hand side of each row until he finds a given word and then look up what's in that row, just as you do with a dictionary.

Of course, the simplest way to tabulate the measurements is just to make them and write down the values. If we measure the position as being the number of miles north and west of a particular point (say, Little Bo Peep's sheepfold), we might find that

$$MilesNorth(here) = 49$$
$$MilesWest(here) = 472$$
$$MilesNorth(Babylon) = 91$$
$$MilesWest(Babylon) = 416$$
$$MilesNorth(Willie) = 49$$
$$MilesWest(Willie) = 416$$

Of course, a table can have many forms, and it's often a good idea to think about different ways of tabulating whatever information you have. Doing so very often makes obvious what you know, and even more obvious what you don't know.

Here's one way:

| Place | MilesNorth | MilesWest |
|-------|------------|-----------|
| here | 49 North, | 472 West |
| Babylon | 91 North, | 416 West |
| WeeWillie | 49 North, | 416 West |

All we've done is take the collection of names and, for each one, write down two coordinates. We can treat the positions as values:

$$MapPlace(here) = [49\ North, 472\ West]$$
$$MapPlace(Babylon) = [91\ North, 416\ West]$$
$$MapPlace(WeeWillie) = [49\ North, 416\ West]$$

Using the table, we can answer questions like "What is the North-South coordinate of Wee Willie's house?" and "What places are at 49 North?"

The set of all possible positions has become the set of all possible pairs [North-South,East-West]: the idea of position has been *decomposed* into a pair (a short sequence) of measurements. It could have been decomposed into other pairs of measurements (such as polar or elliptical coordinates), or even into more than a pair: if we were interested in the eye motion that reads the map, we would have to talk about the distance from the eye to a point on the map, the angle downwards from the eye to that point, and the angle turned left or right by the eye in looking.

Notice that changing the order of the rows makes no difference in the information they convey, so a table is a set rather than a sequence. On the other hand, if I happen to mix up the columns, I could be in big trouble: each row is a sequence, not a set.

Other tables could express the same information, such as

| 49N | 416W | *WeeWillie* | or even | 416/49/W |
|-----|------|-------------|---------|----------|
| 49N | 472W | *here*      |         | 16/91/B  |
| 91N | 416W | *Babylon*   |         | 472/49/h |

We don't even need a table that looks tabular. We just want to know about the way that names and coordinates are related, and the same information about the relation between names and coordinates is present in the "table"

$$\{[W, 49, 416], [h, 49, 472], [B, 91, 416]\}$$

as long as we remember which column means what.

The translation into the model consists of selecting the rows with the right place-names and then reporting the coordinates for each name: [49,472], [91,416], or [49,416]. That doesn't depend on the order of the rows:

$$\{[h, 49, 472], [B, 91, 416]\}$$

shows the same relationship between names and coordinates that you find in

$$\{[B, 91, 416], [h, 49, 472]\}.$$

Of course, looking things up is easier if the rows are in some order, such as alphabetical order, so we may want to represent the map with a table which we represent as an ordered sequence. For now, it doesn't matter. We just need to be able to give a precise description of the thing we want: the real-world question "How far west is Babylon"? is mapped homomorphically into "What are the contents of the third column, in the row whose first column contains 'B'?" This can be answered by a moron trained to read tables, even though he has no idea of what Babylon may be.

The distance in the model is the square root of $(49 - 91)**2 + (472 - 416)**2$, which just happens to be 70.

If we can translate into the model, and solve problems within it, all that's left is to translate the answer back. In this case, the translation from the model is totally trivial: it is the "identity function," which turns 70 (symbolic) miles into 70 (actual) miles.

### Exercise

**4.2-1**   Find the distances from here to Wee Willie Winkie's house and from Wee Willie's house to Babylon.

Notice that we still have an equation of the same form that we had before, viz.

$$RealDistance(x, y) = Scale * MapDistance(MapPlace(x), MapPlace(y))$$

but now the values of the particular expressions are given by

$$MapPlace(here) = [49, 472], MapDistance([3, 0], [0, 4]) = 5, Scale = 1$$

*MapPlace* is the function that looks things up in the model, and *MapDistance* is a calculation which finds the square root of the sum of squares of differences.

We should now extend our table of **TYPES**, **FUNCTIONS**, and so on, adding at least the functions

$$XCoord(x : MapPosition) : Distance$$
$$YCoord(x : MapPosition) : Distance$$

and perhaps also

$$XDiff(x : MapPosition, y : MapPosition) : Distance$$
$$YDiff(x : MapPosition, y : MapPosition) : Distance$$

To define them, we'll want assertions like

$$
\begin{aligned}
MapDistance(x, y) ** 2 &= XDiff(x, y) ** 2 + YDiff(x, y) ** 2 \\
XDiff(x, y) &= XCoord(x) - XCoord(y) \\
YDiff(x, y) &= YCoord(x) - YCoord(y)
\end{aligned}
$$

It would make sense to regard *XCoord* and *YCoord* as components of the points, so that each variable $p : MapPosition$ would really be comprised of two variables $p.x, p.y : Distance$. Then we would define $XCoord(a)$ as $a.x$. However, to put that into a specification amounts to a promise that Cartesian coordinates (rather than radial coordinates or something else) will be used, and it's too soon to promise that. All we need to do is specify the behavior of the functions.

### 4.2.1 A Table Can Have the Same Form
###        as a Picture

It's worth recapitulation: the table we've just been using is a "homomorphic image" of the pictorial map used first, precisely because of the law that determines *RealDistance* from the map constructions. The equation combines the rules for translation, solution, and retranslation, and as long as these work, we have the "same form."

There is more to it than that: the picture itself is just a table. This will be somewhat easier to see if we use yet another variation on the tables in which we looked up coordinates:

$$\{[W, 49, 416], [h, 49, 472], [B, 91, 416]\}$$

could also be written as a table for the *PlaceAt* function such that

$$
\begin{aligned}
PlaceAt(49, 416) &= W \\
PlaceAt(49, 472) &= h \\
PlaceAt(91, 416) &= B
\end{aligned}
$$

Let's write that as we might write a table for any other two-place function: an addition, subtraction or multiplication table, where $PlaceAt(x, y)$ is shown in row $x$ and column $y$. (See Figure 4.5.)

| PlaceAt: | 472W | 416W |
|----------|------|------|
| 91N      |      | B    |
| 49N      | h    | W    |

**Figure 4.5**  An Almost-Full Pictorial Table for *PlaceAt*

There is one blank space in there, because there is no *PlaceAt* $(91N, 472W)$ on this map. If we included more explicit positions, we we have the same *PlaceAt* function but more blanks. (See Figure 4.6.)

This is the original pictorial map, with North-South and East-West distances broken up into blocks 14 miles across. Nonetheless, it is the same conceptual structure, the same relation between names and numbers, as $\{[here, 49, 472], [WeeWillie, 49, 416], [Babylon, 91, 416]\}$.

Even though we have the same structure as before, the details are different and the amount of effort required is different. In programming, we will do a lot of this: find a problem solution by figuring out a model, and then usually work out other solutions by changing models. Usually (as now), we start with a model which is easy to think of, and then develop models which are easier to work with. Most of the time, we will think carefully about how much work each solution involves, but we're not really ready for that yet. (Maybe you are, but I'm not.) At the moment, it's quite enough to think casually about the geometric map as answering

| PlaceAt: | 500W | 486W | 472W | 458W | 444W | 430W | 416W | 402W | 388W |
|---|---|---|---|---|---|---|---|---|---|
| 105N | | | | | | | | | |
| 91N | | | | | | B | | | |
| 77N | | | | | | | | | |
| 63N | | | | | | | | | |
| 49N | | h | | | | W | | | |
| 35N | | | | | | | | | |
| 21N | | | | | | | | | |

**Figure 4.6** An Almost-Empty Pictorial Table for *PlaceAt*

the question by scanning up and down and back and forth across a page to find the names, and then using a ruler and then a multiplication. The second map, listing names and positions, answers the question by scanning down alphabetically to find the names, and then finding squares, a sum, and a square root. For a large map, the second is probably quicker because an alphabetical (binary) search is $\mathcal{O}(\log(N))$ for $N$ names.

Are there any better models for our purpose? Sure... well, maybe. Many road atlases have tables where each place (major city) appears as a label for a row, and also as a label for a column:

|  | Babylon | Here | Oz | Wonderland |
|---|---|---|---|---|
| *Babylon* | 0 | 70 | 492 | 5678 |
| *Here* | 70 | 0 | 450 | 5723 |
| *Oz* | 492 | 450 | 0 | 6187 |
| *Wonderland* | 5678 | 5723 | 6187 | 0 |

Here, each has an implicit position 1,2,3, or 4. *MapDistance* uses two positions, one as a row index, and one as a column index; the *Scale* is still 1, so no arithmetic is required. In effect, we are tabulating all of the measurements for

$$MapDistance(Babylon, Babylon) = 0$$
$$MapDistance(Babylon, Here) = 70$$
$$MapDistance(Oz, Wonderland) = 6187$$

and so on.

**Exercises**

**4.2-2**  Find the distances from here to Wonderland, from here to Oz, and from Oz to Wonderland.

**4.2-3**  Suppose I changed the distance from here to Wonderland on the map to 50, but left the distances from here to Oz and from Oz to Wonderland unchanged. What would be wrong?

This model is just marvelous for looking up distances between a few places, but if we had a large map, it would be very difficult to carry around. No arithmetic is needed at all, but a thousand places would require a thousand rows and a thousand columns. The time requirement is $\mathcal{O}(1)$, but space is $\mathcal{O}(n^2)$.

**Exercise**

**4.2-4**  Suppose that you can put 50 rows and 10 columns on a page. The second kind of map, using only three of the columns, will use just 20 pages for a thousand places. How many pages will be needed to construct the third kind of map for a thousand places?

We have gained some time, but used a lot of space to do it. That's very much worth remembering: a lot of programming effort is spent trading space for time or vice-versa.

Actually, this model does not need to be written in a square; if we think about different ways of tabulating the same data, we can easily come up with variants such as

| | | |
|---|---|---|
| *Babylon* | *Babylon* | 0 |
| *Babylon* | *Here* | 70 |
| *Babylon* | *Oz* | 492 |
| *Babylon* | *Wonderland* | 5678 |
| *Here* | *Babylon* | 70 |
| *Here* | *Here* | 0 |
| *Here* | *Oz* | 450 |
| ⋮ | ⋮ | ⋮ |

This version may make it easier to find entries, and perhaps to find compressed versions of the table such as:

| | | | |
|---|---|---|---|
| *Babylon* | — | *Here* | 70 |
| | | *Oz* | 492 |
| | | *Wonderland* | 5678 |
| *Here* | — | *Oz* | 450 |
| | | *Wonderland* | 5723 |
| *Oz* | — | *Wonderland* | 6187 |

## Exercises

**4.2-5**    Under the same assumptions as before, how many pages would you need for an extension of this table to include a thousand places?

**4.2-6**    State a rule by which you can look up distances in this last table, so that the person asking you will not know that you didn't look them up in the previous (expanded) table. The distance from here to here must be reported as 0, the distance from here to Babylon must be reported as 70, etc.

### 4.2.2  Different Styles of Map Have Different Roles

The maps we've considered have all carried the same kind of data, but in very different ways. They've all been tools for answering the question "What is the (straight-line) distance between A and B?" where A and B are names of places. Despite that basic similarity, they solve different problems. The pictorial map has the nice property that if the mapmaker puts a city in the wrong place it is likely to be obvious, because we can see at a glance how it relates to all the others. The position-table map doesn't have that property, but does have the nice property that we can look up names and then do some arithmetic to get our answers: no searches up and down the map, and no measurements. The distance-table map is not easily checked either, and doesn't even require arithmetic, but with 100 places we need 10,000 entries in the table; it's big.

## Exercise

**4.2-7**    For each of the three kinds of map just described, think of a situation in which it would be best and a situation in which it would be worst.

If it is only to be used for answering distance questions, a map does not need any other collections or relationships than those (e.g., *MapPlace*) we have been using. No matter what it is to be used for, a map does not need anything but sets, sequences, and relations; we can get a lot of mileage out of these ideas. It helps somewhat if we qualify our definitions; e.g., a region is not just any old set, but a set of places, and a relation is not just any old set, but a set of sequences such as $[Place, X, Y]$ all of which have the same length and same structure, so that it can just as well be viewed as a set of records $\{place = S, X = n, Y = m\}$ or $r.place, r.X, r.Y$. To avoid introducing completely new notation, we'll extend the old slightly and say that a region is a *Set(MapPosition)*, i.e., a set which can only contain objects which are *MapPosition*s. If you'd rather write *SetofMapPositions* as one long word, that's all right; just remember that if we take the union of a *SetOfMapPositions* with a *SetOfDoughnuts* we do end up with a set, but it isn't a set of *MapPosition*s or one of *Doughnut*s.

If we want to look up items in tables, we have to find some kinds of rules for defining the process and results. We'll try to deal with the concrete problem of *MapPlace*, given a particular place and a particular table. That means we'd better treat *MapPlace* as depending on both of these: it should be "*MapPlace*($x$ : *Place*, $y$ : *Table*) : *MapPosition*" rather than only depending on $x$. So we think about the table. Just exactly how do we look through it to find the one and only row labelled with x? First, we want to go through one row at a time, which implicitly means we have to treat the table as a sequence, even if we don't really care which row comes first. Now, a table is either empty (it's the sequence []) or it's not empty (it has a first row [a,b,c] and then the rest of the rows; in fact, it is $[a, b, c]@RestOfRows$). Can we cover both cases? If it is empty, then we're in trouble; there is no such place as $x$ here. If it is not empty, it does have a first row $[a, b, c]$ and the *RestOfRows*, so now we're worried about whether $a = x$ or not. If $a = x$, then we want to have $[b, c]$ as the *MapPlace*($x, t$). Otherwise, what can we do? We can forget about that first row, and look at the rest; we want *MapPlace*($x, RestOfRows$).

What we're saying is that

$$MapPlace(x, Table) \quad = \quad Hd([[b, c] : [a, b, c] \in Table])$$

There's no big deal: we've already learned how to handle this kind of situation. The answers come out easily:

$$MapPlace(here, [[here, 49, 416], [Babylon, 91, 472]]) \quad = \quad Hd([[49, 416]])$$
$$= \quad [49, 416]$$

On the other hand, $MapPlace(Chicago, [[here, 49, 416], [Babylon, 91, 472]])$ is undefined; it is $Hd([])$, and a friendly program will produce a helpful error message while an unfriendly one will blow up.

### 4.2.3 Interlude: Mathematical Notation Is Hard to Read

**Q:** Why do you write those horrible expressions like [0N0W,1N1W,1.414...]? Why not write "the distance from 0 North, 0 West to 1 North, 1 West is the square root of 2"?

**A:** Readability is great in English prose, but abbreviation is more important in most modeling. The English description is easier to understand, but the abbreviation is easier to work with: when we want to use the model to answer questions, an absolutely regular structure which has no wasted words at all will speed things up a lot. If you don't believe it, look at your registration choices for this semester. You probably have course schedules described with terms like MWF10:30–11:30, TR14:30–16, and so on. Try to imagine looking for scheduling conflicts in a schedule like this one: "On Monday, Wednesday, and Friday at 10:30, I go to Jabber Hall for introductory computer science. This lasts until 11:30. On Mondays and Wednesdays I go immediately to a lab and don't get lunch until 12:45, but on Fridays I lunch early because of the English composition course at 1PM." You would be able to read it much more easily, but you would need much more work to find things in it.

**Q:** Is there anything I can do to get used to it?

**A:** Yes. Always make sure that you can convert back and forth between words, formulas and diagrams. You'll find that you catch on better and catch mistakes faster. For example, the last "map," which was just a table for distances between four places will make more sense if you sketch a picture with Oz in the lower left corner, Wonderland in the upper right, and Here quite close on Babylon's left, ten times closer to Oz than to Wonderland. Of course, you could just as well make the sketch upside down or backwards; that won't change the distances.

## 4.3 FINDING PATHS IN SEGMENTED MAPS

**Q:** Those maps aren't realistic anyway: what I want to know is the distance by road to Babylon, not the straight-line distance. In looking on a road map, I could try to measure each little segment of road with a ruler, but more often I use maps which have numbers written between the places on the road. If you add up the numbers between the places, that's the distance.

**A:** Fine; let's start thinking about more realistic models. They'll bring in a lot of the basic ideas of specification. It's not very interesting if we have a segmented map with one segment that takes us straight to Babylon, so we'll suppose that the path is actually divided into segments. We have to get to Babylon by going through somewhere nearby; we have to bring Sumer into the problem.

"Sumer is ICumen in, Lhude Sing Cuccu."

*"Cuckoo Song"* [Anonymous, ca. 1250]

### 4.3.1 A Map Can Be Made with Road Segments

The kind of map that you're talking about has a collection of points and a collection of road segments. Each road segment connects two points, at some distance: "There is a road segment from Babylon to Sumer which covers a distance of 38 miles" is written $[Babylon, Sumer, 38]$.

| Start | End | Distance |
|---|---|---|
| Babylon | Sumer | 38 |
| Sumer | here | 32 |
| here | Dorothy'sHouseinKansas | 115 |
| Dorothy'sHouseinKansas | Foxville | 9 |
| Foxville | Dunkiton | 17 |
| Dunkiton | TruthPond | 83 |
| TruthPond | EmeraldCity | 226 |
| here | Jordan | 23 |
| Jordan | Babylon | 96 |

[I've added places from *The Road to Oz*, by L. Frank Baum.] This table, like all the others, can be expressed as a set of measurements, but here the measurements are measurements of road segments, which don't have names. We can invent arbitrary labels for them:

$$Start(s1) \;=\; Babylon; \quad End(s1) \;=\; Sumer; \quad Distance(s1) \;=\; 38;$$
$$Start(s2) \;=\; Sumer; \quad End(s2) \;=\; here; \quad Distance(s2) \;=\; 32;$$

and so on. Since we're really not interested in the individuality of the segments, a better way might be to cluster them like

$$Neighbors(Babylon) \;=\; \{[Sumer, 38], [Jordan, 96]\};$$
$$Neighbors(here) \;=\; \{[Sumer, 32], [Dorothy's, 115], [Jordan, 23]\},$$

and so on. To find the distance from here to Babylon, we can use an addition rule for distances:

> **if** the distance from $A$ to $B$ is $N$ miles,
>     **and** the distance from $B$ to $C$ is $M$ miles,
>     **then** the distance from $A$ to $C$ is $N + M$ miles.

Using that rule twice, with Sumer as midpoint, tells us that the distance from Babylon to here is 70 miles. (Try it.)

**Exercise**

**4.3-1**   How far is it from Foxville to the Emerald City?

That tells us that the distance from here to Babylon is 70 miles. Thus, the addition rule for distances is not always helpful; can you think why?

Consider what happens if we apply it with Jordan as midpoint: the distance from here to Babylon is now 119 miles! Neither 70 nor 119 is now the geometric as-the-crow-flies distance; which is the right answer? Worse yet, consider what happens if we apply it to $[Babylon, Sumer, 38]$ and $[Sumer, Babylon, 38]$. We get

> **if**  the distance from Babylon to Sumer is 38 miles,
> > **and**  the distance from Sumer to Babylon is 38 miles,
> > **then**  the distance from Babylon to Babylon is 76 miles.

The problem is that "distance" in the model is not uniquely defined: if there are many paths from Babylon to here, then there will be many possible distances. We have to be more careful about what we're saying: instead of geometric distance, we need to talk about distance along some particular path. In order to manage that, we need to talk about paths.

### 4.3.2  Paths Are Lists of Places

All right, what is a path? What is $[here, Sumer, Babylon]$? A path is a sequence of places, each of which is connected to the next (if any) by a road segment. The examples just given fit that description, and so do the "empty" paths $[here]$, $[Babylon]$, and $[Dorothy's house]$. Any single road segment also indicates a path: $[here, Sumer]$, $[Sumer, Babylon]$, and so on are certainly paths. Also, the path $[here, Sumer]$ can be joined with the path $[Sumer, Babylon]$ to create a path $[here, Sumer, Babylon]$ which can be joined with the path $[Sumer, here]$ to create a path $[Sumer, here, Sumer, Babylon]$. Thinking about it, we get Figure 4.7.

**Exercises**

**4.3-2**   Fill in some more general assertions, just for practice. (Think about distances.)

**4.3-3**   Invent another useful function.

There's one strange thing about the functions "@" and "+" considered as functions on paths: they don't always work. In principle, there's nothing new about the fact that $Join([here, Sumer], [here, Sumer])$ is meaningless; after all, we found with the cardinal numbers that $3 - 5$ was meaningless too. Still, it looks more upsetting here, because $Join$ is our basic tool for constructing paths. Functions like these are called *partial* functions, because they're not defined in all circumstances. Think

TYPES                    $Place = \{here, Sumer, Babylon, \ldots\};$   —Actually, it doesn't matter.
                         $Path = Sequence(Places);$
CONSTANTS                —None; the empty sequence [] is not a path at all.
FUNCTIONS                $Connected(x : Place, y : Place) : Boolean;$

                         — This is $True$, if a segment connects $x$ and $y$.
                         $EmptyPath(x : Place) : Path;$
                         —For each place $x$, the path $[x]$ goes to itself.
                         $"@"(x : Place, S : Path) : Path;$
                         —For each path S and place x,
                             – **if** $Connected(x, S[1])$ **then** $x@S$ is a path.
                         $Join(A : Path, B : Path) : Path;$
                         —Assuming $A$ ends where $B$ begins produces the path
                         —from $A$'s beginning to $B$'s end.
                         $IsPath(A : Sequence(Place)) : Boolean;$
                         — $True$ if $A$ is a path, $False$ otherwise.
                         $Neighbors(A : Place) : Set(Place);$
                         —Value is $\{B : IsPath(A, B)\}$.
ASSERTIONS               $Connected(here, Sumer) = True;$

                         $Connected(here, Babylon) = False;$
                         $EmptyPath(here) = [here];$
                         $here@[Sumer, Babylon] = [here, Sumer, Babylon];$
                         $Join([here, Sumer], [Sumer, Babylon]) = [here, Sumer, Babylon]$

**Figure 4.7** Objects and Operations for Paths

of *Join* as being a procedure to be carried out without using any intelligence; what should happen when it is used on $[here, Sumer]$ and $[hither, yon]$ as arguments? The usual answers are

a. Blow up: tell the user of the program that something has gone wrong. This is pretty safe, but not always helpful. If *Join* is a program in a module which is used by a program in a module which is used by a program which interacts with unsophisticated users, it's hopeless.

b. Produce some special value which is recognizably not a path, such as "[]". Then other parts of the program can be redefined to deal intelligently with the nonpath. This is potentially very helpful, but it's rather tiresome.

c. Produce one of the arguments unchanged as the result; in this case you might say that

$$Join([here, Sumer], [hither, yon]) = [here, Sumer].$$

This doesn't work in all situations, but if you're building up a path with *Join* it's a pretty good idea: add what you can, don't change anything when you try to add something and can't.

d. Redefine the problem: tell yourself that *Join* isn't really what you wanted anyhow, because it's ill-defined. Change the specification so that it is based on some similar but nicer function such as

$$Joins(AA, BB) = \{A + Tl(B) : A \in AA, B \in BB, Last(A) = Hd(B)\}$$

Given this kind of a definition, you could redefine *Join* as

$$Join(A, B) = X : X \in Joins(\{A\}, \{B\})$$

and then be faced again with options a–c if there is no such $X$, but in most problems you'll simply avoid the issue by using *Joins*.

### Exercise

**4.3-4**    Think of specific examples where each of the four approaches is (a) a good idea; (b) a bad idea. [Don't just think about *Join* or "$-$".]

How can we think about the set of possible paths from here to Babylon? Can we phrase that precisely? The set of all paths $[p_1, p_2, \ldots p_N]$ which take us from here to Babylon is

$$\{p_{1, \ldots N} : p_1 = here, p_N = Babylon, IsPath(p)\}$$

Look at the notation for a moment. The time will come when you can say "I've seen lots of definitions of that general form, and implemented them too. I can start building paths forward from 'here' or backwards from 'Babylon' or inwards from both or outwards from every point in the map all at once, and the outline of the program will come right from that definition."

### 4.3.3 An Exploration Is a Sequence of Sets
### of Sequences of Places

First, let's just think about the paths from here. There is the empty path [*here*]; then we have the one-segment paths [*here, Sumer*], [*here, Dorothy's house*], and [*here, Jordan*]; then we have the two-segment paths [*here, Sumer, Babylon*], [*here, Sumer, here*], [*here, Dorothy's house, Foxville*], [*here, Jordan, Babylon*], and so on. In other words, for each place $P$ and each length $N$, we can find all the paths which go $N$ segments out from $P$. This gives us a sequence of sets of sequences; the distance we want is the distance of one of the paths. (You might prefer to say, in English, that it is the "length" of one of the paths, but remember that we are using the word "length" as a count of the number of items in a sequence. It would be very confusing to say that $Length([here, Sumer])$ was both 2 and 38.

$$PathsFrom(P, 0) = \{[P]\}$$
$$PathsFrom(P, i+1) = \{S + [Q] : Q \in Neighbors(Last(S))\}$$

where

$$Last(X_{1...N}) = X_N$$

## Exercise

**4.3-5**   List all the two-segment paths from Dorothy's house.

Notice that $PathsFrom$ works by $AddToBack$, not "@", because we're adding the new place to the end of the sequence, not the front. If that were a problem, we could work backwards from Babylon with the assertion

$$PathsFrom(P, i+1) = \{P@S : S \in PathsFrom(S_1, i), P \in Neighbors(S_1)\}$$

**Q:** What kind of a definition is that? You've used $PathsFrom(S_1, \ldots)$, in defining $S$, so how could you compute $S$?

**A:** Actually, you'd have to compute all possible paths which happen to have $i$ segments. That's possible, but likely to be expensive; we'll talk more about it later. Part of the trouble is that we're using a definition of $PathsFrom$ a starting point to compute the $PathsTo$ a goal. It's tidier to define

$$PathsTo(X, N) = \{S : S \in PathsFrom(S_1, N), Last(S) = X\}$$

Now we can say

$$PathsTo(B, 0) = \{[B]\};$$
$$PathsTo(B, i+1) = \{P@S : S \in PathsTo(B, i), P \in Neighbors(S_1)\}$$

## Exercise

**4.3-6**   List all the two-segment paths to Babylon.

All right, what exactly do we mean by distance? How about "The distance of a path is the sum of the distances of the road segments on it"? Notice that the distance of any empty path is 0, since it has no road segments. Notice also that

**if** $A$ and $B$ are connected by a path of distance $N$,

**and**   $B$ and $C$ are connected by a path of distance $M$,
**then**   $A$ and $C$ are connected by a path of distance $N + M$.

Now we can define the distance between two points: it's the least possible distance of a path which connects them. This may seem like a lot of work to go through, just to say what we mean by distance. The trouble was that we had a rather fuzzy notion of what distance was, and had to make it (fairly) precise before we could finish the problem. Now, how do we describe finding the distance to Babylon? It's simple to do, but describing it is not really a very easy problem in a fairly realistic model like this one.

The simplest approach is to look over the sequence of sets of paths which was described before. How can we do that? List the paths as they would traverse them:

$[here]$ :      $distance = 0$
************

Now we extend the path to make a set of one-segment paths:

$[here, Sumer]$ :      $distance = 32$
$[here, Dorothy'sHouse]$ :      $distance = 115$
$[here, Jordan]$ :      $distance = 23$
************

Now we extend each path in the set, and combine all the resulting sets of two-segment paths:

$[here, Sumer, Babylon]$ :      $distance = 70$
$[here, Sumer, here]$ :      $distance = 64$
$[here, Dorothy'sHouse, Foxville]$ :      $distance = 124$
$[here, Dorothy'sHouse, here]$ :      $distance = 230$
$[here, Jordan, Babylon]$ :      $distance = 119$
$[here, Jordan, here]$ :      $distance = 46$
************

Now we have two solution paths, and the shorter one is of distance 70.

The paths of distances 124, 230, and 119 may lead us to Babylon, but not in less than 70 miles because they have already used more than that. A path of distance 64 or 46 might lead us to Babylon in less than 70 miles, but we are safe in ignoring those particular paths because each of them visits the same point twice, and

**No path that visits any point twice can be a shortest path.**

(We will prove that, much later.)

**Exercises**

**4.3-7**   Write recursive equations for constructing this sequence.

**4.3-8**   When will this approach fail to find the shortest path? [Hint: What if there were a rest stop halfway to Sumer?]

**4.3-9**   Follow up the previous exercise by suggesting a safer approach.

Even apart from defects in the approach, our model is still not perfect. For example, suppose we had two different road segments

$$[here, Sumer, 38]$$
$$[here, Sumer, 29]$$

That is not an uncommon situation in the real world, and yet our definition of path does not allow us to talk about it: there is no way we can tell whether $[here, Sumer]$ is a 38-mile road around the swamp or a 29-mile road through it. Any question we can translate into the model will be answered within it "homomorphically," but questions about dirt roads vs. yellow brick, questions about wicked witches and enchanted forests, and any other questions about things we left out of the map have been lost.

It is time to think about the maps we've seen.

### 4.3.4  There Are Two Kinds of Maps

In the first map we considered, *MapDistance* was determined by a rule which represents an implicit structure: the structure of Euclidean geometry. The role of *MapPlace* was to translate the distance problem into that abstract mathematical model. This is an *analogy* map; it doesn't require much of a data base, just a bunch of independent (position) measurements and formulas for connecting them. If one position was measured incorrectly then all distances to it will be incorrect, but since the rule carries us directly from one place to another, that error will not affect other pairs of cities (and therefore natural rules about summations of distances can be used fairly easily to check the correctness of the measurements.)

In the second map, *MapDistance* was determined by an explicit problem structure: the recorded distances (and endpoints) of road segments. Almost all of the inferences we want to make about the tabulated map will involve several segments, so it's much harder to figure out where the mistake was.

**Q:** Don't you mean "where the mistake was, *if* there was one"?
**A:** You're still an optimist. Sorry, I meant what I said.

In programming, we often try to find models of the first kind, because they're usually easier to understand, use, and check. Unfortunately, many real problems are defined by complex collections of information, and all we can do is try to keep track of the most important parts. Trying to keep track of it all is not usually a good idea.

### 4.3.5  Bigger and Better Maps Are Usually Worse

Once upon a time[2] there was a country renowned for the excellence of its map-makers. They began with ordinary maps, including a few features of the landscape, where one inch of map might represent many miles of territory. Then they included more detail: one inch for each mile. That was good, but not quite good enough: they went to larger and larger scale maps, until they reached an inch for each yard... an inch for each foot... and finally, an inch for each inch. Their map of their country was a marvel to behold, omitting no detail at all. Unfortunately, whenever it was spread out for examination, farmers complained that it shut out the light. Eventually they found a compromise: they could use the countryside for its own map, and that did nearly as well. This goes to show that

> An absolutely perfect model is worse than none at all.

or

> Model building is the art of choosing what to exclude.

### Exercises

**4.3-10** Very detailed maps have other problems. Explain why they can be a) hard to keep correct, and b) hard to use.

**4.3-11** When would you want one map to include both

- city locations and highways
- population densities and altitude
- precipitation and principal-crop information?

**4.3-12** Why might you avoid a map with all of these together?

**4.3-13** Identify the Carroll and Borges stories mentioned here (Alice is not a character in either). This may take longer than the other exercises here, but it may also be more valuable.

---

[2]In a story by Lewis Carroll, and another by Jorge Luis Borges.

# 5

# Models, Things, and Time

A model—a map, a globe, a blueprint, a pilot plant, a toy truck, a formula, a prototype—is a scaled-down representation of some part or aspect of the world. You're going to spend a lot of time thinking about models, including all the time you spend thinking about programs (because that's what programs are), and also including all the time you think about science, mathematics, art, history, and a few other things.

This chapter is an attempt to make you develop a model of modeling: why are models, and what should we know about them? Sometimes you come to surprising conclusions: the best model may not be the most accurate. Sometimes you come to depressingly obvious conclusions: carelessness with models can be expensive. Sometimes you can easily get confused, especially when we talk about ideas like models of models. Mostly, however, this chapter should be saying things for you that you were almost ready to say for yourself.

Throughout the chapter, we will introduce simple ideas about models by using them. How are they used to answer questions? How they are designed to make such use reasonably easy? Here we will work on the kind of models used in science and business. We will not get very far with the models, but we will introduce some fundamental ideas of three basic kinds of model: small-number, large-number, and medium-number. We will also continue with the ideas of sets, relations, sequences, functions, and homomorphisms.

## 5.1 SCIENCE IS MODEL-BUILDING

A scientific theory (like Einstein's theory of relativity, Newton's theory of gravitation, Boltzmann's theory of statistical thermodynamics, or Darwin's theory of evolution) is often more dynamic and much harder to put into a picture than an ordinary map is, but it is still an exercise in condensation: when Newton talks about a body (yours) in gravitational terms, he forgets about your size, your I.Q., your shape, your age, and your political affiliation and pretends that you have only mass and location (at a single point). You may be attracted to people with your tastes in Mexican food or elephant jokes, but these attractions are totally irrelevant to the gravitational attraction, which depends only on your masses and on the distance between you. In order to calculate the motion of bodies in the solar system, Newton further decided to forget about almost all of them (the asteroids, meteorites, and moons) entirely, concentrating on mass and location for just the Sun and the planets. Finally, he decided to calculate the orbit for each planet as though there were no others. The amount of detail which is left out of the theory is enormous—almost as much as the amount of detail left out of a spreadsheet model of a business.

The value of the model (theory) depends on the condensation of work which it makes possible. With Newtonian mechanics, we can predict where the planets are going to be observed or how long a pendulum will need for each swing; we learn to expect that a long bullet will go further than a short one (other things being equal) and that a lead bullet will go further than a plastic one. A spreadsheet model of a business helps us predict the consequences of strictly financial decisions. Darwinian evolutionary theory leads us to expect to find fossils which could be ancestors of now-disparate species; to expect to find islands with groups of species like the Galapagos finches, which are obviously finches except that some act like woodpeckers and others like other birds; to expect to find that inheritance works by distinct "genes" rather than by blending traits; to find that inheritance isn't perfect, but sometimes involves mutations which themselves can be inherited. Boltzmann's treatment of thermodynamics does lead to new predictions, but a major factor is that it makes the old predictions make sense in a world model of atoms when they had been designed in a world model of continuous fluids.

### 5.1.1 The "Right" Way to Work with Models
### Depends on Model Size

Almost all models can be divided into three kinds: small and simple, huge and simple, and medium-sized and complex. In small, simple models (like Newton's model of gravitation), we pretend that there are only a few things going on and it is possible (with great effort and cleverness) to keep track of them all. The main conceptual tool we need is a thorough understanding of the rules governing those few things, and for physical models this is mostly given by calculus. In huge, simple models (like the atomic theory of gases) we know that enormous numbers of things are going on, and we pretend that they will all average out somehow. (The more

enormous the number, the closer this is to being true.) The main conceptual tool
we need is a thorough understanding of when and how large collections can be said
to average out; this is provided by statistics. In medium-sized, complex systems, we
spend most of our time actually keeping track of large numbers of combinations of
factors, and figuring out which depend upon what. The main conceptual tool is a
thorough understanding of the rules of forming combinations, and this is provided
by discrete mathematics. Computers and computer programs are medium-sized,
complex systems. (So are businesses, organisms, molecules, and ecological systems.)

### 5.1.2 The Importance of Modeling Depends
###         on Problem Size

Once upon a time, an engineer started a large project without any models at all:
no blueprints, no scaled-down construction, no preliminary planning, nothing.

**Exercise**

**5.1-1**   Select a project (jet airplane, bridge, rocket, computer, building, or whatever you
please). Try to finish this story without making worse nonsense than the "perfect"
map of Carroll's story; I can't.

Once upon a time, a couple of kids put a dam across a stream without any
models at all: no blueprints, no scaled-down construction, no preliminary planning,
nothing. They had no real problems, no delays, and the dam was big enough for
both of them to sit on by the time they got hungry. It was useful, too: the pond
wasn't big enough for swimming, but it was big enough to cool off in, and an hour's
work with shovels brought runoff water from the pond to a garden.

**Exercise**

**5.1-2**   Why did it work? What made the project feasible without any explicit modeling?
[Warning: It's not quite as simple as it probably looks; there are several important
differences between the examples. Is it really true that they had no models?]

Once upon a time, a mechanic built a washing machine without any models at
all: no blueprints, no scaled-down constructions, no preliminary planning, nothing.
On the first try, the motor didn't quite fit the cavity provided for it; on the second,
the hose turned out to be smaller than the pipe he meant to go inside it; on the
third, everything worked fine and did the family laundry forever after.

**Exercise**

**5.1-3**   Could you do that? How much experience with washing machines do you think the mechanic must have had? Why? Is it true that he had no models at all?

### 5.1.3  Models Are Always Wrong

The earth is not flat, and flat maps are (somewhat) wrong; a triangle drawn on the earth will have interior angles whose sum is greater than 180 degrees. (For example, if you pick two points on the Equator about 6,000 miles apart, and draw *long* lines to connect them with each other and with the North Pole, you have an equilateral triangle whose interior angles add up to 270 degrees.) Newtonian mechanics is similarly wrong, and we have to view it as an approximation (in one way) to quantum mechanics, but as an approximation (in another way) to general relativity. Either way, problem solutions found with Newtonian mechanics will never be perfectly correct. Basically, a model is useful because it leaves something out, but if it leaves anything out, then it's not the same as the original.

**Exercise**

**5.1-4**   What are the major characteristics that are left out of a toy truck (as a model for a real truck)?

No matter what you're trying to think about, you can't think about all of it at once: you have to simplify somehow, which means you have to find or make something which is like it, but easier to work with. In trying to prepare these notes, I have to write an outline first; the outline is like the notes, but simpler. In trying to drive to a city I haven't visited lately, I use a map; the map is like the countryside, but simpler. In planning a program, I often make diagrams which are somehow like the program, but simpler. Even when I'm just throwing a ball, I have some kind of an image of it which is much simpler than the ball itself: I am aware of its size and weight and texture, but certainly not of its molecular constituency. If I tried to think about the full complexity of the ball's structure, the lifetime of the universe would be far too short to finish all the calculations involved in tossing it to my sons or daughter.

Basically, in order to understand anything, we think about something else which is like it but "simpler" because we think we understand it already. This "simpler" thing is a model.

Of course, simplicity is very much in the eye of the beholder. We sometimes speak of what a program "knows" or "plans" or "wants," and that means we are using a human as a model for understanding the program. On the other hand, almost every program is a model for human behavior.

**Q:** I know that some people try to write programs which will be models of human behavior, but I've written some programs and they certainly weren't any kind of model for anything but themselves. They were just plain ordinary programs.

**A:** When you write a program to do something, you generally already know how to do that something yourself, right?

**Q:** Not always. I just start out coding.

**A:** By the end of this course, we'll have done a lot of work devoted mainly to curing you of that. It is true that you can just start writing code and seeing what happens, tinkering with it until it does something interesting; you then have a program which you don't understand and which probably doesn't do much, or do it reliably.

The basic idea of this course is that the way to write a computer program is to write a people program first, and make sure it works; then put it into whatever computer language is appropriate for the computer to be able to simulate you solving the problem. (After that, you write another people program which is a little closer to what you really wanted, and make sure it works; then put it into computer talk. After that, you write another people program... and so on.) Generally speaking, it's a lot simpler to teach a human to do something than to tell a computer how to do it; we use computers because they can do it faster and cheaper, without making careless errors.

### 5.1.4 In Search of the Elephant's Ballroom

In order to develop an understanding of the different kinds of models and of the mathematical rules which govern them, we are going to consider three elephantine examples, selected (or rather constructed) to typify three basically different styles of modeling. First, we will think about models for one elephant sliding down-hill over wet grass on a particularly rainy African afternoon. These models are governed by "small-number" laws and lead us toward calculus. Second, we will think (in somewhat less detail) about models for elephant life-insurance policies. These models are governed by "large-number" laws and lead us toward statistics. Third, we will think (in much less detail) about the celebrated elephant's square dance, with eight pachyderms and a banyan tree for each square. These models are governed by "medium-number" laws, which usually turn out to be variants of Murphy's Law; they will lead us toward discrete mathematics, the dominant conceptual tool for computer science.

## 5.2 THE ELEPHANT'S SLIDING BOARD

Our problem is to understand the motion of "one elephant sliding downhill over wet grass on a particularly rainy African afternoon." Is that a well-defined problem? Not really. It does tell us that we are not supposed to understand why the elephant likes to slide or how soon the grass will recover, but it doesn't really tell us what questions will be translated into our model. "Understanding" may be what we really want, but it doesn't define a problem. Let's be more precise: we want to be able to predict where the elephant will be at particular times, perhaps so that we can set up automatic movie cameras to photograph him from several angles; this is one home movie that won't bore anybody. We may also want to predict when he will be at particular places, so that we can set up still cameras to catch the best shots.

### 5.2.1  A Sketch in Time Saves Ninety

What does a model look like? Well, the first model might look like a very crude sketch of an elephant sliding down a hill. That's the structure of the problem: it shows us the shape of the hill and suggests strongly that we'd better not need to think much about the shape of the elephant. Another sketchy map will indicate the structure of the solution, the changing altitude of the elephant as time goes on: how far down the hill is he? If these maps (in Figure 5.1) were perfect, we could use them to tell almost what we want to know.   Of course, that sketch is not perfect,

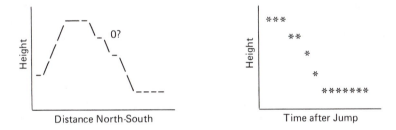

**Figure 5.1** State-Space Sketches

but it does focus our attention on the shape of the problem: we want to know how far down the elephant is at a given time, and we want to know at what time he will reach a given height. We know that he speeds up as he goes along, and then stops at the bottom.

Is that right? Will that let us focus our cameras? Does he *really* stop at the bottom? No: he no longer goes down, but he will keep moving out from the base of the hill. We were asking the wrong question: measuring the height throws away too much information, but we can use either distance north-south or distance along the grass. Either will give us a curve much like the height-time curve, except that it will slow down gradually before stopping. Errors like that are easy to fix when we just find that we've done the wrong sketches, but harder if we start working on a model which turns out to answer the wrong questions, and worst of all if we write, test, debug, and proudly present (to an instructor or employer) the wrong program.

Thinking about that, we make a better sketch, using total distance along the grass; it goes in Figure 5.2.

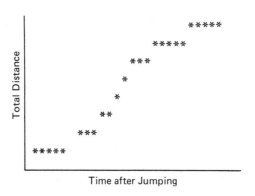

**Figure 5.2** The Elephant's Sliding Distance

This sketch tells the story of an elephant's slow start, speeding up as he slides down the hill, and then beginning to slow down again after he reaches the bottom.

### 5.2.2  Mapping a State-Space

It's obviously not enough to make a map of the hill. What we need is a map of the "state" the elephant is in—not Arkansas vs. Alabama or Oz vs. the Land of Nod, but his current status: how far up the hill he is, how far north-south and east-west, how happy he feels, the time, his weight, whether he is right-side up, how fast he is going, whether he is speeding up or slowing down, and so on.

The diagram we just drew is a map in which the dimensions are $TotalDistance$ and $Time$ rather than distance north-south and east-west; trajectory is described by his path in this map. It is an oversimplification of a "state-space" map which would include all of the dimensions of the problem.

### Exercise

**5.2-1**   List all of the dimensions of that problem.   [Hint: Take a year off to do this exercise.]

What are the important dimensions? Think about how we might get the elephant to go faster or slower: we could speed things up by making the hill steeper or wetter, we could slow things down by making the elephant's hide rougher, we might change things in either direction by making the elephant heavier or by changing the amount of elephant hide in contact with the grass. Why would these work? Because what makes the elephant go faster is the force of gravity pushing him down the hill, and what makes him go slower is the friction of his skin against the grass.

**Q:** When is a dimension (i.e., a possible measurement) important?
**A:** Whenever it will help us to distinguish between states which lead to different answers to the questions we want to ask. As an observer, you don't usually

want to measure dimensions which you could either (a) determine from the things you are observing, or (b) ignore without hurting your ability to answer questions.

Remember, to choose your dimensions is to decompose the state, asserting that its description can be broken down into some particular set of measurements. If I decompose the state into height and east-west distance when the elephant is sliding from north to south, that's a bad decomposition: I'm observing something irrelevant, and my observations won't help me determine where he is when his slide flattens at the bottom of the hill. If I decompose the state into his pulse rate, temperature, carbon-dioxide level at the base of the brain, and time, then I may learn a lot but not the answers to my questions.

If you know that the elephant's altitude (and latitude and longitude) can be determined from the single dimension of total distance along the grass, and that the adrenaline level in his earlobe will not help determine his position at various times, then it makes sense to include the former and exclude the latter.

In working on physical problems, we usually pay attention to position (space and time), to the rate of change of position (velocity), and to the rate of change of velocity (acceleration); we often can avoid thinking about the rate of change of acceleration because of Newton: the acceleration itself, at any given moment, is the force at that moment divided by the mass. Understanding the problem becomes a matter of understanding the forces.

After a great deal more thought like this, we will end up reducing our elephant to a physical model in which we slide a simple block down a ramp, or a mathematical model in which we consider the mass $M$ of the block, the angle $A$ of the ramp, and the "coefficient of friction" $C$ between block and ramp. The motion of the elephant depends upon gravity and friction. The gravitational force seems to depend upon $M$ and $A$, because even without friction we would get no acceleration if there were no slope. The frictional force seems to depend upon $M$ and $C$.

Is that true? Can we vary gravitational force by varying $C$? No. Can we vary the friction by varying $A$? Yes: there will be no friction at all if the elephant is falling off a cliff. Really, then, the frictional force depends on $M$, $C$, and $A$. Are there any other dependencies? Notice that $M$, $C$, and $A$ are constants (until the elephant reaches the bottom of the hill). The gravitational pull on the elephant does not change with time, but the frictional force does: there's no friction if you don't move. Frictional force depends upon velocity, which changes with time due to acceleration, which comes from combining the two forces.

The state-space, then, is a set of states, but a state (or "place") is more complicated than it was on a static map: just as we once described a *MapPlace* by a pair of measurements like $[49N, 416W]$, we now describe an *ElephantSituation* by nine measurements: the state-space is a set of tuples [*Mass, Coefficientoffriction, Angle, Time, Distance, Velocity, Acceleration, Gravforce, Fricforce*], and the elephant travels through that state-space on a path determined by the laws of physics. We don't need to draw all of those things, but we do need to keep track of them all. When we draw a "subspace" which has only a few dimensions, we must remember that it is not a complete map. It is not fair to ask if there is a "road segment" connecting points like {*distance=35, time=47*} with {*distance=38, time=48*} unless you know the other coordinates; the answer depends upon them.

To finish building the model, we would need an elementary knowledge of physics, which is not intended as a prerequisite for this course. If you happen to have that knowledge, then I suggest that you finish the model yourself. If not, read on: you will be reading equations which you are not yet able to write, but you should still be able to draw graphs of them and see how they relate to the original problem.

### 5.2.3 Small-Number Models Can Be
###        Sets of Equations

At this point, we should express the model as a set of equations, defining the state of the problem, i.e. defining the total distance, velocity, acceleration, and both forces as functions of time. For example, the total distance at a particular time is equal to the total distance at the "previous instant" (a very, very short time before) plus the distance covered in between (a very, very small distance, dependent on the velocity at that previous instant). If this were an elementary calculus course, we could then try to solve those equations. Since this is an elementary programming course, we'll take an approach which would lead toward a program.

The solution is going to be a *path* through a state-space: a sequence of states, each of which is connected to the next (by an equation rather than by a stored road segment). Of course, a path is really a continuous curve with an infinite number of points, but you should be used to the idea of drawing many points and then connecting them. Our idea is to plot graphs for each of the changing items as time goes on. We will just draw points at small intervals of time, defining the elephant's state at one moment after another. Therefore, we find the *TotalDistance, Velocity, Acceleration,* etc., for *Time*=0, then for *Time*=1, then for *Time*=2, and so on until the elephant stops sliding or we get bored.

It would be safer to explicitly list the types *Time, Distance, Speed, Angle,* and so forth, but for the moment we will just deal with these as numbers and define the elephant's state at the start, and then at each moment as a function of his state during the previous moment.

At the beginning of the elephant's adventure, he has covered no distance, and is moving at zero velocity. So

$$TotalDistance(0) = Velocity(0) = 0$$

After that, his distance increases with each time step, just as shown in Figure 5.2, until he stops; and his velocity will increase and then decrease, constantly changed by the acceleration, so that

$$\begin{aligned} TotalDistance(t+1) &= TotalDistance(t) + Velocity(t) \\ Velocity(t+1) &= Velocity(t) + Acceleration(t) \end{aligned}$$

The acceleration at any time is generated by the opposing forces of gravity (forward) and friction (back):

$$Acceleration(t) = (GravForce(t) - FricForce(t))/M$$

Until the elephant gets to the end of the slope, the gravitational force pulling him downhill is proportional to the mass and to some function of the angle, which turns out to be the sine. [No, you will not be tested on trigonometry in this course, and you don't really need to know what a sine is except that it's obviously some function of the angle (and it's important enough to be included in most programming languages), but how are you going to figure out how to photograph the next elephant slide you see unless you learn some trigonometry?]

$$\begin{aligned} GravForce(t) \quad &= \quad 0, \qquad\qquad\qquad\qquad\qquad\qquad \text{if } DoneSlope \\ &= \quad GravityConstant * M * sin(A), \quad \text{otherwise} \end{aligned}$$

where

$$DoneSlope \quad = \quad TotalDistance(t) > SlopeLength$$

The frictional force is proportional to the "roughness" of the elephant hide and to the mass pushing that hide downwards, as well as to the velocity pushing hide past grass:

$$\begin{aligned} FricForce(t) \quad &= \quad M * C * Velocity(t), \qquad\qquad \text{if } DoneSlope \\ &= \quad M * C * Velocity(t) * cos(A), \quad \text{otherwise} \end{aligned}$$

(The *cos*ine, like the *sin*e, is a magical function of the angle.)

### Exercises

**5.2-2**  Now you can graph the model, supposing that $M$ is 100, $C$ is 1, *GravityConstant* is 1, *SlopeLength* is 100, and $sin(A)$ and $cos(A)$ are both 0.7.

**5.2-3**  Graph it again, supposing that $C$ is 2.

**5.2-4**  State and justify some of the algebraic properties of these functions.

Like the first map of the distance to Babylon, this problem solution consists of omitting all but a few factors so that we can then use some rather subtle mathematical ideas to calculate an answer. If the hillside's irregularity is confusing, then we simplify by pretending that it's smooth. If the elephant's shape is too complex to handle, we pretend that it's just a simple block. Such ideas led to great successes in physics over the last few centuries: there are many physical systems which behave approximately as if they were simple.

Most of the successes have depended on clever use of mathematical ideas rather than simply drawing graphs of functions. It might be possible to find a simple formula which represents *TotalDistance* as a function of time by carefully analyzing the equations. Nonetheless, computers have extended these successes by making it possible to draw graphs of more complex functions. You might find that the slope changed as the elephant went down, or that the elephant would start to roll if friction was strong enough. That would probably make it impossible to find a simple formula which solves the problem, and the calculations for graphing a solution might be too tedious for a human, but computers (the electronic kind, at least) don't care much about simple formulas and they don't get bored by tedious calculations.

## 5.3 THE ELEPHANT'S LIFE INSURANCE

You have just been called in as a consultant by an insurance company, which has been asked to write a life-insurance policy for the world's largest acrobatic elephant, Jumpo. You are supposed to determine Jumpo's probable lifespan: if he is likely to die soon, the premiums will have to be very high to make his policy a good risk. They understand that you cannot predict his exact death date, but they want to know how likely it is that they will have to pay off the policy in one year, two years,..., or 100 years.

### 5.3.1 Model Designs Need Pictures

Being a good modeler, you quickly sketch some possible curves into Figure 5.3.   If

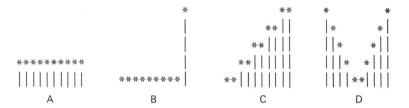

**Figure 5.3** Elephantine Death Rates

you are plotting probability of death against time, then curve A might represent Jumpo's having a 10 percent chance of death in any given year; curve B suggests that he is definitely not going to die until some particular year (say, age 107); curve C is a compromise, suggesting that his probability of death rises steadily as he gets older and weaker; and curve D suggests that he may die early, perhaps from accidents while learning to work on a trapeze, or he may die from illness or accident as he gets older, but his probability of death in mid-career is lower than it will be at the beginning or the end.

Now what? After you do anything, always, the next thing is to try to find what mistakes you could have made so far. There is at least one: we haven't been careful about what is meant by "probability of death." Philosophically speaking, nobody knows what probability is, but in practice we can say that the insurance company wants to know what would happen if it had 10,000 policies like this. With this idea, curve A could mean either of two things: 10,000 in the first year, 9,000 in the second, 8,000 in the third, 7,000 in the fourth, and so on; or else 10,000 in the first year, 9,000 in the second, 8,100 in the third, 7,190 in the fourth, and so on. In the first interpretation, 10 percent of all the original elephants die each year, so that they are all dead after 10 years, but in the second interpretation we have 10 percent of all the remaining elephants dying each year, so that after 10 years there are still some left. These are very different models, with very different results in company profitability.

### THE ROAD TO BANKRUPTCY IS PAVED
### WITH FUZZY THOUGHTS.

It is perfectly fine to begin a model with fuzzy notions, but you must eventually interpret it in terms of real quantities.

### Exercise

**5.3-1**  Figure out exactly how many elephants out of 10,000 are left after 10 years, in the second interpretation.

## 5.3.2 You Can't Keep Track of Everything

Now that you've decided what you're talking about, you realize that you can't possibly write a set of equations that gives a precise answer to the question "How many elephants are left after $N$ years?" In the analogy with physics, we don't know what the forces are; we don't know how many dimensions there should really be to the state-space. We might argue that Jumpo's probability of death at any given moment has a lot to do with his age, his pulse and blood pressure, exposure to diseases, acrobatic risk taking, exposure to cigarette smoke, risks of accidents while being driven from one circus to another, frequency of bathing, nutritional and medical care, and the degree to which he feels loved by his keeper, but it's very hard to measure some of these, and it seems impossible to measure the importance of any of them.

## 5.3.3 Sometimes Knowledge Can Substitute
##        for Understanding

Simulating 10,000 acrobatic elephants looks tough. That's all right: insurance companies don't study things that way in any case. They'd rather keep track of a bunch of elephants (say, 10,000), wait for them to die, and then assume that if 3,842 of the bunch lived to be 97, then about 3,842 of another 10,000 elephants will live as long.

Just assume that every elephant is an average elephant, and—on the average—it will all work out. (Yes, that's an oversimplification.)

That approach has an obvious problem: the policy for Jumpo is needed now.

So you go look for information on how long elephants live. The IBGHA (International Big Game Hunters Association) is delighted to show you their cumulative records, which just happen to include the estimated ages of 10,000 elephants at their deaths: you quickly learn that elephants never die before the age of 25, and rarely after the age of 50. You now write up a quick report on elephant mortality and apply for another consulting position.

## Exercise

**5.3-2**   Before reading onward, list some of the errors in the approach just described.

Unfortunately for you, the insurance company reads your report carefully and quickly arranges for Jumpo to jump on you. The consultant who replaces you is much more careful; she finds that members of the IBGHA hunt mostly in Pachydermia, where shooting elephants under 25 is illegal, and most elderly elephants live in the Old Elephant's Home where no guns are allowed. (Many elephants may have been shot before age 25, or even within the Old Elephant's home, but they wouldn't be listed in official records.) In any case, there would be no reason to suppose that 10,000 circus elephants, in the midst of noise, stress, crowds, and medical care, had life spans close to those of 10,000 jungle cousins who were shot. She starts to look for 10,000 acrobatic elephants, but finds that only five have died, at ages 1,1,2,3, and 83. She reports that acrobatic elephants, on the average, live to be 18 years old.

## Exercise

**5.3-3**   Point out some of the errors in her approach. [Hint: Read *How to Lie with Statistics* [11]]

The third consultant prepares a report which carefully points out the limitations of the statistical approach.

He finds the mean (the arithmetic average), the mode (most common value), and median (midpoint) of various populations: in the acrobats mentioned by his predecessor, the mean was 18, but the mode was 1 and the median was 2. This suggests that there have been dangers associated with being a baby acrobatic elephant, but Jumpo is already 6. Should it be predicted that he'll live to be 82? No. That's like predicting your own age at death by looking at one random grave.

## 5.3.4  Large-Number Techniques Involve Looking for Patterns

This third consultant now looks for "correlations" between age and other factors, using well-known formulas which will not be explained here. He points out that larger elephants seem to live shorter life spans in the IBGHA data, but that this may well be due to hunters' predelictions for shooting the biggest available elephant. His data suggests that larger elephants live longer in captivity; physically active elephants live longer in captivity; and elephants whose commercial value is high seem to live longer (he attributes this to better medical care, but part of the effect may be due to the fact that the most valuable elephants seem to be physically active). He also finds a correlation between life span and ear size, which could have several explanations.

In the end, he comes up with an elephant mortality formula for captive elephants which starts with 63 years, adds 1 year per ton of extra size, adds 2 years for extra activity levels, subtracts 5 years for life near cities, subtracts 2 years for life in crowds, adds 3 years for high commercial value, and so on. The formula predicts that Jumpo will most probably live around 68 years. It is a "good" formula because it matches the captive-elephant data quite well, but of course it says nothing about whether Jumpo will die tomorrow. Separately, he comes up with formulas indicating Jumpo's probabilities for dying accidentally or becoming disabled in his act on a year-by-year basis, depending on the kind of work he's doing—probabilities of death from disease, from train or trailer wreck, and so on. Each of these is based on a smaller collection of data than the first, overall prediction formula, and thus they are even less reliable. The consultant collects all the alternative explanations for the data and hands them over to the life insurance executives, who prepare not one but several policies: they will lower Jumpo's premiums if given assurance that his medical care is indeed adequate, that he will stop performing whenever he seems sick, that he will be kept away from possible contagion, that the vehicles he rides in are carefully maintained, and so on. The circus people accept most of the recommendations, and everybody's happy; but Jumpo still might die tomorrow. These models are governed by "large-number" laws and lead us toward statistics. They never give us any certainty, but thus far they are the best we have.

For a readable explanation of what the third consultant was looking for (and for the errors which tend to crop up in such approaches), read Stephen Jay Gould's *The Mismeasure of Man* [8]. The chapters on factor analysis, as a statistical technique created to bolster hereditarian views of human intelligence, are entertaining as well as intelligible. The surrounding chapters say a lot about the frightful consequences of some scientific investigations. Statistical modeling is an important application area for computers, but the detail we've given is not sufficient to do much computing. Suffice it to say that the third consultant had a great many formulas to get through, and only a mechanical moron should have to do the work.

## Exercises

**5.3-4**  The following *Avg* definition produces an average for a sequence of numbers:

$$Avg(S) \quad = \quad Sum(S)/\max(Length(S), 1);$$

Thus, $Avg([1, 2, 3, 4, 5]) = (1 + 2 + 3 + 4 + 5)/5 = 3$

(a)  What are the time and space requirements of the algorithm?

(b)  Why is $\max(Length(S), 1)$ used instead of merely $Length(S)$?

**5.3-5**  The following *Med* definition should produce the "median" of a sequence, i.e., a number $n$ such that $Length(More(n, S))$ and $Length(NoMore(n, S))$ are approximately equal (a middle member of the sequence):

$$Med(S) \quad = \quad Sort(S)[Half(1 + Length(S))];$$

(a)  Justify the definition given; use an example.

(b)  Why is $Half(1 + Length(S))$ used to find the middle element instead of $Half(Length(S))$? When would the answer otherwise be drastically wrong?

**5.3-6**  Here are equations leading up to the *Mode* definition, which defines the most frequently occurring member of $S$. Justify the definitions.

$$
\begin{aligned}
Count(n, S) &= |\{i : S[i] = n\}| \\
Freqs(S) &= \{[n, Count(n, S)] : n \in S\} \\
HiFreq(S) &= Max(\{f : [n, f] \in Freqs(S)\}) \\
Mode(S) &= Hd([n : [n, HiFreq(S)] \in Freqs(S)])
\end{aligned}
$$

**5.3-7**  Discuss the algebraic properties of *Avg*, *Med*, and *Mode*. When are all three the same? When are they very different from each other?

**5.3-8**  Write a set of simple recursive equations to find the mode of a sequence. Test them carefully.

## 5.4  THE ELEPHANT'S BALLROOM

Here, we want to model "the celebrated elephant's square dance, with eight pachyderms and a banyan tree for each square." The specific question we want to answer is; Will a particular herd of elephants be able to dance in a particular banyan grove? Sometimes this question is easy: if there are more than eight times as many elephants as trees, then the answer is obviously no, and if the trees are plentiful and widely spaced, then it may be obvious that the answer is yes. However, we might easily find an apparently over-crowded grove which could be rearranged to make room for more elephants; it is very hard to tell whether the grove is full. This could be very important if we're trying to hire the smallest grove which will do.

### 5.4.1  Models Need Pictures

Let's start by drawing a picture (Figure 5.4) of a fairly full grove, with O's for trees and X's for pairs of elephants.

```
    X           X               O    X          O  O
   XOX     O   XOX          X        XOX            X      O
    X           X         X  XOX    O  X  O   O XOX
                        XOX  XO                   O      X
                         X        O           O
               X
              XOX
               X
```

**Figure 5.4**   The Elephant's Ballroom

## 5.4.2  Medium-Sized Numbers Don't
## Average Out

Here, we cannot assume that one herd is much like another: a herd of elephants might have only a few members, or it might have dozens, even if we could assume that one elephant is much like another. We cannot simplify to a simple set of equations: big elephants need widely separated trees, smaller elephants can do with trees closer together. The model will have to include the spacing of the trees, the number of elephants, and the space required by each elephant, at the least.

One way to build a model is to visualize the space required by each set of elephants as they dance. For this, we need to think about the dance positions. Figure 5.5 has some sample square-dance positions:[1]

There's food for much thought in Figure 5.5 (and even for nightmares about tidal waves of elephants), but our objective is to isolate those details that we *must* worry about from those which we can forget. If we assume that each set has its own space reserved at the start and can never use any other set's space, then we can find a figure that covers each position for a given square. A large diamond shape, with enough room N-S and E-W for the tidal wave positions but enough room NE, NW, SE, and SW for the square figures will do; it will be a square with its corners pointing N,E,S, and W.

Now we have reduced the ballroom to a list of measurements: a table of the form $\{[x, y, s]\}$, where each $[x, y, s]$ indicates a diamond of side $s$ pinned with center at $(x, y)$. We're supposed to find a table which has all of the diamonds on different pins and which doesn't include any conflicts, if any such table exists. We can pretend for convenience that we start out with all of the diamonds on one pin and all the other pins covered with diamonds of side 0, or we can avoid such a pretence; the problem is solvable either way, but the obvious methods involve enormous cost. If $N$ is the number of diamonds, and $M$ is the number of pins, then the number of possible diamonds-on-pins placements to be checked out is $P(N-M, N)$, where $P$ is the $P$ascal's-triangle function we visited briefly in Chapter 1. This is exponentially large. Another way of looking at it is that each state has about $N * M$ neighbors, and each neighbor has that many neighbors, all of which must be checked. Any way you think about it, the number of combinations is immense. Still, we can begin

---

[1]Contributed by Art Smith, a square-dancing graduate student who also wrote some of the software for the first version of this course.

O = tree,  M = Man,  W = Woman;  Face '*';  handhold = '—',   'I', '/', or '\'.

Square:  (if all hands are joined W--M then it's a circle)

```
                M - - W
                *     *

        M*              *W                     *        *        *        *
        |       O       |       Tidal Wave: M - - W - - W - - M - - M - - W - - W - - M
        W*              *M                        *        *        *        *

                *     *
                M - - W


Facing Couples:     W-   -M          Column:        *     *
                    *     *                        M-   -W


                    *       *                      *       *
                    M-    -W                        M-    -W

                        O                               O

                    W-    -M                        *       *
                    *       *                      M-    -W


                    *       *                      *       *
                    M-    -W                        M     W


Promenade:     *W              Alamo style:            *
               |                                     W - - - M
               *M                                   /        *\
                                                   M*          W*
        W - - M   O    *     *                     |     O      |
        *     *        M - - W                     *W           *M
                                                    \ *        /
               M*                                    M - - - W
               |                                          *
               W*


Thar:        *W              Diamonds:            *M        *
             |                                  W  |   W
             M*                                  *    M*
        *          *
    W - - M - - - O - - - M - - W                    O
    *          *
             |                                    *M        *
             *M                                 W  |   W
             |                                   *    M*
             W*
```

**Figure 5.5** The Elephant's Dance Patterns

to analyze and think about it; the elephants will wait for us, at least for a little while. . . .

### Exercises

**5.4-1**    Define the *In* relation on points and diamonds such that $In(p, D)$ is *True* if the point $p = (x, y)$ falls inside the region covered by $D = [x', y', s]$

**5.4-2**    Define the *Overlap* relation on diamonds so that $Overlap(x, y)$ will be *True* if $x \neq y$ but $x$ and $y$ overlap geometrically. Discuss its algebraic properties.

**5.4-3**    Define the *Conflict* predicate on tables so that $Conflict(S)$ will be *True* if $S$ contains overlapping diamonds.

**5.4-4**    Define the *Badness* measure on tables so that $Badness(S)$ is the total area lost to overlap, i.e., it should be the difference between the actual area and the potential (overlap-free) area.

**5.4-5**    Define the *Swap* operation on tables which exchanges the diamonds on two positions.

### 5.4.3  We Can Picture an Oversimplified State-Space

We can sketch the state-space, but only by drastically oversimplifying it: there are variables for each elephant and variables for each tree which really do make a difference, so all we can do is sketch interesting regions of the state-space rather than individual points in it. For example,

A:  All elephants are outside the grove.

B:  All elephants are in the grove.

C:  The grove is full.

D:  The elephants are packed as tightly as possible into part of the grove.

These regions, like the state-space itself, are sets: they are subsets of the state-space.

With that approach you can draw a state-space of four overlapping circles, as in Figure 5.6.   Notice that there can't be any situations in the overlap between A and B, unless there aren't any elephants.

### Exercise

**5.4-6**    When will there be an overlap between A and C?

To describe that state-space, we have to consider regions which combine the basic ones in several ways:

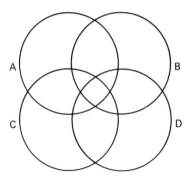

**Figure 5.6**  Elephant-Packing Situations

- We are successful if B is true.

- We are unsuccessful if B is false and C and D are both true.

- If B is false but either C or D is also false, then we're not finished.

We have to introduce some notation for these constructions, so that we can describe sets like the set of paths which lead us to some state satisfying B.

That will help organize the problem, but it does not help us get around the fact that sometimes, just sometimes, it will turn out that by exchanging a large elephant at the southwest corner with a small elephant near the middle, we will be able to barely fit the last square rather than not quite fit the last square. One small change can make the difference between overall success and overall failure.

### 5.4.4  Medium-Number Problems Are Still Too Hard to Handle Perfectly

Do we have to try all possible arrangements to see if they fit? If so, we may need hundreds of years of computer time to find the answer for a medium-sized herd in a just barely adequate grove. This particular problem bears a strong resemblance to some members of the family of "NP-complete" problems, which are widely believed to be "computationally intractable": in principle we can solve them, but it just takes too long. Sad to say, many of those are quite practical problems: finding a multicourse examination schedule with a minimal number of conflicts is very similar to the elephant's difficulty just now. Is it hopeless? Not unless you're a real perfectionist. Many such problems have approximate solutions, just as our simulation of the elephant sliding downhill is an approximate solution. For example, we might try to put the elephants in largest first, squeezing them toward the southwest corner of the grove. When the grove is full, we shuffle them around a bit at random and then (if that doesn't improve matters) give up. In effect, we apply the *BubbleSort* idea: pick two diamonds (including one which may be a 0-size dummy), consider the effects of swapping, and if it doesn't reduce the *Badness*, then don't do it. When you don't see any improvement for a while, stop. Of course, we'll be very embarrassed when some other modeler shows how to put them all in the grove, but we can save face if we can show (a) that a perfect solution is not feasible, and (b) that our solution is always close (say, within 5 percent) of perfect.

### Exercise

**5.4-7**   Write equations defining some reasonable approximation to a solution for this problem. [Warning: This is an extremely difficult exercise.]

These models are governed by "medium-number" laws, which usually turn out to be variants of Murphy's Law: irregularity in the data is expected and almost always makes a difference. Keeping track of such irregularities will lead us toward discrete mathematics, the dominant conceptual tool for computer science.

## 5.5 THE KINDS OF MODELS

In this chapter, we've seen three kinds of models and the beginnings of their use in problem solving. It's time to recapitulate briefly.

**Small-number models:**   These are models that try to forget about all but a very small number of factors, and then develop relatively simple formulas for describing relationships between these factors. Usually the simplifications depend on assumptions such as "a small change in the initial situation will produce only a small change in the final situation," which justify the tools of calculus. Usually the relationships involve ideas such as one numerical measurement being proportional to the sum or product of other measurements. Straight-line and parabolic motion are small-number phenomena; a radio wave, a current in a lamp, or a planet in orbit around the sun come fairly close. Computers help deal with these models by simulations; computers also (sometimes) help create these models by algebraic manipulation.

**Large-number models:**   These are models which try to forget about individuality, assuming that one large group will roughly resemble another, even though members of the groups may differ. The problem is reduced to considerations of a few populations, so huge that no individual member of those populations can be considered significant. This assumption justifies the tools of statistics. Means, medians, and standard deviations are large-number concepts, useful for large-number phenomena like the motion of the atoms in a gas. The number of people in a nation or stars in a galaxy is large enough to justify these for some purposes. Computers help deal with these models by finding the resemblances and differences between large groups; computers are also used for simulations of them.

**Medium-number models:**    These are models which try to keep track of many details, because there are many factors which really make a difference. The problem is "reduced" to considerations of many or all possible combinations of collections of factors, in which the collections are still small enough that each individual is potentially important. Instead of models of simple quantities, we have models of structure: the structure of road segments connecting places, the structure of elephants arranged in dancing groups, the structure of an encyclopedia or of problem solving itself. To get anywhere with models like these, we have to be able to deal with "all possible ways of arranging 29 elephants in a row" as easily as the small-number models deal with acceleration. We have to be able to express the fact that having 20 large and 9 small elephants is different from having 20 small and 9 large elephants, but that both are smaller problems than dealing with 29 elephants of 29 different sizes.

In order to work toward these ideas, we've begun to explore the notions and notations of sets, sequences, relations, functions, and homomorphisms.

Sequences seem somehow the most basic of these, just because sequences are what you write down, one letter after another. Sets look like sequences when written out, but with sets we pretend that ordering and duplications of items are unimportant: only presence or absence matters. A relation seems to be a special kind of set of sequences, which we use for looking up relationships between values; a function is a method for getting one value from others. Obviously, relations and functions are related somehow, but we've been using them so far in quite different ways. A homomorphism is a translation that somehow preserves the structure of what's being translated.

Our map of the country we will be traveling through, the world of system specification, implementation, and analysis, is notable mainly for large blank spaces; it will remain that way for quite a while. In the next chapter, we'll be working through some famous examples of systematic problem solving.

# 6

# Problem Solving
# With State-Spaces

In this chapter, we will construct models and solutions for several problems which are often used to illustrate problem-solving techniques for computer science.

## 6.1 THE WOLF, THE GOAT, AND THE CABBAGES

Once upon a time, there was a farmer named Joe. Joe lived alone in an isolated mountain area. He sold his cabbages (and an occasional goat) at a village on the other side of a river, so he kept a small rowboat to cross back and forth. One day, he planned to take a basket of cabbages and a goat to the village to sell, although the rowboat was so small he could only take one across the river at a time. The night before he left, he trapped a wolf, and decided to take it too. He now had a big problem: he couldn't leave the wolf and goat alone any more than he could leave the goat and cabbage alone, but he could only take one at a time across the river. What could he do?

### 6.1.1 Problem Solving Needs Pictures

Being a general problem solver, he began with a sketch—the rather crude sketch of Figure 6.1.

Obviously, most of that didn't matter. He immediately redrew it as the somewhat more abstract Figure 6.2.

```
          Joe, Cabbages,              |R| /river                  Village
 House     Wolf, Goat.            Boat |i |-\path                                *
                                  /---/ |v |    \
  \-------\ to river             |      |e |    |           village path   |- - -►
    my path \---------|                 |r |    |--------------| to City
```

**Figure 6.1** Wolf, Goat, and Cabbages: First Sketch

```
 Joe, Cabbages,          |
   Wolf, Goat.    Boat |              Village     Figure 6.2  Wolf, Goat, and Cab-
                      | River                     bages: Reduced Sketch
```

When you're given a problem to solve (or a program to write), try to find some way to put it into a diagram. You'll probably need more than two tries, but it's very much worthwhile: your visual cortex is a large fraction of your brain, and you should always make an effort to give it a chance.

### 6.1.2 Modeling Requires Selection

The fact that the goat's name is Edward didn't enter into the solution process any more than the number (12) of cabbages in the basket (which was wooden with a broken handle). Being a fairly good problem solver, Joe asked himself

What observations define the state-space?

He decided that the only important dimensions of the state-space were the positions of his cargo, his boat and himself—not the North-South coordinates, not even the East-West coordinates, but just whether each variable was east or west of the river. He could tabulate states as values for the variables *Joe*, *Cabbages*, *Wolf*, *Goat*, and *Boat* so that states would look like this:

| Joe | Cabbages | Wolf | Goat | Boat |
|------|----------|------|------|------|
| East | West | East | East | West |
| West | East | West | East | West |

He's starting in the state [West, West, West, West, West] and wants to end in the state [East, East, East, East, East]. In effect, Joe is saying that the only function he needs to check out a variable v in a state S is a *Side* function which is defined as

$$Side(v, S) \quad = \quad West, \text{ if } v \text{ is west of the river in } S$$
$$= \quad East, \text{ otherwise}$$

In refusing to include anything else, he was using a basic principle:

**If** a state-space description includes an observation
which is not needed for the problem,
**then** neither the state-space nor
the state-space description are minimal.


**Q:** Minimal? Who said anything about minimal?
**A:** Remember the countryside serving as its own map?


That state-space description is something that we're trying to use to solve a problem, and one of its most important characteristics is that it be no bigger than it has to be for that problem. That's because *all problem solvers are lazy*. If they weren't lazy, they wouldn't solve enough problems to qualify as problem solvers.

Of course, Joe could have used entirely different measurements and thus decomposed the system differently. For example, he could have said that the important dimensions were not measurements of location east or west, which amount to asking "Is it on the same side as the village?" for each variable. That's a village-oriented state-space. Instead, he might have asked "Is it on the same side as I am?" and come up with states in Joe-oriented space, tabulating the variables *Village*, *Cabbages*, *Wolf*, *Goat*, and *Boat* with Boolean values *True* and *False*. In this state-space, the first state of the table given above would be written [*True*, *False*, *True*, *True*, *False*]. (Check it.)


**Exercise**

**6.1-1**    Convert the state description [East, East, East, West, West] of the village-oriented state-space into the corresponding Boolean description of the Joe-oriented one.


As it happens, he did not think of the Joe-oriented state-space, or of a goat-oriented state-space, or of a state-space of answers to

[Am I on the village's side?
Is the boat on my side?
Is the goat on my side?
Is the wolf on the goat's side?
Is the cabbage on the goat's side?]

but any of these would have been reasonable decompositions, and you should think about them now and then.

This village-oriented state-space is actually a table, a set of all possible 5-tuples (sequences of length 5) whose elements are *East* and *West*:

$$Space \quad = \quad \{S : Length(S) = 5, x \in S \Rightarrow x \in \{East, West\}\}$$

It is the Cartesian product of the possible positions, and has $32 = 2*2*2*2*2$ states in it. Joe just needed to find a path in that five-dimensional state-space from the starting state [West, West, West, West, West] to the final state [East, East, East, East, East].

### 6.1.3 Problem Solving Requires
### Path-Finding

To find the path, Joe started writing:
*Initial State*: Wolf, goat, cabbage, boat and man on the west.
*Final State*: Wolf, goat, cabbage, boat and man on the east.
*Operations*: Move man, boat, and any one of the others from one side to the other.
*Examples*:

| S = [j,c,w,g,b] | | $Row(x, S)$ |
| --- | --- | --- |
| $[E, E, E, E, E]$ | $[W, W, E, E, W]$ | if x=Cabbage |
| $[W, E, W, W, W]$ | $[E, E, E, W, E]$ | if x=Wolf |

This operation is actually a way of making new states from old; we describe it more fully by giving it a name, like *Row*, so that if $S$ is a state and $x$ is an item then $Row(x, S)$ is a state, where Joe has rowed across in the boat with $x$:

> **if** the man, the boat, and $x$ are all on one side in $S$
> > **then** they are all on the other side in $Row(x, S)$
> > **and** the other two are on the same side in $Row(x, S)$ as in $S$.
> Otherwise, $Row(x, S)$ is meaningless.

Most people won't find it worthwhile to define *Row* more carefully than that. The goal is to have a definition that is just precise enough so that we can fill in a table of examples like those above.

### Exercises

**6.1-2**   What is $Row(Goat, [\dot{E}, E, W, E, E])$? Explain in terms of the **if-then** rule.

**6.1-3**   Describe some algebraic properties of *Row*.

Now Joe tried to think of constraints: rules describing sets of states which for one reason or another are simply not going to happen—for example, wolf and goat together alone on the east; goat and cabbage together alone on the west; boat on the east, man on the west; boat on the east, boat on the west. He listed them:

*Constraints*:

**1.** If wolf and goat are together, then I'm with them.

**2.** If goat and cabbage are together, then I'm with them.

**3.** I'm always with the boat.

**4.** Any of the five which are not west are east.

Each of these is easily expressed as an **if-then** rule; for example, constraint 3 becomes " **if**  Side(Boat) = x  **then**  Side(Man) = x".

### Exercise

**6.1-4**   Express the other constraints as **if-then** rules.

### 6.1.4  Dependent Information Can Be Excluded

Then he stared at that and thought: **simplify**! All that information is relevant, but it might be redundant if there's a way of deriving part from the rest.

> **if**  *an observation in a state can be predicted*
> *from other observations in the state,*
> **then**  *neither the state-space nor*
> *the state-space description are minimal.*

**Q:** Why? I guess I see that the state-space description isn't minimal, but what do you mean by saying that the state-space isn't?

**A:** The state-space itself now includes "possibilities" that aren't really available in the problem, such as a state in which Joe and the boat are on opposite sides. That can't happen as long as we include a constraint which amounts to saying that the boat's location is dependent on Joe's. Thus, by constraint 3, Joe can leave the boat variable out of the state description (i.e., he can omit that column from the table). This is a case of an *explicit* constraint from a list turning into into an *implicit* constraint built into the model, so it could be forgotten. The state-space is now only a four-dimensional state-space with 16 elements, and there are only three constraints left to be remembered. Joe is applying another basic principle:

### Don't Measure What You Can Deduce.

Think about those constraints in the alternative state-spaces. If his questions had been to relate the village and goat and boat to himself and the wolf and cabbage to the goat, constraint 3 would have been even more obvious because there would have always been a "yes" for the boat. Constraints 1 and 2 would probably have been expressed as the single constraint "The goat is either alone or with me." The last constraint would have been harder to keep track of, and might be best transmuted (not just translated) into "Any of the answers which are not no must be yes."

Now he tried to abbreviate: how can he remember what a situation is? One method is to use a vertical bar "|" to represent the river, and initial letters of Wolf, Goat, Cabbage and Man to represent objects. The initial state is then WGCM| and the final state is | WGCM. Can you tell what state is written as WG| CM? Does it violate any constraints? Is it the same as GW| MC? Is it the same as MC| WG?

Now he tried again to simplify. Looking at each constraint more carefully, he saw that constraint 4 guarantees that in reading GW|MC he didn't need to look past the "GW| . . ." because if only the goat and the wolf are on the west then the cabbage and man must be on the east. Now the initial state would still be WGCM| , but the final state would be | with no letters at all. Having fewer letters to write was nice, but the main point was that another explicit constraint has become implicit and could be forgotten. Now MW| would abbreviate "The man and wolf are on the west, goat and cabbage on the east", and CM| would stand for "The cabbage and man are on the west, goat and wolf on the east." There are only two explicit constraints remaining.

Finally, he noticed that there was a regularity in his situation descriptions: they all end with a "|". Using the rule that

### Regularity is Redundancy, Redundancy, Redundancy

he decided not to write down the "|": MG would stand for "The man and the goat are on the west, the cabbage and wolf on the east," CGMW would stand for "All are on the west, none on the east," and rather than leaving a blank to stand for "None are on the west, all on the east" he decided to put in a dash.

Now he tried to make a map of the state-space. The state-space is the set of all possible states:

—, C, G, M, W, CG, CM, CW, GM, GW, MW, CGM, CGW, CMW, GMW, CGMW

There are no others. How do I know there are no others? Because a state just specifies east and west for each variable, and the size of the Cartesian product is the product of the sizes: $2 * 2 * 2 * 2 = 16$. Since I've written 16 states and they're all different, I can be sure that didn't skip any.

Next, Joe eliminated the states that broke the constraints against having the goat and cabbage or the goat and wolf together without him: M, CG, CM, GW, MW, and CGW. Being a careful problem solver, he didn't just cross them off, which might lead to careless mistakes: he thought about it and realized that these constraints said nothing about east or west, so such situations had to come in pairs: M is the same problem as CGW, CG is the same problem as MW, and CM is the same problem as GW. He's applying a "symmetry criterion," also known as a "don't care principle":

**if** *a rule doesn't care about some difference between states,*

**then** *it will always apply to groups of states.*

That collapsed 12 of the states into 6, (check it!), so he put the 10 remaining states on a picture:

—,C, G, W, CW, GM, CGM, CMW, GMW, CGMW

Being a well-organized problem solver, he put all of those with himself on the left in one line and all of those with himself on the right in another line:

He then drew lines from each state to any state that could be reached from it by his one operation: crossing himself with one item.

**Exercise**

**6.1-5**   Draw the lines on the figure.

Actually, he could just as well indicate his lines by tabulating the pairs of *Connected* states:

$$\{ [\texttt{CGMW,CW}] , [\texttt{GM,--}] ,...\}$$

Unfortunately, no matter how you indicate the connections, there's a little problem. On the map as he drew it, the only place he could go from the initial state CGMW is CW, and the only place to go from CW is back to CGMW.

**6.1.5  Remember: Models Are Always Wrong**

Stalemate ... Bankruptcy looms ... Perhaps he should jump in the river himself. Aha! Perhaps he should put the wolf and the cabbage into the boat, and then swim across, pushing or pulling the boat instead of rowing it .... Or perhaps he should make the wolf or the goat swim across while he stays dry with the cabbage .... Hmm, will cabbage in a wooden basket float?

In this case, our problem solver had found that he could not solve the problem in the original model. Fortunately, despair prompted an inspiration which violated the model altogether, forcing him to see in it all kinds of unstated constraints on the set of possible operations. After a while, he remembered that this particular river happened to be infested with crocodiles, and he discovered by experiment that his particular cabbages didn't float, but by now he realized that what he needed was a larger set of operations. He therefore considered the Useless Move Principle: **If** you can't think of any way to get what you want, **then** you should think about ways to get what you don't want and try working from there.

[Perhaps the best-known popular exposition of this principle is the song "If You Can't Be with the One You Love, Love the One You're With."]

In this case, our hero thought about overloading the boat (it would sink and he would be eaten), pushing it off without him (he would never get to the village himself), and rowing back and forth with no load at all (that's silly). Reflecting that silliness is an essential part of being a problem solver, he proceeded to add the *RowBack* operation which would take any state with himself (and boat) on one side, to a state which would be just the same except that he (and the boat) would be on the other side.

**Exercise**

**6.1-6**   Redraw the 16-place state-space with all the edges on it.

After drawing the new figure, Joe immediately (well, almost immediately) observed a path from CGMW to —. Do you see it? It goes like this: [CGMW, CW, CMW, C, CGM, G, GM, —]. The Useless Move Principle saved the day.

### Jumping outside the model

is what he started to do when contemplating suicide: suicide wasn't one of the operations he had defined. It's always possible that your model has excluded the wrong things: perhaps he should have included the possibility of building a raft, or laying a rope-bridge across the river, or any of millions of other conceivable variations. Being an experienced problem solver, our farmer would have considered such things eventually if the simple model had failed. Being an experienced problem solver, he knew better than to try to build a model more complex than he needed to solve the problem.

### 6.1.6 Pathfinding Occurs in Many Problems

In the farmer's problem, we skipped the explicit definition of the type *Path* and the functions *PathsFrom* and *PathsTo* which we had developed while working with maps; nonetheless, that's what we had to use to solve the problem. The concrete problem of getting a wolf, a goat, and a basket of cabbages across a river was "reduced" to the abstract problem of finding a path in a state-space map, which could have been represented as a table. This will occur again and again (for the rest of your involvement with computers, or even with explicit discussion of problem solving).

### 6.1.7 Problem Solving: Morals and Methods

The farmer showed us several principles of setting up a model to solve a problem. First, he isolated the relevant variables: a state of the problem was described as the position (east or west of the river) of himself, the boat, and the cargo. This implicitly gave him a state-space, or set of possible states. Second, he considered the operations, or relations between states of the problem. Third, he considered the constraints, or conditions to be left invariant by the operations:

**Any operation changes some conditions and
leaves others invariant.**

Also

**Any condition is changed by some operations and
left invariant by others.**

By thinking about these, he was able to simplify his description of a state so that it became very abstract: hard to read, but easy to work with. This provided a smaller state-space, which he made explicit: there were no states in which the boat was across from him, as there would have been if he had tried to describe the state-space at an earlier stage. Now he made a map of the state-space, with connections from one "position" to another wherever there was an operation which changed the state. Finally, he looked for a path.

At every stage he looked for possible errors, and often found them. When he found that the model did not permit a solution, he constructed a small extension of it. If that had not worked, he would again have constructed a small extension or a different small model, so that he would never have lost track entirely.

The same ideas can be used to describe the other problems we have discussed: the distance problem, the elephant's slide, and so on. In each case, there is a state-space in the model. For the distance problem, it involves only space, for the elephant's slide it involves space and time. For the elephant's square dance, it involved so many variables that it was too hard to draw without extreme oversimplification. A lot of problems are like that: we cannot actually draw the state-space itself, but we can draw our decomposition of it into subspaces.

### 6.1.8 Problem Solving Is a Skill

Some take notes well, others throw footballs well, others solve problems well. Curiously, even though the people who can run a business may not be able to read a scientific paper, the same people who can run one business can often run a very different one, and the same people who can solve technical problems in business can often solve technical problems in science. Like other skills, this appears to involve some "innate talent" (that's a code phrase for a difference between people that we don't yet understand), and it definitely involves a lot of practice. There is an analogy with chess playing and long-distance running: different people have different limits and different starting points, but everybody can benefit by working at it.

It may seem very odd to think of problem solving as a skill. We can have courses which teach you to write English compositions, or prove theorems in geometry, or analyze chemicals, or touch-type; can we have a course which teaches you to solve problems? Any problems? "Hey, Joe: I've got this problem communicating with my girl friend Jill. You're a general problem solver, can you solve it?" "Excuse me, Mr. Smith; I need a solution for the problem of nuclear disarmament, and I need it quick!" It sounds somewhat silly at first, but the authors of problem solving books (you should find several in the nearest library or bookstore) will claim that there are general principles which apply to all or almost all different kinds of problems, and that you can learn to use these principles.

Of course, that doesn't mean that a general problem solver can solve all problems; it doesn't even mean that Joe will do as well as Harry (who knows nothing about general problem solving but lots about communication) or as well as Jack (Jill's brother). In household repairs, pliers are very general tools, but a nice specialized set of socket wrenches will often do a better job and do it faster. In problem solving, specialized knowledge is usually helpful and often absolutely necessary. Still, a skilled problem solver should usually do better than an unskilled problem solver with the same specialized knowledge: if Joe knew what Harry knows about communication, or what Jack knows about Jill, then his suggestions would generally be better than theirs.

### 6.1.9 Problem Solving Needs Models

The essence of "general" problem solving is the bag of tools that all problem solutions share: the mental tools you need for building and working with different kinds of models.

Problems with maps are usually of two kinds: you're using it the wrong way, or it's the wrong map. We cannot teach you the one best way to use all maps, but we can help you teach yourself systematic ways which will work pretty well on most maps. We cannot teach you the one right way to make a map for a given problem, but we can help you teach yourself some systematic ways to criticize a map: to look for redundancy, to seek out irrelevant variables, to find an alternative decomposition which would let you look for the solution with fewer explicit variables or logical constraints to keep track of.

### Exercises

**6.1-7**   Check out the equations for path construction; does anything need to be changed for Joe's purposes? Why or why not?

**6.1-8**   Comment on the fact that once the problem was set up correctly, the procedure was almost trivial. How would you begin to describe the problem setup itself

through a collection of rules? [Warning: Don't kill yourself trying to finish. The
mechanization of setting up problems for procedural solution is an open research
area in artificial intelligence.]

## 6.2 EIGHT QUEENS

The "Eight Queens" problem is simple enough to describe: place eight queens on
a chessboard without letting any threaten another. Since any queen in chess can
threaten any other piece located on the same row, column, or diagonal, it turns out
that this can be quite difficult.    On the board in Figure 6.3, the queens labelled

```
* A * * * * * *
* * * * * * * *
* * * * * * * E
* * * * B * * *
* * * * * * * *
* * * * * * * *
* C * * * D *
* * * * * * * *
```

**Figure 6.3**   Queens in Conflict

A and C threaten each other because they share a column. C and D threaten each
other because they share a row. A and B share a downward diagonal (one which
slants downwards from left to right) and C and B share an upward diagonal. Only
E is safe.

The problem is often discussed in the literature of computer science as one requiring a fairly sophisticated level of program development methodology. Nonetheless, it requires no programming knowledge whatsoever; your author encountered
(and solved) it as a chess problem several years before writing his first computer
program. In this section, we will develop models and solutions for the problem.

Before reading onwards, try to solve it for yourself: If you don't have a chessboard handy, sketch an 8 × 8 grid on paper and use coins or pebbles for the queens.

Did you solve it? Stop that! Go back and try. At the very least, you should have
some kind of chessboard sketch to play with as we proceed. Actually, our problem
is not so much to solve it, as to describe the solution in such (almost) perfect detail
that a mechanical moron could solve it. Even if you've got the answer, read on.

### 6.2.1 The State-Space Contains Possible
Observations

What is the state-space? Presumably, we are given eight queens and an 8 × 8
chessboard, so we might quite reasonably say that the dimensions of the problem
are exactly the observations we make on the queens: any possible combination of
properties for the queens is a state. Another way of saying that is to say that the
state-space for the problem is the Cartesian product of the state-spaces for the
queens.

The individual queen's state-space is defined by the observations we make of her: her row, column, upwards diagonal and downwards diagonal. (A diagonal is called "upwards" if it slopes upwards from left to right; geometrically all the diagonals have slopes of 1 or −1, so you may prefer to think of "upwards" as "positive".) The row and column observations each have eight possible values, the diagonal observations each have fifteen, so each queen is in one of $8 * 8 * 15 * 15 = 14,400$ possible states. The Cartesian product of these state-spaces has $14,400 * 14,400 * 14,400 * \ldots * 14,400$ overall states, which is larger than $10000^{**}8 = 10^{**}32$. With a very fast computer, we might check out a million of these positions each second; we would need $10^{**}26$ seconds or $10^{**}20$ years to finish, and that's several billion times more than the probable age (or remaining lifetime) of the universe.

## 6.2.2 Most Measurements are Redundant

Fortunately, it is easy to simplify this if we notice that the diagonals can always be determined by the row and column numbers. The row and column numbers have eight possible values each, so a queen has only 64 possible positions. The Cartesian product of these state-spaces has $64 * 64 * 64 * 64 * 64 * 64 * 64 * 64$ members, or $64^{**}8$, which is a few hundred trillion. With our hypothetical big computer trying out a million positions every second, we would need a few hundred million seconds to finish, which is about 10 years. The improvement is enormous, and we got it entirely by applying the principle of simplifying the state-space to remove redundancy. Still, we have just moved from the realm of the utterly impossible into the ludicrously expensive; surely there's a better way.

Let each queen's state be written as a [row, column] pair, and then the board state will be written as

$$[[r1, c1], [r2, c2], [r3, c3], \ldots, [r8, c8]]$$

The state-space is then the set of all possible combinations. In a solution, however, we know that no two queens can share the same row, column, upward diagonal, or downward diagonal:

> **if**  i ≠ j
>> **then**  r[i] ≠ r[j]
>> **and**  c[i] ≠ c[j]
>> **and**  updiag[i] ≠ updiag[j]
>> **and**  downdiag[i] ≠ downdiag[j]

This is written from the point of view of the queens: for each queen there is a row, column, etc. From the measurement point of view, we're defining the state of the world by making measurements for each queen. Let us try to invert that point of view: can we define the state of the world by making measurements for each row?

for each column? for each diagonal? If for each queen there is a row, then for each row there must be a set of queens. What is that set? How big is it?

The no-conflict rule implies that for each row there is at most one queen; likewise for each column and upwards or downwards diagonal. The fact that there are eight queens, and each must be on some row, and no two can be on one row, implies that every row must have exactly one queen; this simple idea is called the "Pigeonhole Principle," and you'll see it often.

That means that we can fully determine the state by looking at each row and finding the one and only queen in it. What column is it in? Equivalently, we can look in each column to find the row number for the one and only queen in that column, or we can look in each up or down diagonal to see if there is a queen there, and if so where. We do not need to know which queen in any of these cases.

There are only eight rows, so we can do it with eight measurements, each of which can yield one of eight values: the state-space is the Cartesian product of the row-spaces, so there are only $8*8*8*8*8*8*8*8$, or $8**8$, possibilities; a little more than 16 million. The very fast computer we were supposing a few minutes ago would do that in 16 seconds.

This further improvement (from 10 years to 16 seconds) was achieved by another general principle: always consider the other guys' points of view. In this case, the state-spaces of the rows (or columns) were enormously smaller than the state-spaces of the queens. It is worth noticing that they were only somewhat more helpful than the state-spaces of the diagonals.

### Exercise

**6.2-1**  Suppose we decided to let the state be determined by position along one of the fifteen upwards (or downwards) diagonals. How big would the state-space be, and how much time would our very fast computer need?

Of course, the microcomputer on which I am typing this is a lot slower; can we find further improvements? The answer is probably no, if we insist on the idea that we generate all members of the state-space and then test them. The answer is certainly yes, if we think carefully about incremental testing of incrementally generated solution states: it will turn out that we can reject huge blocks of the state-space without testing their individual members.

### 6.2.3  Simple Exploration Involves Sequences
of Sets of Sequences

Suppose, for example, that we were about to try out states such as [8,7,5,3,1,4,2,6] or [8,7,6,6,7,5,2,8] or any other of the $8**6$ (about a quarter of a million) states of the form [8,7,...]. It is not necessary to write down even one of these states, because we can tell before we get past the [8,7...] that the state will contain a conflict. For example, the two boards in Figure 6.4  can both be "rejected" without ever being

```
Q * * * * * * *        Q * * * * * * Q
* Q * * * * * *        * Q * * Q * * *
* * * * * * * Q        * * Q Q * * * *
* * Q * * * * *        * * * * * Q * *
* * * * * Q * *        * * * * * * * *
* * * Q * * * *        * * * * * * * *
* * * * * * Q *        * * * * * * Q *   Figure 6.4  Multiple-Conflict Chess-
* * * * Q * * *        * * * * * * * *   boards
```

generated; whichever conflict arises first on a board should cause it to be rejected
without ever adding more queens. There appear to be 64 ways of putting down the
first two queens, but actually there are only $6*5+2*6 = 42$ ways without conflicts.

## Exercises

**6.2-2**  Justify (or disprove) the claim that there are only 42 ways of setting down the
first two queens without conflicts.

**6.2-3**  Figure out how many ways there are of setting down the second and third queens
if the first queen was in position 3.

In fact, we are expanding the state-space somewhat, allowing each column to
have a queen in any position or to be empty. In effect, however, we get a much
reduced problem world.

We can describe a partial solution as being a sequence of queen positions
which does not contain any conflict: [8,1] is a partial solution, and so is [8,6], but
[8,1,6] is not because the first and third queens conflict. A complete solution is a
partial solution of length 8. Thus, we could define the set of partial solutions as
follows:

$$PS = \{S : Conflicts(S) = \{\}\}$$
$$Solutions = \{s : s \in PS, length(s) = 8\}$$

Of course, we then need to define $Conflicts(S)$, which finds the set of all bad pairs
of queens on a given board. These conflicts might in principle be along diagonals,
rows, or columns:

$$Conflicts(S_{1...n}) = \{[i,j] : i,j \in 1\ldots n, Bad(S,i,j)\}$$
$$Bad(S,i,j) = BadDiag(S,i,j) \vee BadRow(S,i,j) \vee BadCol(S,i,j)$$

The sources of conflict can then be further broken down:

$$
\begin{aligned}
BadRow(S,i,j) &= i = j \\
BadCol(S,i,j) &= S_i = S_j \\
BadDiag(S,i,j) &= BadUpD(S,i,j) \vee BadDownD(S,i,j) \\
BadUpD(S,i,j) &= (S_j - j) = (S_i - i) \quad\quad \text{(slope = 1)} \\
BadDownD(S,i,j) &= (S_j - j) = -(S_i - i) \quad\quad \text{(slope = -1)}
\end{aligned}
$$

Each formula is simple geometry: a queen can conflict with another on a diagonal or row or column....

**Q:** Whoa! How can two queens conflict on their row when you've set up the state-space so that they have to be on different rows?

**A:** You're right; you could delete the *BadRow* test altogether, but the others are required. At any rate, we can now talk about the set of all partial solutions, at least as a subset of the set of all sequences of cardinals. Still, we'd rather not construct all sequences of cardinals and then filter out the bad ones; we need operations which work on partial solutions.

A partial solution can be extended by adding one more queen (i.e., by adding one more number in the range $1 \ldots 8$). For example, [8,1,6] is an extension to [8,1], as is [8,1,5]. Such an extension may or may not be a partial solution, but all partial solutions (conflict-free boards) of length $n + 1$ are extensions of partial solutions (conflict-free boards) of length $n$. Think about it.

Now if we think of the really interesting state-space as being the space which contains sequences of queen-placements as states, like [8,1,4] and [1,2,1,2,1,2], we find an interesting fact about paths in the space: the partial solution [8] is connected to the partial solution [8,1] by this simple operation of extension. It is also connected to the state [8,8] by the same operation.

An extension to a partial solution is a partial solution if there are no conflicts in it: [8,1,6] is not a partial solution, but [8,1,5] is. This idea of partial solutions makes the problem enormously smaller, because instead of having more and more partial solutions as the sequences get longer, you may actually get fewer. Since the length of a partial solution is obviously important, we could consider the sets of partial solutions of various lengths:

$$Trials(n) \quad = \quad \{s : s \in PS, Length(s) = n\}$$

Moreover, if you have a sequence which might be a partial solution, and you know that it is an extension of a partial solution, then you don't need to look at all possible pairs of queens to see whether or not they conflict: you have already tested all except for the last queen. Therefore, we can build the successful trials of length 4 in terms of the successful trials of length 3, and so on:

$$
\begin{aligned}
Trials(0) \quad &= \quad \{[\,]\}; \\
Trials(n + 1) \quad &= \quad \{S + [i] : S \in Trials(n), S + [i] \in Neighbors(S)\}
\end{aligned}
$$

In this problem, the state *is* the path, i.e., the state is always just a state of having made certain placements.

$$Neighbors(S) \quad = \quad \{S + [i] : i \in 1 \ldots 8, Conflicts(S + [i]) = \{\}\}$$

**Exercises**   As a first version, the preceding solution is fine, but notice that we now look all over $S + [i]$ for conflicts after we've already made sure that $S$ contains none. Accordingly,

**6.2-4**   write an incremental version of $Conflicts$ to be called $IC(S, i)$ which assumes as a precondition that $S$ is conflict free and therefore that only conflicts of queens in $S$ against the new queen $i$ need to be considered.

**6.2-5**   Compare the asymptotic complexities of the two versions of $Conflicts$.

Now we (or a mechanical moron) can solve the problem by writing down the set of $Trials$ of length 0, which is $\{[\,]\}$, and then looking that up when necessary to form the $Trials$ of length 1 (there are eight of them), then using that again while writing out the $Trials$ of length 2 (there are 42), and so on until we get to the $Trials$ of length 8.

The procedure is exactly the same as it was for building paths in the explicitly given maps that we used before, but since this map is too big to be given explicitly, we extend a path by thinking about eight possible extensions and then crossing off the bad ones. One way to see what's going on is to imagine the 8**8-element state-space as being split into eight subsets:

1.  The subset of the form $[1,\text{—},\text{—},\text{—},\text{—},\text{—},\text{—},\text{—}]$,
2.  The subset of the form $[2,\text{—},\text{—},\text{—},\text{—},\text{—},\text{—},\text{—}]$,

$\vdots$

The set of solutions to the overall problem is the union of the sets of solutions to these subproblems.

Each of these subspaces contains one-eighth of the state-space, but some of them may have more solutions than others. Some may have no solutions at all, but we can't be sure yet. Each of the eight subsets are then split into eight subsets, for a total of 64, 22 of which can be immediately rejected because we can see immediately that they have no solutions. Each of the 42 remaining subsets are then split into eight parts, most of which can be rejected because their solution sets are obviously empty.

**Q:** How much work will it take our computational moron to do this?

**A:** It depends on the number of paths he actually finds. Suppose $Trials(6)$ has 298 possibilities. For each one of these, he has to consider eight extensions, and for each extension he has to check for conflicts with (no more than) six queens. That comes out to a worst-case of $298 * 8 * 6 = 14,304$ required checks, each of which takes him a few steps. Is that any help?

Generalize again. To check for conflicts in extending a trial sequence with $n$ queens, he has to try $8 * n$ conflict checks. Thus, if $|Trials(n)| = T_n$, then he has to perform $T_n * 8 * n$ tests, each with a few steps. He has to repeat this eight times to reach $Trials(8)$ from $Trials(0)$, so if there is a worst-case $Trials$ value, say $T$, then he has no more than $T * 8 * 8 * 8$ total checks. Unfortunately, that's not a very helpful guide, because we've said nothing about how many solutions (or $Trials(3)$, or $Trials(5)$, etc.) there may be, and we can't suggest any limit on $T$. If there were never any conflicts, there would be 8\*\*8 solutions and our moron would have performed somewhat less than $512*8**8 = 2**32$, or about one billion unsuccessful checks. If $Trials(n)$ is never more than 100, then he will perform less than 50,000 checks. Moreover, if he uses eight squares of graph paper to write down each trial, then he might need $8 * 8**8$ or about 60,000,000 squares of graph paper just to write down $Trials(8)$ if there were few conflicts. On the other hand, if $Trials(n)$ is never more than 100, then he would need no more than 800 squares at each stage. Quite a difference!

Is this an ideal solution? No. Is this the best solution we can expect to come up with? No. We have not yet considered the tactic of trying to find a simpler but related problem to solve.

Suppose that there were only three queens on a $3 \times 3$ board, so that the state-space had only 27 elements. If we apply exactly the same tactics as we have up to now, we find that we get exactly the same kind of results, but there are not so many of them: the $Trials$ construction will begin with the empty trial $\{[\,]\}$, then continue with the three unit trials $\{[1], [2], [3]\}$, and then go on to find the length-two trials $\{[1,3], [3,1]\}$. (There are no others.) There are no length-three trials, and therefore no solutions. We can improve this oversimplified model by simplifying further: let us ignore diagonal threats, and just forbid states in which queens (or perhaps rooks) share a row or column. Now the $Trials$ construction will begin with $\{[\,]\}$ and then $\{[1],[2],[3]\}$ as before, but it will continue with $\{[1,2],[1,3],[2,1],[2,3],[3,1],[3,2]\}$ and then produce

$$\{[1,2,3],[1,3,2],[2,1,3],[2,3,1],[3,1,2],[3,2,1]\}$$

as solutions. The structure of the successive decomposition is now small enough to sketch. (See Figure 6.5).

In this diagram, there are no first-level conflicts; second-level conflicts are those with no descendants in the tree, and third-level conflicts are left out altogether. We can write the tree in this form:

$$
\begin{aligned}
A &= [1@A_1, 2@A_2, 3@A_3] \\
A_1 &= [1@A_{11}, 2@A_{12}, 3@A_{13}] \\
A_{11} &= [\,] \\
A_{12} &= [1@A_{121}, 2@A_{122}, 3@A_{123}]
\end{aligned}
$$

and so on; the idea is that $A_S$ is a way of writing the tree that you reach by putting queens down in the order specified by $S$, and thus that it will be $[\,]$ if there are any repeated digits in $S$ or if there are three digits in $S$ already. Otherwise, it will be

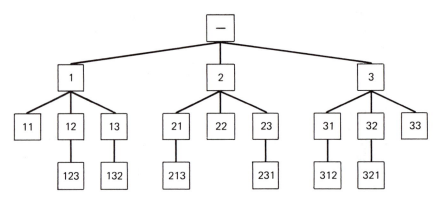

**Figure 6.5** Quasi-Queen Problem Tree

$[A_{S+[1]}, A_{S+[2]}, A_{S+[3]},]$. It all expands out to a large and messy construction which does have the information we need.

**Q:** What have we gained?

**A:** We want to describe every problem with words, formulas, and pictures: this problem simplification lets us construct pictures.

### 6.2.4 Reorganized Exploration Can Be Easier to Manage

The solutions we have been working out with *Trials* can be organized in several different ways. *Trials* is organized by levels: all of the tests with three queens are considered as one large group. Such a level-by-level grouping is called a "breadth-first" search. Another possibility would be to group them according to "subtree" structure: for a given incomplete board, we can consider the set or sequence of all the solutions which could come from it, and which would therefore come below it on the problem tree. For example, the sequence [1] would lead us to the set of all of solutions beginning with 1, and they would all be generated before considering the sequences [2] and [3] at all. Equationally, we could write that what we want is $EQ([])$, where

$$
\begin{aligned}
EQ(S) &= [], & &\text{if } Conflicts(S) \neq \{\} \\
&= [S], & &\text{if } Length(S) = 8 \\
&= EQ(S + [1]) + \ldots + EQ(S + [8]), & &\text{otherwise}
\end{aligned}
$$

Perhaps more computably, although less neatly, we could ask for $EQ'([\,], 1)$ where

$$
\begin{aligned}
EQ'(S, q) &= [\,], & \text{if } q > 8 \\
&= EQ'(S, q + 1) & \text{if } Conflicts(S + [q]) \neq \{\} \\
&= (S + [q])@(EQ'(S, q + 1)) & \text{if } Length(S) = 7 \\
&= EQ'(S + [q], 1) + EQ'(S, q + 1) & \text{otherwise}
\end{aligned}
$$

**Exercises**

**6.2-6**   Explain why $EQ(S) = EQ'(S, 1)$.

**6.2-7**   Carry $EQ'([\,], 1)$ through 20 replacement steps, and see what you get.

It is easy to lose control of such a "tree-style" definition; it is a very useful one, and later on you'll turn it directly into a program, but it's more important to understand what's going on, and it's very hard for you to keep track of all the different $EQ'$ expressions at once. Here the complete picture given for the oversimplified 3-queens problem of the previous subsection becomes very useful: just think of the picture, and reinterpret the equations accordingly (e.g., replace $q > 8$ with $q > 3$.)

The set which this state-space hierarchy gives us is the set

$$\{[\,], [1], [2], [3], [1, 1], [1, 2], [1, 3], \ldots\}$$

with 28 elements. A set, however, is an unordered collection: there are a number of ways (an enormously large number) in which this set could be listed; it does not have to be in order of length. One common and useful way is lexicographic order, in which a word beginning with "a" will always precede a word beginning with "b", no matter what their lengths. Here, we can usefully say that a sequence beginning with "1" can always come before a sequence beginning with "2". The result looks something like Figure 6.6.

```
[]
      [1]
                      [1,1]   X
            [1,2]
                              [1,2,1]
                      [1,2,2]  X
                      [1,2,3] –Solution!
            [1,3]
                      [1,3,1]  X
                      [1,3,2] –Solution!    Figure 6.6  Lexicographic Order of
                      [1,3,3] X              Partial Solutions
```

Using *Trials* requires that we keep track of a fairly large set of sequences at any given moment. It turns out that we can find the next trial position in dictionary order, without doing that.

We have several kinds of situations to consider in finding a successor to a given situation:

**1.** No conflicts, but not a solution:

$$[1, 2] \quad \rightarrow \quad [1, 2, 1]$$
$$[1, 3] \quad \rightarrow \quad [1, 3, 1]$$

Here it seems that we extend the path with a 1.

**2.** Conflicts and solutions:

$$[1, 1] \quad \rightarrow \quad [1, 2]$$
$$[1, 3, 2] \quad \rightarrow \quad [1, 3, 3]$$

Here we add 1 to the last element on the path.

**3.** End of range:

$$[2, 1, 3] \quad \rightarrow \quad [2, 2]$$
$$[1, 2, 3] \quad \rightarrow \quad [1, 3]$$
$$[1, 3, 3] \quad \rightarrow \quad [2]$$

Now, suppose we have a sequence $S = [S[1], \ldots S[N]]$, and we want to find the successor.

- If $S$ has no conflicts but is not a solution, then the successor is $S + [1]$.

- If $S$ has a conflict or is a solution, and $S = X + [n] + Y$, where $Y$ is a (possibly empty) sequence of 3's and $n \neq 3$, so that $n$ is actually the last item in $S$ which is not a 3, then the successor is $X + [n + 1]$.

### Exercises

**6.2-8**   Rephrase the definition of successor to work on the eight-queens problem as originally defined.

**6.2-9**   Mark off a piece of paper with 64 squares in eight rows and columns; use coins or bits of paper for queens. Find the first solution to the problem. Now explain why this method is easier than the generation suggested by the definition of *Trials*.

**6.2-10**  Note that the rules above do not define any successor to [3,3]. Why not?

**6.2-11**  Write rules defining the sequence of all successors generated starting from [].  Explain the space and time requirements of your rules.

### 6.2.5  More Understanding Means Less Work

Now, is this the best solution to the eight queens problem? No. There are several possible improvements we could work on. One is to try to consider symmetry, as

Joe did to check his elimination of bad states in the WGC problem. The conflicts on a chessboard remain the same if we reverse the rows, the columns, or the diagonals, just as the conflict between wolf and goat remained the same whether they were east or west of the river.

### Exercise

**6.2-12** Describe the use of symmetry in finding the solutions. How much difference does it really make?

Another improvement is to add bookkeeping information. We described our moron as always forming eight extensions to each state, but we could describe a state as containing an explicit set of the rows which weren't occupied: instead of the state [8,1,3], we would have [[8,1,3],{2,4,5,6,7}]. Now only those rows need be tried, and row conflicts are impossible. Instead of a maximum number of checks being 7 possible conflicts with 8 extensions, we find that a trial of length 7 has only one extension and the maximum is actually found with 4 possible conflicts and 4 extensions. That's a considerable improvement, even though the size of the state-space appears to have grown.

To use this improvement with the idea of generating states with a *Successor* function, we need to find the *Successor* for the set of free rows when we pick up a queen as well as when we put one down.

### Exercises

**6.2-13** Redefine the *Successor* rules to deal with this.

**6.2-14** Explain the time and space requirements of the revised rules.

**Q:** Well, is that the best possible?

**A:** No. By thinking carefully about the forms of solutions to the problem, it is possible to come up with clever "Knight's Tour" strategies which do substantially better still. However, the Knight's Tour solution is not very general; to study it would teach more about chess than about problem solving. The importance of the solutions we have been working out is that the methods used for their development are extremely general and can be used for finding roads across quite a number of seemingly unrelated state-spaces. In the next section, we will use exactly the same technique (with an abbreviated presentation) for finding a path through a maze; later you will see it as a fundamental tool for algorithm design.

## 6.3 MAZE SEARCH

Here your problem is to systematize a process that you probably learned in or before kindergarten: trace a line through a simple maze, such as you find in Figure 6.7.

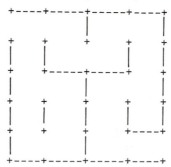

**Figure 6.7**  Simple Maze

As always, the approach is to systematically describe the state-space and then to find paths through it. In this case, the state-space looks very much like an ordinary plane, in which $X$ and $Y$ coordinates give position, as in Figure 6.8.

```
+----+-----+-----+----+
   5,1   5,2  |  5,3    5,4  |
+      +       +      +      +
   4,1  |  4,2    4,3  |  4,4  |
+       +-----+-----+      +
|  3,1     3,2  |  3,3    3,4  |
+      +       +      +      +
|  2,1  |  2,2  |  2,3  |  2,4  |
+      +       +      +----+
|  1,1     1,2  |  1,3    1,4
+----+-----+-----+----+
```

**Figure 6.8**  Simple Maze with Coordinates

Now we can describe the geometric map with a symbolic one.

### 6.3.1  Tabulate the Map

In this case all connections are connections to adjacent positions, but adjacent positions may or may not be connected to one another. An equivalent map could be written by tabulating the set S = $\{[c, c']] : Connected(c, c')\}$, where the predicate $Connected(c, c')$ is *True* if there is a direct route (open wall) between the cell $c$ at $[x, y]$ and the cell $c'$ at $[x', y']$.

[1,1],[1,2]; [1,3],[1,4]; [1,1],[2,1]; [1,2],[2,2]; [1,3],[2,3];
[2,1],[3,1]; [2,2],[3,2]; [2,3],[3,3]; [2,4],[3,4]; [3,1],[3,2];
[3,3],[3,4]; [3,1],[4,1]; [3,4],[4,4]; [4,2],[4,3]; [4,1],[5,1];
[4,2],[5,2]; [4,3],[5,3]; [4,4],[5,4]; [5,1],[5,2]; [5,3],[5,4];

In either case, the task is to find a path from [5,1] to [1,4].

Obviously, the second map is much harder to read than the first, but we can simplify it. The reduction in the state-space of the eight queens problem came from reducing the measurements we were making, first because some of them could be found from others, and then because we did not need some of the information (namely, "Which queen are we talking about?") carried along automatically when measuring from the queen's point of view. Here we are measuring from the points of view of geometric coordinate axes, and yet we don't really care about the geometry of the situation: only the connections matter.

Let's give a name (a letter) to each of the 20 places: row 1 will have letters A,B,C,D; row 2 will have E,F,G,H; row 3 gets I,J,K,L; 4 gets M,N,O,P; and 5 gets Q,R,S,T.

## 6.3.2 Construct the Paths Systematically

Now the task is to find a path from Q to D given connections

{[A,B], [C,D], [A,E], [B,F], [C,G], [E,I], [F,J], [G,K], [H,L], [I,J]
[K,L], [I,M], [L,P], [N,O], [M,Q], [N,R], [O,S], [P,T], [Q,R], [S,T]}

and a rule saying that the *Connected* predicate is symmetric.

As in Chapter 4, we note that either a path is empty or it is the extension of a shorter path by a single segment, and we start forming the paths from Q, hoping to reach D. So we form the sets of:

empty paths          {[Q]};
unit paths           {[Q,R],[Q,M]};
length-two paths     {[Q,R,Q],[Q,R,N],[Q,M,Q],[Q,M,I]};
length-three paths   {[Q,R,Q,R], [Q,R,Q,M], [Q,R,N,R], [Q,R,N,O],
                     [Q,M,Q,R], [Q,M,Q,M], [Q,M,I,M], [Q,M,I,E], [Q,M,I,J]};

and at this point the bookkeeping becomes difficult.

## 6.3.3 Simplify the Model to Represent
##       the Problem Better

**Q:** What's making it take so long?

**A:** There are at least three problems. First, the formulas have a lot of brackets and commas; surely we could write the length-two paths as {QRQ, QRN, QMQ, QMI} and make it somewhat easier to read. Second, looking up paths in both directions from "R" requires scanning the whole list of pairs to see all the places where an "R" occurs, and we ought to have the list organized better. Here's one way. Note that in the table the position A is related to all members of the set {B, E}; the position B is related to all members of {A, F}; and so on. Simply list the letters in alphabetical order, and for each one write (in alphabetical order) all the letters related to it in the original table.

A:BE, B:AF, C:DG, D:C, E:AI, F:BJ, G:CK, H:L, I:EJM, J:FI,
K:GL, L:HKP, M:IQ, N:OR, O:NS, P:LT, Q:MR, R:NQ, S:OT, T:SP.

This abbreviates a description of the form

$$\begin{aligned}
Neighbors(A) &= \{B, E\} \\
Neighbors(B) &= \{A, F\} \\
Neighbors(C) &= \{D, G\}
\end{aligned}$$

$$\vdots$$

Now the information contained in the relation table is represented by the single function of looking up one entry in this new table. [Note: In constructing a new table, errors are always possible. One simple check is that the sum of the sizes of the sets {B,E}, {A,F}, etc., should be twice the number of pairs in the original table.]

## Exercise

**6.3-1**   Why?

After dealing with abbreviation and table organization, we have the third problem, which is the presence of cyclic paths (those which visit the same point more than once), such as QRQ, QRQR, QRQRQ, etc.

**Q:** Can we omit them?
**A:** Yes, because

If we get from Q to D by a cycle [Q, $X_1$, ..., $X_i$, A, $Y_1$, ..., $Y_j$, A, $Z_1$, ...,$Z_k$, D],
   **then** [Q, $X_1$, ... $X_i$, A, $Z_1$, ... $Z_k$, D] is also a path (and a shorter one).

It has to be a path, because every connection it uses is also needed by the cyclic path.

**Q:** I guess I can see that that means that **if** there is an answer, **then** there is an answer with no cycles. Are you sure that you can therefore ignore cycles along the way? After all, with the eight-queens problem you had empty columns in partial solutions and then lost them at the end.
   **A:** Hmm.... This case is different. In the eight-queens problem, a final solution with no empty columns was constructed from a partial solution with empty columns, but in this problem every final solution without cycles can be constructed from a

partial solution without cycles. It has to be, because if the partial solution had repetitions, then the same repetitions would be present in the final form.

**Q:** Is that a proof?

**A:** Not really, but it does give the crucial idea of a proof. Let's just call it a pretty plausible argument and ignore cyclic paths. Starting over, we find that the set of length-0 paths is still [Q], but then we get to

length-1: QR, QM
length-2: QRN, QMI
length-3: QRNO, QMIJ, QMIE
length-4: QRNOS, QMIJF, QMIEA
length-5: QRNOST, QMIJFB, QMIEAB

Notice that the two paths ending in B form a cycle when taken together, but neither considered separately is a cycle. Continuing, we have

length-6: QRNOSTP, QMIJFBA, QMIEABF
length-7: QRNOSTPL, QMIJFBAE, QMIEABFJ
length-8: QRNOSTPLK, QRNOSTPLH

Notice that the set of possibilities suddenly shrank: the paths ending in E and J can each be extended in two ways, but all four of the resulting paths have cycles.

## Exercises

**6.3-2**  Complete the construction to find the path to D.

**6.3-3**  Find the number of paths of length 6 which would be required if we did not eliminate cyclic paths.

**6.3-4**  To estimate the most time our moron might need for the problem, notice that every cell has a maximum of four neighbors—three if you don't count the way you come in. Also, notice that if there is a path to the exit in an $M \times N$ maze, then there is an acyclic path no longer than $M \times N$. How many paths could there be?

**6.3-5**  Suppose I give you a rectangle of graph paper. Show how you could construct a maze in which the path to the exit would go through almost half the cells.

## 6.3.4  The Paths Fit into a Hierarchy

Just as the eight queens problem gave us a choice of rows in which to put the next column's queen, the maze problem gives us a choice of boxes to be explored next. They could be organized as follows:

A:BE, B:AF, C:DG, D:C, E:AI, F:BJ, G:CK, H:L, I:EJM, J:FI,
K:GL, L:HKP, M:IQ, N:OR, O:NS, P:LT, Q:MR, R:NQ, S:OT, T:SP.

Here they are alphabetized overall, and each entry has the sequence of successors in alphabetical order. If we now draw a tree of successors with Q at the root, M and R below it, I and Q below M, N and Q below R, and so on, we'll have the same sort of structure which we had for the eight queens.

## Exercise

**6.3-6**   Draw the tree, crossing off any nodes which repeat nodes above them. How large can it be?

Once again, we can simplify the process of finding a solution to the maze by specifying a sequence of paths in very close analogy to the lexicographic order of partial solutions for the eight queens problem:

$$[Q], [Q,M], [Q,M,I], [Q,M,I,E], [Q,M,I,E,A], \ldots$$

## Exercise

**6.3-7**   Go back to the eight queens problem, and generalize the **if-then** rules which defined the successor of a partial solution so that they can be used to define the successor of a maze path. Try to abbreviate your generalization as much as possible.

### 6.3.5  More Understanding, Less Work

**Q:** Are there better solutions?
   **A:** Of course. Let's look at the picture in a different way, with Figure 6.9.

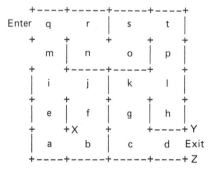

**Figure 6.9**   Simple Maze

We were thinking of the blanks (the holes in the walls) as being the important things, so we essentially described this picture as a pattern of holes. If you think of the maze as a set of tunnels in rock, we were finding paths that didn't have to go right through anything solid. We could instead think of it as a pattern of lines, and consider the structure of rock, not air. Problem solvers sometimes call this a "foreground-background shift" and pass out famous pictures which look like different things depending on how you look at them. (The collected works of M.C.Escher [6] are very good for computer science students; also, remember to read *Gödel, Escher,Bach; An Eternal Golden Braid*, which was mentioned in the introduction.) In this case, the foreground-background shift tells us that rather than thinking about the paths forming one long wiggly line with a loop on the lower left, we could think about a lot of blocks forming three blobs of solid rock, now labelled X, Y, and Z. Blob X is all the way inside the maze, and the other two blobs form its borders. In this case, we want to get from one border point which touches Y and X to another border point which touches Y and Z.

**Q:** What use is it to talk about paths here? You can't walk through blobs; that's why they're marked.

**A:** No, but you can walk through cells beside or around a blob; remember that it's not connected to anything, or that would be part of the same blob. If you walk beside blob Y or Z, you'll eventually reach the exit point.

**Q:** You're cheating. You defined blobs X and Z as stretching from beginning to end, and now you're saying you can get from beginning to end by following them. How do you know when you're inside a maze which way to go to keep following Y?

**A:** Imagine keeping your left hand on it. If you always take every left-hand turn, you will stay with the blob which was on your left when you began, and you know that blob goes to the outside because you were outside with it. You'll be going counterclockwise around blob Y. Similarly, you could stay with blob Z by always taking every right-hand turn, and then you'll be going clockwise around it. Try it.

**Q:** I guess I see how I could do it, but now how would I explain it to the moron with his graph paper?

**A:** He needs a version of the model we built in which the constraint on the states which is to be unchanged (left invariant) by the operations is that the path which defines the state forms a partial border for a blob. Another way of putting that is that at each point, he takes an outgoing path immediately to the right of the path he came in by. Actually, it's the same lexicographic sequencing as before, with a few minor differences.

When you list the cells connected to a given cell, you shouldn't list them alphabetically, because you don't have a set of neighbors any longer. Instead, you have a sequence: write them in clockwise order. (Or counterclockwise, but you have to be consistent). For example, if we list the successors to Q as [Entrance, M, R] then we're doing a counterclockwise ordering, just as if we had listed them as [M,R,Entrance] or [R,Entrance,M]; this says that if you enter Q from M you should leave by R, or if you enter Q from R you should leave by the entrance, or if you enter Q from the entrance you should leave by M.

All in all, we should write a list like

$$
\begin{array}{llllll}
a:eb, & b:af, & c:gd, & d:c<Out>, & e:ia, & f:jb, & g:kc, \\
h:l, & i:mej, & j:if, & k:lg, & l:pkh, & m:qi, & n:ro, \\
o:ns, & p:tl, & q:mr<In>, & r:qn, & s:to, & t:ps.
\end{array}
$$

This simply abbreviates a function of the form

$$
\begin{aligned}
LeftNeighbors(A) &= [E, B]; \\
LeftNeighbors(B) &= [A, F]; \\
&\vdots
\end{aligned}
$$

We'd also better add <In>q and <Out>d, for consistency. Notice that unless a space has at least three successors, there is no difference between clockwise and counterclockwise; if you reach a space with one successor, then you must go out the way you came in; and if you reach a space with two successors, then you came in by one and must necessarily go out by the other.

### Exercise

**6.3-8**  Suppose I had a space with no successors. (For example, I could put a wall between H and L.) Would that create a problem? Explain.

So, back to our counterclockwise ordering: we came into Q from the entrance, so must leave by M.

**Q:** But going from Q to M is not the right way!
**A:** So what? It is part of the right way if we are going around Z.

The successors of M are [Q,I], so if we come in by Q we must leave by I;
the successors of I are [M,E,J], so if we come by M we must leave by E;
the successors of E are [I,A], so if we come by I we must leave by A;
the successors of A are [E,B], so if we come in by E we must leave by B;
and on through F, J, and back to I.

**Q:** But now we're going in a circle! I thought we were going to forget cyclic paths.
**A:** Not this time. Now we're back to I, but this time we come to I from J. The successors of I are [M,E,J], so if we come in by J we must leave by M; the successors of M are [Q,I], so if we come in by I we must leave by Q; the successors of Q are [M,R,Entrance], so if we come in by M we leave by R; and on through the rest of it.

**Exercises**

**6.3-9**  Complete the path construction. Be careful at L.

**6.3-10**  Define the successor operation with **if-then** rules as before. [Hint: you do not have to check for cycles, and you never have to back up.]

**6.3-11**  Figure out at most how many steps the moron must consider. (The longest path is no longer $M * N$; or is it? Different answers to this question are acceptable, but you should be able to find some limit.)

### 6.3.6  Once More, We Hunted for Paths

Of course, it's hardly surprising to find that the problem of finding a path in a maze gets turned into a pathfinding problem. What you should realize is that the translation from concrete problem to abstract model is just as big a step in the solution to the maze as in WGC or in placing the eight queens. It might be an even bigger step, because in describing the right-hand rule we used a constraint on states which is very hard to translate into the model: each state (partial solution) has to form a border on a blob, but the blobs haven't been translated into the model at all; they're simply invisible, unless you start making lists of what connections might be present but aren't.

Building paths incrementally, one step at a time, is a very powerful method. We've seen it work in maps, we've seen it work as the elephant went downhill, we've seen it work across rivers and on chessboards and with mazes. In the next section, we'll be looking at a problem which is best approached by incremental design along another dimension.

## 6.4  THE TOWERS OF HANOI

Another famous puzzle, also used to illustrate principles of computer science although it existed before computers, is called the Towers of Hanoi.

This one goes with a story.

> Once upon a time, in the Far East, a temple was constructed, with a secret room for a table on which were three ivory poles, labelled ARLN, NGREK, and FRULSTIJ.[1] When the poles were put in place, 64 golden disks were made, each with a hole in the middle just large enough for a pole. The first was just big enough to make a ring around a pole, and each one afterwards was a little bigger than the one before it. The rings were placed on the pole labelled ARLN in order of size with the largest on the bottom. The priests were then given their instructions: move the rings to the pole labelled NGREK, but never move more than one ring at a time (the top one), and never put any ring on top of a smaller ring.

---

[1]Perhaps you never heard about the labels, even if you've heard the story. They're magic...but that's another tale, which shall be told another time.

They're still at it: when they finish, the world ends.

Even after you know how to do it, the problem of the towers of Hanoi is sufficiently tedious that with 64 rings, the world is not likely to last long enough for the priests to finish their work. Even with only eight rings, the puzzle can often keep a reasonably bright adolescent going for half an hour or so.


## Exercises

**6.4-1**   Draw a picture of the situation.

**6.4-2**   Cut out eight paper circles of different sizes; try to solve the problem.


### 6.4.1   Describe the Model

What is the state-space? In this case, it seems to be the Cartesian product of the three poles' states, or the Cartesian product of the 64 rings' states. Let's try both: for pole $X$, "What rings do you have?" and for ring $Y$, "Which pole are you on?".

If we ask each ring "Which pole are you on?" we find that it is in one of three states: $\{A, N, F\}$. That gives us a state-space with 3**64 elements, where a state will be written as a sequence of length 64. Thus,

$$[A, A, A, A, N, F, A, F, A, A, F, A, A, N, N, F, A, A, \ldots] \text{ is a state.}$$

Alternatively, we ask each pole "What rings do you have?" and find that each pole contains a sequence of rings. The state is then a sequence of three poles, each of which is a sequence of 64 numbers all in the range $0 \ldots 64$. (We use the zero to represent an empty position; writing a dash "—" is probably more readable.)

If we consider all sequences of 64 numbers to be equally likely, then what we have here is a state-space with 65 possibilities for each of 192 positions, which is 64**192. In this state-space, a state might look like

$$[[-, -, -, 1, 3, 5, 9, 17, \ldots], [-, -, -, \ldots, -, 2, 10, 12, \ldots], [-, \ldots, -, 4, 6, \ldots]$$


## Exercises

**6.4-3**   How much bigger is the second state-space than the first?

**6.4-4**   List some invalid "possibilities" of the larger space.

**6.4-5**   Does the smaller space include any invalid possibilities? Justify your answer. (Your answer doesn't actually have to be right. It does have to be well thought out.)


Actually, for any particular pole we need not ask what order the rings are in, because we know that already. We can treat the rings on a given pole as a set. Further, if we know which rings are on two of the poles, we need not ask which are on the third: all of the other rings will be. In fact we can describe the problem of picking a state as being that of picking a subset of the rings to rest on pole $A$, then a subset of the remainder to rest on pole $N$; whatever's left will be on pole $F$. Think about it a while: this has to yield 3**64 possible states.

### Exercise

**6.4-6**   Why?

Another way of saying that is that we can write a state as a sequence of two sets: $[\{62, 63\}, \{61, 64\}]$ could represent the state in which the four largest disks are divided between the poles $A$ and $N$, while all others are on pole $F$.

Is it reasonable to write this state down? No; it just takes too long to deal with that many numbers. As we did with the eight queens problem, let us define a smaller problem whose state we can write out explicitly: instead of 64 disks, we'll only write out eight.

The initial configuration is $[\{1, 2, 3, 4, 5, 6, 7, 8\}, \{\}, \{\}]$; we need to get from there to the final configuration, which is $[\{\}, \{\}, \{1, 2, 3, 4, 5, 6, 7, 8\}]$. Even this can be abbreviated: as with the man, wolf, cabbages, goat becoming CGMW, we can see how to write these as $[12345678, —, —]$ and $[—, —, 12345678]$. We could abbreviate it further by leaving out the last, but that's not necessary—in this case, that just seems to make it harder to read.

What are the operations? Try an example:

$$[12345678, —, —] \longrightarrow [2345678, 1, —]$$

We can move any digit from the front of the first sequence to the front of the second or third, from the front of the second to the front of the first or third, and from the front of the third to the front of the first or second. What are the constraints? Just that this first digit being moved must not cover a lower digit.

### 6.4.2  Describe the Problem

Now, what exactly is the answer to the "problem"? Clearly it is not the solved puzzle itself (for that, you could cheat); the important factor is the sequence of moves required: as in the puzzles before, we are looking for a path which would take us from the initial state to the final state. The only operation on states is a disk move: a move takes (1) a particular (numbered) disk from (2) a particular pole (where it was the smallest) to (3) another pole (where it will also be the smallest). To describe a move, you must include all three of those factors. The simplest way is just to list them in a triple: "$[5, A, N]$" could be read as "Move disk number 5 from pole $A$ to pole $N$". As long as we stick to single-digit problems, we can abbreviate that as $5AN$ and still know what's meant. A sequence of moves like $[1AN, 2AF, 1NF]$ is then "Move #1 from $A$ to $N$, then move #2 from $A$ to $F$, then move #1 from $N$ to $F$." That sequence would take us along the state-sequence

$$[[1\ldots8,-,-],[2\ldots8,1,-],[3\ldots8,1,2],[3\ldots8,-,12]]$$

which doesn't violate any constraints, but doesn't seem to get us very far. Evidently the sequence of moves has to be somewhat irregular, since a move from $A$ to $N$ cannot possibly be immediately followed by another move from $A$ to $N$, and can only uselessly be followed by a move from $N$ to $A$.

We could generalize that last observation and discover (for example) that if a move from $A$ to $N$ is followed by a move from $A$ to $F$, then the next move cannot be a move from $A$ to $F$ or $N$, cannot be from $F$ to $N$, could only uselessly be a move from $F$ to $A$, and therefore must either be from $N$ to $A$ or $N$ to $F$. Further generalizations will get us deeper and deeper into complicated bookkeeping.

Are there any other principles left to be applied? Yes: in the eight-queens and maze problems, we tried to define partial solutions as abstractions from the complete solution.

In both of those puzzles, we defined a path of length $N+1$ in terms of a path of length $N$, and a solution was given as a path which satisfied a particular property.

### Exercise

**6.4-7**  Define the $Trials(n)$ solutions for the Towers of Hanoi as they were defined for the other puzzles. What is a solution? How do you recognize a cycle?

The idea of incremental growth of a path towards a solution can be made to work in this case as it did in the others, and even to give a solution which always determines exactly which way to go as with the right-hand rule for the maze, but it requires considerably more effort and considerably less generality. As with the Knight's Tour solutions to the eight queens problem, we won't be following it up.

### Exercise

**6.4-8**  Try to find a definition of state so that you can work out a successor function, with each partial path of length $N$ being extended into a path of length $N+1$.

However, there is a more general way to look at describing partial solutions.

### 6.4.3  Generalize the Problem

**Q:** What is a partial solution to the problem of moving 64 disks from $A$ to $N$, using $F$ for temporary storage?

**A:** Clearly, we want to move $D$ disks from $X$ to $Y$, using $Z$ for temporary storage. All I did was turn the obvious constants into variables: I have made the problem apparently harder in order to make the solution more flexible.

We still want to define the solutions incrementally, but the size of the path isn't the only thing we could be incrementing. Instead of building a path out of a path whose length is one less, maybe we could build a solution for moving a bunch of disks out of a solution for one less disk. If we could move $D - 1$ disks from $X$ to $Y$ using $Z$, could we move $D$ disks from $X$ to $Y$ using $Z$?

Moving 7 disks from $A$ to $N$ using $F$ for temporary storage does not seem helpful: that will just get us to a state described by $[8, —, 1 \ldots 7]$. That seems almost worse than before: we would now have to slip the "8" underneath "1 \ldots 7", which appears to be against the rules. However, we have seen the Useless Move Principle before. From this state, we can do one thing that we couldn't do before: we can move disk 8. In particular, we can move to $[—,8,1 \ldots 7]$.

**Q:** So what?

**A:** Well, we just assumed that we could move seven disks from $X$ to $Y$ using $Z$; we can now move seven disks from $N$ to $F$ with $A$, getting $[—,1 \ldots 8,—]$.

**Q:** So what? That's not what we wanted.

**A:** But it looks like what we wanted, it's just shuffled around a little. We can shuffle it back: in order to get from $[1 \ldots 8,—,—]$ to $[—,—,1 \ldots 8]$, we will first get to $[8,1 \ldots 7,—]$ with the One Less principle, then to $[—,1 \ldots 7,8]$, and then to $[—,—,1 \ldots 7]$ with the One Less principle again.

This is a more general way to look at the problem of building paths. Instead of adding a single element to the front or back of a sequence, we can build paths out of smaller paths by sticking them together.

Let's say that again more carefully: the sequence of moves that takes $D$ disks from $X$ to $Y$ with $Z$, or $Hanoi(D, X, Y, Z)$, is the concatenation of the following.

1. The sequence of moves that takes $D - 1$ disks from $X$ out of the way to $Z$ using $Y$, i.e., $Hanoi(D - 1, X, Z, Y)$,

2. The single move that takes the disk numbered $D$ from $X$ to $Y$, $[D, X, Y]$ (written "DXY"), and

3. The sequence of moves that takes the $D - 1$ disks from their storage on $Z$ to $Y$ using $X$, i.e., $Hanoi(D - 1, Z, Y, X)$.

Should the starting point be $D = 0$ or $D = 1$? Either will do; it is rather nice saying that if $D = 0$, then the sequence of required moves is just $[\,]$.

In formal notation, we can say

$$
\begin{aligned}
Hanoi(D, X, Y, Z) \quad &= \quad [\,], \qquad\qquad\qquad\qquad\qquad \text{if } D = 0\\
&= \quad Hanoi(D - 1, X, Z, Y)\\
&\quad\; +[[D, X, Y]]\\
&\quad\; +Hanoi(D - 1, Z, Y, X), \qquad \text{otherwise}
\end{aligned}
$$

That means that $Hanoi(0, A, N, F)$ is $[\,]$. We can then work out a level-1 *Hanoi* problem:

$$
\begin{aligned}
Hanoi(1, A, N, F) \quad &= \quad Hanoi(0, A, F, N) + [1AN] + Hanoi(0, F, N, A)\\
&= \quad [\,] + [1AN] + [\,]\\
&= \quad [1AN]
\end{aligned}
$$

Now we can try a level-2 problem:

$$
\begin{aligned}
Hanoi(2, A, N, F) \quad &= \quad Hanoi(1, A, F, N) + [2AN] + Hanoi(1, F, N, A)\\
&= \quad [1AF] + [2AN] + [1FN]\\
&= \quad [1AF, 2AN, 1FN]
\end{aligned}
$$

and so on.

**Exercise**

**6.4-9**   Calculate $Hanoi(3, A, N, F)$.

### 6.4.4   Examine the Cost of the Solution

How expensive is the solution? There are actually two questions here: one is asking about the solution itself (how big is it when the moron gets it finally written out on graph paper, with one square for each "[", each "1", each ",", etc.?); and the other is asking how much had to be written along the way. For this problem, the size of the answer is $L * S$, where $L$ is the length of the move sequence and $S$ is the size of a move. $S$ is just three spaces, as in "1AF" or "2AN", but $L$ depends on $D$. In fact,

$$
\begin{aligned}
L(D) \quad &= \quad 0, \qquad\qquad\qquad\qquad\quad\;\; \text{if } D = 0\\
&= \quad L(D - 1) + 1 + L(D - 1), \qquad \text{otherwise}
\end{aligned}
$$

Accordingly, we can find that $L(1) = L(0) + 1 + L(0) = 0 + 1 + 0 = 1$, and $L(2) = L(1) + 1 + L(1) = 1 + 1 + 1 = 3$.

**Exercise**

**6.4-10** List $L(3), L(4) \ldots L(8)$. Are you surprised? Look at the pattern and compute $L(64)$. [Hint: All values are very close to powers of two.]

For this problem, the total number of things to be written down for $Hanoi(D, X, Y, Z)$ when found by the strategy suggested above is

- 14 or 15 graph-paper spaces for the expression "$Hanoi(D, X, Y, Z)$" itself,

- 2 spaces for the two characters in "[]" if $D = 0$, or else 7 spaces for the characters in "$+[DXY]+$" and all of the spaces for "$Hanoi(D-1, \ldots)$" twice.

This again is a function of $D$, described as

$$
\begin{aligned}
TotalSpace(D) \quad &= \quad 17, &&\text{if } D = 0 \\
&= \quad 23 + 2 * TotalSpace(D - 1), &&\text{otherwise .}
\end{aligned}
$$

**Exercises**    For the ambitious reader:

**6.4-11** Find $TotalSpace(64)$.

**6.4-12** Note that the $TotalSpace$ formula is not perfect; it assumes that the "$+[DXY]+$" is only written once, whereas if you keep copying it as I did in the example of $Hanoi(2, A, N, F)$, then you will actually use not 9 spaces but $9 * (D - 1)$ because it will be written out $D - 1$ times. Fix the $TotalSpace$ formula.

**6.4-13** Generalize the solution, defining the sequence of moves which will take the start state to an arbitrary goal state. [Hint: think about the biggest disk which is *not* on pole $A$ in the goal state.] What is the $TotalSpace$ requirement for this problem?

**6.4-14** Generalize again, defining the sequence of moves which will take an arbitrary state to an arbitrary state. (Use your solution to the last problem.)

### 6.4.5  Our Problems Are Getting Trickier

... and the solutions are getting more complicated. In the problems like *Paths, Sum, Length,* and even back to table lookup, we had a sequence of steps which was growing incrementally: one step at a time, so that you could write a moron's procedure which amounted to "as long as you haven't come to the end, generate the next step." Now we have a sequence of steps which is not that simple; the solution to $Hanoi(n + 1, x, y, z)$ is a concatenation of sequences, not just a steady growth. We can still use the moron's procedure for simplifying a goal description, just as we did before, but it can be quite difficult to get him to work without keeping that description explicitly written out; try it yourself with eight "rings," keeping track mentally of what you should do next.

**Exercise**

**6.4-15** Write a simple recurrence for the *Hanoi* problem, so that $Hanoi(n, x, y, z) = f([], n, x, y, z, \ldots)$ and $f(a, n, x, y, z, \ldots)$ either is $a$ or is $f(a', n', x', y', z', \ldots)$. [Warning: This is quite difficult.]

If you haven't had doubts about the correctness of some of the steps we've been taking, then either you're afflicted with excessive respect for authority figures like textbook authors (i.e., you haven't read many texts) or you haven't been reading carefully. In order to argue convincingly for (or against) some point of view, (such as "This won't work!") you need some accepted rules for argument. When you formalize those rules, you call them proof techniques, and that's what the next chapter will be about. Proof techniques seem to require a certain amount of "maturity," whatever that is; they don't necessarily go over very well in the first course.

**Q:** You mean the first computer science course?

**A:** No, I mean the first course to try to teach proof techniques—whatever course that may be for you. Proof techniques are necessary in a large part of computer science and in the related mathematical disciplines, and if you skip them or skimp them now, then you'll just be leaving yourself more to do later.... I'm just warning you to expect some internal resistance.

# 7

# Proofs: Reasoning Carefully Through Program Design

What goes wrong with programs? There are two kinds of errors: first, we don't get the right answer; second, we get the right answer but it's too expensive.

## 7.1 CLASSIFYING ERRORS

There are two reasons for not getting the right answer: first, we might actually give a wrong answer; second, we might not be able to produce any answer. Both of these problems are common in programming. There are also two reasons for excessive expense: first, we might be instructing the moron to go through too many steps, so that it takes too much time to finish; second, we might be telling him to keep more on his desk (or in his filing cabinets) than will actually fit. Each of these reasons is common in programming. In this section we will consider some of the particular kinds of errors that can arise at different stages of program development; in this chapter, we will try to develop tools for preventing them.

### 7.1.1 Bad Models

First, we can have a bad model; one which is not a homomorphic image of the part of reality we need, so that the solution in the model is not a solution in the world. That's what happened when we used a pictorial model with implicit or explicit straight-line distance when what was needed was distance by road. All we can do to avoid this situation is to make the model we use be as simple as possible, as understandable as possible, and as explicit as possible, and then ask what's wrong with it.

### 7.1.2  Bad Solutions

Second, we can have a bad solution within the model. For example, the shortest path from here to Babylon is not necessarily one of those with the fewest road segments, as the construction we used implicitly assumed. (If necessary, go back and reread the solution method, and think about the case where there are two paths from A to B; one is composed of three 100-mile country-road segments, and the other is composed of two 1000-mile super-highway segments, one going far out of the way and the other coming back. The method given will find the distance as 2000 miles, not 300.) To avoid this, we have to make the description of the solution as good as possible and then think about what properties it has; a careless description of "the shortest path" will probably be ambiguous about which of those two paths is shortest.

### 7.1.3  Bad Procedures

Third, even if we have a correct solution within the model, we can still have a procedure which fails to construct that solution. Here there are two kinds of failure: we can produce the wrong answer, or none. As an example of producing the wrong answer, we could easily describe the solution of the shortest path correctly, but actually design a procedure which will construct the path with the shortest number of segments rather than the least total length. As an example of producing no answer at all, we could have a procedure for pathfinding which goes around and around in circles rather than going on with the path. (This would have happened in the maze if we had gone ahead with lexicographic ordering of paths but kept to an alphabetic ordering of successors. In that case, we actually went back and changed the model so that it would have the information required for a particular kind of procedure.)

### 7.1.4  Bad Coding

Fourth, we could make a mistake in actually writing code for our procedure in a particular programming language. We can't give examples of that yet, since we haven't done anything with a particular programming language, but you should realize that the mistakes can range from simply mispelling or omitting a required word to misinterpreting the meaning of a programming language construct. The kind of thinking which goes into finding and fixing the first three sorts of errors is different from the kind required to find and fix incorrect coding; in fact, if the first three have been done carefully, the last is a relatively trivial step for each version of a program. (In fact, the mechanical moron can do much of the work of this phase: I have been slow to learn the syntax of *Modula-2*, because I have been using a special kind of editor program called a "syntax-directed editor," which makes many of these mistakes impossible.) This chapter will therefore deal only with the first three kinds of error.

How can we prevent errors in programming? There is no absolutely reliable way, but we have to try. We do it by explicitly writing and criticizing the model, explicitly writing and criticizing the solution, explicitly writing and criticizing the procedure, and finally of course explicitly writing and criticizing the code. In effect, we try to prove (to ourselves, to our instructors, to our teammates) that the whole thing works. Normally, it doesn't (at least at first); this process results in uncovering a variety of errors.

## 7.1.5 Proving Means Different Things in Different Contexts

To prove something is to test it, as when you "prove" armor by hitting it with an ax and then sell "proven" armor, being the armor that doesn't have holes in it, or when you seek the proof of the pudding by tasting it. Similarly, you might "prove" the alchoholic content of a beverage by mixing in some gunpowder and then trying to light it; a liquor with 50% alcohol will burn with a clear blue flame and is thus 100% proven, or 100 proof.[1]

The usual use of the word refers only to successful tests: a proof of an assertion is an argument that convinces the audience of the truth of that assertion. Over the last few thousand years, people have been fooled many times by obviously convincing arguments that turned out to be wrong, and some of them are getting skeptical, not only about some assertions but about some kinds of argument. The worst of these are called mathematicians. Of course, they aren't necessarily skeptical about politics, religion, or art, but they are very skeptical about their own chosen fields.

Similarly, over the past few decades, programmers have been fooled many times by obviously correct programs that turned out to be wrong, and some of them are getting skeptical too. Some have even come to believe that program design and analysis are mathematical disciplines, rather than engineering disciplines which happen to require mathematical skills. We won't take a position on that, but we will teach you to build some proofs, and we'll do it in algorithmic terms. Even a mechanical moron can construct proofs: telling it how to do so is sometimes important, but at the moment it's more important to get you to construct proofs, to understand proofs, to know when some omitted detail could easily be filled in, and to know when an attempted proof has gone bad.

---

[1] I first encountered this history in Dick Francis's thriller, *Proof*; if you don't think the source is authoritative, prove it for yourself.

## 7.2  A FEW KINDS OF ARGUMENT SERVE MOST PURPOSES

We'll work on four basic kinds of argument: substitutions, direct proof, proof by contradiction, and proof by induction. A substitution proof merely replaces equals by equals, as we've been doing all along; a direct proof takes us from *if* to *then*; a contradiction carries us backwards from *then* to *if*; and an inductive proof is actually a kind of program by which we can construct arbitrarily large, specialized proofs of the other kinds. (This classification is oversimplified, of course.)

### 7.2.1  Substitution Is Simple

A proof by substitution can work like this:

> John's height = Mary's height;
> John's height > Joe's height; so
> Mary's height > Joe's height.

If you know that $A = B$, then you can substitute either one for the other. You've been doing this kind of reasoning for a long time, and of course we've depended upon it fairly strongly in the last few chapters. It's time to think about what makes it work ... and when it doesn't.

### 7.2.2  Substitution Isn't Always Safe

The usual problem with this kind of reasoning is that people start thinking about substitutions that are true in one context, and then they apply them to another. If (in 1985) I write that "Ronald Reagan is the President of the United States," and I also note that the President of the United States is the supreme commander of the armed forces, I can reasonably conclude that Ronald Reagan is the supreme commander of the armed forces. If I then report that I heard on short-wave radio that the President of the United States was assassinated in Dallas, then I am telling the literal truth but I am guilty of imprecise phrasing and incomplete state-description. A reader who inferred that I heard that Ronald Reagan was assassinated in Dallas might be justifiably annoyed at me when she realized that I was talking about an event two decades before. To be exact, I have to have some way of distinguishing between them; one would be to say that the United States of 1985 is different from the United States of 1963, and the same applies to the armed forces. I could model this symbolically with the equations

$$RonaldReagan = President(UnitedStates(1985))$$
$$WasAssassinated(President(UnitedStates(1963))) = True$$
$$Commander(ArmedForces(UnitedStates(n))) = President(UnitedStates(n))$$

From this we can conclude that

$$RonaldReagan = Commander(ArmedForces(UnitedStates(1985)))$$
$$WasAssassinated(Commander(ArmedForces(UnitedStates(1963)))) = True$$

But there's not much farther we can go. Many programming errors arise from this sort of confusion: substitutions that are not only valid but essential to the job at one moment, turn out to be subtly wrong in the next.

### 7.2.3  Direct Proofs Are Simple

A simple direct proof works like this:

> John loves Mary;
> Mary despises anyone who is dumb enough to like her; so
> Mary despises John.

As I said, it's simple, it's direct, and it's generally convincing. Direct proofs often use equational steps; the difference is that in a direct proof, we are sometimes working with **if-then** rules rather than just equations. In this case, we could write the assertions formally as

> $Loves(John, Mary)$;
> **if** $Loves(x, Mary)$ **then** $Despises(Mary, x)$; so
> $Despises$(Mary, $John$).

### 7.2.4  Direct Proofs Aren't Always
###         Safe Either

The trouble with a direct proof usually comes when we lose track of what the state(ment) is and argue as in

> (John says that) Bill is tall.
> (Joe says that) Joe resents tall people, so
> Joe resents Bill.

That is quite likely, but not at all certain: John and Joe might disagree about just how tall Bill is, or one of them might even be lying.

### 7.2.5  Proofs by Contradiction Aren't
###         Very Natural

A proof by contradiction works like this:

> Mary despises John.
> Mary loves everyone who doesn't love her, so
> John loves Mary.

That's not quite so simple or direct: in proof by contradiction, we take the view that coming from there is half the fun. The missing idea is that **if** John didn't love Mary, **then** Mary would love him, **but** she doesn't **so** he does. Got it?

*Not*(*Loves*(*Mary*, *John*));
**if** *Not*(*Loves*(*x*, *Mary*)) **then** *Loves*(*Mary*, *x*); so
*Loves*(*John*, *Mary*).

Don't worry, we'll try again later.

### 7.2.6 Proofs by Contradiction Are Often Misleading

Unfortunately, it's easy to miss the assumptions hidden in a proof like this: with
real people, it's perfectly possible that John doesn't love Mary, but Mary both
despises John and loves him. By making an explicit symbolic model, we can see
that "*Despises*(*Mary*, *John*)" can be related to "*Loves*(*Mary*, *x*)" only if we have
a rule relating "*Despises*" to "*Loves*".

### 7.2.7 Inductive Proofs Conceal Repetition

A proof by induction works like this:

Charlemagne was human;
all the children of a human are human; so
any modern-day descendants of Charlemagne must be human.

In this argument, we are concealing some indefinite number of direct proofs:
Charlemagne's humanity implies that each of his children were human, so each of
his children's children were human, so each of his children's children's children were
human, and so on. We don't know how many of these proofs would be required
to cover the actual modern-day descendants of Charlemagne, but we do know that
given a particular descendant and her genealogy, even a mechanical moron would
be able to construct the proof.

### 7.2.8 Inductive Proofs May Also
###       Conceal Errors

Inductive proofs may be the most important kind for computer science, because
almost everything in computing works by constructing or at least traversing some
sort of inductive construction; paths are the ones we've used most so far. Inductive
proofs are also the trickiest and can go wrong most easily, because they include
the other kinds of proofs half-buried inside. Even with the Charlemagne argument,
you can see the beginnings of a problem: if this kind of argument worked perfectly,
there could be no such thing as evolution, as you see on writing

Ichthy Gluck (an ancestor of ours, one billion years back) was a fish;
all the children of a fish are fish; so
any modern-day descendants (including all humans) must be fish.

Similarly, I could write

My one-year-old son is quite small;
**if** a person is small in one minute,
   **then** he will still be small in the next minute; so
he will obviously be small forever.

In each of these, the problem is obviously with the second line: no single step changes the situation recognizably, but they do add up.

### Exercise

**7.2-1**   Think of some other argument with the same structure which goes wrong in the same way. Over what time scale is your argument reliable?

Articles which mathematicians write to amuse each other sometimes describe the use of proof by intimidation, Proof by circular cross-reference (and by nonexistent reference, and indefinitely delayed lemma), proof by exhaustion, etc.; these are sometimes called "Generalized Proof Techniques" because ordinary proof techniques are restricted to proving valid assertions whereas these can be used to prove anything. The *Journal of Irreproducible Results* frequently contains such articles; see if your library subscribes to it.

### 7.2.9 Reasoning Through Examples

In this chapter, we will proceed to develop each of the tools for careful reasoning as we work through a few examples. In each example, we will try to examine first the model itself, within which the problem occurs, then the specification of the solution, and finally the solution procedure.

## 7.3 MODELING PATHS

In this section, we will reconsider the model of the road segment maps developed earlier in the course. We need to think carefully of how to convince a real skeptic of the proposal.

### 7.3.1 Models Leave Things Out

The model proposed had a set of road segments of the form $[place_1, place_2, SegmentLength]$, and a set of rules for constructing paths from those road segments.

1. **if** $x$ is a place **then** $[x]$ is a path of *PathLength* 0.
2. **if** $X = [x_1, \ldots, x_N]$ is a path of *PathLength* $L$ **and** $[y, x_1, K]$ is a segment. **then** $y@X = [y, x_1, \ldots, x_N]$ is a path of *PathLength* $L + K$.
3. Nothing is a path unless it can be made by rules 1 and 2.

**Q:** Why should we be so restrictive? Obviously, there are other ways of making paths: **if** $[x_1, \ldots, x_N]$ is a path of *PathLength L* **and** $[x_N, y, K]$ is a segment **then** $[x_1, \ldots, x_N, y]$ is a path of *PathLengthL + K*.

**A:** Yes, but any path that you can make in another way *could* have been made with rules 1 and 2. This is the same idea as we had with sorting sequences long ago: you can form a permutation of a given sequence in many ways, but it's nice to be able to say that any permutation could have been formed by swaps alone.

If we're going to find the shortest of all possible paths, we need to describe the set of all possible paths. If you start out by including every way of making a path, you're going to get very confused when you try to say why no path can be shorter than the one you've got. Let's take a very simple argument: we want to be sure that "[ ]" is not a path.

**Q:** That's obviously true: every path has at least the place you start.

**A:** Yes, but that sort of verbal argument can get you in trouble sometimes: you might say that every path has at least the place you start and the place you stop, so $[a]$ is not a path. That's obviously false.

**Q:** All right, why is "[ ]" not a path in the model?

**A:** To prove it, you need to consider that rules 1 and 2 never generate an empty sequence, and rule 3 says that any path you could think of can be created by rules 1 and 2 alone, so "[ ]" is never generated at all. Every extra method for creating paths requires another check to make sure that it can't generate an empty path.

All of those other ways of making paths can be added to the model, but if they don't add new sequences as paths, then we don't want them yet. (And if they do add new sequences, e.g., [ ], then we really don't want them.) Certainly we'll use other path generators later, but right now they would just make extra work.

Think about going through a path; either it's empty because you're already there, or you follow one road segment and when you've done that, there's still a path to follow.

The **if-then** rules are one good way to describe a model. Another good way is to define the collection of types, constants, functions and assertions which work on objects in the model. We are working on places and paths, where we previously described a path as a sequence of places. Suppose we are given a *SegmentTable* as a set of triples $[place_1, place_2, SegmentLength]$. We might (or might not) also include segments as a type. We have to ask ourselves what functions can we have on these types. Given a place, we can ask what segments include it—what places are its neighbors—or what places are reachable from it—what paths stretch from it or to it. Given a pair of places, we might ask ourselves what paths connect them. Given a set of places, we might generalize on both of those by asking what paths interconnect them and what places are reachable from some place within the set.

Given a path, we might ask where it starts and ends, what its length is, how many places are involved, or whether it is cyclic. Given a pair of paths, we might ask what places they have in common, whether one is an extension of the other, or whether they can be juxtaposed. Given a set of paths, we might ask what places they interconnect, what subset of those paths have a given length, what are the longest or shortest paths, or what extensions of the set (e.g., by juxtaposition of two paths within the set) are possible. Given a model, we might ask what paths are possible, what shortest paths are possible, what places exist.

These questions are strongly interconnected: once we asked what paths extended from or to a given place, it was inevitable that we would ask what place begins or ends a given path. Once we asked for the length of a given path, it was almost inevitable that we would ask for the paths in a given set which have a given length.

## Exercise

**7.3-1**    Think of a few more questions, suggested by the previous ones.

The simplest functions are selections and projections on the $SegmentTable$.

$$Neighbors(x : Place) : Set(Place)$$
$$Neighbors(x) = \{y : [x, y, K] \in SegmentTable\}$$

Here we are using the function's argument to select rows by the first column, and then we project the second column to form a set. (You may see an inadequacy in this definition and some of those which follow. If so, don't worry about it yet; we'll fix it later.)

The $SegmentLength$ for any given pair of places is a cardinal number (i.e., $0, 1, 2, 3, \ldots$) if there's a segment connecting them, and it's undefined otherwise:

$$SegmentLength(x, y : Place) : Cardinal;$$

$$
\begin{aligned}
SegmentLength(x, y) \quad = \quad & K, & & \text{if } [x, y, K] \in SegmentTable; \\
& \text{undefined}, & & \text{otherwise .}
\end{aligned}
$$

Here we use the arguments to select rows by the first two columns, and then project the third column to find (we hope) a single value. Notice that this presupposes that there is at most one appropriate value for $K$: if we had a map with segments $[a, b, 9]$ and $[a, b, 27]$ then there would be no way for $SegmentLength$ (which only produces a single number) to provide a model for that ambiguity.

To see if these functions are providing a model of the segments, we check to see if we can use them to reconstruct the $SegmentTable$. In fact,

$$SegmentTable = \{[x, y, K] \quad : \quad x \text{ is a Place},$$
$$y \in Neighbors(x),$$
$$K = SegmentLength(x, y)\}$$

You should be able to see from this what you need to do (e.g., in terms of writing rules) to get back where we started from.

**Q:** I guess I can see how that's true, but you've only given me the operations $Neighbors$ and $SegmentLength$; I need the set of all places in order to start.

**A:** You're absolutely right: we must add the constant

$$Places : Set(Place) = \{x : [x, y, K] \in SegmentTable\}$$

Now we have a set of basic functions which seem to encode the information which $SegmentTable$ had explicitly, and we can now use them to find which sequences of places are actually paths:

$$IsPath(A : Sequence(Place)) : Boolean$$
$$IsPath([]) \quad = \quad False$$
$$IsPath([x]) \quad = \quad True$$
$$IsPath([x, y] + S) \quad = \quad (y \in Neighbors(x)) \wedge IsPath(y@S)$$

And of course, for any given path we may want to know the total distance:

$$PathLength(A : Path) : Cardinal$$
$$PathLength([x]) \quad = \quad 0$$
$$PathLength([x, y] + S) \quad = \quad SegmentLength(x, y) + PathLength(y@S)$$

These definitions split up rules 1, 2, and (implicitly) 3 into a somewhat clumsy-looking set of declarations and equations. There are three primary advantages of this approach: first, that we can make more use of proofs by equational substitution; second, that the functions we are defining in the model can frequently be converted directly into code; and finally, that there are simple checks we can perform on this model which will catch errors frequently missed in the **if-then** structure. Rule 3 requires rules 1 and 2 to be complete; if you made an error in writing them, then rule 3 may conceal that error. For example, it would be easy to write down rules 1 and 2 without ever thinking about whether the empty sequence was to be a path or not. In the equational system, to omit $IsPath([])$ in the definition of $IsPath$ is a much more obvious mistake.

In either system, we can reason forward along a path. Given the rules, we can take the set of distinct places $\{a, b, c, d, e\}$ with the set of segments $\{[a, b, 2], [b, c, 4], [c, d, 9]\}$. We can then show that

| | |
|---|---|
| 1. [c] is a path of *PathLength* 0 | 1. Rule 1. |
| 2. [b,c] is a path of *PathLength* 4 | 2. Step 1, rule 2. |
| 3. [a,b,c] is a path of *PathLength* $2 + 4$ | 3. Step 2, rule 2. |
| 4. [a,b,c,d] is a path of *PathLength* $9 + 4$ | 4. Step 3, rule 2. |

This is a direct proof; in each step, we've used the idea that

**if**  "$X$" is true,
**and**  " **if**  $X$  **then**  $Y$" is true,
**then**  "$Y$" is true.

Formally speaking, we are using the logical rule of *modus ponens*.

## Exercises

**7.3-2**  Prove that $[b, c, d]$ is a path.
**7.3-3**  Prove that **if** $[x, y, K]$ is a segment **then** $[x, y]$ is a path.

Equivalently, we can note that

$$
\begin{aligned}
IsPath([a, b, c]) &= (b \in Neighbors(a) \land IsPath([b, c])) \\
&= (c \in Neighbors(b) \land IsPath([c])) \\
&= True
\end{aligned}
$$

and similarly that

$$
\begin{aligned}
PathLength([a, b, c]) &= SegmentLength([a, b]) + PathLength([b, c]) \\
&= 2 + (SegmentLength([b, c]) + PathLength([c])) \\
&= 2 + (4 + 0) \\
&= 6
\end{aligned}
$$

The reasoning in the model does seem to follow an intuitive sense of what goes on in the world during the trip from here to Babylon, but what about going back? We have no rule which says you can go backwards along a segment, much less a path. In fact, we can prove that it is not possible in this model to get from $d$ to $a$, as long as $d$ and $a$ are distinct points—that is, we'll prove that there is no path $[d, \ldots, a]$. First, we prove that rule 1 for path construction could not be the one to produce such a path; next we prove that rule 2 could not be the one to produce it; and finally, we prove that there could not be any such path.

Suppose that rule 1 did produce it; then

| | |
|---|---|
| 1. Rule 1 produced the path $[d, \ldots, a]$ | 1. Supposition. |
| 2. $[d, \ldots, a] = [x]$, for some $x$ | 2. Step 1, rule 1. |
| 3. $d = a$ | 3. Step 2. |
| 4. $d \neq a$ | 4. $d$ and $a$ are distinct points. |

The supposition has led us to contradict what we already knew, so it must be false. Therefore, rule 1 did not produce such a path.

Now suppose that rule 2 produced the path in question; then

| | |
|---|---|
| 1. Rule 2 produced the path $[d, \ldots, a]$ | 1. Supposition. |
| 2. $[d, \ldots, a] = [x, y_1, \ldots, y_N]$ where $[x, y_1, K]$ is a segment and $[y_1, \ldots, y_N]$ is a path | 2. Step 1, rule 2. |
| 3. There is a segment $[d, y_1, K]$ | 3. Step 2. |
| 4. There is no segment $[d, y_1, K]$ | 4. Look at the segment list. |

The supposition has led us to contradict what we already knew, so it must be false. Therefore, rule 2 did not produce such a path.

Now suppose that there is such a path; then

| | |
|---|---|
| 1. There is a path $[d, \ldots, a]$ | 1. Supposition. |
| 2. Rule 1 or Rule 2 produced it. | 2. Rule 3. |
| 3. Neither Rule 1 nor Rule 2 did. | 3. Previous proofs. |

The supposition has led us to contradict what we already knew, so it must be false. Therefore, there is no such path.

This reasoning backwards is a proof by contradiction.

**if** "$X$" is false,
**and** " **if** $Y$ **then** $X$" is true,
**then** "$Y$" is false.

We rarely use contradictions as directly in the equational model, but the same principle holds:

$$1. IsPath([d] + S + [a]) \quad = \quad (S = [] \wedge IsPath([d] + S + [a]))$$
$$\vee (S = x@R \wedge IsPath([d] + S + [a]))$$

**Q:** It does? You could have fooled me.

**A:** The first step works because $S$ is a sequence, so $(S = [] \vee S = x@R)$ is true. (Notice that "$x$" and "$R$" are new symbols: they have to be, because they are being defined now: $x$ is $Hd(S)$, and $R$ is $Tl(S)$.) The logical justification of this step is the rule

$$P = (P \wedge Q) \vee (P \wedge \neg Q)$$

It's just as if we had written that

John is tall $=$ Mary is shorter than John **and** John is tall
  **or** Mary is as tall as John **and** John is tall
  **or** Mary is taller than John **and** John is tall.

or simply

$$(x > y) = ((x > z) \wedge (x > y)) \vee ((x \leq z) \wedge (x > y))$$

You want to prove something from the fact that John is tall, so you work it out with all possibilities for other factors. You won't have to write proofs like that for a while, but you should understand them: since S is a sequence, it is either empty or non-empty, and in either case we have said only that $IsPath([d] + S + [a]) = IsPath([d] + S + [a])$. Think about it, and go on to

2.$IsPath([d] + S + [a]) = IsPath([d, a]) \vee IsPath([d] + (x@R) + [a]$

That one comes from simplifying the expression using $S$, plus some rules for sequences.

3.$IsPath([d] + S + [a]) = IsPath([d, a] + []) \vee IsPath([d, x] + (R + [a]))$

Step 3 comes from 2, using a few manipulations on sequence descriptions.

4.$IsPath([d] + S + [a]) = (a \in Neighbors(d) \wedge IsPath([a]))$
  $\vee (x \in Neighbors(d) \wedge IsPath(x@R + [a]))$

Step 4 comes from 3, using the definition of IsPath twice.

5.$IsPath([d] + S + [a]) = False \vee False$

6.$IsPath([d] + S + [a]) = False$

Step 5 comes from a quick check of $SegmentTable$: we know that "$a \in Neighbors(d)$" or even "$x \in Neighbors(d)$" will be $False$, because with the definitions we have given, $Neighbors(d) = \{\}$. Step 6 uses the fact that $False$ is an identity for $\vee$ in Boolean algebra.

Of course, we don't really want the model to have no path from $c$ to $a$, so we go back and add to the definition of segments;

1. An explicitly listed segment is a segment;

2. if $[x, y, K]$ is an explicitly listed segment **then** $[y, x, K]$ is a segment;

**3.** Nothing else is a segment.

### Exercises

**7.3-4**  Prove that **if** $[x, y, K]$ is a segment **then** $[y, x, K]$ is a segment.

**7.3-5**  Prove that even with the extended definitions there is no path from $a$ to $e$.

**7.3-6**  Prove that **if** $[x]$ is a path **then** $x$ is a place.

**7.3-7**  Prove that **if** $x@[y_1, \ldots, y_N]$ is a path **then** for some $K$, $[x, y_1, K]$ is a segment **and** $[y_1, \ldots, y_N]$ is a path. (This is the Path Decomposition Lemma, which will be used later.)

**7.3-8**  Go back and add to the equational definitions of *Neighbors, Places,* and *Segment-Length* so that the equational version of the model will also work backwards along segments.

### 7.3.2 You Cannot Prove that You Have the Right Model of the World

Somewhere along the line, proving things within the model and thinking about the world, we may begin to think that the model probably works. It would be nice to "prove" that it works, with the same kind of convincing argument that we can use to show that there is no path in the model from $a$ to $e$. That's not possible, except in the sense described at the beginning of this chapter: if you've banged on the current version of the model very hard and long, and you haven't seen any holes, you can sell it as pretty well "proven." It nonetheless remains possible that somebody will point out a problem tomorrow, the next day, or ten years later. Therefore, there are limits to the value of proof techniques; they help us find problems, and they give us almost absolute confidence in some kinds of statements, but they can never give us real confidence that we're solving the right problem, or that the world behaves the way the model describes.

All we can do is keep saying to ourselves: design the model so that any problems will be as obvious as possible. Remember the KISS principle: Keep It Simple, Stupid! Think: if we had allowed several kinds of path-forming operations, there would have been so many cases to consider that we might never have completed the proofs that certain kinds of paths did not exist (because none of the mechanisms for creating paths could have created them.) That doesn't mean that we can't go ahead and define new ways of forming paths, just as we did when we weren't worried about proof. We will, but we won't consider them as being fundamental. We'll show how to construct them from our basic methods of building paths, and then proofs will be feasible.

### 7.3.3 Operations Can Be Inductively Extended

When we considered the world of segmented maps before, we noted that paths could be constructed in several ways: if we have the path $X = [x_1, \ldots, x_N]$, we can extend it to $[a, x_1, \ldots, x_N]$ by definition if there is a segment $[a, x_1, K]$, but we can also in practice extend $X$ to $[x_1, \ldots, x_N, b]$ if there is a segment $[x_N, b, K]$, and we can even extend it to a case which covers all of those preceding—there is a path $[x_1, \ldots, x_N, y_2, \ldots, y_M]$ if there is a path $Y = [y_1, \ldots, y_M]$ and $x_N = y_1$. Rather than include this notion of juxtaposing paths as part of the basic idea of what a path can be, we just present a proof that path length calculation distributes over path juxtaposition as a derived operation.

> **if** $X = [x_1, \ldots, x_N]$ is a path of *PathLength* $L_x$
> **and** $Y = [y_1, \ldots, y_M]$ is a path of *PathLength* $L_y$
> **and** $x_N = y_1$
> **then** $[x_1, \ldots, x_N, y_2, \ldots, y_M]$ is a path of *PathLength* $L_x + L_y$

Equivalently,

> **if** $X$ is a path of *PathLength* $A$, with $N$ elements,
> **and** $Last(X)@S$ is a path of *PathLength* $B$
> **then** $X + S$ is a path of *PathLength* $A + B$.

First, we prove this when $X$ has only one element ($N = 1$);

> **if** $[x_1]$ is a path (of *PathLength* $A = 0$)
> **and** $x_1@S$ is a path of *PathLength* $B$
> **then** $x_1@S$, which is $[x_1] + S$, is a path of *PathLength* $A + B = 0 + B = B$.

That's obviously true, right? **if** $a$ is true **and** $b$ is true **then** $b$ is true. Now we prove it for paths with two elements: $[x_1, x_2]$.

> **if** $[x_1, x_2]$ is a path of *PathLength* $A$
> **and** $x_2@S$ is a path of *PathLength* $B$
> **then** $[x_1, x_2] + S$ is a path of *PathLength* $A + B$.

That's pretty obvious, because

> **if** $[x_1, x_2]$ is a path of *PathLength* $B$
> **then** $[x_1, x_2, K]$ is a segment of *SegmentLength* $B$; we've proven that.

Also, we already know that

> **if** $[x_1, x_2, K]$ is a segment of *SegmentLength* $B$
> **and** $x_2@S$ is a path of *PathLength* $L$
> **then** $x_1@(x_2@S)$ is a path of *PathLength* $L + B$.

That's by rule 2 for making paths.

Finally, we know that $[x_1, x_2] + S$ is the same as $x_1@(x_2@S)$; that's what "+" means in this case. So, juxtaposition works with $N = 2$. Next, we prove it for $N = 3$:

> **if** $[x_1, x_2, x_3]$ is a path of *PathLength A*
> **and** $x_3@S$ is a path of *PathLength B*
> **then** $[x_1, x_2, x_3] + S$ is a path of *PathLength A + B*.

We start out observing (just as with $N = 2$) that

> **if** $[x_1, x_2, x_3]$ is a path of *PathLength A*
> **then** $[x_1, x_2, K]$ is a segment of *SegmentLength K*
> **and** $[x_2, x_3]$ is a path with two elements of *PathLength A − K*.

Now we have to prove that **if** all those are true **then** $X + S$ is a path of *PathLength A + B*, presumably by rule 2; but rule 2 insists that we first show that $[x_2, x_3] + S$ is a path of *PathLength A + B − K*. Why should $[x_2, x_3] + S$ be a path? Clearly, because it falls under case $N = 2$ which we have just proven: it is a two-place path ending in $x_3$, which starts the path $x_3@S$. Using that fact, we can say that $[x_2, x_3] + S$ must be a path of *PathLength (A − K) + B*, and so $X + S$ is a path and has *PathLength K + (A − K) + B = A + B*.

**Q:** Would you run that by one more time?

**A:** Sure; we'll write it out, step by step:

| | |
|---|---|
| 1. $[x_1, x_2, x_3]$ is a path of *PathLength A* | 1. Given. |
| 2. $x_3@S$ is a path of *PathLength B* | 2. Given. |
| 3. $[x_1, x_2, K]$ is a segment (*SegmentLength K*) | 3. Path Decomposition. |
| 4. $[x_2, x_3]$ is a path of *PathLength A − K* | 4. Path Decomposition. |
| 5. $[x_2, x_3] + S$ is a path of *PathLength (A − K) + B* | 5. Steps 2,4 and case $N = 2$ above. |
| 6. $[x_1, x_2, x_3] + S$ is a path of *PathLength A + B* | 6. Steps 3,5 and rule 2. |

Here, the important idea is that we had already shown that we could combine two paths if the first one was of length (not *PathLength*) 2, and so step 5 is guaranteed to work. Next, we prove the hypothesis for paths with four elements:

> **if** $[x_1, x_2, x_3, x_4]$ is a path of *PathLength A*
> **and** $x_4@S$ is a path of *PathLength B*
> **then** $[x_1, x_2, x_3, x_4] + S$ is a path of *PathLength A + B*.

That works, because we find that $[x_1, x_2, K]$ is a segment and $[x_2, \ldots, x_4]$ is a path with three elements of *PathLength A − K*, so $[x_2, \ldots, x_4]@S$ is a path of *PathLength A − K + B*, (remember, we just showed that it works for paths of three elements) which means that $[x_1, \ldots, x_4, y_1, \ldots, y_M]$ is a path of *PathLength* $A + B$ by rule 2.

Notice that the proof for a path of four elements is almost an exact copy of the proof for a path of three elements, except that rather than relying on a proof for a path of two elements, it relies on a proof for a path of three elements. Now think about what we've been doing. First we had to start out showing that the idea works for very simple paths; then we had to show that it works for more and more complex paths, but when we did so we could use the fact that we had already written down a proof for the paths that the complex ones were built from.

## Exercises

**7.3-9**  Prove that the idea works for paths with five elements.

**7.3-10**  Prove that it works for paths with six elements.

### 7.3.4  Procedures Can Generate Proofs

We can now reasonably write rules to generate a proof for paths with 6,799,234 elements. First we define the string $A$ to be the first proof written above. Then we define $B(N)$ to be a string of the form

> **if** $X = [x_1, x_2, \ldots, x_N]$
>   **then** $[x_1, x_2, -]$ is a segment
>   **and** $[x_2, \ldots, x_N]$ is a path of $N - 1$ elements,
>     by the Path Decomposition Lemma.
> So $[x_2, \ldots, x_N, y_1, \ldots, y_M]$ is a path by the previous proof.
> So $[x_1, \ldots, x_N, y_1, \ldots, y_M]$ is therefore a path by rule 2.

Now we can define

$$
\begin{array}{rcl}
Proof(1) & = & A \\
Proof(i+1) & = & Proof(i) + B(i+1)
\end{array}
$$

You know how to apply such rules mechanically at this point, so you know (at least, you know in principle) how to go about finding $Proof(6799234)$, which will be the proof desired.

## Exercises

**7.3-11**  Prove that **if** $[a, b]$ is a path **then** $[b, a]$ is a path.

**7.3-12**  Prove that **if** $[a, b, c]$ is a path **then** $[c, b, a]$ is a path.

**7.3-13**  Prove that **if** $[a, b, c, d]$ is a path **then** $[d, c, b, a]$ is a path.

**7.3-14** Write rules defining the string which proves that **if** $X$ is a path of one million elements **then** the reversal of $X$ is a path, where

$$Reverse([a]) \quad = \quad [a]$$
$$Reverse(x@S) \quad = \quad Reverse(S) + [x]$$

**7.3-15** Extend those rules to show that **if** $X$ is a path of one million road segments, with total *PathLength* $L$, **then** the reversal of $X$ is a path of *PathLength* $L$.

**7.3-16** The joining of paths would be represented in the equational formulation by a simple equation:

$$IsPath([a] + P + [b] + Q + [c]) = IsPath([a] + P + [b]) \wedge IsPath([b] + Q + [c])$$

What does the equation assert which is *not* asserted directly by the **if-then** formulation?

This kind of reasoning is called inductive reasoning:

**if** you can show that something is true for paths with 1 place
   **and** you can show that
     **if** it is true for paths with $N$ places
     **then** it is true for paths with $N + 1$ places
   **then** you can write a procedure to write proofs
     for paths with 1 place, 2 places, 3 places, ...
   So it must be true for any paths at all.

That's an induction on the number of places in a path. Similarly, we can prove things about arbitrary sequences:

**if** you can show that something is true for [ ]
   **and** you can show that
     **if** it is true for all sequences of length $N$
     **then** it is true for all sequences of length $N + 1$
   **then** you can write a procedure to write proofs ...
   So it must be true for sequences of any length.

That's an induction on the Length of a sequence. Notice that the only difference between these was that any shortest possible path has one place, where the one and only shortest possible sequence has no elements. The same principle is being used, and it applies to any kind of domain $D$ in which we start with some set of rules $B$ which define simple objects and some set of rules $C$ which then build objects from simpler objects.

**if** you can show that something is true for all objects defined with $B$
   **and** you can show that
     **if** it is true for all members of a set $S \subseteq D$ of objects
     **then** it is true for any $X$ built by $C$ out of objects in $S$
   **then** it must be true for all objects in $D$.

We will spend a great deal of time with inductive reasoning, for two reasons. First, it's important: most of computer science is devoted to starting with simple objects, and then building more complex ones out of them—sets, sequences, expressions, programs. Inductive definitions and proofs will often turn directly into programs. Second, many students find it quite difficult. If you're having a hard time right now, you should be concerned but not frightened: we expect many good students to pick this up gradually. As your intuitions of programming become stronger, so should your intuition of induction, because an inductive proof is just an outline of a procedure which will generate as many proofs as you need.

The skills needed in coming up with an inductive proof are therefore very much like those needed in programming. First you have to describe your objective carefully. (Usually, that involves thinking up some examples to make sure that you know what you mean). The next step is to rephrase that objective so that you can define a partial solution; we need some notion like $Trials(n)$ from Chapter 6, where we know what $Trials(0)$ is and we can find the relationship between $Trials(n)$ and $Trials(n+1)$. When I wrote out " **if** $[x_1, \ldots, x_N]$ is a path with $N$ elements, **and** $x_N @ S$ is a path, **then** $X + S$ is a path," the reason that I specified the number of elements in $X$ was that I knew I would be performing an induction on that number.

**Q:** Why didn't you do an induction on the number of elements in $S$ instead of $X$?

**A:** Because I thought about it and couldn't see how to make it work. Rule 2 justifies adding places in front of paths, so I can have a proof based on adding things to the front of $S$, but I don't see how to make a proof based on adding things to the back of $X$. Just because induction is a powerful hammer doesn't mean mean that every problem you see is a nail. Think about it.

To return to induction-as-programming; the next step is to provide a proof for each simple case. With paths, there are as many simple cases (empty paths) as there are places, but there's just one rule to cover them all, so there's just one proof. The final step is to provide a proof for each incremental case, which means in this example that you prove that **if** it works for all paths of $N$ places (or fewer), **then** it works for all paths of $N + 1$ places.

Of course, the very fact that inductive reasoning actually works like programming can often get us bogged down in tedious details, where we run the risk of having a proof which works, but which doesn't particularly make sense. You may be able to prove step by step that something is true without being able to understand why it is true, or whether something that sounds similar to it is likely to be true.

One way to avoid this is to minimize the use of induction in models. Rather than building things incrementally, with heavy dependence on **if-then** rules, we can try to work as much as possible with models which treat structures all at once, as sets of components connected by equations.

### 7.3.5 Structures Don't Always Need Induction

In the case of *Reverse*, it may be better to look at an alternative representation of a sequence of values. We'll do it pictorially first. Take a piece of paper, and draw three circles on it, labelled arbitrarily: "$s_1$", "$s_2$", and "$s_3$" will do fine. Inside the circle labelled $s_1$, write "here"; inside the circle labelled $s_2$, write "Sumer"; inside the circle labelled $s_3$, write "Babylon". Now draw an arrow from $s_1$ to $s_2$, and another from $s_2$ to $s_3$. You have specified a sequence, right? The first element of the sequence is the one which has no arrow going in, and the last one is that which has no arrow coming out. This sequence is a path, because each arrow corresponds to a segment. To reverse it, just change the direction of every arrow. Informally, we now know that the reversal of a path is still a path because the reversal of a segment is still a segment.

How do we represent this formally? Use a pair of tables, as in

$$
\begin{aligned}
Successors(S) &= \{[s_1, s_2], [s_2, s_3]\} \\
Values(S) &= \{[s_1, here], [s_2, Sumer], [s_3, Babylon]\}
\end{aligned}
$$

Now we can represent $Hd$ and $Tl$ for this one sequence and its successive tails:

$$
\begin{aligned}
Hd(x) &= v : [x, v] \in Values \\
Tl(x) &= y : [x, y] \in Successors, \text{ if any; [], otherwise}
\end{aligned}
$$

Given those tables and those definitions, it's simple enough to start with $s_1$ whose $Hd$ is *here* and whose $Tl$ is $s_2$, and proceed onwards to stop with $s_3$; in between we list the *Values* $[here, Sumer, Babylon]$. We can certainly treat this as a way of representing nonempty sequences, or empty ones if we needed to: just leave the Values set empty.

**Q:** How can you tell which are the first and last nodes of $S$ without thinking about the picture?

**A:** The arrows are still there, but they are embedded in $Successors(S)$. The *First* element of $S$ is the one with no precedecessor; the *Last* is the one with no successor.

$$
\begin{aligned}
First(S) &= y : \neg([x, y] \in Successors(S)) \\
Last(S) &= x : \neg([x, y] \in Successors(S))
\end{aligned}
$$

Sequence reversal is suddenly as trivial to define as to imagine:

$$
\begin{aligned}
Values(Reverse(S)) &= Values(S), \text{ and} \\
Successors(Reverse(S)) &= \{[y, x] : [x, y] \in Successors(S)\}
\end{aligned}
$$

In this model, we can find that

$$
\begin{aligned}
First(Reverse(S)) &= Last(S), \text{ because} \\
First(Reverse(S)) &= y : \neg([x, y] \in Successors(Reverse(S))) \\
&= y : \neg([y, x] \in Successors(S)) \\
&= Last(S)
\end{aligned}
$$

Renaming makes this hard to read, but no induction is needed. We can also define $IsPath$ in this model:

$$
IsPath(S) = (Successors(S) \leq \{[x, y] : x \in Places, y \in Neighbors(x)\}
$$

From this it follows that $IsPath(Reverse(S)) = IsPath(S)$.

### Exercise

**7.3-17** Prove that $IsPath(Reverse(S)) = IsPath(S)$ in this model; do not use induction.

Of course, we have done nothing to justify the assumption that the two models are equivalent. Since one of them uses induction, a translation would also require induction. To represent an ordinary sequence as a pair of tables, we would need a source of symbols $s_1, s_2, s_3, \ldots$, which we could then use in some definition such as

> $Rep(S : Path) : TablePair$
> **if** $S = [x]$
>     **then** $Successors(Rep(S)) = \{\}$,
>             $Values(Rep(S)) = \{[s_0, x]\}$,
>               and $s_0$ is a new symbol.
> **if** $S = [x, y] + R$
>     **then** $Successors(Rep(S)) = \{[s_0, First(RSP)]\} \cup Successors(RSP)$,
>             $Values(Rep(S)) = \{[s_0, x]\} \cup Values(RSP)$,
>             $RSP = Rep(y@R)$,
>             $s_0$ is a new symbol.

Of course, it would make sense to have $Rep$ produce a record $r$ comprised of $r.Succ$ and $r.Val$, but it's not a requirement of the problem.

### Exercises

**7.3-18** Write down several short paths, and translate each into a table pair.

**7.3-19** Write down several small table pairs, and translate each into a path.

**7.3-20** Write an inverse function $Ab$ such that for any path $P$, $Ab(Rep(P)) = P$. (Hint: You might use not only $First(S)$ on the representation, but also $AllButFirst(S)$, defined as $\{[x, y] : [x, y] \in Successors(S), x \neq First(S)\}$.)

**7.3-21** When will $Rep(Ab(TP)) = TP$?

Of course, to test the model you might need induction: first you would need to prove that the $Ab$ function really did satisfy $Ab(Rep(P)) = P$, and then you would need to prove that $X$ is a path by the inductive definition if and only if the table pair $Rep(X)$ is a path by the definition on representations.

## Exercises

**7.3-22** What is the representation of $Find$ in this model of sequences?

**7.3-23** What is the representation of the juxtaposition of two paths in these tables? Why (without induction) is the juxtaposition $X + [a] + Y$ of two paths $X + [a]$ and $[a] + Y$ always a path?

**7.3-24** Use induction to prove that $Ab(Rep(P)) = P$, with your definition of $Ab$.

**7.3-25** Define $EqPath(x, y : TablePair) : Boolean$ so that $EqPath(x, y) = (Interp(x) = Interp(y))$. Do **not** construct $Ab(x)$ or $Ab(y)$: that's too easy. [Hint: $x@S = y@T$ if and only if $x = y$ and $S$ and $T$ are the same sequence; you can use $First$ and $AllButFirst$.]

### 7.3.6 Cross-Fertilization

At this point, you should feel that you have begun to get acquainted with two different "model worlds," as spaces of possibilities within which you could search for a path. As we said before, there is never going to be any guarantee that either model is right; someone might discover tomorrow that the real-world idea of distance is not simply a sum of segments. All we can say is that if you don't even think about your model—if you're unable to reason about the properties of the objects it contains— then you're most unlikely to find mistakes in it. If you do have a formal model in which your problem is expressible, then you can reason about it, prove to yourself that your first few attempts to solve it won't work, prove to your friends that some later attempted solution does work, and then reason similarly about the procedure which you design to find the solution and the code which you write to implement that procedure. If you think about at least two different models, you are that much more likely to see defects in each, and to realize that a third or fourth or fifth model would serve your purposes better, leading to a simpler and clearer analysis or else to a more efficient implementation. (The $TablePair$ model we have just been using was actually modified several times in order to clarify the presentation.)

We now have a pair of models. Since they are intertranslatable, we can express the shortest-path problem in either. The model of paths as sequences seems some- what more natural, while the model of paths as $Values$ and $Successors$ sets seems to shorten some of the proofs. Actually, it is desirable to do as much as possible with- out commitment to any particular model by using only functions (like $Neighbors$, $IsPath$, and juxtaposition) which can be constructed in any given model. Later in this course (and in other computer science courses), you will find that sort of "data abstraction" to be helpful, but for now we will not be very consistent about it; such functions will be emphasized, but we will go on imagining that we are simply working with sequences.

### 7.3.7 Model Completion

We have previously described the model as allowing certain kinds of questions to be asked and answered. Given a place, we can ask what segments include it: this information is available by combining the *Neighbors* and *SegmentLength* functions. We can ask what places are reachable from it, what paths stretch from it or to it. Given a pair of places, we might ask ourselves what paths connect them. Given a set of places, we might generalize on the obvious questions by asking what paths interconnect them and what places are reachable from some place within the set. Given a path, we might ask where it starts and ends, what its length is, how many places are involved, or whether it is cyclic. Given a pair of paths, we might ask what places they have in common, whether one is an extension of the other, or whether they can be juxtaposed. Given a set of paths, we might ask what places those paths interconnect, what subset of those paths have a given length, what are the longest or shortest paths, or what extensions of the set (e.g., by juxtaposition of two paths within the set) are possible. Given a model, we might ask what paths are possible, what shortest paths are possible, or what places exist.

These questions are strongly interconnected: once we asked what paths extended from or to a given place, it was inevitable that we would ask what place begins or ends a given path. Once we asked for the length of a given path, it was almost inevitable that we would ask for the paths in a given set which have a given length.

### Exercise

**7.3-26**  Think of a few more questions, suggested by the previous ones.

The basic functions which we have been using are *Neighbors*, *SegmentLength*, *Places*, *IsPath*, and *PathLength*. Everything else must be built out of these and ordinary operations on sequences.

## 7.4  REASONING ABOUT A SOLUTION'S SPECIFICATION

Supposing we have a model, we can begin to describe a problem solution. The first description will almost invariably be wrong, but if we are careful to keep it simple, then it isn't likely to have any subtle or hard-to-find errors. As with the models themselves, we aren't going to be able to prove that we are describing the right answer; as with the models themselves, we will be able to make conjectures about properties of objects, and we will be able to prove them in the formal model world. A programmer can use these properties in several ways: first, to keep track of what needs to be true, to simplify her understanding of the problem; second, to express her assumptions explicitly to teammates, thus diminishing the number of communication problems; third, to discover alternative paths to the solution and compare their respective costs; and finally, to justify steps in the procedure which constructs the solution.

### 7.4.1 Specification by Trial and Error

In this case, what we want is the shortest possible path between a given pair of points, which we might express as

> $ShortestPath(x, y) = S,$
> **if**  $S$ is a path from $x$ to $y$ of $PathLength\,L$
> **and** ( **if**  $P$ is a another path from $x$ to $y$ of $PathLength\,L'$
> **then**  $L' > L$).

For example, if we have the SegmentTable {[a,b,2],[b,c,3],[a,c,97]}, then it is pretty clear that the value of $ShortestPath(a, c)$ is $[a, b, c]$. That looks like a pretty good specification. Is it? Try to find an error before continuing.

Suppose that there are exactly two paths from x to y: [x,a,y] of $PathLength$ 52, and [x,b,y] of $PathLength$ 52. Each is an acceptable answer, but neither satisfies the specification given. How about

> $S = ShortestPath(x, y),$
> **if**  $S$ is a path from $x$ to $y$ of $PathLength\ L$,
> **and** ( **if**  $P$ is any path from $x$ to $y$ of $PathLength\,L'$
> **then**  $L' \geq L$).

That seems to fix it; now both satisfy the specification. Is it, then, all right? Try to find an error before continuing.

Well, we can now prove that [x,a,y] = $ShortestPath(x, y)$ and that [x,b,y] = $ShortestPath(x, y)$, and since things equal to the same thing are equal to each other, [x,a,y] = [x,b,y]. That's just not so: the specification has led us into a contradiction. The problem is that if we just want a shortest path, then we don't really care which shortest path we get, so that what we have to specify is the set of shortest paths:

> $S = ShortestPaths(x, y),$
> **if**  $S$ is the set of paths from $x$ to $y$ of $PathLength\,L$,
> **and** ( **if**  $P$ is a path from $x$ to $y$ of $PathLength\,L'$
> **then**  $L' \geq L$).

Well there, we now have a set which clearly includes both of the acceptable answers, so we can pick either. We're surely all done now, aren't we? No! The specification given makes it possible to give a direct proof that {} = $ShortestPaths(x, y)$

as long as $x \neq y$ and there are no segments of length zero:

1. $x \neq y$                                                  1. Hypothesis.
2. $PathLength([x] + S + [y]) > 0$                             2. $a, b > 0 \Rightarrow (a + b) > 0$.
3. $\{\} = \{P : P \text{ from } x \text{ to } y \text{ of length } 0\}$   3. 2, $PathLength(P) \neq 0$.
4. ( **if** $P$ is a path from $x$ to $y$ of length $L'$
    **then** $L' \geq 0$)                  4. 2.
5. $\{\} = ShortestPaths(x, y)$                                5. 3,4, and definition.

Nonetheless, the empty set is not an acceptable answer unless there really are no paths $[x \dots y]$. Like many careless specifications, this one allows a trivial but useless answer. We want to be describing the set of *all* paths which get where we want to go, and are no longer than they have to be. The set of shortest paths from $x$ to $y$ is then a *nonempty* set of all paths $P$ which satisfy the conditions that $P$ begins with $x$ and ends with $y$, $P$ is of length $L$, and there are no shorter paths which begin with $x$ and end with $y$. If there is no nonempty set of shortest paths, then there is no shortest path.

## Exercises

**7.4-1**  Prove informally that there can only be one set of shortest paths according to this definition. (Hint: Assume that there are two different sets, $A$ and $B$, each of which satisfy the definition; then prove they are the same.)

**7.4-2**  When will there be no such set?

Consider the formalization

$$ShortestPaths(x, y) = S :\{P :P = [x] + Q + [y], IsPath(P),$$
$$PathLength(P) = L,$$
$$\{\} = ShorterPaths(x, y, L)\},$$
$$S \neq \{\}$$

This uses the the function $ShorterPaths(x, y, L)$, which produces those paths from $x$ to $y$ which are shorter than $L$:

$$ShorterPaths(x, y, L) = \{Q : Q = [x] + S + [y], IsPath(Q), PathLength(Q) < L\}$$

## Exercise

**7.4-3**  Think up several examples to try this out on.

### 7.4.2 Cleaning Up the Description

**Q:** Why do you have a separate definition of *ShorterPaths*?

**A:** Because when I wrote *ShortestPaths* first, its definition was too complicated and too hard to read; I looked for a part of it that I could give a name.

**Q:** It's still too complicated. Isn't there any way to simplify it further?

**A:** Probably. If you look at the definitions of *ShortestPaths* and *ShorterPaths*, they have a lot in common. We can "factor out" the common part, which involves being a path where we know something about the beginning and end and length, by writing

$$PathsOfLength(x, y, L) = \{P : Hd(P) = x, Last(P) = y, IsPath(P),$$
$$PathLength(P) = L\}$$

and then we can use this to redefine

$$ShorterPaths(x, y, L) = \{P : P \in PathsOfLength(x, y, L'), L' < L\}$$
$$ShortestPaths(x, y) = S : \{P : P \in PathsOfLength(x, y, L),$$
$$\{\} = ShorterPaths(x, y, L)\},$$
$$S \neq \{\}$$

Notice that the description of *ShortestPaths* is no longer dominated by symbols; the complexity is buried inside *PathsOfLength* and *ShorterPaths*. We can clean it up further with a little more thought as follows:

$$ShortestPaths(x, y) \quad = \quad PathsOfLength(x, y, MinDistance(x, y))$$
$$MinDistance(x, y) \quad = \quad Min(\{L : PathsOfLength(x, y, L) \neq \{\}\})$$

or equivalently

$$MinDistance(x, y) \quad = \quad L : PathsOfLength(x, y, L) \neq \{\},$$
$$ShorterPaths(x, y, L) = \{\}$$

Notice how in this development we have slowly gotten further and further from ordinary English words. That's not always good, but it's necessary.

### Exercise

**7.4-4**   Take the examples you constructed in the last exercise, and use them to make some examples of *PathsOfLength*, *ShorterPaths*, and then again *ShortestPaths*.

**Q:** Those are simpler, but they're still rather messy. Isn't there some better way to go about constructing them?

**A:** Often there is. There is a simple principle to remember:

*Never do in one step what you can split into two.*

In this case, we are making too many compound concepts: too many ideas for defining sets of paths from several pieces of information all at once. It's better at this stage to define functions which do only one thing: that way you can put them together in different ways when the time comes to do so. For example, we can define the functions

$$
\begin{aligned}
Paths &= \{P : IsPath(P)\};\\
ComesFrom(x, S) &= \{P \in S : Hd(P) = x\}\\
GoesTo(x, S) &= \{P \in S : Last(P) = x\}\\
LengthIs(L, S) &= \{P \in S : PathLength(P) = L\}\\
LengthLess(L, S) &= \{P \in S : PathLength(P) < S\}\\
MinLength(S) &= Min(\{L : P \in S, PathLength(P) = L\})
\end{aligned}
$$

These simple functions are more manageable because they only do one job at a time. We must, however, combine them occasionally, creating functions like

$$
\begin{aligned}
FromTo(x, y, S) &= GoesTo(y, ComesFrom(x, S))\\
Shortest(S) &= LengthIs(MinLength(S), S)\\
Extensions(S) &= S \cup \{P + [x] : P \in S, x \in Neighbors(Last(P))\}
\end{aligned}
$$

**Q:** How do you think of those?

**A:** Usually by noticing that some combination is being used repeatedly. For example, the original definition of $Extensions(S)$ was just

$$
\{P + [x] : P \in S, x \in Neighbors(Last(P))\}
$$

I then realized that it was always used in the form $X \cup Extensions(X)$. The concept that the discussion was based on was that of adding new elements to a set by extending paths, so the definition was changed to reflect it.

**Exercises**   Prove that

**7.4-5**   For any nonempty set $S$ of paths, the *MinLength* definition gives exactly one value for $L$.

**7.4-6**   $LengthIs(L, GoesTo(x, S)) = GoesTo(x, LengthIs(L, S))$;

**7.4-7**   $PathsOfLength(x, y, L) = LengthIs(L, FromTo(x, y, Paths))$;

**7.4-8**   $ShorterPaths(x, y, L) = LengthLess(L, FromTo(x, y, Paths))$;

**7.4-9**   $ShortestPaths(x, y) = Shortest(FromTo(x, y, Paths))$;

**7.4-10**   $MinLength(Shortest(S)) \leq MinLength(Extensions(S))$;

**7.4-11**   $ComesFrom(x, Extensions(S)) = Extensions(ComesFrom(x, S))$

**Q:** All right, I can see how the specification of *ShortestPaths* works, or at least I can see that we have a bunch of statements which are pretty much compatible with each other. Before we had a bunch of statements which weren't, so I guess things have improved, but have we proven it works?

**A:** Well, we have used counterexamples to *dis*prove all the previous specifications, but we cannot actually *prove* the correctness of this one any more than we can prove the correctness of a model. All we can really do is to use our proof techniques to show properties of the specification in the model world, and then ask ourselves if those properties are appropriate for a solution in the problem world.

### 7.4.3 Exploring a Specification's Logical Consequences

**Q:** What sort of properties should we be trying to prove?

**A:** Almost anything at first. Look for trivial cases: you can easily prove that

$$ShortestPaths(x, x) = PathsOfLength(x, x, 0) = \{[x]\}$$

Look for symmetries; for example, try to prove

$$ShortestPaths(x, y) = ShortestPaths(y, x).$$

**Q:** You mean, by induction or whatever?

**A:** First try it out to see if it makes sense. Structure your examples systematically; try examples like *ShortestPaths(here, here)*, then *ShortestPaths(here, Sumer)*, then *ShortestPaths(here, Babylon)*,... and so on.

**Q:** *ShortestPaths(here, Sumer)* = {*[here, Sumer]*}, but *ShortestPaths(Sumer, here)* = {*[Sumer, here]*}. The assertion is false. Shouldn't the shortest paths from $x$ to $y$ be the reversals of the shortest paths from $y$ to $x$?

**A:** Looks good; can you prove it?

**Exercises**  Prove that

**7.4-12** $ShortestPaths(x, x) = PathsOfLength(x, x, 0) = \{[x]\}$

**7.4-13** $ShortestPaths(x, y) = \{Reverse(P) : P \in ShortestPaths(y, x)\}$
   [Hint: You can refer to proofs done in previous exercises, whether you actually did those exercises or not. You cannot refer to proofs done in later exercises.]

**Q:** Is that all? I mean, when do I stop?

**A:** The pure hacker would never have gotten this far, the pure mathematician would never stop. In computer science, we look for orderly, simple properties which might help construct an answer. For example, is it true that shortest paths are built only from shortest paths? More precisely, do you believe that

**if**  $A + [x] + B \in ShortestPaths(y, z)$

**then**  $A + [x] \in ShortestPaths(y, x)$
**and**  $[x] + B \in ShortestPaths(x, z)$?

**Q:** Of course. Well, maybe not. I'm not sure.

**A:** Let's try a related proposition: do you believe that juxtaposition adds path lengths? More precisely, do you believe that

**if**  $A + [x] + B \in PathsOfLength(y, z, L)$,
   **and**  $A + [x] \in PathsOfLength(y, x, K)$
   **then**  $[x] + B \in PathsOfLength(x, z, L - K)$

**Q:** Sure; we did something a lot like that already, although it wasn't talking about sets.

**A:** Exactly.

## Exercises

**7.4-14** Prove that juxtaposition adds path lengths. (Use induction on the number of places in $A + [x]$, or go back over previous propositions.)

**7.4-15** Prove that shortest paths are built only from shortest paths. (Use proof by contradiction, with the result of the previous exercise.)

**7.4-16** Prove that the juxtaposition of two shortest paths is *not* necessarily a shortest path. (Think of a counterexample.)

**7.4-17** Prove that

   **if** $K < L$ **then** $ShorterPaths(x, y, K) \subseteq ShorterPaths(x, y, L)$

**7.4-18** Using the second exercise of this set, prove that

   **if** $[x, y] + S \in ShortestPaths(x, z)$
   **and** $[x, y, K] \in SegmentTable$
   **then** $y@S \in ShortestPaths(y, z)$.

**7.4-19** A "cyclic path" is one in which some place is visited twice, as in $A+[x]+B+[x]+C$. Prove that for any such path there is a shorter path with the same source and destination, namely $A + [x] + C$.

**7.4-20** From the previous problem, we can define the auxiliary function

$$Acyclic(S) = \{P \in S : \textbf{if } 0 < i < j \leq Length(P) \textbf{ then } P[i] \neq P[j]\}$$

Prove that $Shortest(S) = Shortest(Acyclic(S))$.

**7.4-21** Suppose we have a total of *PlaceCount* possible places on the map. Using the previous exercise, prove that no shortest path has more than *PlaceCount* places in it. (Think about the Pigeonhole Principle.)

**Q:** I guess I can see that it's useful to make sure that the model and specification really do have properties that they ought to have, but I don't see how we're much closer to finding the procedure. All we've got is a lot of proofs, mostly based on induction. Can't we go on to the next section?

**A:** Not yet. The boundary between specification and procedure is actually quite fuzzy. The purest of specifications describes the final object, which we have done, and it is not obligated to describe any other objects. The purest procedure involves a description of every action to be performed in constructing that final object. In practice, however, a useful specification will also relate the goal to subgoals, in order to see what useful properties it has and what alternative descriptions are available, while a procedure description in a higher level language will also describe some of the subgoals as objects. We will break off when we find ourselves describing objects which really make sense only when considered as part of a procedure. That's a subjective decision.

For now, we have to think about the relationships of the goal to other definable objects. So far, we have indeed been doing proofs by induction, which means we have been using induction to relate certain objects to other objects. Induction on what?

**Q:** Induction on the number of places in a path. So what?

**A:** If we're doing induction on the number of places in a path, that usually means that we will later proceed by construction of paths with more and more places in them. Before we actually do that construction, we will define the objects in it: these are objects like the sets of paths with one place, with two places, and so on; the sets of paths with no more than one place, no more than two, and so on; the sets of paths to or from a given place, with constrained numbers of places; sets of shortest paths within a given set of paths; and so on.

**Q:** Do we really need all those?

**A:** Not usually. For most problems, you will find a reasonable answer without trying all possible approaches, and that's fine.

## 7.4.4 Constructing a Trial Solution

In many problems, we can easily rephrase the specification in a "constructive" way without thinking about particular algorithms. For example, we can say confidently that we could find

$$ShortestPaths(x, y) = Shortest(ComesFrom(x, GoesTo(y, Paths)))$$

if only we were given the set of all paths as a starting point. We don't have *Paths*, but we do know that

$$
\begin{aligned}
ShortestPaths(x, y) &= Shortest(ComesFrom(x, GoesTo(y, Paths))) \\
&= Shortest(Acyclic(ComesFrom(x, GoesTo(y, Paths)))) \\
&= Shortest(ComesFrom(x, Acyclic(GoesTo(y, Paths)))) \\
&= Shortest(ComesFrom(x, GoesTo(y, Acyclic(Paths))))
\end{aligned}
$$

and we know that the acyclic paths are all of length less than or equal to *PlaceCount*. That means that we could find the answer with

$$
Acyclic(Paths) \quad = \quad Acyclic(AllPaths(PlaceCount))
$$

where

$$
AllPaths(i) \quad = \quad \{P \in Paths : Length(P) \le i\}
$$

or inductively

$$
\begin{aligned}
AllPaths(0) &= \{\} \\
AllPaths(1) &= \{[x] : x \in Places\} \\
AllPaths(i+1) &= Extensions(AllPaths(i))
\end{aligned}
$$

**Exercises**

**7.4-22**  Prove that **if** $P$ is a path of $i$ places **then** $P \in AllPaths(i)$.

**7.4-23**  For the *SegmentTable* $\{[a, b, 2], [b, c, 3], [a, c, 97]\}$ construct the sets *AllPaths(i)* for $i \in \{1 \ldots 3\}$. (The definition requires that you include cycles as well as the reversal of every included path.)

**7.4-24**  Find *ShortestPaths(a, c)* for the previous problem.

A simple procedure could be outlined as follows: find all paths with *PlaceCount* or fewer places, prune out those with cycles, prune out those that don't go towards our destination, prune out those which don't come from our starting point, and finally prune out all but the shortest.

That would be a perfectly correct solution, easy to define, easy to convert into a program, and fairly obviously correct. Still, it may not be satisfactory. It does more work than is really necessary to solve the problem, simply in the sense that it involves many unnecessary objects. Even without thinking about how these stages will be passed through, you can tell that a program based on this will not be as cheap to run as one based on a more carefully focused specification. In this problem, as in many others, it will be worthwhile to rethink the problem carefully, finding a description of the goal which does not involve more subgoals than we need.

### 7.4.5 Pruning the Specification

Given the previous "pure" specification and the simple "constructive" specification, we want to work onwards toward descriptions of the ShortestPaths set which will not include any descriptions of unnecessary objects. This does not require that we think in terms of a procedure for construction, but it does require that we assume that each object which takes part in the description will at some point be constructed. Surely we need not construct *AllPaths*(PlaceCount); that's a *huge* set.

### Exercise

**7.4-25** How big is the set *AllPaths*(*PlaceCount*) if each place can be directly connected to $N$ others?

**Q:** But wasn't that construction a basically silly one anyway? The whole idea of looking for shortest paths by finding all possible paths is like burning down a forest to cook dinner; it's ludicrous. I thought you were just showing another bad idea.

**A:** Not necessarily. First, there is a lot to be said for a program which is easily written and obviously correct, even if the computer ends up doing extra work. Also, you can't really tell whether a program is ludicrously expensive or the most economical for the job without knowing when it's to be used. The context can make a lot of difference. Are you using one map over and over again, trying to find the shortest paths connecting $A$ to $D$, $B$ to $F$, $A$ to $F$, $D$ to $A$, $C$ to $F$, ..., all in the same neighborhood? In that case, it makes sense to prepare a table of all shortest paths for frequent use: you may want to define the set of all paths of no more than $N$ places, such that if $[x] + A + [y]$ is in the set, then every shorter path from $x$ to $y$ has more than $N$ places.

**Q:** Would you run that by again?

**A:** Sure. Suppose SegmentTable $= \{[a, c, 20], [a, b, 3], [b, c, 2], [c, d, 9]\}$, and we often go from a to c, from a to d, and from b to d. We have a picture something like Figure 7.1.

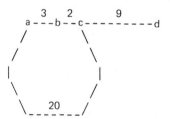

**Figure 7.1** A Simple Cycle and Shortest Paths

What we really want to find is the set of all shortest paths, and we'd like to define it as something like the set of all shortest paths of no more than *PlaceCount* places, where the set of all shortest paths of no more than $N$ places is somehow defined inductively. How about $AllShortestPaths(N)$, or $ASP(N)$, defined this way:

$$ASP(N) = \{P = [x \ldots y] : P \in ShortestPaths(x, y), Length(P) \leq N\}$$

Can you see the problem here?

**Q:** If you then go ahead and define $ShortestPaths$ as $ASP(PlaceCount)$, it looks rather circular; you can't tell if something is a shortest path of no more than $N$ places until after you've constructed all the paths.

**A:** Right. We need a less ambitious definition for $ASP$. Specifically, $ASP(N)$ ought to be the set of all the shortest paths found without even considering any paths with more than $N$ places: $ASP(2)$ might contain a path such as [a,c] which is not really a shortest path, but which appears to be until you get to paths with more places.

$$
\begin{aligned}
ASP(n) &= MinConnectors(AllPaths(n)) \\
MinConnectors(S) &= \{P = [x \ldots y] : P \in Shortest(FromTo(x, y, S))\}
\end{aligned}
$$

**Q:** Could you say that again, a little more slowly?

**A:** Sure. The *minimal connectors* in a set $S$ of paths are exactly those paths whose endpoints are not joined by any shorter paths within $S$. Thus,

$ASP(0)$ is necessarily $\{\}$.
$ASP(1)$ is the set of all shortest paths of no more than one place:
    $\{[a], [b], [c], [d]\}$, each with length 0.
$ASP(2) = \{[a], [a, b], [a, c], [b, a], [b], [b, c], [c, a], [c, b], [c], [c, d], [d, c], [d]\}$.

The new ones are just the segments, and you should notice that although $[a, c]$ is not really the shortest path from $a$ to $c$, it is the shortest path with no more than two places.

We can already see that it is not necessary to write down the one-place paths or the reversals of multi-place paths: we don't need $[a]$ or $[b]$ or $[c]$ or $[d]$, they have to be there no matter what the $SegmentTable$ says, and if we have $[a, b]$ then $[b, a]$ *must* be present. It's convenient to define the Abbreviated $ASP(n)$ set which ignores these, so that $AASP(0) = AASP(1) = \{\}$, and $AASP(2) = \{[a, b], [a, c], [b, c], [c, d]\}$. Here I chose to retain $[a, b]$ rather than $[b, a]$ somewhat arbitrarily, because the starting point "$a$" precedes the end "$b$" lexicographically; that just means that we're keeping the lexicographically lesser member of $\{p, Reverse(p)\}$ for each path $p$. Formally, the rule defining *Abbreviated All Shortest Paths* of no more than $n$ places is:

$$AASP(n) = \{P_{1\ldots N} : P \in ASP(N), 1 < N, P_1 < P_N\}$$

(Remember that if $P_1 = P_N$, then we're in a cycle, which couldn't be in $ASP(N)$ to begin with.) Now if we still need $ASP$ (we do), we can reconstruct it from the abbreviated version this way:

$$\begin{aligned} ASP(0) &= \{\}, \\ ASP(i+1) &= \{[x] : x \in Places\} \cup AASP(n) \cup \{P : Reverse(P) \in AASP(n)\} \end{aligned}$$

We now find that $AASP(3) = \{[a,b],[a,b,c],[a,c,d],[b,c],[b,c,d],[c,d]\}$; the path $[a, c]$ has disappeared because $[a, b, c]$ is shorter. However, $[a, c]$ is still apparently visible within $[a, c, d]$.

### Exercises

**7.4-26** List the shortest paths of no more than four places.

**7.4-27** Prove that for a map with $P$ places, $ASP(P) = ASP(P + 1)$.

**7.4-28** Prove $ASP(i + 1) = MinConnectors(Extensions(ASP(i)))$

We can always find all shortest paths by constructing $ASP(0)$, $ASP(1)$, $ASP(2)$, ..., and so on up to $ASP(PlaceCount)$. That usually isn't necessary; a little more analysis suggests that we can stop as soon as we find that we're making no progress.

### Exercises

**7.4-29** Prove that **if** $[x, y \ldots z]$ is an $N + 2$-place shortest path (i.e., one which does not occur in the set of shortest paths of no more than $N + 1$ places) **then** $[y \ldots z]$ is an $N + 1$-place shortest path (which therefore does not occur in the set of shortest paths of no more than $N$ places). Use previous exercises.

**7.4-30** Using the previous exercise, prove that **if** $ASP(N + 1) = ASP(N + 2)$ **then** it is the set of all shortest paths.

Think about what that means: we could design a procedure based on the observation that when we reach the point that no extension produces a new or shorter path—say that the shortest paths of no more than eight places are just the same as the shortest paths of no more than seven places—we can stop. It would be easy to improve somewhat on such a procedure, even without giving any of the details about *how* its results are achieved, but let's think about it for a moment: how expensive is it? To deal with a map of $P$ places, our mechanical moron may need as many as $P$ stages, each of which involves checking a few extensions for every current path; there may be as many as $P * P$ of these, connecting each place with every other. In other words, this is an $\mathcal{O}(P^3)$ or *cubic* algorithm: if there are 100 places, then he has 1,000,000 steps ahead of him.

## Exercise

**7.4-31** There is a careless assumption in the analysis just given. Can you find it? (If not, you'll see it explained in a few pages.)

Another important thing to look at in this problem approach is that it is problem solving by successive approximation. You begin with a very poor but easy-to-find approximation of the set of all shortest paths: namely, the set of paths having only one place. At each stage, you try to improve the approximation, and when you have reason to believe that the approximation is good enough, you stop. That puts us into the same framework that we have been using for computation since near the beginning of the course: just as we began finding values by algebraically simplifying until no further simplifications were possible, we now find paths by making small improvements until none are possible.

**Q:** I suppose so, but isn't it silly to go to all the trouble of finding all possible shortest paths, when you only want one?

**A:** Yes; if we are only using the map once, then constructing $ASP$ makes no sense: we should be able to find a shortest path from x to y in fewer than $P^3$ stages by restricting our attention to paths from $x$ or paths to $y$. As with $AllShortestPaths$, we will do it by building paths of more and more places:

$$PathsTo(x,n)  =  GoesTo(x, AllPaths(n))$$

From this we can find that

$$\begin{aligned} PathsTo(x,0) &= \{\} \\ PathsTo(x,1) &= \{[x]\} \\ PathsTo(x,i+1) &= ExtensionsBack(PathsTo(x,i)) \end{aligned}$$

where

$$ExtensionsBack(S)  =  \{y@P : P \in S, y \in Neighbors(Hd(P))\}$$

## Exercises

**7.4-32** Prove each of the three equations just listed from the definition.

**7.4-33** Prove that $GoesTo(x, PathsTo(x,i)) = PathsTo(x,i)$.

**7.4-34** Give the corresponding definition and constructive equations for $PathsFrom(x,n)$.

**7.4-35** Prove that $ExtensionsBack(S) = \{Reverse(x) : x \in Extensions(\{Reverse(x) : x \in S\})\}$.

Now we could define

$$PathsFromTo(x, y, n) = ComesFrom(x, PathsTo(y, n));$$

**Exercises**   Prove that

**7.4-36**  $PathsFromTo(x, y, n) = PathsFrom(x, n) \cap PathsTo(y, n)$
**7.4-37**  $PathsFromTo(x, y, n) = \{P \in PathsFrom(x, n) : y = Last(P)\}$

The union of all such sets is the set of all paths from $x$ to $y$, but we don't want all paths from $x$ to $y$; there will be infinitely many of them, anyway. One approach would be to construct a finite set which includes what we need, then throw away what we don't want. For example, knowing that all the shortest paths from $x$ to $y$ are acyclic, we could define all paths which get from $x$ to $y$ with no cycles. Given a finite set of places, that would be a finite set of paths.

**Exercise**   Assume that $AcyclicPathsFrom(x, i) = Acyclic(PathsFrom(x, i))$.

**7.4-38**  Prove that $AcyclicPathsFrom(x, i + 1) =$
$Acyclic(Extensions(AcyclicPathsFrom(x, i)))$

In order to find the shortest paths from $x$ to $y$, we could now construct $S = AcyclicPathsTo(y, P)$ or $S_2 = AcyclicPathsFrom(y, P)$ where $P =$ the number of places, and in either case find the shortest paths in $S$ which started with $x$.

**Q:** All right, that will obviously work and obviously be better, since it never constructs any acyclic paths and never constructs any paths which don't involve the place you're interested in getting to. Do we need to consider more detail than that? Can't we just write the procedure and get to the code?

**A:** No. The construction just given is a really terrible idea, and it's better to find that out without actually writing the code. It is really much more expensive than it would be to construct $ASP$ and then look up the answer.

**Q:** Why? It looks like it's focused on just one piece of the map. How can it possibly be as expensive as $ASP$?

**A:** Imagine a map of the border between two countries, where cities are paired one on each side and the roads make a sort of ladder. (See Figure 7.2.) One country uses lowercase letters to name its cities, the other prefers uppercase; by treaty they have arranged to give corresponding names to neighboring cities.

We first find two acyclic paths from $a$ to $B$, and then two from $B$ to $c$, so there are (at least) four from $a$ to $c$; in fact, there are (at least) eight from $a$ to $d$, (at least) 16 from $a$ to $e$, and so on. Repeat this 10 times, and we have a thousand

```
a --- b --- c --- d --- e --- ......
|     |     |     |     |     ......
A --- B --- C --- D --- E --- ......
```
**Figure 7.2**    Too Many Acyclic Paths

paths; 20 times, and we have a million; 30 times, and we have a billion. If we have $N$ places between $a$ and $z$, then $2**N$ paths are possible. For some problems the idea would work well, because we would never get long ladders; for others it would be disastrous. Please, Please, PLEASE, don't implement before you analyze.

**Q:** But can't this problem arise with the $ASP$ construction?

**A:** Yes, but any shortest path from $x$ to $y$ is as good as any other; at any stage, between any two points, we can remember just one. (Yes, that's a modification of what we've done: the point is that it's a modification which works on the $ASP$ idea, but doesn't work on the acyclic version.) That assumption is really necessary for the construction to need only $P**3$ steps; at each step of our $P$ steps we have only $P**2$ *sets* of shortest paths (one set for each pair of points), but if the sets are large, then finding the extensions of each set can be difficult.

**Q:** But that isn't what you said! You said it would take $P**3$ steps to find *all* of the shortest paths, and now you're telling me that it might be much more than that.

**A:** True. I deliberately lied to you, but my intentions were good, and at least I warned you (in the exercise immediately following the lie) that there was a careless assumption hidden in the analysis. The construction described can produce some shortest path within $P**3$ steps; it can certainly find the length of the shortest path within $P**3$ steps; it cannot actually write out all of the shortest paths within $P**3$ steps because there might be far more than $P**3$ shortest paths.

At this point, we know that shortest paths are always constructed from shortest paths; we can construct the shortest paths from $x$ to $y$ given the set of shortest paths from $x$, which we could find by approximation: construct the shortest paths from $x$ with no more than one place, then the shortest paths from $x$ with no more than two places, and so on. The set of shortest paths from $x$ with no more than $P$ places is the set of shortest paths from $x$.

### Exercise

**7.4-39**  Define $SPF(x, n) = $ "the set of shortest paths from $x$ with no more than $n$ places" formally; prove that, as with $ASP$, **if** $SPF(x, N+1) = SPF(x, N)$ **then** it is the set of shortest paths from $x$.

**Q:** Are these sets really smaller than the ones for $ASP$, or are you tricking me again?

**A:** These are really (a little bit) smaller, and a procedure which constructed them might really work (a little bit) faster than one which constructed all of $ASP$. Still, they will sometimes have elements which could be eliminated by a little thought; we have not defined minimal sets. Suppose we are going from here to Babylon, and we have found a 70-mile path already; it is one of the shortest paths from here with no more than three places. We have also found a 250,000-mile path to the moon; it too is one of the shortest paths from here with no more than three places. Any procedure which tried (on that basis) to construct all the shortest paths from here would go on looking for paths from the moon to Babylon.

**Q:** But that couldn't possibly be the shortest path from here to Babylon; why bother?

**A:** No reason at all, except that it was easier to define the sets that way.

**Q:** You mean, we want the shortest paths of no more than N steps which go from here, except for those which can be left out because they're already longer than some path we've already found: some path that gets all the way from here to Babylon in $N$ steps or less.

**A:** Right. You're getting hold of a very important principle here:

> **if** a series of sets $S_1, S_2, \ldots,$ is defined in a problem,
> **and** the definition of $S_{i+1}$ proceeds by induction on $i$,
>    **then** it will often appear that each set $S_i$ contains
>       1. "dead" elements, of no real use;
>       2. "live" elements, used in S[i+1] or perhaps S[i+2];
>       3. "sleeping" elements, which are not required in the induction
>          but which may be used in the final result.
>          In a solution developed by approximation, these are often just
>          the "old" values, which are present in some earlier set.

In fact, it is often worthwhile to split up each set into subsets. Here we are building a sequence of sets of acyclic paths, hoping to find one from $x$ to $y$. **if** $S_i$ contains a path from $x$ to $y$ of length $L$, **then** any path of greater length in $S_i$ is "dead": no extensions of it will be found in the final solution. **if** $S_{i+1}$ contains a path $P$ which was already in $S_i$, **then** its occurrence in $S_i$ is "sleeping": it may be part of the final answer, but its extensions need not be checked again. The remaining items are "live": they might actually be worth extending.

**Q:** Aren't you really talking about procedures, now?

**A:** Yes. Defining these sets will contribute nothing to our understanding of the problem; they are bookkeeping entities, meaningful only as parts of a particular solution process, and that's what we have to think about next.

### 7.4.6 An End to the Paths

**Q:** Is that all, then?

**A:** Yes; that's all for now.

**Q:** Can we go implement it now?

**A:** Almost. Before we do that, you need to get familiar with a lot of the grungy-detail parts of implementation. It is time to shift examples, to work with the details of table manipulation, with sequences of numbers and sequences of characters; but this time we do it in a programming language.

**Q:** This is very depressing. In high school I wrote a hangman program, a math drill, and then a checkers game, and I never went through all this.

**A:** You won't go through all of it for most of your programming in the future, either. Long ago you had to learn explicit rules for adding multidigit numbers, and you had to write out all the steps. Few adults write out all the steps, because it's too much trouble (even though it would save a few errors). The same principle applies here. Eventually you will just write descriptions (or pictures) of the objects you need to create, then you'll describe the states you need to reach, and then you'll use those descriptions as invariant assertions, inserted into the code. It is rare for a programmer to have to write a proof about his programs; it is not so rare for a programmer to have to adapt procedures from an algorithms book which requires an understanding of proof techniques.

# PROGRAMS

# 8

# Induction, Recursion, and Iteration

In the first two parts, our emphasis was on understanding computation and the objects it works with; if you wrote and ran equational programs along the way, that's good, but it's not crucial. Now it's time to develop programming techniques. Chapter 8 begins with *Modula-2* program development by transliteration from equations; we then proceed through all of the control structures of *Modula-2*, rewriting the first-draft programs one step at a time for efficiency's sake. The programs involving sequences are to be carried out using modules which define sequence types (and operations) which behave like those you've seen in specifications. In Chapter 9, we work out the details of those representations and many others... there is a tremendous variety of methods available to represent sequences and trees, and each has advantages and disadvantages. The list is not exhaustive, but it is extensive, and it does cover many of the lower level parts of the language. That's as far as we go in programming techniques, and it's enough to make you ready to start making yourself a good programmer; it's not enough to really have a feeling for what the underlying machine is like. In Chapter 10, we look at how it all works: we start with switches and move up, through layer after layer of representation, up to support the level at which we've been programming... and beyond.

In this chapter, we begin to implement the specifications as "real" programs. The language used is *Modula-2*, but the principles would apply in related languages such as *ADA*, *Pascal*, *C*, and others.

This chapter is **not** a substitute for a good language manual; simple facts such as the use of ">=" and "#" for "≥" and "≠" are necessary, but they will not be emphasized here. There is quite enough to be covered while sticking with fundamental concepts like the notions and notations of "assignment", by which a state is changed.

Up until now, we have tried to develop coherent *descriptions* of states (and sequences of states). Most programming languages emphasize *prescription* as well: instead of drawing a picture of a house and saying "build this," we say "pick up the hammer; put it on the table; find the right nails; find the right size board; . . . ." In other words, instead of describing a new state as a function of an old state, we transform the old state into the new one by changing the values of variables within it. Expressions (which have values within a given state) are still important, but statements (which alter values, thus forcing the program into a new state) are usually just as important—and much more likely to lead to errors. The use of statements means that an assertion which is true at one moment may be false the next; we have to be much more careful about keeping track of the assertions we make.

In forming a program which implements a specification, you should keep as close as you can to the specification itself. It turns out that some kinds of specifications are very easy to implement, others very difficult. Often, the easiest way to implement one of the latter kind is to think about the program for a while and then go back to work on the specification; you can redo it as (or extend it with) a set of definitions which are equivalent to the ones you had, but which can be easily implemented. Parts of the specification will remain as comments within the program, and these comments can be used as guides in finding errors. We are coming back to the notion of an "invariant assertion," i.e., a claim which is to be true of the state at a particular point in a program.

## 8.1 OUTLINE

The chapter will deal first with code which is a straightforward translation of specification; most programming languages allow you to do this (sometimes rather awkwardly), and it's a good way to develop an understandable prototype. In *Modula-2*, this works best with operations on simple objects (numbers, characters, Boolean values, and enumerations). You'll compile and test your programs with the aid of "library modules" provided for the purpose. (Try to think of them as working by magic, at least for the moment; you can't learn everything at once.) With structured objects, we'll make use of more library modules which define the familiar sequence operations; these are not primitive in *Modula-2*. Your programs will generate output, but only for aid in debugging; a systematic treatment of communication with the outside world will have to be left until later.

After we've developed some prototype programs, we'll go over the reasons that they don't work well in *Modula-2*. You must understand the way that your system represents abstract objects and functions (i.e., an abstract state) in terms of "concrete" objects in space and time. We'll need concepts like "assignment statements" and "control structures" and "VAR parameters." They are likely to seem quite intuitive; unfortunately, they provide marvelous opportunities for subtle bugs.

Now we can look at parts of the magical modules for testing and tracing functions; we'll add output and then input for debugging and for communication with the outside world. The ideas here were almost all presented earlier; all we have to do is put them into *Modula-2*.

The chapter moves through examples from previous chapters, dealing with issues of control structure but not of data representation. We will write procedures which deal with sequences, but just how those sequences are stored is not yet an issue. Operations such as *Put*, *Tl*, and *AddItem* are available; some of these are primitive in the programming language, and others aren't. It doesn't matter yet which, because we are not yet interested in methods for defining *Put* from *AddItem* or vice versa; these will be left for the next chapter. Whether truly primitive or not, some operations will be limited: there may be a maximal allowed value for a cardinal number, or a maximal allowed length for a sequence. These limits are implementation dependent, and will not be discussed in this chapter.

## 8.2 SIMPLE TRANSLATIONS OF FUNCTIONS

Given a specification of a simple recursive function, we can normally put it into programming-language syntax without much difficulty. That means that all operations we define must be prefix, it means that certain key words like PROCEDURE and BEGIN and END will  be scattered liberally around the page, and it means a few other things, but it presents no great difficulty. We'll begin as usual with operations on numbers, but move on quickly from there.

### 8.2.1 Numeric Functions

Let's look at a trivial example first:

$$Double(n) \quad = \quad n + n$$

This specification of a function on integers leads immediately to the program

```
PROCEDURE DOUBLE(n:INTEGER):INTEGER;
  (* post: result = Double(n) = n + n *)
  BEGIN
    RETURN n+n;
END DOUBLE;
```

Think about each item here. In outline, the procedure begins with a keyword to say that it *is* a procedure. The procedure definition should now continue with a name (in this case, DOUBLE), and it includes everything after that up to and including the END DOUBLE which marks the end of that procedure's definition. In between, we have an *argument list* which is very much like that of the specification, except that it has a type INTEGER as well as a name for the argument. After that, we find that there's a type for the result of the procedure as well; it's also an integer. Then comes a semicolon, and we're done with the "header" of the procedure. The line which begins with (* and ends with *) is a *comment line*. The programming-language implementation will ignore it, but it does say something to the human reader of the program: it says that this is a *post*condition, an assertion to be true as the procedure completes its activity, and that the condition is that the result of the procedure DOUBLE is to be the value of the function *Double*, which is $n + n$.

**Q:** But aren't *Double* and DOUBLE the same thing?

**A:** No, the first is a mathematical object and the second one is a computational object, but the closer we can keep them the less confused we're likely to get. Later, we will usually use the same name for the *Modula-2* construct which we used for the mathematical function, even when they have different numbers of arguments or appear different in other ways. Usually this turns out to be helpful rather than confusing, because either you can tell which is which or they're supposed to be the same. In this book, we won't even be careful to keep the capitalization different: if we talk about the "mathematical function 'double'" and the "procedure 'double,'" it should be clear which is which.

The only comment to this procedure is a postcondition: there is no precondition to state what ought to be true at the beginning, so we assume that any argument of the right type should be all right.

After the comment line, the procedure continues. There's a BEGIN and an END, and in between there's a sequence of statements—well, actually there only seems to be one statement, a RETURN which is evidently producing the value we want, followed by a semicolon.

**Q:** My manual says that the semicolon is a delimiter, which goes between two statements.

**A:** That's true; the semicolon is optional.[1] When I write a sequence of statements (even a sequence of length one), I often—but not always—try to think of the semicolons as terminators (like periods or exclamation points in English) rather than delimiters (like English semicolons). The reason is simple; it's easier to turn "Walk; Run; Jump;" into "Jump; Walk; Run;" than it is to turn "Walk; Run; Jump" into "Jump; Run; Walk" and such reshufflings (not to mention insertions and deletions) are extremely common in programming. My goal is to get you to think hard about every character and every punctuation mark in your programs.

---

[1] *Modula-2* interprets "RETURN x;" as a sequence of two statements, the second one being empty.

The best way to get familiar with such issues is to look at another example (or ten)...

$$gcd(x,y) \quad = \quad Max(i): \qquad mod(x,i) = 0, mod(y,i) = 0$$
$$= \quad y, \qquad\qquad \text{if } x = 0$$
$$= \quad x, \qquad\qquad \text{if } y = 0$$
$$= \quad gcd(x-y,y), \quad \text{if } x > y$$
$$= \quad gcd(x,y-x), \quad \text{otherwise}$$

From this, we can immediately (well, after a little practice) write down

```
PROCEDURE GCD(x, y : INTEGER) : INTEGER;
  (* pre: x, y ≥ 0 *)
  (* post : result = gcd(x,y) = Max(r) : mod(x,r) = mod(y,r) = 0 *)
  BEGIN
    IF x=0 THEN RETURN y;
      ELSIF y=0 THEN RETURN x;
      ELSIF x>y THEN RETURN GCD(x−y, y);
      ELSE RETURN GCD(x, y−x);
    END;
END GCD;
```

Here we have fundamentally the same kind of recipe, but almost all the details are different. Instead of one argument, there are two: both INTEGER. Instead of one human-directed comment, there are two: one specifies the *precondition* that this procedure assumes that the arguments are nonnegative, and the other specifies the result as before. The comments do not say anything at all about what will happen if the precondition is false. (Very soon, you can try it and find out.) After them, we have condition-oriented key words IF... which are evidently implementing the conditional rules just as required by the specification.

Let's try another:

$$fact(n) \quad = \quad 1, \qquad\qquad\quad \text{if } n = 0$$
$$= \quad n * fact(n-1), \quad \text{otherwise}$$

This too transcribes quite neatly into *Modula-2*:

```
PROCEDURE FACT(n : CARDINAL) : CARDINAL;
  (* post: result = fact(n) = 1 * 2 * 3 * ... n *)
  BEGIN
    IF n=0 THEN RETURN 1 ELSE RETURN n*FACT(n-1) END ;
END FACT;
```

Here there is no precondition at all, but since $n$ is described as being a CARDINAL number, we know that $n \geq 0$ is true in any case.

**Q:** Then why didn't you use the same idea with GCD in the previous example?
**A:** In this case, because I wanted to show you these two almost-equivalent approaches to the same idea. In general, I might reasonably write an initial version of GCD which would only work on nonnegatives, with the expectation that a later version would work on arbitrary integers... that kind of reasoning is not so likely to apply to FACT. Meanwhile, I certainly can write a CARDINAL-oriented version of GCD, and make other changes at the same time.

The *Modula-2* language we're using contains MOD and DIV as infix primitives on cardinal and integer values; we can rewrite the *gcd* function as

$$gcd(x, y) \quad = \quad \textbf{if } x < y \textbf{ then } g(y, x) \textbf{ else } g(x, y)$$

where

$$\begin{aligned} g(q, r) \quad &= \quad q, & \text{if } r = 0 \\ &= \quad g(r, mod(q, r)) & \text{otherwise} \end{aligned}$$

From this, we write

```
PROCEDURE GCD(x, y : CARDINAL) : CARDINAL;
  (* post : result = gcd(x,y) = Max(r) : mod(x,r) = mod(y,r) = 0 *)
  PROCEDURE G(q, r:CARDINAL):CARDINAL;
    (* pre: q ≥ r ≥ 0 *)
    (* post : result = gcd(q,r) *)
    BEGIN
      IF r=0 THEN RETURN q
        ELSE RETURN G(r, q MOD r)
      END
    END G;
  BEGIN (* GCD *)
    IF x<y THEN RETURN G(y, x) ELSE RETURN G(x, y) END
  END GCD;
```

Nested definitions in programming languages are just like the ones you've seen in specifications. The definition of G is hidden "internally" or "locally" to the definition of GCD. G therefore can't be used except by GCD or by some other procedure which is local to GCD.

**Exercises**   Now you should write some, taking specifications from the Part I rules for cardinal numbers and using appropriate preconditions for these procedures on INTEGERs:

**8.2-1**   *Up*
**8.2-2**   *Down*
**8.2-3**   *min*
**8.2-4**   *SqrRt*
**8.2-5**   *Mul*, with *MulAcc* as a local function.

If these were written as CARDINAL procedures they wouldn't need preconditions about arguments being nonnegative, but *Down* would still need a precondition to specify its strictly positive argument. *Modula-2* also provides the type REAL, with the usual operations $(+, *, /, -,$ etc.), and comparisons $(>, <, =,$ and so on).

**Exercises**   Using "*" and "/" on REAL numbers,

**8.2-6**   Define a function $SqrRt(n, d)$ which assumes that $n \in 0.0 \ldots \infty$ and $0.0 < d < 1.0$ so that $\sqrt{n}$ is between 0.0 and $max(1.0, n)$. Use binary search on that range to find the square root of $n$ to within error-tolerance $d$. You must provide rules as well as code.

**8.2-7**   Define a function $Exp(r : \text{REAL}, n : \text{INTEGER})$ which finds $r^{**}n$. You must deal with negative $n$ as a special case.

### Getting It to Run

**Q:** Wow! I wrote a program... finally. How do I run it?

**A:** That's system-dependent. The purpose of a program (or MODULE) is to provide (or EXPORT) types, objects and operations which satisfy certain constraints. The routines you write go into a library module which EXPORTs them so that they can be used in (IMPORTed by) other programs, which may in turn EXPORT types, objects and operations which will be IMPORTed into other programs, which may in turn...

**Q:** But doesn't it *do* anything? Don't I ever get to look at something happening on a screen?

**A:** Yes; in fact each routine you write may be used to do many things in many contexts. For each use, there will be a different top-level which IMPORTs definitions but never EXPORTs anything because its purpose is activity. At the moment, you just want to test your routines, so you need a TestFns module which IMPORTs them and which then tests them and talks to you about it. Don't try to write it yourself; it's provided with the book. Insert your solutions into the SimpleFns module which is already set up to EXPORT them, and then you can compile and run... and find out what went wrong, and recompile and rerun, and generally act like a computer science initiate. If you look over the TestFns module, you will find that it contains very similar tests for many quite different functions; you'll also find that it contains a good deal of code which you can't yet understand. Often, you'll be able to delete tests which you don't want, or alter tests which you think are testing the wrong thing, or add new tests which you think would be useful. You may feel nervous about doing it without really understanding much of the module. Do it! It's a very good way to begin, as long as you don't lose an original (unaltered) version. A lot of what you will learn will be related to your particular system (e.g., a "post-mortem debugger") rather than to the programming language. It will be hard for you to tell at first what's important and what isn't, but all you can do is try. One useful kind of test involves actually changing the code, to make it report what it sees. For example, you could insert two lines at the top of FACT to read as follows:

```
WriteString("FACT("); WriteCard(n, 0); Write(")"); WriteLn;
WriteString(" Argument n must be > 0 "); WriteLn;
```

If you do that, and then test FACT(3), you'll see the following output on the screen:

```
FACT(3)
Argument n must be > 0
FACT(2)
Argument n must be > 0
FACT(1)
Argument n must be > 0
FACT(0)
Argument n must be > 0
```

At this point, the inner call on FACT concludes, and the overall result of 6 is given to the testing routine. Meanwhile, you've seen a conflict: the assertion which was printed out was wrong when FACT(0) was called. In this particular case, FACT is correct and the assertion was wrong; it should have been "...must be $\geq 0$." In many cases you will find that such a conflict is the easiest way to find a bug in your program. We are not going to cover output systematically now. You have just seen that there are procedures which generate it, and that they have different names depending on what kind of thing is to be printed. As you deal with other data types, you'll find other procedures for printing them.

You will soon find differences between what ought to work and what actually does work: if you use the FACT definition to find the value of $1*2*\ldots*1000$, you'll get an error message indicating that there are too many digits in some intermediate product. If you use the first definition of GCD to find the greatest common divisor of 1,000,000 and 2, you'll get an error message indicating that the system has run out of "stack" space; in effect, it indicates that one of the expressions it built up was too long.

**Q:** That's impossible: this is a simple recurrence, and you've been saying from the start that simple recurrences don't grow. In fact, it's obvious that they don't:

$$gcd(1000000, 2) = gcd(999998, 2) = gcd(999996, 2) = \ldots = gcd(2, 2) = gcd(2, 0) = 2$$

Each of those is the same size as the last, or smaller if you worry about the number of digits.

**A:** The expressions don't need to grow, but *Modula-2* adds some bookkeeping information with each substitution, and it doesn't go away until we finally get a value. It's as if each substitution comes wrapped in parentheses—

$$gcd(1000000, 2) = (gcd(999998, 2) = ((gcd(999996, 2))) = (((gcd(999994, 2)))) \ldots$$

By the time we get a few hundred or a few thousand parentheses deep, we're in trouble. Don't worry about it; there's a simple way to avoid it, which we'll cover soon. I'm only mentioning it now because you may encounter the problem now.

**The Types of the Number 5**    As we've noted, *Modula-2* insists that every expression should have a type like CARDINAL or INTEGER or REAL. One problem with that is that many values, such as the number 5, appear to have more than one type. This can sometimes be quite confusing. Suppose we want to implement the *AbsVal* absolute value function, which produces a nonnegative integer from an arbitrary integer:

$$
\begin{aligned}
AbsVal(n) \quad &= \quad n, \qquad \text{if } n \geq 0 \\
&= \quad -n, \qquad \text{otherwise}
\end{aligned}
$$

This can be translated trivially into *Modula-2* as the AbsVal procedure.

```
PROCEDURE AbsVal(n:INTEGER):INTEGER;
  (* post: result = AbsVal(n₀) *)
  BEGIN
    IF n >= 0 THEN RETURN n
      ELSE RETURN -n
    END;
END AbsVal;
```

**Q:** Why doesn't it return a CARDINAL number?

**A:** There is very little difference between a CARDINAL number and a non-negative INTEGER, but there is some. A CARDINAL number has no sign to mark it as nonnegative; the corresponding integer needs space for one. That means that the largest cardinal number may well be larger than the largest integer. (The space which would be left blank for a sign can be used for a digit.) In most programming languages, there is some simple way to convert back and forth between corresponding CARDINALs and INTEGERs, not to mention other types. Sometimes it's actually implicit: if you just change the result type of AbsVal from INTEGER to CARDINAL, the conversion will happen. In *Modula-2*, the RETURN statements should also be changed to "RETURN CARDINAL(n)" and "RETURN CARDINAL(-n)", respectively; a type-name like CARDINAL can be treated as a function name, which converts values of other types to corresponding values of its type (if possible). If you want to add the INTEGER n to the CARDINAL i and get an INTEGER, it's a good idea to say n+INTEGER(i).

## Exercise

**8.2-8**   Suppose that you wanted to add the (nonnegative) INTEGER n to the CARDINAL i and get a CARDINAL. What could you write?

### 8.2.2  Boolean Operations

Again, we'll work with an example. Let's suppose that we're trying to find out whether the three numbers [12, 5, 13] could make the sides of a right triangle. (They could.) This happens to be part of a library of tests on geometrical figures, including such fascinating constructions as a test on number trios to see if they could be the sides of isosceles triangles.

A trio of cardinal numbers can make a triangle if they're all nonzero, and if the sum of any two is greater than the third. (Think about it; we are not accepting [0, 0, 0] as a triangle, and no side may be too long to connect the other sides.) The numbers can make an isosceles triangle if they can make a triangle **and** two of the numbers are equal. They can make a right triangle if they can make a triangle **and** the square of one of the numbers is the sum of the squares of the other two. In the case under consideration, it just happens that the square of 12 is 144, the square of 5 is 25, and the sum of these two squares is 169—the square of 13.

We can specify triangle predicates as follows:

$$
\begin{aligned}
IsTriangle(x, y, z) \;\; &= \;\; ((x > 0) \wedge (y > 0) \wedge (z > 0)) \\
&\qquad \wedge ((x + y > z) \wedge (y + z > x) \wedge (z + x > y)) \\
IsIsosceles(x, y, z) \;\; &= \;\; IsTriangle(x, y, z) \wedge ((x = y) \vee (y = z) \vee (x = z)) \\
IsRightTri(x, y, z) \;\; &= \;\; IsTriangle(x, y, z) \wedge (H(x, y, z) \vee H(y, z, x) \vee H(z, x, y))
\end{aligned}
$$

where

$$
H(a, b, c) \;\; = \;\; ((Sqr(a) + Sqr(b)) = Sqr(c))
$$

In this case, *IsRightTri* uses both $H$ and *IsTriangle*, but *IsTriangle* is a function useful in other contexts, such as *IsIsosceles*, where $H$ is just an abbreviation, meaningful only within *IsRightTri*. The following IsTriangle procedure corresponds directly to it.

```
PROCEDURE IsTriangle(x, y, z:CARDINAL):BOOLEAN;
(* post: result = IsTriangle(x, y, z) *)
BEGIN
    RETURN( (x>0) AND (y>0) AND (z > 0) AND
            ((x+y)>z) AND ((x+z)>y) AND ((y+z)>x) );
END IsTriangle;
```

Having defined this procedure, we can use it in other programs, just as we used its specification within their specifications. However, we would like the program which finds $H$ to be concealed within the program for *IsRightTri*, just as the corresponding specification was concealed. The IsRightTri program illustrates this:

```
PROCEDURE IsRightTri(x, y, z:CARDINAL):BOOLEAN;
    (* post: result = (they are the lengths of sides of a right triangle) *)
    PROCEDURE H(a, b, c:CARDINAL):BOOLEAN;
        (* pre: a, b, and c are cardinals *)
        (* post: result = (a*a + b*b = c*c) *)
        BEGIN
            RETURN(Sqr(c) = Sqr(a)+Sqr(b));
        END H;
    BEGIN (* IsRightTri *)
        RETURN(IsTriangle(x, y, z) AND (H(x, y, z) OR H(y, z, x)
                OR H(z, x, y)) );
    END IsRightTri;
```

As before, the change is primarily cosmetic: the operations in the programming language are just exactly those of the specification language.

### Exercises

**8.2-9** Write the IsIsosceles procedure in *Modula-2*; as you can see, there is a space for it in the SimpleFns module.

**8.2-10** Specify and write an IsEquilateral operation (predicate) which is *True* of three cardinal numbers, provided that they describe an equilateral triangle.

**8.2-11** Specify and write an IsRightIsos operation which is *True* of three cardinal numbers, provided that they describe an isosceles right triangle. Comment on whether or not the operation makes sense.

The Boolean operations are primitive in *Modula-2*, but it may be reassuring to realize that all the old relationships still hold: AND, OR, and NOT can be defined by the conditional statement just as they were definable with the conditional expression. For example, we could implement AND by the following And2 procedure.

```
PROCEDURE And2(x, y:BOOLEAN):BOOLEAN;
  (* post: result = x ∧ y *)
  BEGIN
    IF x THEN RETURN(y) ELSE RETURN(x) END ;
END And2;
```

### Exercises

**8.2-12**  Implement Or2 as ∨, using conditional statements.

**8.2-13**  Implement Not as ¬ using conditional statements.

**8.2-14**  Implement XOr as ≠ using conditional statements.

### 8.2.3 Characters and Other Enumerations

Conditional operations on characters look very much the same in programs as in specifications. Thus, *IsUC* becomes IsUC with no real surprises.

```
PROCEDURE IsUC(c:CHAR):BOOLEAN;
  (* post: result = IsUC(c), as previously specified *)
  BEGIN
    IF (c >='A') THEN RETURN(c <= 'Z');
      ELSE RETURN(FALSE );
    END;
END IsUC;
```

### Exercises

**8.2-15**  Rewrite IsUC without IF...END as an operation, using a single **and**  to combine the comparisons. Which version is more readable?

**8.2-16**  Write IsLC.

**8.2-17**  Write IsLetter.

**8.2-18**  Write IsDigit.

**8.2-19**  Write IsVowel.

**8.2-20**  Write LexOrder.

As an example of a function which produces a character as its result, let's consider *UC*:

```
PROCEDURE UC(c:CHAR):CHAR;
  (* post: result = UC(c), as previously specified *)
  CONST CaseDiff = 32; (* CaseDiff = ORD('a') - ORD('A') *)
  BEGIN
    IF IsLC(c) THEN RETURN CHR(ORD(c)-CaseDiff);
      ELSE RETURN c;
    END;
END UC;
```

Here we know that the difference between an *ASCII* lowercase letter and the corresponding uppercase letter is 32, but some maintainance programmer might be confused by finding ORD(c)-32 in the middle of a program. Instead, we use the name CaseDifference which is defined as a constant, and we put a comment beside its definition to explain the motivation.

**Exercise**

**8.2-21** Write LC, which converts letters to lowercase as UC did to uppercase.

In *Modula-2*, there are two quotation marks for characters: the we can represent the letter '**X**' with the single-quote '**X**' or the double-quote "**X**". They are equivalent, and either can be used to quote the other: "'" is the single-quote character which (in the *ASCII* system) is *CHR*(39).

Other enumerations are easy to use, but must be explicitly defined as we've been doing in specifications. The syntax is pretty close to the specification as well, as you see in Figure 8.1.

Of course, this kind of function would be better represented as a table; the "if-then-else" idea is a fairly clumsy way to describe the regularity of what's going on here. *Modula-2* does provide a syntax which we can use for function tables inside procedures, and we could write the same idea as shown in Figure 8.2. This kind of tabulation is often more readable and more reliable than the equivalent conditional construction. Also, it can be more efficient, because it hints to the programming system that the 'S' for Saturday can be found without checking the days beforehand, using some version of *Get*. One way or another, we have the FirstLetter function, and now we can use it (as seen on the top of page 351).

```
TYPE
    Language = (English, Spanish);
    DayofWeek = (Sun, Mon, Tues, Wed, Thurs, Fri, Sat);
PROCEDURE FirstLetter(L:Language, D:DayOfWeek):CHAR;
  (* post: result is first letter of D's name in L *)
  BEGIN
    IF L=English
      THEN IF D=Sun THEN RETURN 'S'
        ELSIF D=Mon THEN RETURN 'M'
        ELSIF D=Tues THEN RETURN 'T'
        ELSIF D=Wed THEN RETURN 'W'
        ELSIF D=Thurs THEN RETURN 'T'
        ELSIF D=Fri THEN RETURN 'F'
        ELSIF D=Sat THEN RETURN 'S'
      END
      ELSIF D=Sun THEN RETURN 'D'       (* Domingo *)
      ELSIF D=Mon THEN RETURN 'L'       (* Lunes *)
      ELSIF D=Tues THEN RETURN 'M'      (* Martes *)
      ELSIF D=Wed THEN RETURN 'M'       (* Miercoles *)
      ELSIF D=Thurs THEN RETURN 'J'     (* Jueves *)
      ELSIF D=Fri THEN RETURN 'V'      (* Viernes *)
      ELSIF D=Sat THEN RETURN 'S'      (* Sabado *)
    END
END FirstLetter;
```

**Figure 8.1** FirstLetter as IF...THEN...ELSIF

```
PROCEDURE FirstLetter(L:Language, D:DayOfWeek):CHAR;
  (* post: result is first letter of D's name in L *)
BEGIN
  IF L=English THEN
    CASE D OF
      Sun : RETURN 'S'
      Mon : RETURN 'M'
      Tues : RETURN 'T'
      Wed : RETURN 'W'
      Thurs : RETURN 'T'
      Fri : RETURN 'F'
      Sat : RETURN 'S'
    END
    ELSE
    CASE D OF
      Sun : RETURN 'D'       (* Domingo *)
      Mon : RETURN 'L'       (* Lunes *)
      Tues : RETURN 'M'      (* Martes *)
      Wed : RETURN 'M'       (* Miercoles *)
      Thurs : RETURN 'J'      (* Jueves *)
      Fri : RETURN 'V'      (* Viernes *)
      Sat : RETURN 'S'      (* Sabado *)
    END
  END FirstLetter;
```

**Figure 8.2** FirstLetter as list of CASEs

**FirstLetter function**

PROCEDURE FixedFirst(D:DayOfWeek):BOOLEAN;
   (* returns TRUE if *FirstLetter(D)* is the same in English and Spanish *)
   BEGIN
      RETURN (FirstLetter(English, D) = FirstLetter(Spanish, D))
   END FixedFirst;

**Exercises**   After a quick trip to the library, if needed...

**8.2-22**  Add French to the languages handled by *FirstLetter*.

**8.2-23**  Even if you didn't do the previous exercise, add French to the languages checked
by *FixedFirst*. (This should not require any trip to the library.)

## 8.2.4 Strings

Here *Modula-2*, like many languages, appears to restrict us somewhat. You've seen
that there are strings provided as part of the language, but they don't act like the
strings of our specification language; they are more like the graph paper on which
the moron writes rather than like the values he's trying to represent. Thus, it's
convenient to write

$$\text{WriteString(``gcd(x, y)=gcd}(x_0, y_0)\text{'', x, y=''); WriteInt(x, 9); WriteInt(y, 9);}$$

but it's not so convenient (in many *Modula-2* implementations) to write a procedure
which returns a string as a value. But in the end, that's no problem: if I provide a
Strs library module which EXPORTs the Str type and the required operations on
it, then your programs can simply use that. The only trouble is that they will take
more time and space than is strictly necessary. For the first few versions (of your
first programs or of any programs) you shouldn't worry about that. Later, you can
rewrite those programs so that they work with strings as they are presented in the
programming system.

    We can't arbitrarily choose notation now; we're constrained by syntactic
rules designed into *Modula-2*. Some expressions which we've gotten used to, like
$S[i \ldots j] + (a@Y)$ are no longer meaningful. Still, we can always fall back on prefix
format and say the same thing with

$$\text{Append(Mid(S, i, j), AddItem(a, Y))}$$

That's not a problem, although it can be a nuisance. Study the *Capitalize* function and the corresponding Capitalize procedure:

$$Capitalize(S) \quad = \quad "", \qquad\qquad\qquad\qquad\qquad \text{if } S = ""$$
$$= \quad UC(Hd(S))@Capitalize(Tl(S)) \quad \text{otherwise}$$

```
FROM Strs IMPORT IsNull, AddItem, Hd, Tl;
PROCEDURE Capitalize(S:Str):Str;
  (* post: result= Capitalize(S) = [UC(c) : c ∈ S] *)
  BEGIN
    IF IsNull(S) THEN RETURN S
      ELSE RETURN AddItem(UC(Hd(S)), Capitalize(Tl(S)))
    END
END Capitalize;
```

In order to test the procedure, we insert the code into the SimpStrs module already defined as EXPORTing it, and then we can use the TestStrs module to test it.

**Exercises**   Using the SimpStrs and TestStrs modules, write and test

**8.2-24** $Reverse(S) = [S[Length(S) + 1 - i] : i \in 1 \ldots Length(S)]$

**8.2-25** $Letters(S) = [c \in S : IsLetter(c)]$

**8.2-26** $IsPalindrome(S) = (S' = Reverse(S')) : S' = Capitalize(Letters(S))$

**8.2-27** $CardToStr$

**8.2-28** $StrToCard$

**8.2-29** $IntToStr$

**8.2-30** $StrToInt$

**8.2-31** $Delete(S, n, k) = S[1 \ldots n - 1] + S[n + k \ldots Length(S)]$

**8.2-32** $FindPat(p, S) = \max(0, Min(\{i : p = S[i \ldots Length(p)]\}))$

**8.2-33** $Subst(new, old, S)$

## 8.2.5  Sequences

With sequences in general we have the same problem as with strings only more so: the kinds of sequences provided in the language aren't very close to the kinds we use in specification. The solution is the same: use modules IntSeq, RealSeq, StrSeq, and BoolSeq for sequences of integers, reals, strings, and Booleans, respectively. Each one should export functions named Eq, Hd, Tl, Put, Get, Len, Mid, Append, Find, and IsNull, as well as the NewNull function, which generates a new empty sequence of the right type.

Let's try a sample IntSeq function; later we'll use the other types.

$$Range(i, j) \quad = \quad [], \qquad\qquad\qquad \text{if } i > j$$
$$\quad = \quad i@Range(i + 1, j) \quad \text{otherwise}$$

This becomes (surprise, surprise)

```
FROM IntSeq IMPORT NewNull, AddItem;
PROCEDURE Range(i, j:CARDINAL):IntSeq;
  (* post: result= [i..j] *)
  BEGIN
    IF i>j THEN RETURN NewNull();
      ELSE RETURN AddItem(i, Range(i+1, j));
    END;
END Range;
```

**Exercises**    Now you should have no special trouble writing

**8.2-34**  *Reverse*

**8.2-35**  *Sum*

**8.2-36**  *Count*

**8.2-37**  *IntSeqToStr*

**8.2-38**  *StrToIntSeq*

**8.2-39**  $SwapOrd(S, i, j) =$ **if** $S_i > S_j$ **then** $Swap(S, i, j)$ **else** $S$

**8.2-40**  $Bubble(S, i, j) =$ **if** $i \geq j$ **then** $S$ **else** $Bubble(SwapOrd(S, i, i+1), i+1, j)$

**8.2-41**  $MinFirst(S, i, j) =$ **if** $i \geq j$ **then** $S$ **else** $MinFirst(SwapOrd(S, i, j), i, j - 1)$

**8.2-42**  *Sort*, using the *Bubble* function

**8.2-43**  *Sort*, using the *MinFirst* function

**8.2-44**  *Merge* and Merge*Sort*

As you can see, we're using an *AddItem* function, and all the others that we used with strings; it just happens to be a different *AddItem* function, one which works on sequences of integers rather than sequences of characters. So far as *Modula-2* is concerned, they are completely separate objects, and it must always know which one is in use. To you, they are really the same concept, just applied in different places—and the places do have to be separate, too: if you try to have two different *AddItem* functions at the same time, *Modula-2* is going to get very confused.

**Q:** Hey, wait a minute. What if I have one problem where I need to work with more than one kind of sequence?

**A:** This is the same problem we've always had with multiple objects having the same name; as always, you solve it by renaming (nicknaming) or by adding something to the name, like a family name. If you need to use the procedure *Mid* exported by IntSeqs and—in the same module—the *Mid* procedure exported by Strs, then you can import IntSeqs and Strs as entire modules and then refer to the procedures IntSeqs.Mid and Strs.Mid. This is mildly awkward, but not a real problem.

Here's a sample which we saw near the beginning of our work with sequences:

$$Tails(S) \quad = \quad [], \qquad\qquad\qquad \text{if } S = []$$
$$= \quad S@(Tails(Tl(S)), \quad \text{otherwise}$$

To deal with this, we write

```
IMPORT Strs, StrSeqs;
PROCEDURE Tails(S:Strs.Str):StrSeqs.StrSeq;
  (* post: result = Tails(S) = [S, Tl(S), Tl(Tl(S)),..., [Last(S)]] *)
  BEGIN
    IF StrSeqs.IsNull(S) THEN RETURN StrSeqs.NewNull()
      ELSE RETURN StrSeqs.AddItem(S, Tails(Strs.Tl(S)))
    END
END Tails;
```

**Exercise**    Use the same kind of overall IMPORT statement to write

**8.2-45** $AppendAll(S_{1...n}) = S_1 + S_2 + \ldots + S_n$, for any sequence $S$ of strings.

**Q:** That's pretty ugly. Why can't we just have a single Seq type which can include any of those types?

**A:** We can and we do, but it's not really easy to use. We can't put arbitrary objects all over the place and expect the system to make sense of them as a human reader might. *Modula-2* needs to know the type of every variable and every expression, and '**X**' has a different type than that of 9. If we tried to use mixed-type objects like $X = [5, \text{'A'}, 42, \text{"seventeen"}]$ or even $Y = [\text{"\textbf{What}"}, \text{'a'}, \text{"mess"}]$, [2] then it would be impossible to tell the type of $Get(X, i)$ without knowing the value of $i$ and our system doesn't like that.

**Q:** So how can you have a single Seq type?

---

[2]In the notation of Part I, the '**a**' is a character rather than a string because of the kind of quote-mark used. In *Modula-2*, it is still a character rather than a string simply because it is a single item.

**A:** It's actually not called a Seq at all; it's called a Tree, and it's exported by the Trees module. A tree (in this module) is either a cardinal number, or an integer, or a string, or a sequence of trees.

The virtue—and misery—of dealing with the Tree type is the availability of— and need for—conversion functions which transform other things into trees and back again. The CardToTree procedure converts a cardinal number into a tree, while the TreeToCard procedure is its inverse. You may now guess what the IntToTree and StrToTree procedures do and what their inverses are called.

**Q:** How about IntSeqToTree and so forth?
**A:** It's perfectly possible, but not required. If we wanted an IntSeqToTree function, we could do it by something like

```
FROM IntSeqs IMPORT IsNull, Hd, Tl;
FROM Trees IMPORT NewNull, AddItem, IntToTree;
PROCEDURE IntSeqToTree(S:IntSeqs.IntSeq):Tree;
   (* post: result=[IntToTree(x): x in S]; i.e is S, converted to Tree type *)
   BEGIN
     IF IsNull(S) THEN RETURN NewNull()
        ELSE RETURN AddItem(IntToTree(Hd(S), IntSeqToTree(Tl(S))))
     END
END IntSeqToTree;
```

If we want to add all the integers in a tree containing only integers, we could write

```
IMPORT Trees;
PROCEDURE SumTree(T:Tree):INTEGER;
   (* post: result = T, if T is an integer; result = Sum(SumTree(x):x in T) *)
   (* if T is a sequence; result = 0, otherwise *)
   BEGIN
     IF Trees.TreeType(T) = Trees.Int THEN RETURN Trees.TreeToInt(T)
        ELSIF Trees.TreeType(T) # Trees.Seq THEN RETURN 0
        ELSIF Trees.IsNull(T) THEN RETURN 0
        ELSE RETURN (SumTree(Trees.Hd(T))+SumTree(Trees.Tl(T)))
     END
END SumTree;
```

**Exercises**  Look back over the discussion of trees, and then write and test

**8.2-46** InsTree

**8.2-47** Flatten

**8.2-48** TreeSort, which carries you from IntSeq to (sorted) IntSeq

Now's a good time to think about where we are and how far we've come. You can now define and implement all kinds of operations on simple objects; the process you use for this can also be carried out for operations on strings, sequences, and trees. You are now able—in principle—to define any conceivable behavior for sequences, sets, or trees as a *Modula-2* program. You can reason about that program and even compute with it by hand, because it's so very close to the specification which you had already learned to reason about and compute with.

The only major problem with this kind of programming is that it yields relatively slow programs which don't work well on large input. We're going to work a little more with such programs, and then go on to learn how to rewrite them into programs with higher performance. We'll study the problems of Chapter 6; in particular, the eight-queens problem, the maze, and the towers of Hanoi. (The wolf, goat, and cabbages problem is less interesting merely because the search is so short that it is easier to carry out by hand than mechanically.) We'll go through the eight queens problem, and then leave the other two as exercises.

First, let's consider the tree-structured solution:

$$\begin{aligned}
EQ'(S,q) &= [], & \text{if } q > 8 \\
&= EQ'(S,q+1) & \text{if } Conflicts(S+[q]) \neq \{\} \\
&= (S+[q])@(EQ'(S,q+1) & \text{if } Length(S) = 7 \\
&= EQ'(S+[q],1) + EQ'(S,q+1) & \text{otherwise}
\end{aligned}$$

The only difficulty in implementing this is that it produces a sequence of sequences of integers, which is not one of the types provided. (actually, I left it out on purpose.) We can represent them easily:

- We could convert integers to Trees, and not worry about it.

- We could convert each integer sequence into a string, e.g., [3, 1, 4, 7, 5, 8, 6] as "**3147586**"; then the StrSeq type would be sufficient.

- We could simply concatenate the sequences, representing $S = [S_1, S_2, \ldots S_n]$ with $S' = S_1 + S_2 + \ldots + S_n$; since each sequence was originally of length 8, we would still know that

$$S_i = Mid(S', 8*(i-1)+1, 8*i)$$

In that case, the "@" in the preceding equations would be replaced by "+", and the whole would be easily translated into *Modula-2*.

These representation issues make a good excuse to bring in an obvious point: we've been assuming that "@" is the more fundamental primitive, but the board is, in effect, being constructed with "*AddToBack*". It's perfectly possible to represent each board by the reverse of the sequence of queen positions. If we do that, then the $S + [q]$ operation will be replaced by $q@S$, and we just *Reverse* each solution in the final answer (or simply read off the answers in reverse order). Sometimes trivial things like that can make a significant difference; in this case, it depends on the relative costs of "@" and "*AddToBack*". A few minutes work with a text editor produces the following:

$$
\begin{aligned}
EQ'(S, q) &= [\,], & \text{if } q > 8 \\
&= EQ'(S, q+1) & \text{if } Conflicts(q@S) \neq \{\} \\
&= (q@S)@(EQ'(S, q+1)) & \text{if } Length(S) = 7 \\
&= EQ'(q@S, 1) + EQ'(S, q+1) & \text{otherwise}
\end{aligned}
$$

We'd also like a good (i.e., cheap) solution for the *Conflicts* problem (which now works on reversed sequences). All we want is a Boolean value, and of course when we compute $Conflicts(n@S)$ we assume that there were no conflicts in $S$. Look back at the discussion of rows and of upward and downward diagonals, and then consider the equations:

$$
\begin{aligned}
HasConflict(n@S) &= NoKay(S, n+1, n-1, n) \\
NoKay(S, up, dn, ro) &= False, & \text{if } IsNull(S) \\
&= True, & \text{if } Hd(S) \in \{up, dn, ro\} \\
&= NoKay(S, up+1, dn-1, n) & \text{otherwise}
\end{aligned}
$$

### Exercises

**8.2-49**  Explain why $Conflicts(q@S) \neq \{\}$ can be replaced by $NoKay(S, q+1, q-1, q)$ in the definition of $EQ'$.

**8.2-50**  Write and test the *IntSeqToStr* function required for the first solution to the representation problem.

**8.2-51**  Justify the $Mid(S', 1 + 8 * (i-1), 8 * i)$ formula used in the second solution.

**8.2-52**  Complete and run the solution of the eight queens problem.

What we're doing, of course, is program maintenance: we had a solution already, but it wasn't satisfactory; so we keep on changing it in hopes of finding something better. An alternative idea would be to have a version of the program that just generates a single solution: it produces the $Hd$ of the sequence we've been talking about and then stops. We can still produce this by a variation of the same idea, as

$$
\begin{aligned}
EQ1(S, q) &= [\,], & \text{if } q > 8\\
&= EQ1(S, q + 1) & \text{if } NoKay(S, q + 1, q - 1, q)\\
&= q@S & \text{if } Length(S) = 7\\
&= L, & \text{if } L \neq [\,]\\
&= EQ1(S, q + 1) & \text{otherwise}
\end{aligned}
$$

where

$$
L \;=\; EQ1(q@S, 1)
$$

To construct this, I looked at the places where $EQ'$ was constructing a sequence of sequences beyond the first solution; the first two lines didn't need to be
changed at all. On the third line, it was pretty obvious that the $Hd$ of the overall
answer was going to be $q@S$, so I just produce that $Hd$ without going to the trouble
of building the sequence of all answers. On the fourth line, I had a problem: I didn't
know whether $EQ1(q@S, 1)$ was going to produce a solution or not. Therefore I just
gave the name $L$ to whatever it did produce, and moved on accordingly. I could
just as well have said that the last two lines are really expressing a function $EQC$
which depends on the values $L$, $S$, and $q + 1$. I could then write

$$
\begin{aligned}
EQ1(S, q) &= \ldots \text{first three clauses unchanged}\\
&= EQC(EQ1(q@S, 1), S, q + 1) & \text{otherwise}
\end{aligned}
$$

where

$$
EQC(L, S, q) \;=\; \textbf{if } L = [\,] \textbf{ then } EQ1(S, q) \textbf{ else } L
$$

This is easily turned into a program, with or without the reversal of sequences.

**Exercises**    Write and run solutions to

**8.2-53**  The $EQ1$ problem using $EQC$ just given.

**8.2-54**  The simple-recurrence version of eight-queens presented in Chapter 6; you will
need to work out some more equations first.

**8.2-55**  The maze problem; you will want to tabulate the maze connections, perhaps as a
sequence of strings. (Look at the various versions of $LookUp$ given equationally
in previous chapters.)

**8.2-56**  The towers-of-Hanoi problem. (Have this one produce a sequence of strings; label
the towers "**a**", "**b**", and "**c**", and use CardToStr to find answers like ["**a1c**"] for
$H(1, \text{"}\mathbf{a}\text{"}, \text{"}\mathbf{b}\text{"}, \text{"}\mathbf{c}\text{"})$.

At this point you are well able to develop fairly complex programs through
specification to almost-code, and you've gotten used to programming-language syntax at its closest approximation to our specification language. It's time to look at
the other side of programming—the underside.

## 8.3 STATES, TIME, AND REUSABLE SPACE

Up to this point, you have learned a great deal about what to do with a pencil, but we've made very little use of erasers. We've assumed that the moron will follow us around, somehow clearing up the paper we're no longer using for our calculations. Since the *Modula-2* system does very little cleanup, this has a predictable effect on our programs: they don't make very good use of space. In the previous section, I suggested that the sequence $gcd(1000000, 2)$, $gcd(999998, 2)$, $gcd(999996, 2)$, $gcd(999994, 2)$, ... would run out of space because it was getting deeper and deeper within nested parentheses. That's an oversimplification: in fact, it's getting deeper and deeper into nested environments. In this section, you'll start to get a feeling for the *Modula-2* environment structure. You'll learn to create a time sequence of environments in a fixed amount of space, using assignment statements and control structures. Intuitively, you're going to be changing the contents of specific squares of graph paper which were already in use. Then you'll write procedures which make such changes to some of their parameters, rather than returning any result. At that point, we will no longer be able to talk about equality between procedures: procedure calls P(x, y) and Q(x, y) may have identical effects, but we cannot say that they are equal when they do not have values. Still, they can be equivalent, in which case we'll write P(x, y) == Q(x, y) and we'll feel free to substitute one for the other. As you'll see, these are ideas to be applied with great caution: all of the opportunities for mistakes with equations are still available, but you also have the chance to make new kinds of mistakes which are much harder to find. At our present level of technology, however, these constructions are necessary to writing efficient programs.

### 8.3.1 Environments and Virtual Substitution

From the beginning, we've assumed computation works by substitution just as it did in high school algebra. In the trivial example of multiplication, we assume that the text of the program is actually copied and then simplified at each step, with the leftmost simplifiable term being the "active" one:

$$Mul(n, m) \quad = \quad \textbf{if } n = 0 \textbf{ then } 0 \textbf{ else } m + Mul(n - 1, m)$$

so

$$
\begin{aligned}
Mul(1, 7) \quad &= \quad \textbf{if } 1 = 0 \textbf{ then } 0 \textbf{ else } 7 + Mul(1 - 1, 7) \\
&= \quad \textbf{if } \textit{False} \textbf{ then } 0 \textbf{ else } 7 + Mul(1 - 1, 7) \\
&= \quad 7 + Mul(0, 7) \\
&= \quad 7 + (\textbf{ if } 0 = 0 \textbf{ then } 0 \textbf{ else } 7 + Mul(0 - 1, 7) \\
&= \quad 7 + (\textbf{ if } \textit{True} \textbf{ then } 0 \textbf{ else } 7 + Mul(0 - 1, 7) \\
&= \quad 7 + 0 \\
&= \quad 7
\end{aligned}
$$

Actually, a programming system normally simulates this sequence while avoiding the expense of making a copy of the program. Instead of forming many substitution instances of an expression, the system keeps one encoded version of that expression somewhere and then forms the environments which would give the right values to variables in it. Here is a simplified model of the process it goes through:

$$
\begin{aligned}
Mul(1,7) \quad &\rightarrow & [\{n = 1, m = 7\}] \\
&\rightarrow & [\{n = 0, m = 7\}, \{n = 1, m = 7\}] \\
&\rightarrow & [\{res = 0, n = 1, m = 7\}] \\
&\rightarrow & 7
\end{aligned}
$$

This description is incomplete, but it should be helpful. $Mul$ is to be evaluated in an environment in which $n = 1$, and $m = 7$. In order to perform that evaluation, $Mul$ (the **same** copy of $Mul$) is to be evaluated in an environment in which $n = 0$, $m = 7$; this will be an "inner call" on the procedure. The inner call returns 0 as a $result$, and the space used for its environment is simultaneously freed. The 0 is then used in the outer call, which returns 7 as $result$ and its environment space is also freed.

At any given moment, we have a sequence of environments, each corresponding to a procedure which has not yet finished its computations. Gone is the idea of writing out a substitution instance of a function's definition; instead, we have the 'virtual' substitution created by noting what the environment is that would create that substitution. Gone in the same way is the simple notion of simplifying an expression to find its value: instead, we have the complex act of the RETURN, which produces the value and simultaneously deletes an environment.

**Exercises**    Test your understanding of the simplified program execution model.

**8.3-1**    Write exponentiation as a procedure Exp, and show the sequence of steps (each one as a sequence of environments) for Exp(2, 5).

**8.3-2**    Do the same for sequence reversal (assuming that Append is a primitive operation on sequences.)

**Q:** What's missing from the model?
**A:** The main omission is the place marker which the computer has to keep explicitly with each call on a program, to be able to remember where it left off. It's not enough to know that you're working on an expression representing $Mul$, in an environment where $n = 1$ and $m = 7$; you have to know what part of the expression you were working with. As a secondary issue, the computer needs some systematic way of dealing with values like the $result$ being returned. We'll get to some of these issues in Chapter 10. For the present, it's enough to have an explicit notion of environment.

## 8.3.2  Simple Recurrences with Assignments and Loops

Now we can use the same execution model with a simple recurrence like the original *gcd*:

$$gcd(n, m) \quad = \quad \textbf{if } n = 0 \textbf{ then } m \textbf{ else } \textbf{if } \ldots \textbf{ else } gcd(n, m - n)$$

This gives us computation sequences like the following:

$$
\begin{aligned}
gcd(100000, 7) \quad &\rightarrow &&[\{n = 100000, m = 7\}] \\
&\rightarrow &&[\{n = 99993, m = 7\}, \{n = 100000, m = 7\}] \\
&\rightarrow \quad [\{n = 99986, m = 7\}, &&\{n = 99993, m = 7\}, \{n = 100000, m = 7\}] \\
&\rightarrow \\
&\ \ \vdots &&\ \ \vdots
\end{aligned}
$$

It's pretty obvious what will go wrong here: more and more environments will pile up until we run out of space, long before we get to the result (which is 1).

**Q:** But isn't that pretty stupid? These environments are being saved for no purpose at all. Why can't some clever programmer design a programming system which won't save environments unless they're going to be used?

**A:** That has been done, and several of the languages mentioned as being close to specification languages (*Scheme, Prolog, ML, Hope*) are normally implemented with such tricks. The "TEX" document-preparation system used for this book is based on a special-purpose language with the same kind of cleverness. Maybe someday it will be the usual approach to developing computer programs. The choice is somewhat like the choice of automobile transmissions: an automatic shift is less trouble, but if you're a professional driver, you can probably do significantly better by shifting manually. *Modula-2* is a language for serious programmers: it doesn't even give you an automatic transmission suitable for general-purpose use. You are expected to use the same environment space over and over again, changing the values stored in it. For a sample, we'll go back to GCD, first repeating the pseudo-specificational definition:

```
PROCEDURE GCD(n, m:CARDINAL):CARDINAL;
   (* post: result = gcd(n, m) *)
   BEGIN
     IF n=0 THEN RETURN m
       ELSIF m=0 THEN RETURN n
       ELSIF m>n THEN RETURN GCD(n, m−n)
       ELSE RETURN GCD(n−m, m)
     END
END GCD;
```

What we'd like to do is go around and around and around with **one** environment until we get the answer we want: GCD(10000, 7) by this style of definition may still take a long time, but it should only require space for two variables at any given moment. The way we go around and around in *Modula-2* is with a LOOP, and it looks almost like this:

```
PROCEDURE GCD(n, m:CARDINAL):CARDINAL;
  (* post: result = gcd(n, m) *)
  BEGIN
    LOOP
      IF n=0 THEN RETURN m
      ELSIF m=0 THEN RETURN n
      ELSIF m>n THEN [n, m] := [n, m − n]   (* parallel assignment *)
      ELSE [n, m] := [n − m, m]            (* parallel assignment *)
      END
    END
  END GCD;
```

Look at the two versions of GCD very, very carefully: they're almost identical. The idea is to go around and around and around the LOOP until we hit a RETURN statement; each time that we don't hit one, we come instead to a statement which defines new values for $n$ and $m$. A statement of the form "x:=E" is called an *assignment* statement; it assigns a new meanings to the variable x. $[n, m] := [n, m − n]$ takes us from an environment $\{n = 6, m = 9\}$ to an environment $\{n = 6, m = 3\}$. The form that you see here is called a *parallel assignment* statement because it assigns new meanings to more than one variable simultaneously. That's not legal in *Modula-2*, so you see these statements written in a different typeface. Although the parallel assignment statement is not legal, it is a helpful intermediate step because it is very very close to the function call which we are rewriting as an assignment statement. (We'll get to the 'real' answer shortly.) This almost-program describes the environment sequence

$$gcd(100000, 7) \quad \rightarrow \quad [ \quad \{n = 100000, \quad m = 7\}]$$
$$\rightarrow \quad [ \quad \{n = 99993, \quad m = 7\}]$$
$$\rightarrow \quad [ \quad \{n = 99986, \quad m = 7\}]$$
$$\rightarrow \quad \vdots$$

We might well get tired of waiting for this program to finish, but it won't run out of space. The idea applies to any simple recurrence: if we've written

$$SR(i, j, a) \quad = \quad Sum(Range(i, j)) + a,$$

so that

$$SR(i, j, a) \quad = \quad \textbf{if } i > j \textbf{ then } a \textbf{ else } SR(i + 1, j, i + j)$$
$$SR(1, 4, 0) \quad = \quad SR(2, 4, 1) = SR(3, 4, 3) = SR(4, 4, 6) = SR(5, 4, 10) = 10$$

this then becomes

    PROCEDURE SR(i, j, a:INTEGER):INTEGER;
      (* post: result $= i + (i + 1) + (i + 2) + \ldots + j + a$ *)
      BEGIN
        IF i>j THEN RETURN a ELSE RETURN SR(i+1, j, i+a) END
    END SR;

which in turn becomes

    PROCEDURE SR(i, j, a:INTEGER):INTEGER;
      (* post: result $= i + (i + 1) + (i + 2) + \ldots + j + a$ *)
      BEGIN
        LOOP
          IF i>j THEN RETURN a ELSE $[i, j, a] := [i + 1, j, i + a]$ END
        END
    END SR;

## Exercises

**8.3-3**   Write the sequence of environments for SR(5, 9, 0).

**8.3-4**   Consider the factorial function $f(n) = 1 * 2 * \ldots * n$ for $n > 0$ and $f(0) = 1$. Edit the $SR$ definition into a simple recurrence which computes the factorial, and then rewrite the procedure with a LOOP.

**8.3-5**   Describe multiplication as a simple recurrence using $MulAcc$, and rewrite it with a LOOP.

**8.3-6**   Describe sequence reversal as a simple recurrence, and rewrite it also with a LOOP.

This is almost *Modula-2*; the only violation we've made is to allow more than one thing to be redefined simultaneously, just as appears to happen in function evaluation. Actually, we can only redefine one thing at a time in a *Modula-2* program: the statement x:=y can have a complicated expression on the right, but on the left x must indicate a single place to put the value of that expression. Instead of writing $[x, y] := [a, b]$ we must write something like x:=a; y:=b or perhaps y:=b; x:=a; they are no longer simultaneous, so we have to order them. With this version of GCD, it's easy, because the order makes no difference:

```
PROCEDURE GCD(n, m:CARDINAL):CARDINAL;
  (* post: result = gcd(n,m) *)
  BEGIN
    LOOP
      IF n=0 THEN RETURN m
        ELSIF m=0 THEN RETURN n
        ELSIF m>n THEN n:=n; m:=m−n
        ELSE n:=n−m; m:=m
      END
    END
END GCD;
```

**Q:** Why do you redefine n as n?

**A:** You don't have to; n:=n and m:=m can be deleted from this program without changing it.

### Exercises

**8.3-7**    Enter and test this definition of GCD.

**8.3-8**    Create, enter, and test the corresponding definitions for factorial and multiplication.

**8.3-9**    Create, enter, and test the corresponding definitions for CardToStr and StrToCard.

**8.3-10**   Create the corresponding definition for **Reverse** using $Reverse(x) = R(x, [\,])$, $R([\,], y) = y$, and $R(a@x, y) = R(x, a@y)$.

**Loop Invariants**    So far, so good: you now have learned to make some simple programs which don't run out of space easily, and in the process you've picked up a tremendously useful execution model for future programming. However, you've also picked up a delightful way to generate programming errors. Let's try the same process on SR, to get:

```
PROCEDURE SR(i, j, a:INTEGER):INTEGER;
  (* post: result = i + (i+1) + (i+2) + ... + j + a *)
  BEGIN
    LOOP
      IF i>j THEN RETURN a ELSE i:=i+1; a:=i+a END
    END
END SR;
```

Here I've omitted the reassignment j:=j, which obviously doesn't change anything. Look now at the sequence of states:

$$
\begin{array}{lll}
1. & SR(1,2,0) & \rightarrow \quad [\{i=1, j=2, a=0\}] \\
2. & & \rightarrow \quad [\{i=2, j=2, a=0\}] \\
2'. & & \rightarrow \quad [\{i=2, j=2, a=2\}] \\
3. & & \rightarrow \quad [\{i=3, j=2, a=2\}] \\
3'. & & \rightarrow \quad [\{i=3, j=2, a=5\}] \\
4. & & \rightarrow \quad 5
\end{array}
$$

That's the wrong answer: SR(1, 2, 0) should produce 3. With parallel assignment, we went directly from [i, a] to [i+1, i+a]. Now we go in two steps: replace i by i+1 and then replace a by i+a. Unfortunately, the two-step version is wrong: we want to increase a by the *old* value of i, not by the new value. The two-step version needs to be replaced by a:=i+a; i:=i+1. Now we get the sequence

$$
\begin{array}{lll}
1. & SR(1,2,0) & \rightarrow \quad [\{i=1, j=2, a=0\}] \\
2. & & \rightarrow \quad [\{i=1, j=2, a=1\}] \\
2'. & & \rightarrow \quad [\{i=2, j=2, a=1\}] \\
3. & & \rightarrow \quad [\{i=2, j=2, a=3\}] \\
3'. & & \rightarrow \quad [\{i=3, j=2, a=3\}] \\
4. & & \rightarrow \quad 5
\end{array}
$$

Here we get to state 1 just by entering the program, to state 2 by a:=i+a, to state 2' by incrementing i, and then we reach the end of the loop. Beginning over again in state 2', we get to state 3 by changing a, and to state 3' by changing i, and we reach the end of the loop once more. Beginning over one more time, we find that i>j, and so we can return the value of a.

### Exercises

**8.3-11** Show how the simple recurrence for factorial can be done either correctly or incorrectly by reordering.

**8.3-12** Show how the simple recurrence for multiplication can be done either correctly or incorrectly by reordering.

**8.3-13** Show how the simple recurrence for sequence reversal can be done either correctly or incorrectly by reordering.

In all of your programming with assignment statements, you will have to guard against this kind of mistake. It wasn't possible to make such a mistake with specifications, because you didn't think at that level of detail. In programming, it's fundamental. To guard against it, we bring in the old notion of an invariant, which we developed to describe a sequence of states of a computation. It now becomes a comment inside every loop of a program, with assertions involving the current values variables like $i$ and $j$ and also their original values $i_0, j_0$.

```
PROCEDURE SR(i, j, a:INTEGER):INTEGER;
  (* post: result = i + (i + 1) + (i + 2) + ... + j + a *)
  BEGIN
    LOOP (* 1, 2', 3' :   SR(i_0, j_0, a_0) = SR(i, j, a) *)
      IF i>j THEN
              (* 3' :   i > j, SR(i_0, j_0, a_0) = SR(i, j, a) = a *)
            RETURN a
      ELSE
      (* 1, 2' :   i ≤ j, SR(i_0, j_0, a_0) = SR(i, j, a) = SR(i + 1, j, i + a) *)
            a:=i+a;
      (* 2, 3 :   i ≤ j, SR(i_0, j_0, a_0) = SR(i + 1, j, a) *)
            i:=i+1
      (* 2', 3' :   SR(i_0, j_0, a_0) = SR(i, j, a)) *)
      END
    END
END SR;
```

Look carefully over the example sequence of environments in this example; you'll see that each comment is true every time that we construct a state for it. It may look confusing, but actually it's quite easy to construct these assertions. The comment at the very beginning of the loop is obvious: it says that we're doing a simple recurrence. It's the same as the comment at the end of the loop, because each time we get to the end we go back to the beginning without changing the state. To get the others, we go *backwards* through the loop statements:

- If $SR(i, j, a)$ has a particular value in 2' or 3', then $SR(i + 1, j, a)$ must have had that value in 2 or 3 because the value of $i$ after i:=i+1 is the same as the value of i+1 beforehand.

- Similarly, if $SR(i + 1, j, a)$ has a particular value after a:=i+a, then $SR(i + 1, j, i + a)$ must have had that value before.

The rest of the comments are reasonably obvious: within the **then** part of a conditional, you can assume that the condition was true, and within the **else** part you can assume that it was false.

**Exercises**    Write similar comments for your solutions (in the preceding exercises) to

**8.3-14**  Factorial.

**8.3-15**  Multiplication.

**8.3-16**  Sequence reversal.

It is quite unusual to put comments which are this detailed into real code: as you develop a feeling for the relationships between the states at different points of a program, you will find that a *loop invariant*, a comment describing the state at the head of each loop, is almost always sufficient.

**Q:** Sufficient for what?

**A:** Sufficient for debugging and code extensions or revisions. The loop invariant gives the assumptions the programmer (hey, that's you!) needed to make about the state while writing the code.

- In debugging, you'll find that you can detect programming errors by examining the state to see if the assumptions are correct. In a correct program, the invariant is invariantly true, right? Keep testing it: as long as it is true, you're safe (unless it leaves out some crucial assumption). If it's ever seen to be false, you know that the program is incorrect. You also know exactly when the program violated the assumptions, and you know what part of the program did the evil deed, and you know what needful relationship ceased to be true. Reread the relevant piece of the specification, and then go fix it.

- In extending or revising the program, you usually want to leave almost everything alone. Ideally, you don't even want to reread more than a small fraction of the program. Change the specification first: it's shorter than the code, and (if you've done it well) it's clearer. Only those procedures whose specifications have changed need to be touched, and most of those will usually have large parts which can be left alone. Part of the state (i.e., some values and representations of variables) will be irrelevant to your revision, and only those statements which involve relevant parts of the state need to be studied. The invariants identify the parts of the state involved in a given block of code.

Suppose that we're working on the eight queens problem, and we find that it does not run well enough.

**Q:** Isn't that pretty silly? All we need to do with that one is run it once to get all the answers, and then there's no need to run it ever again.

**A:** Yes, but there are many similar problems to be solved; that was the point of Chapter 6. If you can improve the eight queens performance, you are likely to see how to work on the others. Consider

$$
\begin{aligned}
EQ1(S, q) &= [], & &\text{if } q > 8 \\
&= EQ1(S, q+1) & &\text{if } NoKay(S, q+1, q-1, q) \\
&= q @ S & &\text{if } Length(S) = 7 \\
&= L, & &\text{if } L \neq [] \\
&= EQ1(S, q+1) & &\text{otherwise}
\end{aligned}
$$

where

$$L = EQ1(q@S, 1)$$

Here we have a rather complex situation: there are two simple recurrences, but there's also a recurrence which isn't simple (the inner call on $EQ1$ within the calculation of $L$). Furthermore, we have an environment component ($L$) which is not a parameter. We can start with the EQ1 program of Figure 8.3.

EQ1 is a fairly substantial program, but it's one you've already spent a good deal of time thinking about and you should have little trouble seeing what we've done with it. NoKay is reasonably satisfactory; you can't ask it to do less work than it's doing, and it's quite clear. EQ1 is more worrisome: this is definitely a program which can best be understood by going back and forth between it and the specification. There is one new feature of *Modula-2*, namely the VAR declaration of L as an IntSeq. We want to have that variable in the environment of the program, and so we need to tell *Modula-2* that there should be a space for it in the environment. Notice that it does not occur in the loop invariant (which is the same as the precondition of the procedure). At the point in the code where the invariant is written, the value of L is completely irrelevant. Of course, if we had placed assertions just before (or inside) the conditional statement which ends the LOOP, then the value of L would be crucial, but if we go back to the beginning of the loop then L is obviously being discarded. As I said before, the invariant directs your attention to relevant parts of the state and to relevant relationships between them. A good way to debug a program like this is to stick in Write statements for the appropriate types, so that you print out the current environment and the assertions you're making about it, once for each loop. I've done that; if you try running the program as it is, you will see a lot of output, which does a fairly good job of tracing the decision-making of the program.

**Exercises**    Develop LOOPing solutions of the same sort for

**8.3-17** The maze problem.

**8.3-18** The Towers of Hanoi problem.

**Local Variables and Functions**    In the EQ1 solution, the local list-variable L is just for bookkeeping: we use it to avoid having two copies of the expression EQ1(q@S, 1). It is often possible to improve performance by having helpful information in the environment. For example, the loop of EQ1 finds the length of S once each time through, but S has not changed in between. We could declare the local variable n : INTEGER, write n:=Length(S) before the LOOP, and then test n=7 as the condition for which $q@S$ is to be returned. In this case, $n = Length(S)$ is a necessary part of the loop invariant. If the assertion is false (e.g., if some clever programmer changed n and neglected to change it back), then the loop is no longer correct.

PROCEDURE EQ1(S:IntSeq; q:INTEGER):IntSeq;
  (* pre: S is a sequence of queen positions 1...8; *Length*$(S) \leq 7$ *)
  (* reverse(q@S) is lexicographically $\leq$ any eight-queens solution *)
  (* post: reverse(result) is first eight-queens solution. *)
  VAR L : IntSeq; (* a sequence of queen positions 0...8 *)
  PROCEDURE NoKay(S:IntSeq; up, dn, ro:INTEGER):BOOLEAN;
    (* pre: reverse(S) is conflict-free, but a queen threatens the column of *)
    (* Hd(S) horizontally in ro, diagonally up and dn *)
    (* post: result = (the queen threatens some queen in S) *)
    BEGIN
      LOOP (* a queen threatens the column of Hd(S) in ro, up, dn *)
        IF IsNull(S) THEN RETURN FALSE
          ELSIF (Hd(S) = ro) OR (Hd(S) = up) OR (Hd(S) = dn)
          THEN RETURN TRUE
          ELSE S := Tl(S); up := up+1; dn := dn-1
        END
      END
  END NoKay;
  BEGIN
    LOOP (* precondition of EQ1 *)
      WriteString("S="); WriteSeq(S); WriteLn;
      WriteString("q="); WriteInt(q, 0); WriteLn;
      WriteString("rev(S) is a Queen-pos seq, Len<8, elts 1..8, no conflicts");
      WriteLn; WriteString("q is candidate queen, 1..8"); WriteLn; WriteLn;
      IF q > 8 THEN RETURN NewNull()
        ELSIF NoKay(S, q+1, q-1, q) THEN q:=q+1
        ELSIF Length(S)=7 THEN RETURN AddItem(q, S)
        ELSE L:= EQ1(AddItem(q, S), 1);
            IF IsNull(L) THEN q:=q+1 ELSE RETURN L END
      END
  END EQ1;

**Figure 8.3** Eight Queens with LOOP

**Exercises**    Follow up this idea:

**8.3-19** Enter and test the change just suggested, and try to measure the performance gain. Is it significant?

**8.3-20** Edit the specification and code so that $EQ1$ takes three arguments: the sequence $S$, the queen $q$, and the length $n$ of $S$; the initial call will then be $EQ1([\,],1,0)$, and there will never be any call on *Length* as an operation although it must be mentioned in the precondition and loop invariant. Is the performance gain significant? Is the program more or less readable?

Local variables are also sometimes required in the shift from parallel assignment statements to sequential assignment statements. Consider the definition

$$
\begin{aligned}
gcd(x,y) \quad &= \quad x, & &\text{if } y = 0 \\
&= \quad gcd(x-y,y) & &\text{if } x \geq y \\
&= \quad gcd(y,x) & &\text{otherwise}
\end{aligned}
$$

With this definition, $gcd(18,24)$ goes through the sequence

$$[18,24],[24,18],[6,18],[18,6],[12,6],[6,6],[0,6],[6,0]$$

and then produces 6 as the answer. Coding it as a LOOP, we have a problem:

```
LOOP (* gcd(x,y) = gcd(x0,y0) *)
    IF y=0 THEN RETURN x
       ELSIF x >= y THEN x:=x-y
       ELSE [x, y] := [y, x]
    END
```

In this LOOP, we can't write either x:=y; y:=x or the other way around: both are incorrect. We have to say something like

```
(* let's call x's value a, and y's value b: x, y = a, b *)
    z:=x; (* x, y, z = a, b, a *)
    x:=y; (* x, y, z = b, b, a *)
    y:=z (* x, y, z = b, a, a so x = b, y = a *)
```

Think of $x,y$ as being two names in an address book, each with its own row and each with its own telephone number $(a,b)$. If you need to swap their numbers, then you must copy $x$'s number from $x$'s row to a third row $(z)$ before you can move $y$'s number into $x$'s row. The same problem would occur with swapping two cars' parking spaces: three spaces are necessary. When you call on a function, the programming language will probably use four spaces by copying both numbers (or cars) to new spaces, then ignoring the old spaces—some other part of the program may still be using and changing them.

We sometimes use local variables to avoid local functions altogether. Look at the definition of *gcd* which used a subfunction $g(x, y)$ with precondition $x \leq y$:

$$gcd(x, y) = \text{ if } x \leq y \text{ then } g(x, y) \text{ else } g(y, x)$$

where

$$g(x, y) = \text{ if } x = 0 \text{ then } y \text{ else } g(mod(y, x), x)$$

This can obviously be written (as in the previous section) as a procedure GCD with local procedure G. We can easily make the local procedure into a LOOP, as shown in the following code.

```
PROCEDURE GCD(x, y:INTEGER):INTEGER;
  (* pre: 0 ≤ x, y; post: result= gcd(x, y) *)
  PROCEDURE G(x, y):INTEGER):INTEGER;
    (* pre: 0 ≤ x ≤ y; post: result= gcd(x, y) *)
  VAR r:INTEGER;
  BEGIN
    LOOP (* gcd(x, y) = gcd(x0, y0 *)
      IF x=0 THEN RETURN y
        ELSE r:=x; x:=y MOD x; y:=r
      END
    END
  END G;
  BEGIN
    IF x<=y THEN RETURN G(x, y) ELSE RETURN G(y, x) END
END GCD;
```

Programs like this one are common: the work is mostly done by some procedure inside, which itself is just a LOOP. In such cases, it may be easier to read a revised version such as GCD2, which has essentially replaced the procedure with its code. In GCD2, at the top of the following page, the code of G has been expanded "inline," so that no procedure call is visible.

**Exercises**    In order to compare GCD and GCD2,

**8.3-21**  Try to measure the performance difference between them.

**8.3-22**  Try to explain each to a friend, and estimate the relative difficulties involved.

**8.3-23**  Edit each to handle negative numbers (remembering that $gcd(x, y) = gcd(x, -y)$) and estimate the relative difficulties involved.

Very similar problems are easily found in the context of sequence operations (generators, accumulators, mappings, filters, scanners, and so forth). To find the

```
PROCEDURE GCD2(x, y:INTEGER):INTEGER;
  (* pre: 0 ≤ x, y; post: result= gcd(x, y) *)
  VAR r:INTEGER;
  BEGIN
    IF x>y THEN r:=x; x:=y; y:=r END ;
    LOOP (* gcd(x, y) = gcd(x₀, y₀ *)
      IF x=0 THEN RETURN y
        ELSE r:=x; x:=y MOD x; y:=r
      END
    END
  END GCD2;
```

sum of a sequence $S$, write

$$SumSeq(S) \quad = \quad SA(S, 0)$$

where

$$
\begin{array}{llll}
SA(S, a) & = & a, & \text{if } S = [\,] \\
         & = & SA(Tl(S), a + Hd(S)) & \text{otherwise}
\end{array}
$$

**Exercises**   Using the idea of GCD2,

**8.3-24**  Write SumSeq to find the sum of an IntSeq using a two-argument subfunction SA.

**8.3-25**  Rewrite SumSeq so that SA appears only as a nameless inline LOOP, using a as a local variable.

**8.3-26**  Rewrite Mul with MulAcc expanded into an inline loop, with a local variable.

In these examples, we have been working with code which is executed after a procedure BEGINs but before entering the LOOP. It's also possible to have code after the LOOP comes to an END but before the PROCEDURE does so; this is where we would write the inline expansion of a function called inside a RETURN statement. Suppose, for example, we had written out the summation of a range as

$$SR(i, j) \quad = \quad SumSeq(Range(i, j))$$

and we then expanded Range as a loop. We could write the SR procedure as shown in Figure 8.4.

In this design, the code for Range is expanded inline, and then the value returned by Range is passed to SumSeq explicitly. We could now expand the loop for SumSeq right there between the THEN and ELSE, to RETURN directly to

```
PROCEDURE SR(i, j:INTEGER):INTEGER;
  (* post: result = Sum([i..j]) *)
  VAR S: IntSeq;
  PROCEDURE SumSeq(S:IntSeq):INTEGER;
  (* post: result = Sum(S) *)
END SumSeq;
BEGIN
  S := NewNull();
  LOOP (* SR(Range(i, j) + S) = SR(Range(i₀, j₀)) *)
    IF i>j THEN RETURN SumSeq(S)
      ELSE S := AddItem(j, S); j := j-1
    END
END SR;
```

$$LOOP\ (*\ SR(Range(i,j) + S) = SR(Range(i_0, j_0))\ *)$$

**Figure 8.4** Sum of Range: combining LOOPs

SR's caller. Alternatively, we could write the loop for SumSeq after the loop you see displayed, and replace the RETURN SumSeq(S) statement with the keyword EXIT.

Either approach is correct, but both present a grave danger: we are now talking about working with procedures containing multiple loops and lots of code. In general, long procedures (especially procedures with multiple loops) can cost you a great deal in debugging time. If every loop continues until you reach a RETURN statement (where you leave the procedure and can check its postcondition), you will end up with simpler loop invariants, better use of run-time tracing and debugging facilities, and more easily modified code. The fourth or fifth version of your program may justifiably add some percentage points in speed by expanding many procedures inline, but it's a mistake to do this early. Therefore, this book contains very few EXIT statements and few exercises which require them; after your project not only works but has undergone some maintenance, look for EXITs to make it marginally faster.

**Special Kinds of** LOOPs    *Modula-2* contains other kinds of looping construction. These are not crucial components of program design, but as you read other people's code, and as you edit your own code for greater readability, you should be aware of what the language allows you to say.

To illustrate, I'll write a few functions with WHILE and REPEAT. The WHILE loop looks like this:

```
WHILE expr DO (* loop invariant and expr both TRUE *)
  statements for loop body
END
```

This is just the same as

```
LOOP IF NOT expr THEN EXIT END ;
    statements for loop body
END
```

We will write this equivalence relation as "==":

WHILE P DO S END; == LOOP IF NOT P THEN EXIT END; S END;

The WHILE loop has one condition which is repeatedly tested, and one block of code which is repeatedly performed while that condition continues to be true. After the WHILE reaches its END, we can be sure that the loop invariant is still true, as in GCDW of Figure 8.5.

```
PROCEDURE GCDW(x, y:INTEGER):INTEGER;
    (* pre: 0 ≤ x, y; post: result = gcd(x, y) *)
    BEGIN
        WHILE (x # 0) AND (y # 0) DO (* gcd(x, y) = gcd(x₀, y₀) *)
            IF x < y THEN y := y-x ELSE x := x-y END
        END ;
            (* gcd(x, y) = gcd(x₀, y₀), x = 0 ∨ y = 0 *)
        IF x=0 THEN RETURN y ELSE RETURN x END
    END GCDW;
```

**Figure 8.5** Greatest Common Divisor with WHILE loop

Clearly, we have not gained much: after we finish the loop we must figure out why we finished it and act accordingly. However, for a LOOP which finishes only at the top and only for one reason, a WHILE may have some readability advantage. Compare the following three definitions of "factorial": a simple recurrence, a LOOP, and a WHILE.

```
PROCEDURE Factorial1(n:INTEGER):INTEGER;
    (* pre: 0 ≤ n; post: result = i! *)
    PROCEDURE F(i, s:INTEGER):INTEGER;
        (* pre: 0 ≤ i ≤ n, s = i!; post: result = i! *)
        BEGIN
            IF n=i THEN RETURN s ELSE RETURN F(i+1, (i+1)*s) END
        END F;
    BEGIN RETURN F(0, 1) END Factorial1;
```

The Factorial1 program is a simple bottom-up recurrence which searches for the right value of $i$ so that it can return $i!$. It's easy to put that into LOOP form, as Factorial2:

```
PROCEDURE Factorial2(n:INTEGER):INTEGER;
  (* pre: 0 ≤ n; post: result = 1 * 2 * ... n *)
  VAR i, s: INTEGER;
  BEGIN
    i:=0; s:=1;
    LOOP (* i ≤ n, s = i! *)
      IF i=n THEN RETURN s ELSE i:=i+1; s:=s*i END
    END
  END Factorial2;
```

The Factorial2 procedure is exactly in the form of a WHILE loop: there is only one test leading to loop termination, and it occurs before any code is executed to change the environment. Therefore, we can try the Factorial3 solution:

```
PROCEDURE Factorial3(n:INTEGER):INTEGER;
  (* pre: 0 ≤ n; post: result = 1 * 2 * ... n *)
  VAR i, s: INTEGER;
  BEGIN
    i:=0; s:=1;
    WHILE i # n DO (* i < n, s = i! *)
      i:=i+1; s:=s*i
    END ;
        (* s = i!, i = n *)
    RETURN s
  END Factorial3;
```

The difference between Factorial2 and Factorial3 is not major, but it is worth thinking about. The major danger for them both is that you may be tempted into multiple-loop procedures.

A very similar construct in *Modula-2* is the REPEAT loop, which looks like this:

```
REPEAT(* loop invariant here *)
  statements which preserve invariant
UNTIL expr;
    loop invariant and expr are both true here
```

This is not a fundamentally distinct concept;

REPEAT S UNTIL P;      ==      LOOP S; IF P THEN EXIT END; END;
or simply
REPEAT S UNTIL P;      ==      S; WHILE NOT(P) DO S END;

For the computation of $n!$, we can try Factorial4 as an illustration of REPEAT:

```
PROCEDURE Factorial4(n:INTEGER):INTEGER;
  (* pre: 0 ≤ n; post: result = 1 * 2 * ... * n *)
  VAR i, s: INTEGER;
  BEGIN
    i:=1; s:=1; (* Consider n = 0 as a special case *)
    REPEAT(* i ≤ n, s = (i − 1)! *)
      s:=s*i; (* i ≤ n, s = i! *)
      i:=i+1; (* i ≤ n + 1, s = (i − 1)! *)
    UNTIL i>n
        (* s = (i − 1)!, i = n + 1 *)
    RETURN s
  END Factorial4;
```

Look closely at the difference between the WHILE and REPEAT loops; the design for the latter has been carefully redone to match the logical pattern of a REPEAT construction, and it does not match the specification given as closely. WHILE and REPEAT loops are sometimes clumsier than the equivalent LOOP constructions, and sometimes more elegant; there are no significant differences in efficiency unless you twist a program around to force it into an unnatural mold, as when I twisted the GCD program around. (I could have twisted it further to make the WHILE loop look less clumsy, but I wanted to keep as close to the original design as possible.) The LOOP construct offers greater flexibility for maintenance. (Even if the loop now exits only at the top, it may exit in several places in the next version.) On the other hand, the WHILE and REPEAT constructs have a more obvious relationship to assertions which you can test on exiting the loop.

## Exercises

**8.3-27** Rewrite *Mul* with a WHILE loop.

**8.3-28** Rewrite *Reverse* with a WHILE loop.

**8.3-29** Rewrite *Mul* with a REPEAT loop.

**8.3-30** Rewrite *Reverse* with a REPEAT loop.

**8.3-31** Rewrite GCD with a REPEAT loop.

One final kind of LOOP is extremely valuable in writing readable code; with this one, we often skip recursive equations altogether to work at the level of set or sequence expressions with embedded rules.

FOR n := E1 TO E2 DO S END;
is equivalent to
n:=E1; TmpVar:=E2; WHILE n <= TmpVAR DO S END;

except that the final value of n is not necessarily available after the end of the loop (and TmpVar never appears explicitly at all). As usual, the best presentation is probably an example: Factorial5.

```
PROCEDURE Factorial5(n:INTEGER):INTEGER;
    (* pre: 0 ≤ n; post: result = n! = Product([i ∈ 1 ... n]) *)
    VAR i, s:INTEGER;
    BEGIN
        s := 1;
        FOR i := 1 TO n DO s := s*i (* s = i! *) END ;
        RETURN s
    END Factorial5;
```

The FOR loop is even more restricted than the WHILE, but it fits this problem well.

In a similar manner, a great many accumulators,    generators, mappings, filters, and scanners can be written as simple FOR loops with very little thought and little chance of confusion. The summation of a sequence of integers is shown in SumSeq:

```
PROCEDURE SumSeq(S:IntSeq):INTEGER;
    (* post: result = Sum(S) = Sum([S[i] : i ∈ 1 ... Length(S)]) *)
    VAR i, a:INTEGER;
    BEGIN
        a:=0;
        FOR i:=1 TO Length(S) DO a:=a+Get(S, i) (* a = Sum(S[1 ... i]) *)
            END ;
        RETURN a
    END SumSeq;
```

**Exercises**    SumSeq, of course, is much like other sequence accumulators. Write

**8.3-32** MinSeq, to find the minimum of a sequence

**8.3-33** MaxSeq, to find the maximum of a sequence

**8.3-34** MinLoc, to find the location of the minimum.

For most purposes,

FOR i := $A$ TO $B$ DO S END

is equivalent to a LOOP using the local variable "v":

i := A; v := B; LOOP IF i > v THEN EXIT END; S; i := Succ(i) END

In this kind of programming, i can be an integer, a cardinal, a character, or a member of an enumeration type; as long as Succ(i) is well defined, it will work.

The typical generator we have used is Range, which is a good way to introduce the one common variation on the FOR loop.

```
PROCEDURE Range(i, j:INTEGER):IntSeq;
   (* post: result = [i ... j] *)
   VAR k:INTEGER; R:IntSeq;
   BEGIN
     R:=NewNull();
     FOR k:=j TO i BY -1 DO
       R:=AddItem(k, R) (* R = [k ... j] *)
     END ;
     RETURN R
END Range;
```

The meaning of "BY -1" should be clear: we are counting down, not up. Mappings and filters can work the same way, counting down from the length of the input.

**Exercises**   Using FOR, write and test

**8.3-35** Find
**8.3-36** IsIn
**8.3-37** Capitalize
**8.3-38** Letters

As a final example of this kind of loop, we will go over a version of **QuickSort**.

```
PROCEDURE QuickSort(S:IntSeq):IntSeq;
  (* post: result = Sort(S) *)
  VAR Lo, Hi:IntSeq; i:INTEGER;
  BEGIN
    IF 2 > Length(S) THEN RETURN S END ;
    Lo := NewNull(); Hi := NewNull();
    FOR i:= 2 TO Length(S) DO
      IF Get(S, i) < Get(S, 1) THEN Lo := AddItem(Get(S, i), Lo)
        ELSE Hi := AddItem(Get(S, i), Hi)
      END
            (* [[x ∈ S[1]@(Lo + Hi + S[i + 1, . . .])]] = [[x ∈ S₀]] *)
    END
    RETURN Append(QuickSort(Lo), AddItem(Get(S, 1), QuickSort(Hi)))
  END QuickSort;
```

**Exercises**   Using FOR as much as possible, write and test

**8.3-39** MergeSort

**8.3-40** TreeSort

Feeling out of sorts? Take a rest, and then go on to the next section.

### 8.3.3 Procedures Which Change the State

You've learned to use built-in functions, and you've learned to define new ones as PROCEDUREs. You've also learned to use statements to change variables—the simplest statement, which is just an assignment statement, and the compound statements which involve IF, LOOP, and so on. All of these work by changing the state; but you have not yet written a procedure which changes the state. The reason for that is simple. It's very easy to get lost in a jungle of state-changing procedures, and it's much safer to have the habit of doing what you can do without them. However, there are limits to the efficiency which can be achieved without procedures that change their state. Let's think about the EQ1 procedure we worked on for finding the eight-queens solution. Depending on the memory space available to your *Modula-2* system, you may be able to run that once, twice, even a dozen times, but certainly you will not be able to run it ten thousand times without running out of memory. The reason is simple. When you call on AddItem, new space is taken: it's needed for the new item. On the other hand, when you call on Tl, no space is freed, even if you write S := Tl(S). Therefore, if you go on and on generating sequences, for example with a

S := NewNull(); LOOP S := Tl(AddItem(1, S)) END

you can expect to run out of space sooner or later. (Try it.)

**Q:** Why don't you free the space used by the Hd of S whenever you take the Tl?

**A:** Because there's no way of telling whether we still need the whole sequence S, including the Hd; there may be some other part of the program which is just about to use it.

**Q:** But can't the moron look over his collection of graph paper and tell which parts are still in use?

**A:** The *Modula-2* moron isn't designed for that; this is a stick-shift language. The same languages which detect simple recurrences and generate iterative code for them tend to have "garbage collectors" which analyze all available space to see how much of it is in use, and they also have the problem that the language implementation is usually not quite as clever as a professional programmer would have been. That situation may well change, but for the moment we need operations which change the value of a variable. It would be good to have one which corresponds to S:=Tl(S), another which corresponds to S:=a@S, another for S:=NewNull(), another for S:=Put(S, i, x), and so on. We may even want operations like S:=Append(S, X) or S:=Reverse(S). Programs like these, which change variables, have to be told what variables to change just as our existing procedures have to be told what values to work on. Their descriptions are simple:

PROCEDURE Push(n : INTEGER; VAR S : IntSeq);
(* post: $S = n@S_0$ *)

PROCEDURE Pop(VAR S : IntSeq);
(* pre: $S \neq [\,]$; post: $S = Tl(S_0)$ *)

PROCEDURE Create(VAR S : IntSeq);
(* post: $S = [\,]$ *)

Equivalently, we could specify them through equivalences such as Push(n, S) == S:=AddItem(n, S).

**Exercises**    Write equivalences to specify

**8.3-41** Create
**8.3-42** Pop

These can now be used in a program such as Reverse1, and we can edit the whole thing into Reverse2.

```
PROCEDURE Reverse1(S:IntSeq):IntSeq;
  (* post: result = reverse(S) *)
  VAR A:IntSeq;
  BEGIN
    A := NewNull();
    LOOP (* reverse(S) + A = reverse(S₀) *)
      IF IsNull(S) THEN RETURN A
        ELSE A := AddItem(Hd(S), A); S := Tl(S) END
    END
  END Reverse1;
```

```
PROCEDURE Reverse2(S:IntSeq; VAR A:IntSeq);
  (* post: A = reverse(S) *)
  BEGIN
    Create(A);
    LOOP (* reverse(S) + A = reverse(S₀) *)
      IF IsNull(S) THEN RETURN
        ELSE Push(Hd(S), A); Pop(S) END
    END
  END Reverse2;
```

As you can see, the programs are practically the same; Reverse2 is somewhat shorter and quite possibly more readable. Notice that although it contains a RE-TURN statement, nothing is being RETURNed and there is no overall type for the procedure (on the right of the header). This procedure is changing a parameter, not producing a result. The VAR S annotation tells the system (and you) that the parameter S had better be a variable and will be treated as such; if X is an IntSeq, then Push(5, X) will be meaningful, but Push(5, NewNull()) is useless; it corresponds to

NewNull() := AddItem(5, NewNull())

and *Modula-2* will treat it as a program error. With that restriction, however, any of the programs you've worked with using the standard sequence primitives can be translated into these new ones.

**Exercises**    Use Push, Pop, Create, and IsNull for

**8.3-43** SquareEach(S, A) == A := $[x^{**}2 : x \in S]$

**8.3-44** RangeV(i, j, S) == S := $[i \ldots j]$

**8.3-45** VecSum(X, Y, A) == A := $[X_i + Y_i : i \in 1 \ldots Length(X)]$

**8.3-46** MoreThan(a, X, Y) == Y := $[n \in X : n > a]$

Such procedures are parameterized statements rather than parameterized expressions; all of the bugs which can happen with expressions are still with us, and some new ones come in to join them. Still, the basic policy of gradual, multiversion software development works pretty well: if you have a program which works well with the techniques we've developed thus far, and you edit pieces of the code and of the invariants to introduce these new ideas, then you should find that only a few bugs will be introduced... and the same test cases will help you find them.

There are limits to gradualism; in fact, when we write a real "stick-shift" program the programmer may then be forbidden to write an expression whose value is a sequence, and thus forbidden to write any procedure which returns a sequence value. The IntSeq module we are using allows both, at the price of inefficiency. (In fact, Push is defined by a call on AddItem.) Thus, you can write your programs (recursively) at a level close to the specifications, edit those programs to introduce more and more efficient use of control structures, reedit the same programs to make use of VAR parameters, and finally—after you have no more procedures which treat sequences as values—shift to another module IntSeqVars which provides Push but not AddItem and does so more efficiently than IntSeq could manage with either.

That requires some caution; for example, the Reverse2 procedure above treats A as a variable, but it treats S as a value. This is legal; ideally, it means that the changes forced on S inside the procedure do not actually affect anything outside.

Once we've either accepted or evaded its constraints, we can use IntSeqVars and our programs will not readily run out of storage. In that case, the loop

Create(A); LOOP Push(5, A); Pop(A) END

is simply an infinite loop; it will use as much time as you give it, but will not run out of space.

**Exercises**    Convert from value sequence to VARiable sequence, using Create, Push, and Pop:

**8.3-47** The eight queens problem

**8.3-48** Quicksort

The VAR parameter idea is applicable to any type of variable; we can write procedures which change integers just as easily. Consider SumSeqV(S, a), specified as being equivalent to a:=SumSeq(S):


PROCEDURE SumSeqV(VAR S:IntSeq; VAR a:INTEGER);
  (* post: a $= Sum(S)$ *)
  VAR i:INTEGER;
  BEGIN a:=0;
    FOR i:=1 TO Length(S) DO a:=a+Get(S, i)    (* $a = Sum(S[1 \dots i])$ *)
    END
END SumSeq;



This procedure does treat the unchanging sequence S as a VAR parameter, so that an expression like SumSeq(Range(1, 10), n) will be rejected by the *Modula-2* system even in a context where sequences as values are allowed. It can neither be included in, nor include, an expression. With that exception, it is just as general as the SumSeq procedure which it closely resembles.


**Exercises**    Following the SumSeqV example, write and test

**8.3-49**  MinSeqV

**8.3-50**  MaxSeqV

**8.3-51**  MinLocV

**8.3-52**  PopTop(a, S) as equivalent to [a, S] := [Hd(S), Tl(S)]. (This is sometimes necessary in dealing with sequences of sequences, since we may not want Hd(S) to be used as an expression if it corresponds to a sequence.)


There are many other operations which we can reasonably perform as VAR parameter operations on sequences, but you should be able to see by now that we already have an adequate set for most purposes. The most immediately useful extensions to the list are operations we'll call PutV, SwapV, and CreateN:


PutV(S, i, x) == S := Put(S, i, x)
SwapV(S, i, j) == S := Put(Put(S, i, Get(S, j)), j, Get(S, i))
CreateN(S, N, x) == S := [x, x, ...x] (of length N)



Given these operations, we can manage mappings, but our ability to write generators and filters is limited by our ability to predict in advance the size of the sequences required. For example, we can write a Reverse algorithm with PutV and

CreateN:

```
PROCEDURE Reverse(VAR S, A:IntSeq);
(* post: A = Reverse(S) *)
VAR N, i:INTEGER;
BEGIN
  N := Length(S);
  CreateN(A, N, 0);
  FOR i:= 1 TO N DO (* A[1...i-1] = Reverse(S[N+2-i...N]) *)
    PutV(A, i, Get(S, N+1-i))
  END
END Reverse;
```

In this algorithm, we create a sequence of the right size and then put its elements in place. Notice that here S is a VAR parameter because we have no intention of changing any of its elements. (But see the next section for a warning!)

**Exercises**    After studying the Reverse example,

**8.3-53** Write the loop invariant as it would appear *after* the PutV statement. Why is it simpler? Look over previous examples: you'll see that almost all FOR loops are commented at the bottom, although almost all other loops are commented at the top. Explain.

**8.3-54** Write a procedure Copy(S, A) which creates a new sequence A and then copies all the items in S into it.

**8.3-55** The EqSeq(A, B) procedure is to return TRUE if $A = B$ and FALSE otherwise; the central statement is
IF Get(A, i) # Get(B, i) THEN RETURN FALSE. Complete and test the procedure.

SwapV, which just rearranges the items in a sequence, is best known for its use in sorting. Let's try a version of MaxFirst:

```
PROCEDURE MaxFirst(VAR S:IntSeq; N:Integer);
(* post: Perm(S, S_0), Hd(S) = Max(S[1...N]) *)
VAR i:INTEGER;
FOR i:=1 TO N DO
  IF Get(S, i) > Get(S, 1) THEN SwapV(S, 1, i) END
        (* Perm(S, S_0), Hd(S) = Max(S[1...i]) *)
  END
END MinFirst;
```

It's now easy to write a sorting program; all we need is

FOR i:=Length(S) TO 1 BY −1 DO MaxFirst(S, i); SwapV(S, i) END

**Exercises**

**8.3-56** Finish and test the sorting program just outlined; in particular, add the required invariant to the loop.

**8.3-57** Write the corresponding version of MinFirst, and use it in a sorting program.

**8.3-58** Write and test an insertion sort.

The QuickSort solution shown in Figure 8.6 is of course radically better than the quadratic sorting methods; it is also significantly better in time and space than the previous solutions to QuickSort, although all are $\mathcal{O}(Nlog(N))$ if Get and SwapV are $\mathcal{O}(1)$. QuickSort is not an easy program to follow because so much is going on all at once. However, it's an important program because it brings together a lot of what we've done.

```
PROCEDURE QuickSort(VAR S:IntSeq; lo, hi:INTEGER);
  (* post: S[lo..hi] = Sort(S_0[lo..hi]) *)
  VAR mid: INTEGER;
  PROCEDURE Partition(VAR S:IntSeq; x, lo, hi:INTEGER;
    VAR mid:INTEGER);
    (* post: Perm(S, S_0), S[lo..mid] <= x, S[mid+1..hi] > x *)
    BEGIN
      LOOP (* S[lo_0 ... lo-1] <= x, S[hi+1 ... hi_0] > x, Perm(S, S_0) *)
        IF lo > hi THEN mid := hi; RETURN;
          ELSIF Get(S, lo) <= x THEN lo := lo+1;
          ELSIF Get(S, hi) > x THEN hi := hi-1;
          ELSE SwapV(S, lo, hi); lo := lo+1; hi:= hi-1;
        END ;
      END ;
  END Partition;
  BEGIN
    IF lo >= hi THEN (* postcondition holds *) RETURN END;
    Partition(S, Get(S, lo), lo+1, hi, mid);
    SwapV(S, lo, mid); (* S[lo..mid-1] <= S[mid] <= S[mid+1..hi] *)
    QuickSort(S, lo, mid-1);
    QuickSort(S, mid+1, hi);
  END QuickSort;
```

**Figure 8.6** QuickSort

## Exercises

**8.3-59** How badly does QuickSort do if the input is already sorted? (Answer this both theoretically and with timing figures.)

**8.3-60** How badly does QuickSort do if the input is sorted in reverse?

**8.3-61** How badly does QuickSort do if the input is a sequence of zeros?

**8.3-62** What would happen in each of the preceding questions if QuickSort began by swapping $S[lo]$ with $S[(lo + hi)DIV\,2]$ just before the call to Partition?

### 8.3.4  Aliasing Bugs and Other Joys of a Programmer's Life

At this point, you should have a fairly good feeling for the virtues of VAR parameters; we have skimped on their vices. Let's go back to the procedure Reverse(S, A), which was supposed to achieve the effect of A:=Reverse(S). The core of the procedure was

        N := Length(S); Create(A, N, 0);
        FOR i:=1 to N DO PutV(A, i, Get(S, N+1−i)) END

Now, let's just suppose that some innocent programmer happens to want to use this as a utility and calmly writes Reverse(X, X) in order to reverse a sequence into itself. Being thoroughly confident of this, she includes it in a large and complex program; after all, Reverse has already been tested on small, medium, and large sequences. When things blow up, she tests all of the other program components. After she finds that they seem to work when tested separately, but don't work when put back together, she starts another approach altogether. When this one fails for similar reasons, she looks for another career. Her problem, in fact, is that what she was executing was

        N := Length(X); Create(X, N, 0);
        FOR i:=1 to N DO PutV(X, i, Get(X, N+1−i)) END

This code replaces X with a sequence of zeros of equal length, because the input parameter S and the output parameter A are both VAR parameters identified with X.

The VAR parameters of a procedure must be distinct!

Equivalently, we can just say "No object may have two names!" because the problem raised by the VAR parameter usage in Reverse(X, X) is that the object (variable) X is known by the two names S and A. That is *aliasing*; it is not criminal in itself, but it is often associated with criminal behavior. When you don't obey this rule, you will be lucky when your errors come as close to being obvious as this one. Here, at least, the program will never even appear to work except on sequences of zeros. Sometimes you'll find that your programs work perfectly well... except on Thursdays after 11P.M. on nights with a three-quarter moon. Here's a famous example: we swap two integers in place, with SwapInt.

```
PROCEDURE SwapInt(VAR i, j:INTEGER);
    (* post: i, j = j₀, i₀ *)
    BEGIN
        (* i, j = i₀, j₀ *)          (* e.g., i, j = 3, 7 *)
        i := i+j;
        (* i, j = i₀ + j₀, j₀ *)     (* e.g., i, j = 10, 7 *)
        j := i−j;
        (* i, j = i₀ + j₀, i₀ *)     (* e.g., i, j = 10, 3 *)
        i := i−j
        (* i, j = j₀, i₀ *)          (* e.g., i, j = 7, 3 *)
    END SwapInt;
```

If you study the invariant assertions carefully, you can see why it works; alternatively, study the example. It so happens that swapping within a sorting algorithm can be done this way; you'll see how in the next chapter. As long as distinct items are swapped, there's no problem at all, and this can even be a good way to do the swapping: it may correspond to better machine code than the apparently more straightforward swapping method we've already gone over in SwapV. Unfortunately, it's quite possible to look over a sorting program and not realize that it will, very, very occasionally, swap an item with itself.

**Exercise**

**8.3-63** Explain what happens when you call on SwapInt(n, n).

The moral of this example is simple: be very wary of overuse of VAR parameters, and be very careful of the use of repeated parameters in any program which uses VAR parameters at all. As long as you're just editting a program which has already been tested as a prototype, and as long as you test systematically with each edit, you'll know where your difficulties are coming from.

Aliasing can also happen in the context of *global variables*, but this is less common. As a silly example, we could have a procedure SI which is exactly like SwapInt except that the parameter j is omitted from the header. Now SI(i) swaps i with the variable j, which is meaningless unless j has been declared outside the new version of SI. So in this case, SwapInt(x, y) is equivalent to SI(x); SI(y); SI(x)... usually.

## Exercises

**8.3-64** When will aliasing cause SI to go wrong? Why?

**8.3-65** The three-SI solution to SwapInt given above will sometimes work even though the original solution did not. When and why is this so?

Aliasing involving global variables can happen in realistic situations, but rather than an example to show it happening, we'll go over an example of how to design code so that it won't happen. Suppose, for example, that our specification involves a dictionary which changes in time, i.e., a sequence of dictionaries each of which is logically a set of pairs of strings. Each name is a string, and each definition is also a string. At any given moment, we can access information in the dictionary with a LookUp procedure, and we can get to the next dictionary in the sequence by a Define procedure. We can easily write a module Dict with a definition module as follows:

```
DEFINITION MODULE Dict;
(* This module manages a dictionary, initialized as {} *)
IMPORT Strs;
EXPORT QUALIFIED Define, LookUp;
PROCEDURE Define(VAR Name, Val:Strs.Str);
    (* pre: the dictionary (= D) is not full *)
    (* post: D = D_0 ∪ {[Name, Val]} *)
PROCEDURE LookUp(VAR Name, Val:Strs.Str);
    (* post: Val = def : [Name, def] in D if any; else Val = Name *)
```

Now you can maintain an environment containing definitions for as many symbols as you like. You do it by importing the Define and LookUp operations from this module and then using them. (The initialization code which sets the dictionary to {} will be executed before your code begins to work.) Define and LookUp share an invisible state: the contents of the dictionary. Since the global variable or variables which represent the dictionary are private, no other procedures can have access to that state except through these operations.

**Q:** That's pretty neat, but what does it have to do with aliasing?

**A:** The dictionary is a very long-lived global variable... possibly more than one global variable. If we mixed the code which defines it in with other procedures, we'd be very likely to end up with procedures which "consciously" changed it as a VAR parameter, even while using it indirectly through LookUp or even Define. Indirect aliases are very hard to track down.

But we're safe: we haven't mixed that code in. It's all in a nice little module, and nobody can even tell from the DEFINITION module how many global variables are used to do the storage, much less what their names are. Aliasing can't happen.

It is very easy to provide an implementation module for the definition module given; we can represent a dictionary as a sequence of names with a matching sequence of definitions, and both of those are sequences of strings, which we already have procedures for working with. Examine the implementation module closely.

```
IMPLEMENTATION MODULE Dict;
FROM StrSeqs IMPORT StrSeq, Push, Find, Put, Get, NewNull;
VAR NameSeq, DefSeq : StrSeq;
PROCEDURE Define(VAR Name, Val:Strs.Str);
   (* pre: the dictionary (= D) is not full *)
   (* post: D = D_0 ∪ {[Name, Val]} *)
   VAR i : CARDINAL;
   BEGIN
      i := Find(Name, NameSeq);
      IF i=0 THEN Push(Name, NameSeq); Push(Val, DefSeq)
        ELSE DefSeq := Put(DefSeq, i, Val)
      END
END Define;
PROCEDURE LookUp(VAR Name, Val:Strs.Str);
(* post: Val = def : [Name, def] in D if any; else Val = Name *)
   VAR i : CARDINAL;
   BEGIN
      i := Find(Name, NameSeq);
      IF i=0 THEN Val := Name ELSE Val := Get(DefSeq, i) END
END LookUp;
BEGIN (* initialization code for module *)
   NameSeq :=NewNull();
   DefSeq := NewNull()
END Dict.
```

## 8.4  WRITING AND READING

In Part I, you learned to convert structures to strings and back again quite systematically. In the previous sections of this chapter you learned to use library routines which do it for you, in order to trace your programs in execution. It's time to put the two together, so that you can write output and input routines for each data type you implement.

The new concept here is one that may not seem new at all: the *file* is a potentially unbounded sequence, and we can think of input and output as having more to do with time than with space. Let's suppose we have a type T, and we're writing procedures WriteT and ReadT. They should have preconditions and postconditions much like the following:

```
PROCEDURE WriteT(x : T);
   (* post : OutputFile = OutputFile₀+ Rep(x) *)
PROCEDURE ReadT(VAR x : T);
      (* pre : InputFile = Rep(v) + S *)
      (* post: x=v, InputFile = S *)
```

In other words, to write an object is to tack its (string) representation onto the output file, and to read an object is to pull its (string) representation off of the input file. They correspond naturally to the *Ab* and *Rep* functions which we worked with before, but they have to deal with context (past for output, future for input). Of course, the files may exist in time rather than space, but these procedures neither know nor care.

**Q:** There's something strange about the idea of ReadT dealing with the whole input file as "Rep(v)+S" when S hasn't even been generated yet. Don't you have to do it differently for reading from the keyboard than for reading from a file?

**A:** Not usually; in fact it's often very important not to think of these as different cases, and the underlying library modules of your *Modula-2* implementation work hard to make it unnecessary. Of course, the physical activities of the machine are quite different in the two cases (and different again when we read input through a modem, from a mouse, or from a graphics tablet), but in each case we end up with a sequence of characters (not necessarily confined to *ASCII*'s $0...127$ range). Somehow, we tell the program what the "standard input" and "standard output" files are; it then knows where to read and write. For most purposes, you should be able to do this without any special *Modula-2* code. The system which runs your program can be told to "redirect" the input and output; in the very common *MS-DOS* and *Unix* environments, the line

   myprog < infile.dat > outfile.dat

means "run the program 'myprog' which I have compiled, but read input from 'infile.dat' instead of from the keyboard and write to 'outfile.dat' instead of to my screen." Other systems have other methods; learn yours. If you must use more than one file, you will find that *Modula-2* has procedures OpenInput and OpenOutput (and others) by which you can change the redirection, but the more you do this the harder it will be to combine your programs with one another as tools. In fact, it is crucial that you learn to translate (almost) all input/output thinking into thoughts about one pair of streams.

**Q:** But what about graphics? What about doing things with the screen that you just can't do on a simple output file? What about pulling data from a program associated with one window and giving it to a program locked to another? Don't we have to have a procedure that moves the cursor to a given $x, y$ position on the screen?

**A:** You generate (two-dimensional) pictures by sending a (one-dimensional) signal sequence to an output device. The logical screen (like any window) is a sequence of rows; each row is a sequence of elements which may be characters or Boolean values or colors or brightnesses or some combination of these; the logical cursor has a pair of coordinates, and probably some status mark like BlinkingUnderscore or Invisible. The programs you write don't read from the light on the screen itself (unless you're using a light pencil or a digitizing camera); they work with logical windows, not optical ones, and they'll generally run just as well with the monitor turned off. What I'm trying to say is that the problems you're thinking of aren't primarily input/output problems at all; they are difficult problems, they are lots of fun, and I hope you learn about them in some course not too long after this one, but they simply aren't input/output problems. In this book, we won't get much further than the basics of dealing with standard input and output; that's all you should need for writing some quite substantial programs.

### 8.4.1 Printing Values

The basic *Modula-2* notion of output starts with the Write procedure we've been using to write single characters to the output device. We can build on that with WriteStr:

```
FOR i:=1 TO Length(S) DO
    Write(Get(S, i))
    (* OutputFile = OutputFile_0 + S[1..i] *)
END
```

You've already learned to convert a number, a Boolean value, a sequence, or even a tree into a string. In a way, that solves the whole problem: to write an object, convert it into a string and then write the string. For simple types like integers and cardinals, this is highly desirable in any case because you often write these into spaces of known size. Thus, WriteInt(12, 4) will first convert 12 to "**12**" and then pad it out to four spaces: "  **12**". The space may be too small: WriteInt(938772, 4) converts 938772 to "**938772**" and then writes it out anyway (it takes up six spaces), but at least it does try. That's not all there is to say, however. If we are going to write a long, long, long, long sequence, we may not have room for the sequence and its string representation simultaneously. It would even be nice to be able to write out the sequence $[1, 2, \ldots, 1000000]$, which probably won't fit in our computer's memory. Therefore, we use a distribution law: sequence printing distributes over sequence generation. More particularly, suppose that we want the effect of

```
WriteIntSeq(Range(9, 90))
```

The "natural" approach is to generate and then print:

1. Generate the number 9,

2. Continue on to generate $Range(10, 90)$; we have the value.

3. Write the number 9, (the head),

4. Continue on to write $Range(10, 90)$; we're all done.

We can fold the two together with $WriteRange(1, 100)$ just as we folded generation and summation together in $SumRange$ $(SR)$. All you need to do is generate and write the head, and then generate and write the tail; this will turn into a simple loop:

```
Write( "[" );
IF lo > hi THEN Write( "]" ); RETURN ELSE WriteInt(Get(S, lo), 0) END ;
LOOP (* OutFile = OutFile_0 + "[" + S[lo_0] + ", " + ... + S[lo] *)
   IF lo = hi THEN Write( "]" ); RETURN
      ELSE lo:= lo+1; WriteString( ", " ); WriteInt(Get(S, lo), 0)
   END
END
```

That's a nice second draft, and it does save space and time over the first, but it is not as easy to modify. If the third draft were to involve a lot of formatting (for example, trying to set the output numbers into neat columns whose positions might depend on the actual sizes of the numbers), then you'd want to go back to the first draft rather than work from this one. That's a common problem with second drafts, or in general with folding procedures together.

### Exercises

**8.4-1**  Specify, write, and test WriteIntSeq so that the output will be laid out nicely in columns if it doesn't fit on one line. Assume that you are restricted to 80 characters per line. [Hint: look at each integer to find how much space the longest one needs; consider how many will fit on each line.]

**8.4-2**  Specify, write, and test WriteDict for the Dict module of the previous section.

A very interesting and very common kind of output is simply a document: a sequence of "words" delimited by blanks and end-of-line markers. Often we'd like to have our words formatted, as they are on this page. The formatter which generates these pages is a huge program called TEX, written in the *Pascal* language to transform documents into pictures; we're not going to duplicate it here. On the other hand, it's easy enough to define more limited formatters, which transform a document by filling up lines with blanks. For example, I can take the input

```
This is a series
    of lines, which are not going to match up very well,
because some are
short
and some, on the other hand, are reasonably (or unreasonably) long,
while some start on the left
                              and others are over on the right.
```

and easily generate the (60-column) output

```
This is a series of lines, which are not going to match up
very well, because some are short and some, on the other
hand, are reasonably (or even unreasonably) long, while some
start on the left and others are over on the right.
```

It's somewhat harder to construct a version that lined up (justified) on both left and right:

```
This   is a series of lines, which are not going to match   up
very   well,   because some are short and some, on   the   other
hand, are reasonably (or even unreasonably) long, while some
start on the left and others are over on the right.
```

(Notice that I didn't do anything to the last line.) To manage anything like this, I need to transform the document $D$ into a sequence $W$ of words, and then I need to construct a sequence $L$ of lines from $W$. The first stage might go like this:

$$
\begin{aligned}
Wrds(D) &= D, & &\text{if } D = [\,] \\
&= Wrds(Tl(D)), & &\text{if } IsBlank(Hd(D)) \\
&= InWrd([Hd(D)], Tl(D)) & &\text{otherwise} \\
InWrd(w, D) &= [w], & &\text{if } D = [\,] \\
&= w@Wrds(Tl(D)), & &\text{if } IsBlank(Hd(D)) \\
&= InWrd(w + [Hd(D)], Tl(D)] & &\text{otherwise}
\end{aligned}
$$

For example, output for $Wrds(\textbf{“this is a silly sequence of words.”})$ is

$$[\text{“\textbf{this}”}, \text{“\textbf{is}”}, \text{“\textbf{a}”}, \text{“\textbf{silly}”}, \text{“\textbf{sequence}”}, \text{“\textbf{of}”}, \text{“\textbf{words.}”}].$$

The *IsBlank* test should be true for blanks, tabs, and end-of-line markers. (This last may be a carriage return, a line feed, both, or something else; it tends to vary among different systems. The standard EOL symbol stands for "end of line" in *Modula-2*; it is defined differently on different machines, but can always be used.)

## Exercises

**8.4-3**  Write and test $Wrds$ and $InWrd$ as recursive procedures.

**8.4-4**  Write and test them as iterative procedures.

Given the sequence of words $W$, the next stage would be to define the sequence of partially *or* completely filled lines $PL$: from the seven words found above and a $MaxLen$ of 14, we could say

```
i  PL                Full
1.                |   F
2. this           |   F
3. this is        |   F
4. this is a      |   T
5. silly          |   F
6. silly sequence |   T
7. of             |   F
8. of words.      |   T
```

and from this the output should evidently be [**"this is a"**, **"silly sequence"**, **"of words."**]. We can describe this equationally as

$$
\begin{aligned}
PL[i] &= [\,], & \text{if } i = 1; \\
&= W[i-1], & \text{if } Full[i-1] \\
&= PL[i-1] + \text{``\;''} + W[i-1], & \text{otherwise} \\
Full[i] &= Length(PL[i] + \text{``\;''} + W[i]) \geq MaxLen \vee Length(W) = i - 1 \\
L[i] &= [s \in PL : Full[s]]
\end{aligned}
$$

In this specification, $PL$ is described as a sequence of lines, but of course it can exist in time rather than space: only one line, called the "output buffer," needs to exist at any given moment.

## Exercises

**8.4-5**  Write procedures to generate this result as a StrSeq.

**8.4-6**  Write procedures to generate this result as output.

At this point, we need to worry about blank spaces. We'd like to add blanks equally to each existing blank, but of course they may not go evenly. There are two common rules of thumb:

- Add spaces symmetrically (alternately) from the ends of the line.

- Add spaces preferentially after punctuation marks.

Since we don't want to get into the rather serious complications involved in getting the right answer, we'll just add spaces symmetrically from the front and back of an incompletely full line. The easy way is to count the blanks which are already there ($B = Length([i : L[i] = \text{' '}])$), and the number needed, which is $N = MaxLen - Length(S)$. Each of the $B$ blanks already present should have $div(N, B)$ blanks adjoined to it, and the remaining $r = mod(N, B)$ blanks should be split up; one for each of the first $div(r, 2)$ blanks on the line, and one for each of the last $div(r + 1, 2)$ blanks on the line.

### Exercise

**8.4-7**    Specify, write, and test the full space-adding formatter we've just described.

We could now begin an enormous number of variations and extensions; we won't. Hyphenation could be dealt with by treating each word as a sequence of hyphenatable strings and revising *IsFull* and the response to it accordingly. Paragraph indentation, centering and right alignment, multiple spacing between lines or paragraphs, underlining by backspaces, skipping to a new page, page numbers and running titles and index facilities... all of these are interesting, a moderate selection of them would make a good first-semester project, but none of them are essential to our current objectives. At this point in your reading and programming, you should be able to deal with writing the necessary output routines for any data structures you want to tell the user about.

## 8.4.2  Reading In Values

Like output, input is based on an operation for single characters: Read(VAR c:CHAR) has the precondition that the input file is of the form $a@S$, where $a$ is a character, and the postcondition that $c = a$ and the input file is $S$. There's one trouble about that: with reading, it's perfectly possible to fail (e.g., because the input file is empty). Therefore the InOut module we've been using also exports a variable called Done, which is set to FALSE when an operation fails.

### Exercise

**8.4-8**    Describe the pre- and postconditions for Read carefully; obviously it does not actually assume that the file is nonempty.

As with output, we can build an operation for strings on top of the single-character operation. The problem is that we don't necessarily know when to stop.

We could read in one whole line, as in the following ReadLn procedure.

```
PROCEDURE ReadLn():Str;
  (* post : if InputFile_0 = [] then result = [] *)
  (*       else result+EOL+InputFile = InputFile_0 *)
  VAR c : CHAR;
  BEGIN
    InOut.Read(c);
    IF NOT(InOut.Done) OR c = InOut.EOL THEN RETURN NewNull()
      ELSE RETURN AddItem(c, ReadLn())
  END ReadLn;
```

This is nicely structured (although not very efficiently coded) and quite usable; sometimes we'll use it. However, there are often better choices. The basic *Modula-2* utilities assume that the input file will be composed of numbers and strings delimited by "white space": blanks and control characters whose *ASCII* order is less than the blank, and which can be thrown away. To read a string, we skip over white space, then collect characters until we encounter more white space. The characters we've collected form a string, which (in ReadInt or ReadCard or ReadReal) will then be transformed into a number. Each of these is also responsible for setting the variable InOut.Done to TRUE or FALSE to reflect success or failure.

## Exercises

**8.4-9**   Specify, write, and test versions of ReadInt and ReadCard based on Str.ReadStr rather than on InOut.ReadString.

**8.4-10** Specify, write, and test ReadQuotedStr, which skips until it finds a quotation mark (single or double), then reads input until it finds a matching quotation mark, and returns everything in between.

As things get more complicated, we can't keep reading big gobs of stuff without paying attention to delimiters like parentheses, brackets, commas, and the symbols of arithmetic. Here there are two reasonable alternatives:

- Get yourself a parser generator, which will split the input into pieces according to a grammar you specify, or

- Write your own parsing routines.

We'll go over the latter.

The first requirement is that we have a grammar. For integer sequences, we can write that a sequence is either empty, or else it's nonempty; if it's nonempty then it has a first number and a sequence tail, which either is empty or has a comma followed by another number:

$$IntSeq \quad ::= \quad \text{"[]"} \mid \text{"["} \; Int \; IntSTl$$
$$IntSTl \quad ::= \quad \text{"]"} \mid \text{","} \; Int \; IntSTl$$

Now, for each collection of choices, we have to make sure that the program will be able to make the right choice; that is, the first thing to be read has to tell it which choice to make. In this case they don't; both choices for *IntSeq* begin with a "[". That's no problem: we can rewrite the grammar a little bit, stretching our notation to say

$$IntSeq \quad ::= \quad \text{"["} \; (\text{"]"} \mid Int \; IntSTl)$$

Now we can write the code: ParseIntSeq and ParseIntSTl follow the grammar exactly, in a way which you can learn to read.

```
PROCEDURE ParseIntSeq():IntSeq;
   (* pre : InputStream = Rep(S)+ F *)
   (* S is an IntSeq; IntSeq ::= "[" ("]" | Int IntSTl) *)
   (* post : result = S, InputStream = F *)
   BEGIN
     IF NOT(Match("[")) THEN RETURN NewNull() END ; (* failure *)
     IF Match("]") THEN RETURN NewNull()
       ELSE RETURN AddItem(ParseInt(), ParseIntSTl())
     END
END ParseIntSeq;
PROCEDURE ParseIntSTl():IntSeq;
(* pre : InputStream = Rep(S) + F *)
(* S is an IntSTl; IntSTl ::= "]" | "," Int IntSTl *)
(* post : result = S, InputStream = F *)
BEGIN
   IF Match("]") THEN RETURN NewNull()
     ELSIF Match(",") THEN RETURN AddItem(ParseInt(), ParseIntSTl())
     ELSE RETURN NewNull() (* failure *)
   END
END ParseIntSTl;
```

They work fine; you just need to call InitParse before you run any of them. These procedures use two other procedures: Match and ParseInt. They also use rather oddly phrased conditions, which refer to an InputStream rather than to an InputFile. In fact, these are closely related issues. The lower level procedures mentioned have to be aware that the logical InputStream is very slightly different from the input file with which we were just starting to get familiar. That's the way it is in modular programming: before you really get used to one thing, you build something else on top of it and conceal it altogether. Meanwhile, we can write other parsing procedures without much trouble. Suppose that we want to parse tree structures, still involving only numbers, so that we can get "[3, -2, [2, 9], 18]" or "98" read in as a tree. There are two differences in the grammar: first, a tree can be a number all by itself; second, the head of a tree can be a tree rather than just a number. That gives us a quick editing job:

$$Tree \qquad ::= \qquad Int \mid \text{``[''} (\text{``]''} \mid Tree \; TreeSTl)$$
$$TreeSTl \qquad ::= \qquad \text{``]''} \mid \text{``,''} \; Tree \; TreeSTl$$

Based on the edited grammar, we can easily edit the code:

```
PROCEDURE ParseTree():Tree;
   (* pre : InputStream = Rep(S)+ F *)
   (* S is an Tree; Tree ::= Int | "[" ("]" | Int TreeSTl) *)
   (* post : result = S, InputStream = F *)
   BEGIN
     IF NOT(Match("[")) THEN RETURN IntToTree(ParseInt()) END ;
     IF Match("]") THEN RETURN NewNull()
        ELSE RETURN AddItem(ParseTree(), ParseTreeSTl())
     END
   END ParseTree;
```

The programs may look odd, but you should already be able to write some programs in this style.

**Exercise**    For example,

**8.4-11**  Specify, write, and test ParseTreeSTl. Then compare your answer with the code provided in the module.

At this point, we should study the Match and ParseInt functions, as well as others related to them. The idea is evidently that Match(c) somehow matches c against the "head" of the input and either succeeds (and returns TRUE, and pops off the head) or fails and returns FALSE. Also, it seems clear that ParseInt reads one integer from the input.

It is not clear how they can possibly work: before we call ParseInt, we must know that the next item is an integer. Before we can know that, we must read the first digit of that integer. If we read a digit from a file, it is gone from that file.[3] If the first digit is gone from the file before we even call ParseInt, then ParseInt can't possibly get the right answer by reading from the file.

---

[3]This is not always true, and *Modula-2* does have special-purpose tools for evading the problem, but we're going to meet it head-on.

What this means is just that there must be more to the InputStream than there is to the InputFile; in fact, the input stream (for this collection of problems) is a sequence whose head is the character NextChar and whose tail is the input file. Match is then quite easy to write:

```
PROCEDURE Match(c:CHAR):BOOLEAN;
  (* pre: NextChar@(blanks)+F = InputStream *)
  (* post: if c=NextChar then InputStream=F, result = TRUE *)
  (*       else InputStream=InputStream_0, result = FALSE *)
  BEGIN
    IF c=NextChar
      THEN Read(NextChar); SkipBlanks(); RETURN TRUE
      ELSE RETURN FALSE
    END
  END Match;
```

**Exercise**    Without reading further than Match,

**8.4-12**  Specify and write the SkipBlanks procedure.

In order to write ParseInt, we need to be able to distinguish digits from nondigits. Writing 10 calls on Match is not an ideal way to do this. The simplest is probably to use a MatchDigit(c) procedure which returns TRUE and sets c to NextChar if it is a digit and otherwise returns FALSE. We can then have MatchLetter for letters, MatchBinOp for binary operators like "+" and "*", and so on.

**Exercises**    Without reading further,

**8.4-13**  Specify and write MatchDigit(c).
**8.4-14**  Specify and write ParseInt().
**8.4-15**  Specify and write MatchLetter(c).
**8.4-16**  Specify and write ParseName().
**8.4-17**  Specify and write MatchBinOp(c).

These procedures are not ideal; for example, MatchBinOp obviously can't match a binary operation like "**" or ">=". You could get around this by having it match a string rather than a single character, or by having the grammar deal with "53<=-219" as a sequence ["53", "<", "=", "-219"]. Think about it. A better solution is common: we deny that sentences are sequences of characters. Instead, a sentence is a sequence of words, and the words are sequences of characters. The simplest and most regular parts of the grammar are placed into one module which knows how numbers, names, and other symbols are made out of characters. This module is called a *lexical analyzer*, and it would include all of the programs in the last set of exercises. The parser then works on a somewhat higher level; parsing routines can be as simple as ParseTree, even when the input is very complex.

There are still some major problems. What about ambiguous grammars? What about precedence, where the grammar doesn't tell us what to do? There are a variety of answers to such questions. The simplest (not always the best) is that we can generally force the grammar to contain the information we want, in unambiguous form. For example, the grammar of expressions which we started out with contains some ambiguity which is resolved by precedence: "$1*2*3+4*5*6-7*8/9$" is to be parsed as if it were "$(A + B) - C$", where $A$ is $(1*2)*3$, $B$ is $(4*5)*6$, and $C$ is $(7*8)/9$. In other words, we assume that multiplication and division take precedence over (have a higher precedence than) addition and subtraction, but that equal-precedence operators associate to the left. We can express this by giving different names to groupings at different levels of precedence. The tightest groups are numbers and parenthesized expressions like "418" and "(3+9)"; we'll call this kind of expression an $E0$. The next-tightest kind is an $E1$, connected by multiplications or divisions; it looks like

$$E0 \; MulOp \; E0 \; MulOp \; E0 \; MulOp \; E0 \ldots ,$$

which can be described as an $E0$ followed by a sequence of $MulOp \; E0$ pairs. Finally we have the loosest kind of expression, which we'll call an $E2$, which is one or more $E1$s connected by additions or subtractions; it looks like

$$E1 \; (AddOp \; E1) \; (AddOp \; E1) \; (AddOp \; E1) \ldots ,$$

so the overall grammar is

| | | |
|---|---|---|
| $E0$ | ::= | $Int \mid$ "(" $E2$ ")" |
| $E1$ | ::= | $E0 \; E1'$ |
| $E1'$ | ::= | "" $\mid MulOp \; E0 \; E1'$ |
| $E2$ | ::= | $E1 \; E2'$ |
| $E2'$ | ::= | "" $\mid AddOp \; E1 \; E2'$ |

### Exercises

**8.4-18** Write and test a parser for the grammar as given.

**8.4-19** Extend the grammar to deal with exponentiation as an infix operation of higher precedence than multiplication or division; you'll want to have $E1$, $E2$, and $E3$.

For now, we've done enough with input; you can work with grammars, and you can write prototype parsers.

## 8.5 PUTTING IT ALL TOGETHER

If you've gotten this far through the text, you can write prototypes for more than parsers; you can handle a number of text-processing projects. Here are some samples which you could reasonably start building at this point:

- A simple "macro-substitution" facility reads input one line at a time. A line of the form
  "**@def blip=uzzle wuzzle**"
  defines the string "**@blip**" as a macro—an abbreviation for "**uzzle wuzzle**". There is no output from a definition line. Any other line is a data line. The output from a data line is the result of expanding any abbreviations on that line, as substitutions. Specify, write, and test this facility. You'll find that there are ambiguities in the specification given, so there are choices you have to make. [Hint: Keep the dictionary module separate, keep the parsing module separate, and keep the multisubstitutions module separate. Put them together with a small module which calls on the parser to produce either a command or a data line, and then may call on the dictionary or else on the multisubstituter and on output.]

- (Extension) A parametrized macro-substitution facility looks just like the one above, except that a line of the form
  "**@def f#2=(#1 AND #2)**"
  defines "**@f'first'2nd'**" as "**(first AND 2nd)**". Again this is ambiguous; specify, write, and test. (Notice how different modules grew in different ways; this would be much harder if they had been kept together.)

- A simple database consists of a single table which is a sequence of lines. Each line is a sequence of columns, and each column is a string which may or may not represent a number. There is also a header line containing a label for each column. The input which controls the data base is a sequence of command lines:

```
ReadTable;
AddRow John Jacob Smith, 34, 111-22-3456, $54321;
AddRow Mary Jones, 26, 057-66-9876, $78200;
DeleteIf Salary < $35000;
SortBy Age;
...
```

Typical operations include reading a table (header and data) from a file. (For this you use OpenInput, which prompts for the file name.) Similarly, you can write a table out to a file, initialize a table, add a row to a table, delete all rows for which a given column does (or does not) contain a given entry, sort the table so that a given column will be in order, and add or delete a column with

its header. Specify the sequence of data bases as a function of the sequence
of input lines (and data-file contents); write and test. (The breakdown into
modules should be almost identical with that suggested for the macro facility.)

- (Extension) Allow multiple tables in the database project. Look up the database
  concept of the Join of two relations (i.e., two tables). Specify it in the context
  of your own project, write, and test.

- A text editor looks very much like a database, except that the lines are not
  organized into a fixed-column structure. The editor state consists of the document (a sequence of lines) and three positions: the current "logical cursor"
  position $C$, and the positions of the beginning $B$ and end $E$ of the current
  block. Each position consists of two numbers: a line and a position within that
  line. There should be commands

  - To set $B$ or $E$ to $C$,
  - To shift $C$'s line or column count forwards or backwards

    * To some absolute position (go to line 5)
    * Changing by a fixed amount (9 spaces back, please)
    * Shifting to a pattern (on to the next "**Henry**")

  - To delete the current block, or write it as a file, or print it
  - To delete (part of) the current line, or print it
  - To insert a file at the current position as a new block
  - To delete lines which do/do not have a given string
  - To substitute one string for another on the current line, in the current
    block, etc.

This list is intended to be suggestive, not exhaustive, and it is quite unusual
for two people to agree on what combination of editor commands are desirable.
Notice that I haven't said anything about desirable syntax: you can specify this
with long words, single letters, funny symbols or whatever you please. The joy
of a project like this is that you get to add to the specification yourself, then
work on the prototype, then decide you don't like the "feel" of the commands,
then go back to the specification, and so on. After it's all settled (say, a year or
so from now) you can replace the parser modules and shift to a screen-oriented
display, with little change (at first) to the internal data structures except for
the addition of a representation of the screen itself. Then (or perhaps before
then) you rewrite many small chunks of code to make it perform reasonably
well.

# 9

# Alternative Representations

Throughout the early chapters, we paid attention to the problem of representing one kind of object by another. In the previous chapter, we wrote prototype programs dealing with scalars and sequences, not worrying about their representations. It's time to deal with representation issues at the level of programming languages. The emphasis of the chapter is expressed by the title: we're not satisfied with finding some representation; we want to find some *good* representation, and it turns out that no one representation is best for all situations.

We'll go through increasingly complex issues of representation, most of which have been encountered before somewhere. We can represent a Boolean value by a cardinal number, we can represent a character (or any other enumerated type) by a cardinal, we can represent a cardinal by an integer, and so on. In each case we find that the *Ab*straction function has to throw some information away, and the inverse *Re*presentation function has some arbitrary choices to make, and therefore that a test for equality on abstract objects is an equivalence relation (but usually not equality) on their representations. In order to choose a good representation (i.e., one which allows you to translate and ask your questions cheaply), you need a feeling for the range of representations which will work.

The same kind of issue occurs when we go from sequences, to bags, to sets: the equations may look quite different because they're inductive, but the *Ab*straction still throws information away, and *Re*presentation still has to decide what to put back.

None of that helps much when we want to represent cardinals by Booleans, or integers by cardinals, or real numbers by integers, or "Employees" by the types we have defined or can enumerate. Here we need to record several aspects of each abstract object we want: a cardinal is a Cartesian product (or just a sequence) of Booleans (or digits), an integer is a Cartesian product of a Boolean sign and a cardinal magnitude, and so on. Recording such attributes is straightforward because almost all the programming languages you will use have specific constructs called RECORDs for dealing with Cartesian products. Now the *Abstraction* function is hiding information about several objects at once, and the programmer designing a *Representation* function has to decide how many objects to use in her representation as well as what values to give each.

In dealing with sequences, a number of quite complicated issues come up. Frequently it's not that we have sequences and want to represent bags, but that we have sequences which behave in one way and we want to represent sequences which behave in another way. For example, the most common kind of sequence in most programming languages is the array, a sequence whose size is determined before you ever begin putting values into it. The reason is simple: most computers are designed so that the physical memory itself is viewed as such a sequence. The *Modula-2* moron begins work by letting all of that space "belong" to a module called Storage; other programs can then (implicitly or explicitly) request fixed-size chunks, which they can then use for values. You can think of an array as an abstract sequence, or as a function from an enumeration into some type, or as a collection of variables; this last is quite important, because it turns out to be useful to let array locations serve as VAR parameters at times.

Most generators, filters, and even simple operations like concatenation are obviously going to be impossible with sequences of fixed length, but it turns out that we can avoid the problem by using sequences of fixed length as storage places for sequences of varying length. Many such schemes are possible, and a few of them will be covered. Most of these are only good for "flat" sequences: sequences of scalars, or at least sequences whose depth of nesting is known in advance. However, some are so flexible that they can be used for trees without much trouble.

## 9.1 SIMPLE REPRESENTATION MAPPINGS: EQUIVALENCE RELATIONS

Suppose you have some information which you need to store or process in some way. The basic idea of a representation is that *some* of the information in the representation is used to cover *all* the information you need to represent.

**Q:** But that can't be true: if I draw a map to represent Antarctica, it seems to me that *all* of the information on the map is being used to represent *part* of my information about Antarctica.

**A:** No, you're not using all of the information on the map: a map of Antarctica has a certain color scheme and a certain thickness of paper, but another map with different colors and thickness might convey exactly the same information.

Furthermore, the rest of your information about Antarctica is simply not in the model: if there is nothing there about the thickness of the ice, then ice thickness is not part of the problem. You're not storing it, so you'd better not be planning on processing it. If you want to store it or process it, put it on the map.

Normally, this means that many different representations are equivalent as models: many sequences can represent the same bag, many bags can represent the same set, many cardinals can represent the same boolean value. In this section, we'll use representations of this "simplification" kind: the abstract objects are actually simpler than some kind of object you already have, so you can represent it through some equivalence relation on that kind of object.

### 9.1.1 Simple Representations Using "Scalars"

Suppose that we want to represent the Boolean values *True* and *False* by the cardinal numbers 0 and 1.

**Q:** Why? We already have the Boolean values; they're basic in the language.
**A:** Well, suppose that we had a very incomplete implementation of the language, which doesn't happen to include conjunction, disjunction, or negation. Conditional statements are made from a fixed set of comparisons, like

```
IF x=y THEN ... ELSE ... END
IF x#y THEN ... ELSE ... END
IF x>y THEN ... ELSE ... END .
```

(As we'll see in Chapter 10, that really is the case at the conventional machine level.) The question is, How can we add the ordinary operations?

From the first chapter, we already know how to do this from a mathematical perspective: we define functions *Ab* and *Rep*, and translate all the operations on Boolean values into operations on the cardinal numbers which represent them. For example,

$$Rep(p \wedge q) = (Rep(p) \min Rep(q))$$

From a programmer's point of view, we want to apply this idea so that we can have programs written as if the Boolean values were primitive: we want to provide a "module" which will define the **TYPE** CBool with values CTrue and CFalse and the operations CAnd, COr, and CNot satisfying the normal properties of Boolean algebra. It's very simple: we write a DEFINITION MODULE which describes the requirements, and an IMPLEMENTATION MODULE which achieves them, as shown in Figures 9.1 and 9.2.

DEFINITION MODULE CBoolean;
    (* Provide the type CBoolean, satisfying Boolean algebra rules *)

EXPORT CBoolean, CTrue, CFalse, CAnd, COr, CNot;

TYPE CBoolean;

VAR CTrue, CFalse : CBoolean;

PROCEDURE CAnd(x,y:CBoolean):CBoolean;
(* post: result = $x \wedge y$ *)

PROCEDURE COr(x,y:CBoolean):CBoolean;
(* post: result = $x \vee y$ *)

PROCEDURE CNot(x:CBoolean):CBoolean;
(* post: result = $\neg x$ *)

PROCEDURE CGtr(x,y:CARDINAL):CBoolean;
(* post: result = $x > y$ *)

PROCEDURE CEq(x,y:CARDINAL):CBoolean;
(* post: result = $x = y$ *)

END CBoolean.

**Figure 9.1**

A programmer can then import any of the objects in the export clause without knowing or caring how they were defined. She can then write prefix expressions like

**if** COr(CGtr(x,y), CAnd(CNot(CEq(y+1,z)), p)) = CTrue **then**  ...

which looks ugly, but is equivalent to

**if** $(x > y) \vee (\neg(y + 1 = z) \wedge p)$ **then**  ...

**Q:** I can see how to use it, but your program doesn't even say that the TYPE CBoolean is to be represented by cardinal numbers, and it doesn't mention what CTrue and CFalse are.

**A:** That's right. The specification module just says what is being represented; only the implementation module (e.g., in Figure 9.2) knows what the representation is.

Study it carefully; you should be able to see that there are many ways of writing the implementation module which would have satisfied the requirements of the specification module.

### Exercise

**9.1-1**    Redefine the implementation module so that $x \wedge y$ is implemented as $x * y$, $\neg p$ is implemented as $1 - p$, and $x \vee y$ is implemented as $(x + y) - (x * y)$.

In languages like *Modula-2*, an implementation change such as that of the previous exercise could be carried out without even recompiling the module with the IMPORT statements. The specification has not changed, so the programmer who IMPORTed the specified procedures need not know that they are now realized in a different way.

In fact, we didn't have to make CTrue and CFalse be 1 and 0; the implementation module could have ended with CTrue:=0; CFalse:=1; or even CTrue:=96; CFalse:=37;. As long as they are different values, the idea would work. In other circumstances, it's desirable to make CTrue be greater than CFalse, but we've made no use of that here.

### Exercise

**9.1-2**    Redo the previous exercise so that $\wedge, \vee, \neg$ are implemented as arithmetic operations, but CTrue is represented by 0 and CFalse by 1. [Hint: This is quite trivial if looked at correctly.]

IMPLEMENTATION MODULE CBoolean;

TYPE CBoolean = [0..1]
   (* or CBoolean = CARDINAL, but let's be precise *)

PROCEDURE CAnd(x,y:CBoolean):CBoolean;
  (* post: result = $x \wedge y$ *)
  BEGIN
    IF x=CTrue THEN RETURN(y); ELSE RETURN(x); END;
END CAnd;

PROCEDURE COr(x,y:CBoolean):CBoolean;
  (* post: result = $x \vee y$ *)
  BEGIN
    IF x=CTrue THEN RETURN(x); ELSE RETURN(y); END;
END CAnd;

PROCEDURE CNot(x:CBoolean):CBoolean;
  (* post: result = $\neg x$ *)
  BEGIN
    IF x=CTrue THEN RETURN(CFalse); ELSE RETURN(CTrue); END;
END CAnd;

PROCEDURE CGtr(x,y:CARDINAL):CBoolean;
  (* post: result = $x > y$ *)
  BEGIN
    IF x>y THEN RETURN(CTrue); ELSE RETURN(CFalse); END;
END CAnd;

PROCEDURE CEq(x,y:CARDINAL):CBoolean;
  (* post: result = $x = y$ *)
  BEGIN
    IF x=y THEN RETURN(CTrue); ELSE RETURN(CFalse); END;
END CAnd;

BEGIN
  CTrue := 1;
  CFalse := 0;
  END CBoolean .

**Figure 9.2** CBoolean: Cardinals representing Booleans

Thinking about the code given, you should also be able to see that the solution does not protect anyone from the malicious or too-clever programmer: since CTrue and CFalse are defined as variables, it is possible for the programmer to write CTrue := CFalse. Still, we have gained a lot: it is also possible for the programmer to go on using these values correctly, with no concern for their implementation.

### 9.1.2 Enumerations and Representations

Like most languages of its family, *Modula-2* provides somewhat more elegant ways to handle the CBoolean representation problem; the best is probably to define

TYPE CBoolean = (CFalse,CTrue);

which, as an *enumeration*, will implicitly define

$$
\begin{aligned}
ORD(CFalse) &= 0 \\
ORD(CTrue) &= 1 \\
VAL(CBoolean, 0) &= CFalse \\
VAL(CBoolean, 1) &= CTrue
\end{aligned}
$$

Here and in all *Modula-2* enumerations, $ORD$ is a special *Representation* function and $VAL$ is an *Abstraction*. It follows that

$$
\begin{aligned}
VAL(CBoolean, ORD(x)) &= x, && \text{if } x : CBoolean \\
ORD(VAL(CBoolean, i)) &= i, && \text{if } 0 \le i \le | CBoolean | -1
\end{aligned}
$$

**Exercises**    Assume that the specification above is changed so that CBoolean = (CFalse,CTrue). CFalse and CTrue are evidently no longer variable names and cannot be assigned; they are constants like TRUE and 17.

**9.1-3**    The implementation can now catch your error if you try to change CFalse or CTrue; when could that happen without malice on your part? [Hint: Think about VAR parameters.]

**9.1-4**    With this new representation, what needs to be changed in the implementation module given?

**9.1-5**    Repeat the exercise of implementing the logical operations with arithmetic ones, such as $\wedge$ with $*$. [Hint: Use ORD.]

Other enumerations can also be represented by cardinals (or ranges of cardinals) in the same way: characters of the *ASCII* set, days of the week, months of the year, employee classifications, and so on. In each case, the ORD and VAL operations will carry us back and forth between the items and their ordering.

**Exercises**

**9.1-6**    Specify and implement modules for an enumeration type giving the days of the
week with the predicate IsWorkDay which will be *True* for Monday...Friday but
*False* otherwise, and the successor function NextWorkDay, which carries us from
Monday to Tuesday, from Tuesday to Wednesday, ... and from Friday to Monday.

**9.1-7**    Specify and implement modules for enumeration types giving the months of the
year as the enumeration (January...December) and the seasons as (Spring...Winter)
with the Season function which finds the correct season for each month (e.g., Sea-
son(December)=Winter), and the DaysIn function, which finds the number of
days in a given month, ignoring leap-year issues. [Hint: DaysIn should be a CASE
statement.]

The ORD and VAL operations are obviously useful, but they weren't included
in the original CBoolean specification. To add *Ab* and *Rep* operations which take 0
and 1 to CTrue and CFalse is quite trivial:

```
PROCEDURE Ab(n : CARDINAL) : CBoolean;
(* pre : 0 <= n <= 1 *)
(* post : result = if n=1 then CTrue else CFalse *)
BEGIN IF n=1 THEN RETURN(CTrue) ELSE RETURN(CFalse) END ;
END ;
```

**Exercise**

**9.1-8**    Write the *Rep* procedure to go with *Ab*, and add both to your specification and
implementation modules.

### 9.1.3 Multiple Representations

It is perfectly legitimate to represent CTrue by all the numbers except 0, or by all
the odd numbers, or by all the prime numbers; this kind of solution is sometimes
necessary, but it always causes some trouble. If we accepted every odd number as
*True* and every even number as *False*, we could still implement $p \wedge q$ as $p * q$, and
we could implement $\neg p$ as $p + 1$. In effect, we would be choosing

$$\begin{aligned} Ab(n) &= True, & \text{if } odd(n) \\ &= False, & \text{otherwise} \end{aligned}$$

*Rep* is now no longer uniquely defined: we can choose $Rep(True) = 1$ or $Rep(True) =$
57; it just doesn't matter. Now we've lost the ability to say $x = CTrue$ or $x =$

$CFalse$ or even $x = y$, for CBoolean values. The specification has changed, and the program which imports the type CBoolean would have to change, but the change would not be hard to introduce. We would represent the test $x = CTrue$ with $IsTrue(x)$ as a predicate on CBoolean values. We would represent $x = CFalse$ with another predicate, $IsFalse(x)$. More generally, we would represent $x = y$ on CBooleans with $Equal(x, y)$, where

$$
\begin{aligned}
IsTrue(x) &= Equal(x, CTrue) \\
IsFalse(x) &= Equal(x, CFalse) \\
Equal(x, y) &= (mod(x, 2) = mod(y, 2))
\end{aligned}
$$

$Equal$ is an equivalence relation on the cardinals just as $Perm$ was an equivalence relation on sequences, which gave us the conception of bags. In the Boolean case, we don't seem to gain anything for the extra confusion, because it's just as easy to have a unique cardinal value representing each Boolean value just by choosing 1 to represent CTrue and 0 to represent CFalse.

**Q:** It sounds like you're saying that you've got to choose the right representation at the beginning: if I decided that all odd numbers would be *True* and all even numbers would be *False*, then I could go on trying to fix up my definitions forever but they would never be as good as if I'd done it with TYPE  CBoolean = (CTrue, CFalse).

**A:** That can be true in some cases, but not in this one. If you think hard enough about an unnecessarily complex representation, you can be led to a simpler one. In many cases, a way to get a unique representation (so that $Equal$ on the type CBoolean will be = on CARDINALs) is to think about the $Equal$ relation. If it simplifies objects (by $mod(n, 2)$) and then compares them, we can simplify them in advance: if we take each number $Rep(p)$ and replace it with $mod(Rep(p), 2)$, then we'll always end up with the number 1 representing *True* and the number 0 representing *False*.

**Q:** Could you run that by two or three more times?

**A:** Sure. We've just been saying that 5 and 3 represent *True* under this idea, and 4 and 220 represent *False*, and $*$ represents $\wedge$ because $x * y$ is odd (represents *True*) exactly when $x$ and $y$ are both odd (represent *True*). The distribution of *mod* over multiplication and addition tells you that to ask whether $5 * 3$ is odd is the same as to ask whether $mod(5, 2) * mod(3, 2)$ is odd:

$$
mod(mod(5, 2) * mod(3, 2), 2) = mod(5 * 3, 2)
$$

In other words, when you have an object that is just a *Rep*resentation of an object like CTrue, you should think about changing it to be the simplest or smallest *Rep*resentation of the same object.

### 9.1.4 More Numbers

To represent a cardinal, we can use a nonnegative integer; to represent an integer, we can use a real (floating-point) number. The representation is almost trivial in each case, but not quite. If we represent cardinals with integers, we must watch out for negative values; thus, $Subtract(x, y)$ might have to make sure that $x \geq y$ before performing $x - y$ as an integer operation. The $Ab$ and $Rep$ functions here are just a change in the point of view. *Modula-2* allows "type transfer" between cardinals and integers, so that if $c$ is a cardinal number, then INTEGER(c) is the corresponding integer. Similarly, if $i$ is a nonnegative integer, then CARDINAL(i) is the corresponding cardinal. There is nothing much surprising about that; the only question would be whether CARDINAL should try to do something with negative integers, such as produce their absolute values.

### Exercises

**9.1-9** Write conditional equations for the inverse relationship between the transfer functions CARDINAL and INTEGER.

**9.1-10** Argue for and against having CARDINAL($-5$) produce the cardinal number 5.

In representing a cardinal with a real number, we have a larger conceptual gap with more problems. We can almost get by with representing division by division, but we have to truncate the result somehow. In effect, $Trunc(n) = n - mod(n, 1)$, if *mod* is calculated in the way we have discussed so many times. TRUNC is provided in *Modula-2* and other languages as an operation which takes a real number and produces the corresponding cardinal, throwing away some information; thus TRUNC(3.14159)=3. TRUNC is thus an *Ab*straction operation, with the corresponding *Rep*resentation produced by FLOAT; FLOAT(3)=3.0. As you might expect,

$$\begin{aligned} TRUNC(FLOAT(n)) &= n, \text{ but} \\ FLOAT(TRUNC(n)) &\sim n, \text{ although} \\ FLOAT(TRUNC(FLOAT(n))) &= FLOAT(n) \end{aligned}$$

### Exercise

**9.1-11** State when the "$\sim$" of the second rule will be "$=$".

Here FLOAT cannot be more than a partial inverse for TRUNC, because it cannot create the information which TRUNC throws away. Once more, we have an abstraction which interprets many different real numbers as the same cardinal:

$$Equal(x, y) = (TRUNC(x) = TRUNC(y))$$

**Exercise**

**9.1-12** Write a specification and implementation for the cardinal numbers, to be represented by (prefix functions on) real numbers.

In each of these representation problems, we've seen one simple type used to represent another, even simpler, type. The same idea crops up with aggregate objects: if type $X$ is simpler than type $Y$, then we can represent objects of type $X$ by objects of type $Y$ and implement the corresponding operations. Equality on type $X$ will turn out to be an equivalence relation on type $Y$.

### 9.1.5  Simple Representations with Aggregates

We have already described the representations of bags by sequences and of sets by bags; given the type IntSeq, it is perfectly simple to write the specification in Figure 9.3.

DEFINITION MODULE IntBags;
(* provides bag-of-integer abstraction *)
TYPE Bag;

EXPORT NewBag, AddItem, EqualBag, Max, Min, DeleteItem, Count;

PROCEDURE NewBag():Bag;
(* post: result = [[]] *)

PROCEDURE EqualBag(VAR A,B:Bag):BOOLEAN;
(* post: result = (A=B) *)

**Figure 9.3** Bags of Integers

The programmer who wants to use bags can go right ahead and use them from this specification; inside the implementation module, it would be admitted that

TYPE Bag = IntSeqs.IntSeq;

and that $NewBag() = IntSeqs.NewNull()$, while $EqualBag(A, B) = Perm(A, B)$.

**Exercises**

**9.1-13** Complete the specification and implementation modules for *Bag*.

**9.1-14** Without changing the specification module, modify the implementation module so that a bag is always represented by an ordered sequence. *NewBag()* =

*IntSeq.NewNull*() is still true, but

$$Bag.AddItem(x, A) = IntSeq.InsertItem(x, A)$$

because to add an item to an ordered sequence, we have to find the right place for it. *AddItem* has thus become more complicated, but *Min*, *Max*, and *EqualBag* will all be simpler. For example, $Min(B) = IntSeq.Hd(B)$. For each of your modified procedures, discuss the change in cost.

**9.1-15** Write specification and implementation modules for *Set* based on the type *IntSeq*.

**9.1-16** Without changing the specification module of the previous problem, modify the implementation module to base it on the type *Bag*. Discuss the change in cost if *Bag* is revised as above.

**9.1-17** Again without changing the specification module, modify the implementation module so that a set is always represented by an ordered sequence without repetition. Discuss the cost.

### 9.1.6  Representations within Structures

We can now represent Boolean values by cardinal numbers, or characters by numbers, and we have been using a type IntSeq which is limited to use with integers. How can we develop sequences of Booleans or of characters? It's actually reasonably simple, as shown in Figure 9.4.

SPECIFICATION MODULE CBoolSeq;

(* provides the type CBoolSeq, with the normal sequence operations *)

FROM CBoolean IMPORT CBoolean;

EXPORT CBoolSeq, NewNull, IsNull, AddItem, Hd, Tl, . . .;

TYPE CBoolSeq;

PROCEDURE NewNull() : CBoolSeq;
(* post : result = [], an empty sequence of CBoolean values *)

PROCEDURE Hd(S : CBoolSeq) : CBoolean;
(* pre : Length(S) $\geq$ 1 *)
(* post : result = S[1] *)

**Figure 9.4** Sequences of CBooleans

In the implementation module, we just have to IMPORT IntSeqs to get all the sequence operations, and probably IMPORT CBooleans as well, and then use them to define things correctly. Some operations, like Hd and AddItem, will be trivial:

PROCEDURE Hd(S : CBoolSeq) : CBoolean;
BEGIN RETURN IntSeqs.Hd(S); END Hd;

Others are closely related to sequence operations, but require some thought:

PROCEDURE AllTrue(S : CBoolSeq) : CBoolean;
    BEGIN
        IF IsNull(S) THEN RETURN CTrue
            ELSE RETURN IntSeqs.Min(S);
        END ;
END AllTrue;

**Q:** But what if *Min* doesn't happen to be exported by the IntSeqs module?

**A:** So *add* it already! Of course, you can work entirely within the CBoolSeq framework, and specify

$$
\begin{aligned}
AllTrue(S) &= IsNull([b \in S : b = False]) \\
           &= True, &&\text{if } S = [\,] \\
           &= False, &&\text{if } Head(S) = False \\
           &= AllTrue(Tail(S)), &&\text{otherwise}
\end{aligned}
$$

If you write that, you will have achieved the capability you wanted—and nothing else. If instead you define *IntSeqs.Min* and use it to produce *AllTrue*, you will have done a very small amount of extra work now and saved yourself doing similar tasks within the *CBoolSeq* module, the *Bag* module, the *Set* module, and quite a few others.

**Q:** I see... you want me always to solve every problem in the most general way possible.

**A:** That's almost it. I want you always to *plan* the most general solution possible, and usually to write some quite general solution as your first version. It won't be the last. When you write and rewrite later versions, you will often find that specialization leads to better control of behavior as well as higher efficiency. Generality leads to more reusable code, which means you can finish that first draft sooner, with less debugging effort and a higher confidence level because the same code has already been used in other applications.

Implementing *Hd* required no thought at all; implementing *AllTrue* required a little bit. Still others, like *ReadSequence* and *WriteSequence*, would need to be changed substantially, but all would be easier because we already had the IntSeq type.

## Exercises

**9.1-18** Complete and implement the CBoolSeq modules, including only the operations NewNull, CreateN, AddItem, Head, Tail, Put, Get, Swap, Length, IsNull, EqSeq, and Find.

**9.1-19** Add the operations AllTrue, AllFalse, CountTrue, and CountFalse, where

$$CountTrue(S) = \|\{i : S[i] = \text{CTrue}\}\|$$

and the others work analogously.

**9.1-20** Copy the code for IntSeqs.WriteSeq, and then adapt it so that it prints out readable CBoolean values, e.g., "[CTrue, CFalse, CFalse]" when given the numeric sequence [1,0,0].

The next task is to represent strings as sequences of characters, with each character being represented by a cardinal number. This is no problem at all: the CharSeq definition module will export operations on character sequences $[c_1 \ldots c_n]$, and the implementation module will keep track of cardinal sequences $[ORD(c_1) \ldots ORD(c_n)]$; thus, the implementation module will say that the type CharSeq = Sequence, and we have

```
PROCEDURE Hd(S : CharSeq): CHAR;
   (* pre : Length(S) >= 1 *)
   (* post : result = S[1] *)
   BEGIN RETURN(CHR(IntSeqs.Hd(S))) END Hd;
```

## Exercises

**9.1-21** Finish the CharSeq modules, including only the operations NewNull, CreateN, AddItem, Hd, Tl, AddItem, Put, Get, Swap, Length, IsNull, EqSeq, Find.

**9.1-22** Add the operations AllBlank and CountBlanks where

$$CountBlanks(S) = |\{i : S[i] = \text{' '}\}|$$

and the others work analogously.

**9.1-23** Add the operations WriteCharSeq and ReadCharSeq, adapted to print out and read in string values, e.g., "**abcde**" $\leftrightarrow$ [97,98,99,100,101]
You can define ReadCharSeq with the preconditions $input = [qc] + X + [qc] + S$ and $\neg(qc \in X)$ and the postconditions $result = X$ and $input = S$. The "quotation character" $qc$ can thus be any $ASCII$ character which doesn't occur in the string being quoted.

**9.1-24** Add FindPat to the IntSeqs module, so that you can import it for characters here.

## 9.2 COMPOUND STRUCTURE: CARTESIAN PRODUCTS

These representation operations are quite useful, but they are in rather the wrong direction. We are now able to represent simpler objects by the use of more complex objects; we still have the problem of building up more complex objects out of simpler ones. How can we do this?

The basic idea is to represent "aspects" or "attributes" of the complex objects we need, using collections of the objects we have. The basic tools are the sequence, as a variable-size collection of objects of a fixed type, and the Cartesian product, as a fixed collection of objects of various types. As before, we will begin with simple constructions with numbers and Boolean values, and move up to sequences, bags, and sets.

### 9.2.1 Representing Cardinals

If we are given Boolean values and want to represent cardinal numbers, it's reasonable to treat the numbers as collections of digits. This is how an electronic computer does it: a number is a sequence of on-off switches, and operations on numbers are encoded as circuits.

**Q:** But sequences already involve cardinal numbers as indices. This is circular!
**A:** Not necessarily. We can represent a sequence of eight elements by using separate names for separate variables $b_0, b_2, \ldots, b_7$. We can explicitly indicate the dependencies of each variable, just as we did back in Chapter 2. We can have a cluster of such variables lumped together and call it a RECORD, as in Figure 9.5. $b_0$ represents the binary digit in the units place (to be multiplied by $2^{**}0 = 1$), and $b_7$ represents the bit in the 128s place (to be multiplied by $2^{**}7 = 128$). If all of them are *False*, then the number is 0; if all are *True*, then the number is 255. We give a name to this maximal value: call it $MaxCard8$. It is precisely analogous to the upper limit on CARDINAL values provided by *Modula-2*; this upper limit will also be a number of the form $2^{**}N - 1$, and for the same reason.

Of course, if we want to convert from the cluster into a CARDINAL as the *Modula-2* language represents it, it is convenient to use cardinals, but these are for partial results rather than for indexing. (It's still cheating, but we'll deal with it shortly.)

Of course, it would be a good idea to avoid using CARDINALs, as the language provides them in the implementation of the operations on Card8 objects. For example, we can have the procedure *Incr*, as in Figure 9.6, which increments the number represented by a Card8 variable.

TYPE Card8 = RECORD b0,b1,b2,b3,b4,b5,b6,b7 : BOOLEAN; END;

PROCEDURE Card8ToCard(n : Card8) : CARDINAL;
  (* post : result = $Sum(\{2^{**}i : n.b_i\})$ *)
  VAR r,wgt : CARDINAL;
  BEGIN
    r := 0; wgt := 1;
    IF n.b0 THEN r := r + wgt; END ; wgt := Double(wgt);
    (* k = 1 => wgt = $2^{**}k$, r = $Sum(\{2^{**}i : i < k, n.b_i\})$ *)
    IF n.b1 THEN r := r + wgt; END ; wgt := Double(wgt);
    (* k = 2 => wgt = $2^{**}k$, r = $Sum(\{2^{**}i : i < k, n.b_i\})$ *)
    IF n.b2 THEN r := r + wgt; END ; wgt := Double(wgt);
    (* k = 3 => wgt = $2^{**}k$, r = $Sum(\{2^{**}i : i < k, n.b_i\})$ *)
    $\vdots$
    IF n.b7 THEN r := r + wgt; END ;
    (* k = 8 => wgt = $2^{**}(k\text{-}1)$, r = $Sum(\{2^{**}i : i < k, n.b_i\})$ *)
END Card8ToCard;

PROCEDURE CardToCard8(r : CARDINAL; n : Card8);
  (* post : $result.b_i$ = (1 = Digit(r,i,2)) *)
  BEGIN
    n.b0 := (1 = (r mod 2)); r := r div 2;
    n.b1 := (1 = (r mod 2)); r := r div 2;
    n.b2 := (1 = (r mod 2)); r := r div 2;
    (* k=3 =>$(i < k => n.b_i = (1 = Digit(r,i,2)), r = r_0 div 2^{**}k$ *)
    $\vdots$
    n.b7 := (1 = (r mod 2));
END CardToCard8;

**Figure 9.5** Eight-Bit Cardinals as RECORDs

```
PROCEDURE Incr(VAR n : Card8);
  (* pre : Ab(n) < MaxCard8 *)
  (* post : Ab(n) = 1+Ab(n₀) *)
  VAR c:Card8;
  BEGIN
    c.b0 := TRUE ;
    c.b1 := c.b0 AND n.b0; n.b0 := (c.b0 # n.b0);
    c.b2 := c.b1 AND n.b1; n.b1 := (c.b1 # n.b1);
    c.b3 := c.b2 AND n.b2; n.b2 := (c.b2 # n.b2);
    ⋮
    c.b7 := c.b6 AND n.b6; n.b6 := (c.b6 # n.b6);
    (* if c.b7 AND n.b7 then pre-condition was not satisfied: ERROR *)
    n.b7 := (c.b7 # n.b7);
  END Incr;
```

**Figure 9.6** Incrementing Eight-Bit Cardinals

## Exercises

**9.2-1**  Write an assertion to go after the line c.b3 :=.... Make sure that it describes the state adequately: e.g.,

$$c.b3 = n_0.b0 \wedge n_0.b1 \wedge n_0.b2$$

is a good start, but not very general.

**9.2-2**  Write and document the procedure Decr, which decrements the number represented by a Card8 variable.

**9.2-3**  Write and document the procedure IsZero(n:Card8):BOOLEAN, which tests if a given Card8 number represents 0.

**9.2-4**  Write and document the procedure Add(n,m:Card8; VAR r:Card8) which finds the "sum" of a pair of Card8 numbers, provided that this sum is less than 256; your procedure should use *Incr* and *Decr* to follow the specification

$$
\begin{aligned}
Add(n, m) &= n, & \text{if } m = 0 \\
&= Add(n + 1, m - 1) & \text{otherwise}
\end{aligned}
$$

**9.2-5**  Rewrite and document Add so that it determines the sum by an explicit series of statements n.b0 :=..., n.b1:=.... You will need an explicit Boolean carry variable $C$ such that

$$C_0 = \text{FALSE}, C_{i+1} = \textbf{if } C_i \textbf{ then } n.i \wedge m.i \textbf{ else } n.i \vee m.i$$

Once you have numbers in a limited range, such as the $Card8$ numbers in the range $0 \ldots 255$, it is possible to use them to represent larger numbers in several ways.

A cardinal number of $N$ digits can be modeled by a sequence of digits, indexed by numbers in the range $1 \ldots N$, which have $log(N, 2)$ binary digits. That means that if we have somehow modeled four-bit numbers, with values in the range $0 \ldots 15$, we can therefore use these to model 15-bit numbers, with values in the range $0 \ldots 32,000$. These, in turn, can be used to model numbers as large as we are likely to want.

It is also possible to represent a cardinal of $2*D$ digits using two cardinals with $D$ digits. Suppose that you know that the maximal cardinal your system can handle is $MaxCard$, which happens to be $2**D - 1$. Then you can represent numbers up to $MaxLongCard$, which will be $2**(2 * D) - 1$ by defining

$$
\begin{aligned}
Ab(n) &= n.left * 2**D + n.right \\
Rep(n).left &= div(n, 2**D) \\
Rep(n).right &= mod(n, 2**D)
\end{aligned}
$$

and then writing the following procedures:

```
TYPE LongCard = RECORD left,right:CARDINAL END;

PROCEDURE Incr(VAR n:LongCard);
   (* pre: Abs(n) < MaxLongCard *)
   (* post: Abs(n) = 1 + Abs(n0) *)
   BEGIN
      IF n.right = MaxCard THEN n.right := 0; INC(n.left);
            ELSE INC(n.right); END ;
END Incr;
```

### Exercises

**9.2-6**   Write Decr to decrement a LongCard variable.

**9.2-7**   Write Add to add a pair of LongCard variables.

### 9.2.2  Other Kinds of Numbers

An integer has two attributes: sign and magnitude. 539 and 79 are both positive, but have different magnitudes. 539 and $-539$ have the same magnitudes, but different signs. The two attributes are the answers to the questions "Are you nonnegative?" and "How big are you?". We will therefore consider the integer type to be represented by a Boolean sign which is *True* for positive numbers and for 0, and *False* for negatives. The sign of 78 is *True*, and its magnitude is 78; the sign of 0 is *True*, and its magnitude is 0; the sign of $-78$ is *False*, and its magnitude is 78. The type is given by

> TYPE Int = RECORD sign:BOOLEAN; magnitude:CARDINAL; END;

We can now write *IntToINTEGER* and *INTEGERToInT*, so that

$$
\begin{array}{rcll}
IntToINTEGER(n) & = & INTEGER(n.magnitude) & \text{if } n.sign \\
 & = & -INTEGER(n.magnitude) & \text{otherwise} \\
INTEGERToInt(i).sign & = & i \geq 0 & \\
INTEGERToInt(i).magnitude & = & CARDINAL(Abs(i)) &
\end{array}
$$

With these as guides, we can now write operations on the Int type to simulate INTEGER operations while making use only of CARDINAL arithmetic. For example, we can look at the Incr operation:

```
PROCEDURE Incr(VAR n:Int);
  (* post: Ab(n) = 1 + Ab(n0) *)
  BEGIN
    IF n.sign THEN INC(n.magnitude);
      ELSIF n.magnitude = 1 THEN DEC(n.magnitude); n.sign := TRUE;
      ELSE DEC(n.magnitude);
    END ;
END Incr;
```

**Exercises**

**9.2-8**   Write and document Decr, Add, and Mul for type Int.

**9.2-9**   Write and document Sub and Div for type Int.

**9.2-10**  Define and document the Rational type, with operations Add, Sub, Div and Mul as described in the second chapter.

**9.2-11**  Define and document the Real number type, with the same operations as for Rational.

**Q:** Is that really how the computer represents integers?

**A:** Not usually; this is one of the options, but not the best for most purposes. Instead of a separate sign bit and a recognizable magnitude, it is common to represent integers as a different structure of Boolean values $b0, b1, \ldots bN$. Without going into it in detail, we can give a decimal analogy.

Suppose that we are going to represent integers by sequences of 3 decimal digits: 000 will represent 0, 001, 002, ... 499 will represent positive numbers, and any negative number $-i : 1 \leq i \leq 500$ will be represented by $1000-i$, i.e. by $999-i+1$. $-1$ is thus represented by 999; $-2$ is represented by 998, $-13$ is represented by 987, $-314$ is represented by 686, $-493$ is represented by 507, $-500$ is represented by 500, and $-501$ has no representation. We can count down from 10: 010, 009, 008, 007, 006, 005, 004, 003, 002, 001, 000, 999, 998, 997, . . . .

**Q:** I guess I can see how to do it, but I don't see that it makes any sense.

**A:** We can then use the fact that $x - y = x + (-y)$ to do subtraction by doing addition.

**Q:** Huh?

**A:** Sure: to find $213-046$, we first find $-046 = 953+1 = 954$; now we add 213 + 954 and get . . . hmm, we get a number larger than 999. In fact, we get exactly 1000 more than the answer we want: 1167. If we now throw away the 1000, we will end up with 167, which is the right answer.

**Q:** This is sheer magic.

**A:** Not at all. Remember that $-i$ is represented by the cardinal $1000 - i$; if we want to find $a - b$, one way of doing it is to find $a + (1000 - b)$ and then throw away the inevitable leftmost digit. Subtraction works, and so does negation (which is only subtraction from 0): $--i$ is represented by $-(1000-i)$, which is represented by $1000 - (1000 - i)$, which is $i$. It's also important to check that 0 is the same as $-0$, which is $1000 - 0$, which is correct after we throw away the leftmost digit. Stop now and do a few examples this way: if we want to subtract 236 from $-73$, we write

$$927 - 236 = 927 + 764 = 1691 = 691$$

which represents $-309$.

## Exercises

**9.2-12** Find $444-75$ this way.

**9.2-13** Find $-444-75$ this way.

**9.2-14** Find $57-75$ this way.

**Q:** All right, it's not magic, but it's still silly because in order to do a subtraction you end up doing a subtraction and an addition; you've only made things worse.

**A:** That would be true if we didn't have a special way to find $1000 - i$ for any cardinal in the range $0 . . . 499$. But we do have a special method for it, because $1000 - i = 999 - i + 1$, and we know how to find $999 - i$ for any three-digit number. Just change the digits 0123456789 to 987654321 respectively, and then increment. In order to find $-379$, change the 3 to 6, the 7 to 2, and the 9 to 0; that gets us to 620. Add one and get 621, which is the right answer. In order to find $-(-379)$, i.e. −621, we change the 6 to 3, the 2 to 7, and the 1 to 8; that gets us to 378. Add one and get 379, which is the right answer.

**Q:** It sounds like magic to me. I can keep track of it as long as I'm thinking about nothing else, but if you asked me to solve a real problem using this kind of arithmetic I'd get totally lost.

**A:** That's reasonable, and that's why data representations have to be hidden. You should be able to work on objects of type INTEGER without worrying about how they are represented, and you should be able to work on objects of type Sequence or Employee or Expression without worrying about how they are represented.

If you want to represent a student as a record of variables representing first name, middle initial, last name, major, grade point average, date of birth, and so forth, you can. If you want to represent a car as a record of variables representing model, make, year, mileage, and so forth, you can do that. In each case you can create a module which defines the type and EXPORTs procedures which work on that type. Normally, only those procedures will care about the representation. Everybody else can use the procedures as black boxes which satisfy a specification. In fact, nobody else will notice if the representation is replaced by a new representation, as long as the procedures are simultaneously changed so that they will still look the same from the outside. That's what representation is all about.

## 9.3 REPRESENTING SEQUENCES BY SEQUENCES

One major gap remains in our treatment of elementary representation. We have filled chapters with operations on sequences, bags, and sets of objects, and we have shown how to represent bags and sets with sequences. However, we have defined sequences as variable-length constructions, like the words and sentences and paragraphs in a book. These are logical constructions, not physical ones. The physical representation of a sentence is somehow laid out on a page with a fixed number of lines, each line having a fixed number of columns. In order to achieve literacy, we have to look at the sequence of things in the physical book and find the subsequences which somehow represent the logical entities we need.

As humans, we use all kinds of cues: sentences begin with capital letters and end with periods, exclamation points, or question marks. A paragraph begins with indentation or just after an empty line, and ends at the beginning of the next paragraph. A chapter or section begins with some kind of emphasized title and number. On an envelope, we see addresses for which the street address is always found in one fixed position, the city and state right below it, and the zip code to the right of the state. A telephone-book entry is delimited in one way, a dictionary entry in quite another; we get used to all of them.

In conventional programming languages like *Modula-2*, the language includes primitives by which you can ask for a blank piece of paper of a given size; you are then responsible for keeping track of the logical sequences you use. Once you decide

on a method for doing this, you can then encapsulate it in a Sequence module such as
the one you've been using. The module will try to EXPORT procedures such as Put,
Get, Length, Hd, Tl, AddItem, Push, Pop, Find, ReadSequence, WriteSequence,
and so on. Sometimes the representation will make it easy to implement some of
those operations, but impossible to implement others; it won't be feasible for every
such module to EXPORT all of the procedures. The discussions will mostly be
oriented toward sorting and editing, but actually the examples are quite general in
their applicability. Life is full of sequences, and so is programming.

### 9.3.1 The Basic Array as Sequence Representation

The basic sequence construct provided by languages like *Modula-2* is the ARRAY.
Given a type Item for which we want to form sequences, and an arbitrary upper
limit on the length of a sequence, we can say

```
CONST MaxLen = 100;
TYPE Item = CARDINAL;
TYPE Index = [0..MaxLen+1]; (* Find can return 0, *)
      (* and we sometimes carry a loop one past its upper limit *)
TYPE FixedSeq = ARRAY [1..MaxLen] OF Item;
```

With these definitions, standard procedures like PutV and Get are fairly straightforward, as seen in Figure 9.7.

```
PROCEDURE PutV(VAR S : FixedSeq; i : Index; x :Item);
  (* pre : 1 ≤ i ≤ MaxLen *)
  (* post : S = Put(S₀,i,x) *)
  BEGIN S[i] := x; END PutV;

PROCEDURE Get(VAR S : FixedSeq; i : Index):Item;
  (* pre : 1 ≤ i ≤ MaxLen *)
  (* post : result = S[i] *)
  BEGIN RETURN(S[i]); END Get;

PROCEDURE Length(VAR S : FixedSeq):CARDINAL;
  (* post: result = Length(S) *)
  BEGIN RETURN(MaxLen); END Length;
```

**Figure 9.7** Fixed-Length Sequences

## Exercises

**9.3-1**    Write DEFINITION and IMPLEMENTATION modules for FixedSeq. What procedures should be EXPORTed?

**9.3-2**    Add the definition of SwapV(VAR S:FixedSeq;i,j:Index) to this module, as a procedure equivalent to S:=Swap(S,i,j).

**9.3-3**    Add the definitions of Min and Find, i.e., Min(S:FixedSeq; i,j:Index):Item, and Find(x:Item; S:FixedSeq; i,j:Index):Index.

The obvious problem is that all these sequences are of the same length MaxLen. What use is a QuickSort procedure that insists on a parameter of length 100 when you have a sequence of length 103 or 78? *Modula-2* has an extension appropriate for this and many other problems: the *open array parameter*. The assumption is that every array has a fixed length, indeed, a length which is fixed by the source text of the program and not variable at run time, but that nonetheless a procedure like those above may work on sequences of different lengths and just ask them how big they are. For example, we can write

```
PROCEDURE Sum(VAR A:ARRAY OF INTEGER):INTEGER;
   (* pre: A : ARRAY [L..H] OF INTEGER *)
   (* post: result = A[L]+A[L+1]+...A[H] *)
   VAR i,s : INTEGER;
   BEGIN
      s := 0;
      FOR i:= 0 TO HIGH(S) DO s:=s+A[i] (* s = A[L]+...+A[L+i] *) END
   END Sum;
```

Here there is some inevitable confusion: an array with an index range declared as [1..5] or as [5..9] or as [−2..2] will be seen by this procedure as having an index range [0..4]; the size of the array is fixed, but information about its beginning is lost. An internal reference to A[k] is like an outside reference to A[L+k], which can be confusing. It makes the comments a little bit hard to read in context, and also requires great caution in any redefinition of Sum into the form used in the previous exercises, with a beginning and ending index given explicitly. Let's try one:

```
PROCEDURE Sum(VAR A:ARRAY OF INTEGER;i,j:INTEGER):INTEGER;
   (* pre: A : ARRAY [L..H] OF INTEGER, A[i..j] a legal subrange of A *)
   (* post: result = A[i]+A[i+1]+...A[j] *)
   VAR k,s : INTEGER;
   BEGIN
      s := 0;
      FOR k:= i TO j DO s:=s+A[j] (* s = A[i]+...+A[k] *) END
   END Sum;
```

This has a major bug: $i$ and $j$ are going to be used as offsets, not as indices. Consequently, we *must* change the pre- and postconditions here:

(* pre: A : ARRAY [L..H] OF INTEGER, 0 <= i,j <= H-L *)
(* post: result = Sum(Take(1+j-i,Drop(i,A)))

In this particular case, we're changing the conditions—the specification—to match the code. Normally we do it the other way around, but here there's no way to implement the specification as it's given because there's no way for the Sum procedure to tell what the original meaning of A[i] was. It has to start with the beginning of A as A[0], because the language is defined that way.

Nonetheless, this is a very important language extension: a great many algorithms on arrays can be written with this technique which are very hard to manage without it. Sorting is perhaps the most important example, followed (for some programmers, preceded) by string manipulations. The WriteString procedure within InOut might be defined as

PROCEDURE WriteString(S:ARRAY OF CHAR);
   VAR i:CARDINAL;
   BEGIN FOR i:=0 TO HIGH(S) DO Write(S[i]) END
   END WriteString;

In fact, there's another part of the definition, which we'll get to later.

Even after this extension, it is not possible to perform any operation which changes the length of a sequence. Thus, we cannot define *AddItem* and *Tail* so that

$$Tail(AddItem(x, S)) = S$$

Similarly, we cannot define Take, Drop, Mid, Append, or any other operations which might produce sequences of length other than MaxLen. The problem is real, but many solutions are available. The simplest ones are based on the idea of keeping the logical sequence within a physical sequence, remembering the beginning and ending positions. The lowest-level solution would be to require that the procedures themselves remember the required information, and often this works nicely. If we want to write a procedure to *Take* the first $n$ items from $X$, we might have expected to write

Take(n,X,Y) == (Y := *Take(n,X)*)

Instead, we may say that $X$ is a physical sequence, and that the logical sequence we're interested in is some given subrange, say, $X[a \ldots b]$. We want to put the result in a $Y[c \ldots d]$, where $c$ is given and $d$ is a result of the computation, i.e., a VAR parameter. Thus we get the Take procedure with seven (yes, seven!) ugly parameters, as follows:

$$Take(n,X,Y,a,b,c,d) == Y[c..d] := Take(n,X[a..b])$$

The output parameters are thus $Y$ and $d$, but $X$ is also declared as a VAR parameter. As always, we write a first version (Take1) which is as close to the specification as possible and then edit it into a more economical form.

```
PROCEDURE Take1(n:CARDINAL; VAR X,Y:FixedSeq;
                    a,b,c:Index; VAR d:Index);
  (* pre: X[a ... b] and Y[c ... d'] are legal ranges, where *)
  (*      d' = Length(Take(X[a ... b])]) *)
  (* post: d = d', Y[c ... d] = Take(X[a ... b]) *)
  BEGIN
    IF a > b THEN d := c-1
      ELSE PutV(Y,c,Get(X,a)); Take1(n-1,X,Y, a+1,b,c+1,d);
    END
END Take1;

PROCEDURE Take2(n:CARDINAL; VAR X,Y:FixedSeq;
                    a,b,c:Index; VAR d:Index);
  (* pre: X[a ... b] and Y[c ... d'] are legal ranges, where *)
  (*      d' = Length(Take(X[a ... b])]) *)
  (* post: d = d', Y[c ... d] = Take(X[a ... b]) *)
  BEGIN
    d := c-1;
    LOOP (* Y[c ... d] = Take(X[a_0 ... a - 1]) *)
      IF a > b THEN RETURN
        ELSE d := d+1; PutV(Y,d,Get(X,a)); a := a+1
      END
    END
END Take2;
```

Of course, this kind of programming can lead to problems involving aliases: we may want to shift data from part of a fixed sequence into another part of the same fixed sequence, and if the parts overlap, then we may or may not be in trouble. (It often depends on the order in which we go over the sequence; in other words, whether we thought of the procedure as being top-down or bottom-up.) There are lots of things to think about, but as usual, one of the best things to think about is "Can we imagine a tool which would make this and many other problems easier?"

PROCEDURE Take3(n:CARDINAL; VAR X,Y:FixedSeq;
a,b,c:Index; VAR d:Index);
(* pre: $X[a \dots b]$ and $Y[c \dots d']$ are legal ranges, where *)
(*     $d' = Length(Take(X[a \dots b])])$ *)
(* post: $d = d', Y[c \dots d] = Take(X[a \dots b])$ *)
BEGIN
  IF 1+b-a < n
    THEN Copy(X,Y,a,b,c,d)
    ELSE Copy(X,Y,a,a-1+n,c,d) END
END Take;

## Exercises

**9.3-4**  Add the definition of Copy (six parameters).

**9.3-5**  Add the definition of Drop (seven parameters again).

**9.3-6**  Add the definition of Reverse (only six parameters).

**9.3-7**  Add the definition of Append (nine parameters!).

**9.3-8**  Create a module Sort which imports the preceding definitions from FixedSeq and
exports the predicates Ordered(X,i,j) and Perm(X,Y,a,b,c,d) as well as ISort(X,i,j),
which uses insertion sort to reach the goal
post : Ordered(X,i,j), Perm($X_0$,X,i,j,i,j), i=$i_0$, j=$j_0$

The approach is quite general; the trouble is that these procedures are very
clumsy to use. Merge takes two sequences into one; are you really sure that you can
remember the effect of

$$Merge(X, Y, X, 5, i + 9, j - 3, k, 19, 20 + k)?$$

**Q:** It looks to me as though it's saying

$$X[19 \dots 20 + k] := Merge(X[5 \dots i + 9], Y[j - 3 \dots k])$$

with the abstract interpretation of *Merge*, but I admit that I don't want to live
with it if I don't have to. How can I do it more easily?

**A:** Simple. We have a record which remembers its own beginning and end, so
it keeps track of the midrange all by itself. That's an important long-range trend
in computer programming: we're moving slowly from "procedural" programming
in which all the information is encapsulated in the procedures, towards "object-
oriented" programming in which an object like a sequence is loaded with information—including, quite often, the definitions of procedures which can be applied to

that object. We're not going that far in this course, but we are going to have more information with our sequences than the traditional array wants to remember.

### 9.3.2 "Mid" as a Representation

Given fixed-size $S$, we can represent $Mid(S, i, j) = S[i..j-1]$ by

    TYPE MidSeq = RECORD A:FixedSeq; i,j:INDEX END;

Now we can provide a considerable number of familiar-looking operations:

```
Put(R,k,x) == (R.A[R.i + k - 1] := x;)
Get(R,k) = RETURN R.A[R.i + k - 1]
Len(R) = RETURN (R.j - R.i + 1)
SetNull(R) == (R.i := MaxLen DIV 2; R.j := R.i - 1;) == (R:=NewSeq();)
IsNull(R) = RETURN (0=Len(R))
Hd(R) = (RETURN R.A[R.i])
Pop(R) == (R.i := R.i + 1;) == (R := Tl(R);)
PopHd(x,R) == (x := R.A[R.i]; R.i := R.i + 1; )
Push(x,R) == (R.i := R.i-1; R.A[R.i] := x;)
PushOnBack(x,R) == (R.j := R.j+1; R.A[R.j] := x;)
Copy(R,S) == (S.i := R.i; S.j := R.j; FixedSeqs.Copy(R.A,S.A,...) )
NewNull() == (VAR R; SetNull(R); RETURN(R);)
Tl(R) = (VAR S; S:=R; Pop(S); RETURN(S))
AddItem(x,R) == (VAR S; S:=R; Push(x,S); RETURN(S);)
```

The last three are effectively reduced to pseudocode: they return arrays.

    **Q:** Wait a minute; I've seen that notation before, but that doesn't mean I can deal with this as the whole description of the MidSeq module.
    **A:** Each of these "simple operations" can be converted very straightforwardly into code; for example,

```
PROCEDURE Put(VAR R:MidSeq,k:Index,x:Item);
  (* pre: 0<k<=Length(R) *)
  (* post: R = Put(R_0,k_0,x_0) *)
  BEGIN R.A[R.i+k - 1] := x END ;
```

In using MidSeq.Put, we need not be conscious of the fact that it's quite different from FixedSeq.Put. MidSeq.Put and MidSeq.Get relate to one another in exactly the way they're supposed to. The Sort module of the last exercise in the previous section needed only Put and Get; it will sort MidSeqs just as well as FixedSeqs, although you need to make a copy of it which imports its definitions from the new representation and change the name FixedSeq to MidSeq everywhere in it.

## Exercises

**9.3-9**  Convert the rest of the simple operations into code.

**9.3-10**  Copy the code for the compound operations Min and Sum; since these only depended on the simple operations, the editing of FixedSeq.Min into MidSeq.Min, for example, should be quite trivial.

**9.3-11**  Rewrite Take, Drop, and Append; they should be significantly simpler. (E.g., they shouldn't need extra parameters: Take(n:Index; VAR S,R:MidSeq) is adequate.

**9.3-12**  Edit the Sort module so that it works on MidSeqs.

If we were sure that this code would always be used correctly, that would be the end of the job. However, someone is sure to use your procedures erroneously, and it might be you.

Put(S,Length(S)+1,x) should really do something intelligent, but the specification does not say what. One reasonable possibility is to start out Put by testing the precondition as follows:

IF k=0 OR k > Length(R)
THEN start printing out error messages, and don't Put

This could be used in Get as well.

## Exercises

**9.3-13**  Add error checking to the rest of the simple functions.

**9.3-14**  Add error checking to those compound functions which still need it (even though the simple functions are checking for some errors).

There are several minor variations on the MidSeq idea. It would be perfectly possible to change all of the definitions so that instead of using the record [R,i,j] to represent $R[i \dots j]$, we could use it to represent $R[i \dots i + j - 1]$; in this case, the $j$ component is being used to represent a length rather than an index. Most of the definitions would not change much, whether simple or compound; e.g.,

Length(R) = R.j;
Take(n,R,C) = (Copy(S,R); IF S.j > n THEN S.j:=n; END; RETURN(S);)

### Exercises

**9.3-15**  Edit the simple functions (Put, Get, etc.) for this representation.

**9.3-16**  Edit the compound functions (Min, Sum, Append, etc.) for this representation.

### 9.3.3 Adjustable Sequences

An important variation on the MidSeq idea comes from consideration of the fact that a given sequence "grows" downward towards 1 with Push or upwards toward MaxSeq with PushOnBack, and then fails even though the array may be only half full. For example, if we try to create a MidSeq of length MaxSeq-3 by successive calls on Push, we will fail: each time we call Push(x,S), we find that S.i is reduced by one.

> **Q:** Well, can't you start S.i at MaxSeq?
> **A:** In that case you would find that PushOnBack fails immediately.
> **Q:** Well, when Push discovers that there's no room left, can't it try to shift the whole midrange?
> **A:** Yes; here's a possible answer.

PROCEDURE Push(x:Item,VAR S:MidSeq);
  (* pre: Length(S)$\leq$MaxSeq *)
  (* post: S=x@S$_0$* *)
  BEGIN
    IF S.i=1 THEN (* we would have reported an error, before *)
        IF S.j=MaxSeq THEN Error code goes here... precondition failed
            ELSE RightAlign(S); DEC(S.i); S.A[S.i]:=x; END ;
  END Push;

RightAlign is now a procedure which does not change the abstract value of $S$, but does shift the representation so that S.j=MaxSeq. Since we will also want to have LeftAlign to use when PushOnBack runs out of room, we had better make a Shift procedure: Shift(S,i,j,n) produces a version of $S$ in which the entire range

$S[i \ldots j]$ has been shifted $n$ places. Thus,

$$Shift(S, i, j, k)[i + k \ldots j + k] \quad = \quad S[i \ldots j] \quad \text{if } i, j, i + k, j + k \in 1 \ldots Length(S)$$

Accordingly,

$$
\begin{aligned}
Shift(S, i, j, 0) \quad &= \quad S; \\
Shift(S, i, j, k) \quad &= \quad S, && \text{if } i > j \\
&= \quad Put(Shift(S, i + 1, j, k), i + k, S[i]) && \text{otherwise}
\end{aligned}
$$

Suppose now that $S = [a, b, c, d, e]$ and $k = 2$; we find that

$$
\begin{aligned}
Shift(S, 1, 3, k) \quad &= \quad Put(Shift(S, 2, 3, k), 1 + k, a) \\
&= \quad Put(Put(Shift(S, 3, 3, k), 2 + k, b), 1 + k, a) \\
&= \quad Put(Put(Put(Shift(S, 4, 3, k), 3 + k, c), 2 + k, b), 1 + k, a) \\
&= \quad Put(Put(Put(S, 3 + k, c), 2 + k, b), 1 + k, a) \\
&= \quad Put(Put(Put([a, b, c, d, e], 5, c), 4, b), 3, a) \\
&= \quad Put(Put([a, b, c, d, c], 4, b), 3, a) \\
&= \quad Put([a, b, c, b, c], 3, a) \\
&= \quad [a, b, a, b, c]
\end{aligned}
$$

If defined recursively, Shift works for either positive or negative values of $k$. The top-down solution will Put the first value wherever it should go and then continue with the tail:

```
PROCEDURE ShiftTop(VAR S:Sequence;i,j:CARDINAL; k:INTEGER);
  (* pre: i, j, i + k, j + k ∈ 1 ... Length(S) *)
  (* post: S≐Shift(S₀,i₀,j₀,k₀) *)
  BEGIN
    LOOP (* Shift(S₀,i₀,j,k) = Shift(S,i,j,k) *)
      IF i>j THEN RETURN;
          ELSE Put(S,i+k,Get(S,i));
          INC(i);
          END ;
      END ;
  END ShiftTop;
```

There is one small problem with this solution: it doesn't work. If $S = [a, b, c, d, e]$ then

ShiftTop(S,1,4,k) == (S:=[a,a,a,a,a])  if $k = 1$
ShiftTop(S,1,3,k) == (S:=[a,b,a,b,a])  if $k = 2$

What happened? If you trace through, you find that this actually implements

$$
\begin{aligned}
ShiftTop(S, i, j, k) &= S, & \text{if } i > j \\
&= ShiftTop(Put(S, i + k, S[i]), i + 1, j, k) & \text{otherwise}
\end{aligned}
$$

The two are not the same. Shift was defined as Putting in values from the original sequence $S_0$; ShiftTop Puts them from the current $S$. Careful testing or careful reasoning will suggest that you consider the possibility that the value found by Get(S,j) is not the same as that found by Get($S_0$,j). $S$ differs from $S_0$ in the range $[i_0 + k \ldots i + k - 1]$, and an increasing $i$ will reach this range after $k$ steps...if $k$ is positive. Think about it: ShiftTop will work for $k \leq 0$; it can be used for LeftAlign, but not RightAlign.

Similarly, we consider a bottom-up implementation. The obvious bottom-up solution will just construct solutions for successively longer subsequences of $S[i \ldots j]$:

$$
\begin{aligned}
Shift(S, j + 1, j, k) &= S \\
Shift(S, j, j, k) &= Put(S, j + k, S[j]) \\
Shift(S, j - 1, j, k) &= Put(Shift(S, j, j, k), j - 1 + k, S[j - 1]) \\
Shift(S, j - 2, j, k) &= Put(Shift(S, j - 1, j, k), j - 2 + k, S[j - 2])
\end{aligned}
$$

The recursive definition thus turns into the following program:

```
PROCEDURE ShiftBottom(VAR S:Sequence;i,j:CARDINAL; k:INTEGER);
   (* pre: i,j,i + k,j + k ∈ 1 ... Length(S) *)
   (* post: S=Shift(S₀,i₀,j₀,k₀) *)
   BEGIN
      LOOP  (* S = Shift(S₀,j+1,j₀,k) *)
         IF i>j THEN RETURN;
            ELSE Put(S,j+k,Get(S,j)); (* S = Shift(S₀,j,j₀,k) *)
                 DEC(j);
                 END ;
      END ;
END ShiftBottom;
```

Now, does this always work? No. Careful testing or careful thinking will show that it works only if $k \geq 0$, because

$$
\begin{aligned}
Shift(S, i, j, k)[n] &= S[n], & \text{if } \neg(n \in i + k \ldots j + k) \text{ so} \\
Shift(S_0, j, j_0, k)[j] &= S_0[j] & \text{if } \neg(j \in j + k \ldots j_0 + k)
\end{aligned}
$$

As $j$ diminishes through the program, you can count on $Get(S, j)$ producing the right value only if $k \geq 0$. From this you can see that if $ShiftBottom$ is used then RightAlign will work, but LeftAlign will not.

## Exercises

**9.3-17** To finish these procedures, we must remember that we are working on representations: the midrange represented by $[S.A, S.i, S.j]$ should be transformed into $[Shift(S.A, S.i, S.j, k), S.i + k, S.j + k]$ where $k = MaxLen - j$ for RightAlign and $k = 1 - i$ for LeftAlign. Rewrite ShiftBottom and ShiftTop so that they will perform these transformations. (You should replace each abstract $Get(R, n)$ by the corresponding specific expression R.A[R.i-1+n], and similarly with $Put$.

**9.3-18** Justify the names ShiftRight for the bottom-up schedule and ShiftLeft for the top-down; write a single Shift program which works in either direction by calling on ShiftRight or ShiftLeft as appropriate.

**9.3-19** Write RightAlign and LeftAlign; rewrite Push and PushOnBack so that they perform alignment when appropriate.

Realignment works, but it can be fairly expensive. Suppose that we have a sequence $S$ which we use to keep a list of things to do; the operations are PopHd, which finds the next thing to be done, and PushOnBack, which adds a task to be accomplished when we're through with the previous commitments. (This is common in breadth-first searching; such a list is called a *queue*.) For example, we could have a program to implement

$$Search(S) \quad = \quad \{y : x \in S \wedge Reachable(x, y)\}$$

so

$$
\begin{aligned}
Search(\{\}) \cup R &= R \\
Search(\{x\} \cup S) \cup R &= Search(S \cup (Neighbors(x) - R)) \cup R
\end{aligned}
$$

Assuming that Neighbors(x,A) puts the neighbors of $x$ into sequence $A$, we can proceed with the Search program of Figure 9.8.

In this case, we take items from the front of $S$ but add them to the back; this is fundamentally characteristic of a breadth-first search. Empty space is always created in front, but needed in back. LeftAlign will solve the problem each time, but LeftAlign may take Length(S) steps to enable us to add a single item; that's not very good. A better solution is to let the sequence wrap around so that

$$Ab([[g, h, x, x, x, a, b, c, d, e, f], 6, 2]) = [a, b, c, d, e, f, g, h]$$

```
PROCEDURE Search(VAR S:Sequence):Sequence;
  (* post: result= Search(S_0) *)
  PROCEDURE AddDiff(VAR S,N,R:Sequence);
    (* post: S = S_0+[x ∈ N : ¬(x ∈ R)], N=[] *)
    VAR x:Place;
    BEGIN
      LOOP (* N_0= A+N,S= S_0+[x ∈ A : ¬(x ∈ R)] *)
        IF IsEmpty(N) THEN RETURN; END ;
        PopHd(x,N); IF NOT(IsIn(x,R)) THEN PushOnBack(x,S); END ;
      END ;
  END AddDiff;
  VAR R,N:Sequence; x:Place;

  BEGIN (* Search *)
    R:=NewSeq();
    LOOP (* Search(S_0) = Search(S) ∪ R *)
      IF IsEmpty(S) THEN RETURN; END ;
      PopHd(x,S); Push(x,R); Neighbors(x,N); AddDiff(S,N,R);
    END ;
END Search;
```

**Figure 9.8** Breadth-First Search

All we have to do to achieve this is to make 1 be the successor of MaxLen as an index, i.e., by counting

$$1, 2, 3, \ldots, MaxLen, 1, 2, 3, \ldots, MaxLen, \ldots$$

We can do that by replacing each incrementation $i + 1$ of an index by $1 + mod(i, MaxLen)$, or by replacing each use of an index $i$ by $Adj(i) = 1 + mod(i-1, MaxLen)$ in the definitions of simple sequence operations. $Adj$ has the nice properties that

$$
\begin{aligned}
Adj(i+1) &= i+1, & \text{if } i < MaxLen \\
&= 1, & \text{if } i = MaxLen \\
Adj(i + MaxLen) &= Adj(i) & \text{if } i \in 0 \ldots
\end{aligned}
$$

With $mod$ properly defined on the integers, we will also find that $Adj(0) = MaxLen$. This allows us to rewrite the simple sequence operations, as shown in Figure 9.9.

```
Put(R,k,x) == (R.A[Adj(R.i + k - 1)] := x;)
Get(R,k) = R.A[Adj(R.i + k - 1)]
Len(R) = Adj(MaxLen+R.j - R.i + 1)
SetNull(R) == (R.i := MaxLen DIV 2; R.j := R.i - 1;) == (R:=NewSeq();)
IsEmpty(R) == (0=Len(S))
Hd(R) = (R.A[R.i])
Pop(R) == (R.i := Adj(R.i + 1);) == (R := Tail(R);)
PopHd(x,R) == (x := R.A[R.i]; R.i := Adj(R.i + 1);)
Push(x,R) == (R.i := Adj(R.i-1); R.A[R.i] := x;)
PushOnBack(x,R) == (R.j := Adj(R.j+1); R.A[R.j] := x;)
```

**Figure 9.9**

At this point, we don't need alignment at all: the precondition for Push(x,S) is the same as the precondition for PushOnBack(x,S). Both require that Len(S) < MaxLen, and as long as that's true, we can go ahead and add to the sequence. If all of the compound operations have been defined in terms of these simple ones, their definitions need not be changed.

### Exercise

**9.3-20** Implement and test this adjusted MidSeq representation.

### 9.3.4 Sequences of Sequences

In constructing an editor, text formatter, calculator, or other program which will deal with a sequence of lines, we have to consider the representation of a sequence of sequences. One possibility is just to remember that a sequence of lines is "really" just a sequence of characters, delimited by some control character called EOL, the end-of-line signal. The first line is the subsequence of characters ending at the first EOL, and the 93rd line is simply the subsequence of characters beginning after the 92nd EOL and ending at the 93rd.

This approach can certainly be made to work, but it can be awkward. Suppose that there are 233 lines in a file being edited. (E.g., Suppose this sentence began on line 233 of a file.) Suppose, then, that we want to delete one character in line 3. In this representation, every single character afterwards must be moved up by one space. That's not what we would do as humans working on paper; an operation on a line should normally affect only that line.

Equally important, it will be easier to specify and debug the operation of deleting an item in a sequence, and then use the operation at two levels: to delete characters within a line, and to delete lines within a file.

So how do you implement that? Make a version of the MidSeq module in which the Item type is CHAR; then call this the EdString module, which exports the sequence type EdString and the required operations on EdStrings: Find, Delete, Subst, Take, Drop, Append and so on, as well as Put and Get.

Now make a version of MidSeq in which the Item type is EdString. Call this the EdBuf module, which exports the sequence type EdBuf and the required operations on EdBufs. These will be the basic operations of a text editor; for example,

> Find(x: EdString; VAR B: EdBuf; i, j: Index): Index

will (if possible) produce the index of the first line in $B$ within which we can EdString.Find $x$ as a substring. Similarly,

> Delete(VAR B: EdBuf; i, j: Index);

will delete all lines in $B$ between $i$ and $j$ inclusive, and

> Subst(VAR B: EdBuf; i, j:Index; Old, New: EdString);

will look at every line in $B[i \ldots j]$ and replace, on each line, the first occurrence (if any) of *Old* by *New*. And so on; an exhaustive list of editor operations would be extremely long, but a small sample makes a good project.

Of course, sequences of sequences arise in many contexts. If we want to construct a dictionary, it makes some sense to have two sequences of strings: $N$, which contains names; and $V$, which contains the corresponding values. Once more, we get

$$\begin{aligned} LookUp([N, V], name) \quad &= \quad N[Loc], \quad \text{if } Loc \neq 0; \\ &= \quad name, \quad \text{otherwise }, \end{aligned}$$

where

$$Loc \; = \; Find(name, N);$$
$$Def([N, V], name, val) \; = \; [name@N, val@V]$$

This gives us the basic property that

$$LookUp(Def(Dict, y, a), x) = \textbf{ if } x = y \textbf{ then } a \textbf{ else } LookUp(Dict, x)$$

**Q:** This is just about the same as *Put* and *Get*, isn't it?

**A:** Yes; the axioms are identical. *Put* associates values with numbers, *Def* associates them with names. The only other difference is that we're making *LookUp* return a value even if the *name* is undefined, where *Get* just pulls out whatever is there.

**Q:** Why do you have *LookUp* return the *name* as its own definition if that name is undefined?

**A:** Mainly to encourage questions like that. It's perfectly reasonable to have an error message at that point, or to produce some standard value like "", but it's also worthwhile to think of other possibilities. Suppose that we had a dictionary *Abbr* of abbreviations, representing

```
ACM=Assoc for Computing Machinery;
JACM=Jrnl of the ACM;
USA=US of America;
Jrnl=Journal;
cmp=computer;
thry=theory;
sci=science;
US=United States;
Assoc=Association;
```

Notice that we could create a dictionary from that input sequence, assuming that *name* and *val* are not allowed to contain "=" or ";", using something like

$$ReadDict([N, V], S) \; = \; [N, V] \hspace{3em} \text{if } S = []$$
$$= \; ReadDict([a@N, v@V], S') \hspace{1em} \text{if } S = a + \text{``=''} + v + \text{``;''}$$
$$+ S'$$

We'd like to use this dictionary in substitution, so that

$$ReSubst(Abbr, \text{``The JACM is on cmp sci thry''})$$

would become

> **"The Journal of the Association for Computing Machinery is on computer..."**

Here is a sample solution:

$$First(S) \quad = \quad S[1 \ldots k-1]$$
$$Rest(S) \quad = \quad S[k+1 \ldots Length(S)],$$

where

$$k \quad = \quad Find(`\,\text{'}, S + ``\,\text{''})$$

so that

$$First(``\textbf{THIS IS SILLY.''}) \quad = \quad ``\textbf{THIS''}$$
$$First(Rest(``\textbf{THIS IS SILLY.''})) \quad = \quad ``\textbf{IS''}$$
$$First(Rest(Rest(``\textbf{THIS IS SILLY.''}))) \quad = \quad ``\textbf{SILLY.''}$$

This enables us to define *ReSubst*:

$$ReSubst(D, S) \quad = \quad S, \qquad\qquad\qquad \text{if } S = S'$$
$$\qquad\qquad\quad = \quad ReSubst(D, S') \qquad \text{otherwise ,}$$

where

$$S' \quad = \quad SubstAll(S);$$
$$SubstAll(S) \quad = \quad S, \qquad\qquad\qquad\qquad\qquad \text{if } S = ``\text{''}$$
$$\qquad\qquad\quad = \quad LookUp(D, First(S))$$
$$\qquad\qquad\qquad\quad + ``\text{ ''} + SubstAll(Rest(S)), \qquad \text{otherwise}$$

The definition given is not ideal from the point of view of efficient implementability. It would be better to compute depth-first rather than breadth-first:

$$ReSubst \quad ( \quad D, ``\textbf{The JACM is on cmp sci thry''})$$
$$= \quad ``\textbf{The ''} + ReSubst(D, ``\textbf{JACM is on cmp sci thry''})$$
$$= \quad ``\textbf{The ''} + ReSubst(D, ``\textbf{Jrnal of the ACM is on cmp sci thry''})$$
$$= \quad ``\textbf{The ''} + ReSubst(D, ``\textbf{Journal of the ACM is on cmp sci thry''})$$
$$= \quad ``\textbf{The Journal ''} + ReSubst(D, ``\textbf{of the ACM is on cmp sci thry''})$$
$$= \quad ``\textbf{The Journal of ''} + ReSubst(D, ``\textbf{the ACM is on cmp sci thry''})$$
$$\cdots$$
$$\vdots$$

This idea works because *ReSubst* distributes over sequences of words; i.e., it is usually true that

$$ReSubst(D, X + ``\text{ ''} + Y) = ReSubst(D, X) + ``\text{ ''} + ReSubst(D, Y).$$

**Exercises**

**9.3-21** Specify and implement the operation EqDict, so that EqDict($x, y$) is *True* if and only if all names defined in either of the dictionaries are also defined in the other, with the same definition. (Notice that a dictionary is a table: the order of the "rows" is unimportant.)

**9.3-22** Specify and implement the operations NewDict, ReadDict, and WriteDict so that NewDict will produce an empty dictionary, ReadDict will take a dictionary and add definitions to it from the input file, and WriteDict will print the definitions in a given table on the output file. You should define the abstract functions in such a way that it is always true that

$$EqDict(ReadDict(NewDict, WriteDict(D)), D)$$

(Of course, the procedure WriteDict will generate output rather than returning a value, and ReadDict will read from input rather than from a string parameter; ReadDict may also change a VAR parameter rather than returning a value. The pre- and postconditions will clarify this relationship, as usual.)

**9.3-23** Implement ReSubst according to the definition given.

**9.3-24** Work with the specification of ReSubst to find a version which will be depth-first rather than breadth-first; i.e., it should finish finding ReSubst(First(S)) before doing anything with Rest(S), using the distribution of ReSubst. Implement your specification.

**9.3-25** Find counterexamples to the "usually true" distribution law stated for ReSubst. When would they matter?

**9.3-26** Suppose that the type Dictionary was to be represented with a sequence of [*name, def*] pairs rather than with a pair of sequences. How much would change?

## 9.4 IMPLICIT REPRESENTATION

In the midrange representations of sequences, we have a record with three components: an array and two index values (one for the beginning, one for the end). The array is used only for one sequence, even if only a small part of it is needed for that sequence. When you read sentences on this page, there are no index values at all to tell you where to begin or end. Furthermore, one page (as a regular array of positions) serves to represent many sentences, each of which occupies only a small part of the total space. In programming, it is often worthwhile to let the indicator for the beginning or end of a sequence be implicit in the situation, without keeping track of extra numbers as MidSeq does. The same can apply to the array itself, which may thus be shared among many sequences. In this section, we will take pieces out of the representation type and consider the advantages and disadvantages of having done so.

### 9.4.1 Fixed Bounds: Lower or Upper

In the FixedSeq representation, we had no markers: the lower bound was always 1, and the upper bound was always MaxLen. Here we'll consider the consequences of having a compromise: one bound can be rigid, and the other can be explicitly indexed. For example, if we have subsequences represented by $A[i \ldots j]$ where $i = 1$, then we are using the "initial slice" $A[1 \ldots j]$. Similarly, if we require that $j = MaxLen$, we get the "final slice" $A[i \ldots]$. Can you see the problem?

With the initial slice, it appears that you can't do Push because you've already come to the very beginning of the available space. With the final slice you have the same problem with PushOnBack. Nonetheless, both of these representations are quite common precisely because there are times when you only want Push (and PopHd) or when you only want PushOnBack (and PopOffBack, which you should now be able to define by analogy: PopOffBack is to PushOnBack as PopHd is to Push.)

In either case, we have a sequence which can only be extended or shrunken at one end. Such a sequence is called a *stack*, by analogy with a stack of dinner plates so arranged that you can only add at the top or take off from the top. We can define

```
TYPE PreSeq = RECORD
     A : ARRAY [1..MaxLen] OFItem;
     j : [0..MaxLen+1]; END;
(* Ab([A,j]) = A[1..j] *)

PROCEDURE PushOnBack(x : Item; VAR S : PreSeq);
   (* Pre: Length(S) < MaxLen *)
   (* Post: S = PushOnBack(x,S₀) *)
   BEGIN INC(S.j); S.A[S.j] := x; END PushOnBack;
```

Other procedures from MidSeq can be copied here, with the simplifying assumption that the lower bound to the midrange is always 1. Thus,

```
Length(S) = S.j;
Hd(S) = S.A[1];
Take(n,S,C) == (Copy(S,C); C.j := min(C.j,n); )
```

It appears impossible to define PopHd or Push. However, this appearance is illusory; such procedures are awkward, but not at all impossible in this representation. Try to think how to solve them before going on.

Actually, all you need to realize is that $Tl(S)[i] = S[i+1]$ while $AddItem(S)[i+1] = S[i]$. That suggests a FOR loop:

```
PROCEDURE PopHd(VAR x:Item; VAR S : PreSeq);
(* post : x = Hd(S₀), S = Tl(S₀) *)
VAR i : CARDINAL;
BEGIN
  x := S.A[1];
  R.j := S.j - 1;
  FOR i := 1 TO S.j-1 DO (* S[1..i-1] = S₀[2..i] *)
    S.A[i]:=S.A[i+1];
  END ;
END PopHd;
```

$$(* \text{ post} : x = Hd(S_0), S = Tl(S_0) *)$$

$$(* \ S[1..i-1] = S_0[2..i] \ *)$$

## Exercises

**9.4-1**   What does PopHd do when Length(S)=0? Think of something more sensible, and fix it to do that instead.

**9.4-2**   Write Push as a bottom-up LOOP construction whose loop invariant is
(* $S[i..j] = (x@S_0)[i..j]$, $j=j_0+1$ *).

**9.4-3**   Complete and test enough of the PreSeq module so that the sorting procedures defined for IntSeqs will work with this type as well.

**9.4-4**   Define the PostSeq type so that the upper bound of the sequence is always MaxLen, but the lower bound is explicitly stored in the record. Repeat the previous exercise for this representation.

### 9.4.2 Implicit Global Store

In the previous section, we omitted one of the bounds from the MidSeq representation and found that we could still represent sequences by the assumption that the missing bound was a constant or global variable. We can do the same for the array itself, as seen in Figure 9.10. We can have a global variable Memory declared as an array big enough to hold all the sequences we'll want as subsequences, and then represent any sequence as a midrange of this one.

## Exercise

**9.4-5**   Write Put, IsNull, and Reverse for this representation. [Hint: Only the first involves code you haven't seen before.]

**Q:** I can see how most of the operations work, but where do we start an empty sequence? What does SetNull do?

```
VAR Mem : ARRAY [1..VeryBigNumber] OF Item;
TYPE Seq = RECORD i,j:CARDINAL; END;
(* Ab([i,j]) = Mem[i..j] *)

PROCEDURE Length(S : Seq):BOOLEAN;
   (* post: result = Length(S) *)
   BEGIN RETURN(S.j + 1 - S.i); END Length;

PROCEDURE Push(x : Item; VAR S : Seq);
   (* post: S = x@S *)
   BEGIN DEC(S.i); Mem[S.i] := x; END Push;

PROCEDURE Get(S : Seq; i : CARDINAL): Item;
   (* post: result = S[i] *)
   BEGIN RETURN(Mem[S.i+i-1]); ENDL Get;
```

**Figure 9.10**

**A:** Presumably, you want the new sequence to be somewhere apart from all
the sequences that have already been created. It would be perfectly all right to put
an empty sequence anywhere; the problem that you're working towards is caused
by procedures like Push and PushOnBack. Think about what happens when you
have two sequences in one space and they both grow. Imagine that they are a pair
of idiots writing on a blackboard, completely unaware of one another's presence.

**Q:** Can't they end up writing all over one another's work?

**A:** Exactly. This representation makes Push and PushOnBack unsafe; it is
up to the programmer to make sure that no two procedures are going to mess
each other up. We can make sure that there is enough room to start out with by
associating the global array Mem with an index NextFree which starts out at 1,
but which is changed by each procedure that creates a new array:

```
PROCEDURE NewSeq():Seq;
   (* post: result = [] *)
   VAR S:Seq;
   BEGIN
      S.i := NextFree + MaxLen/2;
      S.j := S.i-1;
      NextFree := NextFree+MaxLen;
      RETURN(S);
   END NewSeq;
```

With this idea, the big array Mem is automatically broken up into small arrays, each of size MaxLen. Every procedure which would have worked on MidSeq as we originally defined it will still work; the only problem is that some procedures which would generate error messages when run on the previous representation will now generate erroneous results instead.

**Exercise**

**9.4-6**  Implement CreateN(S,n,x) to work on this representation, generating an array of length $n$ and increasing NextFree by $n$, not by MaxLen. What have you gained in efficiency? What programs which would have run correctly with the Mid representation will now run incorrectly? What programs which would have generated error messages with the Mid representation will now run correctly?

There is only one more simplification to make in this direction: we can represent a midrange of Mem by indicating *only* its starting (or ending) point, as long as we know how long it is. Thus, if we will accept Length(S)=MaxLen as a constant, we can say

```
VAR Mem : ARRAY [1..BigNumber] OF Item;
VAR NextFree : CARDINAL;
TYPE SimpleSeq = CARDINAL;
(* Ab(i) = Mem[i...i-1+MaxLen] *)

PROCEDURE CreateN(VAR S:SimpleSeq);;
   (* post : S = Copies(MaxLen,GarbageValues) *)
   VAR S : SimpleSeq;
   BEGIN S := NextFree; NextFree := NextFree+MaxLen;
END CreateN;

PROCEDURE Get(S:SimpleSeq; i:CARDINAL) : Item;
   (* post: result = S[i] *)
   BEGIN RETURN(Mem[S+i-1]); END Get;

PROCEDURE Put(S:SimpleSeq; i:CARDINAL; x:Item);
   (* post: S = Put(S_0,i,x) *)
   BEGIN Mem[S+i-1] := x END Put;
```

**Q:** Isn't this a little bit weird? You're saying that a sequence of cardinal numbers is represented by one cardinal number.

**A:** That's right—represented by one cardinal number in a context which includes a big Memory. With this representation, Push and PushOnBack don't really make much sense; they involve changes to our implicit constants. Put and Get work just fine, but we can't check them for invalid arguments. If you Get(1000,3) you will presumably get something, even if no sequence has been allocated at that point in Mem. If you Put(499,7,3), then a 3 will be placed in Mem[505], even if that space is being used by another program for some other purpose. Here we are imitating the lowest level of machine representation of sequences.

## Exercises

**9.4-7**   Using this representation, implement the Sort operations.

**9.4-8**   Using this representation, implement the versions of Push, PopHd, and Append which take three explicit arguments for each abstract sequence. That is,
Push(x:Item; VAR A:SimpleSeq; VAR i,j:CARDINAL);
should satisfy Push(x,A,i,j)==([A[i-1],i]:=[x,i-1]); and analogously for PopHd and Append.

This appears to exhaust the possibilities of implicit midrange selection, but it does not. One major possibility remains: rather than having an end point which is implicit because it is a constant, we can have an end point which is implicit in the data. In effect, we want a definition of the form

$$Ab(S, i) = S[i \ldots j], \text{ where } j = \ldots$$

We are given the starting point, but we want a rule by which to recognize the end point when we see it. For example, in reading a sentence, we proceed onwards until we reach a "." to indicate the end; English has a rule which says that sentences can end that way.

**Q:** Excuse me, but didn't you just contradict yourself? You put a period in the middle of that sentence, within quotation marks. The rule you're talking about would require that the sentence end just before the closing quotes!

**A:** English has lots of rules, some of which are very difficult to mechanize. Periods are used for several purposes, only one of which is to mark a sentence end. Moreover, other marks can be used to end a sentence: question marks, exclamation points, and so on. In sequence representation for a moron, we need to keep to simple rules. We'll start with

$$j = First(Mark, S, i) = Min(\{k \geq i : S[k] = Mark\})$$

This rule simply ends the sentence at a period:

$$
\begin{aligned}
Ab(S, i) \quad &= \quad [], & \text{if } S[i] = Mark \\
&= \quad S[i]@Ab(S, i + 1), & \text{otherwise}
\end{aligned}
$$

Clearly, the idea works just as well if we end a numeric sequence with 0 or with 999999999, or if we end a character sequence with CHR(0) or CHR(127), or if we substitute anything else for Mark. The rule given can easily be stretched to include the possibility of an implicit starting point (position 1 in $S$, so that we are dealing with a PreSeq which has an implicitly computed endpoint) or an implicit global sequence Memory.

**Q:** Well, doesn't that mean that you can have a sequence represented by nothing at all? You've just said that the beginning, the end, and the array can all be implicit.

**A:** Yes, you can have one such sequence: it will begin at position 1 in the global array Mem, and it will end at the first occurrence of Mark. That's not a very useful type; we want to be able to have many variables of each type which we create. The most useful case is the representation of text by strings, each of which is a sequence of fixed size but for which the end of the string is indicated by the null character Chr(0):

CONST MaxLen = 81; Low = 1; NullCh = 0C;

TYPE Index = [Low-1...MaxLen+1];
    MString = ARRAY [Low...MaxLen] OF CHAR;

(* Ab(S) = Ab(S,Low) where Ab(S,i) = S[i..j], j=First(NullCh,S,i)-Low *)

PROCEDURE SetNull(VAR S:MString);
  (* post: result = "" *)
  BEGIN S[Low]:= NullCh; RETURN(S); END SetNull;

PROCEDURE Length(VAR S:MString):Index;
  (* post: result = Length(S) *)
  VAR i:Index;
  BEGIN
    FOR i:=Low TO MaxLen DO
      IF S[i]=NullCh THEN RETURN (i-Low) END
      (* $NullCh \notin S[Low...i]$ *)
    END ;
    RETURN (MaxLen-Low)
END Length;

**Q:** I have a problem with this: STRING is already a type in *Modula-2*, and it may be terminated with NullCh but it isn't indexed by [1...81]. In fact, the manual says that a string is an "open array" [0...]. What does that mean?

**A:** Simply that strings are given as arguments to many kinds of procedures, which may not "know" what the original indexing range was. If you have one kind of string which is indexed by [1...81] and another type [2...37] for some reason, a procedure like InOut.WriteString will perceive the first string as indexed by $[0 \ldots 80]$ and the second as indexed by $[0 \ldots 35]$. So far as WriteString is concerned, the string begins at location 0 and goes on until it stops in a manner which is implementation dependent. NullCh is often used. All you really need to know at this point is that WriteString will work correctly on objects of type MString.

**Q:** Well, how can you say that a string begins at location 1 when the manual says that it begins at location 0?

**A:** The type MString is different from the type STRING, that's all. Actually, we can bring the two together by changing Low to 0 and MaxLen to 80. The definitions just given have been written so that they will still work even if you make that change by hand, but when you pass an open array parameter A, all information about the actual declared values of the index bounds is lost. Only the length of A is remembered at run time, and that is HIGH(A)+1.

### Exercises

**9.4-9**   Define Take, Drop, and FindPat on this representation. Make sure that they will work even if Low=0. [Hint: You should be copying code from previous representations, with only trivial revision.]

**9.4-10**  Define Append as a function satisfying Append(X,Y) = X+Y. Again, be sure it will work even if Low=0.

The rule which ends a sequence at the first Mark is extremely simple, but it fails to allow for the possibility of a sequence which contains "Mark" as an item. Thus, if 0 is an end-marker for a sequence of cardinal numbers, then we cannot represent the abstract sequence $[5, 0, 5]$. One way of allowing for this is to incorporate a special mark which says "The item which follows is not really a special marker, even if it looks like one". Thus, we can try the rule

$$j = Min(\{k \geq i : S[k] = Mark \wedge S[k-1] \neq UnMark\})$$

and implement the $Ab$ function

$$
\begin{array}{llll}
Ab(S, i) & = & [], & \text{if } S[i] = Mark \\
& = & S[i+1]@Ab(S, i+2), & \text{if } S[i] = UnMark \\
& = & S[i]@Ab(S, i+1), & \text{otherwise}
\end{array}
$$

Suppose we are using 0 as an end $Mark$ and 999999999 as an $UnMark$: we can represent the abstract sequence $[5, 0, 5]$ with the physical sequence $[5, 999999999, 0, 5]$, and we can even represent the sequence $[999999999, 999999998, 999999997]$ by writing the first element twice. This method is fully general, but awkward to use.

**Exercises**

**9.4-11** Redefine the MString type based on the constants Mark and UnMark; Mark should still be 0C, and UnMark should be a backslash "\" (134C).

**9.4-12** Provide the functions Length, Head, Tail, Get, and Put.

### 9.4.3 Sequences of Sequences

There is really nothing new to be considered here, except to realize that putting things together will still work. At this point you should go back over the idea of the editor, but now using the MString type. You can still describe operations like 'between 32 and 547, delete all lines containing the string "**bad**".' Each operation means exactly what it did before; only the implementation (algorithm) and the representation (data structure) will be changing. The same idea holds for the Dictionary type; the discussion did not depend on the representation of strings, and you should be able to substitute a different representation without changing—or even recompiling—the code.

## 9.5 REPRESENTATION BY REFERENCE

In the physical world, if I want you to work with my list of telephone numbers, either I can hand you the list, telling you to hand it back when you're done, or I can make a copy of it for you, or I can simply tell you where it is. If you don't change the list, they are all equivalent; if you do, the first and last options are likely to be equivalent, since in either case any changes you make will be present when I next look at the list. The VAR parameter is commonly implemented in the last way; I tell you where the list is by giving you a POINTER to it. Almost anything can serve as a pointer; all we need is a way of interpreting it as a reference to something else. A street address, the name of a person, the title of a book, or an unambiguous description such as "the maple tree in my front yard" or "the *IBM* logo on my keyboard" are all pointers to specific objects. "The computer in my house" is not a reasonable pointer, because there are three; "the ashtray in my house" also fails, because there aren't any. In computer science, we usually use three kinds of pointers:

- A name which is defined in some dictionary can be treated as a pointer to the definition. If I say "Change '**TaxRate**' to 27%", where '**TaxRate**' is entered in a dictionary somewhere, I probably mean to change the *definition* of '**TaxRate**' rather than the string itself.

- An index into some sequence can be treated as a pointer to the corresponding object in the sequence. If I say "Change line $i$ to '**zippety-doodah**'", where $i$ happens to be 5, I probably mean to change the contents of line 5 rather than to change $i$ to be the index of some new line which will contain '**zippety-doodah**'.

- A machine address can be treated as a pointer to whatever is stored at that address in the machine. If the machine is a human brain, this address might be a picture or a scent which brings up some memory. For the kind of machine used to describe most programming languages, the address is a number: a string of binary digits, which can be interpreted as a cardinal number in the range $[0 \ldots MaxAddress]$ and thus as an index into the simple array which is the machine's memory. This is the type POINTER in most programming languages: it is a very low-level, machine-dependent kind of concept, and one which is very prone to promote bugs in programs. We will therefore begin with the somewhat more abstract idea of an index into arrays in general.

### 9.5.1 Arrays of Index Values

Suppose that we have the constant $SEQ = 4$ and a pair of sequences $Val$ and $Nxt$, as shown:

$$\begin{aligned} Val &= [x, silly, x, this, a, is, sequence, x, x, x] \\ Nxt &= [0, 7, 0, 6, 2, 5, 0, 0, 0, 0] \end{aligned}$$

Now suppose we define

$$\begin{aligned} Ab(i) &= [], && \text{if } i = 0 \\ &= Val[i]@Ab(Nxt[i]) && \text{otherwise , i.e.} \\ Hd(i) &= Val[i] \\ Tl(i) &= Nxt[i] \\ IsNull(i) &= (i = 0) \end{aligned}$$

Based on these, we can use existing rules for functions like $Drop$ and $Get$:

$$\begin{aligned} Drop(i, S) &= \textbf{if } i = 0 \textbf{ then } S \textbf{ else } Drop(i-1, Tl(S)) \\ Get(S, i) &= Hd(Drop(i-1, S)) \\ &= Val[Drop(i-1, S)] \end{aligned}$$

With this example, we can find that

$$\begin{aligned} Get(SEQ, 1) &= this \\ Get(SEQ, 2) &= is \\ Get(SEQ, 3) &= a \\ Get(SEQ, 4) &= silly \\ Get(SEQ, 5) &= sequence \\ Drop(SEQ, 5) &= 0 \end{aligned}$$

so that

$$Ab(SEQ) = [this, is, a, silly, sequence]$$

Such a representation looks strange, but all of the familiar access functions (e.g., scanners and accumulators) will work quite well on it. *PutV* can also be defined, using

```
Get(S,i) = Sequence.Get(Val, Drop(i-1,S))
PutV(S,i,x) == Sequence.PutV(Val,Drop(i-1,S),x)
```

In *Modula-2*, we would have to provide declarations like

```
TYPE IntSeq = 0.. 200;
VAR Val : ARRAY [1.. 200] OF Integer;
    Nxt : ARRAY [1.. 200] OF IntSeq;
```

**Q:** Isn't this sort of like the representation you already gave of sequences, using an index into a global array of values?

**A:** Right. The only difference is that instead of finding $Tl(i) = i + 1$ as we did in that representation, we now have to store $Nxt$ explicitly, using two arrays rather than only one.

**Q:** Doesn't that mean that this representation will use more memory than the other?

**A:** Sometimes, but sometimes it will use less. The problem is that all the sequence representations we've used up until now require contiguous storage, allocated in advance: if your program involves fifty sequences, any of which might be of size 100, then you need to grab 5000 spaces in advance. That will be true even if you know for certain that your sequences grow and shrink in complementary ways (some being small while others are large) so that there are never more than 200 objects to store at any given moment. You've wasted a lot of space. With a pointer representation, you could have $Nxt$ and $Val$ each of length 200, and your fifty sequences are actually fifty index values pointing into the same arrays.

## Exercises

**9.5-1**  Take the sequences $Val = [94, 71, 16, 88]$ and $Nxt = [2, 3, 0, 2]$. Explain the calculation of $Max(S)$ if $S = 4$; what is $Hd(2)$?

**9.5-2**  Compare the sequence $S$ of the previous problem with the sequence $Z$ where $Z = 2$, $Val = [0, 88, 71, 16]$, $Nxt = [0, 3, 4, 0]$. In what sense are they the same? Find three representations for the sequence [77,88,99].

As a simple variation of this idea, we could have one array of records rather than a pair of arrays. For example, we could declare

TYPE Index = 0.. MaxList;
VAR ListSpace : ARRAY [1.. MaxList] OF
        RECORD Val : Integer; Nxt : Index END

Val[i] can now be changed to ListSpace[i].Val wherever it occurs in the previous discussion. This has some organizational advantages, but it is somewhat harder to read the expressions.

### Exercise

**9.5-3**    Restate $Ab$ in terms of the ListSpace of records.

**Trees**    All we're doing is using arrays (declared as global variables) to tabulate the information we want for each object. If we want to have recursive sequences, there's no problem: we just need to tabulate more functions. For example, if we want to have an IntTree type where an IntTree either is an integer, or is empty, or has a Head and Tail which are IntTrees, then we can tabulate these functions in arrays and represent any IntTree as an index into the arrays. Here's an example, with the arrays written vertically:

| IsTree | IntVal | Head | Tail |
|--------|--------|------|------|
| TRUE   | ---    | 3    | 6    |
| FALSE  | 417    | --   | --   |
| TRUE   | ---    | 6    | 0    |
| FALSE  | -34    | --   | --   |
| TRUE   | ---    | 1    | 1    |
| TRUE   | ---    | 2    | 0    |

Given these arrays, [0...6] are meaningful IntTrees. I'll write the $Ab$stractions corresponding to them, in the order in which you can figure them out: 0,2, and 4 can be found immediately, 6 can be found based on 2 and 0, 3 can be found based on 6 and 0, then 1 can be found based on 3 and 6, and finally 5 can be found based on 1:

$$
\begin{aligned}
Ab(0) &= [\,] \\
Ab(2) &= 417 \\
Ab(4) &= -34 \\
Ab(6) &= Ab(2)@Ab(0) &= [417] \\
Ab(3) &= Ab(6)@Ab(0) &= [[417]] \\
Ab(1) &= Ab(3)@Ab(6) &= [[[417]], 417] \\
Ab(5) &= Ab(1)@Ab(1) &= [[[[417]], 417], [[417]], 417]
\end{aligned}
$$

## Exercises

**9.5-4**  Define $Ab$ as a collection of rules.

**9.5-5**  Define the data type IntTree with the access functions Hd, Tl, IsNull, TreeToInt, and IsAtomic; don't start on tree construction just yet.

Here we're obviously wasting a considerable amount of space, because we only want to use IntVal when we don't want Head or Tail; IsTree tells us which one is needed. We could save the extra space by storing IntVal in the Head array, but then we're likely to get mixed up about the types of objects we're using. There are two tricks available for keeping track of this:

- You've noticed that different arrays start in different places; some examples have used arrays indexed by $[0 \ldots N]$, others by $[1 \ldots M]$. It's perfectly all right to have an array indexed by $[-9 \ldots 17]$. We could have declarations which avoided confusion, like this:

  > VAR IntVal : ARRAY [1.. 100] OF INTEGER;
  >          Head,Tail :ARRAY [101.. 200] OF Index;

  Now IsNull would not change, but IsTree(i) would just be $i > 100$, with no need for an explicit array. In order to store $n$ integers of size $a$ and $m$ tree cells of size $b$, we no longer need $(n + m) * (a + b)$ as we did before; we only need $n * a + m * b$, which can be a great improvement. The trouble is that we've lost flexibility, because we have to decide in advance how many integers and how many tree cells we'll need since they are allocated separately.

- There's a way around that that's really based on the idea of storing the IntVal in the Head array, but letting the system keep track of the confusion. We can adapt the array-of-records notion, say, that some of these records will be IntVals and some will be tree cells, and they are to be stored in whatever is the right amount of space.

```
TYPE Tree = 0..200;
     Cell = RECORD
CASE IsTree : BOOLEAN OF
     TRUE: Head, Tail : Tree |
     FALSE: IntVal : INTEGER
END ;
VAR TreeSpace : ARRAY [1..200] OF Cell
```

Given these declarations, we can then find $Ab(i)$ as

TreeSpace[i].IntVal, if  NOT(TreeSpace[i].IsTree)
$Ab$(TreeSpace[i].Head)@$Ab$(TreeSpace[i].Tail),  otherwise

Now we can store $n$ integers of size $a$ and $m$ tree cells of size $b$ in a total space allotment of $(n + m) * max(a, b)$; and we don't have to decide in advance on $n$ or $m$ as long as we can set a limit to their sum.

## Exercise

**9.5-6**  Describe the basic access functions on trees in terms of the representations just given.

**Infinite Sequences**    In any of these cross-linked representations, it's perfectly possible to "store" an infinite list: take the sequences $Val = [na, ba]$ and $Nxt = [1, 1]$. We have

$$Ab(2) = ba@Ab(1) = ba@(na@Ab(1)) = [ba, na, na, na, na, \ldots].$$

This is a recursive construction: we've defined a structure which satisfies the rules

$$\begin{aligned} X &= ba@Y \\ Y &= na@Y \end{aligned}$$

It is strongly recommended that you contemplate this and other examples; if you don't feel slightly dizzy, you haven't really gotten the idea.

## Exercises

**9.5-7**  Write a representation for the infinite list $[9,9,9,\ldots]$. [Hint: you need only one entry in $Val$ and one in $Nxt$.]

**9.5-8**  Explain what will happen if you try to compute the $Length$ of such a list using the rule $Length(S) = 1 + Length(Tl(S))$.

**9.5-9**  Explain what will happen if you use $PutV(S, 1000, 3)$ with this infinite list of 9's as $S$. [Hint: The process will take 1000 steps, and $S$ will still be an infinite list.]

This provides a very nice way to implement recursive procedures: they are represented as structures which contain themselves, i.e., as (cyclically) infinite structures. It's a little bit difficult to print them, but you can't have everything.

**Free Space**    Given $Val = [a, b, c, d]$ and $Nxt = [2, 4, 0, 0]$, we can see that $Ab(0) = [\,]$, so $Ab(4) = [d]$ and $Ab(3) = [c]$, so $Ab(2) = [b, d]$ and finally $Ab(1) = [a, b, d]$. If we are really interested only in keeping a representation of the sequence $[b, d]$, then spaces 1 and 3 are actually "free." Let's keep track of free space by marking it: any index $i$ for which $Nxt[i] > Length(Nxt)$ will be considered illegal. If we mark the version of $Nxt$ just given, we can write $Nxt = [99, 4, 99, 0]$; $Ab(2)$ is unchanged, but since $Ab(99)$ is certainly meaningless, $Ab(1) = a@Ab(99)$ is meaningless too. At this point, we can implement $AddItem$ in a strange way: to construct $AddItem(x, S)$, where $x$ is an item and $S$ is a cardinal number representing a sequence, we just find a free space $i$, $PutV$ the value $x$ in $Val[i]$, and $PutV$ the pointer $S$ in $Nxt[i]$; $Ab(i)$ will now be $x@Ab(S)$.

Let's try it. To find $AddItem(e, 2)$, we find that the first 99 in $Nxt$ is at position 1, so we set $Val[1]$ to be $e$ and we set $Nxt[1]$ to be 2. Now we have

$$Val = [e, b, c, d], Nxt = [2, 4, 99, 0], Ab(1) = [e, b, d]$$

as desired. To specify $AddItem$ in this context, we should describe the effect on $Nxt$ and $Val$ as well as the result itself:

$$AddItem(x, S) \quad = \quad i,$$

where

$$
\begin{aligned}
i &= Find(99, Nxt_0, 1) \\
Nxt &= PutV(Nxt_0, i, S) \\
Val &= PutV(Val_0, i, x)
\end{aligned}
$$

Of course, this is meaningless if $Find$ produces 0, since in that case there were no free spaces to be used.

### Exercises

**9.5-10**   Use the remaining free space (position 3) to construct $AddItem(f, 2)$.

**9.5-11**   Based on the preceding problem, consider what will happen if we use $PutV(2, 1, c)$. What will $Ab(1)$ become? What about $Ab(3)$?

**9.5-12**   Provide yet another implementation of the type *Sequence*, EXPORTing all the standard operations, based on these ideas. Your implementation module should contain two arrays called $Val$ and $Nxt$, each of size $MaxNode$; the marker can be the cardinal number $MaxNode + 1$. Procedures such as *Append* can be written recursively, just adapting the definitions from the first part of this book.

It is quite possible to improve the performance of the *Sequence* type in the previous exercises. The number of steps involved in a simple operation like *AddItem* can be as large as $Length(Nxt)$, just because you have to look for a mark like 99, which may be anywhere in $Nxt$. Therefore, constructing a sequence of length $Length(Nxt)$ may involve $(Length(Nxt)^{**}2)/2$ steps... fifty million steps to form a 200-page book as a sequence of ten thousand lines. This expense is not necessary; instead of marking each unused node with an illegal value for $Nxt$, let us begin with

$$Val = [x, x, x, x, x, \ldots], Nxt = [2, 3, 4, 5, \ldots, Length(Nxt), 0], Free = 1$$

Now $Ab(Free) = [x, x, x, \ldots]$; in effect, $Free$ now represents a sequence including all the values in $Val$. We can now implement $AddItem$ with

$$
\begin{aligned}
AddItem(x, S) &= \quad i, \text{ where} \\
i &= \quad Free_0, \\
Val &= \quad PutV(Val_0, i, x) \\
Nxt &= \quad PutV(Nxt_0, i, S) \\
Free &= \quad Nxt[i]
\end{aligned}
$$

Of course, this is meaningless if $Free_0 = 0$, just as the previous version was meaningless if there were no spaces marked with 99.

Suppose that we've defined

$$
\begin{aligned}
Insert(S, i, x) &= \quad S[1 \ldots i-1] + (x@S[i \ldots] \\
&= \quad x@S, &&\text{if } i = 1 \\
&= \quad S[1]@Insert(Tl(S), i-1, x) &&\text{otherwise}
\end{aligned}
$$

and

$$
\begin{aligned}
Delete(S, i) &= \quad S[1 \ldots i-1] + S[i+1 \ldots] \\
&= \quad Tl(S), &&\text{if } i = 1 \\
&= \quad S[1]@Delete(Tl(S), i-1) &&\text{otherwise}
\end{aligned}
$$

It should be clear by paper-and-pencil experimentation that, by these definitions, $Insert(S, i, x)$ and $Delete(S, i, x)$ each take roughly $i$ steps and use roughly $i$ storage spaces. In the array representation, each of them took $Length(S)$ steps and storage spaces for copying, which can be considerably worse. Similarly, if we define $Append(X, Y) = X + Y$ using $AddItem$, it will take roughly $Length(X)$ steps and storage spaces, which can be much better than $Length(X + Y)$ of each.

The same analysis works when we have tree operations; in fact, tree operations can simulate these without changing the asymptotic analysis. The trees are more complicated and require somewhat more bookkeeping, but the overhead is not huge.

**Exercises**    Using the tree type as previously described:

**9.5-13**  Add a *Free* construction, using either the *Hd* or *Tl* space to keep it in.
**9.5-14**  Define the standard tree-construction functions.

**Dangerous Procedures**    A further advantage to dealing with this style of representation is that we can perform common operations like *Delete, Insert, Append*, and so on without moving or copying the sequences we are working on. Thus, if we are given $S = 1$ and the sequences

$$Val = [a, b, c, d, x, x, x], Nxt = [2, 3, 4, 0, 99, 99, 99]$$

we could represent $Delete(S, 3) = S[1 \ldots 2] + S[4 \ldots]$ as

$$Val = [a, b, c, d, x, x, x], Nxt = [2, 4, 99, 0, 99, 99, 99]$$

so that $Ab(1) = [a, b, d]$. The only action required is $[Nxt[2], Nxt[3]] := [Nxt[3], 99]$. If we don't bother to mark $Nxt[3]$ as unused, we can just say $Nxt[2] := Nxt[Nxt[2]]$. Alternatively, we can represent $Insert(S, 3, e) = S[1 \ldots 2] + [e] + S[3 \ldots]$ as

$$Val = [a, b, c, d, e, x, x], Nxt = [2, 5, 4, 0, 3, 99, 99]$$

so that $Ab(1) = [a, b, e, c, d]$. Here the actions required are $[Val[5], Nxt[5], Nxt[2]] := [e, 3, 5]$; or perhaps more precisely, $Nxt[2] := AddItem(2, Nxt[2])$.

In previous examples, we have written operations on VAR parameters with somewhat this effect; suppose that we try now to write

```
Delete(S,i) == (S := (S[1...i-1]+S[i+1...])
            == S := Tl(S), if i = 1
            == [Hd(S),Tl(S)] := [Hd(S),Delete(Tl(S), i-1)] otherwise
```

In other words, we have

```
PROCEDURE Delete(VAR S : Seq; i:Index);
   (* post: S = Delete(S₀,i) *)
   BEGIN
      IF i=1 THEN S:=Tl(S); ELSE Delete(Tl(S), i-1); END;
END Delete;
```

**Q:** Don't VAR parameters have to be variables? Is Delete(Tl(S),...) legal?
**A:** Yes, they do have to be variables, so this program needs to be edited a bit; in this representation, we can use

IF i=1 THEN S:=Tl(S); ELSE Delete(Nxt[S], i-1); END

**Q:** Is $Nxt[S]$ a VARiable?

**A:** In *Modula-2* (and most other programming languages), the answer is yes; an array element is just like a variable in that it exists at a fixed location which can be read and written, so it is all right to use one as a VAR parameter. Another way to say it is that a *Modula-2* array A[1..N] is actually just a collection of variables $A_1, \ldots, A_N$. The crucial question is that of location: anything which can be thought of as a fixed location (rather than a value) can be a VAR parameter. Expressions like $Tl(S)$ or $3 + x$ have values which are put in temporary locations and then thrown away; it doesn't make sense to say 3+x:=y.

Now, let's define an iterative version, satisfying the loop invariant

(* Delete(S,i) = Delete($S_0$,$i_0$) *)

**Q:** But isn't that trivial? This is a simple recurrence: all I need to write is

LOOP (* Delete(S,i) = Delete($S_0$,$i_0$) *).
   IF i=1 THEN S:=Tl(S); RETURN ELSE S:=Nxt[S]; i:=i-1 END
END

How could there be anything wrong with it?

**A:** If you try running it, you'll see that it has the effect of S:=Drop(i,S) rather than a single deletion. The loop invariant is correct, in a manner of speaking, but this procedure tears the walls down in its pursuit of the goal. Don't go into shock; the basic idea of a simple recurrence as an iteration was one we worked out with great care for values, but we edged around the issue for VAR parameters. The answer is not really all that easy. What we want to say is

IF i=1 THEN S:=Nxt[S]
   ELSIF i=2 THEN Nxt[S]:=Nxt[Nxt[S]]
   ELSIF i=3 THEN Nxt[Nxt[S]]:=Nxt[Nxt[Nxt[S]]]
   $\vdots$

Thus if $i = 1$, we are changing $S$; otherwise we are changing a position inside the $Nxt$ array. One good way to express (and solve) the problem is

IF i=1 THEN Pop(S) ELSE Pop(Nxt[Drop(i-1,S)]) END

Since Drop(n,S) is a value-parameter program, its conversion from

IF n=0 THEN S ELSE Drop(n-1,Tl(S)) END

to a simple loop is straightforward.

## Exercises

**9.5-15** Explain why this version of the program is in some respects more efficient than the previous version: How much space does it use? How much time?

**9.5-16** Consider Insert(S,i,x) == Insert(Nxt[s],i-1,x) by analogy with Delete; complete the definition. (Use recursion).

**9.5-17** Explain the space and time requirements of this version of Insert, and define an iterative version. (Use Drop).

**9.5-18** Define a version of Append along the same lines, so that Append(X,Y) == (X := X+Y). (Again, use Drop).

**Q:** I can see that these procedures will sometimes be more efficient than the ones using arrays, and I can certainly see that they're often confusing, but what's dangerous about them?

**A:** The basic problem is that when you change one object with two names, then both names are redefined. If I have defined $X$ as $AddItem(5, Y)$, then $Y$ and $Nxt[X]$ are different names for the same thing, so $Delete(X, 3)$ and $Delete(Y, 2)$ perform the same operation. Again, we're involved with aliases, and strange bugs fly in through the window and through other apertures. (There is a Mexican proverb to the effect that "Flies stay out of a closed mouth;[1]" it's very strange how many programmers get into bug trouble through a failure to close off their data structures.)

It's time for a summary: where are we? Well, you've expanded your ability to deal with sequences, so you can now implement the sequence and tree modules of the previous chapter in terms of fixed-size arrays. Not only that, but you can choose between "mid-slice," "front-slice," and "back-slice" approaches in which a logical sequence is represented by a subsequence of a physical sequence, or between lists linked by $Nxt$ pointers and trees linked by $Hd$ and $Tl$ pointers. Each of these gives drastically different performance results on the same abstract programs, and also drastically different kinds of bugs. You are now able to program independently in *Modula-2*...but don't go away quite yet, there are still a few basic ideas to go over before we're done. I'm not talking about the many features of the language we haven't covered: language features can be picked up pretty easily if you have some grasp of the ideas underneath them. ("Underneath" doesn't always mean low level:

---

[1] *En boca cerrada, moscas no entran.*

the ideas underneath the set constructions of *Modula-2* are ideas which we covered in Part I. In this case, however, the missing pieces are very low-level concepts.)

### 9.5.2 Pointers

We've been dealing with pointers as a way of looking at (or using) arrays of indices. We've used the idea of memory as a large array, but we've used it more as a metaphor than as a tool. We haven't really dealt with pointers as addresses. That limits us in two ways:

- We haven't connected our pointer ideas with those of VAR parameters, even though I've told you (in the original description of the VAR parameter concept) that a variable parameter is passed as a reference to that variable's location.

- We're still limited to advance selection of upper bounds: as long as our program's lists of integers are stored in one array, its lists of strings in another, and so on, the total size of all lists of integers is bounded in advance. It may well be that this program's requirements grow and shrink, while some other program's requirements shrink and grow: as we link many modules together, it is unlikely that they all reach their maximum storage requirements all at once. We don't have any method of sharing space between different types of objects or between modules.

**Allocation and Traversal of Dynamic Structures**    We'll begin by getting away from the second restriction. Any time that we want to create (and perhaps get rid of) objects of a certain type, we just define a POINTER TO that type. If we declare that P is a POINTER TO INTEGER, that means that it can point to an integer; it isn't necessarily pointing to anything in advance. We can create a new integer just by saying NEW(P); after that, P^ is a variable of type INTEGER. Logically speaking, this is just like an index into memory, so when we say P^, think Mem[P]. The NEW procedure takes an object off of Free and lets us work with it; it doesn't have to be a list element.

However, the extension that this technique gives us is not limited to handling new objects which aren't lists. A big difference is that memory now looks rather lumpy, because we can pull out objects of different sizes. There can be pointers to integers, characters, Booleans, records, arrays, or even pointers. As an example, let's look at the IntSeq module, in Figure 9.11.

In this module, an integer sequence is represented as a pointer to a record; each record contains a Head, which is an integer, and a Tail, which is a pointer. The correspondence to the Val and Nxt arrays is exact, with the special pointer NIL taking the role we assigned to 0. We could make it even more obvious by changing the names of the arrays Val and Nxt to Head and Tail, respectively. Then we could simply say that NIL corresponds to 0, while P^.Head corresponds to Head[P] and P^.Tail corresponds to Tail[P]. (In reading this sort of code, it helps to keep

IMPLEMENTATION MODULE IntSeq;

FROM Storage IMPORT ALLOCATE;

TYPE IntSeq = POINTER TO IntSeqNode;
    IntSeqNode = RECORD Head : Item; Tail : IntSeq END ;

PROCEDURE Hd(S:IntSeq):Item;
    (* pre: S = [S1..Sn], n >= 1. post: result = S1 *)
    BEGIN RETURN S^.Head END Hd;

PROCEDURE AddItem(A:Item; S:IntSeq):IntSeq;
    (* post: result is sequence R with Hd(R)=A, Tl(R)=S *)
    VAR R : IntSeq;
    BEGIN
      NEW(R);
      R^.Head := A;
      R^.Tail := S;
      RETURN R
END AddItem;

PROCEDURE IsNull(S:IntSeq):BOOLEAN;
    (* post: result is TRUE if S is empty, FALSE otherwise *)
    BEGIN RETURN (S=NIL) END IsNull;

PROCEDURE NewNull():IntSeq;
    (* post: result is an empty sequence *)
    BEGIN RETURN NIL END NewNull;

END IntSeq.

**Figure 9.11**

remembering that if R is a pointer to a record, then R^ is the record itself, i.e., R^ really is a variable.)

**Q:** What's this about FROM Storage IMPORT ALLOCATE? The name ALLOCATE isn't used anywhere in the program.

**A:** Yes, it is, but it's invisible. NEW is defined as an abbreviation for something involving ALLOCATE; if you change ALLOCATE, you'll change NEW.

Now we can write procedures like Push(a,S), which in this representation is most easily expressed as S:=AddItem(a,S); Pop(S), which is S:=Tl(S); and so on. It's perfectly all right to return these structures as the values of functions: a POINTER is thought of as a simple quantity like an INTEGER or CARDINAL, and any implementation of *Modula-2* will let you return it as a value.

Your ability to express solutions has not changed at all from the previous (array-based) version of linked-sequence definitions. All that has changed is that your IntSeq links did not need to come out of a specific array associated with that type and allocated in advance. That should mean that the program can run with no more space for IntSeq cells than it really needs. Moreover, it can have several different kinds of sequences and trees, none of which need any space allocated in advance; all such space is taken out of a common "heap," as a chunk of memory which is not associated with any high-level type.

Here's a sample IntTree type:

```
TYPE IntTree = POINTER TO IntTreeNode;
     IntTreeNode = RECORD CASE IsTree : BOOLEAN OF
                          TRUE : Head,Tail : IntTree |
                          FALSE : IntVal : Integer
                      END
              END;
```

This should now (with a little work) seem quite comprehensible.

**Exercise**

**9.5-19** Specify, write, and test an IntTrees module based on this data structure, which exports the usual access and construction functions.

As much as we can, we write programs which don't care about the underlying data structure. However, it's a good idea to consider solutions which take advantage of that structure. Now, it's easy enough to construct a SumTree(T:IntTree) algorithm as

```
IF T=NIL THEN RETURN 0
    ELSIF T^.IsTree THEN RETURN (SumTree(T^.Head)+SumTree(T^.Tail))
    ELSE RETURN (T^.IntVal)
END
```

We can even rewrite it as a loop:

```
S := 0;
LOOP (* S+SumTree(T) = SumTree(T₀) *)
    IF T = NIL THEN RETURN S
        ELSIF T^.IsTree THEN S:=S+SumTree(T^.Head); T:=T^.Tail
        ELSE RETURN (S + T^.IntVal)
    END
END
```

There's nothing difficult about designing, debugging, or maintaining these representation-sensitive versions of general tree operations; the only difficulty is that they may need to be rewritten if we want to carry out the same operation on a similar type next month or next year.

Assuming that IntTrees exists, we can then define a module for OrderedTrees, where an ordered tree is either empty, or it has a Mid $n$ which is an integer, a Lo $A$ which is an ordered tree of integers less than or equal to $n$, and a Hi $B$ which is an ordered tree of integers strictly larger than $n$. We would do that by writing the six functions

$$
\begin{aligned}
NewTree(n) &= MakeTree(n, [\,], [\,]) \\
MakeTree(n, A, B) &= [n, A, B] \\
Mid(T) &= TreeToInt(Hd(T)) \\
Lo(T) &= Hd(Tl(T)) \\
Hi(T) &= Hd(Tl(Tl(T))) \\
Insert(n, [\,]) &= NewTree(n) \\
Insert(n, [m, L, H]) &= [m, Insert(n, L), H] \qquad \text{if } n \leq m \\
&= [m, L, Insert(n, H)] \qquad \text{otherwise}
\end{aligned}
$$

As before, we now sort a sequence by putting all its elements into an ordered tree and then flattening. However, we'd like to be able to have the Insert work efficiently; in particular, we'd like it to be a procedure

Insert(n:INTEGER; VAR T:OrderedTree)

which then requires a representation-sensitive program

```
IF T=NIL THEN T:=NewTree(n)
   ELSIF n <= Mid(T)
      THEN Insert(n, T^.Tail^.Head)       (* Insert(n, Lo(T)) *)
      ELSE Insert(n, T^.Tail^.Tail^.Head)       (* Insert(n, Hi(T)) *)
   END
```

That's a very sad situation. It's pretty easy to develop this kind of program from the prototype which used the general-purpose tree (and associated routines for reading and writing general-purpose trees), then modify it this way to make it somewhat more efficient, and then discover that the modification isn't really good enough. We could do better by redefining OrderedTree as

```
TYPE OrderedTree = POINTER TO OrderedNode;
     OrderedNode = RECORD IntVal : INTEGER; Lo, Hi : OrderedTree END
```

Now the Insert code would be simply

```
IF T=NIL THEN NEW(T); T^.IntVal := n; T^.Lo := NIL; T^.Hi := NIL
   ELSIF n <= T^.IntVal THEN Insert(n, T^.Lo)
   ELSE Insert(n, T^.Hi)
```

Such a revision will not change the asymptotic analysis of the algorithm, but it can significantly decrease the amount of work which the program has to do. Unfortunately, if you've already written a heavily representation-dependent algorithm, then it can be very hard to make such changes.

Don't introduce representation-dependence until you must.

The Insert code just presented looks like a simple recurrence, but it's working on VAR parameters.

### Exercises

**9.5-20** Explain what will happen if you simply turn the Insert code into a LOOP using T := T^.Lo as if it were a value parameter.

**9.5-21** (Difficult!) Develop a LOOPing solution by generalizing the Drop-based solution, i.e., write an iterative procedure which (for a nonempty initial tree) finds the node to be altered and perhaps records whether $n$ is to go into the Head or Tail.

The clumsiness of this situation can be partly avoided if we just learn how to think about VAR parameters as pointers, but this situation is very difficult to visualize and the effort to work that way frequently causes very hard-to-find bugs. First, we'll develop our visualizations—and programming skills—a little further, by learning to get rid of space we no longer want.

**The Programmer Proposes, but** DEALLOCATE DISPOSEs    The pointer-based IntSeq definition works well, but eventually it does run out of space. As was noted (without much explanation) in the last chapter,

S := NewNull(); LOOP Push(a,S); Pop(S) END

will eventually run out of space because Push requires that new space be created, but Pop does not release any space. An apparently reliable fix is easy: we import a procedure called DEALLOCATE along with the ALLOCATE procedure from STORAGE, and then we redefine Pop(S) as [S,Free] := [Tl(S), Hd(S)@Free]. In other words, we say

VAR R; BEGIN R := S; S := Tl(S); DISPOSE(R) END

The DISPOSE procedure is an abbreviation for something involving DEALLO-CATE, and the node which AddItem requested is sent back to the "heap" of available storage. Using this, we can write Delete(i,S) as

IF i=1 THEN S:= S^.Tail ELSE R:= Drop(i-2,S); Pop(R^.Tail) END;

Of course, there's a problem. Of course, it involves aliases. The problem is that you may have many pointers to the same storage location, and if you DISPOSE(R) after saying that S :=R, then S will be a pointer to deallocated storage, which may be untouched for a while or may be immediately reallocated and filled with bits representing some other data type. This situation is a great boon to the sellers of headache remedies, not to mention coffee, because the bugs which creep into code like this have a tendency to stay buried for a long time, surfacing only when many complicated things are happening. When they do surface, the problem therefore seems to be somewhere else. The reason for that is simple: the simple test cases will not usually put stress on the allocator, so the data pointed to by S will remain untouched for a while; it's only when you're doing it for real that Murphy's Law gets a chance.

There are at least three things you can do about that:

- Avoid aliases: keep as few variables of each pointer type as you can, and keep them separate (It helps a lot to keep them in separate modules.) Write using nondestructive abstract procedures like AddItem, Hd, and Get as much as possible.

- Test thoroughly: even though you're sure it works, remember the strange bugs that come in with aliases and keep on testing. It can help to replace the

DISPOSE(R) call with the procedure MyDispose(R) defined for each pointer type, which first overwrites the list or tree node pointed to by R and then calls on DISPOSE. That way, early test cases are more likely to come up with problems. As an extension of that idea, you can extend the node to include a Boolean field IsDead, which MyDispose sets to TRUE and which is tested by Hd and Tl or whatever access functions your type requires. Access to a dead node is clearly an error.

- Improve your understanding of the underlying situation. That means that you have to have a good idea of how to deal with pointers as addresses.

**Pointers As Addresses**    For this problem, we really need to look at the VAR parameter idea: what does it mean when we write a procedure like SwapInt?

```
PROCEDURE SwapInt(VAR i,j:INTEGER);
   VAR k:INTEGER;
   BEGIN k := i; i := j; j := k END SwapInt;
```

In fact, different implementations are allowed for different compilers, but the most common is a straightforward pointer construction. What we're really writing is

```
TYPE IntPtr = POINTER TO INTEGER;
PROCEDURE SwapInt(i,j: IntPtr);
   VAR k:INTEGER;
   BEGIN k := i^; i^ := j^; j^ := k END SwapInt;
```

Remember what I said about P^ corresponding to Memory[P]; look at the last line as

```
BEGIN k := Memory[i]; Memory[i] := Memory[j]; Memory[j] := k END
```

You should see that there is actually no difference between this and the Swap idea on sequences. Now, what does a call on SwapInt look like? When we say SwapInt(x,y) with VAR parameters, what we really mean is

```
SwapInt(ADR(x),ADR(y))
```

just as if we were writing Swap(Memory,xNdx,bNdx), where xNdx is the index of x in the Memory sequence. Now, of course, we can write the Delete iteration directly from the recursive version;

```
IF i=1 THEN S:=Tl(S) ELSE Delete(S^.Tail,i-1) END
```

becomes a program on values if we give it P=ADR(S) as argument, so that S=P^. Then we can write (by simple substitution)

```
IF i=1 THEN P^:=Tl(P^) ELSE Delete(ADR(P^^.Tail),i-1) END
```

This is truly a simple recurrence, and we can easily construct

LOOP (* Delete(P^,i) = Delete($P_0$^,$i_0$) *)
    IF i=1 THEN P^:=Tl(P^) ELSE P := ADR(P^^.Tail); i:=i-1 END
END

Of course, it's not very nice to force everyone to use the ADR procedure in order to make use of Delete;[2] it's much better to let Delete(S,i) continue to be a VAR parameter procedure and precede the loop just given with P:=ADR(S), where P is a local variable of type POINTER TO IntSeq.

## Exercises

**9.5-22** Complete and test the Delete definition just suggested.

**9.5-23** Improve the procedure by making it test for premature termination of the sequence: What should Delete([1,2,3],1000) do?

**9.5-24** Using the same principle, write an Insert(S,i,x) procedure for integer sequences with the effect of

S := Append(Take(i-1,S),AddItem(x, Drop(i-1,S)))

(The code you write will not be strictly equivalent to this, because Append andTake construct new list structures; you will only allocate one new node.)

**9.5-25** Specify, write, and test an Insert procedure for ordered trees using this idea.

We haven't covered all of the important ideas of data representation, by any means. However, we have covered many of them, and at this point you can develop and compare good representations for a lot of problems. If you go back to the end of the previous chapter and look at the projects there, you'll realize what the next stage has to be: pick a prototype and improve it. Here are some hints which you might find helpful:

- If you have a sequence type for which you often use PushOnBack(S,x), you can start with a version like

    IF S=NIL THEN S:=AddItem(x,S)
     ELSE R:=Last(S); R^.Tail:=AddItem(x,S) END
    where
    Last(S) = IF IsNull(Tl(S)) THEN S ELSE Last(Tl(S)) END

    Notice that Last is only meaningful on nonempty sequences; notice also that as you do PushOnBack, you determine the value of Last for next time. It's

---

[2]For one thing, it has to be explicitly imported from the SYSTEM module because it's a dangerous thing to have around.

easy enough to record that, if you have a place to do so...and it's a lot better to do it in the sequence itself than in the program. Accordingly, you can define a new sequence type, which many people call a queue, as

TYPE Queue = RECORD Seq, Last : IntSeq END;

and the module defining this kind of sequence will export all the standard operations on sequences, including PushOnBack—which will be a constant-time operation just as it was with some of the array implementations. It's easy enough to define PushOnBack(Q,x):

```
IF Q^.Seq = NIL THEN
        Q^.Seq := IntSeqs.AddItem(x,NIL);
        Q^.Last := Q^.Seq
    ELSE Q^.Last^.Tail := IntSeqs.AddItem(x,NIL);
            Q^.Last := Q^.Last^.Tail
END
```

Now you should be able to define all the other access and construction operations for this fundamental type.

- If you have a sequence type for which you often move slowly forwards (a text editor is a common example) where Get(S,i) is quite likely to be followed by Get(S,i+1), it can equally well help to define a record type which records LastUsed instead of Last. More precisely, whenever you Get(S,i) or Put(S,i) or insert or delete, you want to find Drop(i-2,S) and go on from there. If you've defined Drop to use the LastUsed field, then there's very little code to write as you shift from one linked-list implementation in which

FOR i:=1 TO K DO Delete(S,N) END

requires $\mathcal{O}(K*N)$ operations, to another in which it requires at most $\mathcal{O}(K+N)$ (and may require just $K$ operations if we are already near position $N$).

There are a great many variations on these ideas. You can simplify some of the code I just suggested by sticking a "dummy" node in front of your sequences, so that the logical sequence $S$ is represented by the physical sequence $P^\wedge$.Tail and there is no longer any special code to write for the empty-sequence case since it isn't physically empty. You can tabulate the $Prev$ function as well as the $Nxt$ function, so that you can move backward as well as forward in constant time. You can keep a dictionary with a LookUp procedure which pulls definitions to the front of the dictionary whenever they're used, so that they'll be found more quickly next time. The list goes on forever, but this chapter doesn't. (It just seems that way.) You now have the core of what you need for competent programming. There are many missing pieces, and you will spend much of your programming time trying to fill them in systematically. One useful approach is to look over manuals and see what's there which hasn't been mentioned here, and then work on figuring it out and using it; if you have trouble understanding *Modula-2*'s SET OF constructions, then you should go back to Part I and start all over again. The particular missing piece left over for the final chapter of this book is the basic framework of programming language implementation, which fits together all the work we've done so far (and a few new things) in the attempt to see how it all works.

# 10

# How Does It Work?

In this chapter, we'll put together most of the concepts underlying the programming system itself. Of course, you can use a programming system as a programmer without fully understanding it, but the more you understand your tools the better you'll be able to deal with things that go wrong. Actually, this is just an excuse: the best reason for studying programming-language implementation, Greek philosophy, or evolutionary biology is that it's fascinating. We start with simple physical principles, and we build one representation on top of another, each hiding the details of the one beneath it, until we arrive at a level you've come to understand as suitable for describing arbitrary computations. This is one of the most surprising products of the human mind so far. It is as if we were to come up with physical methods of constructing atoms, and chemical methods of constructing organic molecules, and then package these into functional units of varying sizes (membrane, nucleus, mitochondria,...) and find how to package those units into cells, how to build the cells into organs—such as the units which make up the brain—and finally how to construct a human being who's able to repeat the process. All coexist in the same physical object, but each logical level of design is quite distinct from all the rest. Your intuitive understanding of physics tells you almost nothing about the chemical properties you find at the next layer up, chemistry constrains but does not seem to explain cellular components, and so on up the line.

We won't go over the details of a real *Modula-2* (or comparable language) implementation, or even the details of a real machine. Instead, we'll lay the foundations by working with slightly simplified problems at each level.

- The first step is to talk about machinery: not the physics of silicon vs. gallium-arsenide semiconductor technology, but something logically equivalent and a lot easier to visualize. We'll work out a "physical layer" containing wires and switches and electromagnets.

- Based on this, we can construct a "gate layer" containing the operations of Boolean logic, and a clock.

- From these gates, we can construct a "package layer" containing (mainly) arithmetic operations and memory access (read-only or read/write).

- From the packages, we can build a "microprogramming layer" containing instructions for connecting them; i.e., for using switches to open paths between packages. Here we have something that does look somewhat like a programming language, but all of the statements are assignment statements... and it's easy to intepret each of them as a pattern of ones and zeros, as switches on or off.

- Now we can design a "stack machine," with microprograms which interpret data management instructions somewhat like Push and Pop, arithmetic/logical instructions somewhat like "+" and "∧", and control operations somewhat like "IF..THEN..ELSE" and procedure invocation. The layer involving such instructions is the one which we usually think of as "the machine," and the instructions just mentioned are usually called machine code. Many large programs are written at this level, usually as assembly code, which can be turned into machine code by substitution. Language implementations usually translate the high-level code to this level.

- Now we can translate simple expressions like "$3 * (5 - 8)$" into machine code.

- We can extend the translation in various directions, e.g., to include statements involving arrays, assignment and input/output:

    x:=INPUT; y[3]:=x∗x∗x;
    IF x < z THEN OUTPUT:=y[0]-x ELSE z:=x END;

  (As we do so, we end up adding more features to the machine itself.)

- Now we can extend the translation to include simple functions, without any notion of scope. (At this point, you'll see why simple recurrences shouldn't have to run out of space.)

- Now we can extend again to use nonlocal variables.

- Finally, we consider extensions beyond *Modula-2*... and extensions beyond those.

At each level, we see the issues of representation and implementation arising once more: there is always a layer above, whose objects and operations are closely (but perhaps imperfectly) modeled by the layer below. We pile model on top of model, world over worlds, passing through intermediate logical layers which don't much resemble either the top or the bottom. The images and terminology we use will not be completely standard, but they will be close enough so that as you go on to study computer architecture and compiler design you'll recognize many of the fundamental ideas. Even if you go no further, you should now have some sense of what lies beneath you as you program in a high-level language...and of what might lie ahead.

## 10.1 THE PHYSICAL LAYER

The physics underlying computer operation changes in minor ways every few years, and in major ways from one generation to the next. I don't greatly care whether you understand the principles underlying transistor operation; the logical idea is that a small activity (electrical current) in one place (wire) can control (amplify or inhibit) a larger current in another, and this is something we can look at without thinking about solid-state physics. All we want for now is the "Doorbell Model of Computation"; that's quite enough to build computers with, as long as we don't expect them to work very fast.

Imagine a lamp which can be turned off by either of two switches: one labelled $W$ on the wall, and one labelled $B$ at the base of the lamp. (Both switches must be on for the lamp to be on.) Now replace the switches with buttons, held upwards by light springs, which must be pushed down to be turned on. That's not very convenient: you have to be in two places at once to turn on the lamp. We'll turn $B$ upside down: if I'm at the wall and you're sitting by the lamp, then I can turn the light on by pushing $W$ down unless you turn it off by pulling $B$ up. If you don't like pulling on the button, we'll give you a magnet to do it with. Just hold the magnet close to $B$ and it will overcome the spring, so the light will turn off. (The spring does have to be weaker than the magnet.)

A doorbell (like a light bulb) sits quietly, waiting for electricity to start flowing through it. When I push the wall-button $W$, electricity flows through an electro-magnet which pulls $B$ up. That stops the electricity from flowing through the wire, so the electromagnet turns off, so $B$ drops down, so the electromagnet turns on, so $B$ comes up, so the electromagnet...got it? $B$ is *buzzing* *back* and forth quite noisily, and if it bangs against a bell, the effect can be quite chiming, really.

### Exercise

**10.1-1**    Draw pictures of this. Go to a hardware store and get a coil of wire, some nails, and batteries. (You can use gravity instead of the springs.) Get buzzy. (If you need more explicit directions, do *not* go to your college librarian or physics professor. You'll have better luck with the children's librarian in a public library, or with an elementary-school science teacher.)

**Q:** Why does this stuff belong in an introductory computer science textbook?

**A:** Because that's all you need for a mental model of low-level computation: circuits made of wires and switches, with the switches sometimes opened or shut by currents through other wires—or even the same wires. The doorbell is a particularly elegant example: it's a circuit which insists on turning itself off, just as fast as you turn it on. All it wants is to be let alone... why don't you stop bothering the poor thing and go on to the next section?

## 10.2 GATEWAYS TO LOGIC

Given the doorbell model, we can construct a "gate layer" containing the operations of Boolean logic. We take some wires and label them $A$, $B$, and $C$. Now we think of a wire as representing a Boolean value *True* if current flows along it, and *False* otherwise. Now we try connecting them in various ways, and measure the current flow as we start things up on $A, B$, and $C$ and again an instant later (after giving switches a chance to flip) to find $A'$, $B'$, and $C'$.

- Control $B$ with a switch which is pulled open (off) if $A$ is on, and is shut if $A$ is off. That means that $B' = \neg A$ and we have implemented a NOT gate, or "inverter".

- Alternatively, control $C$ with a pair of switches which are held open with springs, but $A$ closes one of them and $B$ closes the other. Current flows through $C$ if current flows through $A$ and $B$, so $C' = A \wedge B$, and we have implemented an AND gate.

- Again, we could control $C$ with a pair of switches held shut with springs, one of which is opened by $A$ and the other by $B$. In this case $C' = \neg(A \wedge B)$, and that's called a NAND gate.

We don't need any more than these; in fact, we don't even need all of these. Obviously, we could build a NAND gate by combining an AND gate and a NOT gate; we just need one more wire than if we built it directly from switches and springs. Less obviously, we could build a NOT gate from a NAND gate. If both of the springs involved in the NAND gate are opened by the same current, then we're computing $\neg(A \wedge A)$ which is the same as $\neg A$.

### Exercises

**10.2-1**  Explain how to construct an OR gate directly with switches and springs.

**10.2-2**  Explain how to construct an OR gate from two NOT gates and a NAND gate.

**10.2-3**  Explain how to construct an "XOR" (or "$\neq$") gate from NAND gates.

In an ideal world, we might be able to say that we're constructing a Boolean-algebra module and the definition  module is entirely independent of the implementation module. In practice, it's not quite that simple. It takes time for the switches to open and close, and a complex circuit may go wrong because an OR gate which takes a millisecond to close is not really the same as one which takes twice that long. It takes power for a wire to drive an electromagnet, so we can't run an arbitrarily large number of switches from a single wire; we need a COPY gate in which $B' = A$, but $B$'s power source is not a drain on $A$. (We construct it by having $B$ powered through a switch which is normally held open, but which $A$ pulls shut.) If we want to compute a thousand Boolean functions from one wire, we may find that we need to have that wire flip eight copy switches, each of which flips eight copy switches, each of which flips eight copy switches, each of which is used to compute two Boolean functions; this "fanout" again takes time. Even worse, it's not really true to say that a given wire is always "on" or "off": the current varies continuously between minimal and maximum values.

We get around some of these problems by bringing back the doorbell—the circuit that constantly switches itself off, and thus generates a steady on/off/on/off ... buzz. The doorbell's $A' = \neg A$ buzz serves as a clocktick which holds our system to a steady pace, provided that it's slower than any of the system pieces need to be. (We can slow down the doorbell by putting lots of copy switches in it.) Then we can build circuits which look like this:

$$
\begin{aligned}
A' &= A, && \text{if } \neg T \\
&= \neg B, && \text{otherwise}
\end{aligned}
$$

If $T$ is a clock $T$ick, then the circuit defining $A'$ is a clocked inverter: $A$ never changes except when the clock ticks, and then it switches away from $B$'s value. As a Boolean function, we just need $A' = (\neg T \wedge A) \vee (T \wedge \neg B)$, which is tedious but not difficult. We can now develop the whole machine to run in synchronous cycles: the clock ticks and switches start flipping as information propagates through the circuits, but everything settles down before the next clock tick. If it doesn't, then the machine behaves unpredictably and the designer has to put in faster switches, smaller circuits, or a longer time between ticks.

**Q:** Is that really how it works?

**A:** It's an oversimplified version of part of one way that it could work. The issues I'm talking about are real issues, and the images you should be collecting are not too far from realistic images.

The clocked inverter, meanwhile, is not far from being a memory "flip-flop" element, which only changes when the clock ticks and there's a signal instructing it to change, i.e.

$$
\begin{aligned}
A' &= A, && \text{if } \neg T \\
&= A && \text{if } \neg B \\
&= \neg A, && \text{otherwise}
\end{aligned}
$$

That requires the Boolean circuit $A' = (\neg T \wedge A) \vee (T \wedge (B \neq A))$. Actually, we can slowly start to forget the clock: it's going to be in there all the time, but we can just think of $A$ as being a "clocked variable" defined with $A' = A \neq B$, where a "clocked variable" is only redefined when the clock ticks. Now you can imagine connecting the flip-flop in various ways: if you have $B = 1$ (a constant) and start out with $A = 1$, you'll get the sequence 1,0,1,0,....

## Exercises

**10.2-4**  What happens if you have $B = 0$ (again, a constant)?

**10.2-5**  What happens if you have $B = A$ (feed the output back to the input)?

**10.2-6**  What happens if you have $B$ be the output from a flip-flopping flip-flop: 1, 0, 1, 0, 1, 0, 1, 0, ...?

You can construct a lot of things with these. In fact, it's perfectly possible to construct a memory out of flip-flops, but it's nicer to be able to change the "flip-flop" to an honest Boolean variable which can be the target of an assignment statement. Now we need the clock $T$ick, a signal to say "time for a $C$hange in your value," and a third signal for the $V$alue itself":

$$
\begin{aligned}
A' &= A, && \text{if } \neg T \\
&= A, && \text{if } \neg C \\
&= V, && \text{otherwise}
\end{aligned}
$$

This construction will let us model $A := V$ by turning $C$ on but leave $A$ unchanged otherwise.

## Exercises

**10.2-7**  Write the Boolean expression for this kind of memory element, leaving out the clock tick.

**10.2-8**  Assume that the answer to the previous exercise is the expression $X$. Use $X$ (without taking it apart) in writing the full Boolean expression, including the clock tick.

So we can compute Boolean functions. Not only that, but we can have a state which is a collection of clocked Boolean variables $b_0, b_1, \ldots$, and we can have a series of states $S_0, S_1, \ldots$ in which each $b_i$ in $S_{j+1}$ is an arbitrary Boolean function of the values in $S_j$. It's not a computer design, but it certainly looks like a permission slip for starting one.

### Exercises

**10.2-9**    Design a Circuit type, with the appropriate functions. (This is a lot of fun, but it's hard to come up with convincing answers. It can help to think of a "pile" of circuits as having a lot of loose input and output lines: instead of linking two circuits directly, we make a pile of them and select one input and one output line to be linked within the pile.)

**10.2-10**    Implement and test a prototype of your Circuit module.

## 10.3  IT'S ALL IN THE PACKAGING

From these gate constructions, we hope to build a "package layer" with arithmetic operations and memory access (read-only or read/write). We have almost entirely forgotten the doorbell itself: we are working with gates, not the switches which are used to make them. If someone comes tomorrow with a new technology for better switches, then the cost factors of our problem will change, but the problem itself will not because we'll still be building our packages from gates rather than directly from switches. The modularity issue is just the same as in software.

So how can we construct gadgets to handle integers and addresses? Easily (although with prolonged attention to detail); we did this in Part I. We can build a package which has 16 Boolean inputs $b_{15}, b_{14}, \ldots b_0$ representing a binary number between 0 and (2\*\*16-1); another 16 for another binary number; another for the clock; and 16 Boolean outputs to represent the sum of the inputs. That's a 16-bit adder. We can build a package which has 16 Boolean inputs and 16 Boolean outputs, wherein if the input represents $n$, then the output represents $(n + 1)$ mod 2\*\*16. That's a 16-bit counter.

**Q:** Yes, but when we did that in Part I we assumed that the digits were constructed one at a time, as the carry propagated from right to left. To add 18543176 to 31457828 and get 50001004 presumably takes eight steps. Aren't you assuming that it now happens all at once?

**A:** No, I'm just assuming that the carry propagation finishes before the clock ticks again. Arithmetic can be slow: many machines are organized so that different kinds of operations take different amounts of time, but we're going to construct our hypothetical machine so that the fastest parts just wait for the slowest. Therefore our clock will tick several times to make a "minute" long enough for one complete arithmetic operation, and we may (or may not) use several of these to make a "minor machine cycle" and several of these to make a "major machine cycle"; this chapter will not work at that level of detail.

It is worthwhile to mention alternatives. The algorithm suggested in Part I is $\mathcal{O}(N)$ for adding $N$-$bit$ numbers, but actually it can be done faster than that: to add 18543176 to 31457828, we use a single eight-digit adder beginning with a carry of 0, or we can simultaneously start up three four-digit adders. One is adding 1854 to 3145 (the left halves) with an initial carry of 0, the second is adding 3176 to 7828 (the right halves) with an initial carry of 0, and the third—the "just-in-case" adder—is adding the left halves with an initial carry of 1. In this case, the left halves add together to make 4999 with a final carry of 0, and the right halves make 1004 (remember, this was a four-digit adder) with a final carry of 1. If the right halves had added together with a final carry of 0, we wouldn't need the just-in-case adder; the answer would be 49991004. Since they had a final carry of 1, we use the just-in-case adder's value of 5000 (with a final carry of 0), and that gives us the result 50001004 (with a final carry of 0). That required four steps by each of the three smaller adders, and a put-together step; in fact we can apply this idea recursively to define a $\mathcal{O}(log(N))$ adder which uses $\mathcal{O}(N*log(N))$ circuits arranged in a tree to compute the final answer.

**Exercise**

**10.3-1**   Discuss the "parallel adder" concept with words, diagrams, and equations.

Each adder (or counter) presumably has an extra output to indicate a carry from the highest bit; the adder might have other inputs to encode messages like "do subtraction instead," while the counter might have a "reset to 0" input line. The conceptual center of a traditional computer is often an adder extended this way and is called an $ALU$: an arithmetic and logic unit, which can be told to generate several different functions of its input lines. A crucial piece of the machinery for getting the $ALU$ its instructions is a program counter, which can be reset not only to zero but to an arbitrary value provided on its input lines: when we call on a procedure, we want to start executing that procedure's code, wherever it may be.

In each case, the result is that we're constructing a new state (i.e., a new collection of Boolean variables) as a function of the old. There are several other important kinds of packages, but for my limited purposes I can get by with just one more kind. Here's a package which is going to be labelled with a number $n$ between 0 and $2**16-1$; we'll choose 53219, just to be definite. Package#53219 is associated with two Boolean variables: $a$ and $b$. The value of $a$ is one of the package's input lines; it also has a clock input as always, 16 lines of data input called an address, one $C$ontrol line, and one $V$alue line. Despite all this complex input, the only external output is $b$. Now we must define $a$ and $b$ as Boolean functions:

$$a', b' \;=\; a, 0 \quad \text{if address} \neq 53219 \text{ in binary}$$
$$=\; a, a \quad \text{if } C = 0$$
$$=\; V, 0 \quad \text{otherwise}$$

In other words, if the address is not that of this package, then the output is 0 (*False*) and the contents are unchanged. If the address is that of this package and the *C*ontrol signal is off, then somebody's trying to read this datum and not change it. If the address is that of this package and the *C*ontrol signal is on, then somebody's trying to write this bit, so record the *V*alue line!

Now let's construct 2**16 of these packages, each with a different number. After we deal with fanout and fanin, we have a "64K-by-1-bit" memory which will accept any address and either read from it or write to it. This memory still has only a clock input, 16 lines of address, one control line, and one value line... all leading to one output line. We can read and write bits!

Take 16 of these memories connected side by side. The same clock input, 16 lines of address, and one control line should be copied to each of them. However, we'll use 16 value lines... all leading to 16 output lines. Now when we ask "What's at address 53219?" we get 16 distinct answers, which we can interpret as the 16 bits of a binary number. If we want to put 16 bits into address 53219, we can do that too. We can read and write (16-bit) words! When we build a machine with a memory which is "$N$-by-$k$" bits, $N$ is the "memory size," $log(N)$ is the number of bits required for an address, and $k$ is the "word size," A word is just a sequence of bits, and different machines have different word sizes; *Modula-2* has the built-in type WORD but the size of a word is machine dependent. Words are usually made of eight-bit chunks, used to store characters or other information; *Modula-2* therefore has the type BYTE.

Those are the crucial pieces: the ALU, the counter, and the memory. Besides these, we'll need a few numbers; i.e., collections of Boolean variables for keeping track of what's where. These will be called *registers*, and everything will be hooked together with a lot of gates that we won't talk about.

**Exercises**    This system sends a message "Are you it?" to every memory cell.

**10.3-2**    Explain how the fanout process could do part of the address checking, so that most of the memory cells would never be asked and thus would not need to know more than a few of their own address bits.

**10.3-3**    Define the data types ALU, Counter, Memory, Register, and Flag. What are the operations? What are the pre- and postconditions?

Overall, our idea is that we're going to use the ALU to change the state of the memory—one number at a time. The ALU is going to get information out of the memory, change it, and put the results into the memory. That's what gives us our basic moron model: the switches which we have grouped together and called the ALU are going to form the central piece of the moron, and the switches which we have grouped together and called the memory are going to pretend to be graph paper ready for writing and rewriting. That means that we have an enormous number of switches and a lot of wire, and almost all of it sits around doing almost nothing almost all of the time. Most of the switches are memory, so they sit and compute $A' = A$ over and over and over again, waiting for the ALU to come around and turn them into something else. If you write a loop to add 1 to each element of a length-$N$ array, it takes $\mathcal{O}(N)$ steps because we have to copy the first number from one set of switches to the ALU, and copy the result back, then copy the second number from another set of switches to the ALU, and copy the result back.... Meanwhile, each memory cell is a tiny computer, busily computing Boolean functions and running as fast as it can in a circle so that its contents won't change.

**Q:** Why can't you just have each memory element add 1 to itself and get the answer in $\mathcal{O}(1)$?

**A:** It sounds great, and to some extent it can work; it's called parallelism, and each year it becomes useful for a larger range of problems. It would be great if we could have a system that associates full ALU capabilities to each memory cell, or perhaps to every few memory cells; proposals vary from parallel systems with thousands (or millions) of very feeble ALUs with a few cells of memory each, to parallel systems with only a few ALUs but a lot of memory for each one. There are three problems:

- We have to get the results from one processor to another at the right times. The scheme we have now allows us to create a memory which (in $\mathcal{O}(log(N))$ time for an $N$-by-$k$ memory to allow for fanout to $N$ memory cells) will let you read or write $k$ bits as a single unit. To make all the cells of our graph paper active, we might have to make it possible for all of them to get information from all the others. To connect each processor directly to every other requires a quadratic number of wires... almost all of which will usually be wasted. More conservative strategies are possible, and often useful, but they tend to have flaws. For example, you can arrange all of your processors and memory on a tree, so that any two nodes have a common ancestor through which they communicate. This works beautifully for many problems, but can fail disastrously when many nodes try to communicate through the same node simultaneously. Again, you can arrange your processors and memory on a grid and let each communicate with its four neighbors: this is marvelous for some problems, but disastrous for others. More complex solutions are available, but nothing is best for all purposes.

- We have to get the program(s) out to the processors. If we're able to create a path between the ALU and the memory, then the ALU's instructions can sit in the memory; it only does one thing at a time, so getting instructions one at a time is all right too. If we had activity distributed over the memory, we'd have to have programs distributed around the memory too.

- We have to write the program(s). It's hard enough to write a program which does one thing at a time; how are you going to write a program which manages thousands of activities simultaneously?

Each of these problems has many feasible answers in many different contexts. We won't be studying them here; the idea of these remarks on parallelism is to help you see the enormous conceptual step we just took in choosing to develop a one-ALU, one-memory system. There was absolutely nothing in the ideas given up to there which would have suggested it. Now that we've taken that step, we have to control it.

## 10.4  MICROPROGRAMMING

*Microprogramming* does not mean "programming micro(computer)s"; it's a very detailed, very fine-grained kind of programming which often underlies that which underlies the programming-language implementation  we're trying to get to understand. (Some computers don't have a microprogramming level, others have two with the lower level called a nanoprogramming level; we're not going to get into either of those possibilities.) From our point of view, microprogramming is a way of telling the packages how to behave. We want to control the movement of data through the computer; that's a very different kind of thinking than that directed toward controlling the contents of packages. The microprogramming we'll do is not completely realistic, because some issues have been deliberately left out. Nonetheless, the "pseudo-microcode" we'll deal with will be a considerable help in organizing thoughts about the machine.

We do need some way of organizing things here, or we're going to get lost in a maze of wires connecting packages like a gigantic bowl of spaghetti holding together a moderate number of meatballs. We begin to get somewhere if we line the wires up and make them sit down in nice neat rows and columns, like the passengers on a bus. An actual computer may well have more than one bus system, but right now we're worried about the internal bus that carries information back and forth among bookkeeping registers, to and from an ALU. All bits of information flowing between registers have to ride on the bus. That's a nice organizing principle: what it means is that if we have registers $A$ and $B$ in our system, we can write A:=B and expect to figure out how to implement that by moving information from $B$ to the bus and then to $A$. The bus itself is a collection of Boolean variables representing the activity level of those wires.

That A:=B is part of a microprogram instruction, which is just a long sequence of bits which open some switches and shut others. That kind of instruction is very limited, but it's a basic tool in developing a programming system because we use microprogram instructions to control the machine's response to "machine-level" programs. We can only treat an operation as a microprogram instruction if we can reasonably expect it to come down to switches being on or off. For example, suppose that we had a machine with three registers $A$, $B$, and $C$, and the bus $Z$, each register consisting of 16 Boolean variables. We'd like to be able to implement the six statements A:=B, B:=C,. ... We can do this by making sure that the microprogram instruction we invent will have three bits $a, b$, and $c$ to select the information sent to the bus, and three more bits $a'$, $b'$, and $c'$ to select the information taken from it. All we need is the following collection of functions (I'm ignoring the clock, but it's still there):

$$Z'_i = (A_i \wedge a) \vee (B_i \wedge b) \vee (C_i \wedge c)$$
$$A'_i = (A_i \wedge \neg a') \vee (Z_i \wedge a')$$
$$B'_i = (B_i \wedge \neg b') \vee (Z_i \wedge b')$$
$$C'_i = (C_i \wedge \neg c') \vee (Z_i \wedge c')$$

Now control of the six bits $abca'b'c'$ will be sufficient to control the movement of data. If only one of those six bits is on, then only one of our six instructions will be executed. If all but $b$ and $c$ are on, then all three registers are filled with the value which was on the bus, while the former value of $A$ is placed on the bus.

## Exercise

**10.4-1**    What happens if all six bits are on? What other possibilities can you suggest?

So, what are our registers? What are the objects, and what are the operations?

* The memory itself is not on the bus, but there are some registers which are connected to it. The MAR (memory address register) holds the address of the currently interesting location in memory, the address lines we talked of in the last section; the MBR (memory buffer register) holds the value which has just been read from Mem[MAR] or perhaps just written to Mem[MAR]. The control line is MemOp, which is either Read or Write. Suppose again that $A$ and $B$ are registers. Since MAR and MBR are connected to the bus, we can expect

$$\text{MAR} := A, \text{MemOp} := \text{Read}; B := \text{MBR}$$

to have the net effect of B:=Mem[A]. (Here the assignments to MAR and MemOp are connected by commas: they are to take place in parallel, assuming that they are controlled by independent switches in the collection of packages. The semicolon indicates that we must wait for the next cycle because the new assignment depends on the results of previous ones.) Similarly, we have

$$\text{MAR} := A, \text{MBR} := B, \text{MemOp} := \text{Write};$$

to have the net effect of Mem[A]:=B.

* The arithmetic/logic unit has input registers $X$ and $Y$, output register $Z$; the operation it performs is signaled by some lines which we think of as a value

ALU_Op which is Addition, Subtraction, NegationOfX, DoubleX, or others which we'll come up with as we go along. It is associated with some "flag bits" which tell us whether the result was positive, zero, or negative, or perhaps an integer overflow. Now we can say that

$$X := A, Y := B, \text{ALU\_Op} := \text{Addition}; A := Z$$

will have the effect of A:=A+B.

- IC (the instruction counter) holds the address of the current program instruction. (Don't ask what the current program instruction is just yet; you'll see soon.)

- SP (the stack pointer) holds an address which helps us organize our use of memory itself. The "memory slice" Mem[SP...N] is called the *stack*, and we can drastically simplify our work with the machine by having almost all of our computation done on the stack rather than at arbitrary positions in memory. The idea is simply that of the PostSeq "final slice" array representation in which Push and Pop are quite cheap and only change the slice's lower bound by one; we therefore think of SP as having at least the circuitry of a counter which can easily count either up or down.

- There are others. We'll call $U$, $V$, and $W$ scratch registers, and there can be more besides, but we're not providing a complete machine; these will do for now.

At this point, it's a good idea to remember what these packages really are: collections of Boolean variables held together by collections of gates. Every time the clock ticks, those Boolean variables are allowed to change to reflect their inputs, and the gates which depend upon them are buzzy again. Slowly they settle down... and the clock ticks again. It is only in our minds that one or another of them may have meaning.

The microprogram, then, is a sequence of microinstructions, and each microinstruction is a rather long sequence of switch settings, with one switch for each of the necessary control lines for the whole set of registers and for the ALU as well. This program is (for our particular hypothetical machine) stored in a different memory, a special microprogram memory. This memory is not 64K-by-16-bits; it's more likely to be 2K-by-64 bits, with relatively few instructions (and no data) but many switches in each instruction. This system may have its own MAR and MBR (I'll call them the MMAR and MMBR to avoid confusion), but these are not registers on the bus that we've talked about. They are separate circuits which control the switches on that bus. Their sizes will fit the kind of memory they work with. If there are no more than 2K (2048=2**11) words in the microprogram memory, then the MMAR needs only 11 bits, while if there are 64 bits in a microinstruction, then that's how many the MMBR needs. We can normally imagine the MMAR as a counter which steps through a sequence of instructions in the microprogram memory, but it can also be loaded from part of the current microinstruction. Suppose that bits $53 \ldots 63$ of the microinstruction contain an "alternate next instruction," or "failure address." We can make bit 52 into a "carry" test: if it is on, and if the arithmetic instruction fails to cause a carry from either end of the ALU (e.g., doubling the largest number, or taking half of an odd number), then the alternate next instruction is loaded into the MMAR. Otherwise, the MMAR simply counts up. Similarly, we can have several other tests associated with other bits. We can even have separate bits associated with the complement of a given test; we can have a "no carry" test as well as a "carry" test, even though we know that they are not independent. The Boolean logic can simply take the AND of each one with its corresponding flag, and OR the results all together; this gives a signal $s$ which is used to select whether the alternate address or the next address goes into the MMAR. The logic, once more, will be

$$MMAR'_i \quad = \quad (\neg s \wedge (MMAR + 1)_i) \vee (s \wedge FA_i)$$

where FA is the "failure address." We can thus write W:=min(U,V) as

> X:=U, Y:=V, ALU_Op:=Subtraction, Test:=Positive, ElseAddr:=Lbl;
> X:=Y;
> Lbl:   W:=X;

Suppose that we had 10 registers (I've mentioned nine) whose bus motions are controlled by two bits each; suppose we have one bit for the MemOp, 20 bits for possible ALU_Ops, 12 different Tests with one bit each, and 11 bits for the ElseAddr which is the next MMAR if none of the Tests are true. That leads to a sequence of $10 * 2 + 1 + 20 + 12 + 11 = 64$ bits in each microinstruction word. Actually, we would need more bits for other things, and we wouldn't need so many bits for the ALU_Ops or for the Tests.

### Exercises

**10.4-2**   Suppose that we had a total of 20 different arithmetic/logical operations. If we encode them as cardinal numbers $0 \ldots 19$, each is represented by a five-bit binary number. Explain how a 32-bit-by-20-bit memory could be used to extract the switches we want. (No, that's not likely to be the best solution, but it would save us 15 bits in each microinstruction.)

**10.4-3**   Specify an interpreter for microinstructions: given a machine state and a microinstruction, it should generate the next machine state.

## 10.5 THE MACHINE LEVEL

Now we have a collection of rather funny-looking objects and operations on them. We'd like to deal with simple variables, arrays, assignment statements, procedures, and fun things like that. The logical level of design which is usually thought of as the "machine level" gets us partway there.

The basic idea of the machine level (for our simplified hypothetical machine) is that the machine state consists of logical entities like the stack pointer, the instruction counter, the memory contents, and some of the flags, but it does not contain the microprogramming registers. They cease to be visible, just as the possibility of writing microinstructions ceases to be visible: they belong to the implementation, not the definition. In the machine as we define it, we have a program which consists of one or more sequences of words (cardinal numbers) somewhere in memory. It is supposed to act on data which also consist of one or more sequences of words somewhere in memory. It acts on the data by pushing items onto the stack, carrying out arithmetic and logical operations which work on the top of the stack, and then popping the result off of the stack. Here's the way we would find the value of $2 + (3 + 4) - 8$: get the two, then the three, then the four; now add the three and four; now add the two back in; now get the eight; now subtract.

```
LDC 2    ;S =       [2,...]
LDC 3    ;S =     [3,2,...]
LDC 4    ;S = [4,3,2,...]
ADD      ;S =     [7,2,...]
ADD      ;S =       [9,...]
LDC 8    ;S =     [8,9,...]
SUB      ;S =       [1,...]
```

LDC n stands for "LoaD the Constant n onto the stack"; ADD and SUB should be clear. (But notice the order of arguments for SUB!) We try to read this as a sequence of instructions as if they were written in nice neat order on a page, but actually I've said that the program is found in the memory somewhere. Let's imagine that LDC is instruction 7, while ADD and SUB are 3 and 4 respectively: we would represent this program as the sequence

$$[7, 2, 7, 3, 7, 4, 3, 3, 7, 4]$$

Each instruction corresponds to a function which maps the machine state into a new machine state. Here are typical instructions, with their pre- and postconditions:

LDC n           abbreviates  Mem[IC]=7, Mem[IC+1]=n
    pre: SP > 0
    post: IC = $IC_0$+2, SP = $SP_0$-1, Mem[SP]=n

This instruction loads the number given to the top of the stack; we can think of it as Stk:=n@Stk.

ADD
    pre: SP $<$ MaxMem
    post: IC $=$ IC$_0$+1, SP $=$ SP$_0$+1, Mem[SP]=Mem$_0$[SP$_0$]+Mem$_0$[SP$_0$+1],
       Carry=...

This is the addition operation Stk:= (Stk[1]+Stk[2])@Tl(Tl(Stk)). It also changes the Carry flag so that we can write programs which respond correctly to overflow. SUB, MUL, DIV, MOD, and so on can all be assumed to work similarly.

LSH         left-shift the bits at the top of stack
    post: IC $=$ IC$_0$+1, Mem[SP]=Double(Mem$_0$[SP]), Carry=...

The left-shift instruction turns 00101 into 01010, doubling the number represented. We should actually write it as

[Carry@Mem[SP]:=Double(Mem[SP])]

We can then assume that RSH is similarly [n,C]:=[n DIV 2, n MOD 2] with n being Mem[SP] and C being the Carry.

JP n        "jump" to the instructions at n
    post: IC=n
JPZ n       "jump", if $Hd(Stack) = 0$
    post: IC= **if** Mem[SP]=0 **then** n **else** IC$_0$+2, SP=SP$_0$+1

These instructions (and others like JPN, which says to jump if the head of the stack is negative) help us to handle conditionals, loops, and procedure calls in which the focus of activity jumps around from one part of the program to another.

Up to this point, we have ignored the need for moving information to and from the stack. We expect to work on variables stored at particular memory locations; we need a variant of LDC which loads a variable instead of a constant. Here are two:

LDA n
    pre: SP $>$ 0
    post: SP $=$ SP$_0$-1, Mem[SP]=Mem$_0$[n], IC=IC$_0$+2
LDR n
    pre: SP $>$ 0
    post: SP $=$ SP$_0$-1, Mem[SP]=Mem$_0$[SP$_0$+n], IC=IC$_0$+2

The first one pushes a value onto the stack which comes from a specific address in memory; the second actually calculates an address and then finds a value in it.

(LDR 0 is Stk:=Hd(Stk)@Stk.) Thus, if we know that variable $x$ is in location 15 or is the eighth item in the stack, we can get at it and calculate things based on its value. To change it, we'd better have storage operations STA n and STR n which simulate PopHd(Mem[n], Stk) and PopHd(Mem[SP+n],Stk).

## Exercises

**10.5-1**    Write preconditions and postconditions for STA and STR.

**10.5-2**    Explain the effects of STR 0.

**10.5-3**    Explain the effects of LDA n; STA n.

**10.5-4**    Write a sequence of instructions for Mem[i]:=Mem[j]+Mem[k].

**10.5-5**    Specify the instructions JPA and JPR by analogy with LD and ST: A for address, R for relative (to stack).

**10.5-6**    Suppose the code beginning at location 15 is
LDA 93; LDR 0; JPN 23; JP 26; LDC 0; SUB; STA 93
What is the effect on Mem[93]? [Hint: Be careful of the order of arguments for SUB.]

The idea of this is not to teach you assembly-level coding for a specific machine: you should be getting a picture of the way things work on a stack-oriented computer architecture, so that we can move both upwards and downwards from that picture. I'm not interested in having a complete list of instructions: perhaps there should be a SWP instruction which swaps the top two elements of the stack, perhaps there should be a ROT instruction of the form Stk[1,2,3]:=Stk[2,3,1] so that ROT; ROT brings the third stack item to the top and ROT; SWP; ROT; ROT; interchanges the second with the third. On the other hand, perhaps there shouldn't be any such instruction; that depends on whether or not it's useful in supporting a higher level system, and as we go up a level we'll feel quite free to add or alter existing instructions. One nice thing to look for, as you go on thinking up instructions, is to make sure that you can get at every part of the state if you want to: we have JP instructions which set the instruction counter, but we have no instructions which read it. It might be a good idea to have a LDIC n instruction with the effect of Push(IC+n,Stk) and other instructions to read and write whatever flags are available in the system. It might even be a good idea to have an instruction which loads the stack pointer itself onto the stack. It's certainly a good idea to have a NOOP, or "no-operation", instruction, which tells the machine to do nothing until it's time for the next cycle.

Once we have such instructions, we may want to modify them. It turns out that the most common reason for looking at the instruction counter itself is that you're calling a procedure and want its RETURN statement to cause your current activity to continue at the next instruction. The address of that continuation point has to be on the stack, because that's where everything is: you might well want to have the instructions CALL proc, equivalent to LDIC 4; JP proc for procedure call, and RET, equivalent to JPR 0 for the RETURN statement. (We'll discuss both of these in the next section.) If so, you can make your machine-level programs smaller by defining these instructions in microcode.

In order to have this abstract machine work as we've just described it, we need a microprogram which reads and obeys the programs in memory, as found by the instruction counter. The basic outline is simple: we fetch an instruction and execute it...forever (unless we have an opcode which stops the machine).

LOOP OpCode := Mem[IC]; Execute(OpCode) END

That can be transformed into a microprogram, but the process is tedious. The instruction fetching is one microinstruction:

MAR:=IC, MemOp:=Read;

This is sufficient to bring the instruction into MBR, and then we can use it as guide for the next cycle. Some Boolean logic has to take it apart, or just use it as an index into a mini-memory with the initial contents of the MMAR.

Suppose, then, that we have fetched the current instruction from Mem[IC] and find that the current instruction is "LDC"; i.e., Mem[IC]=7. Then we set the MMAR accordingly, let the MMBR be loaded, and start off in a microprogram:

IC:=IC+1, SP:=SP-1;
MAR:=IC, MemOp:=Read;
MAR:=SP, MemOp:=Write, IC:=IC+1

In other words, we make the instruction counter point at the number to be loaded, we make the stack pointer point at the place to put that number, we read from the place indicated by the instruction counter, we write to the place indicated by the stack pointer, and we move on to the next instruction. This is one *fetch-execute* cycle.

The ADD instruction has no arguments; if we find that Mem[IC]=3, we can say

IC:=IC+1, MAR:=SP, MemOp:=Read, SP:=SP-1;
Y:=MBR, MAR:=SP;
X:=MAR, ALU_OP:=Addition;
MBR:=Z, MemOp:=Write;

The other simple arithmetic operations are similar, except that it's probable that multiplication and division are written as microprograms with loops. Remember the old equations:

$$
\begin{aligned}
mul(u, v) &= 0, & &\text{if } u = 0 \\
          &= mula(u, v, 0) & &\text{otherwise} \\
mula(u, v, w) &= w, & &\text{if } u = 0 \\
          &= mula(u/2, v * 2, w) & &\text{if } u \bmod 2 = 0 \\
          &= mula(u/2, v * 2, w + v) & &\text{otherwise ;}
\end{aligned}
$$

These can be turned into a microprogram making heavy use of scratch registers:

```
            IC:=IC+1, MAR:=SP, MemOp:=Read, SP:=SP-1;
            U:=MBR, MAR:=SP, W:=0
            V:=MBR, X:=U, Y:=0, Op:=Sub, Test:=IsZero, ElseAddr:=Mula;
            MBR:=U, MemOp:=Write, END_CYCLE;
Mula:       (* mula(U, V, W) = result needed; U > 0 *)
            X:=U, Op:=HalfOfX, Test:=Carry, ElseAddr:= Mulb;
            X:=V, Y:=W, Op:=Add;
            W:=Z;
Mulb:       (* mula(U/2, V*2,W) = result needed; U > 0 *)
            X:=U, Op:=HalfOfX; Test:=IsZero, ElseAddr:=Mulc;
            MBR:=W, MemOp:=Write, END_CYCLE;
Mulc:       (* mula(Z, V*2,W) = result needed; Z > 0 *)
            U:=Z, X:=V, Op:=DoubleX;
            V:=Z, Test:=FALSE, ElseAddr:=Mula;
```

Clearly, this is not a very nice programming language, and nothing is likely to make it nice. Notice that an END_CYCLE instruction and an always-failing test FALSE have been added, and we can go on adding things for convenience or from necessity, but microcode is not easy to debug or figure out. Fortunately, there's no reason for anyone to write large programs in microcode: it exists only to support the machine level, which exists only (from our point of view) to support high-level languages. If we have use for an instruction that looks like

$$
\text{pre} : \text{Stk} = [x, a, \ldots]; \text{post} : \text{Stk} = [\text{Mem}[a], a + 1, \ldots]
$$

then we can give it a name and some microcode; if not, we won't. If we find that we could do it better by changing the microcode level, we can; if we find that we can do that better by changing the package structure, we can; if we find that we can do that better by making new packages out of gates, we can. Design decisions propagate slowly down this hierarchy of levels, and other kinds of design decisions propagate back up. If someone invents better switches, it's quite possible that they will change (say) the relative cost of AND and OR gates, which in turn will change the costs of different kinds of packages, which... and so it goes.

**Exercise**

**10.5-7**    Choose some machine instructions, and write microprograms for them. If you
want to change the lower level features of the machine, then specify the changes
carefully and justify each one.

Once we have the machine level defined, it is perfectly possible to use it
directly, just as it is possible to use microcode directly. Many large programs have
been written in "assembler," which translates directly into machine codes. What
that means is that the programmer writes a series of "assembler" instructions which
look like this:

```
596   DigVal:                  ; Stk = ORD(c), RetAddr, ...
596           LDC 48           ; Stk = ORD('0'), ORD(c), RetAddr, ...
598           SUB              ; Stk = ORD(c)-ORD('0'), RetAddr, ...
599           SWP              ; Stk = RetAddr, ORD(c)-ORD('0'), ...
600           RET
601
```

This is a version of the *DigVal* function: given a character in the range ['0'...'9']
(represented by its *ASCII* code on the top of the stack) we can now generate its
numeric value (again, on top of the stack) by saying CALL DigVal. The actual
"machine code" program consists of five numbers: [7,48,4,s,r] (with s and r being
the numbers assigned to the SWP and RET instructions). The left-hand column
is not part of the assembler program; it's just a record of where the numbers go—
specifically, in locations 596, 597, 598, 599, and 600. The program that reads the
assembler instructions and writes the machine-code numbers is called an assembler.
It has to keep a dictionary defining the numbers for each instruction, it has to keep
count of the locations used, and it has to record the fact that the name DigVal
is a label for location 596, so that the assembler statement CALL DigVal can be
written as the two numbers [c,596], where c is the CALL instruction number.

When I say "DigVal is a label", I really mean just that the assembler dictionary
remembers that DigVal is 596 just as it remembers that LDC is 7. We could perfectly
well write LDC DigVal to bring 596 to the top of the stack, or even LDA DigVal to
bring 7 to the top of the stack. We could even use LDA DigVal to load the 7, then
increment the top of the stack, and then use STA DigVal to change the 7 to an 8.
(Now what will CALL DigVal do?) This trick can be used to manage variables with
names: they are labels, just like functions, and the "code" associated with them will
be loaded and changed and stored instead of being executed. (It's probably a good
idea to start with NOOP here.) These variables (and functions) are just names for
*absolute addresses* in memory; the lowest-level features of *Modula-2* also allow you

to define such variables, just by adding the address to the declaration. (Of course, that can have very strange effects on your program).

**Q:** That's all very well for scalars, and I suppose you'll just say that characters and Boolean values can be dealt with directly as numbers, but what about real numbers? What about arrays?

**A:** Suppose I want an array A of 10 elements; I can write

A : NOOP; NOOP; NOOP; . . . NOOP

and now LDA A will pick up the first NOOP. Let's call that one A[0] for simplicity. To get to A[1]. . .A[9], or generally to A[i], I'd better be able to add something to A itself as an address, I can say

LDC NOOP; LDC A; LDA i; ADD; STR 1

and there I have it: the value of A[i], right on top of the stack. (Clumsy, isn't it? If we often want A[i], we should define some more instructions to help.)

An assembler to be used for large-scale program development has to provide more facilities than those we've just gone over, but we don't need them: we're just concerned with high-level language support.

### Exercises

**10.5-8**    Specify a simple assembler, and write a prototype. You will need to assign numbers to the instruction codes. Assume that the location counter starts in location 0 and works up from there. (I.e., the code grows up from 0 as a PreSeq, and the stack grows down from MaxMem as a PostSeq. What happens when the code size and stack size together are larger than available memory?)

**10.5-9**    Specify an interpreter for machine codes, and write a prototype.

## 10.6  SIMPLE EXPRESSIONS

We'd like to translate simple expressions like "$3*(5-8)$" into machine code. That's easy enough to do by hand: what we want is

LDC 3; LDC 5; LDC 8; SUB; MUL;

and now the result we want is at the top of the stack, which is probably the best place to keep it anyway. If it's so easy to do by hand, surely we can do it mechanically, modifying or using the parsing procedures from earlier chapters. In fact, suppose that we have an arithmetic expression stored as a tree: the example just given would come out as ["*", 3, ["−", 5, 8]]. All we have to do is a "postfix traversal" of that tree:

$$
\begin{aligned}
Post(n) &= [n] \\
Post([S, A, B]) &= Post(A) + Post(B) + [S]
\end{aligned}
$$

From this we get $Post(3) = [3]$, $Post(["-", 5, 8] = [5, 8, "-"]$, and the overall $Post$fix form of our example is $[3, 5, 8, "-", "*"]$. This looks very close to the result we want, except that it lacks the LDC encoding. No problem. We'll just define $Code$ as a function which takes expression-trees and produces the appropriate assembler-strings (these always end in a ";"):

$$
\begin{aligned}
Code(n) &= \textbf{“LDC ”} + CardToStr(n) + \text{“;”} \\
Code([S, A, B]) &= Code(A) + Code(B) + NameToOp(S) \\
NameToOp(\text{“+”}) &= \textbf{“ADD; ”} \\
NameToOp(\text{“-”}) &= \textbf{“SUB;”}
\end{aligned}
$$

This is postfix assembler code (also called "reverse Polish notation") for arithmetic expressions. (Incidentally, we can easily edit these to generate machine code, just by substituting the numbers for the strings.)

### Exercises

**10.6-1**  Write out *Post* and *Code* as conditional recursive equations.

**10.6-2**  Write and test either *Post* or *Code* as a Modula-2 prototype.

**10.6-3**  Generalize the idea to work on single-argument primitive operations like unary "−", as in "X := −X", and on multiargument operations as well. This will be easy if you write a *Codes(S)* function which accumulates the concatenation of $[Code(x) : x \in S]$.

We've used two very important organizing principles here: first, that the code for an expression (or subexpression) should always have the net effect of leaving the value of that expression on top of the stack; and second, that the machine code for an abstract syntax tree should be a function of the machine codes for the subtrees. Neither of those is always desirable, but they're both often very helpful as guides.

## 10.7 SIMPLE STATEMENTS

We can extend the translation in various directions, e.g., to include statements involving arrays, assignment, and input/output:

```
x:=INPUT; y[3+x]:=x*x*x;
IF x < z THEN OUTPUT:=y[0]-x ELSE z:=x END;
```

Parsing will not be much of a problem; we'll need a grammar which includes assignment, array indexing, and conditionals as well as statement sequencing, but there's nothing really new there: we can generate the abstract syntax trees

```
:=(x,INPUT)
:=(INDEX(y,+(3,x)), *(*(x,x),x))
IF( <(x,z),
    :=(OUTPUT,-(INDEX(y,0),x))
    :=(z,x) )
```

Of course, we need to work on a sequence of input statements and generate a sequence of abstract syntax trees.

### Exercises

**10.7-1**   Write a grammar and prototype parser to generate these trees from this input.
**10.7-2**   Extend it to include precedence-based expressions.

Once we have the abstract syntax trees, we have to worry about what to do with them. The first thing to notice is that INPUT and OUTPUT are being treated like ordinary variables, i.e., ordinary locations in memory. That's because one of the many ways to deal with input and output is to replace some of the words of memory with switches which can be read or written from the outside. That's called *memory-mapped IO*, and it makes it easy for the low-level programmer to begin dealing with input. If INPUT is the name for the memory location which is really under outside control (e.g., its switches are reset from a keyboard), then LDA INPUT will bring the input word (if any) to the top of the stack. Similarly, if x is location 318, STA x will put that input word into location 318. No problem—or is there?

The abstract syntax trees for expressions generate code which leaves values on top of the stack. That's not what we want to do for statements: they should leave nothing on top of the stack. Worse, when we say x:=INPUT we obviously don't want the value of x at all. Worse yet, we have subtrees like INDEX(y,+(3,x)) where it seems we do want the value of 3+x, but we don't yet have any hint as to what should be generated for y and the overall result should not be a value: it should tell us how to store a value at y[3+x]. What principle can be employed?

Life will be easier if we can find a general principle which handles all assignment statements in terms of the abstract syntax trees beneath them. In x:=E, we want the *value* of E to be associated with the *address* of x; very well, let us say that a value is indeed computed from the left-hand side of an assignment statement and placed on the stack, but this value is a "left-value" or "l-value," which is an address. The code we want from x:=INPUT is going to be

LDC x; LDA INPUT; ST;

where ST shifts us from Stk=[n,a]+S to Stk=S; Mem[a]=n;.

**Exercises**    Go back and look over the instruction set; ST isn't there.

**10.7-3**    Explain how to microcode the ST instruction.
**10.7-4**    Explain how to do without it; you may need to allocate a variable to dump the top of stack into.

Now we can write two mutually recursive Code operations, one of which computes a normal value to put on the stack, and the other (called LCode) computes an address. If we want to Code an assignment statement or an indexing expression, then we call on Code for the right subtree and LCode for the left subtree, and then put them together with ST. If we want to LCode an indexing expression, then we want to LCode the left subtree and Code the right subtree, and then add them. (Of course, this assumes that all arrays are arrays of words; if you had an array of larger objects, you would have to multiply the right subtree's value by the object size before adding.)

Similarly, if we want to Code IF P THEN A ELSE B END, we need

$$Code(P) + [\text{``}\mathbf{JPF\ L1;}\text{''}] + Code(A) + [\text{``}\mathbf{JP\ L2;\ L1:\ }\text{''}] + Code(B) + [\text{``}\mathbf{L2:\ }\text{''}]$$

That definition is not quite complete, because we can't actually use the label "**L1**" more than once: we have to use "**L1**", then "**L2**", then "**L3**", and so on.

**Exercises**

**10.7-5**    Without worrying about reuse of labels, write Code and LCode to deal with the language constructions we've seen so far.
**10.7-6**    Extend the definition to deal with a LOOP construction; all you need is a label and a JP. Do not actually extend it to handle the loop EXIT, but describe what would be required to do so.
**10.7-7**    Assuming that NewLbl() always produces a string which is a new label, rewrite Code so that it will use new labels correctly.
**10.7-8**    Write a prototype for Code.

A large part of the effort that goes into writing a language implementation simply amounts to specifying and writing (and respecifying and rewriting) Code (and LCode and Codes); the more features there are in the language, the more complex this task is. *Modula-2* tries to simplify things by moving many concepts out of the domain of Code and into libraries; for example, many languages have special constructions for input/output, frozen into the Code design rather than into a standard library written in the language itself. Another example is storage management. The STORAGE module simply manages an array of words, beginning at the top of the code and going on up to the stack; it keeps a global variable indicating where the next free storage is. When you call on NEW(p), where p is a POINTER TO X and the size required for X is $n$, then p is set to the value of that global variable, which is then bumped up by $n$ just as you saw in the last chapter. There's no special facility in Code for this; there doesn't have to be. There does have to be some information associated with p, namely its type (and therefore, indirectly, the size of the object which it points to). This information is kept in a dictionary by Code as it goes along.

**Exercise**

**10.7-9**    Respecify Code as a function which takes two arguments—a tree and a dictionary—and then yields the resultant code.

## 10.8  SIMPLE FUNCTIONS

Now we can extend the translation to include simple functions, without any notion of scope. (Here you'll see why simple recurrences shouldn't have to run out of space, but often do.)

Our stack-organization principle tells us that the code for an abstract syntax tree F(a,b,c,d,e) should depend on the code for the subtrees; they will evidently leave the values of e,d,c,b, and a on the stack in that (reversed) order. Presumably, we then CALL F, which will leave the value of the whole expression on top of the stack as it RETurns. For example, if we are coding the expression GCD(9,x), and we're starting the code in location 4317, we will presumably get the sequence

```
4317    LDC     9;
4319    LDA     x;
4321    CALL    GCD;
```

and we assume (from the previous description of the CALL statement) that the execution of GCD at a moment when Mem[x]=12 will begin with the stack holding $[4323, 12, 9] + S$ and is supposed to end with a jump to 4323, leaving the stack holding $[3] + S$, just as if those three instructions had been replaced with LDC 3.

That means that when the *Code* for the function GCD is executed, it needs to get the values of its formal parameters from the stack. It also needs to get its continuation point (return address) from the stack. Here is one (somewhat clumsy) approach to generating code for the procedure definition.

Suppose we've defined *Code* as a function which takes an abstract syntax tree and a dictionary, and yields code. The procedure definition

PROCEDURE GCD(a,b:INTEGER):INTEGER;
BEGIN IF a=0...END GCD;

will presumably have ended up as an abstract syntax tree somewhat like

PROCEDURE(INTEGER(GCD(INTEGER(a), INTEGER(b))), IF(= (a, 0) ...));

I'm treating the type-name as a function for purposes of tree construction at least. However, let's simplify this: we're really only worried about words, so we'll forget the type-names and write

PROCEDURE(GCD(a, b), IF(= (a, 0), RETURN(b), IF(= (b, 0), ...)));

We know how to handle everything but the parameter-passing itself, the use of the variable names (which are *not* global variables), and the RETURN statement. We also know that as we begin, the stack will be [RA,b,a,...], where RA is the return address. That means that we could load b with LDR 1, we could load a with LDR 2, and in general we could load the $i$th parameter of an $n$-parameter procedure with LDR $(n + 1 - i)$; the return address counts as the $n + 1$st parameter.

**Exercises**   Using this idea:

**10.8-1**   Define *Code* for value-returning procedures. What has to go into the dictionary as you begin? What code is generated for assignments to local variables? Do *not* implement your solution.

**10.8-2**   Find the bug in the encoding just suggested, without reading onwards.

The problem with this is actually quite easy to see, but not quite as easy to fix. If we code the =(a,0) subtree using LDR 2 for a, that will work quite well. If, on the other hand, we coded =(0,a) using LDR 2 for a, that wouldn't work at all; the stack is higher now, and we'll get b instead. We have to generate different codes for a depending on the stack-manipulation instructions that come before the reference. We can solve the problem by revising Code so that it keeps track of the cumulative changes in SP since the procedure invocation began. For a procedure of $n$ parameters, LVL begins at $n+1$. Every time Code generates a LD instruction, LVL goes down by 1; more generally, every time it generates an instruction which changes SP by $n$, LVL will change by $n$, and the code generated for the $i$th parameter will be "**LDR** "$+StrToCard(LVL - i)$. This solution requires that Code produce more than one result: in particular, it has to produce LVL. A good way to do that is to modify Code so that it actually does produce only one result: an environment including code, LVL, and information about the types of variables and procedures.

Similarly, Code can be written to take only one argument: an environment including abstract syntax tree, LVL, and the same information about variables and procedures. This is not the only solution, but it will work. The resultant compilation for

$$PROCEDURE(F(n),IF(=(n,0),RETURN(1),RETURN *(n,F(-(n,1)))))$$

will closely resemble

```
F:      LDR 1       ; Stk = [n,RetAddr, n, ...]
        LDC 0       ; Stk = [0,n,RetAddr,n,...]
        SUB         ; Stk = [n-0, RetAddr,n...]; subtract to test n=0
        JPNZ L1     ; jump if result is nonzero, i.e., if n≠0
        LDC 1       ; Stk = [1, RetAddr, n,...]
        RET 3       ; IC = RetAddr, Stk = [1,...]
L1:     LDR 1       ; Stk = [n,RetAddr, n, ...]
        LDR 2       ; Stk = [n,n,RetAddr, n,...]
        LDC 1       ; Stk = [1,n,n,RetAddr, n,...]
        SUB         ; Stk = [n-1,n,RetAddr, n,...]
        CALL F      ; IC = F, Stk = [L2, n-1,n, RetAddr, n...]
                    ; on return to L2, Stk = [F(n-1), n, RetAddr, n...]
L2:     MUL         ; Stk = [F(n), RetAddr, n...]
        RET 3       ; IC = RetAddr, Stk = [F(n),...]
```

Notice that I changed the RET instruction so that RET n would assume that the result to be returned is on top of the stack, and the return address is next, followed by the $n - 2$ arguments to the function which is returning. The result should be that all of these are popped off the stack, the result is pushed back onto the stack, and the instruction counter is set to the return address.

## Exercises

**10.8-3**  Show how to do without this, using only the RET instruction previously discussed.

**10.8-4**  Show how to implement this in microcode.

**10.8-5**  Hand-Code the definition of GCD. Trace through the execution of GCD(12,9).

**10.8-6**  Revise the specification and prototype implementation of Code to work on environments and handle functions as described.

The solution given works, but it is not a good solution. As you should see from your work on GCD, the space used on the stack is actually proportional to the depth of the recursion. Here's an example: if we try to implement and then parse

$$G(n,a) = \textbf{if } n = 0 \textbf{ then } a \textbf{ else } G(n-1, n*a)$$

what we get is

PROCEDURE(G(n,a),IF(=(n,0),RETURN(a),RETURN(G(-(n,1),*(n,a)))))

Now if we code this according to the recipe given thus far, we get

```
G:      LDR 2       ; Stk = [n,RetAddr,a,n,...];
        LDC 0       ; Stk = [0,n,RetAddr,a,n...];
        SUB         ; Stk = [n-0, RetAddr,a,n...];
        JPNZ L1     ; if result is 0, continue, else L1; Stk=[RetAddr...]
        LDR 1       ; Stk = [a,RetAddr,a,n,...]
        RET 4       ; IC=RetAddr, Stk = [a,...]
L1:     LDR 2       ; (ELSE) Stk = [n,RetAddr,a,n...]
        LDC 1       ; Stk = [1,n,RetAddr,a,n,...]
        SUB         ; Stk = [n-1,RetAddr,a,n,...]
        LDR 3       ; Stk = [n, n-1, RetAddr,a,n,...]
        LDR 3       ; Stk = [a,n,n-1, RetAddr,a,n,...]
        MUL         ; Stk = [n*a,n-1, RetAddr,a,n...]
        CALL G      ; IC = G, Stk = [L2, n*a,n-1, RetAddr,a,n...]
                    ; after return to L2, Stk= [G(n*a,n-1),RetAddr,a,n...]
L2:     RET 4       ;
```

You know this is a simple recurrence. Then why does it tend to run out of space? The reason is obvious, after you go through an example or two: the (recursive) call on G is immediately followed by a RETurn. The environment (i.e., the return address and two arguments sitting on the stack) which was described in Chapter 8 is thrown away during the RETurn, but not before; it should be thrown away during the call. CALL-RET is a waste of space.

Suppose that we didn't have the arguments and the returned result cluttering up the stack; the CALL instruction would just push the continuation point IC+1 onto the stack, and the RET instruction (with no argument) would just pop the top of stack into the instruction counter. In that case, we'd find that any CALL-RET sequence could simply be replaced by a JP instruction. On many real computers, there are such instructions at the machine level, and it's perfectly all right to go through your assembler code and make that substitution. It works—but it doesn't handle parameters.

One (not very good) way to handle this would be to microcode (or simulate) a DEL n k instruction which would have the effect of deleting $k$ items beginning at level $n$ in the stack:

Stk := Stk[1..n-1]+Stk[n+k..]

This could be used to throw away space, just before the CALL.

**Exercise**

**10.8-7**    Explain how this could work.

A better solution (and a quite common one) is to require that the machine have (or simulate) a sufficient number of scratch registers to hold the arguments and result(s). One problem with this is that if you have a CALL which is *not* followed by a RET, then you can't leave the registers blocked up with your own parameters while the CALL is performed; you have to save the parameters from registers to stack before the call, and restore them from the stack afterwards. (As a refinement, you can save only those parameters which will actually be used after the call.) A less fundamental but sometimes irritating problem is that you may find a programming language implementation which works quite well... until you write a function with more parameters than the number of scratch registers in the machine. Then performance goes down, and you may even find that the program works incorrectly. (Yes, this has happened to your author.)

Another approach (which can be used as a refinement on the register-parameter solution) is to have a global variable (or register) which is the location of the RetAddr on the stack. Instead of loading a location found as Mem[SP+LVL], we load a location found as Mem[EP+LVL], where EP is the "environment pointer," and stays put for the duration of the call. This changes details, but not the fundamentals.

Of course, there are many other solutions as well as refinements on these answers; the main thing is that at this point, the questions—and solution strategies—should be clear.

**Exercise**

**10.8-8**    Suppose that you have 15 scratch registers for procedure parameters and one for the result. What changes will you have to make in the specification of Code?

Here you might expect that we have to begin all over again with the coding of VAR parameters, or generally with procedures which have no results. Actually, these introduce very little new difficulty.

- A procedure with no result is a statement, but then its body is a statement too, and its RETURN statement does not return a value. If we process the RETURN statement correctly, nothing else needs to be done to separate the two kinds of procedures.

- A VAR parameter X is a pointer, an actual address rather than a value. That means that within the procedure body we find that LDA X only gets us the address (the l-value, as desired by LCode) of the "real" variable X, and then we need to load again to get the value of X within Code. Within the actual call on the procedure P(X), we want the l-value of X as the value of the formal parameter. That means that we must use LCode rather than Code on any VAR parameters in an abstract syntax tree, which in turns means that the environment used by Code must contain the declaration to the procedure before Code attempts to generate code for it. That's not a very onerous restriction.

### Exercise

**10.8-9**   Explain how Code can be extended to deal with this case; use at least two examples, show the code you would generate by hand, and trace its effect. (But don't write the new version of Code in full.)

## 10.9 SCOPE

Now we can extend our language to use nonlocal variables, to allow a Partition procedure defined within QuickSort which uses (and changes) variables of QuickSort which are not passed as parameters. There are two general solutions:

- Transform the definitions given into definitions which you already know how to handle. For example, looking at the definition of Partition, we see that it uses these variables, so we change the abstract syntax tree so that it receives them as VAR parameters. Then apply the previous solutions.

- Keep a record of the environments accessible to each procedure, and prepare to find variables from those environments. Here the "environment pointer" solution of the previous section becomes very important. Let us imagine that the dictionary which Code takes as argument contains all the parameters and declared variables as a list of nested environments, each of which is a list of (name, definition) pairs. When Code is called on a procedure, it simply adds a new environment to this list. When a program P includes a procedure Q which includes a procedure R, then Code works on the body R using a list of three environments: the inner environment of R itself, the outer environment of Q, and the global environment of P. If we try to Code the variable X within R, we first check R's own environment. If X happens to be the third variable of the local environment, we generate code which will push $Mem[EP_0+3]$ onto the stack. If it is the eighth variable of Q's environment, we generate code to push $Mem[EP_1+8]$ onto the stack. If it is the first variable of the environment of P, we push $Mem[EP_2+1]$ onto the stack. If it isn't any of them, we produce an error message; this was an attempt to use an undeclared variable.

Both solutions have significant overhead. The first one turns out to require that procedure Q take all the parameters which are globals possibly used by R, just in case Q might call on R. If R is a procedure which reports errors, checking on all of the variables in a complex state, then this can make Q a very much more expensive procedure than it needs to be. The second solution requires that we keep track of all the environment pointers at runtime; this is usually done with an array called a "display." Each call statement and each return must be associated with code to make sure that the table of environment pointers will be up-to-date... even though most procedures don't even use any environments but their own.

There are many ways to make this situation somewhat better, both by clever code generation and by redesign of the machine. Still, the overhead involved in procedure calls is normally nonzero. It is often possible to take a working system and improve its performance by a significant percentage by replacing procedure invocations with edited copies of the procedure bodies. All you're doing is substituting equals for equals, but the performance is not equivalent.

### Exercises

**10.9-1**   Design a collection of "benchmark" programs to compare the performance of code generated by various *Modula-2* compilers. Try to come up with some which will show the relative speeds of integer arithmetic, real-number arithmetic, array access, NEW, and DISPOSE—and procedure invocation. Run each benchmark on at least three compilers, and discuss your results.

**10.9-2**   Specify, write, and test a version of Code which handles nested procedures with nonlocal variables.

## 10.10  EXTENSIONS AND GOODBYE

Do we have to stop at the level of *Modula-2*? Of course not: we can now go on to build levels on top of the conventional programming-language level, and levels on top of those. One obvious direction would be an effort to implement the specification language: can we write programs which compute with rule-sequences like the multiplication rules?

$$
\begin{aligned}
n * m &= n * m + 0 \\
n * 1 &= n \\
n * 0 + a &= a \\
n * (m + 1) + a &= n * m + (a + n)
\end{aligned}
$$

The answer is yes; you learned to use such programs yourself in the first chapter of the book, and you can implement them in *Modula-2* to work on abstract syntax trees. Suppose that we have the abstract syntax tree $*(5, 3)$; the equations tell us that this can be replaced with $+(*(5, 3), 0)$, which can be replaced with $+(*(5, 2), 5)$, which can be replaced with .... The equations also provide other possible replacements: they define neighbors, and we can use those neighbors to carry out a search. In fact, there are four components to the problem: matching a given pattern to a given expression, substituting values for variables in a given expression, (partially) simplifying an expression, and searching.

- Matching: Suppose that we're trying to use the rule $n * 0 + a = a$, expressed as the left-hand tree $+(*(n, 0), a)$ and right-hand tree $a$, on the expression $5 * 0 + 7$. We match the expression with the left-hand tree: it works and gives us the environment $\{n = 5, a = 7\}$.

- Substituting: We then use that environment to find a substitution instance of the right-hand tree $a$, which is the replacement value for this expression. In this case, the substitution instance is simply 7.

- Simplifying: If, instead, we had the rule $n * (m + 1) + a = n * m + (n + a)$ to be used on the expression $5 * 3 + 5$, we would have the environment $\{n = 5, m = 2, a = 5\}$, producing the substitution instance $5 * 2 + (5 + 5)$. We want to simplify this using the "skill" of addition, to produce $5 * 2 + 10$.

- Searching: Suppose that we have the abstract syntax tree $*(5, *(3, 1))$, which has the subtrees $*(5, *(3, 1))$, 5, $*(3, 1)$, 3, and 1; we also have the patterns $x$, $*(n, 1)$, $+(*(n, 0), a)$, and so on—the left-hand sides of the equations. Going back to the procedures of Chapter 1, we can match any patterns against any of the subtrees to find an environment which matches the left-hand side of the rule to the subtree. We don't know which is the right rule to apply; we do know that some rules (in this system, $n * m = n * m + 0 = (n * m + 0) + 0 = \ldots$) could go into cycles. We may have to search in all directions to find an answer to our problem.

Let's consider each of these steps briefly.

In matching, we're given two abstract syntax trees: one of them contains "data", and the other contains "variables." We hope to find an environment $E'$ within which the two trees are equivalent. Let's write $Match(P, V, E)$ as a function which takes a $P$attern, a $V$alue, and an $E$nvironment which is just a dictionary of names, each initially defined as "$Undef$". To make the rules easier to read, we'll split them into cases: the $P$attern can be a $var$iable named in the environment, or it can be a $const$ant, or it can be a sequence $p@S$, where both $p$ and $S$ are patterns. First, we can consider the constants:

$$\begin{aligned} Match(const, V, E) \quad &= \quad E, & \text{if } const = V \\ &= \quad \textbf{FAILURE}, & \text{otherwise} \end{aligned}$$

That part's certainly pretty easy, but obviously we'll need to consider later what to do with failures. Now we can think about variables: a variable is known because we find it in the dictionary. (Here we'll write $LookUp(var, E)$ as $E[var]$ and $Define(E, var, val)$ as $E[var := val]$.) If a variable is unknown, it can be matched to anything; otherwise its value had better match the value you're trying to match it against!

$$Match(var, V, E) \quad = \quad E[var := V] \qquad \text{if } E[var] = Undef$$
$$\qquad\qquad\qquad\quad = \quad Match(E[var], V, E) \quad \text{otherwise}$$

Now, what about sequences? It's pretty straightforward:

$$Match(p@S, x@V, E) \quad = \quad Match(S, V, Match(p, x, E))$$

**Q:** What about the empty sequence?
**A:** It's a constant.
**Q:** In sequence matching, what if the $Match(p, x, E)$ produces a **FAILURE**?
**A:** We do need a rule to handle that:

$$Match(P, V, \textbf{FAILURE}) = \textbf{FAILURE}$$

That rule has to be applied no matter what the pattern may be.
    **Q:** In sequence matching, what if the value is not a sequence?
    **A:** In simple pattern matching, you must consider that a **FAILURE**.

## Exercises

**10.10-1**    Write *Match* as a simple conditional rule sequence.

**10.10-2**    Implement and test a prototype matcher. (You must choose a representation for **FAILURE**.)

**10.10-3**    Extend *Match* so that it can match the pattern $+(n, 1)$ against the simple value 19 and come out with $n = 18$. Try to make this systematic; how many cases can you handle?

Now we can consider the substitution process. Suppose that we have an environment $E$ found from matching the left-hand side of a rule with an expression; i.e., it wasn't a **FAILURE**. Now, we want to take the right-hand side of that rule and substitute. Let's say that $ValOf(x, E)$ is $x$ itself if $x$ is not one of the variables defined in $E$, and it's $E[x]$ otherwise. Now we can define *Subst*itution on trees:

$$Subst(x@S, E) \quad = \quad Subst(x, E)@Subst(S, E) \quad \text{deals with nonatomic objects}$$
$$Subst(atm, E) \quad = \quad ValOf(atm, E) \qquad\qquad\quad \text{deals with the rest}$$

## Exercises

**10.10-4**    Write *Subst* as a simple conditional rule sequence.

**10.10-5**   Implement and test a prototype version of *Subst*, and combine it with *Match* from the previous exercise. What algebraic properties can you easily use to test the two together?

**10.10-6**   Specify, write, and test $TryRule([L, R], E)$ which uses the rule $L = R$ on the expression $E$ and returns the result if $L$ matches $E$, but which returns $E$ unchanged otherwise.

Now it's time to consider simplification of expressions: we want to be able to simplify an expression by applying whatever built-in operations we have to the values of the subtrees. Here's the beginning of a simplifier:

$$
\begin{aligned}
Simp(X) \quad &= \quad X, & &\text{if } IsAtomic(X) \\
&= \quad SimpLevel(Hd(X), [Simp(a) : a \in Tl(X)]) & &\text{otherwise}
\end{aligned}
$$

This pattern will now try to simplify with *SimpLevel* at every level in the tree:

$$
\begin{aligned}
SimpLevel(\text{`+'}, [x, y]) \quad &= \quad x + y, & &\text{if } IsNumber(x) \wedge IsNumber(y) \\
&= \quad [\text{`+'}, x, y] & &\text{otherwise} \\
SimpLevel(\text{`*'}, [x, y]) \quad &= \quad x * y, & &\text{if } IsNumber(x) \wedge IsNumber(y) \\
&= \quad [\text{`*'}, x, y] & &\text{otherwise} \\
&\ \ \vdots
\end{aligned}
$$

## Exercises

**10.10-7**   Use *Simp* on the expressions $5 + (3 + 2)$, $(5 + 3) * x$, and $0 + y$.

**10.10-8**   Write and test Simp.

**10.10-9**   Combine Simp with the previous procedures to write one procedure which takes a rule $[L, R]$, its environment $E$, and an expression $X$, and produces a simplified-as-far-as-possible expression which is equivalent to $X$ after applying the rule (if possible).

**10.10-10**   Extend Simp to include subtraction.

**10.10-11**   Extend SimpLevel to allow algebraic simplifications like

$$SimpLevel(+, [x, 0]) = x$$

so that it does not always call on the primitive operations; simplification can have built-in rules of its own. If you simplify this way, what happens to the $n * m = n * m + 0$ rule which we used to get started?

Now we can apply rules, even conditionally. Suppose, for example, we have a conditional rule $X = Y$ if $P$. We can match $X$ with an input expression to get an environment or **FAILURE**. If we get a failure, we stop; otherwise, we take the environment and use it to find the simplified value of $P$: if $P$'s substitution instance simplifies to *True*, then we can apply the rule, but otherwise we must pretend that there was no match in the first place.

What about searching? We can organize it in many ways; none of them will easily lead us to a small search space in this very open-ended world of possibilities. One possibility is not to search at all: all rules are to be tried, but one after another (in order) at all possible levels. Suppose that *RList* is the name of the sequence of all rules. Then

$$
\begin{aligned}
Eval(atm) &= atm \\
Eval(op@args) &= TryRules(op@[Eval(a) : a \in args], RList)
\end{aligned}
$$

In this definition, *TryRules* is an accumulator:

$$
\begin{aligned}
TryRules(E, [\,]) &= E \\
TryRules(E, [L, R]@S) &= TryRules(TryRule([L, R], E), S)
\end{aligned}
$$

Assuming that *TryRule(LR, E)* tries to apply the rule *LR* to *E* and produces the (possibly simplified) result, this will make an effort to try all the rules in the system.

## Exercises

**10.10-12** Write and test the expression evaluator *Eval* according to this definition.

**10.10-13** Try a different strategy, e.g., by having $Eval(x@s)$ depend on $TryRules(x@s)$. This would be a "top-down" order of rule application.

These definitions avoid the need for a search; they will only try one rule on a given expression, and then they try another rule on the result of that first attempt, and so on. We get an enormously more expensive, enormously more general "evaluator" by trying all the rules at all possible subtrees to generate "neighbors," and then searching onwards from there. You've learned to express problems and solutions as rules; you've also learned to work with searches which go off in all possible directions.

## Exercises

**10.10-14** Specify, write, and test a *Neighbors* function which will try every rule at every subtree.

**10.10-15** Specify, write, and test a search function which will use the *Neighbors* function of the previous exercise.

**10.10-16** Informally, try to analyze the computational complexity of the system you're generating; try to suggest improvements.

The use of sensible search strategies is basic to the study of artificial intelligence. If we associate a collection of rules with a search strategy, we have a "production system." At this logical level, we can build systems of rules which express much of our knowledge about a particular subbranch of medical diagnosis or chemical analysis, about the inferences to be drawn from a particular kind of prepositional phrase, or about methods for writing or debugging a particular kind of program. Now think about what kind of packages could be built from these as components... and about what could be built from those packages.

> *Around and around and around it goes,*
> *and where it stops, nobody knows...*

**Exercises**    Pick one:

**10.10-17**   Specify, write, and test a "DearAbby" program which reads letters (in English) and writes responses to them, in such a way that the correspondent cannot tell whether "DearAbby" is a program or a human being.

**10.10-18**   Prove that a successful answer to the previous exercise is impossible.

# Bibliography

[1] Aho, A., Hopcroft, J., and Ullman, J. 1976. *The Design and Analysis of Computer Algorithms*. Reading, Mass.: Addison-Wesley.

[2] Brooks, F. 1979. *The Mythical Man-Month*. Reading, Mass.: Addison-Wesley.

[3] *The American Heritage Dictionary of the English Language*. 1979. Boston: Houghton-Mifflin.

[4] *The Oxford English Dictionary (Compact Edition)*. 1971. London: Oxford University Press.

[5] Eddington, A. 1968 (Originally published 1928.) *The Nature of the Physical World*. Ann Arbor, Mich.: University of Michigan Press.

[6] Escher, M.C. 1960. *The Graphic Work of M.C. Escher*. New York: Hawthorne Books.

[7] Florman, S. 1981. *Blaming Technology*. New York: St. Martin's Press.

[8] Gould, S.J. 1981. *The Mismeasure of Man*. New York: W.W. Norton.

[9] Haugeland, J. 1985. *Artificial Intelligence: The Very Idea*. Cambridge, Mass.: MIT Press.

[10] Hofstadter, D. 1979. *Gödel, Escher, Bach: An Eternal Golden Braid*. New York: Basic Books.

[11] Huff, D. 1954. *How to Lie with Statistics*. New York: Norton.

[12] McCorduck, P. 1979. *Machines Who Think*. San Francisco: W.H. Freeman.

[13] Parnas, D. L. 1985. "Software Aspects of Strategic Defense Systems." *American Scientist* 73:5,432–40.

[14] Pirsig, R. 1974. *Zen and the Art of Motorcycle Maintenance*. New York: Morrow.

[15] Weinberg, G. 1975. *An Introduction to General Systems Thinking*. New York: Wiley.

[16] ——— 1971. *The Psychology of Computer Programming*. New York: Van Nostrand Reinhold.

[17] ——— 1982. *Rethinking Systems Analysis and Design*. Boston: Little, Brown and Company.

[18] Weizenbaum, J. 1976. *Computer Power and Human Reason*. San Francisco: W.H.Freeman.

# Index

Tear out this card and fill in all necessary information. Then enclose this card in an envelope and mail to:

Book Distribution Center
PRENTICE HALL
Route 59 at
Brook Hill Drive
West Nyack, N.Y. 10995

EQUATIONS, MODELS, AND PROGRAMS:
A MATHEMATICAL INTRODUCTION TO
COMPUTER SCIENCE
THOMAS J. MYERS

Please send the item checked below. The Publisher will pay all shipping and handling charges.

_____ Please send the Program Disk (28368-9) to accompany EQUATIONS, MODELS, AND PROGRAMS: A MATHEMATICAL INTRODUCTION TO COMPUTER SCIENCE which is available free, upon adoption, to instructors for duplication and distribution to students.

NAME _____

DEPT _____

SCHOOL _____

CITY _____ STATE ___ ZIP _____